ERISA

ERISA

PRINCIPLES OF
EMPLOYEE BENEFIT LAW

PETER J. WIEDENBECK

OXFORD
UNIVERSITY PRESS

Oxford University Press, Inc., publishes works that further Oxford University's objective of excellence in research, scholarship, and education.

Oxford   New York
Auckland   Cape Town   Dar es Salaam   Hong Kong   Karachi   Kuala Lumpur   Madrid   Melbourne
Mexico City   Nairobi   New Delhi   Shanghai   Taipei   Toronto

With offices in
Argentina   Austria   Brazil   Chile   Czech Republic   France   Greece   Guatemala   Hungary   Italy
Japan   Poland   Portugal   Singapore   South Korea   Switzerland   Thailand   Turkey   Ukraine
Vietnam

Published by Oxford University Press, Inc.
198 Madison Avenue, New York, New York 10016

Oxford is a registered trademark of Oxford University Press
Oxford University Press is a registered trademark of Oxford University Press, Inc.

Library of Congress Cataloging-in-Publication Data

Wiedenbeck, Peter J., 1953–
  ERISA : principles of employee benefit law / Peter J. Wiedenbeck.
    p. cm.
  Includes bibliographical references and index.
  ISBN 978-0-19-538767-4 (hardback : alk. paper)
  1. Pension trusts—Law and legislation—United States.
  2. Deferred compensation—Taxation—Law and legislation—United States.
  3. United States. Employee Retirement Income Security Act of 1974. I. Title.
  KF3512.W533 2010
  344.7301'252—dc22   2009034703

1 2 3 4 5 6 7 8 9

Printed in the United States of America on acid-free paper

Note to Readers
This publication is designed to provide accurate and authoritative information in regard to the subject matter covered. It is based upon sources believed to be accurate and reliable and is intended to be current as of the time it was written. It is sold with the understanding that the publisher is not engaged in rendering legal, accounting, or other professional services. If legal advice or other expert assistance is required, the services of a competent professional person should be sought. Also, to confirm that the information has not been affected or changed by recent developments, traditional legal research techniques should be used, including checking primary sources where appropriate.

(Based on the Declaration of Principles jointly adopted by a Committee of the American Bar Association and a Committee of Publishers and Associations.)

Contents

Part II

Conduct Controls: Welfare and Pension Plans 55

Chapter 3   Disclosure 57

Acknowledgments

I thank Kris Markarian, legal editor at the Federal Judicial Center, for her continuing support of this work, and for her advice and skillful editing of Chapters 1 to 9. I am especially grateful for the patience and confidence she displayed when the project was repeatedly delayed, first by several stints chairing faculty appointments committees, and then by a four-year term as associate dean. For guiding the proposal for a revised and expanded version of the work through the Oxford University Press acquisition process, I thank Samantha Cassetta and the anonymous peer reviewers who graciously shared their time and expertise.

Thanks also to the many individuals who reviewed prior drafts of parts of this book, including the participants at several faculty workshops at Washington University School of Law. In particular, I am grateful for thoughtful reviews and comments received from Dean Kent S. Syverud, Presidents Russell K. Osgood (Grinnell College) and Joel S. Seligman (University of Rochester), and from Professors Merton Bernstein, Cheryl D. Block, Jonathan Barry Forman, John O. Haley, Daniel I. Halperin, Daniel L. Keating, Pauline Kim, John H. Langbein, Dana M. Muir, and Robert B. Thompson.

For research assistance I thank Jessica I. Rothschild of the Stanford Law School Class of 2011, Jocelyn H.W.C. Chong of the Washington University School of Law Class of 2010, James A. Bloom of the Washington University School of Law Class of 2008, and Hopey A. Gardner of the Washington University School of Law Class of 2007. I am also indebted to Thomas E. Clark (Washington University J.D. 2007, LLM 2008) for comments and suggestions pertaining to participant-directed investments. My assistant, Beverly Owens, deserves credit for revising and correcting the internal cross references.

Earlier versions of parts of this work appeared in: PETER J. WIEDENBECK, ERISA IN THE COURTS (GPO 2008); Peter J. Wiedenbeck, *Implementing ERISA: Of Policies and "Plans,"* 72 WASH. U. L.Q. 559 (1994); Peter J. Wiedenbeck, *ERISA's Curious Coverage*, 76 WASH. U. L.Q. 311 (1998); and PETER J. WIEDENBECK & RUSSELL K. OSGOOD, EMPLOYEE BENEFITS 132–37, 389–96, 443–46, 787–832 (West Pub. Co. 1996), reprinted with permission of West, a Thomson Reuters business. In addition, a portion of the explanations of the tax treatments of health care and of deferred compensation is derived from WILLIAM D. ANDREWS & PETER J. WIEDENBECK, BASIC FEDERAL INCOME TAXATION 119–26, 318–24 (6th ed. 2009), and is used with the permission of Aspen Publishers.

PART I

General Considerations

Chapter 1

Overview of ERISA

The stakes are high in the regulation of employee benefit plans. The aggregate assets held in trust by qualified private retirement savings plans reached $6.2 trillion by the close of 2007, a more than six-fold increase in real terms since the passage of the Employee Retirement Income Security Act of 1974 (ERISA). That extraordinary figure excludes $1.9 trillion in private pension plan assets held by life insurance companies and more than $4.5 trillion held by deferred compensation plans covering government workers.[1] Employer spending for employee health care coverage is now

---

[1]   Employee Benefit Research Institute, EBRI Databook on Employee Benefits, Table 11.3c (Apr. 2009), http://www.ebri.org/pdf/publications/books/databook/DB.Chapter%2011.pdf; *id.* Table 18.2b (Jan. 2009), http://www.ebri.org/pdf/publications/books/databook/DB.Chapter%2018. pdf ($1.16 trillion total assets in federal government retirement pension plans in 2007; *id.* Table 19.3b (Jan. 2009), http://www.ebri.org/pdf/publications/books/databook/DB.Chapter%- 2019.pdf ($3.38 trillion in state and local government plans in 2007). The life insurance asset figure is from 2006, EBRI Pension Investment Report 3rd Quarter 2008, Table 13 (2009), http://www.ebri.org/publications/pir/pdf/PIR_08Q3_Final.pdf. In comparison, total assets in private trusteed plans in 1975 were reported as $260 billion (nominal dollars). Employee Benefits Security Administration, U.S. Department of Labor, Private Pension Plan Bulletin Historical Tables and Graphs, Table E11 (Feb. 2009), http://www.dol.gov/ebsa/pdf/1975-2006historicaltables.pdf. From 1975 to 2007 the consumer price index increased by a factor of about 3.85.

more than $530 billion *annually*.[2] Retirement and savings plan contributions constitute about 3.5 percent of total compensation costs in private industry, while employer-provided health insurance costs constitute 7.1 percent of total compensation (these amounts represent 4.9 percent and 10 percent of average wage and salary cost, respectively).[3] In 2007, 42 percent of private-sector workers were retirement plan participants, while some 74 percent of Americans working full-time were covered by an employer- or union-sponsored group health care plan.[4]

This book provides an overview of the regulation of employee benefit plans under federal labor and tax laws. Part I explores the structure, policy, and scope of federal benefit plan regulation (Chapters 1–2). Part II addresses those aspects of benefit plan regulation that are common to both pension plans, which provide employees with deferred cash compensation, and welfare plans, which provide employees with medical insurance, dental insurance, life insurance, or other benefits. The four common concerns of pension and welfare plan regulation—disclosure, fiduciary obligations, enforcement, and preemption (Chapters 3–6)—have been the focus of much litigation that evinces unresolved discrepancies between several fundamental policies. Part III examines the minimum standards required of certain key terms of the pension contract, specifically those relating to plan participation and vesting, pension distributions, and defined benefit plan funding and termination rules (Chapters 7–9). Part IV traces the influence of federal tax law on retirement savings and health care financing, giving particular attention to who is covered by employer-sponsored programs and the type and amount of benefits provided to participating employees (Chapters 10–11).

The focus of Parts I–III is on the labor law aspects of ERISA, which are codified in Title 29 of the United State Code.[5] Counterparts to several important labor provisions appear in the Internal Revenue Code as conditions on the favorable income tax treatment accorded "qualified" (i.e., tax-subsidized) pension, annuity, profit-sharing, and stock bonus plans (collectively known as qualified retirement plans). In particular, many of the minimum standards governing pension plan content (Part III) are reproduced (verbatim or nearly so) in Subchapter D of the tax Code.[6] This overlap is attributable to a paternalistic or protective policy that is common to some of the tax and labor provisions of ERISA, and in those instances, the interpretation of the qualified plan rules offers guidance for the application of ERISA's labor provisions. Other objectives of the two bodies of law are not shared, and their administration and enforcement are

---

2   *Id.* Table 34.1 (Mar. 2009), http://www.ebri.org/pdf/publications/books/databook/DB.Chapter%2034.pdf ($532.1 billion in 2007).

3   *Id.* Table 3.2c (May 2009), http://www.ebri.org/pdf/publications/books/databook/DB.Chapter%2003.pdf.

4   *Id.* Table 10.10b (Dec. 2008), http://www.ebri.org/pdf/publications/books/databook/DB.Chapter%2010.pdf; *id.* Table 27.4 (Oct. 2008), http://www.ebri.org/pdf/publications/books/databook/DB.Chapter%2027.pdf.

5   29 U.S.C. §§ 1001–1461 (2006). The term "ERISA" as used herein refers only to the labor law provisions of the statute, even though Title II of the original legislation contained extensive amendments to the Internal Revenue Code.

6   I.R.C. §§ 401–424 (2006). Throughout this book, citations to the Internal Revenue Code will be provided where there is a close tax-law counterpart to ERISA's labor provisions.

markedly different.[7] Part IV takes up the additional requirements that the Internal Revenue Code imposes as prerequisites to the favorable tax treatment accorded qualified retirement savings (Chapter 10) and employer-sponsored health care (Chapter 11).

An earlier version of Parts I–III was prepared for the Federal Judicial Center to provide a resource for federal judges handling ERISA cases, which are legion and frequently complex.[8] That function focused the resulting monograph on the kinds of cases and issues most frequently presented to the federal courts.[9] Because tax issues pertaining to employee benefit plans are generally resolved administratively and only rarely come before the courts, they were not addressed in the original study. Outside the courthouse, however, tax law rules have an enormous influence that largely determines the structure and scope of any employer plan (considered singly) and of the entire employment-based pension and health insurance systems of the United States. For that reason, the tax controls addressed in Part IV, while infrequently raised in litigation, are pivotally important to professionals involved in benefit plan design and to anyone seeking to understand the strengths and weaknesses of our semi-private (i.e., massively tax-subsidized) social insurance system.

A. BENEFIT PLAN VARIETIES[10]

Employee benefit plans are categorized in a number of different ways, according to the characteristics of the program. Those characteristics determine the extent of governmental regulation of the program under both ERISA and the tax Code, and so a brief benefit plan typology is essential background.

The type of benefit available under the plan affords the most fundamental basis for classification. ERISA applies only to certain employee benefit plans.[11] The statute defines an employee benefit plan as "an employee welfare benefit plan or an employee pension benefit plan or a plan which is both an employee welfare benefit plan

---

7   In contrast to unified public administration of the qualified plan rules by the Internal Revenue Service, suits by plan participants and beneficiaries (i.e., private enforcement) are the dominant mode of implementing ERISA. *See* ERISA § 502(a), 29 U.S.C. § 1132(a) (2006).

8   In the twelve-month period ending March 31, 2006, 11,391 civil actions under ERISA were commenced in the U.S. district courts, constituting 4.1 percent of all new civil cases. Moreover, ERISA suits were the third largest category of statutory actions commenced during the period, after employment discrimination suits and prisoner civil rights cases. Administrative Office of the U.S. Courts, Federal Judicial Caseload Statistics, Mar. 31, 2006, at 42–44, Table C-2. Over the same twelve-month period, ERISA cases contributed about 2.6 percent of the civil appeals filed in the U.S. Courts of Appeals (5.5 percent if prisoner petitions are excluded). *Id.* at 30–31, Table B-7 (assuming "Other Labor" category of private cases involving federal question jurisdiction is predominately composed of ERISA suits).

9   PETER J. WIEDENBECK, ERISA IN THE COURTS (GPO 2008).

10 The discussion in this section is adapted from PETER J. WIEDENBECK & RUSSELL K. OSGOOD, CASES AND MATERIALS ON EMPLOYEE BENEFITS 132–37 (1996), and is reprinted with permission of West, a Thomson Reuters business.

11 ERISA § 4(a), 29 U.S.C. § 1003(a) (2006).

and an employee pension benefit plan."[12] A program that systematically defers cash compensation until termination of employment (or longer) is an *ERISA pension plan*,[13] while a program that provides any of certain specifically listed benefits is a *welfare plan*, whether the benefit is provided on a current or deferred basis.[14] Health insurance is by far the most costly welfare benefit; other types of welfare benefits include life insurance, disability insurance, and severance pay.[15] Because the definitions of "pension plan" and "welfare plan" are not exhaustive, there is a third category of employee benefits entirely beyond ERISA's reach—any nonpension employee benefit that is not enumerated in the definition of welfare plan.[16]

Whether the program receives preferential income tax treatment provides a second ground for classification. A *qualified* deferred compensation plan obtains the advantage of tax deferral by satisfying numerous conditions; if those conditions are not met, the program is a *nonqualified* arrangement, and the employer's deduction must await inclusion of the benefits in the employee's gross income.[17] Certain types of welfare benefits can also receive preferential tax treatment, typically in the form of outright tax exemption rather than deferral. Both the value of the insurance coverage and the amount of any proceeds received under an employer-provided health care plan may be entirely tax-free; employer-provided group-term life insurance may qualify for similarly advantageous treatment.[18] In addition to such "qualified" welfare benefits, tax exemption is granted to some benefits that ERISA does not regulate, such as educational assistance programs and employer-provided parking or transportation benefits.[19] In each instance, favorable tax treatment does not depend solely on the type of benefit; it is also conditioned on satisfaction of various criteria prescribed by the Internal Revenue Code. Consequently, benefits provided under a program that fails to meet the tax law's requirements are taxable in-kind compensation.

---

12 ERISA § 3(3), 29 U.S.C. § 1002(3) (2006).

13 ERISA § 3(2)(A), 29 U.S.C. § 1002(2)(A) (2006). *See infra* Chapter 2C.

14 ERISA § 3(1), 29 U.S.C. § 1002(1) (2006). *See infra* Chapter 2C.

15 Some welfare benefits, such as employer-provided group-term life insurance, are received by more workers than health care, but are far less expensive. For a comparison of the cost and coverage of health care and other benefits, see Employee Benefit Research Institute, EBRI Databook on Employee Benefits, Table 3.2c (May 2009), http://www.ebri.org/pdf/publications/books/databook/DB.Chapter%2003.pdf; *id.* Table 4.1a (July 2008), http://www.ebri.org/pdf/publications/books/databook/DB.Chapter%2004.pdf; U.S. Department of Labor, Bureau of Labor Statistics, National Compensation Survey: Employee Benefits in Private Industry, March 2007, at 5 (2007), http://www.bls.gov/ncs/ebs/sp/ebsm0006.pdf.

16 ERISA §§ 4(a), 3(1)–(3), 29 U.S.C. §§ 1003(a), 1002(1)–(3) (2006). *See infra* Chapter 2C.

17 *Compare* I.R.C. § 404(a)(1)–(3) (2006) (current deduction for contributions to qualified pension, annuity, profit-sharing, or stock bonus plans), *with id.* § 404(a)(5) (nonqualified arrangements). For an overview of the tax treatment of qualified deferred compensation, see *infra* Chapter 1D; the intricate qualification conditions that must be satisfied to obtain favorable tax treatment are explored *infra* Chapter 10.

18 I.R.C. § 106(a) (2006) (health care coverage), *id.* § 105(b) (2006) (health care proceeds), *id.* § 79 (2006) (group-term life insurance coverage), *id.* § 101(a) (2006) (life insurance proceeds). The tax treatment of employer-provided health care is examined in detail *infra* Chapter 11.

19 I.R.C. § 127 (2006) (educational assistance programs), *id.* § 132(a), (f) (2006) (qualified transportation fringe).

Turning specifically to deferred compensation, the most important determinant of both labor law and tax law regulation is the plan's status as either a defined benefit or a defined contribution plan. A *defined contribution plan* (also known as an "individual account plan" in ERISA's lexicon) means a plan "which provides for an individual account for each participant and for benefits based solely on the amount contributed to the participant's account, and any income, expenses, gains and losses, and any forfeitures of accounts of other participants which may be allocated to such participant's account."[20] Any other sort of deferred compensation program is a *defined benefit plan.*[21] Contributions or benefits need not be set at a stated dollar amount to be "defined"; rather, the plan need only specify a definite formula (which may depend on compensation level, length of service, age, or other factors) for allocating contributions among participants (in the case of a defined contribution plan) or for determining benefits (in the case of a defined benefit plan).[22] The distinction between defined contribution and defined benefit plans is keyed to an important practical difference—whether the employee or the employer (respectively) bears the risk of investment performance. Under a defined contribution plan, the employee is entitled only to the balance in his or her account. Accordingly, the amount of deferred compensation received is diminished by poor rates of return and declines in asset values (possibly impairing the employee's standard of living in retirement), while high yields and asset appreciation increase the employee's wealth. In contrast, the risks and rewards of investment performance fall primarily on the employer under a defined benefit plan.[23] That is, a defined benefit plan is an employer's commitment to make specified future payments; the employer is contractually obligated to make those payments even if the assets set aside to finance them prove to be inadequate. In many respects, defined benefit plans are subject to much more intensive regulation than defined contribution plans.[24]

Among deferred compensation arrangements, the broad categories of defined benefit and defined contribution plans are subdivided further. The Internal Revenue Code provides for qualified pension, profit-sharing, stock bonus, and annuity plans. It is essential to understand that a pension plan within the meaning of the tax law is not the same as a pension plan as defined by ERISA. A *pension plan* in tax usage is "a plan established and maintained by an employer primarily to provide systematically for the payment of . . . benefits to his employees over a period of years, usually for life, after retirement";[25] therefore, it is also a pension plan under ERISA. The ERISA category, however, is broader, including also most profit-sharing, stock bonus, and annuity plans. Compounding confusion is the fact that a pension plan (tax Code sense) may be

---

20   ERISA § 3(34), 29 U.S.C. § 1002(34) (2006); *see* I.R.C. § 414(c) (2006).
21   ERISA § 3(35), 29 U.S.C. § 1002(35) (2006); *see* I.R.C. § 414(j) (2006).
22   *See* Treas. Reg. § 1.401-1(b)(1) (as amended in 1976).
23   In the case of an underfunded plan of an insolvent employer, the Pension Benefit Guaranty Corporation (PBGC) will make good on most pension promises (cost spreading through an insurance mechanism), but employees with large or recently enhanced pension claims may bear part of the loss. And when an overfunded qualified plan is terminated, as much as 50 percent of the excess assets may be claimed by the IRS or the participants. *See infra* Chapter 9.
24   These additional requirements are addressed *infra* Chapters 7B and 9.
25   Treas. Reg. § 1.401-1(b)(1)(i) (as amended in 1976).

of either the defined benefit or defined contribution type. A fundamental difference between a pension plan (tax Code sense) and a profit-sharing or stock bonus plan has to do with the timing of distributions: pension plans must be designed to provide retirement income, while profit-sharing and stock bonus plans may permit in-service distributions after the passage of a fixed number of years or the attainment of a stated age.[26] Today, profit-sharing and stock bonus plans generally provide for distributions upon separation from service or retirement, and so they too are pension plans in the ERISA sense. But in the original intendment of the tax laws, pension plans were conceived as retirement savings vehicles, while profit-sharing and stock bonus plans were seen as shorter-term deferred compensation programs.

A *money purchase pension plan* is a defined contribution plan that requires specified annual contributions (usually a percentage of each participant's compensation) regardless of the employer's profits.[27] The money purchase plan is, in most respects, the simplest qualified deferred compensation arrangement, the "plain vanilla" retirement plan. A *profit-sharing plan* is also a defined contribution arrangement, but the amount contributed may be geared to profits or left to the discretion of the board of directors; indeed, annual contributions are not required, and contributions can be made even if the employer has no current or accumulated profits or is a tax-exempt (nonprofit) organization.[28] The plan must, however, provide a definite formula for allocating any contributions among participants' accounts. A *stock bonus plan* can be a discretionary contribution arrangement like a profit-sharing plan, except that it provides distributions in the form of employer stock.[29] A profit-sharing or stock bonus plan may include a *cash-or-deferred arrangement* (commonly known as a *CODA* or *401(k) plan*) that allows participants to contribute a portion of their pay to the deferred compensation plan or take it all in cash. If the plan is properly structured (i.e., if it meets the requirements of a "qualified" cash-or-deferred arrangement, as specified in I.R.C. § 401(k)), participants are not treated as having constructively received amounts they contribute, and so tax is deferred until distribution.[30]

Two types of formulae are commonly used to specify the amount of the retirement annuity due (i.e., to "define" the benefit) under a defined benefit pension plan. A *unit credit plan* explicitly takes into account job tenure with a three-factor formula: the benefit at retirement age is defined as the product of (1) a service factor (usually either the participant's total years of service with the employer or years of participation in

---

26   *Compare id.* § 1.401-1(b)(1)(i) (first sentence), *with* § 1.401-1(b)(ii) (second sentence). The rule that in-service distributions are prohibited under a pension plan, as defined for tax purposes, is subject to a statutory exception, which was enacted in 2006 to facilitate phased retirement programs. I.R.C. § 401(a)(36) (2006) provides that a pension plan can be qualified even if it permits distributions to be made to an employee who has attained age 62 and who is still employed. Corresponding language was added to the definition of a pension plan for purposes of ERISA (ERISA § 3(2)(A), 29 U.S.C. § 1002(2)(A) (2006) (final sentence)), but because of the greater breadth of the ERISA category, that amendment was probably unnecessary.

27   Treas. Reg. § 1.401-1(b)(1)(i) (as amended in 1976).

28   *Id.* § 1.401-1(b)(1)(ii); I.R.C. § 401(a)(27) (2006).

29   Treas. Reg. § 1.401-1(b)(1)(iii) (as amended in 1976); I.R.C. §§ 401(a)(23), 409(h) (2006).

30   I.R.C. § 402(e)(3) (2006).

the plan), (2) a stated percentage (typically in the range of 1 percent to 3 percent), and (3) a specified measure of compensation. The compensation measure is sometimes career average compensation, but more often it is computed over a shorter period— frequently three to five years—that yields the maximum average (called highest average compensation) or that immediately precedes separation from service (called final average compensation). In contrast, a *flat benefit plan* uses a two-factor formula, specifying the benefit at normal retirement age as the product of (1) a specified measure of compensation (which again may be career average, highest average, or final average), and (2) a stated percentage (typically in the range of 40 to 60 percent). The difference between flat benefit and unit credit formulae is really only a matter of degree, however, because under a flat benefit plan a minimum period of service (typically ten years or more) is invariably required to qualify for the full stated benefit, and the "flat" benefit is reduced proportionately for participants with fewer years of service.

Defined benefit plans present special problems relating to funding. ERISA requires that the employer's commitment to pay specified benefits in the future be backed up by a systematic savings program in the present. Because the amount that will become due is generally contingent on future events (such as final or career average compensation, total length of service, and survival to retirement), the total amount that will become due must be estimated based on reasonable predictions of such factors, and a method must be used to allocate that estimated total cost over the participants' working years. That is, contributions under a defined benefit plan are not specified in the plan (as they are in a defined contribution plan), but must be determined actuarially.

Another important feature of defined benefit plans is the ability to grant or increase benefits retroactively; benefits may be granted based on periods of service prior to institution of the plan. For example, the service factor under a unit credit formula may use total years of service with the employer, both before and after the plan is established, rather than years of participation. The grant of such *past-service credit* necessarily creates an immediate unfunded liability, which the plan's actuarial funding method, as regulated by ERISA's minimum funding rules, must redress.

An *annuity plan* is, in effect, a pension plan (tax law meaning) that is funded by the purchase of annuity contracts from an insurance company rather than by contributions to a trust. Accordingly, to receive preferential tax treatment, an annuity plan must, in general, satisfy all the qualification requirements applicable to pension plans other than those pertaining to the terms and funding of the trust.[31]

The organizational chart in Figure 1-1 (following page) presents an overview of the main types of employee benefit arrangements, categorized according to distinctions in treatment under ERISA and the Internal Revenue Code. (It is oversimplified in some respects; for example, similar subcategories apply to nonqualified pension plans.)

---

31   I.R.C. §§ 403(a), 404(a)(2) (2006). A qualified annuity plan of the sort described in the text is a generally available qualified plan. It must be distinguished from a "403(b) annuity" (also known as a "tax-sheltered annuity"), which is a special retirement savings program subject to relaxed requirements that may be offered to employees of tax-exempt educational or charitable organizations, as well as state and local government educational organization (e.g., public school) employees. *Id.* § 403(b).

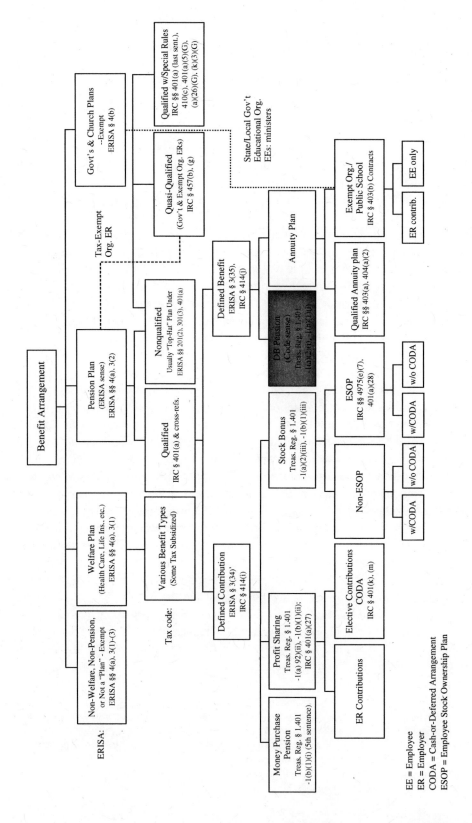

Benefit Arrangement

ERISA:

Non-Welfare, Non-Pension, or Not a "Plan" - Exempt
ERISA §§ 4(a), 3(1)-(3)

Welfare Plan
(Health Care, Life Ins., etc.)
ERISA §§ 4(a), 3(1)

Pension Plan
(ERISA sense)
ERISA §§ 4(a), 3(2)

Gov't & Church Plans
--Exempt
ERISA § 4(b)

Tax-Exempt
Org. ER

Tax code:

Various Benefit Types
(Some Tax Subsidized)

Qualified
IRC § 401(a) & cross-refs.

Nonqualified
Usually "Top-Hat" Plan Under
ERISA §§ 201(2), 301(3), 401(a)

Quasi-Qualified
(Gov't & Exempt Org. ERs)
IRC § 457(b), (g)

Qualified w/Special Rules
--Exempt
IRC §§ 401(a) (last sent.),
410(c), 401(a)(5)(G),
(a)(26)(G), (k)(3)(G)

State/Local Gov't
Educational Org.
EEs: ministers

Defined Contribution
ERISA § 3(34)'
IRC § 414(i)

Defined Benefit
ERISA § 3(35),
IRC § 414(j)

Annuity Plan

DB Pension
(Code sense)
Treas. Reg. § 1.401
-1(a)(2)(i), -1(b)(1)(i)

Exempt Org./
Public School
IRC § 403(b) Contracts

Money Purchase
Pension
Treas. Reg. § 1.401
-1(b)(1)(i) (5th sentence)

Profit Sharing
Treas. Reg. § 1.401
-1(a) 92)(ii), -1(b)(1)(ii);
IRC § 401(a)(27)

Stock Bonus
Treas. Reg. § 1.401
-1(a)(2)(iii), -1(b)(1)(iii)

Qualified Annuity plan
IRC §§ 403(a), 404(a)(2)

ER contrib.

EE only

ER Contributions

Elective Contributions
CODA
IRC § 401(k), (m)

Non-ESOP

ESOP
IRC §§ 4975(e)(7),
401(a)(28)

w/CODA

w/o CODA

w/CODA

w/o CODA

EE = Employee
ER = Employer
CODA = Cash-or-Deferred Arrangement
ESOP = Employee Stock Ownership Plan

The statutory citations provide support for the indicated classifications; they are not intended to designate the regulatory regime that applies to each category (the subject of the remainder of this book). Special shading is applied to defined benefit pension plans to indicate that this type of retirement savings program is subject to intensive regulation to ensure that adequate funds will be available to pay promised benefits (*see* Chapter 9).

Another important characteristic used to categorize benefit plans is the distinction between single-employer plans and multiemployer plans. A *multiemployer plan* is a plan to which more than one employer is required to contribute that is maintained pursuant to a collective bargaining agreement with more than one employer. For this purpose, all businesses that are under common control are treated as one employer.[32] Any plan that is not a multiemployer plan is called a *single-employer plan*, even if several legally distinct entities contribute.[33] A plan may be classified as a single-employer plan because it is, in fact, maintained by only one employer; because it is maintained by multiple employers under common control; or because unrelated multiple employers contribute to a plan that is not the product of collective bargaining. Multiemployer plans grant contributions or benefits for service with any participating employer and are frequently sponsored by unions representing workers in industries such as the construction trades, where workers change employers frequently. Multiemployer plans, although well adapted to employment patterns in certain industries, present special challenges for funding.

B. ERISA'S PATTERN OF REGULATION

ERISA implicitly prescribes four levels of employee benefit regulation. First, certain employer-provided benefits are exempt from federal regulation, either because they are not provided pursuant to a "plan, fund or program," or because they are of a kind that does not fit the description of a pension or welfare benefit.[34] Congress also stipulated that governmental and church plans are to be free of federal oversight, presumably to ease intergovernmental relations (comity) and prevent entanglement.[35]

---

32 ERISA § 3(37), 29 U.S.C. § 1002(37) (2006); *see* I.R.C. § 414(f) (2006).

33 ERISA § 3(41), 29 U.S.C. § 1002(41) (2006).

34 *See infra* Chapter 2.

35 ERISA §§ 3(32), (33), 4(b)(1), (2), 29 U.S.C. §§ 1002(32), (33), 1003(b)(1), (2) (2006); Church Plan Parity and Entanglement Protection Act, Pub. L. No. 106-244, 114 Stat. 499 (2000). In addition to its federalism concerns, Congress also observed that underfunded governmental plans pose less threat to workers' financial security, since public employers have recourse to the tax power to make good on their benefit promises. *See* Rose v. Long Island R.R. Pension Plan, 828 F.2d 910, 914 (2d Cir. 1987). In 1996, however, Congress imposed advance funding as a condition on the favorable tax treatment of certain state and local government retirement plans. I.R.C. § 457(g) (2006). Also expressly excepted from ERISA are unfunded excess benefit plans, which are arrangements maintained for the exclusive purpose of providing pension benefits that exceed the Internal Revenue Code's limits on the amount of deferred compensation that may be provided under a qualified retirement plan. ERISA §§ 3(36), 4(b)(5), 29 U.S.C. §§ 1002(36), 1003(b)(5) (2006).

Although entirely beyond ERISA's reach, benefits in this first category are permissible subjects of state or local regulation because ERISA's preemption clause also does not apply.[36]

The lowest level of federal regulation constrains the administration of all employee benefit plans, both pension and welfare, in three respects. First, reporting and disclosure rules mandate the collection and dissemination of information concerning plan terms and finances to the Secretary of Labor and the participants and beneficiaries.[37] Second, plan fiduciaries are held to exacting standards of conduct derived from trust law.[38] Third, state regulation of pension and welfare plans is preempted, and federal courts are granted exclusive jurisdiction to enforce ERISA's requirements (including fiduciary duties), as well as jurisdiction concurrent with state courts over suits by a participant or beneficiary to enforce the terms of the plan.[39]

Additional requirements apply to pension plans, which provide retirement income or the deferral of income until the termination of covered employment or beyond.[40] These plans are subject to complex, intensive regulation, including minimum standards governing certain terms of the deferred compensation program.[41] The minimum standards generally prevent employers from imposing age or service conditions on plan membership that are more exacting than the attainment of age 21 and completion of one year of service.[42] The minimum standards also demand (among other things) that benefits derived from employer contributions become nonforfeitable within a reasonable period (often five years),[43] that a participant's spouse receive certain protections in the event of death or divorce,[44] and that a participant's interest in the plan be inalienable.[45]

The most stringent regulation is reserved for defined benefit pension plans. Over and above the foregoing, defined benefit pension plans must provide minimum rates of benefit accrual,[46] satisfy minimum funding standards,[47] and comply with the Pension

---

36   ERISA § 514(a), 29 U.S.C. § 1144(a) (2006).
37   ERISA §§ 101–111, 29 U.S.C. §§ 1020–1031 (2006).
38   ERISA §§ 401(a), 404, 406, 29 U.S.C. §§ 1101(a), 1104, 1106 (2006).
39   ERISA §§ 502, 514, 29 U.S.C. §§ 1132, 1144 (2006).
40   ERISA § 3(2)(A), 29 U.S.C. § 1002(2)(A) (2006).
41   ERISA §§ 3(3), 4(a), 201–211, 301–305, 29 U.S.C. §§ 1002(3), 1003(a), 1051–1061, 1081–1085 (2006).
42   ERISA § 202(a)(1)(A), 29 U.S.C. § 1052(a)(1)(A) (2006); *see* I.R.C. § 410(a) (2006) (corresponding tax qualification condition). Exceptions are discussed *infra* Chapter 7 note 2 and accompanying text.
43   ERISA § 203, 29 U.S.C. § 1053 (2006); *see* I.R.C. § 411 (2006) (corresponding tax qualification condition).
44   ERISA §§ 205, 206(d)(3), 29 U.S.C. §§ 1055, 1056(d)(3) (2006); *see* I.R.C. §§ 401(a)(11), (a)(13)(B), 414(p), 417 (2006) (corresponding tax qualification conditions).
45   ERISA § 206(d)(1), 29 U.S.C. § 1056(d)(1) (2006); *see* I.R.C. § 401(a)(13) (2006) (corresponding tax qualification condition).
46   ERISA § 204, 29 U.S.C. § 1054 (2006); *see* I.R.C. § 411(b) (2006) (corresponding tax qualification condition).
47   ERISA §§ 301(a)(8), 302–305, 29 U.S.C. §§ 1081(a)(8), 1082–1085 (2006); *see* I.R.C. §§ 412, 430–432, 436 (2006) (corresponding tax law funding rules).

Benefit Guaranty Corporation (PBGC) termination insurance program,[48] which includes restrictions on plan termination.[49]

The morphogenesis of this graduated system of regulation is straightforward. Congress was primarily concerned about pensions and was persuaded to impose detailed substantive regulation of certain key terms of deferred compensation programs (hereafter, pension content controls). Among pension plans, defined benefit arrangements required greater oversight because of the actuarial funding challenge. Absent systematic advance funding, payment of the stipulated retirement annuity is contingent on the long-term financial health of the employer; funding rules and the PBGC insurance system secure the employer's pension promise. With a defined contribution plan, such security is unnecessary because full performance is rendered upon contribution to the participant's account (i.e., the participant bears the investment risk). Welfare plans generally involve current, rather than deferred, compensation, and so the risks of defeated expectations and employer default are less severe. Consequently, Congress declined to regulate the content of welfare plans,[50] but mandated disclosure of plan terms and finances, imposed uniform fiduciary obligations, and promulgated a detailed scheme of federal judicial enforcement. This three-pronged approach equips participants with tools to safeguard their own interests. Thus, ERISA facilitates private monitoring of privately constituted welfare plans, while pension plans are subject to both private monitoring and limited content regulation.

ERISA's four-tiered system of regulation is modified in two instances, to adapt federal law to the special characteristics of (1) executive deferred compensation programs (discussed *infra* Chapter 2D), and (2) insurance-funded pension and welfare plans. Insurance-funded plans get special treatment to accommodate federal benefit plan regulation to paramount state insurance law. ERISA's minimum funding requirements do not apply to a pension plan funded *exclusively* by the purchase of level-premium individual or group insurance or annuity contracts under which benefits are guaranteed by a state-licensed insurance company.[51] If pension benefits are partially insurer-guaranteed, then funding rules apply, but ERISA's fiduciary responsibility standards do not cover the insurance company's investment and asset-management activities under such a "guaranteed benefit policy."[52] In the case of an insured welfare plan (a health plan financed by the employer's purchase of a group medical insurance policy, for example), federal welfare standards (i.e., reporting and disclosure, fiduciary

---

48   ERISA § 4021(a), (b)(1), 29 U.S.C. § 1321(a), (b)(1) (2006).

49   ERISA §§ 4041, 4041A, 29 U.S.C. §§ 1341, 1341a (2006).

50   In recent years, Congress has responded to public concern over gaps in health insurance coverage by twice extending ERISA to impose certain limited content controls on health care plans. *See infra* Chapter 1 notes 100–105 and accompanying text.

51   ERISA § 301(a)(2), (b), 29 U.S.C. § 1081(a)(2), (b) (2006); *see* I.R.C. § 412(e)(3) (2006); Treas. Reg. § 1.412(i)-1 (1980).

52   ERISA § 401(b)(2), 29 U.S.C. § 1101(b)(2) (2006). *See* John Hancock Mut. Life Ins. Co. v. Harris Trust & Sav. Bank, 510 U.S. 86 (1993) (construing "guaranteed benefit policy" as requiring the allocation of investment risk to the insurer, and concluding that ERISA's fiduciary rules apply to assets held in an insurance company's general account under a participating group annuity contract).

responsibility, and enforcement) are not relaxed, but preemption is limited, with the result that state regulation of the terms of the insurance contract may survive.[53]

C. ERISA'S PRINCIPAL POLICIES

The pattern of benefit plan regulation described above is a response to a number of perceived injustices and breakdowns in the delivery of retirement and insurance benefits as employment compensation. The tax-subsidized but largely unregulated regime that preceded ERISA frequently frustrated workers' expectations, if not their legal rights. ERISA, as one key participant has observed, "was, at its core, a 'reasonable expectations' bill. It gave an ordinary employee the assured right to receive what a reasonable person in his boots would have expected in the circumstances. Primarily, it was a consumer protection bill."[54] This goal of consumer protection is advanced by three of ERISA's general policies: promoting informed financial decision making; preventing mismanagement and abuse of benefit programs; and protecting the reliance interests of plan participants and beneficiaries. At the same time, Congress embraced a fourth policy: preserving substantial employer control over plan sponsorship and design. These four principal policies are briefly described in this section. The tensions among them, however, are not so easily resolved. Subsequent chapters will show that ERISA litigation frequently calls on the federal courts to reconcile conflicts among these competing policies.

Promoting Informed Financial Decision Making

Mandatory disclosure rules are a central component of ERISA. Disclosure of plan terms and finances promotes economic efficiency by giving participants and beneficiaries the information they need to accommodate their personal financial affairs to the employer's program, as, for example, in determining their needs for additional savings or insurance. ERISA requires that the plan administrator supply participants and beneficiaries with a summary plan description (SPD), which "shall be written in a manner calculated to be understood by the average plan participant, and shall be sufficiently accurate and comprehensive to reasonably apprise such participants and

---

53 ERISA § 514(b)(2), 29 U.S.C. § 1144(b)(2) (2006) (the insurance "savings clause"). *Compare* Metro. Life Ins. Co. v. Massachussetts, 471 U.S. 724 (1985) (state law requiring medical insurance contracts to provide minimum mental health coverage applies to group health insurance policies purchased under employer plans), *and* FMC Corp. v. Holliday, 498 U.S. 52 (1990) (state automobile insurance statute barring subrogation from an accident victim's tort recovery cannot be applied to the reimbursement claim of a self-insured health care plan), *with* Pilot Life Ins. Co. v. Dedeaux, 481 U.S. 41 (1987) (state cause of action for bad-faith handling of insurance claims preempted, notwithstanding the insurance savings clause, based on congressional intent that ERISA's civil enforcement scheme be exclusive).

54 Frank Cummings, *ERISA: The Reasonable Expectations Bill*, 65 Tax Notes 880, 881 (1994).

beneficiaries of their rights and obligations under the plan."[55] Congress made the SPD the participants' principal source of information on plan content for the following reasons:

> It is grossly unfair to hold an employee accountable for acts which disqualify him from benefits, if he had no knowledge of these acts, or if these conditions were stated in a misleading or incomprehensible manner in plan booklets. Subcommittee findings were abundant in establishing that an average plan participant, even where he has been furnished an explanation of his plan's provisions, often cannot comprehend them because of the technicalities and complexities of the language used.[56]

Facilitating informed decision making is a pervasive goal of ERISA, extending far beyond the mandatory disclosure rules. Many of ERISA's core requirements of pension plan content (e.g., minimum standards governing vesting and funding) can be understood as a response to the problem of information overload (Chapters 7 and 9).

> For most workers, the cost of evaluating the specialized terms and particular finances of numerous alternative plans (associated with different employment opportunities) may exceed the benefit of a marginally more valuable pension. Information costs may be reduced by limited standardization (i.e., restricting the variance) of key contract terms. By reducing job search costs, such content regulation may increase economic efficiency.

> From the information cost perspective, pension content controls complement the disclosure regime. Disclosure provides access to information, while content controls limit the volume of information to a manageable level. Together, they facilitate career and financial planning.[57]

ERISA standardizes certain *express* terms of the pension promise, but does not stop there. In effect, all *implied* terms of *both* pension and welfare plans are standardized as well. By imposing uniform fiduciary obligations and authorizing the development of a

---

55   ERISA § 102(a), 29 U.S.C. § 1022(a) (2006).

56   S. REP. NO. 93-127, at 11 (1973), *reprinted in* 1 SUBCOMM. ON LABOR OF THE S. COMM. ON LABOR AND PUBLIC WELFARE, 94TH CONG., LEGISLATIVE HISTORY OF THE EMPLOYEE RETIREMENT INCOME SECURITY ACT OF 1974, at 587, 597 (Comm. Print 1976) [hereinafter ERISA LEGISLATIVE HISTORY].

   In *Central Laborers' Pension Fund v. Heinz*, 541 U.S. 739 (2004), the Court construed a plan amendment placing additional restrictions on the receipt of pension benefits as a prohibited reduction in benefits, in part to protect retirement planning decisions:

   > Heinz worked and accrued retirement benefits under a plan with terms allowing him to supplement retirement income by certain employment, and he was being reasonable if he relied on those terms in planning his retirement. The 1998 amendment undercut any such reliance, paying retirement income only if he accepted a substantial curtailment of his opportunity to do the kind of work he knew.

   Id. at 744–45.

57   Peter J. Wiedenbeck, *Implementing ERISA: Of Policies and "Plans,"* 72 WASH. U. L.Q. 559, 574 (1994).

federal common law of benefit plans to replace preempted state law, the unwritten terms of the benefit program are standardized as well (Chapters 4 and 6).[58]

Preventing Mismanagement and Abuse

ERISA imposes uniform federal fiduciary obligations to control mismanagement and abuse of employee benefit programs. While drawing on general principles of trust law, ERISA's fiduciary standards include two fundamental departures from prevailing state law. First, the statutory definition of fiduciary extends far beyond state law trustees, imposing standards of competence and fair dealing on anyone who has or exercises any discretionary authority in the administration of the plan or the management of its assets, and on investment advisors as well.[59] Second, ERISA voids any attempt to relax its stringent fiduciary obligations through the inclusion of exculpatory clauses in the plan,[60] even though such indulgences are common and effective under state law.

Federal fiduciary standards were designed to work in combination with improved disclosure of plan finances and powerful enforcement tools to stem misconduct in plan administration.[61] Particularized reporting of transactions between the plan and certain related parties would give participants and the Labor Department information needed to assert workers' rights,[62] while the federal courts, armed with broad remedial powers and supported by nationwide service of process, would grant effective relief.[63] Moreover, employees would be free to assert their rights without fear of employer retaliation by discharge, demotion, or other adverse employment action.[64]

---

58 *Id.* at 576.

59 ERISA § 3(21)(A), 29 U.S.C. § 1002(21)(A) (2006). *E.g.*, S. Rep. No. 93-127, at 29 (1973), *reprinted in* 1 ERISA Legislative History, *supra* Chapter 1 note 56, at 587, 615 (fiduciary responsibility provisions deemed necessary because "it is unclear whether the traditional law of trusts is applicable" to certain "plans, such as insured plans, that do not use the trust form as their mode of funding"). While the extension of fiduciary obligations to insurance and annuity plans was deliberate and well understood, including as fiduciaries all persons with any discretionary authority in plan administration (in addition to those who have a role in the management or disposition of assets) seems to have escaped congressional attention.

60 ERISA § 410(a), 29 U.S.C. § 1110(a) (2006). *See* S. Rep. No. 93-127, at 29 (1973), *reprinted in* 1 ERISA Legislative History, *supra* Chapter 1 note 56, at 587, 615.

61 *E.g.*, S. Rep. No. 93-127, at 27–28, 29 (1973) ("[W]ithout provisions . . . allowing ready access to both detailed information about the plan and to the courts, and without standards by which a participant can measure the fiduciary's conduct . . . he is not equipped to safeguard either his own rights or the plan assets,"), *reprinted in* 1 ERISA Legislative History, *supra* Chapter 1 note 56, at 587, 613–14, 615.

62 *Id.* at 27–28 (1973), *reprinted in* 1 ERISA Legislative History, *supra* Chapter 1 note 56, at 587, 613–14. *See* ERISA § 103(b)(3)(D), 29 U.S.C. § 1023(b)(3)(D) (2006).

63 *E.g.*, S. Rep. No. 93-127, at 35 (1973) ("[R]emove jurisdictional and procedural obstacles which in the past appear to have hampered effective enforcement of fiduciary responsibilities under state law."), *reprinted in* 1 ERISA Legislative History, *supra* Chapter 1 note 56, at 587, 621; Cummings, *supra* Chapter 1 note 54, at 881–82 (draftsman of ERISA recounts service-of-process problems under prior law).

64 *See* ERISA § 510, 29 U.S.C. § 1140 (2006).

Protecting Reliance

In the case of pension plans, ERISA goes beyond disclosure and regulation of fiduciary conduct to impose minimum standards for certain plan terms. Such substantive regulation ensures that the promise of a pension has some minimum content. Limited content control of pension plans has traditionally been justified as necessary to protect employee reliance interests.[65] But under a regime of mandatory disclosure, is reliance worthy of protection? If, for example, participants are made aware that the plan does not allow for vesting, no legitimate expectation is defeated when a pension is denied an employee terminated before retirement age, however long her service.

Minimum standards of pension plan content "protect" reliance only in the sense that they *prevent* reliance that might often be unwarranted. Hence, the justification for content regulation must lie in a concern that substantial numbers of plan participants would not make proper use of the information available to them. That concern may be well founded, for workers may misevaluate pension promises as a result of an innate bias in human judgment. Investigations in cognitive psychology yield evidence that people systematically underestimate the likelihood of the occurrence of low-probability, long-delayed events.[66] Underestimation of the risk of pension loss from factors such as forfeiture conditions, underfunding, fiduciary misconduct, or employer insolvency would cause workers to overvalue unregulated pension promises. Consistent overvaluation would permit employers to charge more for pension plan coverage, via reduced wages or other benefits, than such contingent retirement savings are really worth. Substantive regulation to reduce the risk of pension loss might bring the real worth of plan coverage into line with workers' inflated estimation, increasing their welfare and improving overall economic efficiency. From this standpoint, ERISA's pension plan content controls could be fairly viewed as an instance of consumer protection legislation;[67] disclosure being ineffective in this area, protection took the form of minimum standards of product quality, similar to automobile safety standards.

There is a second strand to ERISA's worker protections that is distinct from the effort to align expectations and reality. Curiously, ERISA contains elements of a forced savings system, even though plan sponsorship is voluntary, and public subsidy is available only through the Internal Revenue Code. ERISA's restriction on certain

---

65 The congressional findings include: "many employees with long years of employment are losing *anticipated* retirement benefits owing to lack of vesting provisions in such plans" and owing to the termination of plans before requisite funds have been accumulated, employees and their beneficiaries have been deprived of *anticipated* benefits; and that it is therefore desirable in the interests of employees and their beneficiaries . . . that minimum standards be provided assuring the equitable character of such plans and their financial soundness. ERISA § 2(a), 29 U.S.C. § 1001(a) (2006) (emphasis added).

66 *E.g.*, Cass R. Sunstein, *Legal Interference with Private Preferences*, 53 U. Chi. L. Rev. 1129, 1167 (1986); Cass R. Sunstein, *The Laws of Fear*, 115 Harv. L. Rev. 1119 (2002) (reviewing Paul Slovic, The Perception of Risk (2000)); Jeffrey J. Rachlinski, *The Uncertain Psychological Case for Paternalism*, 97 Nw. U. L. Rev. 1165 (2003); Amos Tversly & Daniel Kahneman, *Availability: A Heuristic for Judging Frequency and Probability*, in Judgment Under Uncertainty: Heuristics and Biases 179 (Daniel Kahneman et al. eds., 1982).

67 *See supra* text accompanying Chapter 1 note 54.

age and service conditions[68] ensures that employees who are otherwise eligible begin participation early, making it more likely that they will accumulate adequate retirement savings in spite of any youthful proclivity to over discount future support needs.[69] In addition, the anti-alienation requirement invalidates the sale or transfer of rights under the plan in an effort to prevent participants and beneficiaries from dissipating their savings prior to retirement.[70]

These two protective policies (preventing unwarranted reliance and forcing retirement savings) are fundamentally paternalistic. Paternalism is the conventional understanding of ERISA's primary purpose. Yet there is an alternative justification for limiting the variability of certain plan terms: promoting better decision making. As noted earlier, some standardization of key contract terms, such as vesting or funding, may be necessary to avoid information overload.[71] This information cost perspective views much of ERISA as an effort to facilitate individual career and financial planning, not override it. Many particular rules are subject to wildly divergent interpretations, according to whether they are understood as efforts to liberate or confine employee decision making.

Preserving Employer Autonomy

ERISA does not infringe on employers' freedom to choose whether to sponsor employee benefit programs. Because pension and welfare benefit plans are voluntary employment-based programs, employers will decline to offer retirement or health benefits if costs become too high. By virtue of this opt-out, the regulation of employee benefits entails a delicate balance—measures intended to improve the quality of pension and welfare benefit programs, if taken too far, deter some employers from providing such benefits at all. Hence the imposition of higher and higher standards, while ensuring first-rate coverage for some workers, would cause a larger and larger proportion of the U.S. labor force to receive nothing.[72] This cost/coverage trade-off sets the limits of legislation in this field, as the courts have recognized.[73]

The "minimum standards" approach sets a reliable baseline content for certain key pension plan provisions, such as vesting, that had repeatedly brought workers to grief.

---

68   *See supra* Chapter 1 note 42 and accompanying text.

69   *See* H.R. Rep. No. 93-807, at 43–44 (1974), *reprinted in* 2 ERISA Legislative History, *supra* Chapter 1 note 56, at 3115, 3163–64.

70   ERISA § 206(d)(1), 29 U.S.C. § 1056(d)(1) (2006); *see* I.R.C. § 401(a)(13) (2006).

71   *See supra* Chapter 1 notes 55–58 and accompanying text.

72   This point was made forcefully during Senate debate on ERISA. 119 Cong. Rec. 30,375 (1973) (remarks of Sen. Harrison Williams, principal Democratic cosponsor of pension reform legislation), *reprinted in* 2 ERISA Legislative History, *supra* Chapter 1 note 56, at 1776.

73   *See, e.g.,* Hozier v. Midwest Fasteners, Inc., 908 F.2d 1155, 1160 (3d Cir. 1990) ("Having made a fundamental decision not to require employers to provide *any* benefit plans, Congress was forced to balance its desire to regulate extant plans more extensively against the danger that increased regulation would deter employers from creating such plans in the first place."). *See also infra* Chapter 1 note 76.

These lower bounds can be surpassed or not, as the sponsor chooses, while other plan terms and practices are unconstrained. Most notably, neither the extent of workforce coverage nor the level of plan benefits is fixed by law.

The virtue of the minimum standards approach is the flexibility it preserves for plan sponsors—flexibility to tailor the plan to the unique needs and objectives of the business.[74] With flexibility comes variation and complexity, causing increased costs of plan administration and compliance. This is the vice of the minimum standards approach.[75] (In contrast, the lockstep, take-it-or-leave-it approach to deferred compensation—mandatory plan terms with voluntary employer participation—at least has the virtue of simplicity.) Many experts are worried that the costs of compliance with ERISA's minimum funding and termination insurance rules, which have been repeatedly tightened since the mid-1980s, have contributed to a marked decline in prevalence of defined benefit pension plans.

Supersession of state regulation—federal preemption—is an indispensable counterpart to the minimum standards approach. If state and local governments were permitted to impose additional controls on pension or welfare plans, benefit costs would increase under many plans, while their utility in serving employer personnel policies would diminish.

Policy Interactions

The importance of ERISA's four principal policies varies with the context, as shown by the increasing levels of regulation applied to welfare plans, defined contribution pension plans, and defined benefit pension plans. The absence of welfare plan content controls, for example, indicates that the protective policy (paternalism) has little force in this arena. The disclosure of plan terms and finances serves employees' information needs (as do uniform fiduciary standards), while preemption shields the employer from the costs of state-mandated benefits. With these tools, Congress promotes informed

---

74   As a result, plans can be designed to promote different personnel policies. Some employers may wish to provide an incentive to increase job tenure, thereby reducing recruitment and training costs, while other businesses (especially since the elimination of mandatory retirement) may want to limit job tenure, using the pension plan to ease out superannuated workers. Some pension plans are geared to providing a secure source of retirement income by accumulating regular contributions in a diversified investment portfolio for periodic distribution over the employee's retirement years, while others—such as profit-sharing and stock bonus plans— may provide a productivity incentive by making contributions dependent on firm output or profits, or by investing heavily in employer securities. *See* TERESA GHILARDUCCI, LABOR'S CAPITAL: THE ECONOMICS AND POLITICS OF PRIVATE PENSIONS 15–16, 20 (MIT Press 1992) (flexibility the main attraction of pensions for employers).

75   *E.g.*, Varity Corp. v. Howe, 516 U.S. 489 (1996). In interpreting ERISA's fiduciary duties "courts may have to take account of competing congressional purposes, such as Congress' desire to offer employees enhanced protection for their benefits, on the one hand, and, on the other, its desire not to create a system that is so complex that administrative costs, or litigation expenses, unduly discourage employers from offering welfare benefit plans in the first place." *Id.* at 497.

contracting with respect to welfare benefits, thereby facilitating private autonomy rather than restricting it.

The regulatory implications of these policy concerns are sometimes remarkably consistent. Preemption, for example, is supported both by the employer's interest in controlling costs and the employee's planning interest (via the standardization of implicit plan terms). Frequently, however, ERISA's policies interfere with rather than reinforce one another.[76] Where important problems were foreseen, Congress specially adjusted the balance between competing concerns. For instance, ERISA accommodates the traditional use of profit-sharing and stock bonus plans as a productivity incentive by relaxing generally applicable fiduciary duties (prudence and diversification) to permit concentrated investment in employer securities.[77] Other tensions must be resolved by the courts, as where fiduciary action advances the interests of the employer along with the interests of the participants and beneficiaries.

D. ERISA'S RELATION TO TAX QUALIFICATION

ERISA's graduated regulatory regime (*supra* Section B) applies to welfare and pension plans regardless of whether the program qualifies for preferential tax treatment. Most pension and health care plans are intended to garner special tax benefits— deferral in the case of pensions, and outright exemption in the case of health care. Such favored status is provided to encourage widespread pension and health insurance coverage, but the tax concessions come with strings attached. Numerous conditions must be satisfied to "qualify" for special tax treatment. In the case of retirement savings, some of those qualification conditions track ERISA's pension plan content controls. Indeed, apart from the PBGC insurance system, all the major substantive components of federal pension regulation are reproduced in the Internal Revenue Code, where they function as conditions on the preferential tax treatment granted qualified retirement plans. This section focuses on the overlap between ERISA's pension regulation and the tax Code's qualification criteria, with emphasis on the cause and extent of that correspondence.

---

76 *E.g.*, Mertens v. Hewitt Assocs., 508 U.S. 248, 262–63 (1993) ("There is, in other words, a 'tension between the primary [ERISA] goal of benefiting employees and the subsidiary goal of containing pension costs.'" (quoting Alessi v. Raybestos-Manhattan, Inc., 451 U.S. 504, 515 (1981)).

77 ERISA §§ 404(a)(2), 407(b)(1), (d)(3), 29 U.S.C. §§ 1104(a)(2), 1107(b)(1), (d)(3) (2006). In 2006, however, Congress altered the balance between retirement security and employer autonomy by requiring most defined contribution plans holding publicly traded employer securities to allow a participant who has at least three years of service to switch the investment of his account from employer securities to a diversified investment vehicle. Regardless of length of service, a participant must be given similar investment control over the portion of his account balance that is attributable to employee contributions or elective contributions under a 401(k) plan. ERISA § 204(j), 29 U.S.C. § 1054(j) (2006); *see* I.R.C. § 401(a)(35) (2006); *see also* I.R.C. §§ 401(a)(23), (a)(28), 409(h) (2006) (additional diversification requirements for qualified stock bonus and employee stock ownership plans).

The definition of a qualified plan is set forth in I.R.C. § 401(a)—the longest subsection of the Internal Revenue Code—which incorporates by reference much of the remainder of Subchapter D. Directly or indirectly, the definition of a qualified plan imposes hundreds of conditions. Although the qualification requirements are quite intricate, the operational tax rules are actually very simple.

There are three major components of the preferential tax treatment of qualified deferred compensation. First, the employer receives a current deduction (subject to certain limits) for amounts actually contributed to the plan.[78] Second, the trust that holds the plan assets is generally exempt from taxation on its investment income.[79] Third, any amount contributed on behalf of an individual employee is not included in gross income until actually distributed by the plan; upon distribution, trust earnings are taxable to the recipient as well.[80] In some circumstances, distributions may be eligible for further tax deferral if they are promptly reinvested in another qualified plan or an individual retirement account (IRA).[81] Because the employer is allowed a deduction even though the employee does not simultaneously report income, deferral is the essence of the qualified plan tax preference. In contrast, nonqualified plan contributions are subject to the "matching principle"—the employer's deduction must await inclusion by the employee.[82]

The magnitude of the tax deferral accorded qualified retirement plans is staggering: the annual federal revenue loss is roughly $100 billion. According to the Treasury, the net cost of the preferential treatment of qualified retirement plans is projected to be approximately $97 billion in fiscal year 2010 ($125 billion if IRAs and Keogh plans are included).[83] Going by congressional estimates, the figure is $111 billion for employer plans ($146 billion if IRAs and Keogh plans are included).[84] By either measure, the tax subsidy for qualified retirement savings is certainly one of the top two federal tax expenditures (the other being the exclusion of employer-provided health care benefits), and it may well be the largest. Presumably, tax deferral on such a grand scale is granted for some compelling public purpose. That purpose, principally, is to provide workers an incentive to accumulate an adequate level of retirement income.[85] Social Security alone affords only a base-level or subsistence-level standard of living

---

78   I.R.C. § 404(a)(1)–(3) (2006).
79   *Id.* § 501(a) (2006). Qualified trusts are subject to tax on any unrelated business taxable income, as provided in tax Code sections 511–514.
80   *Id.* §§ 83(e)(2), 402(a) (2006).
81   *Id.* § 402(c) (2006).
82   *Id.* § 404(a)(5) (2006); Albertson's Inc. v. Comm'r, 42 F.3d 537 (9th Cir. 1994).
83   Office of Mgmt. & Budget, Exec. Office of the President, Analytical Perspectives, Budget of the United States Government, Fiscal Year 2010, at 301 (2009), *available at* http://www.gpoaccess.gov/usbudget/fy10/pdf/spec.pdf.
84   Staff of the J. Comm. on Taxation, Estimates of Federal Tax Expenditures for Fiscal Years 2008–2012, at 57 (2008), *available at* http://www.jct.gov/publications.html?func=startdown&id=1192.
85   *See National Pension Policies: Private Pension Plans: Hearings Before the Subcomm. on Retirement Income and Employment of the H. Select Comm. on Aging*, 95th Cong. 228–50 (1978) (statement of Daniel I. Halperin, Tax Legislative Counsel, U.S. Department of the Treasury).

in retirement; middle- and upper-income workers must supplement their Social Security benefits in order to maintain their pre-retirement standard of living. Instead of relying on supplementation via private saving, the government intervenes to encourage accumulation through qualified plans in order to counteract an assumed bias in favor of current consumption.[86] Secondarily, Congress hopes that the qualified plan tax subsidy will promote economic growth by increasing investment and capital formation.

A subsidy is justifiable only to the extent that it induces behavior that would not otherwise occur—in this case, additional savings. The myriad conditions on the preferential tax treatment of qualified retirement savings represent attempts to properly target the tax subsidy to avoid wasted revenue. Some of those conditions ensure that the tax allowance benefits employees rather than the employer; some try to direct the subsidy to the group of employees who would not save on their own (generally lower-paid workers); and some try to restrict subsidized saving to use as retirement income (instead of being used to buy a house or send a child to college, for example).[87] The first of these objectives is shared with ERISA and explains the duplication of ERISA's pension provisions in the tax Code's qualification requirements.[88] The latter two objectives, which try to channel public assistance into additional *retirement* funds for that portion of the workforce that would not otherwise save enough, explain the many qualification conditions that have no ERISA counterparts.

The antidiscrimination norm is the paramount means to this end. A qualified retirement plan cannot discriminate in favor of highly compensated employees, either with respect to plan membership or the proportion of each participant's compensation provided as contributions or benefits.[89] This nondiscrimination principle is the central criterion for qualification because it attempts, through a covert redistribution mechanism, to channel the tax allowance into retirement savings that would not otherwise occur.[90] The nondiscrimination rules are a complex, awkward, and imperfect means of targeting the tax subsidy, however, because their efficacy depends upon variables to

---

86   ALICIA H. MUNNELL, THE ECONOMICS OF PRIVATE PENSIONS 50–51 (Brookings Inst. 1982); Deborah M. Weiss, *Paternalistic Pension Policy: Psychological Evidence and Economic Theory*, 58 U. CHI. L. REV. 1275 (1991); Peter J. Wiedenbeck, *Paternalism and Income Tax Reform*, 33 U. KAN. L. REV. 675, 684–85, 689–91 (1985).

87   Various tax rules restrict the timing of qualified plan distributions in an attempt to ensure that subsidized savings are neither dissipated before retirement nor amassed as a legacy to the next generation. *E.g.*, I.R.C. § 72(t) (2006) (additional tax on early distributions); *id.* § 401(a)(9) (2006) (minimum distributions required to prevent excessive deferral).

88   Conversely, preexisting tax qualification rules sometimes have a bearing on the interpretation of ERISA's labor law rules. Raymond B. Yates, M.D., P.C. Profit Sharing Plan v. Hendon, 541 U.S. 1, 13 (2004) ("Congress' objective was to harmonize ERISA with longstanding tax provisions.").

89   I.R.C. §§ 401(a)(3), 410(b) (2006) (coverage nondiscrimination); *id.* § 401(a)(4), (a)(5)(C), (*l*) (2006) (nondiscrimination in contributions or benefits).

90   *See infra* Chapter 10A, 10B. Bruce Wolk, *Discrimination Rules for Qualified Retirement Plans: Good Intentions Meet Economic Reality*, 70 VA. L. REV. 419, 429–33 (1984); Peter J. Wiedenbeck, *Nondiscrimination in Employee Benefits: False Starts and Future Trends*, 52 TENN. L. REV. 168, 246–49 (1985).

which they are not attuned, particularly the composition of the employer's workforce (factors such as the age, pay level, and savings proclivity of each worker).[91] In addition to nondiscrimination, other tax rules restrict the amount and duration of tax deferral in an effort to minimize wasted revenue, and some regulate the timing of pension plan distributions so that public assistance is devoted to *retirement* support instead of saving for other goals.[92] Because responsible stewardship of public money is the objective, this network of qualified retirement plan tax controls is distinct from, and applies in addition to, ERISA's pension content controls (and the tax qualification criteria that reiterate them), which protect workers whether their pension is subsidized or not.

Preferential tax treatment has also shaped the contours of U.S. health care financing, as described in Chapter 11. Unlike retirement savings, however, an overarching anti-discrimination norm has never emerged in the health care realm, despite the staggering revenue loss associated with the current system. (The tax expenditure associated with the exclusion of employer contributions for medical insurance premiums and medical care is estimated by the Treasury to be $155 billion in fiscal year 2010, or $137 billion according to congressional staff.[93]) Consequently, the tax rules applicable to health care plans largely mirror and reinforce ERISA's labor law standards. There are independent health care tax controls, but they are few.

E. NOTE ON COVERAGE

Before commencing an in-depth examination of employee benefit plan regulation, the limits on the scope of this study should be highlighted.

The subject of this book is the *federal* regulation of employee benefits. State or local law is not systematically addressed. As already noted, a benefit arrangement that does not satisfy ERISA's definition of either a welfare plan or a pension plan is a permissible subject of state or local regulation.[94] Thanks to preemption, state and local law is ordinarily irrelevant to welfare and pension plans, but some general state laws survive, and insured plans must contend with state insurance regulation.[95] In addition, under ERISA's governmental plan exception, welfare and pension benefit programs for employees of a state or local government are also left to the protection of state or local law.[96] On the tax side, special rules (including relaxed or alternative qualification requirements)

---

91   *See infra* Chapter 10B.
92   *See infra* Chapter 10C.
93   Exec. Office of the President, *supra* Chapter 1 note 83, at 301; Staff of the J. Comm. on Taxation, *supra* Chapter 1 note 84, at 56.
94   *See supra* Chapter 1 note 36 and accompanying text.
95   *See infra* Chapter 6B, 6E.
96   ERISA §§ 4(b), 3(32), 29 U.S.C. §§ 1003(b), 1002(32) (2006). The governmental plan exception also extends to Indian tribal governments and their subdivisions, agencies, and instrumentalities, provided that all plan participants are employees substantially all of whose services involve the performance of essential governmental functions and who are not engaged in commercial activities.

apply to governmental deferred compensation plans.[97] While sometimes mentioned in Chapter 10, these special tax regimes for government retirement programs are not examined comprehensively.

Apart from churches and church affiliates, charitable organizations are subject to ERISA's labor law requirements. Their deferred compensation programs may, however, obtain favorable tax treatment under somewhat more lenient standards than apply to taxable employers.[98] *See* Figure 1-1. As with state and local government retirement plans, these rules are alluded to in Chapter 10 but are not explored thoroughly.

The special rules applicable to multiemployer plans, both welfare and pension, are also beyond the scope of this book. In particular, multiemployer defined benefit pension plans are subject to minimum funding obligations that are distinct from the rules for single employer plans, and the PBGC termination insurance program operates differently.[99] In most other important respects, however, multiemployer plans are governed by the same federal labor and tax law rules as single employer plans.

Finally, it was observed in the description of ERISA's pattern of regulation that Congress mandated disclosure of plan terms and finances, imposed uniform fiduciary obligations, and promulgated a detailed scheme of federal judicial enforcement, but generally declined to regulate the content of welfare plans. Since the late 1980s, health care plans have become an exception to the laissez-faire approach to welfare plan content. As health care prices grew by leaps and bounds and non-group health insurance became almost unaffordable, the Consolidated Omnibus Reconciliation Act of 1986 (COBRA) added Part 6 of ERISA Title I, which requires sponsors of group health plans that normally cover twenty or more employees to provide continued access to health plan coverage to workers who would otherwise lose coverage due to termination of employment or reduction of hours. Beneficiaries who would lose coverage due to the death of the employee or certain changes in dependency or family status are also granted a right to elect continuation coverage.[100] In each case, COBRA continuation coverage is for a limited period (typically 18 or 36 months) and may be made contingent on payment of a premium that cannot exceed 102 percent of the plan's cost of covering similarly situated employees or beneficiaries.[101]

---

97 *E.g.*, I.R.C. § 401(a) (2006) (final sentence), *id.* §§ 411(e), 401(a)(5)(G) (relaxed qualification criteria), 403(b) (tax-sheltered annuities for public school employees), 457 (alternative rules for deferred compensation plans of state and local governments).

98 *E.g.*, I.R.C. § 403(b) (2006) (tax-sheltered annuities for educational organization employees), *id.* § 457 (alternative rules for deferred compensation plans of tax-exempt organizations).

99 ERISA §§ 302(a)(2)(C), 304, 29 U.S.C. §§ 1082(a)(2)(C), 1084 (2006) (minimum funding standard for multiemployer plans); I.R.C. §§ 412(a)(2)(C), 431 (2006) (same). ERISA §§ 4201–4402, 29 U.S.C. §§ 1381–1461 (2006) (special termination insurance provisions for multiemployer plans).

100 ERISA §§ 601, 603, 29 U.S.C. §§ 1161, 1163 (2006); *see* I.R.C. § 4980B (2006).

101 ERISA §§ 602, 604, 29 U.S.C. §§ 1162, 1164 (2006); *see* I.R.C. § 4980B(f) (2006). The American Recovery and Reinvestment Act of 2009 provides for temporary premium reductions and additional election opportunities for health benefits under COBRA. Eligible individuals pay only 35 percent of their COBRA premiums and the remaining 65 percent is reimbursed through a tax credit granted the employer. Pub. L. No. 111-5, § 3001, 123 Stat. 115,

The first experiment with health care plan content regulation under COBRA was soon followed by further major inroads. Starting in 1993, group health plans were required to provide benefits to a child of the plan participant in accordance with the terms of a qualified medical child support order, so that children of divorced or separated parents would have reliable access to continued health care coverage.[102] Then, in 1996, Congress added Part 7 of ERISA Title I, which limits exclusions from group health plan coverage based on preexisting health conditions and prohibits certain health status discrimination.[103] Subsequent amendments to Part 7 have expanded its reach to prohibit discrimination on the basis of genetic information; mandate coverage of a minimum hospital stay following the birth of a child; cover post-mastectomy reconstructive surgery; continue coverage of college students while on medical leave of absence; and provide parity in mental health benefits.[104] As with ERISA's pension plan content regulation, the Internal Revenue Code reinforces the message by imposing a parallel set of rules backed by tax sanctions.[105] This deluge of group health plan content regulation is symptomatic of the vastly increased expense and importance of employer-financed health care. While these developments might be a prelude to comprehensive health care reform legislation, health plan content controls are not explored further in this work.

---

455 (2009); I.R.C. § 139C (West Supp. 2010) (subsidy excluded from gross income), *id.* § 6432 (payroll tax credit to the employer). The premium reduction lasts for up to nine months for those eligible for COBRA during the period beginning September 1, 2008 and ending December 31, 2009 due to an involuntary termination of employment that occurred during that period.

102 ERISA §§ 514(b)(7), 609, 29 U.S.C. §§ 1144(b)(7), 1169 (2006). The qualified medical child support order is modeled after the qualified domestic relations order, which provides a mechanism for family law claimants to obtain access to a participant's pension if certain conditions designed to protect the plan and other participants are satisfied. *See infra* Chapter 8B; ERISA § 206(d)(3), 29 U.S.C. § 1056(d)(3) (2006); I.R.C. § 414(p) (2006).

103 ERISA §§ 701, 702, 731–734, 29 U.S.C. §§ 1181, 1182, 1191–1191c (2006); *see* I.R.C. §§ 9801, 9802, 9831–9834 (2006).

104 ERISA §§ 702(c)–(f), 711–714, 29 U.S.C. §§ 1182(c)–(f), 1185–1185b (2006); *see* I.R.C. § 9802(c)–(f), 9811–9813 (2006).

105 Most of the group health plan content requirements of Part 7 of ERISA Title I appear in I.R.C. §§ 9801–9833 (2006). Violation of these rules exposes the employer (or the plan, in the case of a multiemployer plan or a multiple employer welfare arrangement) to an excise tax of $100 per day for each individual affected by the violation for each day that it persists. *Id.* §§ 9834, 4980B. Certain exceptions or limitations of the penalty tax may apply if the failure to comply was due to reasonable cause rather than willful neglect. *Id.* § 4980D(c), (d).

Similarly, the tax version of the COBRA continuation coverage requirements appear in I.R.C. § 4980B.

ERISA's required recognition of qualified medical child support orders (*supra* Chapter 1 note 102 and accompanying text), and ERISA § 713, which mandates coverage of post-mastectomy reconstructive surgery, do not have tax Code counterparts.

Chapter 2

ERISA's Coverage

Congress relied on the Commerce Clause as the basis for regulating employee benefit plans. The labor provisions of ERISA apply to any "employee benefit plan" established or maintained by an employer "engaged in commerce or in any industry or activity affecting commerce," as well as to plans established or maintained by unions representing employees so engaged.[1] The statute broadly defines "commerce" and "industry or activity affecting commerce" to reach most any employer or union, regardless of size.[2]

---

1   ERISA § 4(a), 29 U.S.C. § 1003(a) (2006).
2   ERISA § 3(11), (12), 29 U.S.C. § 1002(11), (12) (2006). *See* Fugarino v. Hartford Life & Accident Ins. Co., 969 F.2d 178, 183 (6th Cir. 1992) (group health insurance provided by small family-owned restaurant subject to ERISA notwithstanding the business's trivial impact on commerce), *overruled on other grounds by* Raymond B. Yates, M.D., P.C. Profit Sharing Plan v. Hendon, 541 U.S. 1 (2004).
     ERISA's definitions of "commerce" and "industry or activity affecting commerce" were carried over verbatim from a predecessor statute, the Welfare and Pension Plans Disclosure

Enterprise size does not seriously restrict ERISA's scope, but federal controls come into play only if there is an "employee benefit plan." The definition of employee benefit plan imposes three important limitations on ERISA's coverage. First, the arrangement for the provision of benefits must constitute a "plan, fund, or program." Second, the plan must provide benefits to employees or their beneficiaries. Third, the benefits provided must be of a type specified in either the definition of a "welfare plan" or a "pension plan."[3] Each of these criteria implicates fundamental interpretive and policy issues that are examined below. The chapter concludes with an exploration of legislative exceptions that render certain employee benefit plans largely or completely exempt from federal regulation.

A. THE "PLAN" PREREQUISITE

To be subject to ERISA, an arrangement for the provision of benefits must be a "plan, fund, or program."[4] The statute offers no definition of those terms. Courts regularly encounter three types of challenges to the existence of a plan: namely that the benefit arrangement is too transient, too indefinite, or too restricted in coverage.

Transience[5]

Where an employee benefit can be provided without establishing an ongoing administrative apparatus, there is no "plan," provided that the obligation is unfunded and non-discretionary. This conclusion follows from a line of cases that has *Fort Halifax Packing Co. v. Coyne*[6] as its source. There, the Supreme Court held that a Maine law requiring one-time severance payments in the event of a plant closing was not preempted by ERISA because it "neither establishes, nor requires the employer to maintain, an employee welfare benefit 'plan.'"[7]

Act of 1958, Pub. L. No. 85-836, § 3(10), (11), 72 Stat. 997, *amended by* Pub. L. No. 87-420, 76 Stat. 35 (repealed by ERISA § 111(a)(1), 29 U.S.C. § 1031(a)(1) (2006)). Those definitions were in turn taken from the jurisdictional provision of the Taft-Hartley Act, 29 U.S.C. § 142(1) (2006). 104 CONG. REC. 16,437–38 (1958) (remarks of Reps. Barden, Frelinghuysen, and Green). Under Taft-Hartley, it is sufficient if the industry as a whole affects commerce; it is not necessary that the particular enterprise in which the employer or unionized employees are engaged affects commerce. *E.g.*, United States v. Ricciardi, 357 F.2d 91, 95 (2d Cir. 1966) (relevant industry "comprises all business activities in the same field").

3   ERISA § 3(3), (1), (2)(A), 29 U.S.C. § 1002(3), (1), (2)(A) (2006).
4   ERISA §§ 4(a), 3(3), (1), (2)(A), 29 U.S.C. §§ 1003(a), 1002(3), (1), (2)(A) (2006).
5   Much of the following discussion is derived from Wiedenbeck, *supra* Chapter 1 note 57, at 586–89, 591–93.
6   482 U.S. 1 (1987).
7   *Id.* at 6.

In *Fort Halifax*, the Court equated an ERISA plan with an "ongoing administrative program for processing claims and paying benefits."[8] That definition was supported by the policy of preemption: conforming a benefit program to a patchwork of state regulation would forfeit the advantages of uniform administrative practice. The Maine law, in contrast, imposed only a contingent one-time obligation to make nondiscretionary lump-sum payments, and so entailed no such inefficiency. The Court acknowledged that it had previously affirmed decisions holding an unfunded severance program subject to ERISA, but in that instance payments were due whenever covered workers left employment. Such an ongoing commitment to pay benefits required a continuing administrative scheme, unlike the one-time obligation in *Fort Halifax*, the case at hand.[9] The Court also observed that the Maine plant-closing law "not only fails to implicate the concerns of ERISA's preemption provision, it fails to implicate the regulatory concerns of ERISA itself."[10] Looking to the legislative history of ERISA's fiduciary responsibility rules (which apply to both pension and welfare plans), the Court concluded that "[t]he focus of the statute thus is on the administrative integrity of benefit plans—which presumes that some type of administrative activity is taking place."[11]

Lower court decisions involving employer-initiated severance programs have fleshed out the scope of *Fort Halifax*. Arrangements to make a readily determinable lump-sum cash payment have been found not to constitute an ERISA plan.[12] Yet some short-term commitments calling for payment in a lump sum have been subjected to federal regulation, notwithstanding the Supreme Court's search for an ongoing administrative program. Comparison of the decisions demonstrates that if there is no continuing administrative apparatus, then ERISA's application turns on the presence or absence of *discretion* in processing benefit claims.

Many of the leading cases involve *unfunded* executive severance ("golden parachute") programs. In *Fontenot v. NL Industries, Inc.*,[13] the employer adopted, as one component of a takeover defense, a plan providing that if the employment of selected senior executives was terminated for any reason within two years of a change in control of the corporation, the affected individuals would receive lump-sum cash

---

8   *Id.* at 12. The *Fort Halifax* majority observed that "Congress intended pre-emption to afford employers the advantages of a uniform set of administrative procedures governed by a single set of regulations." *Id.* at 11. Yet employers could secure the cost advantages of a single set of administrative procedures by including a choice-of-law provision in their benefit plans. This consideration suggests that it is workers who benefit, through lower information costs, from having all plans subject to the *same* set of supplementary rules. *See supra* Chapter 1C.

9   *Fort Halifax*, 482 U.S. at 17–19 (distinguishing Holland v. Burlington Indus., 772 F.2d 1140 (4th Cir. 1985), *summarily aff'd*, 477 U.S. 901 (1986); Gilbert v. Burlington Indus., 765 F.2d 320 (2d Cir. 1985), *summarily aff'd*, 477 U.S. 901 (1986)).

10   *Fort Halifax*, 482 U.S. at 15.

11   *Id.*

12   Young v. Wash. Gas Light Co., 206 F.3d 1200 (D.C. Cir. 2000); Belanger v. Wyman-Gordon Co., 71 F.3d 451 (1st Cir. 1995); Angst v. Mack Trucks, Inc., 969 F.2d 1530 (3d Cir. 1992); Fontenot v. NL Indus., 953 F.2d 960 (5th Cir. 1992); Wells v. Gen. Motors Corp., 881 F.2d 166 (5th Cir. 1989).

13   953 F.2d 960 (5th Cir. 1992).

severance payments equal to three times their highest annual compensation over the preceding three years.[14] The plaintiff, who was not included in the program, was terminated one year after the takeover; he sued for benefits under federal law. The district court granted summary judgment in favor of the employer on the ground that ERISA did not apply, and the court of appeals affirmed.[15]

In contrast, ERISA has been applied to some golden parachute programs. It is startling, and perhaps a little ironic, that a labor law enacted to protect workers' interests is sometimes invoked to protect managers in the event of a change in corporate control. Cases such as *Bogue v. Ampex Corporation*[16] vividly illustrate the breadth of the statute. The program in *Bogue* promised severance pay to any of ten executives of a subsidiary that was slated for sale, if the executive was not offered "substantially similar employment" within ten months after the sale.

> In this case, Allied-Signal, the program's administrator, remained obligated to decide whether a complaining employee's job was "substantially equivalent" to his pre-acquisition job. Although the program, like the plans in *Fort Halifax* and *Wells*, was triggered by a single event, that event would occur more than once, at a different time for each employee. There was no way to carry out that obligation with the unthinking, one-time, nondiscretionary application of the plan administrators in *Fort Halifax* and *Wells*. Although its application was uncertain, its term was short, and the number of its participants was small, the program's administration required a case-by-case, discretionary application of its terms. Whether or not Allied-Signal ever thought [that the program would be subject to ERISA] does not matter. . . . We hold that Allied-Signal was obligated to apply enough ongoing, particularized, administrative, discretionary analysis to make the program in this case a "plan."[17]

Similarly, an arrangement that required a separate determination of each covered executive's eligibility for benefits (specifically, whether post-merger termination was for reasons other than cause) was an ERISA plan.[18] And a Massachusetts

---

14 *Id.* at 961, 963.

15 *Id.* at 961.

16 976 F.2d 1319 (9th Cir. 1992). The Ninth Circuit subsequently distinguished *Bogue* in holding that an individually negotiated executive employment contract that called for readily determinable severance payments in the event of termination "without cause" did not establish an ERISA plan. According to the court, this single discretionary determination—unlike the ten decisions possible in *Bogue*—did not require "ongoing discretionary analysis." Delaye v. Agripac, Inc., 39 F.3d 235, 238 (9th Cir. 1994). This analysis conflates the search for continuing (nondiscretionary) administrative activity with the search for discretionary decision making. ERISA's policies of preventing employer abuse and protecting participants indicate that a single judgment call should result in plan classification, so that federal fiduciary oversight is triggered. *See infra* text accompanying Chapter 2 notes 53–67 for a discussion of restricted coverage.

17 *Bogue*, 976 F.2d at 1323. *Accord* Schonholz v. Long Island Jewish Med. Ctr., 87 F.3d 72, 76 (2d Cir. 1996); Cvelbar v. CBI Ill., Inc., 106 F.3d 1368, 1376 (7th Cir. 1997); Collins v. Ralston Purina Co., 147 F.3d 592, 595–97 (7th Cir. 1998).

18 Pane v. RCA Corp., 667 F. Supp. 168, 170–71 (D.N.J. 1998), *aff'd*, 868 F.2d 631 (3d Cir. 1989). *Cf.* Kulinski v. Medtronic Bio-Medicus, Inc., 21 F.3d 254, 257 (8th Cir. 1994) (agreement calling for severance pay in the event of resignation for good reason within one year of a

"tin parachute" statute, mandating lump-sum severance payments to certain employees who are eligible for unemployment compensation when discharged within 24 months after takeover of their employer, was held preempted because, in contrast to *Fort Halifax*, the payment obligation is triggered separately (by termination) for each worker, and eligibility for unemployment compensation requires a potentially controversial factual determination that the worker was not discharged for cause.[19]

This focus on administrative discretion seems sensible in light of the *Fort Halifax* policy analysis: if preventing mismanagement and abuse by fiduciaries is the central tenet of ERISA, perhaps ERISA should not apply where there are no judgment calls to oversee. ERISA's fiduciary-duty and prohibited-transactions rules apply only to fiduciaries,[20] and the statute provides a broad functional definition that classifies as a fiduciary any person who has or exercises "any discretionary authority" in the management or administration of the plan.[21] This approach is also consistent with the limited abuse-of-discretion standard of review that is applied to benefit claim denials where the plan gives the fiduciary discretionary authority to determine eligibility for benefits or to construe the terms of the plan.[22]

Mishandling of plan assets is as much a threat to the integrity of benefit plans as abusive decision making. ERISA's fiduciary responsibility provisions were intended to prohibit outright thievery and looting of benefit funds by anyone with access to the fund, however exalted or subordinate that person's position. Accordingly, oversight of discretionary decision making alone is not enough to protect workers' interests. ERISA should apply *either* if the benefit obligation involves the exercise of discretion *or* if it is advance funded. ERISA's drafters apparently understood this point: if the plan is funded, any person who "exercises any authority or control respecting management or disposition of its assets" is a fiduciary, whether that authority involves the exercise of discretion or not.[23] Yet the protection Congress intended to afford in the definition of fiduciary becomes illusory if the statute fails to apply for want of a plan. To safeguard workers from *both* oppressive decisions *and* looting of the fund, the core jurisdictional principle should be: where there is a fiduciary, there is a plan.

The severance payments required by the Maine plant-closing statute in *Fort Halifax* were unfunded and nondiscretionary; the employer's obligation could be discharged without the service of an ERISA fiduciary. Yet the Court's opinion indicates that ERISA would apply if there were "an ongoing administrative program for processing

---

hostile takeover did not create an ERISA plan because it gave the *employee* unfettered discretion to decide whether he had good reason to resign; the court noted that a plan exists where the *employer* "must analyze each employee's particular circumstances in light of the appropriate criteria" to determine benefit eligibility or amount).

19   Simas v. Quaker Fabric Corp. of Fall River, 6 F.3d 849, 853–54 (1st Cir. 1993) (relying on *Bogue*). *Accord* United Paperworkers Int'l Union, Local 1468 v. Imperial Home Decor Group, 76 F. Supp. 2d 179 (D.R.I. 1999) (Rhode Island tin parachute statute preempted).

20   ERISA §§ 404(a), 406, 29 U.S.C. §§ 1104(a), 1106 (2006).

21   ERISA § 3(21)(A), 29 U.S.C. § 1002(21)(A) (2006). *See infra* Chapter 4A.

22   Firestone Tire & Rubber Co. v. Bruch, 489 U.S. 101 (1989). *See infra* Chapter 5B.

23   ERISA § 3(21)(A)(i), 29 U.S.C. § 1002(21)(A)(i) (2006). *See generally infra* Chapter 4A.

claims and paying benefits."[24] Apparently, then, a regular or continuing benefit obligation would trigger ERISA even if it were unfunded and nondiscretionary.[25] This connotation of "plan" may take into account that, although "ERISA's central focus [is on] administrative integrity,"[26] fiduciary responsibility is not the only component of federal benefit plan regulation. In particular, workers must be informed of the extent of the benefit obligation (coverage, amount, and timing) and the method for "processing claims and paying benefits" in order to take full advantage of the program. Ongoing administration by itself implicates informational interests, and so should trigger ERISA's reporting and disclosure regime.[27]

This judicially developed definition of plan (requiring either ongoing administration or the presence of a fiduciary) is informed by the goals of ERISA and is moored to the statute's text. Recall that ERISA defines both a welfare plan and a pension plan as a "plan, *fund*, or *program*."[28] Use of the term "fund" indicates that ERISA applies whenever the obligation is advance funded. Funding, of course, requires continuing oversight and ensures that there will be someone with fiduciary status. "Program" implies an ordered sequence of events (such as a procedure for processing claims and paying benefits), which lends credence to the distinction between ongoing administration and a one-time lump-sum payment.

Indefiniteness

To be subject to federal regulation, a welfare or pension plan must be "established or maintained by an employer or by an employee organization."[29] That is, the plan must already have come into existence. A tentative or projected benefit arrangement is not a "plan" or (equivalently) has not been "established."[30]

---

24   Fort Halifax Packing Co. v. Coyne, 482 U.S. at 1, 12 (1987).

25   *Id.* at 18 nn.10, 12 (distinguishing a benefit obligation that entails "regularity of payment").

26   *Id.* at 18.

27   In discussing why the Maine plant-closing statute "fails to implicate the regulatory concerns of ERISA itself," *Fort Halifax*, 482 U.S. at 15, the Court considered *both* fiduciary responsibility and reporting and disclosure. The opinion notes that there was no "administrative activity potentially subject to employer abuse" and that "[n]o financial transactions take place that would be listed in an annual report, and no further information regarding the terms of the severance pay obligation is needed because the statute itself makes these terms clear." *Id.* at 16.

28   ERISA § 3(1), (2), 29 U.S.C. § 1002(1), (2) (2006) (emphasis added).

29   *Id.*

30   Brines v. XTRA Corp., 304 F.3d 699, 701 (7th Cir. 2002) ("The statement in the plan that 'The company will develop and implement an appropriate separation program' did not create a legally enforceable promise." "And the vagueness of the 'will develop' statement is a strong indication that it was not *intended* to be a promise, but merely a prediction, which creates no rights." (citations omitted)); Elmore v. Cone Mills Corp., 23 F.3d 855, 862 (4th Cir. 1994) (employer's preliminary statements of its intentions concerning the terms of a new employee stock ownership plan do not constitute an enforceable plan); James v. Nat'l Bus. Sys., Inc., 924 F.2d 718, 720 (7th Cir. 1991) (Posner, J.) (stating that for ERISA to come into play, the plan must be "intended to be in effect, and not just be something for future adoption" and that documents describing a plan as being tentative, contingent, or *in futuro* should be considered as evidence that no plan was in effect).

Donovan v. Dillingham[31] is the leading authority on the proof required to demonstrate that a plan has been created.[32] The case involved the purchase of health insurance by small employers through a group insurance trust in order to obtain more favorable rates. The Secretary of Labor argued that even if the purchase of health insurance was not itself sufficient to trigger ERISA, the separate determination of each employer to provide benefits to its employees by subscribing to the group trust established a plan.[33] The court held that a plan is not "established" merely by virtue of a *decision* to provide benefits of a type specified in ERISA; rather, the program must have become a reality.[34] A decision implemented by the purchase of insurance, however, creates a plan.[35] Employers who purchased insurance through the group trust were found to have established ERISA welfare plans if the insurance was obtained to fulfill a collective bargaining agreement or under circumstances indicating an intent to provide continuing coverage to a class of employees.[36] More generally, the court observed that "[i]n determining whether a plan, fund, or program (pursuant to a writing or not) is a reality a court must determine whether from the surrounding circumstances a reasonable person could ascertain the intended benefits, beneficiaries, source of financing, and procedure for receiving benefits," recognizing that some of these essential criteria can be incorporated from sources outside the plan, such as an insurance claims procedure.[37]

As the *Dillingham* definition suggests, no particular formality is required to show the existence of a plan. Most important, compliance with ERISA is not essential. (If compliance were a condition of plan classification, then ERISA's standards, which were intended to be mandatory, would be made elective.[38]) Oral arrangements can be

---

31   688 F.2d 1367 (11th Cir. 1982) (en banc).

32   "Every circuit that has since been required to decide whether, on the particular facts before it, a pension plan has come into being has adopted the *Dillingham* approach." Kenney v. Roland Parson Contracting Corp., 28 F.3d 1254, 1257 (D.C. Cir. 1994) (Ginsburg, J.) (citing authorities).

33   Donovan v. Dillingham, 668 F.2d 1196, 1198 (11th Cir. 1982) (opinion before rehearing en banc).

34   *Dillingham*, 688 F.2d at 1373.

35   *Id.* at 1375.

36   *Id.* at 1374–75.

37   *Id.* at 1373.

38   *Id.* at 1372 ("[I]t would be incongruous for persons establishing or maintaining informal or unwritten employee benefit plans, or assuming the responsibility of safeguarding plan assets, to circumvent the Act merely because an administrator or other fiduciary failed to satisfy reporting or fiduciary standards"). *Accord* Brines v. XTRA Corp., 304 F.3d at 699, 701 (7th Cir. 2002) (dicta, explaining cases); Scott v. Gulf Oil Co., 754 F.2d 1499, 1503–04 (9th Cir. 1985) (unwritten plan); Henglein v. Informal Plan for Plant Shutdown Benefits for Salaried Employees, 974 F.2d 391, 400–01 (3d Cir. 1992) (same, but emphasizing that oral representations cannot modify a valid written plan); Phillips v. Brandess Home Builders, Inc., No. 95-C-204, 1995 U.S. Dist. LEXIS 14496, at *6 (N.D. Ill. Oct. 2, 1995) ("The applicability of ERISA standards cannot turn on an employer's compliance with them."); Strzelecki v. Schwarz Paper Co., 824 F. Supp. 821, 826 (N.D. Ill. 1993) ("If an employer could avoid ERISA coverage of its benefit plan simply by violating ERISA's requirements and then claiming that the plan did not function the way ERISA plans typically function, the whole purpose of the statute—to protect employees from employers' mismanagement of benefit plans—would be defeated."

plans even though ERISA requires almost all welfare and pension plans to be in writing.[39] Similarly, unpublicized (secret) benefit programs can trigger the statute, bringing its fundamental tenet of employee disclosure into play.[40] Moreover, if the intended benefits and beneficiaries are clear but the employer is silent as to funding or claims procedure, some decisions find a plan based on the inference that benefits are to be paid out of the employer's general funds, or that application for benefits should be made to the company's personnel department.[41]

Can an informal policy of providing a benefit in individually determined amounts to selected employees be a plan? Arguably, the intended benefits and beneficiaries of such a policy are unascertainable. When faced with evidence that a large employer maintained a long-standing system of ad hoc individualized grants of severance benefits, the Third Circuit held that "the discretionary nature of benefits . . . does not alone deprive a document or program of its status as an employee benefit plan under the *Dillingham* standard, so long as a reasonable person can ascertain the contingent benefit and contingent beneficiaries."[42] The discretionary nature of the benefit would not prevent a disappointed employee from obtaining review of the denial of the benefit, but that review would be limited to the deferential abuse-of-discretion standard.[43] In contrast, the Seventh Circuit has refused to apply ERISA to an accounting firm's informal pension arrangement, where only 3 of 25 retirees received benefits and the amount was determined ad hoc rather than according to an established formula. The court observed that "[w]ith only this evidence, we could not begin to fashion appropriate relief for [plaintiff], since we do not know whether he was the type of employee [the firm] intended to cover, or what benefits are due."[44] Similarly, a district court found that a chief executive officer's practice of occasionally granting severance pay in amounts determined by the application of largely undefined criteria was too unsystematic and indefinite to constitute a plan.[45]

(citations omitted)). *See also* Feifer v. Prudential Ins. Co., 306 F.3d 1202, 1209–10 (2d Cir. 2002) (informal program summary constituted the plan during period before plan instruments were drafted despite attempted disclaimer; crediting disclaimer would permit employers to opt out of ERISA's requirements).

39 *E.g., Dillingham*, 688 F.2d at 1372; Scott v. Gulf Oil Co., 754 F.2d 1499, 1503–04 (9th Cir. 1985).

40 *E.g.,* Brown v. Ampco-Pittsburgh Corp., 876 F.2d 546, 550–51 (6th Cir. 1989) (confidential memorandum to management created severance pay plan); Blau v. Del Monte Corp., 748 F.2d 1348 (9th Cir. 1984) (same, and refusing to interpret secret plan with reference to the employer's secret intentions or past course of conduct).

41 *E.g.,* Deibler v. United Food & Commercial Workers' Local Union 23, 973 F.2d 206, 210 (3d Cir. 1992); Dwyer v. Galen Hosp. Ill., Inc., No. 94-C-544, 1996 U.S. Dist. LEXIS 2921, at **26–27 (N.D. Ill. Mar. 11, 1996).

42 *Henglein*, 974 F.2d at 401.

43 *Id.*

44 Diak v. Dwyer, Costello & Knox, P.C., 33 F.3d 809, 813 (7th Cir. 1994).

45 Spanos v. Cont'l Pub'g Servs., Inc., No. C-93-1624 MHP, 1994 U.S. Dist. LEXIS 6695, at **7–11 (N.D. Cal. May 17, 1994).

The principle that discretionary authority brings ERISA's fiduciary standards into play to safeguard employees[46] clashes with the cases holding that too much discretion negates the existence of a plan by making the intended benefits or beneficiaries unascertainable. If standards or guidelines for the exercise of discretion can be gleaned from the employer's representations, past practice, or surrounding circumstances, then the courts have a basis to review benefit determinations to prevent employer abuse, and the policy of ERISA demands such review. But what if there are no standards, so that discretion is unbounded and benefits are awarded by a series of individualized ad hoc determinations? When discretion becomes prerogative, does judicial review have any role to play?

Under the federal Administrative Procedure Act, there is no jurisdiction to review bureaucratic action where the decision is "committed by law to agency discretion."[47] The Supreme Court interprets this exception to the general rule of reviewability narrowly, holding that judicial review is precluded only where there is "no law to apply"— that is, preclusion applies only where there is no basis for a court to police the exercise of discretion because there is no indication of any standards or guidelines that the agency must use in making the decision.[48] A similar futility concern seems to be present in cases holding that too much discretion negates the existence of a plan by making the intended benefits or beneficiaries unascertainable. ERISA requires that every employee benefit plan "specify the basis on which payments are made to and from the plan."[49] "Plan" is a broader category than "fund," and this rule applies to nearly all plans, including unfunded welfare plans. Where there is no fund, specifying "the basis on which payments are made . . . from the plan" necessarily requires that the plan either expressly define its intended beneficiaries and benefits (either by specification, class description, or formula), or set forth meaningful guidelines to inform the fiduciary's exercise of discretion.

Should a benefit arrangement that does not comply with this aspect of ERISA be exempt from ERISA, any more than, for instance, a program that violates the writing requirement? Because ERISA was designed to protect employees' reasonable expectations, the answer apparently depends on the information available to employees. If the employer's actions or omissions have created a reasonable expectation that benefits might be awarded, a plan might be held to exist, but covering only that group of employees as to which such a reasonable expectation could arise.[50] Using reasonable

---

46 *See supra* text accompanying Chapter 2 notes 12–22.

47 5 U.S.C. § 701(a)(2) (2006).

48 Citizens to Preserve Overton Park v. Volpe, 401 U.S. 402 (1971). *See generally* Ronald M. Levin, *Understanding Unreviewability in Administrative Law*, 74 Minn. L. Rev. 689 (1990).

49 ERISA § 402(b)(4), 29 U.S.C. § 1102(b)(4) (2006).

50 *Belanger v. Wyman-Gordon Co.*, 71 F.3d 451 (1st Cir. 1995), held that severance pay granted under a series of four time-limited early retirement offers made within four years did not create an ongoing severance pay plan because each offer involved only an unfunded, nondiscretionary, one-time payment that was independent on its face, and the company never represented that there was any linkage or continuing commitment. *Id.* at 456. The court observed that in determining the existence of a plan, "[o]ne very important consideration is whether, in light of all the surrounding circumstances, a reasonable employee would perceive an ongoing commitment by the employer to provide employee benefits." *Id.* at 455.

expectations as a guide, ad hoc grants of severance or pension benefits that are unknown to the continuing workforce would not trigger ERISA. On the other hand, if workers become aware (whether by employer information or recurrent practice) that such benefits are granted to selected managerial employees, a plan covering management could be found to exist. This approach would distinguish *Henglein v. Informal Plan for Plant Shutdown Benefits for Salaried Employees*,[51] in which a plan was held to exist where the employer was aware that salaried employees believed there was an ongoing discretionary severance program but made no effort to dispel that impression, from *Diak v. Dwyer, Costello & Knox, P.C.*, in which the court held there was no plan, and where there was no evidence that the claimant was aware of ad hoc unfunded pension payments to three retirees.[52]

Restricted Coverage[53]

Restricted coverage constitutes the third and final ground on which the existence of a plan is frequently challenged. Where a benefit is provided to one or a very small number of employees, the arrangement may be intended only as a "special deal" contained in individual employment contracts and not part of a general program. But does the meaning of "plan" necessarily entail a general program? ERISA's policies strongly suggest that the answer should be "no," although the statutory text offers scant guidance.[54]

---

51   974 F.2d 391, 396, 400 (3d Cir. 1992) (describing relevant evidence of the existence of a plan, including the employer's oral representations, "a deliberate failure to correct known perceptions of a plan's existence, [and] the reasonable understanding of employees").

52   Diak v. Dwyer, Costello & Knox, P.C., 33 F.3d 809, 811, 813 (7th Cir. 1994) (no evidence that claimant expected a pension; he was told that the firm had no pension plan and that payments to a retiree were compensation for services). In the author's opinion, the *Diak* court reached the right result, but the decision should have been founded on the lack of employee reliance rather than the difficulty in ascertaining the intended benefits or beneficiaries. *See also* Gilmore v. Silgan Plastics Corp., 917 F. Supp. 686 (E.D. Mo. 1996), in which an announced company policy of granting severance benefits to employees approved by the plant manager was held not to create a plan, even though the manager's discretionary decision was shown to have been based on production needs. Under the analysis suggested in the text, the *Gilmore* facts are enough to constitute a plan. Had ERISA been applied, the plaintiffs should nevertheless have been denied relief because they were not challenging any discretionary (i.e., fiduciary) decision. Instead, they had been denied benefits pursuant to company announcements (informal plan amendments) that clearly limited program eligibility to employees in other job classifications.

53   Parts of the following discussion are derived from Wiedenbeck, *supra* Chapter 1 note 57, at 576–85.

54   The welfare and pension plan definitions refer in the plural to "participants" and "employees." ERISA § 3(1), (2)(A), 29 U.S.C. § 1002(1), (2)(A) (2006). *But see* 1 U.S.C. § 1 (2006) ("In determining the meaning of any Act of Congress, unless the context indicates otherwise . . . words importing the plural include the singular."). On the other hand, in common usage, the term "plan" normally conveys a sense of prearrangement or design, not generality. *E.g.*, RANDOM HOUSE COLLEGE DICTIONARY 1014 (rev. ed. 1975); AMERICAN HERITAGE COLLEGE DICTIONARY 1045 (3d ed. 1993); WEBSTER'S NEW UNIVERSAL UNABRIDGED DICTIONARY 1372 (2d ed. rev. 1983).

Legislative history suggests that a benefit arrangement covering one or a few employees can be a plan. ERISA's reporting and disclosure rules and its definitions of welfare and pension plans are drawn from the Welfare and Pension Plans Disclosure Act of 1958 (WPPDA),[55] which exempted plans covering 25 or fewer participants from disclosure obligations.[56] However, ERISA did not carry forward any such small-plan exemption.[57] The alteration made to the predecessor definitions of welfare and pension plans is also telling. The WPPDA required that the plan be "communicated or its benefits described in writing to the employees."[58] This writing requirement was designed to "eliminate informal or personal arrangements from the scope of the [WPPDA]," because "[i]ndividual arrangements with executives for benefits are not contemplated as being covered by the [WPPDA]."[59] Under ERISA, certain executive compensation arrangements are excluded in a more targeted fashion, as described below.[60] And while ERISA requires nearly all plans to be "established and maintained pursuant to a written instrument,"[61] the writing requirement is now a consequence of plan classification, not a predicate of it.[62]

A regulation in effect since 1975 indicates that a single-employee arrangement can be a plan subject to ERISA,[63] and several courts agree.[64] Other cases hold that restricted coverage bars ERISA's application, but many of them can be traced to some early Labor Department advisory opinions that announced (without support) that an individual employment contract is not subject to ERISA[65]—a position the Department has since recanted.[66] Cases may also proceed from the assumption that Congress could not

---

55   Pub. L. No. 85-836, 72 Stat. 997 (1958) (repealed 1975).

56   *Id.* § 4(b)(4), 72 Stat. at 999, *amended by* Pub. L. No. 87-420, 76 Stat. 35 (1962).

57   Early versions of pension reform legislation did exempt plans covering not more than 25 employees. *E.g.*, S. 4, 93d Cong. § 104(b)(4) (1973), *reprinted in* 1 ERISA LEGISLATIVE HISTORY, *supra* Chapter 1 note 56, at 93, 117; S. REP. NO. 93-127, at 18–19 (1973) (stating small plans exempted to avoid inhibiting growth of pension coverage), *reprinted in* 1 ERISA LEGISLATIVE HISTORY, *supra* Chapter 1 note 56, at 604–05.

58   Welfare and Pension Plans Disclosure Act of 1958, Pub. L. No. 85-836, § 3(1), (2), 72 Stat. 997, *amended by* Pub. L. No. 87-420, 76 Stat. 35 (1962).

59   S. REP. NO. 85-1440, at 25 (1958), *reprinted in* OFFICE OF THE SOLICITOR, U.S. DEPARTMENT OF LABOR, LEGISLATIVE HISTORY OF THE WELFARE AND PENSION PLANS DISCLOSURE ACT OF 1958, at 206 (1962) [hereinafter WPPDA LEGISLATIVE HISTORY]; H.R. REP. NO. 85-2283, at 11 (1958), *reprinted in* WPPDA LEGISLATIVE HISTORY, *supra* at 207.

60   *See infra* text accompanying Chapter 2 notes 67, 119–130.

61   ERISA §§ 401(a), 402(a)(1), 29 U.S.C. §§ 1101(a), 1102(a)(1) (2006).

62   *See supra* Chapter 2 notes 38–39.

63   29 C.F.R. § 2510.3-3(b) (2009) ("[A] Keogh plan under which one or more common law employees, in addition to the self-employed individuals, are participants covered under the plan, will be covered under title I.").

64   *E.g.*, Cvelbar v. CBI Ill., Inc., 106 F.3d 1368, 1376 (7th Cir. 1997); Biggers v. Wittek Indus., 4 F.3d 291, 298 (4th Cir. 1993); Strzelecki v. Schwarz Paper Co., 824 F. Supp. 821, 827 (N.D. Ill. 1993); Williams v. Wright, 927 F.2d 1540, 1545 (11th Cir. 1991).

65   *E.g.*, Jervis v. Elerding, 504 F. Supp. 606 (C.D. Cal. 1980); Lackey v. Whitehall Corp., 704 F. Supp. 201 (D. Kan. 1988); O'Halloren v. Marine Cooks & Stewards Union, 730 P.2d 616 (Or. App. 1986).

66   *E.g.*, Letter to Mr. Joel P. Bennet (Oct. 19, 1985) (ERISA coverage is "not affected by the fact that the arrangement is limited to covering a single employee, is negotiated between the

have intended to work such a sweeping transformation of employment relations. Applied to individualized benefit commitments, ERISA might seem to swallow up the common law of employment contracts. But this concern is misplaced because ERISA only reaches post-employment compensation (i.e., pensions) and enumerated welfare benefits, not all terms and conditions of employment.

The objection that ERISA's protective policy is unnecessary when a benefit arrangement is specially designed (perhaps even separately bargained for) to meet the needs of one or a few employees is more weighty. In those circumstances, it can be assumed that participation is fully informed and deliberate, and key personnel typically have the education, judgment, and bargaining power necessary to protect themselves. Because such special arrangements grow out of competition for highly skilled labor, the firm's interest is aligned with the participant's, minimizing the risk of employer abuse.

But restricted coverage by itself does not ensure that the program is designed and administered to meet the needs of participants. Consider a financially strapped small firm that promises a pension to one or a few rank-and-file employees in lieu of paying higher wages—the business may fail while the benefit is unfunded, but the participants are not in a position to gauge that risk. As this example illustrates, the identity of the promisees is a better indicator of the need for regulation than mere breadth of coverage. In fact, ERISA excepts unfunded deferred compensation plans for "a select group of management or highly compensated employees" from its fiduciary oversight and pension content controls.[67] This targeted exclusion of certain executive compensation arrangements confirms that an individual employment contract or small-plan exception was not intended and is not necessary.

B. "EMPLOYEE" STATUS

ERISA applies only to plans that provide pension benefits to "employees"[68] or welfare benefits to "participants or their beneficiaries."[69] Where the statute applies, it confers rights and remedies on participants and beneficiaries. "Participant" is defined by reference to employee status,[70] but the statute defines "employee" circularly as "any individual employed by an employer."[71] Perhaps incorporation of the common-law

---

employer and the employee, or is not intended by the employer-plan sponsor to be an employee benefit plan for purposes of [ERISA]"); ERISA Advisory Op. 91-20A (U.S. Dep't of Labor, 1991).

67   ERISA § 201(2), 29 U.S.C. § 1051(2) (2006) (participation, benefit accrual, vesting, spousal rights, and anti-alienation); ERISA § 301(a)(3), 29 U.S.C. § 1081(a)(3) (2006) (funding); ERISA § 401(a)(1), 29 U.S.C. § 1101(a)(1) (2006) (fiduciary responsibility); ERISA § 4021(b)(6), 29 U.S.C. § 1321(b)(6) (2006) (termination insurance). This "top-hat plan" exception is examined *infra* Chapter 2D.

68   A pension plan is defined as a program that provides retirement income to employees or results in a deferral of income by employees until the termination of employment or later. ERISA § 3(2)(A), 29 U.S.C. § 1002(2)(A) (2006).

69   ERISA § 3(1), 29 U.S.C. § 1002(1) (2006).

70   ERISA § 3(7), 29 U.S.C. § 1002(7) (2006).

71   ERISA § 3(6), 29 U.S.C. § 1002(6) (2006).

meaning was expected, but the legislative history offers no clear guidance, and other definitions are plausible. The resulting ambiguity has forced the courts to decide whether federal law governs the benefit rights of certain categories of workers, including business owners and independent contractors.

Working Owners

Labor Department regulations provide that a benefit program that covers *only* individuals who own, or whose spouses own, an interest in an unincorporated business (as partner or proprietor) is not a "plan" subject to federal regulation, but ERISA applies if one or more common-law employees are participants.[72] If a corporation is *wholly* owned by an individual (or by an individual and his or her spouse), a benefit program that does not cover anyone else is also exempt from ERISA, even if the owner is also a common-law employee of the corporation.[73]

ERISA applies if a benefit plan covers at least one common-law employee along with business owners. In that situation, do ERISA's protections extend to the owners? ERISA grants rights and remedies to "participants" and their beneficiaries,[74] and the statute defines "participant" as an "employee or former employee of an employer . . . who is or may become eligible to receive a benefit" under the plan.[75] Reliance on the traditional common-law understanding of the employment relationship would suggest that partners and proprietors cannot be participants and so cannot qualify for ERISA's protections, even if they are covered under a plan that includes common-law employees. If so, their rights and obligations would be defined and enforced by state, not federal, law. Having different bodies of law apply to employees and owners who work side-by-side in an unincorporated business and participate in the same benefit programs seems a strangely inefficient result, yet a circuit split developed on the question. *Raymond B. Yates, M.D., P.C. Profit Sharing Plan v. Hendon* put the matter to rest, holding that:

> If the plan covers one or more employees other than the business owner and his or her spouse, the working owner may participate on equal terms with other plan participants. Such a working owner, in common with other employees, qualifies for

---

72 29 C.F.R. § 2510.3-3(b), (c) (2009). To trigger ERISA, the program must cover a common-law employee who is not an owner's spouse.

73 *Id.* This rule was apparently designed to avoid distortions in the choice-of-business form, but it does not extend to cases where the corporation is closely held and all plan participants are shareholder-employees. Leckey v. Stephano, 263 F.3d 267 (3d Cir. 2001) (ERISA applies to pension plan of corporation wholly owned by participant, his spouse, and his stepdaughter). Accordingly, the incorporation of a sole proprietorship does not affect ERISA's coverage, but the incorporation of a partnership often does.

74 *E.g.*, ERISA § 102, 29 U.S.C. § 1022 (2006) (disclosure); ERISA § 404(a)(1), 29 U.S.C. § 1104(a)(1) (2006) (fiduciary duties); ERISA § 502(a), 29 U.S.C. § 1132(a) (2006) (civil enforcement).

75 ERISA § 3(7), 29 U.S.C. § 1002(7) (2006).

the protections ERISA affords plan participants and is governed by the rights and remedies ERISA specifies.[76]

Yates involved a sole shareholder and president of a professional corporation, but the Court's holding and reasoning apply with equal force to working owners of unincorporated businesses, such as partners, limited liability company members, and sole proprietors.[77] *Yates* avoids the inefficiency, confusion, and perception of unfairness that would flow from letting state law govern the rights and obligations of partners or proprietors, while federal law, with its more limited set of remedies,[78] controls the fate of common-law employees who are covered by the same plan and involved in the same transaction. *Yates* does not preclude another curious result: the benefit rights of the owners of an unincorporated business are given by state law so long as the owners are the only plan participants, but the inclusion of a single employee in the program instantly modifies the owners' rights, making them a creature of federal law.

Independent Contractors

Nationwide Mutual Insurance Co. v. Darden[79] involved a benefit arrangement set up by an insurance company for its independent commission agents. In determining ERISA's reach, the Supreme Court construed the term "employee" to incorporate the traditional test of employee status under the general common law of agency:

> In determining whether a hired party is an employee under the general common law of agency, we consider the hiring party's right to control the manner and means by which the product is accomplished. Among the other factors relevant to this inquiry are the skills required; the source of the instrumentalities and tools; the location of the work; the duration of the relationship between the parties; whether the hiring party has the right to assign additional projects to the hired party; the extent of the hired party's discretion over when and how long to work; the method of payment; the hired party's role in hiring and paying assistants; whether the work is part of the regular business of the hiring party; whether the hiring party is in business; the provision of employee benefits; and the tax treatment of the hired party.[80]

Conceding that the common law offers "no paradigm of determinacy," the Court explained that "all of the incidents of the relationship must be assessed and weighed with no one factor being decisive."[81] The Court rejected the argument that ERISA's

---

76   Raymond B. Yates, M.D., P.C. Profit Sharing Plan v. Hendon, 541 U.S. 1, 6 (2004).

77   The Court's opinion consistently addresses the status of "working owners," not just "shareholder-employees." *See, e.g., Yates*, 541 U.S. at 11, 17.

78   *See infra* Chapter 5D.

79   503 U.S. 318 (1992).

80   *Id.* at 323–24 (quoting Community for Creative Non-Violence v. Reid, 490 U.S. 730, 751–52 (1989)).

81   *Darden*, 503 U.S. at 327, 324 (quoting NLRB v. United Ins. Co. of Am., 390 U.S. 254, 258 (1968)). *Accord* Barnhart v. N.Y. Life Ins. Co., 141 F.3d 1310, 1312–13 (9th Cir. 1998).

broad remedial purposes support a more expansive reading of the term, in part because the purposive approach would engender even greater uncertainty.[82]

In spite of *Darden*, the Seventh Circuit, in *Ruttenberg v. U.S. Life Insurance Co.*,[83] held that a disability insurance policy covering independent commodities traders was subject to ERISA rather than state law. Although the trader was an independent contractor of the trading firm that arranged the insurance, he was named to receive benefits by the policy, and so the court concluded that he fit the statutory definition of a beneficiary, a "person designated by a participant, *or by the terms of an employee benefit plan*, who is or may become eligible to receive a benefit thereunder."[84] If taken seriously, this definition of beneficiary would allow a plan to extend coverage to anyone it wants, perhaps even selling its package of health or disability insurance to individuals unrelated to the employer or union sponsor. The rights and obligations of those unrelated (but named) plan "beneficiaries" would then be governed exclusively by ERISA, potentially obliterating a large area of state insurance law.[85] Before the Supreme Court's decision in *Yates*,[86] some lower courts ruled that sole proprietors or partners covered by a welfare plan were employers, not employees, and could not be participants. As such, state law rather than ERISA would apply to such owners, unless they could somehow be treated as beneficiaries.[87] To avoid the inefficiency of having different bodies of law apply to owners and employees who work side-by-side in an unincorporated business under the same benefit program, some courts seized upon the fact that covered workers were named in the policy as payees of disability and certain other insurance benefits, and hence working owners could be seen as beneficiaries, even if they were not participants. This line of authority was rendered irrelevant by the holding in *Yates*, that working owners covered by a plan are participants subject to ERISA (i.e., employer and employee are not mutually exclusive categories). The idea that there can be a beneficiary when there is no corresponding participant was a convenient but anomalous construct. Having outlived its usefulness, this idea should be disavowed, not used as the foundation for an extension of ERISA's jurisdiction to independent contractors, as was done in *Ruttenberg*.

The increase in the contingent workforce and the rise of telecommuting has blurred the worker classification distinction between employee and independent contractor.

---

82   *Darden*, 503 U.S. at 326–27.

83   413 F.3d 652, 662 (7th Cir. 2005).

84   *Id.*; ERISA § 3(8), 29 U.S.C. § 1002(8) (2006) (emphasis added).

85   In an amicus brief to the Supreme Court, the Justice Department argued that this interpretation of beneficiary "has no logical stopping point, because it would allow a plan to cover anyone it chooses, including independent contractors excluded by [*Nationwide Mutual Insurance Co. v. Darden*]." Raymond B. Yates, M.D., P.C., Profit Sharing Plan v. Hendon, 541 U.S. 1, 11 n.2 (2004).

86   *See supra* Chapter 2 notes 76–78 and accompanying text.

87   *E.g.*, Peterson v. Am. Life & Health Ins. Co., 48 F.3d 404 (9th Cir.1995); Wolk v. UNUM Life Ins. of Am., 186 F.3d 352, 356–58 (3d Cir. 1999). These cases decline to treat partners as "participants" because ERISA restricts that term to employees or former employees. Instead, they hold that a partner who is covered by a benefit program along with one or more common-law employees falls within ERISA's definition of "beneficiary" because the partner is designated by the terms of the plan as a person who may be entitled to benefits. *Peterson*, 48 F.3d at 408–09; *Wolk*, 186 F.3d at 356–58.

Where a plan by its terms covers some or all categories of "employees" (meaning common-law employees), or expressly excludes independent contractors, errors in worker classification can cause wrongful denial of benefits.[88] ERISA, however, does not mandate universal coverage; it allows employees to be excluded from participation based on their mode of payment, job type, work location, or for other reasons.[89] Consequently, workers who are found to have been mistakenly treated as independent contractors are not automatically entitled to participate by virtue of their employee status; plans may, and commonly do, impose other, more restrictive conditions.

Nominal Partners

ERISA does not apply to retirement plans that cover only partners.[90] Yet an appellate court has held that a nominal partner in one of the world's largest accounting firms was more properly classified as an employee for purposes of ERISA and was therefore entitled to statutory protection against discharge intended to prevent pension vesting.[91] While recognizing that the partner-employee distinction is governed by common-law principles codified in the Uniform Partnership Act, the court's analysis was heavily influenced by the traditional test of employee status under the general common law of agency (as enunciated in *Darden*), with particular emphasis on the plaintiff's inability to participate in the management and control of the business.[92] The case presented an extreme example of a partner being frozen out by a self-perpetuating management committee.[93]

C. THE PENSION-WELFARE DICHOTOMY

ERISA applies only to an "employee benefit plan," defined as either an employee welfare benefit plan or an employee pension benefit plan.[94] Consequently, in addition

---

88 *See* Vizcaino v. Microsoft Corp., 120 F.3d 1006 (9th Cir. 1997) (en banc) (unless excluded by another provision, ERISA plan that by its terms applies to "common-law employees" must cover a large staff of "freelance" software developers that the company erroneously treated as independent contractors for employment tax purposes, despite the fact that freelancers were hired under the understanding that they were not eligible for benefits). Besides plan coverage, the worker classification distinction is important because fees paid to independent contractors are not subject to income tax withholding, nor is the payor liable for Social Security taxes or the federal unemployment tax.

89 The only eligibility conditions outlawed by ERISA are certain age and service conditions in the case of pension plans and specified health status factors in the case of group health plans. ERISA §§ 202, 702, 29 U.S.C. §§ 1052, 1182 (2006).

90 29 C.F.R. § 2510.3-3(b), -3(c)(2) (2009).

91 Simpson v. Ernst & Young, 100 F.3d 436 (6th Cir. 1996).

92 *Id.* at 443.

93 See the district court's opinion for a fuller recitation of facts, *Simpson v. Ernst & Young*, 850 F. Supp. 648, 650–53 (S.D. Ohio 1994).

94 ERISA §§ 4(a), 3(3), 29 U.S.C. §§ 1003(a), 1002(3) (2006).

to requiring a "plan" in which at least one "employee" participates, federal regulation applies only if the arrangement provides either welfare or pension benefits. A program that provides retirement income, or systematically defers compensation until termination of covered employment or beyond, qualifies as a pension plan.[95] A program that provides any of certain *specifically listed benefits* is a welfare plan, whether the benefit is provided on a current or deferred basis.[96] Welfare benefits may be provided in kind, but far more commonly, they take the form of cash payments or reimbursements of the cost of designated expenses (e.g., medical care). Any nonpension employee benefit that is not enumerated in the definition of "welfare plan" is wholly exempt from federal regulation. This section examines some curious features of this statutory benefit taxonomy, beginning with pension benefits.

Pension Benefits

Pension plans are subject to the most intensive federal regulation because of the long-term nature of the benefit promise and the resulting potential for changed circumstances and defeated expectations.[97] Because a worker's employment or family circumstances may change, ERISA requires that pension benefits become nonforfeitable (i.e., that they vest) upon the completion of no more than seven years of service and normally provides survivor annuity protection to the participant's spouse. Because the employer's financial condition may take an unexpected turn for the worse, ERISA contains safeguards against default, requiring systematic advance funding and PBGC insurance of defined benefit plans. Although deferral creates the risks to which these rules respond, the statutory definition of a pension plan is not simply keyed to the duration of the commitment. To be a pension plan, the program must "(i) provide[] retirement income to employees, or (ii) result[] in a deferral of income by employees for periods extending to the termination of covered employment or beyond."[98] Consequently, deferral of compensation, even for an extended period, does not create a pension plan (absent special circumstances) if the deferred amounts are payable

---

95   ERISA § 3(1), 29 U.S.C. § 1002(1) (2006).
96   ERISA § 3(2)(A), 29 U.S.C. § 1002(2)(A) (2006).
97   *See supra* Chapter 1B and 1C.
98   ERISA § 3(2)(A), 29 U.S.C. § 1002(2)(A) (2006). ERISA is not a tax statute, and so the definitional references to "retirement income" and "deferral of income" should not be construed as conditioning pension plan classification on the time at which compensation must be included in gross income. Funded nonqualified deferred compensation is taxable upon the elimination of any substantial risk of forfeiture, I.R.C. §§ 402(b), 83(a) (2006), which may occur well in advance of retirement or separation from service, yet such plans were clearly intended to be subject to ERISA. *See, e.g.,* ERISA § 201(2), 29 U.S.C. § 1051(2) (2006) (only certain *unfunded* executive deferred compensation plans are subject to relaxed regulation). Hence, the references to income in the pension plan definition should be interpreted according to the timing of the *distribution* of deferred compensation—in accordance, that is, with the common understanding that the term "income" has reference to receipt.

during the continuance of the employment relationship.[99] Indeed, such in-service deferred compensation arrangements do not even meet the definition of a welfare plan, and therefore are also exempt from federal disclosure and fiduciary obligations.

Retirement income need not be paid in cash,[100] and annuity distribution is not required. A lump-sum payment can be used for support in retirement, and a plan that provides retirement income is a pension plan regardless of "the method of distributing benefits from the plan."[101] The other prong of the statutory definition is even more expansive, for a plan that defers income only to the "termination of covered employment"—that is, until separation from service—is a pension plan, although departing employees may be years away from retirement, in the sense of permanent withdrawal from the labor force. Moreover, a plan that does not, "by its express terms," provide retirement income or defer compensation until separation from service is nevertheless a pension plan if it does so "as a result of surrounding circumstances."[102] Under this rule, a deferred compensation arrangement can be a pension plan if distributions are skewed toward the last years of participants' careers,[103] and even relatively short-term deferral can trigger pension classification if the program's coverage is tilted in favor of older workers nearing retirement.[104] Absent such surrounding circumstances, the mere fact that a fixed-term deferred compensation agreement calls for earlier payment in the event of death, disability, or other termination of employment does not turn it into a pension plan because termination-based distributions are incidental, rather than being the focus of the program.[105]

---

99 A Labor Department regulation provides that the term "pension plan" does not include "payments made by an employer to some or all of its employees as bonuses for work performed, unless such payments are systematically deferred to the termination of covered employment or beyond, or so as to provide retirement income to employees." 29 C.F.R. § 2510.3-2(c) (2009).

100 *See* Musmeci v. Schwegmann Giant Super Mkts., Inc., 332 F.3d 339 (5th Cir. 2003) (vouchers for groceries provided to retired supermarket employees); I.R.C. §§ 401(a)(23), (a)(28), 409(h) (2006) (stock bonus plans and employee stock ownership plans must permit distribution in form of employer securities); *but see* Rathbun v. Qwest Commc'ns Int'l, Inc., 458 F. Supp. 2d 1238 (D. Colo. 2006) (program reimbursing active and retired employees' local telephone expenses does not provide retirement income, distinguishing *Musmeci*).

101 ERISA § 3(2)(A), 29 U.S.C. § 1002(2)(A) (2006) (final clause); ERISA Advisory Op. 75-12 (U.S. Dep't of Labor, 1975) (profit-sharing plan calling for lump-sum distribution on termination of employment is a pension plan under ERISA). A pair of Fourth Circuit decisions can be read as finding long-term payout important to pension classification, but that conclusion is suspect. Wiedenbeck, *supra* Chapter 1 note 57, at 579–81.

102 ERISA § 3(2)(A), 29 U.S.C. § 1002(2)(A) (2006).

103 ERISA Advisory Op. 83-46A (U.S. Dep't of Labor, 1983) (late-career distributions and long payout schedule are factors to be considered in determining whether a deferred compensation arrangement is a pension plan as a result of surrounding circumstances).

104 *E.g.*, ERISA Advisory Op. 89-07A (U.S. Dep't of Labor, 1989) (bonus program under which employee must continue to be employed for five years to receive payment is not a pension plan unless the selection of bonus recipients is skewed toward employees nearing retirement); ERISA Advisory Op. 81-16A (U.S. Dep't of Labor, 1981) (ten-year payout could make oil and gas royalty fund a pension plan, depending on the likelihood that employees permitted to participate will retire or separate from service within that period).

105 Hagel v. United Land Co., 759 F. Supp. 1199, 1202 (E.D. Va. 1991) (bonus that provided for payment in five equal annual installments or earlier in the event of death, permanent disability,

If a participant is given the option of taking payment of deferred compensation after a specified period of time or allowing the amount to remain on deposit for distribution (with earnings) upon separation from service, is it a pension plan? Provided that early payment is not penalized nor delayed distribution subsidized (by the tax law or the employer) so as to bias the participant's choice, the program would not cause compensation to be *systematically* deferred until the termination of employment, and is exempt from ERISA.[106] If, however, the employer administers the program in a way that discourages participants from taking early payment, then it is a pension plan as a result of surrounding circumstances. These circumstances may include the employer's communications (or lack thereof) concerning the program, such as the failure to publicize the early withdrawal option.[107]

Severance pay plans present a unique classification challenge under ERISA. Severance pay is, by definition, compensation deferred until the termination of employment. Thus, it would automatically fall into the pension category, but for a special dispensation. That dispensation takes the form of statutory authorization for the Secretary of Labor to write regulations treating some or all severance pay arrangements as welfare plans rather than pension plans.[108] Pursuant to that authority, if severance payments that do not exceed twice the employee's annual pre-termination compensation are completed within two years, the program will not be treated as a pension plan, provided that the payments are not conditioned, directly or indirectly, on retirement.[109]

---

or change in control of employer held not pension plan because ERISA requires that a plan "generally defer the receipt of income to the termination of employment," which is not satisfied where "under the facts of a particular case, a portion of the withheld income happens to become due after termination"); ERISA Advisory Op. 83-46A (U.S. Dep't of Labor, 1983) ("[The] mere fact that a plan provides that payments which would otherwise be made on a specified date may be paid earlier in the event an employee terminates employment does not automatically mean that the arrangement is a pension plan by its express terms," but is a factor to be considered in conjunction with surrounding circumstances). *See* Murphy v. Inexco Oil Co., 611 F.2d 570 (5th Cir. 1980).

106   29 C.F.R. § 2510.3-2(c) (2009) (bonus program does not constitute a pension plan unless "payments are systematically deferred to the termination of covered employment or beyond, or so as to provide retirement income to employees"); McKinsey v. Sentry Ins., 986 F.2d 401, 406 (10th Cir. 1993).

107   ERISA Advisory Op. 81-18A (U.S. Dep't of Labor, 1981) (employee stock purchase plan, under which participants had the right to sell their stock but were not always given share certificates, could be a pension plan if it is administered or communicated in a way that discourages participants from receiving or selling the stock); ERISA Advisory Op. 90-17A (U.S. Dep't of Labor, 1990) (employee stock purchase plan could be pension plan if communications to participants suggest that it is intended to provide retirement income or defer income until separation from service); ERISA Advisory Op. 83-46A (U.S. Dep't of Labor, 1983) (same).

108   ERISA § 3(2)(B), 29 U.S.C. § 1002(2)(B) (2006). Severance pay is also a welfare benefit by virtue of the cross-reference to benefits described in section 302(c) of the Labor-Management Relations Act in ERISA's definition of a welfare plan. ERISA § 3(1), 29 U.S.C. § 1002(1) (2006); 29 C.F.R. § 2510.3-1(a)(2) (2009). But recall that ad hoc separation payments to selected employees may be so indefinite that the arrangement does not constitute a "plan." *See* *supra* Chapter 2 notes 29–52 and accompanying text.

109   29 C.F.R. § 2510.3-2(b) (2009). The Labor Department has taken the position that severance pay may be indirectly conditioned on retirement and so subject to stringent pension plan

Welfare Benefits

Welfare plans are subject to reporting and disclosure requirements, fiduciary responsibility standards, and a federal enforcement mechanism that includes broad preemption of state law. To be classified as a welfare plan, the program must provide one or more statutorily enumerated benefits, namely:

> (A) medical, surgical, or hospital care benefits, or benefits in the event of sickness, accident, disability, death or unemployment, or vacation benefits, apprenticeship or other training programs, or day care centers, scholarship funds, or prepaid legal services, or (B) any benefit described in section 302(c) of the Labor-Management Relations Act, 1947 (other than pensions on retirement or death, and insurance to provide such pensions).[110]

In general, ERISA applies without regard to whether benefits are financed by the purchase of insurance (group-term life insurance is commonly used to provide employee death benefits, for example) or are paid out of the general assets of the employer (i.e., self-insurance).[111] While a welfare plan may provide benefits of more than one type, a benefit that is not described in ERISA does not become subject to federal regulation merely because it is included with pension or welfare benefits in a multi-benefit plan.[112] Federal preemption does not apply, and employees' rights to such non-ERISA benefits are determined by state courts under state law.

The types of benefits included in the welfare plan definition seem haphazard and unsystematic. In fact, the statute reflects the scope of two earlier pieces of federal legislation. The Welfare and Pension Plans Disclosure Act of 1958 (WPPDA) provided the starting point for ERISA's definition of a welfare plan, but it reached only "medical, surgical, or hospital care or benefits, or benefits in the event of sickness, accident, disability, death or unemployment."[113] Presumably, this definition responded to the perceived prevalence of various sorts of employee benefit programs at the time

---

regulation if the program is limited to employees with many years of service (a group for whom termination of employment is likely to mean withdrawal from the labor force, i.e., retirement) or is conditioned on taking distribution from the company's retirement plan. ERISA Advisory Op. 84-15A (U.S. Dep't of Labor, 1984) (severance arrangement limited to employees with 18 or more years of service); ERISA Advisory Op. 83-47A (U.S. Dep't of Labor, 1983) (severance pay conditioned on employee taking lump-sum distribution from defined benefit pension plan).

110 ERISA § 3(1), 29 U.S.C. § 1002(1) (2006).

111 The fiduciary responsibility provisions (Part 4, Title I) contain an exception for unfunded executive deferred compensation plans, ERISA § 401(a)(1), 29 U.S.C. § 1101(a)(1) (2006) (discussed *infra* Chapter 2D), but not for unfunded welfare plans. The welfare plan definition, however, lists "scholarship *funds*," ERISA § 3(1), 29 U.S.C. § 1002(1) (2006) (emphasis added), not scholarships generally, and so unfunded educational assistance programs are not covered. 29 C.F.R. § 2510.3-1(k) (2009).

112 ERISA § 3(1), 29 U.S.C. § 1002(1) (2006), provides that a benefit program is a welfare plan only "to the extent that" it provides one of the statutorily listed benefits. Kemp v. Int'l Bus. Machs. Corp., 109 F.3d 708 (11th Cir. 1997).

113 WPPDA, Pub. L. No. 85-836, § 3(a)(1), 72 Stat. 997 (1958) (repealed 1975).

of its enactment. ERISA expanded upon this definition by directly listing most of the benefits then described in paragraphs (6) through (8) of section 302(c) of the Labor-Management Relations Act (the Taft-Hartley Act),[114] while incorporating the rest by reference. In 1974, the cross-reference to section 302(c) reached only severance and holiday benefits,[115] but a 1990 amendment of the Taft-Hartley Act brought "financial assistance for employee housing" within the ambit of welfare plan regulation.[116]

The welfare plan definition looks only to the type of benefit. A promise of *deferred* welfare benefits is just a welfare plan, not a pension plan (the benefit is not retirement income). Consequently, retiree health care benefits are subject only to reporting and disclosure, fiduciary obligations, and federal enforcement. Because no vesting requirement applies, employers are generally free to terminate such programs at any time to stem escalating costs or for other reasons, regardless of an employee's length of service or level of need. The employer may, of course, voluntarily obligate itself to provide lifelong health care benefits to retirees, and many cases are founded on the assertion that such a contractual undertaking was made,[117] but such a commitment exceeds ERISA's minimum standards for welfare plans.

---

114   Labor-Management Relations (Taft-Hartley) Act, § 302(c), 29 U.S.C. § 186(c) (2006).

115   29 C.F.R. § 2510.3-1(a)(3) (2009) (1975 regulation observes that Taft-Hartley Act cross-reference expands ERISA's statutory list of welfare benefits only by adding holiday, severance, and similar benefits). As noted earlier, severance programs can also be classified as pension plans because benefits are deferred until "the termination of covered employment." ERISA § 3(2)(A), 29 U.S.C. § 1002(2)(A) (2006). Nevertheless, most severance pay plans are subject only to welfare plan requirements because the Labor Department has exercised its authority to exempt designated severance pay plans from pension controls by regulation. ERISA § 3(2)(B), 29 U.S.C. § 1002(2)(B) (2006); 29 C.F.R. § 2510.3-2(b) (2009). Under that regulation, if severance benefits do not exceed two years' pay and are fully distributed within two years, pension plan treatment is avoided, and almost all severance programs are written to conform to those conditions.

116   29 U.S.C. § 186(c)(7)(C) (2006). ERISA's reliance on the Taft-Hartley Act's list of benefits apparently stems from the fact that notorious abuses in the management of employee benefit funds created the impetus for ERISA's fiduciary standards, and those abuses involved trusts to provide benefits to unionized employees under the Taft-Hartley Act. That act makes it a crime for an employer to contribute to a trust for unionized employees if the trust provides any type of benefit not specifically permitted by section 302(c), and so the Taft-Hartley Act's list of permissible benefits may have been assumed to cover the field of lawful employee benefits. Unfortunately, there are two problems with this assumption. First, other types of benefits may be provided to unionized employees if they are not funded through a trust, and, in general, ERISA was intended to apply regardless of funding. (Even if there is no pot of money to steal, ERISA makes a fiduciary's discretionary decisions subject to oversight.) Second, employers may unilaterally establish benefit plans (funded or not) for their nonunionized workers, and these programs are not constrained by the Taft-Hartley Act's list of permissible benefits. Accordingly, if ERISA's definition of a welfare plan was intended to cover the universe of nonpension benefits—or even if it was meant to cover all *funded* nonpension benefits—its drafters were mistaken.

117   *See infra* Chapter 3B and 3C.

Other Benefits

ERISA's pension and welfare plan definitions fail to reach several types of compensation that can be significant to workers' career and financial planning, such as the decision whether to accept or continue employment, or the determination of the necessary amount of household saving. Or, from a paternalistic perspective, the statute fails to cover a number of benefits that can induce substantial reliance. In-service deferred compensation is among the most glaring omissions. Employer financial assistance that is targeted to dependent care or college costs is usually also exempt.[118] Because such arrangements escape classification as pension or welfare plans, federal preemption does not apply. Consequently, this third category of employee benefits, while exempt from federal oversight, is a permissible subject of state and local regulation.

D. EXCEPTIONS: TOP-HAT, GOVERNMENT, AND CHURCH PLANS

A few benefit arrangements that fit the statutory definition of an employee benefit plan (either pension or welfare) are nevertheless excepted from most or all of ERISA's requirements. The most important exceptions are for unfunded executive deferred compensation arrangements (so-called "top-hat" plans), and for plans sponsored by governmental or religious organizations.

Top-hat plans are unfunded plans "maintained by an employer primarily for the purpose of providing deferred compensation for a select group of management or highly compensated employees."[119] Although they would otherwise be classified as pension plans (the deferral invariably extends at least to the termination of employment), top-hat plans are exempt from all the minimum standards applied to pension plans and are even excused from ERISA's generally applicable fiduciary obligations.[120] Consequently, only the reporting and disclosure rules and the federal enforcement mechanisms (including preemption) apply.[121] Of these, the reporting and disclosure

---

118   The Labor Department takes the position that the welfare plan definition comprehends dependent care benefits only when the employer provides care *in kind* (on-premises child care facilities, for example) or when financed through a trust, not when the company provides financial assistance out of its general assets for employee-arranged care. ERISA Advisory Ops. 88-10A (U.S. Dep't of Labor, 1988) and 91-25A (U.S. Dep't of Labor, 1991). Similarly, the welfare plan definition takes into account "scholarship *funds*" but misses more common, unfunded employer promises to provide education benefits. 29 C.F.R. § 2510.3-1(k) (2009) (unfunded scholarship programs exempt).

119   ERISA § 201(2), 29 U.S.C. § 1051(2) (2006). Language is repeated at ERISA §§ 301(a)(3), 401(a)(1), 4021(b)(6), 29 U.S.C. §§ 1081(a)(3), 1101(a)(1), 1321(b)(6) (2006).

120   ERISA §§ 201(2) (accrual, vesting, spousal rights, and anti-alienation), 301(a)(3) (funding), 401(a)(1) (fiduciary responsibility), 4021(b)(6) (plan termination insurance), 29 U.S.C. §§ 1051(2), 1081(a)(3), 1101(a)(1), 1321(b)(6) (2006).

121   Barrowclough v. Kidder, Peabody & Co., 752 F.2d 923, 929–31 (3d Cir. 1985) (limited application to top-hat plans), *overruled on other grounds by* Pritzker v. Merrill Lynch, Pierce, Fenner & Smith, Inc., 7 F.3d 1110 (3d Cir. 1993) (arbitrability of ERISA claims).

obligations of top-hat plans have been relaxed by regulation,[122] so ERISA's principal effect on unfunded executive deferred compensation arrangements is to provide a mechanism for federal judicial enforcement of the terms of the plan, which (as a result of the ouster of state law) must be interpreted and applied according to federal common law.[123] Congress exempted top-hat plans from ERISA's requirements because high-level executives have the bargaining power to negotiate particular terms and monitor their interest under the plan, and therefore do not need substantive protections (the minimum standards of pension plan content) or fiduciary obligations. If bargaining and informal oversight break down, however, these executives must have access to judicial enforcement to vindicate their rights or the plan becomes an illusory promise.[124]

The definition of a top-hat plan leaves the scope of this exemption unclear. The plan must be unfunded and "maintained by an employer primarily for the purpose of providing deferred compensation for a select group of management or highly compensated employees." Whether "primarily" refers to the type of benefits provided or to the composition of participants was an unsettled issue[125] until the Labor Department issued an opinion in 1990. The Labor Department announced its view that "primarily" refers to the benefits provided under the plan and not to the participant composition,[126] so that the exemption may be lost if any participant is not a member of the "select group." Case law since then has followed this approach,[127] which is more consonant with

---

122   ERISA § 110, 29 U.S.C. § 1030 (2006), permits the Labor Department to prescribe an alternate method of compliance with the statutory reporting and disclosure obligations for any category of pension plans that meet certain criteria. Pursuant to that authority, the Labor Department allows an employer to satisfy its informational obligations by filing a single statement of the number of unfunded top-hat plans it maintains and the number of employees in each, and providing plan documents to the Department on request. 29 C.F.R. § 2520.104-23 (2009); *Barrowclough*, 752 F.2d at 931–34 (relaxed disclosure requirements).

123   *Barrowclough*, 752 F.2d at 935–37 (federal enforcement mechanism and federal common law apply to claim for breach of the plan's terms); Kemmerer v. ICI Americas, Inc., 70 F.3d 281, 287 (3d Cir. 1995) ("[B]reach of contract principles, applied as a matter of federal common law, govern disputes arising out of [top-hat] plan documents" and such plans should be "interpreted in keeping with the principles that govern unilateral contracts.").

124   *Kemmerer*, 70 F.3d at 288. *See* Wiedenbeck, *supra* Chapter 1 note 57, at 581.

125   Early decisions and rulings seemed to follow the latter approach, looking to the percentage of employees covered by the plan and comparing their *average* pay with the rest of the workforce, so that the exemption could apply even if a few rank-and-file employees were covered by the plan. *E.g.*, Belka v. Rowe Furniture Co., 571 F. Supp. 1249 (D. Md. 1983). *See generally* Amorso et al., *SERP Sponsors Beware*, 24 Pens. & Ben. Rep. (BNA) 1001 (1997); Edward J. Rayner, *ERISA's Top-Hat Plan Exemption: A Primer*, 99 Tax Notes 107 (2003).

126   ERISA Advisory Op. 90-14A (U.S. Dep't of Labor, 1990).

127   Gallione v. Flaherty, 70 F.3d 724, 726–28 (2d Cir. 1995) (union plan covering full-time officers, who were responsible for setting policy and negotiating labor contracts, exempt because limited to upper echelon of union management); Duggan v. Hobbs, 99 F.3d 307, 312–13 (9th Cir. 1996) (unfunded pension provided under individually negotiated severance agreement was an exempt top-hat plan because departing employee had sufficient clout to influence the design and operation of the plan).

ERISA's informational and protective policies, although in mixed-membership plans it may "safeguard" executives in ways that they do not need or want.[128]

In order to apply a rule that top-hat status is lost if any member fails to qualify as "management" or a "highly compensated employee," those categories must be specified with precision. Yet the statute leaves both terms undefined. Some practitioners have assumed that satisfaction of the tax law's quantitative definition of the term "highly compensated employee" suffices for top-hat status, but that definition serves other purposes.[129] The Labor Department's 1990 opinion seems to take the view that "the ability to affect or substantially influence, through negotiation or otherwise, the design and operation of their deferred compensation plan" provides a functional definition of "management or highly compensated employees"; and subsequent cases follow that path.[130] Under this approach, many plans that extend coverage to middle-management ranks could be found to violate ERISA's substantive provisions, even though all participants satisfy the tax law's definition of "highly compensated employee." That may be appropriate in light of ERISA's protective policy, but the functional approach requires a fact-intensive inquiry, the outcome of which is far less predictable than bright-line criteria keyed to compensation levels.

Government and church plans, both pension and welfare, are exempt from all of ERISA's labor law requirements, including the reporting and disclosure and federal enforcement provisions.[131] Unlike the top-hat plan exceptions, these exclusions are not conditioned on the plan being unfunded or limited to executives. This is unsurprising, for the absence of need for regulation was not the primary justification for excluding government and church plans from coverage. Government plans were exempted primarily because of the concern that the imposition of the new standards "might entail unacceptable cost implications to governmental entities."[132] Costs to state and local

---

128 If the top-hat plan exemption is forfeited because of the inclusion of rank-and-file employees, then ERISA's pension funding and vesting requirements would come into play, which (in the case of a nonqualified plan) would cause the participants to be taxed in advance of distribution. *See* I.R.C. §§ 402(b), 83(a) (2006).

129 I.R.C. § 414(q) (2006) (definition of highly compensated employee for purposes of the coverage and amount nondiscrimination rules). *See* Raymond B. Yates, M.D., P.C. Profit Sharing Plan v. Hendon, 541 U.S. 1, 13–14 (2004) (looking to the tax Code's definition of highly compensated employee for guidance in interpreting the top-hat plan exception to ERISA's fiduciary responsibility rules).

130 *E.g.*, Duggan v. Hobbs, 99 F.3d 307 (9th Cir. 1996); Gallione v. Flaherty, 70 F.3d 724 (2d Cir. 1995). *See generally* Amoroso et al., *supra* Chapter 2 note 125.

131 ERISA §§ 4(b), 3(32), 3(33), 4021(b), 29 U.S.C. §§ 1003(b), 1002(32), 1002(33), 1321(b) (2006). In addition, government and church pension plans are excused from compliance with the tax law counterparts of ERISA's minimum standards for pension plan content; they must, however, satisfy pre-ERISA vesting rules to be treated as qualified plans. I.R.C. § 401(a) (2006) (final sentence); *id.* § 411(e) (accrual and vesting), § 412(e) (2006) (funding exception and pre-ERISA vesting requirement), § 4975(g) (2006) (prohibited-transaction excise tax exception). Church plans, but not state and local government plans, must also satisfy the pre-ERISA nondiscrimination rules. I.R.C. §§ 410(c)(2), 401(a)(5)(G), (a)(26)(G) (2006).

132 H.R. REP. No. 93-807, at 165 (1974), *reprinted in* 2 ERISA LEGISLATIVE HISTORY, *supra* Chapter 1 note 56, at 3115, 3285. ERISA did, however, mandate further congressional study of the adequacy of participant protections under governmental retirement plans. ERISA § 3031,

governments were the focus of concern, and so the governmental plan exception is founded on principles of federalism, in the sense of comity or noninterference.[133]

A governmental plan is defined generally as a plan that is "established or maintained for its employees by the Government of the United States, by the government of any State or political subdivision thereof, or by any agency or instrumentality of any of the foregoing."[134] The concept of an agency or instrumentality of a state or political subdivision is broad, but not limitless. The tax law's definition of qualified deferred compensation plans contains corresponding exceptions for government and church plans. The IRS has ruled that a volunteer fire company providing fire protection services by contract with local municipalities was not an agency or instrumentality of the government where the company was under the exclusive control of a board of trustees elected by the volunteer firefighters, was not affiliated with the state under any specific legislation, and was financed by community donations and contract fees rather than tax revenue.[135] The IRS announced a multifactor test that emphasizes the extent of public control over the organization's operations.

> A plan will not be considered a governmental plan merely because the sponsoring organization has a relationship with a governmental unit or some quasi-governmental power. One of the most important factors to be considered in determining whether an organization is an agency or instrumentality of the United States or any state or political subdivision is the degree of control that the federal or state government has over the organization's everyday operations. Other factors include: (1) whether there is specific legislation creating the organization; (2) the source of funds for the organization; (3) the manner in which the organization's trustees or operating board are selected; and (4) whether the applicable governmental unit considers the employees of the organization to be employees of the applicable governmental unit. Although all of the above factors are considered in determining whether an organization is an agency of a government, the mere satisfaction of one or all of the factors is not necessarily determinative.[136]

---

29 U.S.C. § 1231 (2006). Reports by the labor and tax committees of the House and Senate were due by the end of 1976, but no legislation resulted from efforts to develop a "Public Employee Retirement Income Security Act."

133   Rose v. Long Island R.R. Pension Plan, 828 F.2d 910, 914 (2d Cir. 1987). *See* H.R. Rep. No. 93-533, at 9 (1973).

134   ERISA § 3(32), 29 U.S.C. § 1002(32) (2006).

135   Rev. Rul. 89-49, 1989-1 C.B. 117. The tax Code's definition of a governmental plan is identical to ERISA's, except that it requires the plan to be "established and maintained" by a governmental organization rather than "established or maintained." *Compare* I.R.C. § 414(d) (2006), *with* ERISA § 3(32), 29 U.S.C. § 1002(32) (2006). This unexplained and apparently inadvertent discrepancy is discussed in *Rose*, 828 F.2d at 918–21.

136   Rev. Rul. 89-49, 1989-1 C.B. 117. Contrast I.R.S. Priv. Ltr. Rul. 9414007 (Apr. 8, 1994), which applied the same standards to find that a volunteer fire protection district created under specific state legislation was an instrumentality of state government where the bulk of its revenues were received from property taxes, and three of the seven members of the district's board of trustees were elected by property owners or appointed by public officials.

Although the Department of Labor has not adopted this test as an interpretation of ERISA's definition of a governmental plan, it appears to follow a similar approach.[137]

While the test focuses on operational control over the plan sponsor, day-to-day operational control *over the plan* is not required. A plan can be "established or maintained" by a unit of government for its employees without being governmentally administered; a health care plan for state employees is a government plan even though benefits are provided via contractual arrangements with one or more health maintenance organizations, for example.[138] Similarly, welfare and pension plans established by collective bargaining between a governmental unit and a union representing public employees are treated as established or maintained by the government, even if they are administered by a board that is not controlled by the public employer; the exemption is not limited to plans created by the unilateral action of a governmental body.[139]

ERISA also exempts church plans, apparently out of concern for separation of church and state. The exception precludes First Amendment challenges based on entangling government regulation. ERISA accommodates the complex institutional structure of some churches by including as a church any related tax-exempt organization. The related organization need not have a primary religious purpose. As a result, the church plan definition is remarkably expansive. As amended in 1980, it goes far beyond exempting plans covering religious personnel or church employees—exempting plans covering employees of religiously affiliated charitable organizations such as hospitals, schools, and group homes. An employee of a tax-exempt organization is treated as the employee of a church, and his employer is deemed to be a church if the organization is "controlled by or associated with a church or a convention or association of churches,"[140] and sharing "common religious bonds and convictions with the church" is sufficient to show association.[141] Accordingly, benefit plans covering employees of Catholic hospitals or parochial schools (for instance) may be exempt from ERISA, even though their

---

137   *E.g.*, ERISA Advisory Op. 86-06A (U.S. Dep't of Labor, 1986) (City of Milwaukee Firemen's Relief Association's death benefit plan is a governmental plan because the association was established by state statute and municipal charter, its membership is limited to current and former public employees, and the plan is subsidized by the city).

138   Silvera v. Mut. Life Ins. Co. of N.Y., 884 F.2d 423 (9th Cir. 1989); Simac v. Health Alliance Med. Plans, Inc., 961 F. Supp. 216 (C.D. Ill. 1997). Limiting the governmental plan exemption to cases of direct public administration of employee benefit plans would violate the principle of economic neutrality for no apparent purpose. Private employers cannot escape ERISA by contracting out the provision of benefits. *See* 29 C.F.R. § 2510.3-1(j) (2009) (employer may establish or maintain a benefit plan by paying premiums to provide coverage under group insurance arrangements selected by the employees).

139   ERISA Advisory Op. 79-36A (U.S. Dep't of Labor, 1979) (equal numbers of employer and union trustees); ERISA Advisory Op. 86-22A (U.S. Dep't of Labor, 1986) (governmental plan even if administered solely by union representatives).

140   ERISA § 3(33)(C)(ii)(II), (33)(C)(iii), 29 U.S.C. § 1002(33)(C)(ii)(II), (33)(C)(iii) (2006); *see* I.R.C. § 414(e)(3)(B)(ii), (e)(3)(C) (2006).

141   ERISA § 3(33)(C)(iv), 29 U.S.C. § 1002(33)(C)(iv) (2006); *see* I.R.C. § 414(e)(3)(D) (2006).

tax-exempt but nonsectarian counterparts must contend with the full force of federal regulation.[142]

The church plan definition is expansive in two further respects. First, all ministers or clergy engaged in religious work are treated as church employees even if they are technically independent contractors or are actually employed by another institution (e.g., army, prison, or hospital chaplains, or teachers of religious studies at an unrelated university).[143] Second, a retroactive correction mechanism is provided for plans that fail to meet the exemption criteria.[144]

E. CONCLUSION

The scope of federal benefit regulation is remarkably broad—it can reach an oral promise made to a single employee. Yet ERISA's coverage also has significant limitations. Some of those limitations are consistent with the statute's objectives; others are quite anomalous.

It takes a "plan" to trigger the statute. The goal of preventing mismanagement and abuse requires the oversight of discretionary decision making, so the courts have rightly concluded that the presence of discretion is sufficient to justify finding that there is a plan. Stringent fiduciary obligations were also meant to apply to anyone who handles benefit funds, and so advance funding should be enough to find a plan, even absent discretion. In contrast, an unfunded nondiscretionary benefit obligation does not require fiduciary oversight, but in that case another statutory goal may come into play. ERISA promotes economic efficiency by providing workers with the information they need to make better career and financial planning decisions. Where disclosure of the principal features of an ongoing benefit commitment would facilitate planning, that alone should be enough to find a plan.

Uncertainty as to the amount of benefits or the identity of beneficiaries has led some courts to hold that no enforceable plan exists. Often that is the right result. But ERISA was intended to protect employees' reasonable expectations, so if the employer's acts create a reasonable expectation of benefits, that expectation should be enforced notwithstanding documents or practices that purport to give the employer uncontrolled discretion over who will benefit or in what amount.

ERISA was enacted to inform and protect employees. An "employee" (construed by the Supreme Court to mean common law employee) must participate in a benefit program for the law to apply. Where working owners of an unincorporated business are covered under the same program as their common law employees, the owners' rights as plan participants are controlled by ERISA rather than state law, even though the

---

142   *E.g.*, ERISA Advisory Op. 86-03A (U.S. Dep't of Labor, 1986) (plan covering Catholic school employees); ERISA Advisory Op. 94-11A (U.S. Dep't of Labor, 1994) (plan covering employees of Mennonite hospital).

143   ERISA § 3(33)(C)(ii)(I), 29 U.S.C. § 1002(33)(C)(ii)(I) (2006); *see* I.R.C. § 414(e)(3)(B)(I) (2006); 126 Cong. Rec. 20,245 (remarks of Sen. Long).

144   ERISA § 3(33)(D), 29 U.S.C. § 1002(33)(D) (2006); *see* I.R.C. § 414(e)(4) (2006).

owners also sometimes act as employer with respect to the plan. An individual may act in more than one capacitywear multiple hats in relation to an employee benefit plan, with distinct rights and obligations flowing from those different roles.

The applicability and intensity of federal regulation is also keyed to the nature of the program's benefits; only plans providing employees with "welfare" or "pension" benefits are covered. Arguably, ERISA's goals would be best served by classifying deferred compensation of any sort as a pension benefit, with current in-kind compensation designated as a welfare benefit if the compensation is of a sort that is important enough to warrant federal oversight. The history of political and legal attention to employee benefits produced categories that are less functional, however. Pension controls come into play only if the program is designed to provide retirement income or if compensation is deferred to the termination of employment; welfare plans may offer substantial deferred compensation without concern for vesting or funding; and some important fringe benefits, including employer financial assistance with child care or college costs, are exempt from ERISA.

Three important exceptions from ERISA are also surprising in light of legislative objectives. Unfunded executive deferred compensation arrangements must use ERISA's enforcement mechanism, but are otherwise exempt from all federal and state regulation. Top managers typically have access to information and the power to protect themselves; but why limit this exception to *unfunded* deferred compensation? Executives who arrange a special trust fund for their retirement hardly need federal safeguards to reign in their hand-picked trustee. In addition, government and church plans, both pension and welfare, are entirely excluded from ERISA, regardless of the employees' need for information or protection. Although the legal rationales and political expediency of those exclusions are clear, many workers are left without protection, and in some industries ERISA's coverage can be erratic. Retirement plans of both state and church-affiliated institutions of higher education are exempt from federal oversight, for example, while private, nonsectarian colleges and universities must toe the line.

Any comprehensive new statute is bound to contain some mistakes and political compromises. ERISA has its share. ERISA's coverage, while not capricious, is in several ways quite curious.

PART II

Conduct Controls
Welfare and Pension Plans

ERISA entails two very different approaches to the regulation of employee benefits. The administration of all employee benefit plans is subject to federal oversight to promote informed participation and ensure compliance with plan terms. To protect the interests of participants and their beneficiaries (the paternalistic policy), pension plans are also subject to minimum standards governing the terms of the deferred compensation program. Since 1997, limited content controls also apply to certain terms of group health plans. Thus, ERISA monitors only the administration or *conduct* of most welfare plans, while it subjects pension plans and group health plans to both *conduct* and *content* regulation.

ERISA's conduct controls constrain the administration of all employee benefit plans, both pension and welfare, in four respects. First, reporting and disclosure rules mandate the collection and dissemination of information concerning plan terms and finances to the Secretary of Labor and plan participants and beneficiaries (Chapter 3). Second, plan fiduciaries are held to exacting standards of conduct derived from trust law (Chapter 4). Third, a federal enforcement mechanism prescribes remedies and gives the federal courts exclusive jurisdiction to enforce ERISA's requirements (including fiduciary duties), as well as jurisdiction concurrent with state courts over suits to enforce the terms of the plan (Chapter 5). And fourth, state regulation of pension and welfare plans is broadly preempted (Chapter 6).

Chapter 3

Disclosure

This chapter analyzes the major themes that have emerged from the burgeoning appellate case law on disclosure obligations. ERISA grants claimants a private right of action to recover benefits due to them or to obtain "appropriate equitable relief" to enforce the statutory obligations, including disclosure requirements and fiduciary duties. This robust civil enforcement mechanism puts teeth in the disclosure regime, as the courts have found that the employer's misdescription of plan terms can, in some instances, support a contract claim for benefits, estop the plan from denying benefits, or bind the negligent or deceitful fiduciary. The result has been an explosion of disclosure litigation.

There is an obvious functional relationship between disclosure and the other components of ERISA's conduct regulation. Reporting and disclosure of plan finances may deter fiduciary misconduct. Should deterrence fail, disclosure provides plan participants and beneficiaries the information they need to monitor the plan's administration to enforce their rights. Besides working to control mismanagement and abuse of benefit funds, disclosure also promotes economic efficiency. It gives workers the information they need to evaluate alternative employment opportunities, and it allows workers to accommodate their personal financial affairs to the employer's program. For instance, disclosure permits participants to more accurately determine their need for additional savings or insurance.

A. STATUTORY DISCLOSURE OBLIGATIONS

The statutory disclosure obligations imposed by Part 1 of Title I of ERISA apply to all employee benefit plans, both pension and welfare, although they are relaxed by regulation for certain types of plans, including unfunded or fully insured welfare plans that cover fewer than 100 participants, and unfunded or insured pension or welfare plans covering "a select group of management or highly compensated employees."[1] Disclosure obligations are imposed on the plan administrator, a person so designated by the terms of the plan; absent such designation, the plan sponsor is the administrator by default.[2] The obligations run in favor of plan participants and beneficiaries and the Secretary of Labor. Disclosure obligations are enforceable by injunction or civil penalties, and in the case of willful violations, by criminal penalties.[3]

Routine disclosure is required of three kinds of information: (1) the terms of the plan, (2) the current financial status of the plan, and (3) the participant's current entitlement to benefits under the plan. In addition, the instruments under which the plan is operated must be available for examination, and a copy must be provided by the administrator upon written request from a participant.

---

1   ERISA § 104(a)(2), (3), 29 U.S.C. § 1024(a)(2), (3) (2006) (authority to relax certain information requirements by regulation); ERISA § 110, 29 U.S.C. § 1030 (2006) (authority to prescribe alternative method of compliance for pension plans that is consistent with the statute's purposes and provides adequate disclosure); 29 C.F.R. § 2520.104-20 (2009) (small unfunded or insured welfare plans), id. §§ 2520.104-23, -24 (unfunded or insured pension or welfare plans for a select group of management or highly compensated employees).
2   ERISA §§ 101, 104, 105, 29 U.S.C. §§ 1021, 1024, 1025 (2006) (administrator's obligations); ERISA § 3(16), 29 U.S.C. 1002(16) (2006) (administrator defined). The sponsor is the employer in the case of a single-employer plan, the union in the case of a union plan, or the trustees in the case of a jointly administered Taft-Hartley plan. ERISA § 3(16), 29 U.S.C. 1002(16) (2006).
3   ERISA § 502(a)(3), (a)(5), 29 U.S.C. § 1132(a)(3), (a)(5) (2006) (injunctions); ERISA § 502(a)(1)(A), (a)(4), (a)(6), (c), 29 U.S.C. § 1132(a)(1)(A), (a)(4), (a)(6), (c) (2006) (civil penalties); ERISA § 501, 29 U.S.C. § 1131 (2006) (criminal penalties).

Plan Terms

Participants' principal source of information about the terms of the plan is the summary plan description (SPD). The SPD must be furnished to each participant and to each beneficiary receiving benefits under the plan within ninety days after the employee becomes a participant or the beneficiary first receives benefits; and a summary of any material modification or change of the information required to be presented in the SPD must be distributed to participants and beneficiaries within 210 days after the close of the plan year in which the change is adopted. In the case of a material reduction in covered services under a group health plan, notification must be made within sixty days after the change.[4] In addition, notice of a plan amendment that significantly reduces the *rate* of future benefit accrual under a defined benefit or money purchase pension plan must be provided within a reasonable time before the effective date of the amendment.[5] This *advance* notice requirement gives affected employees an opportunity to lobby their employer, seek alternative employment, or take other steps to protect their interests.[6]

Plan Finances

An annual report supplies the Labor Department with extensive information on the financial condition of the plan, including a complete set of audited financial statements and, in the case of a defined benefit pension plan, an actuarial statement detailing the funding status of the plan.[7] (Simplified reporting requirements apply to certain plans, including those covering fewer than 100 participants and unfunded or insured welfare plans.[8]) The annual report consists of a completed IRS Form 5500, the "Return/Report of Employee Benefit Plan," and schedules thereto. Form 5500 must be filed with the IRS within seven months after the close of the plan year; the IRS shares the information in Form 5500 with the Department of Labor.[9] The summary annual report (SAR) provides participants and beneficiaries with basic information on the financial condition of the plan. It is a short document (typically one page) that discloses aggregate plan expenses and benefit payments for the year, the number of participants, the value

---

4   ERISA § 104(b)(1), 29 U.S.C. § 1024(b)(1) (2006); 29 C.F.R. § 2520.104b-2, -3 (2009).

5   ERISA § 204(h), 29 U.S.C. § 1054(h) (2006); *see* I.R.C. § 4980F (006) (excise tax for failure to give advance notice); Treas. Reg. § 54.4980F-1 Q&A-9 (as amended in 2006) (reasonable time generally means 45 days). An amendment that decreases any participant's *total* accrued benefit violates ERISA's minimum standards on pension plan content. ERISA § 204(g), 29 U.S.C. § 1054(g) (2006); *see* I.R.C. § 411(d)(6) (2006). *See infra* Chapter 7B, text accompanying notes 39–50.

6   *See infra* Chapter 7B, text accompanying notes 51–54.

7   ERISA § 103, 29 U.S.C. § 1023 (2006).

8   29 C.F.R. §§ 2520.103-1(c), 2520.104–41, -44, -46 (2009).

9   29 C.F.R. §§ 2520.103-1(b), 2520.104a-5 (2009). *See* ERISA § 3004(a), 29 U.S.C. § 1204(a) (2006) (Labor–Treasury consultation and coordination in the development of forms and regulations under ERISA).

of net assets at the beginning and end of the year, as well as plan income and employer and employee contributions. The SAR also notifies participants of their right to receive, without charge, a copy of the plan's balance sheet and income statement (with notes), or a copy of the full annual report and schedules thereto upon payment of a reasonable copying charge.[10] The benefit plan annual report and SAR serve the same function under ERISA as the traditional trust law duty to periodically render an accounting to beneficiaries: they provide the information necessary to monitor and enforce compliance with fiduciary obligations.[11]

Because of the risk presented by underfunding, additional notification requirements apply to defined benefit pension plans subject to ERISA Title IV, the plan termination insurance program. After the close of each plan year, the administrator of an insured plan must provide a plan funding notice to the PBGC, to each plan participant and beneficiary, and to each union representing participants or beneficiaries; this notice must be written so as to be understandable by the average plan participant. The plan funding notice for a single-employer plan must state whether the plan met its funding target in each of the past three plan years, report the funding target attainment percentage if less than 100 percent in any of those years, and report the assets and liabilities of the plan for each of those years. If any amendment or event having a material effect on plan liabilities (e.g., a plant closing) took effect during the year, the notice must explain the change and provide a projection of its impact on plan liabilities as of the end of the plan year. The funding notice must also summarize the rules governing defined benefit plan termination, describe the nature and limits of the PBGC's guarantee of benefits, explain how to get a copy of the plan's annual report, and alert recipients if the sponsor and members of its controlled group were required to provide detailed financial information to the PBGC as a result of specified indicia of serious underfunding.[12] If the required funding notice is not timely provided, each affected participant and beneficiary may seek a civil penalty of up to $110 per day.[13]

Individual Status

ERISA requires that any participant or beneficiary whose claim for benefits is denied be given individualized notice of the specific reasons therefor, written "in a manner

---

10   ERISA §§ 101(a)(2), 104(b)(3), 29 U.S.C. §§ 1021(a)(2), 1024(b)(3) (2006) (summary annual report requirement); 29 C.F.R. § 2520.104b-10(d) (2009) (contents of summary annual report).

11   *See* RESTATEMENT (THIRD) OF TRUSTS § 83 & cmt. a (2007); RESTATEMENT (SECOND) OF TRUSTS § 172 (1959); 2A AUSTIN W. SCOTT & WILLIAM F. FRATCHER, SCOTT ON TRUSTS § 172 (4th ed. 1987) [hereinafter SCOTT ON TRUSTS].

12   ERISA § 101(a)(2), (f), 29 U.S.C. § 1021(a)(2), (f) (2006) (effective for plan years beginning after 2007; for prior years, ERISA § 4011 (repealed 2006) imposed less stringent notice requirements).

13   ERISA § 502(a)(1)(A), (c)(1), 29 U.S.C. § 1132(a)(1)(A), (c)(1) (2006); 29 C.F.R. § 2575.502c-1 (2009) (inflation adjustment). The funding notice requirement may also be enforced by injunction. ERISA § 502(a)(8), 29 U.S.C. § 1132(a)(8) (2006).

calculated to be understood by the claimant," along with a description of the steps to be taken to obtain review of the claim denial.[14] The notice must indicate what type of information would support the claim and explain why it is necessary so that the participant has a reasonable opportunity to perfect his claim.[15]

Particularized status reports must be provided to pension plan participants and beneficiaries at specified periods or upon written request. These pension benefit statements must report total accrued benefits (i.e., benefits earned by service to date) and either the portion that is nonforfeitable ("vested") or the earliest date on which they will become nonforfeitable. Invoking both the planning and anti-abuse objectives of the statute, one court observed that, were a participant unable to obtain this information on request, "his or her financial planning would be impaired and his or her effort to enforce the rights and fiduciary obligations imposed by ERISA would be severely hampered."[16] In the case of a defined contribution plan, the statement must also report the most recent valuation of any assets in which the participant's account is invested. If the participant has the right to direct the investment of his or her individual account, then the statement must also describe any limitations on that right, explain the importance of diversification to retirement security, warn of the risk of investing more than 20 percent of a portfolio in one entity, and direct attention to investment information on the Labor Department's Web site.[17] Similarly, defined contribution plan participants and beneficiaries are also generally entitled to advance notice of (1) any blackout period during which their right to direct the investment of their accounts or obtain distributions or plan loans will be suspended, and (2) their right to divest their holdings of employer securities.[18] If a pension benefit statement is not timely provided, each affected participant and beneficiary may seek civil penalty of up to $110 per day, but the corresponding civil penalty for failure to provide notice of blackout periods or divestment rights is payable to the Labor Department.[19]

Plan Instruments

Upon written request and the payment of a reasonable charge for copying, any participant or beneficiary may also obtain a copy of "the bargaining agreement, trust agreement, contract, or other instruments under which the plan is established or operated."[20] This disclosure obligation clearly applies to the plan document and any trust agreement, as well as the collective bargaining agreement in the case of a jointly administered plan under the Taft-Hartley Act. But what about a request for other documents

---

14   ERISA § 503, 29 U.S.C. § 1133 (2006); 29 C.F.R. § 2560.503-1(f), (g) (2009) (timing and contents of notice).

15   29 C.F.R. § 2560.503-1(g)(1)(iii) (2009); Wolfe v. J.C. Penney Co., 710 F.2d 388 (7th Cir. 1983).

16   Barrowclough v. Kidder, Peabody & Co., 752 F.2d 923, 934 (3d Cir. 1985).

17   ERISA § 105, 29 U.S.C. § 1025 (2006).

18   ERISA § 101(i), (m), 29 U.S.C. § 1021(i), (m) (2006).

19   ERISA § 502(a)(1), (a)(6), (c)(1), (c)(7), 29 U.S.C. § 1132(a)(1), (a)(6), (c)(1), (c)(7) (2006).

20   ERISA § 104(b)(4), 29 U.S.C. § 1024(b)(4) (2006).

that may be prepared or used in the process of plan administration? Examples include actuarial valuation reports of defined benefit plans, statements of investment policy, proxy voting guidelines, minutes of trustee meetings, schedules of usual and customary charges for reimbursable medical services, and contracts with third-party administrators. This issue has been brought to the attention of the federal courts, and the circuits have split over the necessity of disclosing actuarial reports.[21]

Certain generalizations are safe. Clearly, a participant's access to "instruments under which the plan is established or operated" is less extensive than the Labor Secretary's authority to "require the submission of reports, books, and records" in investigating compliance with ERISA.[22] The objective of disclosure is to ensure "that the individual participant knows exactly where he stands with respect to the plan— what benefits he may be entitled to, what circumstances may preclude him from obtaining benefits, what procedures he must follow to obtain benefits, and who are the persons to whom the management and investment of his plan funds have been entrusted."[23] Consistent with that purpose, information should not be disclosable simply because it is used in the course of plan administration, even if it is essential data, like the names and addresses of plan participants.[24] Accordingly, a "but for" test (i.e., but for the information, the plan could not be operated) is inappropriate. Similarly, although ERISA requires retention of records to permit verification by the Labor Department of required reports,[25] there is no need to disclose such data and backup documentation to participants and beneficiaries.

"[I]nstruments under which the plan is established or operated" contemplates governing instruments. "Congress meant the formal legal documents that govern or confine a plan's operations, rather than routine documents with which or by means of which a plan conducts its operations."[26] The courts' interpretation is consistent with the Supreme Court's observation that paragraphs (2) and (4) of ERISA § 104(b) require access to "a set of all currently operative, governing plan documents."[27] Although ERISA demands that a plan be "established and maintained pursuant to a written instrument," a *single* plan document is not required. Frequently, recourse to a multiplicity of documents is necessary to define the terms of a welfare plan. Even pension plans,

---

21   *Compare* Bd. of Trustees of the CWA/ITU Negotiated Pension Plan v. Weinstein, 107 F.3d 139 (2d Cir. 1997) (release of actuarial report not required), *with* Bartling v. Fruehauf Corp., 29 F.3d 1062 (6th Cir. 1994) (release required).

22   *Compare* ERISA § 104(b)(4), 29 U.S.C. § 1024(b)(4) (2006), *with* ERISA § 504(a)(1), 29 U.S.C. § 1134(a)(1) (2006).

23   S. Rep. No. 93-127, at 27 (1973), *reprinted in* 1 ERISA Legislative History, *supra* Chapter 1 note 56, at 613.

24   Hughes Salaried Retirees Action Comm. v. Adm'r of the Hughes Non-Bargaining Ret. Plan, 72 F.3d 686, 689–91 (9th Cir. 1995) (en banc) (disclosure of names and addresses of retirees not required; section 104(b)(4) does not mandate release of all documents that are critical to the operation of the plan).

25   ERISA § 107, 29 U.S.C. § 1027 (2006).

26   *Weinstein*, 107 F.3d at 142. *Accord* Brown v. Am. Nat'l Life Holdings, 190 F.3d 856, 861 (8th Cir. 1999); Ames v. Am. Nat'l Can Co., 170 F.3d 751, 758–59 (7th Cir. 1999); Faircloth v. Lundy Packing Co., 91 F.3d 648, 653 (4th Cir. 1996).

27   Curtiss-Wright Corp. v. Schoonejongen, 514 U.S. 73, 84 (1995) (dicta).

which are typically maintained pursuant to complex plan documents that often run thirty pages or longer, commonly rely on subsidiary instruments to control certain aspects of their operation, such as an investment policy or claims procedure.

Under this governing instrument interpretation, any documents that "set the rights or obligations of participants or fiduciaries" would have to be disclosed.[28] In private rulings, the Labor Department takes the position that if a document

> establishes or amends the plan in question, establishes a claims procedure, specifies formulas, methodologies, or schedules to be applied in determining or calculating a participant's or beneficiary's benefit entitlement, or does any of the other things described in sections 402(b) and 402(c) of ERISA [which specify certain required and permitted terms of employee benefit plans], it would have to be furnished in accordance with the terms of section 104(b)(4).[29]

Consequently, the Labor Department ruled that access must be given to a schedule of usual and customary fees used as the basis for determining the dollar amount to be paid for health claims under a welfare benefit plan,[30] but that minutes of trustees' meetings need not be released where they concern a review of the investment manager's performance and do not specify plan terms or procedures.[31] In line with this position, in 2000 the Labor Department revised the claims procedure regulation to provide that where a claim is denied under a group health plan or disability benefit plan, and an "internal rule, guideline, protocol, or other similar criterion was relied upon in making the adverse determination," the internal guidance must be disclosed.[32]

Documents that specify benefit entitlements or impose *binding obligations* on plan administrators are a clear case for disclosure. But what about documents that do not control plan operations but limit or *constrain decision making*? And what of documents that, although *purely advisory*, are intended to influence fiduciary judgment, such as the opinions of lawyers, accountants, and other professionals?

Standards that limit discretion rule out certain actions and thereby control plan operations to that extent. Consider investment guidelines (e.g., a maximum percentage of the fund's portfolio that may be invested in common stock), or a nonexclusive list of circumstances in which a hardship distribution from a profit-sharing plan will be allowed. Limits such as these can easily affect a participant's standing in relation to the plan. Therefore, the policy of facilitating better-informed career and financial planning calls for disclosure. That conclusion finds some support in the case law. The Second Circuit has ruled that access must be granted to documents that "govern or *confine* a plan's operations," and the Fourth Circuit ordered disclosure of an employee stock

---

28   *Weinstein*, 107 F.3d at 146.

29   ERISA Advisory Op. 97-11A (U.S. Dep't of Labor, 1997) (ruling that a contract between the plan and a third-party administrator need not be disclosed unless it supplies such terms, procedures, or formulae).

30   ERISA Advisory Op. 96-14A (U.S. Dep't of Labor, 1996).

31   ERISA Advisory Op. 87-10A (U.S. Dep't of Labor, 1987). *See* ERISA Advisory Op. 82-33A (U.S. Dep't of Labor, 1982) (distinguishing minutes of trustees' meetings that would have to be disclosed).

32   29 C.F.R. § 2560.503-1(g)(1)(v) (2009).

ownership plan's (ESOP) funding and investment policies, which ordinarily provide only guidelines or general instructions to fiduciaries but do not direct particular outcomes.[33]

Nonbinding advice or instructions to the fiduciary present the most difficult case for disclosure. Typical of this category are reports or memoranda setting out factors that should (or should not) be considered by a fiduciary in making a decision. Such factors are usually intended to be evaluated in light of all the relevant circumstances and so, standing alone, are not outcome-determinative. Realistically, such advice from the fiduciary's supervisor (commonly, employees of the plan sponsor serve as fiduciaries[34]) or from a professional with special expertise is going to be taken seriously; de facto, it establishes a binding protocol for decision making which, although it does not control the outcome, is certainly intended to influence it. From this perspective, the policy of disclosure applies here with equal force. Trust law also supports disclosure, for section 104(b)(4) is ERISA's counterpart to a trustee's duty to furnish information to beneficiaries upon request, and that duty extends to inspection of opinions of counsel obtained by the trustee to assist in the administration of the trust.[35]

On the other hand, one appellate court held that a report containing recommendations and advice is not subject to mandatory disclosure,[36] and two other courts construed the requirement in ways that seem to compel that result.[37] In addition, documentary disclosure might simply lead to oral communication of such advice and instructions.

A rule requiring disclosure of any protocol for administration or fiduciary decision making, whether it be binding, confining, or merely advisory, seems most consistent with the goals of disclosure. If, however, a distinction is drawn between purely advisory reports or recommendations and more or less binding instructions, courts should pay attention to the function of various plan-related documents. An actuarial report has been kept confidential on the ground that plan fiduciaries were not required to accept its recommendation, and so it was more akin to a status report or advisory opinion.[38]

---

33 *Weinstein*, 107 F.3d at 142 (emphasis added); Faircloth v. Lundy Packing Co., 91 F.3d 648, 656 (4th Cir. 1996). *See* 29 C.F.R. § 2509.94-2 (2009) (definition of statement of investment policy and conclusion that fiduciary's obligation under ERISA § 404(a)(1)(D), 29 U.S.C. § 1104(a)(1)(D) (2006), to act "in accordance with the documents and instruments governing the plan" requires compliance with such guidelines).

34 *See* ERISA § 408(c)(3), 29 U.S.C. § 1108(c)(3) (2006) (officer, employee, or agent of plan sponsor may serve as fiduciary).

35 RESTATEMENT (THIRD) OF TRUSTS § 82(2) & cmt. f (2007); RESTATEMENT (SECOND) OF TRUSTS § 173 (1959); 2A SCOTT ON TRUSTS, *supra* Chapter 3 note 11, § 173. *But see* Varity Corp. v. Howe, 516 U.S. 489, 497 (1996) ("[T]he law of trusts often will inform, but will not necessarily determine the outcome of, an effort to interpret ERISA's fiduciary duties.").

36 *Weinstein*, 107 F.3d at 144–45.

37 *Faircloth*, 91 F.3d at 655 (disclosure of ESOP stock valuation report not required because report not a formal legal document under which plan is set up or managed); Hughes Salaried Retirees Action Comm. v. Adm'r of the Hughes Non-Bargaining Ret. Plan, 72 F.3d 686, 691 (9th Cir. 1995) (en banc) (disclosure limited to documents similar in nature to those specifically listed in ERISA § 104(b)(4)).

38 *Weinstein*, 107 F.3d at 144–45.

In fact, however, an actuarial report effectively determines a defined benefit plan's minimum funding obligation by virtue of the actuary's determination of actuarial assumptions, experience gains and losses, accrued liability, and the actuarial value of plan assets; these critical determinations should be open to examination, for they affect the extent to which participants bear a risk of underfunding.[39] Funding in excess of ERISA's minimum standards is left to the discretion of the employer. To this extent, an actuarial report can be fairly characterized as advisory, and so segregation or redacting may be required if access to nonbinding advice is denied. Similarly, an ESOP stock valuation report has been withheld, apparently with no appreciation of the fact that the appraisal measures the participants' account values, and so effectively sets the level of plan benefits.[40]

B. SPD CONTENTS AND CONSEQUENCES

ERISA requires that participants and beneficiaries be furnished with a summary plan description (SPD) "written in a manner calculated to be understood by the average plan participant [that is] sufficiently accurate and comprehensive to reasonably apprise such participants and beneficiaries of their rights and obligations under the plan."[41] The SPD is intended to give participants accessible, reliable information about the plan, and to serve as their primary source of information concerning the plan's terms.[42] This section analyzes the legal effects of the SPD when it conflicts with the plan document, is internally inconsistent, or is incomplete or ambiguous.

A few preliminary generalizations are in order. First, the SPD was intended to facilitate workers' career and financial planning, and, as such, it must be reliable enough to be the basis of action. As a corollary, language asserting that, in the event the SPD conflicts with the plan document(s) or is incomplete or ambiguous, the terms of the plan document(s) control (an SPD disclaimer clause) cannot be effective in all events, for that would defeat the informational objectives of the statute. Yet a document written to be understood by the average participant cannot be *completely* accurate and comprehensive; it need be only *reasonably* so, in recognition of the fact that generalizations and simplifications are necessary to make the SPD intelligible, and therefore useful, to the intended audience. Accordingly, there can be no categorical answer to the question whether the SPD or the formal plan document(s) should control in cases

---

39 *See* ERISA §§ 302, 303, 29 U.S.C. §§ 1082, 1083 (2006); *see also* I.R.C. §§ 412, 430 (2006); PETER J. WIEDENBECK & RUSSELL K. OSGOOD, CASES AND MATERIALS ON EMPLOYEE BENEFITS 386–437 (1996).

40 *Faircloth*, 91 F.3d at 655. An ESOP of a closely held corporation is required to give participants the right to take cash instead of stock distributions, with the amount determined under a fair valuation formula. I.R.C. § 4975(e)(7) (2006) (ESOP definition), *id.* §§ 401(a)(23), 409(h) (2006) (put option).

41 ERISA § 102(a), 29 U.S.C. § 1022(a) (2006).

42 The comprehensibility of the SPD has recently become an area of policy concern. *See SPDs Are Difficult to Understand, Lack Clarity, Practitioners Tell Council*, 32 Pens. & Ben. Rep. (BNA) 1517 (2005).

of incongruence. The necessity of compromises between precision and understandability demands a more nuanced approach.

The Inaccurate SPD

There is nearly unanimous agreement in the case. law that the purposes of disclosure demand that the SPD have controlling legal effect in the event it conflicts with the terms of the plan, notwithstanding a disclaimer clause.[43] The leading case is *Hansen v. Continental Insurance Co.*:

> Under Continental's proposed rule [that the SPD must yield if it is ambiguous or in conflict with the terms of the plan or insurance policy] the summary would not need to be accurate or comprehensive—if there were an ambiguity in the summary or an inaccuracy that put the summary in conflict with the policy, that ambiguity or inaccuracy would be cured by the policy itself. The result would be that before a participant in the plan could make any use of the summary, she would have to compare the summary to the policy to make sure that the summary was unambiguous, accurate, and not in conflict with the policy. Of course, if a participant has to read and understand the policy in order to make use of the summary, then the summary is of no use at all.

* * *

> [T]his Court holds that the summary plan description is binding, and that if there is a conflict between the summary plan description and the terms of the policy, the summary plan description shall govern. Any other rule would be, as the Congress recognized, grossly unfair to employees and would undermine ERISA's requirement of an accurate and comprehensive summary.

* * *

> Finally, in keeping with our conclusion that statements in the summary plan description are binding this Court must also reject Continental's argument that it can disclaim the binding effect of the summary plan description.

* * *

---

43   Hansen v. Cont'l Ins. Co., 940 F.2d 971, 981–82 (5th Cir. 1991). *Accord* Atwood v. Newmont Gold Co., 45 F.3d 1317, 1321 (9th Cir. 1995) (dicta); Aiken v. Policy Mgmt. Sys. Corp., 13 F.3d 138, 140–41 (4th Cir. 1993); Senkier v. Hartford Life & Accident Ins. Co., 948 F.2d 1050, 1051 (7th Cir. 1991) (dicta); Heidgerd v. Olin Corp., 906 F.2d 903, 907–08 (2d Cir. 1990); Edwards v. State Farm Mut. Auto. Ins. Co., 851 F.2d 134, 136 (6th Cir. 1988); McKnight v. S. Life & Health Ins. Co., 758 F.2d 1566, 1571 (11th Cir. 1985) (alternative holding). *Contra* Kolentus v. Avco Corp., 798 F.2d 949, 958 (7th Cir. 1986); *but see* De Nobel v. Vitro Corp., 885 F.2d 1180, 1195 (4th Cir. 1989) (disclaimer effective, but that conclusion subsequently treated as dictum by *Pierce v. Security Trust Life Insurance Co.*, 979 F.2d 23, 28 n.4 (4th Cir. 1992)). *But cf.* Bergt v. Ret. Plan for Pilots Employed by Mark Air, Inc., 293 F.3d 1139, 1145 (9th Cir. 2002) (if SPD contradicts plan document and plan document is more favorable to employees, then plan document controls).

                                                       ERISA: PRINCIPLES OF EMPLOYEE BENEFIT LAW

[I]f the insurer could escape the binding effect of the summary simply by adding a disclaimer to the summary, the insurer could escape the requirement of an accurate and comprehensive summary plan description. Accordingly, this Court holds, as a necessary corollary to its holding that the statements in the summary plan description are binding, that drafters of a summary plan description may not disclaim its binding nature.[44]

Usually participants receive only the SPD, not the underlying plan document(s). In *Hansen*, by contrast, the terms of the plan were actually distributed to participants as an attachment to the SPD, yet the court found that the summary prevails despite the disclaimer.[45]

The circuits are split over whether a showing of contradictory terms is sufficient to have the language of the SPD trump the plan documents. Some of the decisions explicitly treat the matter as one of estoppel.[46] The Seventh and Eleventh Circuits require the participant or beneficiary to prove detrimental reliance as a condition to recovery.[47] Other courts are more lenient, offering disappointed claimants an alternative. Instead of requiring detrimental reliance, the First, Fourth, Eighth, and Tenth Circuits insist only that the participant "show some significant reliance upon, or possible prejudice flowing from, the faulty plan description."[48]

In contrast, the Third and Sixth Circuits hold that proof of detrimental reliance is not necessary to recover under a defective SPD. The Sixth Circuit stated that "existing precedent does not dictate that a claimant who has been misled by summary descriptions must prove detrimental reliance. Congress has promulgated clear directives prohibiting misleading summary descriptions. This court elects not to undermine the legislative command by imposing technical requirements upon the employee."[49]

---

44   *Hansen*, 940 F.2d at 981–82.

45   *Id.* at 980. An SPD disclaimer clause can be effective *against the employer*: "having represented to its employees that the Plan—not the handbook—governed questions about benefits, [the employer] cannot now repudiate this representation and rely on statements in the handbook that are less favorable to [the participant]." Glocker v. W.R. Grace & Co., 974 F.2d 540, 542 (4th Cir. 1992).

46   *E.g.*, Senkier v. Hartford Life & Accident Ins. Co., 948 F.2d 1050, 1051 (7th Cir. 1991) (Posner, J.); Gridley v. Cleveland Pneumatic Co., 924 F.2d 1310, 1316, 1318–19 (3d Cir. 1991).

47   Health Cost Controls of Ill., Inc. v. Washington, 187 F.3d 703 (7th Cir. 1999) (if "the plan and the summary plan description conflict, the former governs . . . unless the plan participant or beneficiary has reasonably relied on the summary plan description to his detriment"); Andersen v. Chrysler Corp., 99 F.3d 846 (7th Cir. 1996); Branch v. G. Bernd Co., 955 F.2d 1574, 1579 (11th Cir. 1992).

48   Govini v. Bricklayers, Masons & Plasterers Int'l Union, Local No. 5 Pension Fund, 732 F.2d 250, 252 (1st Cir. 1984); Bachelder v. Commc'ns Satellite Corp., 837 F.2d 519, 522–23 (1st Cir. 1988) (following *Govini*); Aiken v. Policy Mgmt. Sys. Corp., 13 F.3d 138, 141 (4th Cir. 1993) (adopting *Govini* test and holding that it requires either reliance or prejudice, not both); Palmisano v. Allina Health Sys., 190 F.3d 881, 888 (8th Cir. 1999); Anderson v. Alpha Portland Indus., 836 F.2d 1512, 1520 (8th Cir. 1988); Chiles v. Ceridian Corp., 95 F.3d 1505, 1519 (10th Cir. 1996).

49   Edwards v. State Farm Mut. Auto. Ins. Co., 851 F.2d 134, 137 (6th Cir. 1988). *Accord* Helwig v. Kelsey-Hayes Co., 93 F.3d 243, 249–50 (6th Cir. 1996) (*Edwards* principle that defective SPD trumps inconsistent language in plan documents applies to welfare as well as pension plans).

The Sixth Circuit seems to be saying that the function of the SPD requires that it be treated as the binding contract between the employer and participating employees, so that the SPD's terms, as far as they go, are the terms of the plan itself. The Third Circuit, which applies an especially strict version of estoppel in ERISA cases, initially held that "a summary plan description is not a 'plan' within the meaning of [ERISA]."[50] It later characterized those comments as dictum, concluding that the better view is that the SPD controls over contradictory plan language as a matter of contract, without proof of reliance.[51] Without explicitly addressing reliance, the Eighth Circuit seems to reach the same result by treating the SPD as one of the plan documents and applying contract interpretation principles to resolve any ambiguity that appears from reading the summary in conjunction with the formal plan contract.[52]

After reviewing the confusion in the appellate courts, the Second Circuit rejected reliance and opted to require a showing of possible or likely prejudice.[53] Acknowledging that the "courts apply the amorphous prejudice standard with varying degrees of stringency," the court applied a presumption of prejudice, which the plan sponsor apparently could overcome only by showing that the plaintiff was actually aware of the plan document's contrary terms.[54] The likely prejudice standard is so lenient that it may differ little in operation from a rule enforcing the SPD as a matter of contract.

If reliance is necessary, the SPD governs as a matter of estoppel; if reliance is not necessary, the SPD is enforced as a matter of contract because it sets forth the principal terms of the "plan" itself. Doctrinally, the importance of distinguishing between the two approaches is the available remedy. ERISA § 502 and the cases interpreting it circumscribe the relief available to a plan participant or beneficiary: he may sue to "recover benefits due to him under the terms of his plan," and may also "obtain other appropriate equitable relief [to redress a violation or to enforce] any provisions of this title or the terms of the plan."[55] If the misleading SPD merely describes but does not

50   Gridley v. Cleveland Pneumatic Co., 924 F.2d 1310, 1316 (3d Cir. 1991).
51   Burstein v. Ret. Account Plan for Employees of Allegheny Health Educ. & Research Found., 334 F.3d 365, 376–77, 380–82 (3d Cir. 2003). *See also* Rhorer v. Raytheon Eng'rs & Constructors, Inc., 181 F.3d 634, 644 n.12 (5th Cir. 1999) ("This Court has never held that an ERISA claimant must prove reliance on a summary plan description in order to prevail on a claim to recover benefits.").
52   Jensen v. SIPCO, Inc., 38 F.3d 945, 949, 950, 953 (8th Cir. 1994); *id.* at 953 ("SPDs are simply part of that interpretive landscape"); Barker v. Ceridian Corp., 122 F.3d 628, 633, 635, 638 (8th Cir. 1997). Each opinion observes that because of the importance of disclosure, the terms of the SPD must prevail in the event of a conflict between the formal plan provisions and the summary. *Jensen*, 38 F.3d at 952; *Barker*, 122 F.3d at 633. The tension in *Barker*, however, was apparently internal to the SPD, and so the case may be better understood as an example of a self-contradictory SPD.
53   Burke v. Kodak Ret. Income Plan, 336 F.3d 103, 111–14 (2d Cir. 2003) (declining to use "harsh common law principles to defeat employees' claims based on a federal law designed for their protection").
54   *Id.* at 113, 114. *See* Weinreb v. Hosp. for Joint Diseases Orthopaedic Inst., 404 F.3d 167, 171–72 (2d Cir. 2005) (following *Burke*, but finding presumption rebutted by actual knowledge of plan requirement).
55   ERISA § 502(a)(1)(B), (a)(3)(B), 29 U.S.C. § 1132(a)(1)(B), (a)(3)(B) (2006). Case law interpreting section 502 is discussed *infra* Chapter 5D.

itself comprise "the plan," then a suit for benefits (recovery on the contract) will fail, for the terms of the plan as set forth in the plan documents have not been breached. Consequently, instead of enforcing the plan, recovery is limited to "appropriate equitable relief" to enforce ERISA in contravention of the plan. A claim of promissory estoppel is equitable in nature and redresses a violation of the statutory requirement that the SPD be accurate.[56] Promissory estoppel is conditioned on proof of reliance. Alternatively, if the SPD is understood to embody the deal, then the SPD (as far as it goes) sets out the terms of the plan itself, and recovery on the contract is available in a suit for benefits, without proof of reliance.

The issue is which remedial approach to an inaccurate SPD is preferable in light of ERISA's policies. In the employee benefits context, proof of reliance can be difficult and costly. Discrete instances in which the employee rejected another job offer, failed to save, or declined to purchase additional insurance because of her understanding of a plan's promised benefits are hard to support with objective evidence. Consequently, conditioning recovery on proof of detrimental reliance may lead to significant under-enforcement of the norm that the SPD provide accurate information. Under-enforcement reduces the sponsor's incentive to take adequate precautions.[57] Accordingly, requiring reliance as a condition of recovery (the estoppel approach) appears less in line with ERISA's underlying policies than directly enforcing the SPD as the plan (the contract approach).[58] Admittedly, treating the summary plan *description* as the *plan* presents a certain linguistic challenge; but if the SPD is to fulfill its role of facilitating planning, it will be treated by workers as the deal. Recognizing the SPD as the central plan document—despite its form—ensures that it will provide accessible, reliable information.[59]

---

56   ERISA § 102(a), 29 U.S.C. § 1022(a) (2006).

57   In principle, intentional deception could be deterred by the threat of criminal or civil penalties, or tort liability for fraud. ERISA offers very little in the way of penalties for deliberate misrepresentation, however. Willful disclosure violations are a crime, ERISA § 501, 29 U.S.C. § 1131 (2006), but public enforcement is too sporadic to provide a substantial deterrent. The common law has traditionally given a bounty to private litigants, in the form of exemplary or punitive damage awards, to stamp out egregious misconduct, but punitive damages are not available under ERISA (*infra* Chapter 5D). That would seem to leave ERISA's civil penalties as the sole instrument of deterrence. But there is a problem here as well—no penalty is automatically triggered by publication of a defective SPD. Even if the courts could craft an adequate deterrent to fraud, the problem of negligent misdescription would remain, and insistence on proof of reliance would lead to under-enforcement of the requirement that the SPD be accurate.

58   *See* Bergt v. Ret. Plan for Pilots Employed by Mark Air, Inc., 293 F.3d 1139, 1145 (9th Cir. 2002) ("[T]he law should provide as strong an incentive as possible for employers to write the SPDs so that they are consistent with the ERISA plan master documents, a relatively simple task.").

59   Another way to describe this approach (that does less violence to the language) is to say that the SPD misrepresentation is grounds for reformation of the underlying plan documents. Traditional contract law would permit reformation if the misrepresentation is fraudulent and material, RESTATEMENT (SECOND) OF CONTRACTS §§ 166, 167 & cmt. b (1979), but ERISA's policy of promoting optimal career and financial planning requires that those limitations be dispensed within the case of SPD misrepresentations. Better still, the SPD may be equated with an express warranty of coverage or benefits, the breach of which gives rise to a right to expectation damages. *Cf.* U.C.C. § 2-313(1) (2003) ("Any description of goods which is made part

The Self-Contradictory SPD

If, instead of contradicting the underlying plan documents, the SPD contradicts itself, the courts generally refuse to impose liability, on the view that reliance is unjustified. If a reasonable participant's careful reading of the SPD alone reveals an inconsistency, further investigation would seem to be the prudent response. Accordingly, where the SPD is obviously defective, the participant arguably has a duty to consult the terms of the underlying plan documents and fails to do so at his peril.

This problem received a great deal of attention during the 1990s in a series of cases involving SPDs that apparently promised no-cost, life-long retiree health care, but also reserved to the employer the unrestricted right to amend or terminate the plan.[60] ERISA does not require vesting of welfare benefits,[61] and retiree health care is classified as a welfare benefit, even though the plan provides valuable long-term deferred compensation. The employer is free, however, to make a commitment to vesting.[62] The employer may, as a matter of contract, unconditionally obligate itself to provide future welfare benefits, or it can extend such benefits subject to any conditions or limitations it chooses. Employers providing retiree health care plans typically condition eligibility for benefits on retirement at specified ages (as opposed to separation from service under circumstances where the employee is likely to work for another firm), and may require completion of an extended period of service. In addition, the plan documents invariably reserve the right to amend or terminate the plan, for ERISA requires every employee benefit plan to contain a procedure for amending the plan.[63] Read broadly, such a "reservation of rights" clause imposes a crucial additional condition on eligibility for benefits: that the company not alter or disavow its commitment before the health care is sought. The real issue in the retiree health plan cutback cases is how broadly *should* such a reservation of rights clause be read?

The matter is noncontroversial if the SPD clearly warns that the employer is obligated to provide retiree health care for the time being only; and while the employer expects the program to continue, it may be altered or discontinued at any time for any reason. Plan sponsors are not always so forthright, however, for they have an interest in obtaining the maximum advantage from such benefit programs, which requires that workers place a high value on them. To obtain that advantage (typically reduced

---

of the basis of the bargain creates an express warranty that the goods shall conform to the description."), *id.* § 2-714(2) (expectation damages for breach of warranty).

60 *E.g.*, Vallone v. CNA Fin. Corp., 375 F.3d 623 (7th Cir. 2004); Sprague v. Gen. Motors Corp., 133 F.3d 388, 403 (6th Cir. 1998) (en banc); Chiles v. Ceridian Corp., 95 F.3d 1505 (10th Cir. 1996); *In re* Unisys Corp. Retiree Med. Benefit "ERISA" Litig., 58 F.3d 896 (3d Cir. 1995); Jensen v. SIPCO, Inc., 38 F.3d 945 (8th Cir. 1994). *See also* Calogera Abbruscato v. Empire Blue Cross & Blue Shield, 274 F.3d 90 (2d Cir. 2001) (life insurance benefits).

61 ERISA § 201(1), 29 U.S.C. § 1051(1) (2006).

62 *E.g.*, *Jensen v. SIPCO*, 38 F.3d at 951–52 (retiree medical benefits vested by contract); Alexander v. Primerica Holdings, Inc., 967 F.2d 90, 95 (3d Cir. 1992); *In re* White Farm Equip. Co., 788 F.2d 1186, 1193 (6th Cir. 1986) ("The parties may themselves set out by agreement or by private design, as set out in plan documents, whether retiree welfare benefits vest, or whether they may be terminated.").

63 ERISA § 402(b)(3), 29 U.S.C. § 1102(b)(3) (2006).

worker turnover and/or lower current compensation), employers want to tout the benefits of the program, and lifetime, no-cost health care coverage is a considerable benefit.

This is all well and good, for benefit plans are voluntary programs that must serve the employer's interest as well as the interests of the participants and beneficiaries.[64] But if the touting appears in the SPD itself, there is cause for concern. And if the glowing description crosses the line to puffing or deliberate deception—as where the SPD makes strong representations as to the future continuance of the program (explicit promises of lifetime medical care, for instance), with the only hint that benefits could be reduced or employee costs increased appearing as an inconspicuous statement concerning amendment authority located in a remote part of the booklet—then that concern should turn to alarm.[65]

Two circuits have squarely held that an unambiguous reservation-of-rights clause in the SPD insulates the plan sponsor from liability for lifetime benefits promised elsewhere in the SPD. *In re Unisys Corporation Retiree Medical Benefit "ERISA" Litigation*[66] involved an SPD that stated, "When you retire . . . the comprehensive medical expense benefits then in force for you and your eligible dependents under this plan will be continued for the rest of your life," with a reservation-of-rights clause in another location. The Third Circuit in *In re Unisys* dismissed the retirees' estoppel claim.

> While we acknowledge that many retirees may have relied to their detriment on their interpretation of the summary plan descriptions as promising vested or lifetime benefits, we nonetheless must reject their estoppel claim. Due to the unambiguous reservation of rights clauses in the summary plan descriptions by which Unisys could terminate its retiree medical benefit plans, the regular retirees cannot establish "reasonable" detrimental reliance based on an interpretation that the SPDs promised vested benefits. The retirees' interpretation of the plans as providing lifetime benefits is not reasonable as a matter of law because it cannot be reconciled with the unqualified reservation of rights clauses in the plan.[67]

That is, estoppel generally requires *reasonable* reliance, and it would seem foolish to credit either of two contradictory statements. The Sixth Circuit, which enforces the SPD as a matter of contract, also refuses relief, holding that an unambiguous reservation-of-rights clause implicitly qualifies representations that the program will

---

64   *See supra* Chapter 1C for a discussion of ERISA's policy of preserving employer autonomy.

65   The problem with which we are here concerned arises only when the SPD is internally inconsistent, and its resolution depends upon the special status of the plan summary. Where the promise of continued benefits does not appear in the SPD, but is made through other oral or written communications, participants may be similarly misled, but the problem should be analyzed in terms of the binding effect of informal communications. *See infra* Chapter 3C.

66   58 F.3d 896 (3d Cir. 1995).

67   *Id.* at 907. *Unisys*, which is founded on estoppel principles, predates *Burstein v. Retirement Account Plan for Employees of Allegheny Health Education & Research Foundation*, 334 F.3d 365 (3d Cir. 2003), in which the Third Circuit repudiated estoppel in the inaccurate SPD context. *See supra* Chapter 3 note 51 and accompanying text.

be maintained as-is in the future.[68] Under either approach, the message is, let the participant beware.[69]

Other courts have criticized these decisions in dicta.[70] The Eighth Circuit held that an internal SPD conflict between a promise of benefit continuation and reserved amendment rights makes the benefit contract ambiguous, allowing resort to extrinsic evidence to resolve the confusion, and preventing summary judgment for the employer.[71]

Because the case law is unsettled, courts may look to ERISA's policies to see if notice of retained amendment authority should negate an SPD promise of lifetime benefits. Three serious considerations strongly suggest that it should not.

First, the contradiction in the SPD, however apparent to judges and lawyers, is seldom obvious to and never highlighted for participants. The inconsistency between representations concerning the value of the plan in the future and a reserved power to amend may be imperceptible to participants, especially if it appears within the context of other employer representations touting the plan.

Second, focusing on the conscientiousness of the participant overlooks ERISA's policies. An SPD containing such a patent ambiguity is defective; it fails to "reasonably apprise . . . participants and beneficiaries of their rights and obligations under the plan."[72] It seems odd to say that participants must bear an additional burden (the costs of investigation or the risks of failing to investigate) because the administrator has violated ERISA. Instead of forcing participants to look behind the SPD when faced with inconsistent terms, they could be permitted to rely on a reasonable interpretation of the document. A reservation-of-rights clause can be read (as the courts do) to qualify representations that the program will be maintained as-is in the future, but the representations may just as reasonably be understood as implicit exceptions to the sponsor's retained amendment authority.[73] Where the SPD ambiguity appears in

---

68   Sprague v. Gen. Motors Corp., 133 F.3d 388, at 400–01 (6th Cir.) (en banc), *cert. denied*, 524 U.S. 923 (1998).

69   Several other decisions are routinely cited for the proposition that a "reservation-of-rights" clause overrides a promise of lifetime benefits. In those cases, however, the vesting language appeared in informal communications, not in the SPD. Hughes v. 3M Retiree Med. Plan, 281 F.3d 786 (8th Cir. 2002); Gable v. Sweetheart Cup Co., 35 F.3d 851 (4th Cir. 1994); Alday v. Container Corp. of Am., 906 F.2d 660 (11th Cir. 1990). *See supra* Chapter 3 note 65.

70   Diehl v. Twin Disc, Inc., 102 F.3d 301, 307 (7th Cir. 1996) (calling *Unisys* a "forced construction" and "interpretive gymnastics"); Stearns v. NCR Corp., 97 F. Supp. 2d 954, 963 (D. Minn. 2000) ("[T]he *Sprague* decision in effect gives [employers] carte blanche license to offer inducements to employees to waive their rights and then to renege on their promises after the employees have irrevocably done so. Nothing in ERISA requires courts to sanction such an unfair result."), *rev'd*, 297 F.3d 706 (8th Cir. 2002), *cert. denied*, 537 U.S. 1160 (2003).

71   Barker v. Ceridian Corp., 122 F.3d 628, 638 (8th Cir. 1997). *See also* Am. Fed'n of Grain Millers v. Int'l Multifoods Corp., 116 F.3d 976, 981 (2d Cir. 1997) ("In this Circuit, to reach a trier of fact, an employee does not have to 'point to unambiguous language to support [a] claim. It is enough [to] point to written language capable of reasonably being interpreted as creating a promise on the part of [the employer] to vest [the recipient's] . . . benefits.'").

72   ERISA § 102(a)(1), 29 U.S.C. § 1022(a)(1) (2006).

73   This argument was made explicit in *Unisys*: "According to the retirees, the plans were ambiguous because they were susceptible to either of two interpretations: the retirees' interpretation that the lifetime language limited the scope of the reservations of rights, or the company's

the context of an employer campaign promoting the promise of lifetime benefits, the latter accommodation seems to be the more natural reading.

Finally, consider the employer's conduct and its consequences. Avoiding a self-contradictory SPD is extremely easy—it requires only a careful reading of the summary description itself. The minimal cost of prevention raises a strong inference that any such repugnancy is the product of a deliberate attempt to mislead. Where the SPD contradicts plan documents, employers are not allowed to expressly disclaim inadvertent misstatements; reading a reservation-of-rights clause broadly permits employers to implicitly disavow deceit and profit by inducing workers to overvalue benefit plans. Workers presented with an equivocal SPD may use it or ignore it, but in either event, society bears the cost of suboptimal career and financial planning. Alternatively, workers may investigate further, which is duplicative and wasteful.[74]

Viewed in this light, refusing relief, where a promise of lifetime benefits appears in an SPD that also reserves amendment authority, could be seen as condoning employer misappropriation and undermining the goal of promoting planning by minimizing information costs. Attention to the origin of the contradiction, its lack of salience to the average plan participant, and the relative costs that the employer and workers would have to incur to avoid the resulting harm, suggest that ERISA's policies would be better served by the rule of *contra proferentem*. Provided that it appears reasonable to the average participant, the interpretation that reconciles the SPD contradiction to the workers' advantage would be enforced as the terms of the plan.[75] In addition, claimants could be awarded attorneys' fees whenever such a patent ambiguity is shown.[76]

---

interpretation that the reservation of rights limited the lifetime language." *In re* Unisys Corp. Retiree Med. Benefit "ERISA" Litig., 58 F.3d 896, 903 (3d Cir. 1995). The opinion concludes, without explanation, that where a reservation-of-rights clause is "broad and unequivocal, it will prevail over a promise of lifetime benefits." *Id.* at 904 n.11.

A distinction might plausibly be drawn between a reservation-of-rights clause that contains explicit overriding language (like "notwithstanding anything in this booklet to the contrary") and one that does not, because such overriding language may eliminate the contradiction. But here again the role of the SPD indicates that the presence of an ambiguity should be determined from the viewpoint of a reasonable participant, not a businessperson, lawyer, or judge.

74 *See* FRANK H. EASTERBROOK & DANIEL R. FISCHEL, THE ECONOMIC STRUCTURE OF CORPORATE LAW 280–81, 287 (1991) (disclosure by the firm prevents redundant production of information), 290–92 (free-rider and standardization problems support mandatory disclosure).

75 Rhorer v. Raytheon Eng'rs & Constructors, Inc., 181 F.3d 634, 642 (5th Cir. 1999); Phillips v. Lincoln Nat'l Life Ins. Co., 978 F.2d 302, 311 (7th Cir. 1992) (holding federal common law of ERISA provides that ambiguous terms in benefit plans should be construed in favor of beneficiaries); *see* Billings v. UNUM Life Ins. Co., 459 F.3d 1088, 1095 (5th Cir. 2006) (involving ambiguity in plan rather than in SPD; court observed, "once we conclude that an ERISA-governed plan is ambiguous, we apply the doctrine of *contra proferentem* to resolve the ambiguities in the insurance contract").

76 *See* ERISA § 502(g)(1), 29 U.S.C. § 1132(g)(1) (2006) (authorizing a discretionary award of fees and costs to the prevailing party in suits under ERISA). *See also* Alan Schwartz, *The Myth that Promisees Prefer Supracompensatory Remedies: An Analysis of Contracting for Damage Measures*, 100 YALE L.J. 369, 395–98, 401–03 (1990) (public action to reduce promisee litigation costs, as by an award of attorneys' fees, is economically superior to punitive damages as a solution to the problem of contract underenforcement).

This approach would bolster the incentive to provide reliable information without requiring separate penalties for defective SPDs.

The Incomplete SPD

The SPD controls where it flatly contradicts the underlying plan documents. Where the SPD is silent on an issue that the plan documents address, however, ERISA does not provide clear guidance. Most courts that have encountered this situation have adopted the rule that, absent a direct contradiction between the SPD and the plan documents, the plan documents control. Under this categorical approach, an inference based on the SPD's silence cannot override more specific provisions in the underlying instruments.[77] While it sometimes yields sensible results, the difficulty with this approach is that the categories are not always readily distinguishable.

In *Mattias v. Computer Sciences Corporation*,[78] the court used a different approach. *Mattias* involved a plan that provided partial disability benefits. The plan document defined partial disability to require that the employee be unable to perform substantial duties of her regular occupation and actually be employed in her regular occupation on a partial or part-time basis. The SPD used, but did not define, the term "partial disability." The district court recognized that "[t]he issue in this case is how a court should interpret an ERISA plan where the SPD uses words with relatively broad definitions, and the Plan Documents contain a more restricted limiting definition of those words."[79] Observing that there were "two doctrines in tension," the court attempted to reconcile them.

> First, where an SPD and the Plan Documents contradict or conflict with each other, the SPD controls. The policy rationale for this rule is that the ERISA statute contemplates that employees will depend on the SPD, and if the Plan Documents are allowed to supersede, then the SPD is useless.

> Second, where an SPD is silent on an issue, the Plan Documents control. The policy rationale for this view is that if silence in the SPD were enough to trump an underlying plan, then SPDs would mushroom in size and complexity until they mirrored the Plan Documents.

---

77   *E.g.*, Mers v. Marriott Int'l Group Accidental Death & Dismemberment Plan, 144 F.3d 1014, 1023–24 (7th Cir. 1998) (accidental death insurance policy limited coverage to accidents that operate directly and independently of all other causes, but SPD did not describe joint causation exclusion); Sprague v. Gen. Motors Corp., 133 F.3d 388, 401 (6th Cir. 1998) (en banc) (holding that the principle that the terms of the SPD control when they conflict with the terms of the underlying plan does not apply when the SPD is merely silent on an issue because "an omission from the summary plan description does not, by negative implication, alter the terms of the plan itself"); Jensen v. SIPCO, Inc., 38 F.3d 945, 953 (8th Cir. 1994); Wise v. El Paso Natural Gas Co., 986 F.2d 929, 938 (5th Cir. 1993).

78   34 F. Supp. 2d 120 (*Mattias I*) (D.R.I. 1999), *rev'd on other grounds*, 50 F. Supp. 2d 113 (D.R.I. 1999) (plaintiff failed to prove significant reliance on or possible prejudice flowing from SPD as required to recover in First Circuit) (*Mattias II*).

79   *Mattias I*, 34 F. Supp. 2d at 125.

At the extremes, these two doctrines work. This Court would have no difficulty applying them if the CSC Summary had made no mention of partial disability coverage or if the CSC Summary included a detailed definition of "partial disability" that conflicted with the CSC Plan. However this case occupies the swath where neither rule controls perfectly and where the two policies are in tension, namely where an SPD uses a term and then the Plan Documents define that term. The [CSC] Summary says that partial disability benefits are available, and the [CSC] Plan defines "partial disability." Using merely common sense, it is not obvious that this situation is either a "conflict" or "silence" on the issue of partial disability benefits.[80]

In light of the language and policy of ERISA, the court rejected the view that a conflict exists only if both the plan and the SPD explicitly define a term and those definitions conflict. Instead, it adopted a common-meaning rule, concluding "conflict occurs where an SPD uses a term and the Plan Documents define it in a fashion inconsistently with the term's common meaning."[81] Because partial disability is ordinarily understood to mean an incapacitating condition that keeps an employee out of her job, but doesn't prevent her from working in any job, the court refused to enforce the plan's undisclosed part-time work requirement.[82]

As *Mattias* illustrates, the dichotomy between contradiction and silence is overly simplistic. While *Mattias* represents a laudable attempt to devise a more satisfactory approach, the defects of the categorical approach are not widely understood, and so courts have not developed an authoritative response. The discussion that follows suggests a systematic solution that is informed by considerations of law and economics. This proposed solution, referred to hereafter as the "material omissions approach," has not been adopted by the federal judiciary. Nevertheless, several aspects of the material omissions approach do find support in the ERISA decisions, and the material omissions approach is followed in the closely analogous field of state insurance law.

Benefit plan documents are complex legal instruments, often running over thirty pages in length, the precise meaning of which can only be determined by giving scrupulous attention to a set of defined terms, and following a large number of internal cross-references. To be useful to its intended audience of participants and

---

80   *Id.* (citations omitted).

81   *Id.* at 126. The opinion cautions that "There would be no conflict where a word has no common meaning or where it would be unreasonable for a plan member to rely thereon. That would include where an SPD explicitly refers to a definition in the Plan Documents, for example, by noting that the specific term was used as defined by the Plan Documents." *Id.* at 127.

82   *Id.* Similarly, in *Heady v. Dawn Food Products, Inc.*, No. 3:03CV-26-H, 2003 U.S. Dist. LEXIS 21634 (W.D. Ky. Nov. 25, 2003), benefit eligibility under a long-term disability plan changed after 24 months from inability to perform one or more essential duties of the employee's previous occupation to the inability to perform essential duties of *any* occupation. The SPD included the former, more liberal definition of disability, but failed to indicate that after two years a more stringent test applied. The court noted that "a fine line can separate differences created by an omission and those created by a conflict." *Heady*, at *7. While the SPD technically omitted the stricter eligibility condition, the court recognized that participants had no reason to believe the SPD's definition was incomplete. Accordingly, the defect was characterized as a case of conflict rather than silence, and the court held that the SPD controls. *Id.* at *7–8.

beneficiaries, the SPD must *summarize* by simplifying and omitting detail.[83] When viewed in isolation, however, a simplified statement can frequently be interpreted to announce a general rule that admits of no exceptions or qualifications.[84] Should such an interpretation be binding?

While ERISA makes certain disclosures mandatory, the level of detail required of the SPD is at best vaguely indicated. Information is costly, and it would be wasteful to induce the employer to provide more than needed. When the benefit of better-informed decision making for some workers (better career and financial planning) is outweighed by the costs of providing particularized information that is relevant to their special circumstances, then inclusion in the SPD would be unwise. Those costs include the costs of drafting, reviewing, and publishing the additional information, and the cost of information overload; other workers will be deterred from making use of the SPD as it becomes more detailed and complex. Hence *optimal disclosure*—not full disclosure—should be the objective of the SPD.[85] That conclusion is consistent with the statutory standard—the SPD need not be comprehensive, only "*sufficiently* . . . comprehensive to *reasonably* apprise . . . participants and beneficiaries of their rights and obligations under the plan."[86] Adjudication is a costly and crude device for identifying this optimum because the accumulation of precedent is likely to sanctify a set of bright-line disclosure rules that are unresponsive to the context of a particular plan and workforce. Instead, the law should seek to provide proper incentives for employers to make optimal disclosure decisions *ex ante*.[87]

---

83   In *Hansen v. Continental Insurance Co.*, 940 F.2d 971 (5th Cir. 1991), the Fifth Circuit observed

> The Court understands that ERISA's requirement of a summary plan description necessarily requires abbreviation or omission of some of the detail of the plan or policy. Indeed, the very idea of the summary is to provide an accurate, but abbreviated, description of the plan provisions; its purpose is to simplify and explain the policy. Thus, it is not inappropriate to refer to the plan or policy itself to fill in details, or to provide other incidental information not included in the summary.

> *Id.* at 982 n.8.

84   Similarly, vague SPD terminology may create a false impression of entitlement if not dispelled by specific notice that some term has a technical meaning in special circumstances. Indeed, this vagueness or latent ambiguity case is merely another instance of implicit overbroad generalizations—the problem of the incomplete SPD, differently described.

85   *See* Mers v. Marriott Int'l Group Accidental Death & Dismemberment Plan, 144 F.3d 1014, 1024 (7th Cir. 1998) ("Clarity and completeness are competing goods."); *Mattias I*, 34 F. Supp. 2d at 125 ("The perfect document would be simple enough for anyone to understand and be complete enough to cover every contingency. The problem is that clarity and completeness are competing goals.").

86   ERISA § 102(a), 29 U.S.C. § 1022(a) (2006).

87   With respect to securities law, Easterbrook and Fischel observe:

> If damages are set correctly, the seller will investigate and disclose up to the point where an additional dollar spent on this activity produces just one more dollar for investors. The person with the best access to information will make the decision on the spot, saving the resources that could be spent on *ex post* inquests years later in court. In many cases it will be much more efficient to establish a damage rule to induce the seller to make the decision than to have a judicial inquiry into the optimal level of disclosure.

> EASTERBROOK & FISCHEL, *supra* Chapter 3 note 74, at 318.

The employer automatically bears the costs of overdisclosure because it pays for the preparation and dissemination of the SPD and pays greater compensation if workers mistakenly undervalue the plan (the likely response to an overly hedged or lengthy SPD). The costs of underdisclosure, however, are felt by the workers who, for lack of information, find their benefit expectations defeated. Consequently, the sponsor will have an incentive to downplay the negative unless it is also liable in cases of material nondisclosure. "The legal system may call some nondisclosure an offense not for the purpose of extirpating all conduct of that class, but for the purpose of bringing home to the decision maker the costs of his conduct."[88] These considerations indicate that optimal disclosure can be achieved by using a material omissions approach under which the sponsor would be bound by the terms of the SPD and reasonable inferences based thereon *unless*: (1) the SPD contained a particularized warning that additional information should be consulted in special circumstances; (2) the omission would not have been material to a person in the claimant's position; or (3) its importance was not known or foreseeable to the plan sponsor.

Courts have held that benefits should be awarded only if a reasonable participant would have understood the SPD to have promised such benefits.[89] If the plan summary cannot reasonably be interpreted as granting some benefit not provided under the plan documents, the claim is frivolous. For example, in *Fuller v. FMC Corp.*,[90] two employees claimed the right to subsidized early retirement benefits after the defendant terminated their employment in connection with the sale of the plant where they worked. The plan documents provided that an employee who retired after attaining age

---

88   *Id.* at 319.

89   *See* Watts v. BellSouth Telecomm., Inc., 316 F.3d 1203, 1207–08 (11th Cir. 2003) (reasonableness "must be judged from the perspective of the average plan participant," and from that perspective exhaustion of administrative remedies not required where SPD said disappointed claimant "may" pursue administrative appeal or "may" file suit); Moriarity v. United Tech. Corp. Represented Employees Ret. Plan, 158 F.3d 157, 161 (2d Cir. 1998) ("[N]othing in the SPD's language, structure or printed layout that could reasonably lead a participant to believe that benefits continue to be available to an employee for a disability that develops after he or she leaves" the employer); Am. Fed'n of Grain Millers v. Int'l Multifoods Corp., 116 F.3d 976, 980 (2d Cir. 1997) ("In this Circuit, to reach a trier of fact, an employee does not have to 'point to unambiguous language to support [a] claim. It is enough [to] point to written language capable of reasonably being interpreted as creating a promise on the part of [the employer] to vest [the recipient's] . . . benefits.'" (quoting Schonholz v. Long Island Jewish Med. Ctr., 87 F.3d 72, 78 (2d Cir. 1996)); Barker v. Ceridian Corp., 122 F.3d 628, 634 (8th Cir. 1997) (holding that "a reasonable person in the position of a plan participant would believe the language of the disability summary plan descriptions assured payment of the various insurance premiums"); Chiles v. Ceridian Corp., 95 F.3d 1505 (10th Cir. 1996):

> An SPD is intended to be a document easily interpreted by a layman; an employee should not be required to adopt the skills of a lawyer and parse specific undefined words throughout the entire document to determine whether they are consistently used in the same context. An employee reading the SPD and believing that upon the termination of the LTD Plan she would be entitled to continued company-paid premiums for health insurance, is not engaging in an "unrealistically narrow" interpretation of the document.

Chiles, 95 F.3d at 1517–18 (citation omitted).

90   4 F.3d 255 (4th Cir. 1993).

55 with ten or more years of service would receive subsidized early retirement benefits, but one who "cease[d] to be an employee before age fifty-five for any reason other than death" would not. The plaintiffs, who had more than ten years of service but were under age 55 when the plant was sold, nevertheless claimed a right to the early retirement subsidy based on the language of the SPD. The summary provided that the normal (unsubsidized) retirement benefit applied "[i]f you leave FMC before you reach age 55." The plaintiffs argued that this did not describe their involuntary termination (*they* did not leave FMC, but vice versa). They contended that they were, therefore, eligible to elect subsidized early retirement once they attained age 55, even though they were no longer employed by FMC. The court was unpersuaded, finding the SPD "neither confusing nor ambiguous" because "[r]etirement by definition presupposes an employer–employee relationship."[91] This sort of strained or unnatural reading of the SPD is rightly rejected, for it is a good indicator of a retrospective attempt to exploit minor misstatements that would not have induced reliance.[92] In such cases, an award of attorneys' fees against the claimant may be in order.

Consistent with this reasonable interpretation predicate, the proposed material omissions approach would permit the employer to avoid liability if the SPD contained a *particularized warning* that additional information should be consulted *in special circumstances*. Some topics are by nature either so specialized or so technical and complex that explanation would detract from the utility of the SPD. Providing everyone information that is only relevant to a few plan members would tend to obscure or divert attention from more important information. Too much specialized information will confuse the average plan participant or dissuade him from using the SPD, yet the details may be vitally important to a few participants who have unusual personal, medical, or financial situations. Optimal disclosure calls for a sensitive balance between these competing needs. To inform the few without bewildering the many, a generalization in the SPD could be coupled with a specific warning that the statement is subject to exceptions or qualifications in some circumstances. For example, a coordination-of-benefits clause in a group health insurance policy might be adequately summarized with the statement: "If you or a dependent covered under this plan is entitled to benefits under another health plan or insurance policy, the amount that would otherwise be paid under this plan may be reduced to take into account that other source of benefits. For further information ask the plan administrator for details." Under the material omissions approach such notice would be considered "*sufficiently* accurate and comprehensive to *reasonably* apprise . . . participants and beneficiaries of their rights and obligations under the plan."[93]

---

91   *Fuller*, 4 F.3d at 261.

92   *See* Joyce v. Curtiss-Wright Corp., 171 F.3d 130, 134 (2d Cir. 1999) ("Referring to several statements that become ambiguous only after extensive linguistic contortion, however—here through fifteen pages of briefing and treatise citation—fails to satisfy this burden [of pointing to specific written language reasonably susceptible to interpretation as a promise to vest retiree health benefits]."). *Accord* Int'l Union, United Auto., Aerospace & Agric. Implement Workers of Am. v. Skinner Engine Co., 188 F.3d 130, 141–42 (3d Cir. 1999).

93   ERISA § 102(a), 29 U.S.C. § 1022(a) (2006) (emphasis added). In contrast, a *global* SPD disclaimer clause does not identify limited circumstances where further inquiry may be needed.

Absent notice that resort to additional information is required in specified, unusual situations, the material omissions approach would still permit undisclosed conditions and limitations to be enforced if the information would not have affected worker behavior had it been known in advance. In that situation, a claim for benefits based on an omission from the SPD is post hoc opportunism.[94] Facilitating planning is the polestar, and so SPD generalizations that are *likely* to induce reliance must be distinguished from those that are not. Assume that a fair reading of the SPD supports the claimant's position that, by virtue of the summary's failure to mention some condition or limitation, it implicitly promises some benefit not provided under the plan documents. Then liability may be appropriate, but only if there is a substantial likelihood that the misrepresentation would influence a reasonable participant's career or financial planning. This is, of course, a materiality test.[95] The precise meaning of materiality must be developed in context, but one aspect is clear: the focus should be on the information's *ex ante* impact on career and financial planning.[96]

Consequently, the traditional disclaimer does not reasonably apprise affected participants and beneficiaries of their potential vulnerability; the planning goal would be defeated if a global disclaimer were treated as sufficient notice that any statement made in the SPD may be subject to extrinsic exceptions and qualifications. Similarly, an employer should not be allowed to eviscerate the reliability of the SPD by commencing its every sentence with "In general." Only where participants and beneficiaries are counseled to seek additional information pertaining to particular and unusual situations would the material omissions approach impose a duty of inquiry.

94   As Judge Posner observed:

[T]he fundamental function of contract law (and recognized as such at least since Hobbes's day) is to deter people from behaving opportunistically toward their contracting parties, in order to encourage the optimal timing of economic activity and (the same point) obviate costly self-protective measures. But it is not always obvious when a party is behaving opportunistically.

RICHARD A. POSNER, ECONOMIC ANALYSIS OF LAW 94–95 (6th ed. 2003) (footnote omitted).

95   The materiality condition amounts to requiring a finding that an SPD generalization is likely to induce reliance by a reasonable participant. This raises the question whether the plaintiff must in addition establish *actual* reliance. As explained in the discussion of inaccurate SPDs, *supra* Chapter 3 notes 43-59 and accompanying text, some circuits apply a rule of estoppel in SPD cases, while others enforce the SPD as a matter of contract without proof of reliance. To avoid problems of proof and align incentives to promote optimal disclosure, the law should not insist on actual reliance (estoppel). Proof of actual reliance guards against windfall recoveries, but this interest is served, to some extent, by the additional condition of foreseeability, discussed below, which ensures that liability is limited to cases where the employer has failed to exercise due care in drafting the SPD.

96   One might follow the Supreme Court's formulation in the securities law context, where the Court has recognized that "[s]ome information is of such dubious significance that insistence on its disclosure may accomplish more harm than good," because fear of liability may cause corporate management "to bury shareholders in an avalanche of trivial information—a result that is hardly conducive to informed decisionmaking." TSC Indus. v. Northway, Inc., 426 U.S. 438, 448–49 (1976). Therefore, under the federal securities laws, an omission is material only if "there is a substantial likelihood that a reasonable investor would consider it important in [decision making]." *Id.* at 449; *see also* Basic, Inc. v. Levinson, 485 U.S. 224, 232, 239–40 (1988). *But see* MICHAEL J. TREBILCOCK, THE LIMITS OF FREEDOM OF CONTRACT 114 (1993) ("Material facts might be understood to refer to those facts the ignorance of which is likely to

For example, the SPD for a group health plan might explain the benefits available in the event of disease or injury but neglect to point out that the plan contains a subrogation clause calling for reimbursement of the plan if medical expenses are recovered from a tortfeasor.[97] The missing information is unlikely to affect participants' behavior, so there is no policy reason to allow the SPD to trump the plan. In contrast, liability is appropriate if the SPD fails to notify participants that the plan's definition of reimbursable medical expenses excludes custodial care. Although the probability of incurring custodial care expenses is low for most workers, the small common risk of very large expenses makes the apparent coverage a feature that reasonable participants would value. As these examples indicate, SPD representations that are likely to affect behavior would be binding under the materiality test, even if they don't concern the basis of the employment bargain or the most important features of the plan. They may not alter the decision whether to take or keep the job, yet such representations can still affect planning (setting personal savings or insurance goals, for example) in ways that implicate ERISA policies.

In the employee benefits arena, a material omissions test arguably should have a foreseeability component. In contrast to the securities markets, where investors are seeking a financial return that is independent of their personal circumstances, benefit plan participants are not all similarly situated. The expected return under an insurance program (including life, health, and disability insurance, and defined benefit retirement plans as well) depends on personal characteristics of the insured, some of which may not be known to or readily ascertainable by the insurer. For instance, a group health plan SPD might fail to describe the exclusion from coverage of an expensive procedure used only in the treatment of one rare genetic disease, and the apparent availability of coverage may be very important to a worker who knows she has a family history of the disease. This sort of inside information leads to the well-known phenomenon of adverse selection. Where an incomplete SPD creates an expectation of benefits in circumstances that are unknown and unforeseeable by the sponsor, the prospect of liability cannot affect the disclosure calculus. Therefore, participants in unusual circumstances can avoid mistakes at lower cost, and it would be more efficient to require them to delve deeper to see how the terms of the plan document affect their situation, rather than relying on an implication drawn from the broad generalizations of the SPD. Accordingly, the suggested material omissions approach would be based upon whether known or reasonably foreseeable participants would attach importance to the information, not upon how someone possessed of unusual information could be expected to respond.

Support for the material omissions approach is found in state decisional law that protects the reasonable expectations of the insured in spite of insurance policy

---

substantially impair the expected value of the transaction to the buyer.") *See also* RESTATEMENT (SECOND) OF CONTRACTS § 162(2) & cmt. c (1979) (misrepresentation material "if it would be likely to induce a reasonable person to manifest his assent, or if the maker knows that it would be likely to induce the recipient to do so").

97   *See* FMC Corp. v. Holliday, 498 U.S. 52 (1990) (ERISA preempts state law prohibiting subrogation).

language that denies coverage.[98] The decisions have established the principle that "the coverage provided by an insurance policy should be determined in accordance with what laypersons would reasonably understand as the scope of the coverage."[99] The reasonable expectations principle recognizes that the detailed meaning of an insurance policy is, as a practical matter, inaccessible to most policyholders; the documents are long and complex, and often are not even made available until after the insurance is purchased.[100] The insurer is held liable according to the insured's reasonable expectations of coverage if the insurer was in some way responsible for creating the inaccurate expectations or failing to dispel them.[101] The reasonable expectations principle is concerned with protecting consumers. But rather than demanding proof of actual reliance, "courts have generally focused instead on whether any reasonable insured might have expected [coverage]."[102] The doctrine strives to promote an efficient insurance market by encouraging disclosure of coverage limitations and is partly based on equitable considerations (relative responsibility for the misunderstanding).[103] The expectations principle offers a striking parallel to the misleading SPD problem. Where a plan summary is allegedly incomplete, the proposed material omissions test would promote optimal disclosure by making the sponsor liable for the reasonable expectations its statements engender, regardless of reliance.[104]

Liability under the material omissions approach is justified as a means of creating the incentives necessary to achieve optimal disclosure. Materiality (whether disclosure would likely have altered worker behavior) and foreseeability (whether the loss was avoidable) are crucial qualifications. Yet imposing liability for an incomplete SPD presents dangers of its own, even under this carefully limited approach. There is some risk that plan sponsors will respond to this liability either by refusing to provide an SPD or by distributing an explanation that is so detailed and complete that it no longer functions as an accessible *summary* of the plan. These evasive strategies can be satisfactorily curtailed.

First, consider outright noncompliance. Overzealous policing of SPD contents could induce sponsors to avoid the risks of inaccuracy and incompleteness by foregoing the summary entirely. That response obviously would undermine the goal of giving participants information on which they may base their career and financial planning. Although ERISA requires the distillation and dissemination of plan terms in an SPD,

---

98   *See generally* Kenneth S. Abraham, Distributing Risk 101–32 (1986); Robert I. Keeton & Alan I. Widiss, Insurance Law § 6.3 (1988).

99   Keeton & Widiss, *supra* Chapter 3 note 98, at 636.

100   *Id.* at 634–35.

101   Abraham, *supra* Chapter 3 note 98, at 104–09, 113–14, 119–22.

102   *Id.* at 103. *Accord* Keeton & Widiss, *supra* Chapter 3 note 98, at 641 (detrimental reliance not required).

103   Abraham, *supra* Chapter 3 note 98, at 114–16, 119–22.

104   *See* Saltarelli v. Bob Baker Group Med. Trust, 35 F.3d 382, 385–87 (9th Cir. 1994) (as matter of federal common law, ERISA-governed insured plans should be interpreted in accordance with the reasonable expectations of the participants).

it offers little in the way of monetary sanctions for noncompliance.[105] Nevertheless, self-interest should keep the employer from simply disregarding the obligation. Employee benefit plans are instituted voluntarily to serve the employer's ends, which may include increasing the firm's attractiveness in relevant labor markets, reducing workforce turnover, or increasing productivity. These objectives cannot be obtained without publicizing the advantages of the program to obtain workers' cooperation. Accordingly, some type of simplified presentation to workers, whether written or oral, is essential. In the absence of an SPD, such presentations, however incomplete or defective, should be treated as de facto SPDs, so that the employer is obliged to perform the undertaking as publicized. That is, the SPD obligation should be enforced by holding informal explanations to the same standard; a de facto SPD would trigger liability if it conflicts with underlying plan documents, is internally inconsistent, or fails to warn of important conditions or limitations.[106] Informal written descriptions

---

105   A participant, beneficiary, fiduciary, or the Secretary of Labor could force preparation of an SPD via suit for an injunction, but there is little incentive to pursue that remedy. Nothing mulcts an administrator for neglecting to furnish participants and beneficiaries with a proper SPD when the statute calls for regular distribution (e.g., within ninety days after becoming a participant or first receiving benefits). Realistically, the sponsor's only financial exposure for ignoring the SPD obligation would come from failing to respond within thirty days to a participant's or beneficiary's written request for an SPD, which would trigger a penalty of up to $110 per day thereafter. *See* ERISA §§ 104(b)(4), 502(a)(1)(A), (c)(1)(B), 29 U.S.C. §§ 1024(b)(4), 1132(a)(1)(A), (c)(1)(B) (2006); 29 C.F.R. § 2575.502c-1 (2009) (inflation adjustment).

106   Currently, there is no clear judicial consensus on the handling of this issue, although the approach recommended in the text has some support in the cases. The Ninth Circuit early held that an employer's deliberate noncompliance with ERISA's disclosure rules was sufficient to justify an order awarding a disappointed worker benefits under ERISA § 502(a)(1)(B), even if the worker was ineligible under the terms of the plan. Blau v. Del Monte Corp., 748 F.2d 1348 (9th Cir. 1984). Other circuits distinguished *Blau* on the ground that it involved egregious and bad-faith disclosure violations. *E.g.*, Kreutzer v. A.O. Smith Corp., 951 F.2d 739, 745 (7th Cir. 1991) (unlike *Blau*, no evidence of active concealment or unfair administration); Simmons v. Diamond Shamrock Corp., 844 F.2d 517, 525 (8th Cir. 1988) (same). So limited, the Ninth Circuit recently reaffirmed *Blau*'s holding. Peralta v. Hispanic Bus., Inc., 419 F.3d 1064, 1075–76 (9th Cir. 2005). In contrast, the Third Circuit rejected nondisclosure as a justification for an award of benefits not provided by the terms of the plan. Hozier v. Midwest Fasteners, Inc., 908 F.2d 1155, 1170 (3d Cir. 1990).

    Even absent evidence of bad-faith nondisclosure, some courts permit recovery in certain circumstances. The Second Circuit holds that complete failure to develop and provide an SPD should be treated like a summary that simply lacks certain required information: triggering liability for benefits if the failing causes "likely prejudice" (*see supra* Chapter 3 notes 53-54 and accompanying text). Weinreb v. Hosp. for Joint Diseases Orthopaedic Inst., 404 F.3d 167, 171 (2d Cir. 2005). The Eighth Circuit follows a similar approach where the SPD is faulty, so long as it is not hopelessly inadequate. *Compare* Dodson v. Woodmen of the World Life Ins. Soc'y, 109 F.3d 436, 439 (8th Cir. 1997) (reliance or prejudice will support recovery under faulty SPD), *with* Palmisano v. Allina Health Sys., 190 F.3d 881, 888 (8th Cir. 1999) (hopelessly inadequate SPD has no legal effect). *See* Antolik v. Saks Inc., 383 F. Supp. 3d 1168, 1174–78 (S.D. Iowa 2005) (explaining Eighth Circuit cases). But note that the Eighth Circuit suggested in *Simmons*, that egregious nondisclosure might trigger liability.

are likely to be crafted with far less care than an SPD, and oral explanations invite misunderstanding. The prospect of liability based on such presentations is daunting and should create a powerful stimulus to comply with the SPD requirement.

Incautious expansion of SPD liability creates a risk that plan sponsors will react by saying too much rather than too little. Absent judicial restraint, the temptation to engage in protective expatiation will obscure plan fundamentals and defeat the purposes of the SPD, because too much information is likely to be ignored rather than sifted and analyzed. The sponsor, however, cannot afford to have workers undervalue the benefits provided, and so the employer will resort to other methods of publicizing the advantages of the plan. Egregious overdisclosure could be prevented by holding that an overly detailed formal description is not an SPD within the meaning of ERISA, and instead treating other informal explanations as de facto SPDs. As with refusal to supply an SPD, the prospect of liability based on such informal presentations should create a powerful stimulus to comply.

C. INFORMAL COMMUNICATIONS

It remains to be seen whether, apart from the summary plan description, the employer may be bound by misleading oral or written communications concerning plan content. Imposing liability for informal communications raises two concerns. First, the employer is held to exacting standards in formulating the SPD to ensure that employees have on hand a reliable source of understandable information about the plan, which suggests that employees should have a reciprocal duty to use it. Second, ERISA requires employee benefit plans to be "maintained pursuant to a written instrument," which must contain a "procedure for amending [the] plan, and for identifying the persons who have authority to amend the plan."[107] Each of these concerns weighs heavily

---

The view that liability cannot be premised on a wholly inadequate SPD stems from *Hicks v. Fleming Cos., Inc.*, 961 F.2d 537 (5th Cir. 1992), which concluded that, in view of the binding effect of the SPD, in order to avoid "a trap for the unwary employer," "there should be no accidental or inadvertent SPDs." *Hicks*, 961 F.2d at 542. That rationale, of course, does not extend to informal explanations provided in instances of deliberate noncompliance with ERISA's disclosure rules.

Although generally overlooked, a viable alternative approach would analyze the failure to provide the required summary as a breach of fiduciary duty. The plan administrator is a fiduciary and usually (and by default in the absence of another designation) is the plan sponsor. A deliberate or negligent disclosure violation would generally transgress the administrator's duty of loyalty or prudence. *See* ERISA § 404(a)(1), 29 U.S.C. § 1104(a)(1) (2006). The remedy for such a breach is limited to "appropriate equitable relief," ERISA § 502(a)(3), 29 U.S.C. § 1132(a)(3) (2006), which ordinarily does not permit recovery of plan benefits (contract damages). *See infra* Chapters 3D and 5D. Promissory estoppel, however, is an equitable remedy, predicated on a "promise which the promisor should reasonably expect to induce action or forebearance," RESTATEMENT (SECOND) OF CONTRACTS § 90(1) (1979). Informal explanations offered in lieu of an SPD (or as a substitute for omitted information that is required to be contained therein) would seem to satisfy this standard.

107 ERISA § 402(a)(1), (b)(3), 29 U.S.C. § 1102(a)(1), (b)(3) (2006).

against enforcement of *oral* statements that *contradict* the summary description. Neither concern prevents recognition of informal communications, whether written or oral, that are consistent with the summary, such as statements interpreting an ambiguous plan provision or reporting an exercise of discretion. *Written* representations that are inconsistent with the SPD present a more difficult case. Arguably, these should be enforced only if, applying the law of agency, they constitute an amendment of the plan.

Inconsistent Oral Statements

Any attempt to hold the employer to assertions that are inconsistent with the plan runs the risk of foundering on ERISA's enforcement scheme. The action is not a claim for benefits "under the terms of the plan,"[108] but in spite of them. Estoppel provides the usual mechanism for obtaining this type of variance. Although promissory estoppel is an equitable remedy, a participant or beneficiary can only invoke equitable jurisdiction to enforce the terms of the plan or the provisions of ERISA.[109] Nothing in ERISA proscribes misleading informal communications by a nonfiduciary.[110] Moreover, because of preemption, estoppel is not available as a state law cause of action.[111] That leaves one possibility: estoppel claims might be recognized as a matter of federal common law.

Starting with *Nachwalter v. Christie*,[112] a long line of cases refuses to apply estoppel to permit oral modifications of employee benefit plans. With one important qualification, that outcome is consistent with ERISA policies. The qualification is that oral representations should be dismissed out of hand only if they are inconsistent with the summary description. If an oral statement conflicts with the underlying plan document(s) but not the SPD, the participant has no reason to know that it is incorrect. Such cases should be analyzed as instances of incomplete SPDs,[113] with the oral representation serving only to buttress the reasonableness of the participant's interpretation of the SPD.

Parol variance claims are properly rejected for two reasons. The first is that the conditions of promissory estoppel cannot be satisfied.[114] Because the SPD gives

---

108   ERISA § 502(a)(1)(B), 29 U.S.C. § 1132(a)(1)(B) (2006).

109   ERISA § 502(a)(3), 29 U.S.C. § 1132(a)(3) (2006).

110   Fiduciary misrepresentations may violate the ERISA duties of loyalty or care. ERISA § 404(a)(1)(A), (B), 29 U.S.C. § 1104(a)(1)(A), (B) (2006). *See infra* Chapter 3D.

111   ERISA § 514(a), 29 U.S.C. § 1144(a) (2006).

112   805 F.2d 956, 960 (11th Cir. 1986).

113   *See supra* Chapter 3B.

114   *See, e.g.*, Curcio v. John Hancock Mut. Life Ins. Co., 33 F.3d 226, 235 (3d Cir. 1994) (reasonable reliance required); *In re* Unisys Corp. Retiree Med. Benefit "ERISA" Litig., 58 F.3d 896, 908 (3d Cir. 1995) ("[A] participant's reliance on employer representations regarding benefits may never be 'reasonable' where the participant is in possession of a written document notifying him of the conditional nature of such benefits."); Schmidt v. Sheet Metal Workers' Nat'l Pension Fund, 128 F.3d 541, 546 (7th Cir. 1997) ("[O]ral representations that conflict with the terms of a written plan [in this case, including the SPD] will not be given effect, as the written

participants ready access to trustworthy plan information, reliance on oral representations that contradict the summary cannot be either reasonable or justifiable. Even oral representations that purport to reflect plan amendments (thereby explaining away the SPD inconsistency) should be dismissed because ERISA requires authentic plan changes to be reported to participants in *writing*, via a summary of material modifications (an SPD addendum).[115] In formulating the SPD, an employer is held to exacting standards of draftsmanship. But a meticulously crafted document is only a means of fostering better employee career and financial planning. To achieve that objective, workers should be given incentives to use its contents. Enforcement of contradictory oral statements is undesirable because it would diminish that impetus.

The second reason parol variance claims are properly rejected is that ERISA's writing requirement stands as a barrier to oral modifications. The obligation to enforce a clear statutory mandate is the most common judicial explanation for rejecting such changes.[116] But that explanation masks a problem. Recall that failure to reduce a plan to writing does not invalidate the program. If an enforceable benefit plan can be instituted without any documentation, it is not obvious why unwritten alterations are intrinsically invalid. Plan establishment and modification have very different consequences, however. Oral programs are treated as employee benefit plans in order to prevent evasion of ERISA's minimum standards, the applicability of which was not intended to be elective.[117] Oral modifications need not be recognized for this reason—with or without the change, participants and beneficiaries will be afforded the baseline legislative safeguards. That leaves courts free to follow the dictates of the writing requirement and the policies it reflects. As a statute of frauds, the central purpose of ERISA's written plan mandate is to guarantee the authenticity of the alleged promise (an evidentiary function), preventing opportunistic plan revisions based on malleable words and fallible memories. A writing also offers some assurance that the commitment was deliberate on the employer's part, but ERISA's requirement that every plan set forth an amendment procedure better serves that end.[118]

---

instrument must control."). *See* Restatement (Second) of Contracts § 90(1) & cmt. b (1979) (reasonableness of promisee's reliance and formality with which promise is made are factors bearing on whether enforcement necessary to prevent injustice).

115 ERISA §§ 102(a), 104(b)(1), 29 U.S.C. §§ 1022(a), 1024(b)(1) (2006).

116 *E.g.*, Nachwalter v. Christie, 805 F.2d 956, 960 (11th Cir. 1986).

117 *See supra* Chapter 2A.

118 Courts also resist oral changes on the ground that such changes may render the plan underfunded, jeopardizing payments to other beneficiaries. *E.g.*, *Nachwalter*, 805 F.2d at 960–61; Armistead v. Vernitron Corp., 944 F.2d 1287, 1300 (6th Cir. 1991). However, under a defined contribution pension plan, a participant is entitled to the balance of her account, and disbursements from that account do not affect other participants' account balances. (If, however, a defined contribution plan allocates forfeitures to the accounts of ongoing participants, oral relaxation of the plan's vesting requirements would reduce such allocations. Nevertheless, it would not jeopardize the payment of amounts already credited to other participants.)

With respect to defined benefit pension plans, it is true that oral modifications ordinarily would not have been taken into account in determining the actuarial cost of the plan and so would negatively impact funding. A defined benefit plan sponsor cannot disclaim liability for unfunded accrued benefits, however, and a solvent sponsor cannot terminate an

Plan Clarification

Holding the sponsor to statements that interpret or apply the provisions of the plan is much less problematic than enforcing statements that are inconsistent with the summary description. Statements that interpret ambiguities or reflect an exercise of discretion merely clarify the plan, without in any way contradicting the SPD. Consequently, such statements can be given effect without undermining the special role of the SPD as the principal and authoritative source of plan information. If written, such clarifying statements are obviously compatible with ERISA's writing requirement. But even oral clarifications involve no real conflict with the writing requirement because only the "plan" must be documented, not its application to every set of facts.

Despite the courts' adamant refusal to permit estoppel to override plan terms (e.g., in *Nachwalter* and its progeny), many courts invoke estoppel when a participant or beneficiary detrimentally relies on a statement interpreting an ambiguous plan provision. *Kane v. Aetna Life Insurance Co.*[119] was the first in this line of cases. There, the wife of a medical plan participant asked whether the plan would pay the substantial hospitalization costs of a premature infant the couple was interested in adopting. In response to her telephone call, a customer service employee of Aetna, the plan administrator, informed Mrs. Kane that the child would be covered under the plan from the time formal adoption proceedings were commenced.[120] An insurance verifier for the hospital in which the child was being treated also telephoned Aetna and was told that expenses would be covered from June 1, 1984, the date the adoption proceedings commenced.[121] The child was hospitalized until July 5, but when the Kanes filed a claim for reimbursement of the child's medical expenses, Aetna denied it based on an exclusion of the costs of any continuous period of hospitalization commencing before the effective date of coverage.[122] The plan's definition of effective date of coverage was susceptible to two interpretations. It could be read narrowly to refer to

---

underfunded plan. *See infra* Chapter 9 notes 73–80 and accompanying text. Consequently, the disbursement of larger benefits to some employees pursuant to an oral modification, even if it creates or increases underfunding, triggers an increase in the employer's cost rather than a reduction in the benefits that have already been earned by other employees. Kimberly A. Krawolec, Comment, *Estoppel Claims Against ERISA Employee Benefit Plans*, 25 U.C. Davis L. Rev. 487, 559–62 (1992). Conceivably, the employer might respond to that cost increase by reducing *future* benefit accruals under the plan, but if it is assumed that the employer's oral modification was deliberate, that response seems unlikely.

Some courts apply estoppel against welfare plans on the ground that actuarial concerns vanish where there is no fund to deplete. *E.g.*, Black v. TIC Inv. Corp., 900 F.2d 112, 115 (7th Cir. 1990) (allowing estoppel against unfunded welfare plan); *Armistead*, 944 F.2d at 1300 (allowing estoppel against insured welfare plan). Yet actuarially unanticipated benefit increases under welfare plans (whether unfunded or insured) lead to the same sort of future cost escalation as underdefined benefit pension plans, which might jeopardize continuance of the program.

119   893 F.2d 1283 (11th Cir. 1990).
120   *Id.* at 1284.
121   *Id.* at 1284–85.
122   *Id.* at 1285.

the single date when an employee becomes covered under the plan upon completing six months of service, or broadly (as Aetna read it) to also include later dates when new family members obtain coverage under the plan as eligible dependents of a covered employee.[123] Finding that the case involved an interpretation of ambiguous plan provisions and not a modification of the plan, the Eleventh Circuit distinguished its earlier decision in *Nachwalter* and applied equitable estoppel.[124] The court stated that enforcing oral interpretations "will not affect the ability of employees and beneficiaries to rely on the written terms of such plans."[125] Several other circuits have followed *Kane*'s distinction between statements that would modify a plan and those that merely interpret it, holding that estoppel prevents the repudiation of interpretations on which claimants have relied.[126]

The extent of this principle is still unsettled. Discretionary decisions, like the interpretation of ambiguities, involve determinations as to the application of plan provisions to specific facts, so estoppel seems equally appropriate. It should apply with at least equal force to written clarifications, for the writing lends weight to the reasonableness of reliance. In line with the approach that emphasizes the primacy of the SPD, the existence of an ambiguity should be determined based on a reasonable participant's reading of the SPD alone, regardless of the clarity of underlying plan documents.[127] The chief difficulty concerns the maker of the statement; not all loose talk should be binding, and so the question is, *whose* statements estop the plan?

Plan interpretation, like other discretionary decisions, is an inherently fiduciary function. The exercise of discretion in the management or administration of the plan is the key indicator of fiduciary status.[128] Yet many representations on which participants and beneficiaries might reasonably rely will be made by executives of the sponsor or staff in its benefits department, people who are unlikely to have the fiduciary responsibility of interpreting the plan or exercising discretion in the subsequent determination of a claim for benefits. If the fiduciary ultimately rejects the claim, estoppel does not enforce the plan as *authoritatively interpreted*;[129] it carves out an exception to its uniform application. And it can hardly be an abuse of discretion for the fiduciary deciding claims to ignore extraneous representations by persons not charged with that task.[130] How, then, does ERISA authorize a cause of action for estoppel?

---

123   *Id.* at 1285–86.

124   *Id.* at 1285.

125   *Id.* at 1286.

126   *E.g.*, Greany v. W. Farm Bureau Life Ins. Co., 973 F.2d 812, 821–22 (9th Cir. 1992); Slice v. Sons of Norway, 34 F.3d 630, 634–35 (8th Cir. 1994); Law v. Ernst & Young, 956 F.2d 364, 369–72 (1st Cir. 1992). *See also* Spink v. Lockheed Corp., 125 F.3d 1257, 1261–63 (9th Cir. 1997) (estoppel available where employee relied on oral and written statements that apparently resolved an inconsistency in the provisions of the plan).

127   *See supra* text accompanying Chapter 3 notes 68–73.

128   ERISA § 3(21)(A), 29 U.S.C. § 1002(21)(A) (2006). *See generally infra* Chapter 4A.

129   *See* ERISA § 502(a)(3), 29 U.S.C. § 1132(a)(3) (2006).

130   The scope of review of discretionary benefit determinations is abuse of discretion. Firestone Tire & Rubber Co. v. Bruch, 489 U.S. 101 (1989). *See generally infra* Chapter 5B.

The answer lies in the fact that the plan administrator is also a fiduciary, because persons providing information about the interpretation or application of the plan exercise discretion (namely, the choice whether to obtain and supply the information) in the administration of the benefit plan.[131] Accordingly, the faithless or indolent acquisition or dissemination of information breaches the plan administrator's duty of loyalty or care, so an action lies to enforce the fiduciary responsibility provisions of ERISA. Although exacting, ERISA's fiduciary duties do not impose strict liability, which means that not all information clarifying the plan's application would give rise to estoppel. Prudent persons responsible for supplying plan information should ascertain past practices or seek the advice of claims administrators before addressing doubtful points. Failing such investigation, liability would be appropriate; but this rationale would not necessarily provide a remedy for information carefully supplied that ultimately proves incorrect. That may, in fact, have been the situation in *Kane* because the Aetna representatives who gave oral assurances of coverage were apparently unaware of the ambiguity and may not have been negligent in overlooking it.[132]

Informal Amendment

Informal *written* communications do not offend ERISA's statute of frauds; but if they contradict the SPD, they should not be enforced unless they qualify as plan amendments, or, in certain cases, where they are issued by a fiduciary. The latter possibility is explored in the next section (*infra* Chapter 3D). The SPD functions as the readily available, understandable source of authoritative plan information. In light of that role, reliance on assertions that contradict the SPD is unjustified unless the summary has been superseded, which requires an effective plan amendment. The validity of plan amendments is determined in the first instance by compliance with plan procedures; but unauthorized amendments may also be binding under the law of agency. This line of analysis suggests that writings at variance with the SPD should sometimes be enforced as a matter of contract, not as a matter of estoppel.

Compared to oral assertions, written representations tend to be more definite and formal; the mode of communication does not convey an implicit caveat respecting dependability. Therefore, it may be natural to credit a writing that contradicts the SPD, especially if the writing is specifically addressed to a particular person or an unusual situation. The SPD is not just another writing, however; it has a special status as the primary source of information about plan terms. This highlights a

---

131   *See* ERISA § 3(21)(A), 29 U.S.C. § 1002(21)(A) (2006); Varity Corp. v. Howe, 516 U.S. 489, 502–03 (1996) ("[A]dministrators, as part of their administrative responsibilities, frequently offer beneficiaries more than the minimum information that the statute requires" and in doing so are engaged in a fiduciary act.).

132   Notice that relief might be available if the information supplied proves mistaken because of a later change of position by the claims administrator. A claim denial based on such a break with past practice or prior advice might (or might not) constitute an abuse of discretion. *See infra* Chapter 5B.

crucial question: can reliance on a document that runs counter to the SPD ever be sufficiently justified to support estoppel?

Most workers probably do not understand the unique role of the summary plan description; any expectation that workers will check other written communications for consistency with the SPD may well be counterfactual. Consequently, reliance may seem reasonable in this circumstance, and the proposition that estoppel is unwarranted is fairly contestable. Refusing estoppel (i.e., holding reliance unjustified as a matter of law) amounts to imposing a duty of inquiry on participants and beneficiaries. For two reasons, such a duty of inquiry is appropriate. First, it reinforces the salience of the SPD and thereby advances the planning function. Second, it promotes uniform plan administration and private dispute settlement.

In an environment where there is easy access to reliable plan information, the burden of verifying employer representations is not great. A rule that encourages utilization of the SPD for independent decision making is more conducive to career and financial planning than is paternalistic application of estoppel. Moreover, disclosure was also intended to promote the self-policing of employee benefit plans. A duty to check the SPD will cause participants to identify errors and ambiguities in the employer's representations, which should lead to corrections or clarifications. Thus, the actions of a few vigilant participants will not only protect the participants but also alert the employer to steps that can be taken to avoid misunderstandings generally. Estoppel, in contrast, would protect unthinking acceptance of any plausible written assertion. Estoppel both promotes litigation and leads to the nonuniform application of plan provisions, as a series of "special deals" arises from enforcement of ill-considered employer representations. Numerous cases hold that other writings cannot override the plan summary, but most involve informal assurances of lifetime health benefits juxtaposed against an SPD that reserves to the plan sponsor the unconditional right to amend or terminate the plan.[133]

It must be emphasized that this no-estoppel principle has a limited scope. As it is premised on a duty to consult the SPD, it should apply only to representations that an average participant (as opposed to an actuary, benefits specialist, lawyer, or judge) would understand to be inconsistent with the SPD. In addition, it should not apply to writings that operate as plan amendments, which include not only formal changes but informal amendments as well. Although overlooked to date, the informal amendment category is potentially quite expansive, including many written representations made by persons with actual or apparent authority to adopt or report plan amendments.

---

133   *E.g.*, Gable v. Sweetheart Cup Co., 35 F.3d 851, 857 (4th Cir. 1994) ("ERISA prohibits informal written or oral amendments of employee benefit plans, and references to lifetime benefits contained in non-plan documents cannot override an explicit reservation of the right to modify contained in the plan documents themselves.") (citations omitted); Alday v. Container Corp. of Am., 906 F.2d 660, 665–66 (11th Cir. 1990) (extending its holding in *Nachwalter* to contradictory written communications); Moore v. Metro. Life Ins. Co., 856 F.2d 488, 492 (2d Cir. 1988) (where filmstrips and articles in employee newspapers referred to lifetime benefits without mention of reserved amendment power, the court held that "absent a showing tantamount to proof of fraud, an ERISA welfare plan is not subject to amendment as a result of informal communications between an employer and plan beneficiaries").

Every employee benefit plan is required to include "a procedure for amending such plan, and for identifying the persons who have authority to amend the plan."[134] Significantly, the SPD is not required to report these terms, but must be supplemented in due course with a summary of any material amendment actually made to the plan.[135] Accordingly, participants and beneficiaries typically have no clear idea of how the plan can be amended or by whom, but they can expect to receive a written report of changes made. This creates the possibility that informal written communications could appear to be plan amendments or reports of plan changes. The question whether a particular writing should have the effect of a plan amendment or SPD supplement should be answered by applying federal common law of agency.

Some written statements may be binding either because they actually comply with the amendment mechanism set forth in the plan document or because they are effective as a contract that institutes a new and distinct plan. To have that effect, representations made by officers or other employees must be attributed to the plan sponsor. The Supreme Court has acknowledged that the general law of agency, as applied specifically to employees' acts while in the service of their corporate employer, should be used for this purpose. *Curtiss-Wright Corp. v. Schoonejongen*[136] involved a plan provision stating, "[t]he Company reserves the right at any time and from time to time to modify or amend, in whole or in part, any or all of the provisions of the Plan."[137] The Court held unanimously that the provision set forth a valid amendment procedure as required by ERISA § 402(b)(3), even though it set forth "the barest of procedures."[138] Observing that "for an amendment procedure that says the plan may be amended by 'the Company' to make any sense, there must be some way of determining what it means for 'the Company' to make a decision to amend."[139] The Court looked to corporate law principles to determine who has authority to make decisions on behalf of the company.[140] The case was remanded "for a fact-intensive inquiry, under applicable corporate law principles" into who possessed amendment authority and whether that person or persons approved the challenged provision.[141] For the many plans that stipulate only such a bare-bones amendment mechanism, benefit representations by top

---

134   ERISA § 402(b)(3), 29 U.S.C. § 1102(b)(3) (2006).
135   ERISA § 102(b), 29 U.S.C. § 1022(b) (2006). In 2000, the SPD content regulation was amended to require that the SPD include "a summary of any plan provisions governing the authority of the plan sponsors or others to terminate the plan or amend or eliminate benefits under the plan and the circumstances, if any, under which the plan may be terminated or benefits may be amended or eliminated." 29 C.F.R. § 2520.102-3(*l*) (2009). This warning of potential loss of benefits apparently does not require disclosure of the plan's amendment procedure or the specific individuals with amendment authority. *See* 65 Fed. Reg. 70226, 70229 (Nov. 21, 2000) (rule intended to codify Labor Department Technical Release 84-1).
136   514 U.S. 73 (1995).
137   *Id.* at 76.
138   *Id.* at 80.
139   *Id.*
140   *Id.* at 80–81.
141   *Id.* at 85, *decision on remand*, 143 F.3d 120 (3d Cir. 1998). *See* Biggers v. Wittek Indus., 4 F.3d 291, 296 (4th Cir. 1993) (plan amendment reducing severance benefits could not be applied to terminations occurring before it was approved by the company president).

management may well constitute authorized amendments. But reference to corporate contracting powers has an even more far-reaching implication: that a benefit promise not conforming to the amendment procedure of an existing plan might create a *new* plan if the maker has authority to set employee compensation.[142]

Sometimes, one or a few key executives are promised a special benefit arrangement. If the employer disavows the promise, litigation may present the question whether a program that is specially designed (perhaps even separately bargained for) to meet the needs of one or a few employees can be effective as a plan amendment or a separate plan. Because such special deals are arranged at the highest level of the corporate hierarchy and typically promise benefits that are not available under extant plans, it is often easy to conclude that the employer authorized establishment of a new one-person plan that supplements existing programs.[143] This seems the proper approach, although it has not been uniformly followed.[144]

---

142   Deboard v. Sunshine Mining & Ref. Co., 208 F.3d 1228, 1237–39 (10th Cir. 2000). *Contra* Sprague v. Gen. Motors Corp., 133 F.3d 388, 402–03 (6th Cir. 1988) (en banc).

   The facts of *Sprague* illustrate the type of situation that generates claims to vested benefits based on informal amendment or the establishment of a new plan. In *Sprague*, the district court found that GM entered into binding bilateral contracts with a class of early retirees pursuant to which the company agreed to provide no-cost lifetime health benefits in return for early retirement. Sprague v. Gen. Motors Corp., 843 F. Supp. 266, 299, 301, 319 (E.D. Mich. 1994). The evidence showed that a series of voluntary early retirement programs was instituted under the direction of GM's chief executive officer and that employees considering early retirement were given information on postretirement benefits, prepared by GM's vice president for industrial relations, promising that full basic health care coverage for the employee and eligible dependents would be continued "for life at no cost to the retiree." *Id.* at 275–78 (adoption of early retirement programs), 279 (principal document summarizing early retiree health benefits). The district court found that the representations made by GM employees concerning continued health care coverage were authorized. *Id.* at 317. Although there was testimony that the company's director of employee benefit plans did not believe that these early retirement programs amended GM's health care plan, the district court held that the corporation had either modified the general health care plan or established a new plan. *Id.* at 299, 319 (lifetime vested health benefits enforceable under ERISA as "independent bilateral contract"—as a new plan, in effect—or as modifications to GM's existing health benefit plan). On appeal, the Sixth Circuit initially affirmed the district court's findings on this point, Sprague v. Gen. Motors Corp., 92 F.3d 1425, 1440 (6th Cir. 1996), but the panel decision was vacated pending rehearing en banc, 102 F.3d 204 (6th Cir. 1996), and the full court reversed based on its reluctance to alter "a welfare plan on the basis of non-plan documents and communications, absent a particularized showing of conduct tantamount to fraud." *Sprague*, 133 F.3d 388, 403 (6th Cir. 1998) (en banc). Despite that reluctance, however, the Sixth Circuit later reached much the same result by applying a fiduciary breach theory, rather than the informal amendment approach. *See infra* Chapter 3 note 225 and accompanying text.

143   *E.g.*, Cvelbar v. CBI Ill., Inc., 106 F.3d 1368 (7th Cir. 1997). *See* Frahm v. Equitable Life Assur. Soc'y, 137 F.3d 955, 957–58 (7th Cir. 1998). *See also supra* Chapter 2A.

144   In *Miller v. Taylor Insulation Company*, 39 F.3d 755 (7th Cir. 1994), the employer agreed to allow its retiring chairman to continue participation in the company's insured medical reimbursement plan, the terms of which limited coverage to full-time employees. Several years later, a new insurer refused coverage, and the retired executive brought suit. The Seventh Circuit, in an opinion by Judge Posner, refused to hold that the agreement created a one-person plan that was identical in all respects to the general plan, save the full-time employee

Where someone without actual authority to amend the plan or institute a new one makes written representations inconsistent with the SPD, the employer can still be held to the change, either as a matter of apparent authority or by ratification.[145] Apparent authority exists where the principal knowingly permits the agent to exercise an unauthorized power or where the principal's acts or declarations give the agent the appearance of authority. Assertion of authority by the agent is not enough: the principal's words or conduct must create a reasonable impression that the agent possesses authority, and such action may include appointment to a position that carries generally recognized duties.[146] Where apparent authority exists, the principal is obligated to third parties to the same extent as if the agent's action were actually authorized, even though the transaction is wrongful as between principal and agent.[147] As applied to a large corporation, the chief executive would normally have apparent authority to establish a benefit plan because the position commonly entails the power to hire employees and establish compensation arrangements. Lower-ranking officers (division managers, for example) who hire workers might also have apparent authority to make benefit commitments. Absent notice to the contrary, managers with actual or apparent authority to institute a benefit program would also have apparent authority to amend the plan.

---

coverage limitation. *Id.* at 760–61. The court did allow the suit to proceed on a promissory estoppel theory, while noting that the plaintiff might encounter some difficulty proving reasonable reliance on a promise that contradicted the plan. *Id.* at 759. This approach, of course, is exactly the reverse of the position advanced here, that estoppel should be rejected (because reliance on a contradictory writing is inherently unreasonable), while a properly adopted writing should be enforced as a plan amendment or a separate plan. The *Taylor Insulation* court seems to have been influenced by the plaintiff's attempt to secure state law contract breach remedies. The court correctly held the state contract claim preempted, but thought it would be "odd, in fact formalistic in the worst sense," to suppose that the asserted contract was nevertheless enforceable as a matter of federal common law. *Id.* at 761.

145 Anderson v. Int'l Union, United Plant Guard Workers, 150 F.3d 590, 592–93 (6th Cir. 1998) (apparent authority to amend early retirement eligibility conditions). *See* Taylor v. Peoples Natural Gas Co., 49 F.3d 982 (3d Cir. 1995) (supervisor of employee benefits had apparent authority, as agent of plan, to counsel retiree on early retirement program).

In *Curtiss-Wright Corp. v. Schoonejongen*, 514 U.S. 73, 85 (1995), the Court observed that an unauthorized plan amendment would be effective if it were subsequently ratified. The opinion does not explicitly refer to apparent authority as a basis for enforcement, perhaps because the modification at issue was unfavorable to employees, and so they contested rather than asserted its validity. The Court did approve the proposition that "principles of corporate law provide a ready-made set of rules for determining, in whatever context, who has authority to make decisions on behalf of a company." *Id.* at 80–81. The treatise on which the Court relied states "[t]he general principles of the law of agency govern the authority of agents and officers of private corporations to enter contracts on behalf of their corporate principal," 2 WILLIAM MEADE FLETCHER, CYCLOPEDIA OF THE LAW OF PRIVATE CORPORATIONS § 466, at 505 (rev. ed. 1990), and explicitly acknowledges apparent authority as one of those principles. *Id.* at §§ 438, 449.

146 RESTATEMENT (SECOND) OF AGENCY §§ 8, 27 & cmt. a, 161 & cmt. d (1958); 2 FLETCHER, *supra* Chapter 3 note 145, §§ 449, 457.

147 RESTATEMENT (SECOND) OF AGENCY §§ 8 cmt. a, 159, 383 (1958); 2 FLETCHER, *supra* Chapter 3 note 145, § 455.

Potentially more far-reaching is the possibility that apparent authority to *report* plan changes could accomplish informal amendments. ERISA obligates the plan administrator to provide participants and beneficiaries with a timely summary of material modifications to a benefit plan (an SPD supplement).[148] A written statement by the administrator that contradicts the existing SPD might therefore appear to be a valid SPD supplement. Under agency law, the employer would be bound to the same extent as under an actual SPD supplement,[149] and an SPD supplement should, like the SPD itself, be enforced as the terms of the deal.[150] The duties of plan administrator are commonly delegated to lower-level managers (such as the company's director of benefits or head of the payroll department) who regularly communicate with workers concerning benefits. Because no particular label, language, or format is required of an SPD supplement,[151] some writings that are inconsistent with the outstanding SPD might bind the employer as informal amendments under this theory—some, but not all, for the theory requires that the incorrect representation reasonably appear to be an SPD supplement. Accordingly, the representation must be in writing (as the SPD and supplements must be), made by one acting as plan administrator, and issued either to all participants and beneficiaries, or to the subset that would be affected by the apparent change.[152] Consequently, erroneous written advice to an individual participant ordinarily would not be binding because it could not be fairly interpreted as reporting a change in the plan.

D. FIDUCIARY DISCLOSURE

Erroneous or misleading statements by fiduciaries cannot support a claim for "benefits due [to a participant or beneficiary] under the terms of the plan," but equitable relief is available if the statement violates ERISA's duties of loyalty or care.[153] While faithless or careless fiduciary communications are actionable, it isn't always easy to know when a person is speaking in a fiduciary capacity. Nor does silence guarantee immunity, for sometimes the fiduciary's role as special protector imposes an extraordinary duty to speak.

---

148   ERISA §§ 102(a), 104(b)(1), 29 U.S.C. §§ 1022(a), 1024(b)(1) (2006).

149   RESTATEMENT (SECOND) OF AGENCY § 159 cmt. f (1958) (where principal refers others to an agent for information, the agent becomes spokesperson with apparent authority to make statements on the subject matter that are binding on the principal).

150   *See supra* Chapter 3B.

151   *See* 29 C.F.R. § 2520.104b-3 (2009) (summary of material modifications).

152   Although 29 C.F.R. § 2520.104b-3 (2009) requires the summary of material modifications to be issued to each participant covered under the plan and each beneficiary receiving benefits, section 2520.102-4 permits different SPDs to be prepared for classes of participants and beneficiaries that are treated differently under the plan.

153   ERISA §§ 502(a)(1), (3), 404(a)(1)(A), (B), 29 U.S.C. §§ 1132(a)(1), (3), 1104(a)(1)(A), (B) (2006).

Identifying Fiduciary Communications

"Fiduciary duties under ERISA attach not just to particular persons, but to particular persons performing particular functions."[154] ERISA assigns employee benefit plan information functions to the plan administrator, who is a fiduciary to the extent that she has "any discretionary responsibility in the administration of such plan."[155] While certain disclosures are mandatory, the detailed content of the SPD is a judgment call, as is the decision to provide additional information. The administrator is a fiduciary in the conduct of these discretionary functions, and her decisions are reviewable as such.[156] But the administrator is usually also an employee of the sponsor, either by plan designation or delegation of authority.[157] Consequently, communications relating to employee benefits made by officers or employees of the sponsor could be made either in the sponsor's business or fiduciary capacity, and a single individual may wear both hats. This sorely complicates the job of sorting out those communications that must be held to exacting standards of honesty and diligence from the mass that can be challenged only under the rules governing those dealing at arm's length.

Varity Corp. v. Howe[158] exemplifies the problem. In the mid-1980s, Massey-Ferguson, a farm equipment manufacturer (and wholly owned subsidiary of Varity Corp.), transferred its money-losing divisions to a new entity in an effort to free itself of various financial obligations, including the liability to pay medical and other welfare benefits to employees of those divisions.[159] Varity could have simply terminated benefits for those workers, but it wanted to avoid the labor problems that would cause. Instead, it took steps to induce employees of the money-losing divisions to accept employment with the new entity, Massey Combines, thereby releasing Massey-Ferguson from further benefit liability.[160] Some 1,500 workers did so, but,

---

154   Hozier v. Midwest Fasteners, Inc., 908 F.2d 1155, 1158 (3d Cir. 1990).

155   ERISA §§ 3(21)(A), 101, 104, 29 U.S.C. §§ 1002(21)(A), 1021, 1024 (2006). Moreover, the statute seems to assume that *all* tasks assigned to the plan administrator, whether discretionary or mandatory, are fiduciary functions. *See* ERISA § 402(c)(1), 29 U.S.C. § 1102(c)(1) (2006).

156   Varity Corp. v. Howe, 516 U.S. 489, 502–03 (1996) ("[A]dministrators, as part of their administrative responsibilities, frequently offer beneficiaries more than the minimum information that the statute requires—for example, answering beneficiaries' questions about the meaning of the terms of a plan so that those beneficiaries can more easily obtain the plan's benefits," and the provision of such additional information is a fiduciary act); *id.* at 504 ("There is more to plan . . . administration than simply complying with the specific duties imposed by the plan documents or statutory regime; it also includes the activities that are 'ordinary and natural means' of achieving the 'objective' of the plan."); *In re* Unisys Corp. Retiree Med. Ben. "ERISA" Litig., 57 F.3d 1255, 1261 n.10 (3d Cir. 1995) ("Our decisions firmly establish that when a plan administrator explains plan benefits to its employees, it acts in a fiduciary capacity.").

157   ERISA § 3(16), 29 U.S.C. § 1002(16) (2006). Such dual status (and perhaps, by implication, the divided loyalties that go with it, *infra* Chapter 4) is expressly permitted by ERISA § 408(c)(3), 29 U.S.C. § 1108(c)(3) (2006).

158   516 U.S. 489 (1996).

159   *Id.* at 492–93.

160   *Id.* at 493.

as expected, Massey Combines failed within two years, causing the workers to lose their welfare benefits.[161] The workers sued for reinstatement in the Massey-Ferguson plan, claiming that the company had breached its fiduciary duties by inducing them to switch employers through deliberate deception.[162] Although Varity was the welfare plan's administrator,[163] it argued that "it was acting only as an *employer* and not as a plan *fiduciary* when it deceived its employees."[164]

The communications made to convince employees to switch to Massey Combines emphasized that benefit programs would remain unchanged and included a detailed, side-by-side comparison of the benefits provided under Massey-Ferguson's plan with those promised by the new, unfunded Massey Combines plan.[165] That plan-related information was true, but it was accompanied by false statements about the financial health of Massey Combines. The restructuring, it was said, would "provide the funds necessary to ensure [Massey Combines'] future viability," giving it "a bright future."[166] Such statements about a new subsidiary's financial prospects, Varity argued, "have virtually nothing to do with administering benefit plans," and therefore cannot be fiduciary acts.[167] But the new plan was unfunded, and so the continuation of welfare benefits would ultimately depend on Massey Combines' performance. The statements about the viability of Massey Combines were closely linked to the statements about plan benefits in a deliberate effort to convey the basic message that "your benefits are secure."[168] The Court held that "making intentional representations about the future of plan benefits in that context is an act of plan administration" subject to ERISA's fiduciary duties.[169] By highlighting the context in which the statements were made, the Court disavowed the notion that all employer statements about the future of benefit plans are fiduciary acts.[170] Three factors were crucial. The statements "came from those within the firm who had authority to communicate as fiduciaries with plan beneficiaries";[171]

---

161   *Id.* at 494.
162   *Id.* at 492, 494.
163   *Id.* at 498.
164   *Id.* at 495.
165   *Id.* at 499–501.
166   *Id.* at 500, 501.
167   *Id.* at 504.
168   *Id.* at 504–05.
169   *Id.* at 505.
170   In addition to the holding quoted above, at two other points the majority opinion expressly conditions its fiduciary finding on the specific context in which the representations were made. "We conclude, therefore, that the factual context in which the statements were made, combined with the plan-related nature of the activity, engaged in by those who had plan-related authority to do so, together provide sufficient support for the District Court's legal conclusion that Varity was acting as a fiduciary." *Id.* at 503. "[I]n the present context [citing the opinion's explanation of the benefit-related information provided to the workers Varity wanted to transfer to Massey Combines], Varity's statements about the security of benefits amounted to an act of plan administration." *Id.* at 505.
171   *Id.* at 503.

those people were in a position to know the correct information;[172] and the statements formed the core content of a carefully scripted presentation.[173]

The *Varity* opinion says little about the relevance of these factors, leaving the ultimate impact of the decision in doubt. While it could be limited to its unusual facts, the logical implication of certain elements of *Varity*'s factual context is potentially far-reaching. Recall that the Court emphasized that the statements were made by people "who had authority to communicate as fiduciaries."[174] Of course, the problem arises precisely because the speaker is wearing two hats (informational fiduciary and corporate employer). But in the next paragraph, the majority observes that reasonable employees "could have thought that Varity was communicating with them *both* in its capacity as employer *and* in its capacity as plan administrator."[175] That is, dual roles created the potential for confusion, and Varity did nothing to dispel that confusion; to the contrary, it deliberately exploited the ambiguity.[176] That participants had no reason to know that representations about the future of plan benefits were not made with their interests at heart suggests that the fiduciary finding is based on apparent authority principles. That is, management representations will be treated as fiduciary acts where the corporate principal creates the impression that its agent is speaking on behalf of persons interested in the plan, and those persons do not know or have reason to know that the agent is pursuing other ends.[177]

Unless workers are told otherwise, many (perhaps most) statements by top executives about benefits could be treated as fiduciary acts under apparent authority principles.[178] On its face, *Varity* doesn't go that far. Its conclusion, the majority says, depends on the context, including factors not obviously related to apparent authority.[179] But what is special about *Varity* may be the nature of the statements attributed to the fiduciary rather than the conditions for attribution. Notwithstanding the Court's characterization, the ultimate message that Varity Corporation intended to

---

172 The statements concerning the financial prospects of Massey Combines were made by its newly appointed president, who was also a vice-president of Varity Corporation. *Id.* at 499. The detailed benefit comparison and a question-and-answer sheet were apparently prepared or approved by high-level Varity management. In fact, the district court had found that the company "purposefully made the questions and answers incomplete, confusing, evasive, and deceptive. Defendants developed more forthright questions and answers, but they opted not to publish them." Howe v. Varity Corp., 36 F.3d 746, 749 (8th Cir. 1994) (quoting from the district court's findings of fact).

173 *Varity*, 516 U.S. at 499–501.

174 *Id.* at 503.

175 *Id.*

176 *See supra* Chapter 3 note 172.

177 RESTATEMENT (SECOND) OF AGENCY §§ 27, 49(a) (1958); 2 FLETCHER, *supra* Chapter 3 note 145, §§ 449, 451.

178 Indeed, in many situations, the efficacy of express notice in dispelling apparent authority could be open to serious question. Where a principal notifies those dealing with an agent that the agent is not authorized to make certain statements, the principal is still liable if he has reason to believe that the third party will not understand or be deterred by the warning. RESTATEMENT (SECOND) OF AGENCY § 166 cmt. e (1958).

179 *See supra* Chapter 3 note 170 and accompanying text.

convey was not that "your benefits are secure," but that your benefits will be secure if you transfer to Massey Combines.[180] That is, although the representation was made by Varity personnel who had authority to speak as plan administrators, *it did not relate to Varity's plan!*[181] Under ordinary circumstances, it would be hard to conclude that a statement about *some other company's benefit program* was made in a fiduciary capacity. For example, an executive who also served as plan administrator might compare a competitor's benefit program with her own company's, but her audience would normally understand the statement to have been made in the employer's interest rather than in the audience's interest, even without special notice to that effect. Representations about other opportunities, in other words, are generally too far afield from the informational responsibilities of a plan administrator to be made with apparent fiduciary authority. In contrast, Varity's representations were not made in a competitive context (Massey Combines was a new subsidiary), so there was no implicit disclaimer. Furthermore, the representations were made by people known to have detailed knowledge of the alternative plan and its sponsor, and formed the core content of a carefully scripted presentation. The scope of apparent authority depends upon the manner in which a corporation holds out an officer or agent as having power to act, and is interpreted in light of surrounding circumstances.[182] Therefore, the peculiar context of *Varity* establishes apparent authority to speak as a fiduciary about a *different* plan, and the Court's repeated attempts to limit *Varity*'s holding actually reinforce the conclusion that apparent authority principles apply in identifying fiduciary communications.

At a minimum, *Varity* clearly establishes that an employer–administrator engages in a fiduciary activity when it provides workers with information about its own plans. That is so even though the information concerns the *future* of plan benefits and involves decisions or events beyond the fiduciary's control, such as the financial outlook of the company or the likelihood that the plan will be amended or terminated.[183] Courts have

---

180   *Compare Varity*, 516 U.S. at 504 ("[The] ultimate message Varity intended to convey [was] 'your benefits are secure'"), *with id.* at 501 ("The District Court concluded that the basic message conveyed to the employees was that transferring from Massey-Ferguson to Massey Combines would not significantly undermine the security of their benefits.").

181   The majority opinion never acknowledges this fact. It frequently describes Varity's statements as providing information about the "future of plan benefits" without noting that Varity was talking about another plan, distinct from the one in which the employees were then enrolled. Of course, information about the Massey Combines plan also supplied information about the relative merits of their current plan. At one point the Court observes that an administrator has the implied power to "offer beneficiaries detailed plan information in order to decide whether to remain with the plan," *id.* at 503, but again does not say that the "detailed plan information" concerned a plan different from the one they were deciding whether to remain with.

182   RESTATEMENT (SECOND) OF AGENCY §§ 34, 49(a) (1958); 2 FLETCHER, *supra* Chapter 3 note 145, § 451.

183   The Supreme Court confronted this objection head on:
    While it may be true that amending or terminating a plan (or a common-law trust) is beyond the power of a plan administrator (or trustee)—and, therefore, cannot be an act of plan "management" or "administration"—it does not follow that making statements about the likely future of the plan is also beyond the scope of plan administration. As we explained above, plan administrators often have, and commonly exercise, discretionary authority to communicate with beneficiaries about the future of plan benefits.

seized upon this principle—that communications concerning nonfiduciary acts can be a fiduciary function—to provide a remedy for intentional deception.[184] The most interesting example is *In re Unisys Corp. Retiree Medical Benefit "ERISA" Litigation*,[185] where the employer made repeated assurances that retirees would receive lifetime no-cost health care, but the SPD contained a reservation-of-rights clause warning that the plan could be altered or ended at any time for any reason. The plan summary itself promised lifetime coverage, but despite the self-contradictory SPD, the Third Circuit refused to impose liability in the face of an "unambiguous" reservations-of-rights clause.[186] Moreover, it rejected the retirees' estoppel claim because their detrimental reliance on the promise of lifetime medical benefits, which the court admitted was real and pervasive, was "not reasonable as a matter of law because it cannot be reconciled with the unqualified reservation of rights clauses in the plans."[187] Nevertheless, the findings that "the company actively misinformed its employees by affirmatively representing to them that their medical benefits were guaranteed once they retired, when in fact the company knew this was not true and that employees were making important retirement decisions relying upon this information, clearly support a claim for breach of fiduciary duty under ERISA."[188] The misinformation, although included in the SPD, was repeated and reinforced by a multitude of informal oral and written communications, and under the fiduciary duty approach, informal communications alone can be the basis of liability, even if the SPD is not deceptive.[189]

Varity, 516 U.S. at 505. Similarly, the Third Circuit has explained that "[w]hen a corporate plan administrator speaks about benefits to its employees, the administrator acts in a fiduciary capacity even if he speaks about a non-fiduciary decision such as the business decision to terminate a welfare plan." *In re* Unisys Corp. Retiree Med. Benefit "ERISA" Litig., 57 F.3d 1255, 1261 n.10 (3d Cir. 1995). Presumably, a corporate spokesperson could avoid this imputation of authority with appropriate caveats, by making clear that certain information (such as profit or loss projections) is not provided on behalf of plan participants and beneficiaries.

184   *E.g.*, Jones v. Am. Gen. Life & Accident Ins. Co., 370 F.3d 1065, 1072 (11th Cir. 2004) (circuits "consistently hold[] that ERISA plan participants may state a cause of action for breach of fiduciary duty based on a plan administrator's material misrepresentations or omissions" (citing numerous cases)).

185   57 F.3d 1255 (3d Cir. 1995). Although published first, this was the second of three opinions issued by the Third Circuit in this litigation, and so is referred to hereafter as "Unisys II." The full appellate history is: *Unisys I*, 58 F.3d 896 (3d Cir. 1995) (defective SPD issue); *Unisys II*, 57 F.3d 1255 (3d Cir. 1995) (fiduciary breach issue), *cert. denied sub nom.* Unisys Corp. v. Pickering, 517 U.S. 1103 (1996), *appeal following remand*; and *Unisys III*, 242 F.3d 497 (3d Cir.) (fiduciary breach issue), *cert. denied sub nom.* Unisys Corp. v. Tonnies, 534 U.S. 1018 (2001).

186   *Unisys I*, 58 F.3d at 903–05. *See supra* Chapter 3B.

187   *Unisys I*, 58 F.3d at 907.

188   *Unisys II*, 57 F.3d at 1266–67; *Unisys III*, 242 F.3d 497.

189   *Unisys II*, 57 F.3d at 1259–61, 1266. The opinion does not in any way suggest that a misleading or deceptive SPD is a necessary condition for liability.

Misleading Information

Under ERISA, fiduciaries are not subject to strict liability; the duty of prudence is a negligence-style standard of reasonable care.[190] Mistaken informal communications by mid- or lower-level managerial employees cannot trump the SPD, regardless of care.[191] Representations that are not inconsistent with the SPD (i.e., those that appear to clarify the summary by resolving an ambiguity or confining the exercise of discretion) would bind the employer under estoppel principles.[192] Recall, however, that promissory estoppel includes, as an element, the requirement that the promise be one that the "promisor should reasonably expect to induce action or forbearance."[193] This reasonable expectation requirement is an objective standard of foreseeability and so imports a negligence test into the estoppel calculus.[194]

In a line of cases beginning with *Berlin v. Michigan Bell Telephone Co.*,[195] the appellate courts have held that material misrepresentations concerning the likelihood of future benefit enhancements breach the administrator's duty of loyalty even though the decision to offer such retirement bonuses is a nonfiduciary business decision.[196] Thus some communications made prior to the ultimate decision to amend the plan, although necessarily predictive and therefore possibly incorrect, may be subject to oversight for fidelity and prudence. *Berlin* involved a severance pay plan that was offered to managers who retired during a window period in order to correct a

---

190   ERISA § 404(a)(1)(B), 29 U.S.C. § 1104(a)(1)(B) (2006). A strict liability standard may apply to the duty to follow plan documents that are not inconsistent with ERISA. *See* ERISA § 404(a)(1)(D), 29 U.S.C. § 1104(a)(1)(D) (2006), which would create a dilemma for fiduciaries forced to interpret an ambiguous provision, either of the statute or their own plan.

191   *See supra* Chapter 3C. Some written representations that are inconsistent with the SPD could be enforced as informal plan amendments upon a showing of apparent authority, but that authority is lacking in the lower-level benefits administrators who regularly communicate with participants and beneficiaries.

192   *See supra* text accompanying Chapter 3 notes 119–132.

193   RESTATEMENT (SECOND) OF CONTRACTS § 90(1) (1979).

194   1 E. ALLAN FARNSWORTH, FARNSWORTH ON CONTRACTS § 2.19, at 142–43 (1990) ("Even if the promisee relied on the promise, the promisor is not liable if the promisor had no reason to expect" reliance of the sort that occurred, but "[t]he standard for testing expectation is an objective one, under which the promisor is bound if the promisor had reason to expect reliance, even if the promisor did not in fact expect it.").

195   858 F.2d 1154 (6th Cir. 1988).

196   *E.g.*, Beach v. Commonwealth Edison Co., 382 F.2d 656 (7th Cir. 2004); Martinez v. Schlumberger, Ltd., 338 F.3d 407 (5th Cir. 2003) (providing an in-depth analysis of the evolution of the case law); Bins v. Exxon Co. U.S.A., 220 F.3d 1042, 1049–50 (9th Cir. 2000) (en banc); McAuley v. IBM Corp., 165 F.3d 1038 (6th Cir. 1999); Hockett v. Sun Co., 109 F.3d 1515 (10th Cir. 1997); Vartanian v. Monsanto Co., 131 F.3d 264, 268 (1st Cir. 1997); Muse v. IBM Corp., 103 F.3d 490 (6th Cir. 1996); Wilson v. Sw. Bell Tel. Co., 55 F.3d 399, 406 (8th Cir. 1995); Mullins v. Pfizer, Inc., 23 F.3d 663, 668–69 (2d Cir. 1994); Fischer v. Phila. Elec. Co., 994 F.2d 130 (3d Cir.) [hereinafter *Fischer I*], *cert. denied*, 510 U.S. 1020 (1993), *appeal after remand*, 96 F.3d 1533 (3d Cir. 1996) [hereinafter *Fischer II*], *cert. denied*, 520 U.S. 1116 (1997); *Berlin*, 858 F.2d at 1163–64. *See also* Barnes v. Lacy, 927 F.2d 539, 544 (11th Cir. 1991).

management surplus.[197] After close of the window period in late 1980, Michigan Bell, after discovering that some managers were delaying retirement in the hopes of a second offering, advised workers considering retirement not to delay because there were no plans for a second general application of the severance program.[198] After a second offering was announced in mid-1982, managers who retired before its effective date brought suit, contending that Michigan Bell breached its fiduciary duty by intentionally misleading them concerning the future availability of enhanced benefits.[199] The Sixth Circuit held that if the administrator communicates with plan participants after serious consideration is given to providing enhanced benefits, then a material misrepresentation would give rise to liability.[200] But as a corollary, the court indicated that the defendant had no duty to say anything at all about the future availability of enhanced benefits and suggested that misrepresentations concerning a future offering would not be actionable if they occurred prior to the time when serious consideration is given to implementing the change because such misrepresentations would not be material.[201]

Later cases have tried to define "serious consideration" in order to identify the point of liability with particularity. The Third Circuit has recognized that "large corporations regularly review their benefit packages as part of an on-going process of cost-monitoring and personnel management"; it would be costly and counterproductive to require disclosure of all proposed changes because "truly material information could easily be missed if the flow of information was too great."[202] Accordingly, the court held that "[s]erious consideration of a change in plan benefits exists when (1) a specific proposal (2) is being discussed for purposes of implementation (3) by senior management with the authority to implement the change."[203]

The first element is designed to distinguish "serious consideration from the antecedent steps of gathering information, developing strategies, and analyzing options."[204] The second factor "protects the ability of senior management to take a role in the early phases of the process without automatically triggering a duty of disclosure"; and the third ensures that adoption of the proposal is sufficiently probable by focusing on the involvement of "those members of senior management with responsibility for the benefits area of the business . . . who ultimately will make recommendations to the Board regarding benefits."[205] In contrast, the Second Circuit has rejected the "bright-line rule that serious consideration . . . is a prerequisite to liability for misstatements

---

197   *Berlin*, 858 F.2d at 1157.

198   *Id.* at 1158, 1160.

199   *Id.*

200   *Id.* at 1164.

201   *Id.* at 1164 & n.7. *Accord* Muse v. IBM Corp., 103 F.3d 490, 494 (6th Cir. 1996).

202   *Fischer II*, 96 F.3d at 1539.

203   *Id. Accord* Hockett v. Sun Co., 109 F.3d 1515, 1523 (10th Cir. 1997); McAuley v. IBM Corp., 165 F.3d 1038, 1043 (6th Cir. 1999); Bins v. Exxon Co., U.S.A., 220 F.3d 1042, 1049–50 (9th Cir. 2000). *See* Mushalla v. Teamsters Local No. 863 Pension Fund, 300 F.3d 391, 398 (3d Cir. 2002) (*Fisher II*'s serious-consideration test applies with equal force to multiemployer plans).

204   *Fischer II*, 96 F.3d at 1539–40.

205   *Id.* at 1540.

regarding the availability of future . . . benefits."[206] From the premise that a misrepresentation is material if it would induce a reasonable person to rely on it, the court concluded that "[w]hether a plan is under serious consideration is but one factor in the materiality inquiry."[207]

> [T]he employer's false assurance that future enhancements have been ruled out for some specific period can be decisive in inducing an employee to hasten retirement, rather than delay in the hope of receiving enhanced future benefits. This aspect of the assurance can render it material regardless of whether future changes are under consideration at the time the misstatement is made.[208]

Challenging Fiduciary Silence

When the administrator, as chief information officer of the plan, acts in a fiduciary capacity, the command of the duty of loyalty is almost automatic: "Put simply, when a plan administrator speaks, it must speak truthfully."[209] But when must the administrator speak? Apart from the statutory disclosure obligations, can the administrator safely stand mute? Or is there, in some circumstances, a fiduciary duty to speak? Challenges to fiduciary silence pose the most difficult questions in the law of ERISA disclosure.

Berlin suggested that the administrator could avoid liability for misleading statements about future benefit enhancements by simply keeping silent.[210] However, later appellate decisions indicated otherwise. In *Eddy v. Colonial Life Insurance Co.*,[211] the plaintiff called the insurer to inquire about maintaining coverage when he learned that his employer's group health plan would terminate on the eve of surgery. The district court found that Eddy had not specifically inquired about a right to convert the group coverage into an individual policy and found no fault in Colonial Life's failure to tell him that such a right existed.[212] Relying on the common law of trusts, the D.C. Circuit ruled that "refraining from imparting misinformation is only *part* of the fiduciary's duty. Once Eddy presented his predicament, Colonial Life was required to do more than simply *not misinform*; Colonial Life also had an affirmative obligation to *inform*—to provide complete and correct material information on Eddy's status

---

206   Ballone v. Eastman Kodak Co., 109 F.3d 117, 123 (2d Cir. 1997).

207   *Id.* at 123–24.

208   *Id.* at 124. *Accord* Wayne v. Pac. Bell, 238 F.3d 1048, 1055 (9th Cir. 1999) ("The fiduciary duty not to deceive plan participants exists at all times, not merely once serious consideration of offering such benefits has begun."); Martinez v. Schlumberger, Ltd., 338 F.3d 407, 428 (5th Cir. 2003) (concluding, after extended analysis of ERISA appellate case law and consideration of the Supreme Court's definition of materiality in the securities fraud context, that *Ballone* represents the better approach). *Contra* Beach v. Commonwealth Edison Co., 382 F.3d 656, 660–61 (7th Cir. 2004) (rejecting *Ballone* and *Martinez* in favor of the serious-consideration test).

209   Fischer v. Phila Elec. Co., 994 F.2d 130, 135 (3d Cir. 1993).

210   *Berlin*, 858 F.2d at 1164 ("[P]laintiffs are not arguing, nor do we hold, that defendants had any duties, under the circumstances, to say anything at all or to communicate with potential plan participants about the future availability of [early retirement severance benefits].").

211   919 F.2d 747 (D.C. Cir. 1990).

212   *Id.* at 749, 751.

and options."[213] Relying on *Eddy*, the Third Circuit ruled that an ERISA fiduciary who is aware of a beneficiary's situation has a "duty to convey complete and accurate information that [is] material to [that] circumstance," even if asked the wrong question.[214] In each of these cases, an inquiry from the plan participant or beneficiary initiated the obligation.

Potentially more far-reaching is *Shea v. Esensten*,[215] which indicates that an inquiry is not necessary to trigger a duty to speak if the fiduciary otherwise has reason to know that silence may be harmful. *Shea* involved a health plan participant who died of heart failure after his primary care physician refused, in the face of an extensive family history of heart disease and existent symptoms, to refer him to a cardiologist.[216] The Eighth Circuit held that the HMO breached its duty of loyalty in failing to disclose that its "doctors were penalized for making too many referrals and could earn a bonus by skimping on specialized care," even though no request for this information had been made.[217] The Eighth Circuit has since given *Shea* a limiting interpretation, asserting that the employer was required to disclose the referral disincentives in the SPD but failed to do so.[218] Other circuits have flatly rejected a duty to disclose in the absence of an inquiry.[219]

---

213   *Id.* at 751.

214   Bixler v. Cent. Pa. Teamsters Health & Welfare Fund, 12 F.3d 1292, 1302–03 (3d Cir. 1993). *Accord* Krohn v. Huron Mem'l Hosp., 173 F.3d 542, 548 (6th Cir. 1999); Hamilton v. Allen-Bradley Co., 244 F.3d 819, 827 (11th Cir. 2001). *See In re* Unisys Corp. Retiree Med. Benefit "ERISA" Litig., 57 F.3d 1255, 1264 (3d Cir. 1995) ("[W]hen a plan administrator affirmatively misrepresents the terms of the plan or fails to provide information when it knows that its failure to do so might cause harm, the plan administrator has breached its fiduciary duty to individual plan participants and beneficiaries."); *id.* at 1266 (employer's knowledge that employees were accelerating retirement decisions on the mistaken belief that they would thereby qualify for free lifetime health care created a duty to disabuse them because "the trustees had to know that their silence might cause harm"). *Accord In re* Unisys Corp. Retiree Med. Benefit "ERISA" Litig., 242 F.3d 497, 509–10 (3d Cir. 2001).

215   107 F.3d 625 (8th Cir. 1997).

216   *Id.* at 626.

217   *Id.* at 629. *See also Unisys II*, 57 F.3d at 1264 (plan administrator breaches its fiduciary duty if it "fails to provide information when it knows that its failure to do so might cause harm"; but employer had engaged in concerted program of deception); Barker v. Am. Mobil Power Corp., 64 F.3d 1397, 1403 (9th Cir. 1995) (alternative holding or dicta) ("[A] fiduciary has an obligation to convey complete and accurate information material to the beneficiary's circumstance, even when a beneficiary has not specifically asked for the information"). *But see* Ehlmann v. Kaiser Found. Health Plan of Tex., 198 F.3d 552, 556 (5th Cir. 2000) (no duty to disclose HMO incentives to ration care absent inquiry from plan member or "other special circumstances," while expressing skepticism of *Shea*); Horvath v. Keystone Health Plan E., Inc., 333 F.3d 450, 460–63 (3d Cir. 2003) (HMO does not breach fiduciary duties by failing to disclose incentive to ration care absent either a member request for such information or circumstances putting the HMO on notice that the member needed such information to avoid making harmful decisions about health care coverage).

218   Ince v. Aetna Health Mgmt., Inc., 173 F.3d 672, 676 (8th Cir. 1999) ("*Shea* involved a breach of the plan administrator's duty to publish an accurate description of plan benefits to participants and beneficiaries.").

219   Martinez v. Schlumberger, Ltd., 338 F.3d 407, 428 (5th Cir. 2003) (employer has no fiduciary duty to affirmatively disclose whether it is considering amending its benefit plan);

Evaluating Fiduciary Liability

The special status of the SPD as a source of accessible, reliable information about the plan supports a reciprocal duty on the part of participants and beneficiaries to consult the SPD, with the consequence that informal communications contradicting the SPD should not give rise to liability unless, under agency principles, the communications constitute an amendment or institute a new plan (*supra* Chapter 3C). After this review of the expanding law of fiduciary disclosure, it is fair to ask if a solemn incantation of "fiduciary responsibility" is all that is needed to swallow up those limitations. Are the courts applying two incompatible legal standards to disputes over misleading informal communications, according to whether the complaint asserts "estoppel" or "breach of fiduciary duty"? Admittedly, some of the decisions and the language of many of the opinions seems to point in that direction, yet principled limits on fiduciary disclosure liability are available.

In approaching this problem, two situations deserve separate analysis. The first involves misinformation concerning the content or meaning of the *current* plan. Fiduciary liability is *generally* inappropriate in this class of cases, although other bases of liability may offer some relief. The second involves representations about the plan's *future status*, such as *Varity Corp.* and the *Berlin* benefit enhancement line of cases. Because the SPD describes only the content of the current plan, participants have no check on statements relating to future developments. In situations involving prospective information, both doctrine and policy support fiduciary liability for fraudulent misrepresentation (i.e., deceit).

The cases involving misinformation concerning the content or meaning of the current plan may be subdivided into two types. One category involves wide-scale dissemination of false or misleading information by fiduciaries. In the second common scenario, courts grapple with mistaken or unhelpful answers to individual questions about a current plan's application to a particular set of facts.

Preliminarily, it should be noted that several of the most far-reaching fiduciary disclosure cases could have been decided under a nonfiduciary theory of liability. *Shea*, the case involving nondisclosure of HMO disincentives for specialist referrals, is really a defective SPD case.[220] The summary failed to "reasonably apprise" the participant of his (limited) rights under the plan, and the incomplete SPD would have supported a claim for benefits under the material omissions approach presented earlier.[221] Similarly, *Unisys* involved systematic misrepresentation of a health plan's

---

Pocchia v. NYNEX Corp., 81 F.3d 275, 278 (2d Cir. 1996) (If prior acts of the fiduciary have not created confusion, "a fiduciary is not required to voluntarily disclose changes in a benefit plan before they are adopted."). The Fifth Circuit suggested that there is also no duty to respond to employee inquiries about possible plan changes. *Martinez*, 338 F.3d at 407 n.171.

220 *See supra* Chapter 3 note 218 and accompanying text.

221 *See supra* text accompanying Chapter 3 notes 83–106. Of course, the participant had died, and so the claim for benefits (such as cardiologist fees and the costs of tests and prescription drugs) had become moot. What the plaintiff (the participant's widow) really wanted was a wrongful death recovery. Presumably, she believed that broader remedies might be obtained in a fiduciary breach action under ERISA § 502(a)(3), but that overlooks the limitation to equitable relief. *See infra* Chapter 5D.

terms (specifically, whether benefits vested upon retirement), but that atmosphere of deception was facilitated by an ambiguous or self-contradictory SPD.[222] While liability was grounded on a breach of fiduciary duty, that dependence would be unnecessary if courts construed self-contradictory SPDs against the drafter, as explained above.[223]

But what if the SPD in *Unisys* had *not* been defective? Is fiduciary liability appropriate where the SPD unambiguously denies benefits, but the plan administrator (typically the employer) systematically disseminates false or misleading information? To ensure uniform plan administration and reinforce the primacy of the SPD, oral statements at variance with the summary are generally unenforceable.[224] The rationale that reliance on contradictory assurances cannot be reasonable or justifiable evaporates if the message originates at the highest level of the company and is broadcast deliberately. Where general fiduciary communications are issued in a way that makes them appear authoritative, workers will naturally credit them; because that response is entirely foreseeable, the fiduciary's conduct is necessarily imprudent (if not disloyal).[225] In addition to the fiduciary's personal liability, a concerted campaign of deception emanating from the highest levels of the corporate hierarchy would also support plan liability under the informal amendment theory explored earlier.[226]

Now, consider the fiduciary disclosure cases that involve mistaken or unhelpful answers to individual questions about the current plan's application to a particular set of facts. This category of faulty responses overlaps the erroneous informal communication cases discussed earlier (*supra* Chapter 3C), where the question was whether the plan could be held to statements that promised more than the SPD and plan documents in fact provided. There, the usual answer was no, except where the statements clarify the plan without contradicting the SPD, or work an informal amendment of the plan. That approach is needed to obtain the certainty and uniformity benefits of the writing requirement and to encourage resort to the SPD as the authoritative source of plan information. Those goals would be undercut by allowing routine recovery on a fiduciary breach theory. ERISA fiduciary law does not mandate that result. Although intentional or negligent misrepresentation would clearly breach a fiduciary's obligations, fiduciaries typically do not give individual advice concerning the application of the plan to a specific set of facts. Instead, such information normally is provided by lower-level employees who perform ministerial functions within a framework of

---

222   *See supra* text accompanying Chapter 3 notes 185–189.
223   *See supra* text accompanying Chapter 3 notes 60–76.
224   *See supra* Chapter 3 notes 112–118 and accompanying text.
225   *See* James v. Pirelli Armstrong Tire Co., 305 F.3d 439, 453–56 (6th Cir. 2002). In *James*, the court distinguished its en banc decision in *Sprague v. General Motors Corp.*, 133 F.3d 388 (6th Cir. 1998), and relied on the Third Circuit's *Unisys II* decision to hold that, despite a reservation of amendment rights in the SPD, "an employer or plan administrator fails to discharge its fiduciary duty to act solely in the interest of the plan participants and beneficiaries when it provides, on its own initiative, materially false or inaccurate information to employees about the future benefits of a plan." *James*, 305 F.3d at 455.
226   *See supra* text accompanying Chapter 3 notes 133–152.

policies, interpretations, and procedures set by others. Lacking discretionary authority, such persons are not fiduciaries, and any misinformation they offer, however disloyal or imprudent, is not actionable.[227] Consequently, fiduciary breach claims can generally be dismissed, together with their estoppel counterparts, where informal communications promise more than the language of the SPD will support. An exception must be recognized, however, for actions of the administrator or other fiduciary that facilitate the provision of misinformation by the nonfiduciary agent, as where the fiduciary fails to exercise due care in hiring, training, or supervising the agent. In such circumstances the fiduciary, of course, would be directly responsible for his own carelessness.[228]

Fiduciary disclosure litigation is not always premised on promising too much. Some cases seek redress for misleading or unhelpful responses that prevent claimants from qualifying for benefits to which they would have been entitled under the terms of the plan.[229] A fiduciary who has been advised of a participant's situation has an affirmative duty to provide *complete* information, regardless of whether the fiduciary is asked the right question.[230] Nevertheless, a showing that the misleadingly incomplete response was given by a fiduciary is still required.[231] Where the incomplete response is given by a lower-level ministerial employee (and is not facilitated by a fiduciary), fiduciary responsibility is not implicated. Denying relief in that situation maintains the incentive to use the SPD.

Other considerations come into play where the fiduciary is alleged to have misrepresented the plan's future—as opposed to current—status, such as the likelihood that it will be amended or terminated. ERISA does not mandate disclosure, in the SPD or otherwise, of possible future plan changes. Consequently, there is no need to restrict liability for misleading communications in order to maintain the primacy of the SPD. Nevertheless, participants have an interest in obtaining information about the future of employee benefit programs because that information has an important bearing on long-term decision making—it can affect job and career choices, as well as decisions on retirement timing, insurance, and investments. Misinformation is likely to cause some workers to make poor choices. Relief seems justified by ERISA's policy of using information to promote better career and financial planning. Yet ERISA contains no express anti-fraud rule, and it preempts state law actions for fraud or deceit. Careless or faithless statements by a fiduciary do, however, breach statutory obligations. As noted earlier, *Varity* establishes that an employer–administrator engages in a

---

227   29 C.F.R. § 2509.75-8, Q&A D-2 (2009); Schmidt v. Sheet Metal Workers' Nat'l Pension Fund, 128 F.3d 541, 547–48 (7th Cir. 1997); Easa v. Florists' Transworld Delivery Ass'n, 5 F. Supp. 2d 522 (E.D. Mich. 1998).

228   *See Schmidt*, 128 F.3d at 548; *see also* ERISA § 405(a), 29 U.S.C. § 1105(a) (2006) (liability for breach by cofiduciary based on facilitation).

229   *E.g.*, Eddy v. Colonial Life Ins. Co., 919 F.2d 747 (D.C. Cir. 1990) (discussed *supra* text accompanying Chapter 3 notes 211–213). Typically, such failure to inform claims cannot be cast as an estoppel.

230   *Id.* at 751 (relying on Restatement (Second) of Trusts).

231   In *Eddy*, the court assumed without discussion that an unidentified agent's unhelpful telephone response constituted a *fiduciary* breach despite evidence that the insurer had policies in place to provide complete responses to telephone inquiries. *Id.* at 752.

fiduciary activity when it provides workers with information about the *future* of plan benefits, even if the information involves decisions or events beyond the fiduciary's control.[232] This principle offers a possible remedy for misrepresentations concerning the plan's future status.

Statements relating to the future of plan benefits often consist of predictions of future events rather than reports of existing facts. This inherent element of uncertainty does not prevent a finding of fiduciary breach, for tort law has long recognized that a misrepresentation of intention[233] or opinion[234] may be fraudulent.[235] Deceptive predictions breach an ERISA duty (as distinguished from a preempted tort duty) only if they can be attributed to a fiduciary. This again rules out liability for most misrepresentations made by lower-level personnel or benefits office employees performing ministerial functions. That limitation is not troublesome, for redress is appropriate only for misrepresentations made or orchestrated by higher officials. Reasonable workers would rely on predictions only if the information comes from people in a position to monitor the sponsor's policy-level benefits decisions (including plan design and amendment), and inevitably these people will be managers with discretion—fiduciaries, that is. The shocking instances of benefit fraud, such as *Varity* and the *Berlin* benefit enhancement line of cases, are all of this nature. And of course, fiduciary liability would attach to misrepresentations made by ministerial employees at the behest of managers or as a result of policies that deliberately insulate contact people from vital information.

Fiduciary liability for future-sounding misinformation is compatible with ERISA's policy of promoting worker career and financial planning in that it ensures the sponsor's voluntary disclosures are reliable without undermining the primacy of the SPD. It also finds support in the analytical tools of law and economics.[236] Absent an anti-fraud rule, some firms would attract and retain workers with informal prospective promises that they did not intend to keep, thereby paying lower compensation than truthful firms (and effectively misappropriating labor). That behavior arguably will

---

232 Varity Corp. v. Howe, 516 U.S. 489, 505 (1996). *See supra* Chapter 3 note 183 and accompanying text.

233 RESTATEMENT (SECOND) OF TORTS §§ 525, 530(2), 526, 544 (1977).

234 At common law, reliance on a statement of opinion is only justified in limited circumstances, apparently on the theory that adversaries in a bargaining transaction will recognize and appropriately discount puffing. Recovery is allowed in situations where the recipient of the representation of opinion would not be on his guard, including where the maker of the representation stands in a fiduciary relation to the recipient. RESTATEMENT (SECOND) OF TORTS §§ 525, 526, 542 (1977); W. PAGE KEETON et al., PROSSER AND KEETON ON THE LAW OF TORTS § 109 (5th ed. 1984).

235 According to the RESTATEMENT (SECOND) OF TORTS, a misrepresentation is fraudulent where the maker knows or believes that the matter is not as represented, does not have confidence in the accuracy of the representation, or knows that he does not have a basis for the representation. RESTATEMENT (SECOND) OF TORTS § 526 (1977).

236 *See generally* EASTERBROOK & FISCHEL, *supra* Chapter 3 note 74, at 279–85; Kent Greenfield, *The Unjustified Absence of Federal Fraud Protection in the Labor Market*, 107 YALE L.J. 715, 738–54 (1997) (arguing that fraud protections may be more important to the efficient operation of labor markets than it is for the capital markets).

cause workers to discount the promises of all firms unless truthful firms can distinguish themselves to attract better workers. Verification of information about the future of employee benefit programs is difficult for workers because only the sponsor has the necessary information (e.g., profit projections or actuarial cost data). Truthful firms may take steps to give credence to their representations by independent certification or adopting enforceable plan amendments, but these devices entail additional costs. A rule against fraud, if properly enforced, functions as an informational warranty and makes it unnecessary for workers to verify information or for sponsors to undertake expensive certification. It decreases the cost of providing truthful prospective information while increasing the cost of falsehood. This cost reallocation to mendacious employers permits sponsors of higher-quality plans to compete more effectively in the labor market.

E. CONCLUSION

Several major themes can be distilled from the burgeoning and confused appellate case law on disclosure obligations. The central issue concerns the role of the summary plan description vis-à-vis the underlying plan documents. The SPD is designed to provide participants and beneficiaries with an accessible, reliable source of information about the plan. But because it is a simplified explanation of the principal features of the plan, it is necessarily incomplete and may be inconsistent with the plan documents, which are typically lengthy, complex, and technically worded legal instruments. Where the SPD contradicts the plan documents, the sponsor is held to the advertised terms even if the summary disclaims binding effect, but the courts are divided on the question whether the SPD should govern as a matter of contract or estoppel. In view of its special role, the better view is that the SPD should be treated as the "deal," and its terms, as far as they go, should be treated as the terms of the plan itself. This approach eliminates the need for proof of reliance, the uncertainty and expense of which could cause significant under-enforcement of the disclosure rules.

If, instead of contradicting the underlying plan documents, the SPD contradicts itself, the courts generally refuse to impose liability on the view that reliance is unjustified. Attention to the origin of the contradiction, its lack of salience, and the relative costs that the employer and workers would have to incur to avoid the resulting harm, shows that ERISA's policies would be better served by the rule of *contra proferentem*. That is, the interpretation that reconciles the SPD contradiction to the workers' advantage should be enforced as the terms of the plan.

Where the SPD is silent on an issue that the plan documents address, workers may interpret the simplified presentation, viewed in isolation, as the announcement of a general rule that admits no exceptions or qualifications. To bind the sponsor to that interpretation would defeat the purposes of the SPD: to be useful, a summary must necessarily generalize and simplify, and the details omitted will frequently impose technical (but important) limitations and qualifications. The SPD obligation presents an inherent trade-off, for if disclosures are made more detailed and complex, so that they are more informative to participants in unusual circumstances, they also become correspondingly longer, more difficult to understand, and therefore less useful to workers generally. To promote *optimal disclosure*, the plan sponsor should be bound by the terms of the SPD and reasonable inferences based thereon *unless either* (1) it would be apparent to an average participant, based only on a careful reading of the SPD itself, that the particular provision of the SPD at issue is incomplete (typically because the SPD contained a particularized warning that additional information should be consulted); (2) the omission would not have been material to a person in the claimant's position; or (3) its importance was not known or foreseeable to the sponsor.

Informal (that is, non-SPD) communications that are at variance with the plan present a somewhat different set of considerations. The courts refuse to apply estoppel to permit oral modifications of employee benefit plans. (If, however, the oral statement conflicts with the underlying plan documents but not the SPD, the matter should be analyzed as an incomplete SPD case, under the approach summarized in the prior paragraph.) Upon an adequate showing of reliance, many courts will prohibit the plan from reneging on an informal communication that clarifies an ambiguous plan provision, but not one that would override clear plan terms. Reliance, and therefore estoppel, is ordinarily unjustified where an informal written communication contradicts the SPD. If, however, the writing is made by someone who has the authority to amend the plan, to institute a new plan, or to report such developments, then the writing could be given effect as an informal plan amendment by applying apparent authority principles from the law of agency.

Plan fiduciaries are subject to exacting standards of loyalty and prudence that can trigger liability for misinformation even if the plan could not be bound as a matter of contract or estoppel. Under ERISA's broad functional definition of fiduciary, corporate officers advising workers on the future of employee benefit plans might be speaking as fiduciaries, rendering incautious or deceitful remarks actionable. Not only must a plan fiduciary speak truthfully, in some circumstances the fiduciary cannot safely stand mute. Sometimes, that is, a fiduciary has a duty to say more than the statutory disclosure obligations require. A fiduciary who is aware of a beneficiary's special situation has a "duty to convey complete and accurate information that [is] material to [that] circumstance," even if asked the wrong question.[237] Moreover, an inquiry from a participant or beneficiary may not be required to trigger the obligation—the fiduciary has a duty to speak if he has reason to know that his silence may be harmful.

---

237   Bixler v. Cent. Pa. Teamsters Health & Welfare Fund, 12 F.3d 1292, 1302–03 (3d Cir. 1993).

Chapter 4

Fiduciary Obligations

"The focus of the statute thus is on the administrative integrity of benefit plans."[1]

---

[1]   Fort Halifax Packing Co. v. Coyne, 482 U.S. 1, 15 (1987).

Assurance of integrity is the heart and soul of ERISA. Federal fiduciary standards were designed to work in combination with improved disclosure (*see* Chapter 3) and powerful enforcement tools (*see* Chapter 5) to stem misconduct in plan administration.[2] Experience suggests that this convergence of means to the end of controlling mismanagement and abuse is no overreaction, for claims of fiduciary misconduct are presented in most cases litigated under ERISA.

ERISA's fiduciary rules were abstracted from state trust law. In combination with preemption, federal fiduciary standards avoid the conflicts, costs, and complications that would arise from local variations in the law of trusts. But ERISA's fiduciary responsibility provisions serve an interest in addition to, and more important than, uniformity. To tailor administrative requirements to the special circumstances of employee benefit plans, Congress prescribed several departures from conventional trust law.

Three modifications are central to ERISA's mission. First, Congress adopted a broad functional definition of fiduciary so that all benefit plan decision makers—not just asset managers (traditional trustees)—can be called to account. Second, to hold their feet to the fire, ERISA not only specifies a stringent set of fiduciary duties, but it also outlaws plan provisions (known as exculpatory clauses) that would relax their force. Third, certain transactions involving insider dealings with the plan are banned without regard to fairness or whether loss ensues. This chapter explores each of these departures from traditional state trust law and then takes up the phenomenon of participant-directed investments under defined contribution pension plans—including most 401(k) plans—paying particular attention to the extent to which employee decision making insulates plan fiduciaries from liability for poor investment choices, including losses from substantial holdings of stock in the employer corporation.

A. DEFINITION OF FIDUCIARY

General Principles

Liability for misconduct in the affairs of an employee benefit plan is generally limited to fiduciaries.[3] Fiduciaries are also granted standing to enforce the duties of other fiduciaries and to seek equitable relief for violations of the terms of the plan or ERISA.[4] Status as a plan fiduciary is determined under ERISA § 3(21), which provides in part

[A] person is a fiduciary with respect to a plan to the extent (i) he exercises any discretionary authority or discretionary control respecting management of such

---

2   *E.g.*, S. Rep. No. 93-127, at 27–28, 29 (1973) ("[W]ithout provisions . . . allowing ready access to both detailed information about the plan and to the courts, and without standards by which a participant can measure the fiduciary's conduct . . . he is not equipped to safeguard either his own rights or the plan assets."), *reprinted in* 1 ERISA Legislative History, *supra* Chapter 1 note 56, at 587, 613–14, 615.

3   ERISA § 409(a), 29 U.S.C. § 1109(a) (2006).

4   ERISA § 502(a)(2), (3), 29 U.S.C. § 1132(a)(2), (3) (2006).

plan or exercises any authority or control respecting management or disposition of its assets, (ii) he renders investment advice for a fee or other compensation, direct or indirect, with respect to any moneys or other property of such plan, or has any authority or responsibility to do so, or (iii) he has any discretionary authority or discretionary responsibility in the administration of such plan. Such term includes any person designated under section 405(c)(1)(B) of this title.[5]

Several aspects of this definition are noteworthy. Comparing the first part of clause (i) with clause (iii), it is apparent that *discretionary* authority over plan administration, whether or not exercised, is sufficient to ensure fiduciary classification ("exercises" versus "has"). In contrast, any reference to discretion is notably absent from the second part of clause (i), which provides that the exercise of "any authority or control respecting the management or disposition of [plan] assets" also triggers fiduciary status. Finally, payments for investment advice can bring automatic fiduciary classification, even if the ultimate discretionary investment decision lies in other hands, and even if the investment advisor does not handle plan assets.

This definition brings fiduciary duties to bear on those persons whose venality or neglect could injure plan participants. Discretionary authority, large or small, could be abused to the detriment of participants, and so all judgment calls are monitored under the law's most exacting standards. Persons who are not involved in operational decision making cannot ordinarily do much damage, unless they are in a position to loot the fund. For that reason, the statute indicates that anyone who handles the money will also be held to the strictest standards of loyalty and care, even in the absence of decision-making authority. Investment advisers who don't make final decisions and don't have access to plan assets would not be subject to fiduciary obligations absent their express inclusion in clause (ii), and, in fact, other paid professional advisors, such as lawyers, accountants, and actuaries, ordinarily are not fiduciaries.[6] The legislative history does not explain this discrepancy, but a Labor Department regulation substantially narrows it.[7]

---

5   ERISA § 3(21)(A), 29 U.S.C. § 1002(21)(A) (2006).

6   29 C.F.R. § 2509.75-5, D-1 (2009) (attorney, accountant, actuary, or consultant is not a fiduciary solely by virtue of rendering legal, accounting, actuarial, or consulting services to the plan). The ERISA conference report observes

> While the ordinary functions of consultants and advisers to employee benefit plans (other than investment advisers) may not be considered as fiduciary functions, it must be recognized that there will be situations where such consultants and advisers may because of their special expertise, in effect, be exercising discretionary authority or control with respect to the management or administration of such plan or some authority or control regarding its assets. In such cases, they are to be regarded as having assumed fiduciary obligations within the meaning of the applicable definition.

H.R. REP. No. 93-1280, at 323 (1974), *reprinted in* 3 ERISA LEGISLATIVE HISTORY, *supra* Chapter 1 note 56, at 4590.

7   29 C.F.R. § 2510.3-21(c)(1)(ii)(B) (2009) provides that paid investment advisers who lack discretionary authority will be classified as fiduciaries only if they render advice on a regular basis, pursuant to an understanding that their "services will serve as a primary basis for investment decisions with respect to plan assets," and that they will render "individualized investment advice . . . based on the particular needs of the plan." Where there is such a special

De Facto Fiduciaries

ERISA's functional definition of fiduciary extends not only to those who are authorized to perform the designated task, but also to those who wield power de facto. A person who "exercises any discretionary *authority*" over plan management, or who "exercises any *authority* . . . respecting management or disposition of [plan] assets," is a fiduciary. But so is anyone who, absent authority, "exercises any . . . discretionary *control*" or "exercises any . . . *control*" over plan assets.[8] That is, anyone who actually exercises control, regardless of legitimacy, is a fiduciary.[9]

The courts have repeatedly held such de facto fiduciaries accountable for their conduct. For example, the sponsoring employer is often found to be a de facto fiduciary where, by deliberately failing to provide necessary information (a ministerial duty), the employer prevents a participant from presenting her claim for benefits to an independent fiduciary.[10]

Discretion and Funding

Fiduciary classification under ERISA is founded on functions performed, not on formal designation. It also does not depend on satisfaction of the requirements for creation of a valid trust. The existence of some trust property, a "res," is essential to the creation of a trust,[11] yet some unfunded employee benefit programs are welfare plans,[12] and their decision makers are ERISA fiduciaries even though there are no plan assets to protect or invest. So, for example, decisions about benefit claims (coverage determinations) under a self-insured health care plan are fiduciary acts subject to review under ERISA's duties of loyalty and care.

Oversight of discretionary decisions is a primary concern of the fiduciary rules, but it is not the exclusive concern. Where a plan is funded, anyone who handles the money is a fiduciary, even absent decision-making responsibility.[13] Unfortunately, courts have

---

relationship, reliance is to be expected, and the advisor can price his services to account for the increased exposure. Such ongoing individualized investment advice is akin to de facto delegation of discretionary authority, which is the case where other paid professionals can be held liable as fiduciaries. *See supra* Chapter 4 note 6.

8   ERISA § 3(21)(A)(i), 29 U.S.C. § 1002(21)(A)(i) (2006) (emphasis added).

9   *See* Explanation of H.R. 12906, 120 Cong. Rec. 3983 (1974), *reprinted in* 2 ERISA Legislative History, *supra* Chapter 1 note 56, at 3293, 3309 ("Conduct alone may in an appropriate circumstance impose fiduciary obligations.").

10 *E.g.*, Blatt v. Marshall & Lassman, 812 F.2d 810 (2d Cir. 1987) (employer's failure to provide insurer with confirmation of employee's separation from service, delaying pension plan distribution, held to be exercise of actual control over disposition of plan assets); Hamilton v. Allen-Bradley Co., 244 F.3d 819 (11th Cir. 2001) (employer exercised actual control over claim process by failure to timely provide application for long-term disability benefits).

11 Restatement (Second) of Trusts § 74 (1959); Restatement (Third) of Trusts § 2 & cmt. i (2003).

12 *See supra* text accompanying Chapter 2 notes 110–116.

13 In *Chao v. Day*, 436 F.3d 234 (D.C. Cir. 2006), an insurance broker misappropriated premium payments from 29 health plans, to which he issued fake insurance policies. In a suit brought by

sometimes overlooked this prong of the fiduciary definition, holding that discretion is the sine qua non of fiduciary status.[14] Judicial confusion over the fiduciary status of directed trustees and other ministerial asset handlers may have its origin in an early and misguided Labor Department pronouncement. Issued in 1975 and still in effect, Interpretive Bulletin 75-8[15] provides, in part, that persons who have no power to make decisions about plan policy, interpretation, practices, or procedures, but who merely perform certain administrative tasks under a framework of policies, interpretations, rules, and procedures established by others, are not fiduciaries. Most of the listed tasks involve the processing of information (such as recordkeeping, communicating, reporting, and initially applying plan rules determining eligibility for participation or benefits) and advisory functions. As to these tasks, it is clearly correct to conclude that purely ministerial acts conducted under rules set and overseen by others (persons who unquestionably have discretion and are fiduciaries) will not bring fiduciary classification. Unfortunately, however, the list of nonfiduciary ministerial tasks includes "[c]ollection of contributions and application of contributions as provided in the plan," which entails handling the money. The proposition that a person with access to plan assets who performs only ministerial duties could loot the fund without being subject to robust fiduciary remedies would surely have startled the Congress that enacted ERISA.[16] As the Supreme Court has observed, "[a] fair contextual reading of the statute makes it abundantly clear that its draftsmen were primarily concerned with the possible misuse of plan assets, and with remedies that would protect the entire plan. . . ."[17]

---

the Secretary of Labor, the defendant argued that he could not be held liable as a fiduciary because he lacked discretion in the use of the funds. The court found no statutory support for this defense: "Because the disposition clause [of ERISA's definition of fiduciary] contains no 'discretion' requirement, it is irrelevant whether [the defendant] exercised 'discretion' in his thievery. 'Any authority or control' is enough." *Id.* at 236. *See also* IT Corp. v. Gen. Am. Life Ins. Co., 107 F.3d 1415, 1421–22 (9th Cir. 1997) (check-writing control over plan bank account may trigger fiduciary status despite lack of discretionary authority because "[t]he statute treats control over the cash differently from control over administration"); Coldesina v. Estate of Simper, 407 F.3d 1126, 1132 (10th Cir. 2005) ("Discretion is conspicuously omitted from the fiduciary function of controlling plan assets. . . . As other courts have recognized, this distinction evidences Congress's intent to treat control over assets differently than control over management or administration.").

14   *E.g.*, Maniance v. Commerce Bank, 40 F.3d 264, 267 (8th Cir. 1994) ("[D]iscretion is the benchmark for fiduciary status under ERISA."). The problem has been particularly pronounced in the case of directed trustees. *See generally* Patricia Wick Hatamyar, *See No Evil? The Role of the Directed Trustee Under ERISA*, 64 TENN. L. REV. 1, 41–52 (1996), and cases cited and discussed therein.

15   29 C.F.R. § 2509.75-8, D-2 (2009).

16   Federal fiduciary standards were an early and noncontroversial component of legislative proposals for benefit plan regulation. The consensus grew out of spectacular revelations in the mid-1960s of the diversion of more than $4 million from the welfare funds of two small local unions to the unfettered command of the union boss. *See* S. COMM. ON GOVERNMENT OPERATIONS, DIVERSION OF UNION WELFARE-PENSION FUNDS OF ALLIED TRADES COUNCIL AND TEAMSTERS LOCAL 815, S. REP. NO. 89-1348, at 33–39 (1966).

17   Mass. Mut. Life Ins. Co. v. Russell, 473 U.S. 134, 142 (1985).

Multiple Hats

Discretionary authority relating to employee benefits is not alone sufficient to trigger fiduciary classification. It must be discretion of a certain type, namely, that involved in the management or administration of the plan. Judgments respecting the design, establishment, or modification of an employee benefit plan are not fiduciary acts, for they do not implicate program management. This fundamental distinction between design and implementation is often referred to as the difference between "settlor" and "trustee" functions, an analogy to private trust law counterparts. Long recognized by lower courts, the Supreme Court has affirmed that when a plan sponsor adopts, amends, or terminates an employee benefit plan (either welfare or pension), it is not acting in a fiduciary capacity.[18] Consequently, the obligation to act "solely in the interest of the participants and beneficiaries" does not attach to plan design decisions, leaving employers free (subject to ERISA's content controls) to structure the program to maximal business advantage. That flexibility to tailor benefit plans to best promote the sponsor's personnel policies is crucial to the maintenance of ERISA's delicate balance between public regulation and private sponsorship.[19]

Under ERISA, settlor or design functions can be conducted for the sponsor's benefit, but trustee or administrative functions must generally be carried out for the "exclusive purpose of providing benefits to participants and their beneficiaries and defraying reasonable expenses of administering the plan."[20] ERISA, however, permits one person to act in both roles. An individual who is a fiduciary because of certain activities does not thereby become a fiduciary for all purposes nor in all of her dealings with the plan. Rather, one is a fiduciary only "to the extent" she has or exercises managerial discretion, handles plan assets, or provides investment advice for a fee.[21] Consequently, a sometimes-fiduciary can, at other times, be a plan participant serving her own interest in obtaining pension or welfare benefits. Likewise, a fiduciary may be an employee, officer, or director of the sponsor, carrying out plan-design functions or business-management functions that affect benefits (hiring, firing, or transferring employees, for example). Or she may even serve in all three capacities, as fiduciary, participant, and agent of the sponsor.[22]

> [T]he statute does not describe fiduciaries simply as administrators of the plan, or managers or advisers. Instead it defines an administrator, for example, as a fiduciary

---

18 Curtiss-Wright Corp. v. Schoonejongen, 514 U.S. 73, 78 (1995) (welfare plan); Lockheed Corp. v. Spink, 517 U.S. 882, 890–91 (1996) (pension plans); Hughes Aircraft Co. v. Jacobson, 525 U.S. 432, 443–44 (1999) (rule applies regardless of whether employees have contributed to the plan).

19 *See generally supra* Chapter 1C.

20 ERISA § 404(a)(1)(A), 29 U.S.C. § 1104(a)(1)(A) (2006).

21 ERISA § 3(21)(A), 29 U.S.C. § 1002(21)(A) (2006).

22 *See* ERISA § 408(c)(1), (3), 29 U.S.C. § 1108(c)(1), (3) (2006) (multiple roles not barred by prohibited-transaction rules).

only "to the extent" that he acts in such a capacity in relation to a plan. 29 U.S.C. § 1002(21)(A). In every case charging breach of ERISA fiduciary duty, then, the threshold question is not whether the actions of some person employed to provide services under a plan adversely affected a plan beneficiary's interest, but whether that person was acting as a fiduciary (that is, was performing a fiduciary function) when taking the action subject to complaint.[23]

Where a fiduciary wears "multiple hats" in her various dealings with the plan, it is sometimes difficult to determine in which capacity a particular action was undertaken. If confusion surrounds the role in which one deals with the plan, the Supreme Court has indicated that the ambiguity should be resolved in favor of fiduciary status, at least in cases where the confusion is deliberately fostered.[24]

Health maintenance organizations (HMOs) and other managed care plans bring cost-containment considerations to bear on the central fiduciary function of determining eligibility for benefits. In *Pegram v. Herdrich*,[25] the Supreme Court was asked to decide whether mixed eligibility and treatment decisions made by HMO doctors are fiduciary acts. Costs are, of course, always relevant to plan design (a nonfiduciary "settlor" function). Under a traditional indemnity-based health care plan, costs are restrained by limiting covered conditions or procedures, requiring participants to pay a portion of their health care costs (coinsurance features), and by imposing annual or lifetime caps on coverage. These cost-containment devices are separate from the medical treatment decision. Managed care plans typically employ some or all of these strategies, but they also enlist physicians in the cost-containment effort by making benefit eligibility dependent upon the necessity of a particular diagnostic or treatment program, a matter of professional judgment, and by providing financial incentives to exercise that judgment conservatively.

Pegram began as a medical malpractice case in which the patient, Cynthia Herdrich, sued her physician for failing to properly diagnose and treat appendicitis. The patient initially presented with pain in the midline area of her groin, and when she returned six days later, Dr. Pegram discovered an inflamed mass in her abdomen. Nevertheless, Dr. Pegram did not order an immediate ultrasound at the local hospital, but decided that the patient could wait another eight days to have the procedure performed fifty miles away at a facility run by the for-profit HMO of which Dr. Pegram was a physician-owner. In the meantime, Ms. Herdrich's appendix ruptured, causing peritonitis. Ms. Herdrich won a jury award on her malpractice claims, but the question brought before the Supreme Court was whether treatment decisions made by an HMO acting through its physician-employees are fiduciary acts subject to ERISA.[26]

---

23   Pegram v. Herdrich, 530 U.S. 211, 225–26 (2000).
24   *See* Varity Corp. v. Howe, 516 U.S. 489 (1996), discussed *supra* Chapter 3 notes 158–183 and accompanying text.
25   530 U.S. 211 (2000).
26   *Id.* at 214–15.

The *Pegram* Court held *unanimously* that HMO physicians' mixed eligibility and treatment decisions are *not* fiduciary acts within the meaning of ERISA.[27] The Court was persuaded that Congress did not intend these decisions to be measured against fiduciary standards, both because such suits would undercut a long-standing congressional policy of promoting HMOs, and because they would boil down to medical malpractice claims of the sort already available under state law.[28] Moreover, recognition of such fiduciary claims might even federalize medical malpractice law by triggering ERISA's preemption provision.[29]

Does *Pegram* portend a more general relaxation of fiduciary oversight in dual status (multiple hat) situations? Or are HMO eligibility decisions sui generis?[30] It is noteworthy that the Court did not adjust fiduciary obligations; it found them wholly inapplicable to the situation. While conflicted decision making is endemic to some other plan types that Congress has promoted,[31] federal protections would still be needed where an effective state law remedy (akin to medical malpractice in the HMO situation) is lacking. In *Aetna Health Inc. v. Davila*,[32] the Court clarified that a "benefit determination under ERISA . . . is generally a fiduciary act," and the "fact that a benefit determination is infused with medical judgments does not alter this result."[33] Thus, the exception in *Pegram* is a narrow one, which applies only "where the underlying negligence also plausibly constitutes medical treatment by a party that can be deemed to be a treating physician or such a physician's employer."[34]

---

27   *Id.* at 237.

28   *Id.* at 235–36.

29   *Id.* at 236–37.

30   *See* Marks v. Watters, 322 F.3d 316, 324–27 (4th Cir. 2003) (distinguishing *Pegram*; utilization review under preferred provider organization health plan not a mixed eligibility and treatment decision; state law claims for negligent utilization review subject to complete preemption).

31   *E.g.*, Grindstaff v. Green, 133 F.3d 416 (6th Cir. 1998) (voting of employee stock ownership plan stock by directors to perpetuate their own incumbency not breach of fiduciary duty in light of dual nature of ESOPs as retirement plans and method of corporate finance); Moench v. Robertson, 67 F.3d 553, 571 (3d Cir. 1995) (purpose of ESOP supports conclusion that fiduciary investment in employer stock entitled to presumption of prudence); Edgar v. Avaya, Inc., 503 F.3d 340, 347 (3d Cir. 2007) (same reasoning applies to other eligible individual account plans).

32   542 U.S. 200 (2004).

33   *Id.* at 219.

34   *Id.* at 221 (quoting from Judge Calabresi's dissent in *Cicio v. Does*, 321 F.3d 83, 109 (2d Cir. 2003)). Land v. CIGNA Healthcare of Fla., 381 F.3d 1284 (11th Cir. 2004) (medical malpractice claim preempted because adverse medical necessity determination by HMO approval nurse was benefit decision by ERISA fiduciary; *Pegram* exception for mixed eligibility and treatment decisions does not apply where decision maker is not treating physician); Mayeaux v. La. Health Serv. & Indem. Co., 376 F.3d 420 (5th Cir. 2004) (ERISA preempts state law claims against health plan administrator based on denial of benefits under plan's experimental therapy exclusion).

Multiple Fiduciaries

Another consequence of ERISA's functional definition of fiduciary is the proliferation of limited-role fiduciaries. Just as one person may deal with the plan in multiple capacities, multiple people may deal with the plan in a fiduciary capacity, with either overlapping or distinct responsibilities. Certain responsibilities are statutorily defined. Foremost is the named fiduciary, who has "authority to control and manage the operation and administration of the plan."[35] The named fiduciary functions as the chief executive officer of the plan, with ultimate authority over operations. The plan may, however, call for multiple named fiduciaries, having either joint or divided responsibilities.[36] For a funded plan, the trustee is the fiduciary who is legal owner of the assets and generally has exclusive authority over investment decision making.[37] The plan administrator is the person designated by the plan (or in default of which, the plan sponsor), who is assigned statutory responsibility for satisfying reporting and disclosure requirements. Thus, the administrator is a fiduciary who functions, in effect, as the chief information officer of the plan.[38]

Beyond the roles of named fiduciary, trustee, and administrator, other fiduciaries abound. Recall that any actual involvement in the management or disposition of plan assets, even if only by an underling (agent or employee) who lacks discretionary authority and is answerable to the trustee, suffices to bring about fiduciary classification. And ERISA permits the plan instrument to establish a procedure by which named fiduciaries may allocate fiduciary responsibilities among themselves or delegate their

---

35   ERISA § 402(a)(1), 29 U.S.C. § 1102(a)(1) (2006). ERISA calls for the named fiduciary to be named in the plan instrument or identified by a procedure set forth in the plan. ERISA § 402(a) (2), 29 U.S.C. § 1102(a)(2) (2006). Since no trust fails for want of a trustee, RESTATEMENT (SECOND) OF TRUSTS § 108 (1959), RESTATEMENT (THIRD) OF TRUSTS § 31 (2007), failure of the plan instrument to provide for a named fiduciary presumably would not invalidate the plan, just as breach of the requirement of a written instrument does not, *see supra* Chapters 2A and 3C.

36   ERISA §§ 402(a)(1) ("jointly or severally"), 405(c)(1) (plan procedures for allocation responsibilities), 29 U.S.C. §§ 1102(a)(1), 1105(c)(1) (2006).

37   ERISA § 403(a), 29 U.S.C. § 1103(a) (2006). ERISA recognizes three exceptions to the trustee's exclusive authority to manage and control plan assets. First, the plan may provide the named fiduciary with authority to appoint one or more investment managers to manage plan assets. ERISA §§ 402(b)(3), 403(a)(2), 29 U.S.C. §§ 1102(b)(3), 1103(a)(2) (2006). Second, the plan may provide that trustees' dealings with plan assets will be subject to the direction of a named fiduciary who is not a trustee (the directed trustee). ERISA § 403(a)(1), 29 U.S.C. § 1103(a)(1) (2006). Third, a defined contribution pension plan may permit a participant to exercise investment control over the assets in his account (a "404(c) plan"). ERISA § 404(c)(1), 29 U.S.C. § 1104(c)(1) (2006); 29 C.F.R. § 2550.404c-1 (2009). Trustees are immunized from liability for the acts or omissions of investment managers, provided the trustee does not knowingly participate in or try to conceal the investment manager's breach. ERISA § 405(d)(1), 29 U.S.C. § 1105(d)(1) (2006). The potential continuing liability of a directed trustee is analyzed in Hatamyar, *supra* Chapter 4 note 14. Exposure of fiduciaries under a participant-directed 404(c) plan is examined *infra* Chapter 4D, and in Colleen E. Medill, *Stock Market Volatility and 401(k) Plans*, 34 U. MICH. J.L. REFORM 469 (2001).

38   ERISA §§ 3(16)(A), 101, 104, 105, 29 U.S.C. §§ 1002(16)(A), 1021, 1024, 1025 (2006). *See supra* Chapter 3D.

responsibilities to others.[39] Even if a delegation does not conform to ERISA's requirements, the delegate would nevertheless "have" or "exercise" discretionary authority regarding some aspects of plan management or operations, and would, to that extent, satisfy ERISA's definition of fiduciary.

Diffuse responsibility raises the question, who is to be held accountable? Speaking broadly, fiduciary liability under ERISA is premised on personal fault, not on notions of joint or vicarious responsibility. An act or omission in breach of duty by one fiduciary does not by itself render a cofiduciary liable. Instead, the cofiduciary is ordinarily liable only if his own breach of duty enabled the other fiduciary to commit the breach, or if, *knowing* that the other's act or omission is a breach, he knowingly participates in, knowingly undertakes to conceal, or fails to make reasonable efforts to remedy the other's breach.[40] In each of these cases the cofiduciary's own misconduct is a proximate cause of the loss that flows from another fiduciary's breach.

Conversely, if such personal responsibility is lacking, then a cofiduciary is ordinarily not held liable for another fiduciary's breach. As noted earlier, ERISA permits the plan instrument to establish a procedure by which named fiduciaries may allocate fiduciary responsibilities (other than asset management) among themselves or designate others to perform those responsibilities. If a plan provides such a procedure, and if a named fiduciary does not breach her own duties in making or continuing an allocation or delegation of responsibilities thereunder, then ERISA insulates her from liability for the acts or omissions of the person assigned to carry out the tasks.[41] Similarly, the ERISA Conference Report observes that fiduciaries may sometimes hire agents to perform ministerial acts, in which case "the liability of the trustees (or other fiduciaries) for acts of their agents is to be established in accordance with the prudent man rule."[42] In other words, a fiduciary principal must be shown to have been negligent in hiring or supervising the agent to become liable to participants for the agent's acts. In suits to enforce fiduciary obligations, ERISA does not adopt a rule of respondeat superior: fiduciaries are not generally subject to imputed or vicarious liability.[43]

---

39   ERISA § 405(c), 29 U.S.C. § 1105(c) (2006). Named fiduciaries are not permitted to allocate or delegate asset-management functions, *id.*, but asset management is normally the exclusive province of the trustee rather than the named fiduciary, except in the case where the plan expressly provides that the trustee is subject to proper direction by a named fiduciary who is not a trustee. *See* ERISA § 403(a)(1), 29 U.S.C. § 1103(a)(1) (2006).

40   ERISA § 405(a), 29 U.S.C. § 1105(a) (2006); H.R. CONF. REP. No. 93-1280, at 299–300 (1974), *reprinted in* 3 ERISA LEGISLATIVE HISTORY, *supra* Chapter 1 note 56, at 566–67 (liability for failure to take reasonable steps to remedy a breach requires more than mere knowledge of a cofiduciary's act or omission; it requires actual knowledge that it is a breach).

41   ERISA § 405(c), 29 U.S.C. § 1105(c) (2006).

42   H.R. CONF. REP. No. 93-1280, at 301 (1974), *reprinted in* 3 ERISA LEGISLATIVE HISTORY, *supra* Chapter 1 note 56, at 4568. This observation seems to indicate that Congress expected ordinary trust law principles to govern an ERISA fiduciary's liability for an agent's acts. *See* RESTATEMENT (SECOND) OF TRUSTS § 225 (1959); 3 SCOTT ON TRUSTS, *supra* Chapter 3 note 11, §§ 225, 225.1.

43   *See, e.g.*, Schmidt v. Sheet Metal Workers' Nat'l Pension Fund, 128 F.3d 541, 547–48 (7th Cir. 1997) (fiduciaries not liable for misinformation provided by ministerial agent where fiduciaries exercised due care in hiring, training, and supervising agent).

There is an important situation in which one fiduciary is accountable for a breach of duty committed by another, even though the first neither participated in nor had knowledge of the other's breach. ERISA permits the allocation or delegation of fiduciary functions (other than asset management) only if the plan expressly allows it and provides a procedure for doing so.[44] If, in contravention of those rules, a named fiduciary assigns some responsibility to another person, the named fiduciary remains on the hook for any breach committed by his deputy.[45] It seems that Congress sought to deter such informal delegations, even if not imprudent or disloyal, "so the employees may know who is responsible for operating the plan."[46] Thus, the named fiduciary is a proper defendant and remains subject to liability unless there is a paper trail showing proper delegation of authority to someone who can be readily identified.

Making significant personal involvement a necessary element of cofiduciary liability is consistent with traditional state trust law.[47] While it may deny injured

---

44   ERISA § 402(b)(2), 29 U.S.C. § 1102(b)(2) (2006).

45   Fiduciary duties always include the obligation to follow the terms of the plan insofar as they are consistent with ERISA. ERISA § 404(a)(1)(D), 29 U.S.C. § 1104(a)(1)(D) (2006). Consequently, the act of allocating or delegating responsibilities would entail a breach of the named fiduciary's own obligations if it is not authorized by the plan or fails to conform to plan procedures. Under ERISA § 405(c)(2)(A)(i), 29 U.S.C. § 1105(c)(2)(A)(i), a named fiduciary who violates his own duties in allocating or delegating fiduciary functions is not exempt from liability for the acts of the deputy. Moreover, ERISA § 405(a)(2), 29 U.S.C. § 1105(a)(2), provides that if a fiduciary's failure to comply with his own duties in carrying out the specific responsibilities that give rise to his fiduciary status enables another fiduciary to commit a breach, then the first is liable for the other's breach. The ERISA Conference Report observes that "[a]llocation or delegation (and the consequent elimination of liability) can only occur" where the plan expressly provides for it. H.R. CONF. REP. NO. 93-1280, at 301 (1974), *reprinted in* 3 ERISA LEGISLATIVE HISTORY, *supra* Chapter 1 note 56, at 4568.

     ERISA's rule of derivative liability based upon improper delegation is consistent with, and apparently derived from, state trust law. A trustee is liable to the beneficiary if he "improperly delegates the administration of the trust to his co-trustee," or if he delegates to an agent acts, the performance of which the trustee "was under a duty not to delegate." RESTATEMENT (SECOND) OF TRUSTS §§ 224(2)(b), 225(2)(b) (1959); 3 SCOTT ON TRUSTS, *supra* Chapter 3 note 11, §§ 224.2, 225.1. *See* RESTATEMENT (SECOND) OF TRUSTS, *supra*, §§ 171 (duty not to delegate), 184 (where there are several trustees, each is under a duty to participate in the administration of the trust, to use reasonable care to prevent a cotrustee from committing a breach of trust, or to compel a cotrustee to redress a breach); RESTATEMENT (THIRD) OF TRUSTS §§ 80 & cmts. d–h, 81 (2007).

46   H.R. CONF. REP. NO. 93-1280, at 297 (1974), *reprinted in* 3 ERISA LEGISLATIVE HISTORY, *supra* Chapter 1 note 56, at 4564.

47   RESTATEMENT (SECOND) OF TRUSTS § 224 (1959) provides

     (1) Except as stated in Subsection (2), a trustee is not liable to the beneficiary for a breach of trust committed by a co-trustee.

     (2) A trustee is liable to the beneficiary, if he

         (a) participates in a breach of trust committed by his co-trustee; or

         (b) improperly delegates the administration of the trust to his co-trustee; or

         (c) approves or acquiesces in or conceals a breach of trust committed by his co-trustee; or

         (d) by his failure to exercise reasonable care in the administration of the trust has enabled his co-trustee to commit a breach of trust; or

         (e) neglects to take proper steps to compel his co-trustee to redress a breach of trust.

participants access to a deep pocket, as between multiple fiduciaries, fairness seems to demand such a restriction because a fiduciary in breach is "personally liable to make good to [the] plan any losses to the plan resulting from" the breach.[48] More important, in passing ERISA, Congress sought to promote plan sponsorship, and some such limit on exposure to risks imposed by the actions of other persons is necessary to keep monitoring, insurance, and plan-administration costs within acceptable bounds.[49]

B. FIDUCIARY DUTIES

In General

ERISA's general standards of fiduciary conduct were derived from trust law. There are four major imperatives: (1) the exclusive benefit rule, which is based on the trust law duty of loyalty;[50] (2) the prudence requirement, often referred to as the Prudent Man Rule, which follows the trust law duty of reasonable care;[51] (3) the diversification rule, which under state trust law is a specific application or corollary of the general duty of reasonable care;[52] and (4) a requirement that the fiduciary act in

---

Accord RESTATEMENT (THIRD) OF TRUSTS § 81 cmt. e (2007).

The five instances in which *Restatement (Second) of Trusts* § 224(2) authorizes cotrustee liability correspond, respectively, to (a) ERISA § 405(a)(1), participation; (b) § 405(c)(2)(A), improper delegation; (c) § 405(a)(1), concealment; (d) § 405(a)(2), enablement; and (e) § 405(a)(3), failure to remedy. Unlike the *Restatement*, however, in cases of participation, concealment, or failure to remedy, ERISA demands *actual* knowledge, not just reason to know, that the other's conduct constitutes a breach, and that one's own act or omission facilitates injury.

48   ERISA § 409(a), 29 U.S.C. § 1109(a) (2006).

49   Rather than performing different functions, multiple fiduciaries may act at different times. Taking an approach similar to the limits on cofiduciary liability, section 409(b) broadly absolves a successor trustee from liability for breaches committed by his predecessor. ERISA § 409(b), 29 U.S.C. § 1109(b) (2006). In contrast, trust law imposes a duty on a successor trustee to examine his predecessor's accounts and take steps to redress any breach. RESTATEMENT (SECOND) OF TRUSTS § 223 (1959).

50   ERISA § 404(a)(1)(A), 29 U.S.C. § 1104(a)(1)(A) (2006). *See* RESTATEMENT (SECOND) OF TRUSTS § 170(1) (1959); RESTATEMENT (THIRD) OF TRUSTS § 78 (2007). The language of ERISA's exclusive benefit rule is similar to a long-standing qualification criterion (i.e., condition on obtaining preferential tax treatment) applicable to pension, profit-sharing, and stock bonus plans. I.R.C. § 401(a)(2) (2006) provides that it must be "impossible [under the trust instrument] at any time prior to the satisfaction of all liabilities with respect to employees and their beneficiaries under the trust, for any part of the corpus or income to be . . . used for, or diverted to, purposes other than the exclusive benefit of his employees or their beneficiaries."

51   ERISA § 404(a)(1)(B), 29 U.S.C. § 1104(a)(1)(B) (2006). *See* RESTATEMENT (SECOND) OF TRUSTS § 174 (1959); RESTATEMENT (THIRD) OF TRUSTS § 77 (2007).

52   ERISA § 404(a)(1)(C), 29 U.S.C. § 1104(a)(1)(C) (2006). In certain circumstances an ESOP, profit-sharing plan, or stock bonus plan is permitted to invest heavily in employer securities or employer real estate notwithstanding the diversification rule (or the prudence requirement, to the extent that it would require diversification). ERISA §§ 404(a)(2), 407(d)(3)–(6),

accordance with plan documents, insofar as they are consistent with the requirements of ERISA.[53]

Despite its trust law origins, ERISA's specification of fiduciary duties entails three striking departures from traditional trust administration principles. First, ERISA does not explicitly impose a duty to deal impartially with multiple plan participants and beneficiaries.[54] Second, unlike their trust law counterparts, ERISA's fiduciary duties are *mandatory*; they do not serve merely as default rules that can be overridden by agreement (here, the plan instrument).[55] Third, ERISA's exclusive benefit rule looks to subjective motivation, unlike the trust law duty of loyalty.

Even where ERISA's fiduciary obligations follow state trust law, Congress understood that the traditional duties were being imported into a very different environment and that they might have to evolve differently in their new surroundings. Employee benefit plan administration bears little resemblance to the main function of private trusts, which is to provide a vehicle for ongoing management of intergenerational transfers of family wealth. "The conferees expect that the courts will interpret this prudent man rule (and the other fiduciary standards) bearing in mind the special nature and purpose of employee benefit plans."[56] The Supreme Court explained the appropriate analytic approach as follows:

> [W]e recognize that these fiduciary duties draw much of their content from the common law of trusts, the law that governed most benefit plans before ERISA's enactment.

---

29 U.S.C. §§ 1104(a)(2), 1107(d)(3)–(6) (2006). In plan years beginning after 2006, defined contribution plan participants must in some cases be allowed to direct the plan to switch their account investments from employer securities to diversified investment options. ERISA § 204(j), 29 U.S.C. § 1054(j) (2006); *see* I.R.C. § 401(a)(35) (2006). *See* Restatement (Second) of Trusts § 228 (1959); Restatement (Third) of Trusts § 227(b) (1990) (Prudent Investor Rule); Restatement (Third) of Trusts § 90(a), (b) (2007).

53 ERISA § 404(a)(1)(D), 29 U.S.C. § 1104(a)(1)(D) (2006). *See* Restatement (Third) of Trusts § 76(1) & cmt. b(1) (2007).

54 *See* Restatement (Second) of Trusts § 183 (1959) ("When there are two or more beneficiaries of a trust, the trustee is under a duty to deal impartially with them."); *id.* § 232 ("If a trust is created for beneficiaries in succession, the trustee is under a duty to the successive beneficiaries to act with due regard to their respective interests."); Restatement (Third) of Trusts § 79 (2007).

55 *See* Restatement (Second) of Trusts § 164 (1959): "The nature and extent of the duties and powers of the trustee are determined: (a) by the terms of the trust, except as stated in §§ 165–168; and (b) in the absence of any provision in the terms of the trust, by the rules stated in §§ 169–196." *Accord* Restatement (Third) of Trusts §§ 76, 77 cmt. d, 78(1) (2007). It is significant that the Restatement treats the general fiduciary duties of trustees as a set of default rules that can be modified by the trust agreement, while ERISA sections 404(a)(1)(D) and 410(a) forbid such modifications. *See infra* Chapter 4 note 63 and accompanying text.

56 H.R. Rep. 93-1280, at 302 (1974) (Conf. Rep.), *reprinted in* 3 ERISA Legislative History, *supra* Chapter 1 note 56, at 4569. *See* H.R. Rep. 93-533, at 12, 13 (1973), *reprinted in* 2 ERISA Legislative History, *supra* Chapter 1 note 56, at 2359, 2360 ("[T]he typical employee benefit plan, covering hundreds or even thousands of participants, is quite different from the testamentary trust both in purpose and in nature," so the "principles of fiduciary conduct are adopted from existing trust law, but with modifications appropriate for employee benefit plans.").

We also recognize, however, that trust law does not tell the entire story. After all, ERISA's standards and procedural protections partly reflect a congressional determination that the common law of trusts did not offer completely satisfactory protections.

Consequently, we believe that the law of trusts often will inform, but will not necessarily determine the outcome of, an effort to interpret ERISA's fiduciary duties. In some instances, trust law will offer only a starting point, after which courts must go on to ask whether, or to what extent, the language of the statute, its structure, or its purposes require departing from common-law trust requirements. And, in doing so, courts may have to take account of competing congressional purposes, such as Congress' desire to offer employees enhanced protection for their benefits, on the one hand, and, on the other, its desire not to create a system that is so complex that administrative costs, or litigation expenses, unduly discourage employers from offering welfare benefit plans in the first place.[57]

Impartiality

Temporal division of property ownership always creates the potential for conflict between current and future claimants. Left unsupervised, the owner of the current interest may be inclined to consume the whole; common law responded by protecting future interest holders with the doctrine of waste. Where property is held in trust, current and future beneficiaries typically have very different preferences regarding investment policy. The current income beneficiary wants to generate the maximum short-term return, and so favors high-risk investments, while the principal beneficiary prefers maximum security, even though minimizing risk of loss will reduce or eliminate current yield. The duty of loyalty enjoins the trustee to act for the exclusive benefit of the beneficiaries, yet on matters of investment policy, beneficiaries' interests inevitably conflict. Trust law handles this dilemma by imposing a duty of impartiality, which prohibits favoritism and instructs the trustee (in effect) to fairly compromise the beneficiaries' conflicting interests. Similar conflicts arise between current and future retirees under pension trusts, yet ERISA does not explicitly impose a duty to deal impartially with multiple plan participants and beneficiaries.

Some differences of opinion between pension plan participants present classic impartiality questions. Retirees and older workers under a defined contribution plan will tend to favor more secure investments bearing a lower yield, while younger participants ordinarily have a greater risk tolerance and seek higher rates of return. Under specified conditions, it is now possible to let participants exercise investment control over their own individual accounts, and so make separate decisions in line with their own personal risk tolerance.[58] But where a named fiduciary, an investment manager, or the trustee is in charge of investment decision making, the fiduciary must

---

57   Varity Corp. v. Howe, 516 U.S. 489, 496–97 (1996).
58   ERISA § 404(c), 29 U.S.C. § 1104(c) (2006); 29 C.F.R. § 2550.404c-1 (2009). *See infra* Chapter 4D.

select appropriate risk and return objectives for the fund as a whole, and participants will differ over that collective decision. In such a case, the traditional trust law duty of impartiality is clearly the correct approach, and the federal courts should have little difficulty imposing it, despite ERISA's silence. The interpolation of a duty of impartiality would be an appropriate exercise of the courts' power to craft a federal common law of employee benefit plans. Moreover, a duty of impartiality is implicit in the general standard of care, for a prudent person charged with representing conflicting interests would pursue a reasonable accommodation of those interests.[59]

Many cases involving inter-participant conflicts do not present true impartiality issues; they only masquerade as such. These pseudo-impartiality cases are of two types. The first consists of situations where participants' interests conflict, but the fiduciary is also a plan participant. As to these, loyalty is usually the real issue.[60]

The second type of case that presents conflicts of interest between classes of participants involves interests other than plan benefits. Consider the takeover defense cases, where the issue is whether employer stock held in a pension trust should be tendered for sale at a substantial premium over the current market price for the shares. Retirees and older workers are likely to favor tendering the plan's shares, while younger workers, fearing that the change in ownership will entail corporate restructuring with attendant job losses through downsizing, are likely to oppose the takeover. Employment security (and with it, the prospect of future pension accruals) is likely to be much more important to younger participants than is the security of previously accrued pension benefits, while only the latter consideration is relevant to workers who are already out the door. In these instances there is a clear-cut difference of opinion among participants, but it is not just about plan benefits—it is also about other important interests (here, continued employment). The trouble with approaching the issue from the perspective of impartiality is that an ERISA fiduciary is not empowered to promote the interests of the participants at large. Far from having a general warrant to do good, a fiduciary must discharge his duties for the exclusive purpose of providing plan benefits and defraying reasonable expenses of administration. Consequently job security, although vitally important to young workers, is not a cognizable interest under ERISA. Nor should it be, for in cases of this sort, the younger workers who are opposed to the takeover are, in substance, seeking to trade a portion of their accumulated pension

---

59 In *Varity Corp. v. Howe*, 516 U.S. 489 (1996), after observing that ERISA's "fiduciary duties draw much of their content from the common law of trusts," *id*. at 496, the Court said that recognizing an ERISA "fiduciary obligation, enforceable by beneficiaries seeking relief for themselves, does not necessarily favor payment over nonpayment. The common law of trusts recognizes the need to preserve assets to satisfy future, as well as present, claims and requires a trustee to take impartial account of the interests of all beneficiaries." *Id*. at 514. *See* Morse v. Stanley, 732 F.2d 1139, 1145 (2d Cir. 1984) ("[A] trustee has a duty to deal impartially with beneficiaries. In this case there are working Plan participants and retired beneficiaries and/or their families. The trustee must deal even-handedly among them, doing his best for the entire trust looked at as a whole."). *See* RESTATEMENT (THIRD) OF TRUSTS §§ 79 cmt. b, 90 cmt. c (2007) (duty of impartiality derivative of general duties of prudence and loyalty).

60 *See, e.g.*, Foltz v. U.S. News & World Report, Inc., 865 F.2d 364 (D.C. Cir. 1989) (no breach of duty found where plan administered in favor of future rather than past retirees, but the court took no note of the fact that the fiduciaries were themselves members of the favored class).

wealth for increased job security, which clearly violates the protective policy of ERISA's anti-alienation rule. A worker cannot directly trade a portion of her accrued pension benefit for a no-cut clause in her contract, and the exclusive benefit rule prohibits her from accomplishing the same result indirectly through fiduciary decision making. The lesson here is that not every dispute between participants should be analyzed as an impartiality question: only the interest in plan benefits is statutorily cognizable.[61] A compromise that takes into account other illegitimate interests necessarily undermines ERISA policies.

Exculpatory Clauses

The settlor of a private trust may, by an express provision in the trust instrument, relax otherwise applicable obligations, including the trustee's stringent duties of loyalty and care.[62] ERISA outlaws such exculpatory provisions, both implicitly, by the stipulation that the fiduciary must follow plan documents only insofar as they are consistent with ERISA, including ERISA's specification of fiduciary duties, and explicitly, by declaring such indulgences "void as against public policy."[63] Setting high standards of administrative integrity and competence would accomplish little if they could be gutted in the fine print of the plan document.

Instead of barring exculpatory clauses, Congress might have simply demanded prominent notice, leaving it up to employees to decide how much confidence to put in a plan that excuses faithless or foolish management. In taking the matter out of the hands of individual decision makers, the prohibition of exculpatory clauses can be viewed as another instance of ERISA's protective policy. But an alternative explanation is that uniform fiduciary standards may facilitate career and financial planning by reducing information costs.

Disclosure provides access to information, but a rational worker will not use the information if the cost of evaluating it exceeds the benefit likely to be gained from it. Comparing the health care, group life insurance, and retirement plans sponsored by several potential employers is a daunting task. The task is greatly complicated if one must delve beyond the plan terms governing participation and benefits to assess the

---

61   *E.g.*, Summers v. State St. Bank & Trust Co., 104 F.3d 105, 108 (7th Cir. 1997) (favoring active over retired participants "would be picking and choosing among beneficiaries, in violation of the traditional duty imposed by trust law of impartiality among beneficiaries," but that principle does not apply to a trade-off between wages and employee stock ownership plan benefits because the "trustee's sole duty is to the participants as participants").

62   RESTATEMENT (SECOND) OF TRUSTS § 222 (1959); RESTATEMENT (THIRD) OF TRUSTS §§ 77 cmt. d, 78(1) & cmt. c(2), 87 & cmt. d (2007).

63   ERISA §§ 404(a)(1)(D), 410(a), 29 U.S.C. §§ 1104(a)(1)(D), 1110(a) (2006). The labor committees of both the Senate and House singled out exculpatory provisions as the reason that "reliance on conventional trust law is often insufficient to adequately protect the interests of plan participants and beneficiaries." S. REP. No. 93-127, at 29 (1973), *reprinted in* 1 ERISA LEGISLATIVE HISTORY, *supra* Chapter 1 note 56, at 615; H.R. REP. No. 93-533, at 12 (1973), *reprinted in* 2 ERISA LEGISLATIVE HISTORY, *supra* Chapter 1 note 56, at 2359.

extent to which the apparent benefit promise is undermined by fiduciary rules that absolve negligent or disloyal decisions. To identify the most valuable plan, workers would have to discount nominal benefits by the probability of nonreceipt through fiduciary misconduct. The cost of ferreting out and computing the effect of such differences may be so high that the rational response to variation in fiduciary standards is simply to ignore it and assume that all plans, whatever their nominal participation and benefit rules, are of average quality.

In contrast, limited standardization of benefit plan terms might reduce information costs enough to make it worthwhile for workers to attend to the remaining important differences between plans. If so, plans would become more valuable to employers and employees alike, because differences in plan terms could be used to compete for labor, and better-informed workers would make better career and financial planning decisions.

The ban on exculpatory clauses ensures that ERISA imposes *uniform* fiduciary obligations, and thereby standardizes the key unwritten terms of employee benefit plans. That standardization may well be paternalistic, but the information cost perspective suggests that it could actually enhance efficiency.[64] Of course, the validity of the information cost hypothesis is an empirical question that requires further investigation.

Despite its central role in the scheme of fiduciary oversight and the important policy ambiguity underlying it, the ban on exculpatory clauses has received very little judicial attention. Apparently, plan drafters got the message and have shied away from the more blatant attempts to limit fiduciary duties. But the courts have not always recognized covert exculpatory clauses when they encounter them. From one perspective, the question of the proper scope of review of fiduciary plan interpretations concerns the enforceability of a well-disguised exculpatory clause, but the Supreme Court did not approach the question as such.[65]

The Exclusive Benefit Rule

ERISA demands that a fiduciary discharge his duties "solely in the interests of the participants and beneficiaries and for the *exclusive purpose* of providing benefits to participants and their beneficiaries and defraying reasonable expenses of administering the plan."[66] This standard of integrity is the third momentous discrepancy between the obligations of private trustees and employee benefit plan fiduciaries. The exclusive

---

64 Wiedenbeck, *supra* Chapter 1 note 57, at 570 ("A single set of interstitial rules (contract and trust) governing all plans would limit information costs and increase the efficiency of the labor market."); *id.* at 576 ("By imposing uniform fiduciary obligations and authorizing the development of a federal common law of benefit plans (conduct controls) the unwritten terms of the benefit arrangement are standardized as well [referring to the standardization achieved by the pension plan content controls]."). As suggested by the last-cited source, this information cost perspective may also provide an economic justification for several important pension plan content controls, including the minimum standards governing benefit accrual and vesting. *See infra* Chapter 7B and 7C.

65 *See* Firestone Tire & Rubber Co. v. Bruch, 489 U.S. 101 (1989), discussed *infra* Chapter 5B.

66 ERISA § 404(a)(1)(A), 29 U.S.C. § 1104(a)(1)(A) (2006) (emphasis added).

benefit rule looks to the decision maker's purposes, and therefore the duty turns upon subjective motivation. This perspective is reiterated by ERISA's anti-inurement rule, which provides that "the assets of a plan shall never inure to the benefit of any employer and shall be held for the *exclusive purposes* of providing benefits to participants in the plan and their beneficiaries and defraying reasonable costs of administering the plan."[67] ERISA's acceptance of divided loyalties apparently reflects a concession to the practice of benefit plan management by representatives of the plan sponsor. Congress expressly provided that the prohibited-transaction rules do not bar a fiduciary from also serving as an "officer, employee, agent or other representative of a party in interest," which includes the employer.[68] By permitting a fiduciary to wear multiple hats in his relation to the plan, ERISA accepts the existence of pervasive conflicts of interest, while at the same time the exclusive benefit rule purportedly demands that those conflicts never influence decision making.

Professors Daniel Fischel and John Langbein call the exclusive benefit rule "ERISA's fundamental contradiction" and convincingly demonstrate how it "bedevil[s] a remarkable array of the main issues in modern pension trust administration: takeover cases, social investing, employee stock ownership schemes, asset reversion from terminated plans, and judicial review of benefit denials and other plan decisions."[69] They warn that a "rule favoring employees that overrides the initial understanding between the parties, whether explicit or implicit, will actually harm employees by discouraging plan formation."[70] Their proposed solution is to recognize that the employer is, in important respects, also a beneficiary of the plan,[71] and their analysis suggests that the exclusive benefit rule should be construed to permit the courts to take into account the employer's interests.

The statutory language presents a stumbling block to such an expansive interpretation of the exclusive benefit rule, as Fischel and Langbein acknowledge.[72] Although the employer obviously benefits from the program by deriving advantages such as lower compensation costs or reduced worker turnover, the employer is neither a "participant" nor a "beneficiary" as those terms are used by ERISA to designate the

---

67   ERISA § 403(c)(1), 29 U.S.C. § 1103(c)(1) (2006) (emphasis added).

68   ERISA §§ 408(c)(3), 3(14), 29 U.S.C. §§ 1108(c)(3), 1002(14) (2006). From the perspective of trust law, section 408(c)(3) functions as a statutory exculpatory clause for employee benefit plan fiduciaries, permitting them to proceed under a conflict of interest so long as they seek to advance only the interest in plan benefits of participants and their beneficiaries (i.e., they act in good faith). *See infra* Chapter 4 note 75.

69   Daniel Fischel & John H. Langbein, *ERISA's Fundamental Contradiction*: *The Exclusive Benefit Rule*, 55 U. Chi. L. Rev. 1105, 1107, 1126–57 (1988).

70   *Id.* at 1158.

71   *Id.* at 1117 ("it is best for many purposes to conceive of employer and employee as both settlor and beneficiary"); *id.* at 1118 ("plans are established for the mutual advantage of employer and employee, not for the exclusive benefit of one."); *id.* at 1158 ("We believe that ERISA permits the courts to be more forthright in recognizing the employer's interest as beneficiary.").

72   *Id.* at 1118, 1158 (language of the exclusive benefit rule "appears to preclude recognition of the employer as a beneficiary").

protected class under the exclusive benefit rule.[73] Moreover, the exclusive benefit rule does not permit any action that is designed to promote some interest of participants and beneficiaries (e.g., continued employment); instead it authorizes only actions directed to providing participants with plan benefits. When, on matters of administration, the employer's and employees' interests diverge, the employer is typically seeking either to deny benefits (contain costs) or to use the plan for other purposes (e.g., to finance an acquisition or a takeover defense).

Trust law generally avoids these problems by prohibiting the trustee from entering into any transaction in which she would have a conflict of interest.[74] Such an objective prohibition on divided loyalties forestalls questions of good faith or fairness.[75] In contrast, ERISA's acceptance of nonneutral fiduciaries often makes it impossible to assume that a fiduciary's act proceeds from a purity of motives. In making the fiduciary's "exclusive purpose" the touchstone, ERISA demands assessment of a conflicted decision maker's state of mind. Subjective purpose, of course, is necessarily inferred from objective facts. Because people are assumed to intend the natural consequences of their actions, the extent to which the fiduciary's decision actually promotes some competing interest is often the most relevant evidence of purpose. Mutually beneficial outcomes are the hardest cases. A decision that promotes the participants' and beneficiaries' interests in plan benefits, as well as some conflicting interest, creates a strong inference of improper motivation if another decision would have *better* served participants and beneficiaries. On the other hand, if results appear optimal from the standpoint of providing plan benefits, one cannot automatically condemn a decision that also serves the employer's or fiduciary's interest, because an unbiased decision maker would have reached the same conclusion.[76]

---

73   ERISA §§ 3(7), (8), 404(a)(1), 29 U.S.C. §§ 1002(7), (8), 1104(a)(1) (2006). "Beneficiary" means a person designated to receive plan benefits either by the participant or the terms of the plan. *See also* Treas. Reg. § 1.401-1(b)(4) (1976) (definition of beneficiary for purposes of the qualified plan rules).

74   *See, e.g.,* RESTATEMENT (THIRD) OF TRUSTS § 78(1), (2) & cmt. b (2007); 2A SCOTT ON TRUSTS, *supra* Chapter 3 note 11, § 170 at 311; GEORGE G. BOGERT & GEORGE T. BOGERT, THE LAW OF TRUSTS AND TRUSTEES § 543 at 264, 267–68 (rev. 2d ed. 1993).

75   Where the settlor authorizes the trustee to enter into a transaction in which she has a conflict of interest, the trustee must act in good faith. RESTATEMENT (THIRD) OF TRUSTS § 78 cmt. c(2) (2007) (despite exculpatory clause, "a trustee violates the duty of loyalty to the beneficiaries by acting in bad faith or unfairly"); RESTATEMENT (SECOND) OF TRUSTS §§ 170 cmt. t, 222(2) (1959) ("[A] provision in the trust instrument is not effective to relieve the trustee from liability for breach of trust committed in bad faith."). That is, an exculpatory clause that implicates the duty of loyalty is interpreted to lift the objective prohibition but substitute an inquiry into subjective purpose. Correspondingly, ERISA § 408(c)(3), the authorization of nonneutral fiduciaries, functions as a statutory exculpatory clause, and the exclusive benefit rule imposes the good-faith criterion.

76   A qualification is in order here. If the optimal result from the standpoint of participants' and beneficiaries' interests in a plan benefit could also have been achieved by means of another decision or course of action that would not have benefited the employer or fiduciary, then the fiduciary's selection of the mutually beneficial means necessarily reflects a prohibited purpose.

The leading takeover defense case, *Donovan v. Bierwirth*,[77] illustrates both the practical difficulty of identifying improper motivation and the approaches taken by the federal courts. In the fall of 1981, LTV Corporation attempted to acquire Grumman Corporation by making a tender offer at a price of $45 per share for 70 percent of Grumman's stock, which, prior to the offer, had been trading for about $25 per share. Two days after the tender offer was announced, the Grumman board unanimously voted to oppose it and issued a press release stating that the LTV offer was "inadequate, and not in the best interests of Grumman, its shareholders, employees or the United States."[78] At the time of the offer, Grumman's defined benefit pension plan owned 525,000 shares of the company's stock. The trustees of the Grumman pension plan consisted of Grumman's chairman of the board (Bierwirth), the company's chief financial officer, and the treasurer of Grumman Aerospace; the first two were directors, and all of them worked feverishly in their capacity as management employees to defeat the LTV tender offer. When they met as plan trustees, they voted not to sell the plan's Grumman shares to LTV, and then quickly authorized the plan to purchase additional Grumman shares up to the 10 percent limit imposed by ERISA's prohibited-transaction rules.[79] The plan bought about 1,275,000 additional shares for a cost of about $44 million. A few days later, Grumman's request for a temporary injunction of LTV's tender offer based on alleged securities and antitrust violations was granted, and the value of the Grumman shares bought by the plan dropped to $32.5 million. The Secretary of Labor (Donovan) brought suit against the plan trustees for breach of fiduciary duties, despite the fact that the Grumman plan participants overwhelmingly supported the trustees' actions.

Judge Friendly's opinion establishes several important points. First, fiduciary action that advances a conflicting interest and does not also promote (or even harms) the participants' interest *in benefits* almost necessitates finding a breach of the exclusive benefit rule. The trustees' decision to purchase additional Grumman shares at a price greatly inflated by the LTV tender offer was of this sort, for it advanced management's interest in blocking the takeover, while exposing the plan to a substantial risk of loss.[80]

---

77   680 F.2d 263 (2d Cir. 1982). The case is discussed at length by Fischel and Langbein, *supra* Chapter 4 note 69, at 1126–28, 1138–41.

78   *Bierwirth*, 680 F.2d at 266.

79   *See* ERISA § 407(a)(2), 29 U.S.C. § 1107(a)(2) (2006).

80   Judge Friendly explained:

> [I]n purchasing additional shares when they did, the trustees were buying into what, from their own point of view, was almost certainly a "no-win" situation. If the LTV offer succeeded, the Plan would be left as a minority stockholder in an LTV-controlled Grumman—a point that seems to have received no consideration. If it failed, as the Plan's purchase of [an] additional 8% of the outstanding Grumman stock made more likely, the stock was almost certain to sink to its pre-offer level, as the trustees fully appreciated. Given the trustees' views as to the dim future of an LTV-controlled Grumman, it is thus exceedingly difficult to accept Bierwirth's testimony that the purchase of additional shares was justified from an investment standpoint—or even to conclude that the trustees really believed this. Investment considerations dictated a policy of waiting. If LTV's offer were accepted, the trustees would not want more Grumman shares; if it failed, the shares would be obtainable at prices far below what was paid. Mid-October 1981 was thus the worst possible time for the Plan to buy Grumman

On the other hand, Judge Friendly agreed with the defendants' argument that fiduciaries do not *necessarily* violate their duties by following a course of action that actually benefits *both* the corporation and the participants. But the court cautioned that, to avoid liability where a decision incidentally benefits the corporation or themselves, the fiduciaries must conclude that the action is "*best* to promote the interests of participants and beneficiaries," and the decision "must be made with an eye single to the interests of participants and beneficiaries."[81] This is in line with the earlier conclusion that if results appear optimal from the standpoint of providing plan benefits, one cannot automatically condemn a decision that also serves the employer's or fiduciary's interest. Consistent with the statutory "exclusive purpose" standard, Judge Friendly's formulation confirms that one also cannot automatically approve it.

When a fiduciary asserts that some challenged action was in fact best for participants and beneficiaries, and only incidentally benefited a conflicting interest, how can one determine if the decision was "made with an eye single to the interests of participants and beneficiaries"? As a practical matter, how can a court put the subjective loyalty standard into effect? *Bierwirth* typifies the judicial response, which is to abandon the exclusive benefit rule and fall back on prudence. In contrast to the exclusive benefits rule's focus on motivation, the prudence rule, being a negligence-based, reasonable person standard, is an objective test. Under ERISA case law, the prudence rule has a predominantly procedural cast, for neglect in monitoring, fact-gathering, or obtaining expert advice is ordinarily a surer sign of careless decision making than is any particular judgment on the merits.[82] Often a decision that promotes the employer's or fiduciary's interest is arrived at without full information and deliberation because the illegitimate consideration drives the process. The record in *Bierwirth* revealed numerous failures to investigate facts that were clearly relevant to the trustees' decision not to tender the plan's Grumman stock.[83] But the Friendly opinion goes further,

---

stock as an investment. It is almost impossible to believe that the trustees did not realize this and that their motive for purchasing the additional shares was for any purpose other than blocking the LTV offer.

Bierwirth, 680 F.2d at 275 (footnote omitted).

81 *Id.* at 271.

82 *See* ABA SECTION OF LABOR AND EMPLOYMENT LAW, EMPLOYEE BENEFITS LAW 667–70 (2d ed. 2000); Beck v. Pace Int'l Union, 427 F.3d 668, 678 (9th Cir. 2005). In principle, of course, a decision made upon full information after adequate deliberation could seem so illogical as to be imprudent. With respect to investment decision making, ERISA does not assess the prudence of a particular investment in isolation; instead, the propriety of the investment is gauged by its role (with respect to risk, return, and liquidity) in the portfolio as a whole. 29 C.F.R. § 2550.404a-1(b)(1), -1(b)(2) (2009). In this, ERISA fiduciary law substantially predated trust law's incorporation of modern portfolio theory. RESTATEMENT (THIRD) OF TRUSTS § 227(a) (1990) (Prudent Investor Rule) (prudence of investment assessed "not in isolation but in the context of the trust portfolio and as part of an overall investment strategy, which should incorporate risk and return objectives reasonably suitable to the trust"); RESTATEMENT (THIRD) OF TRUSTS § 90(a) (2007).

83 *Bierwirth*, 680 F.2d at 272–74. For a recent example of the application of the "eye single" standard by resort to a procedural test, see *Beck v. Pace International Union*, 427 F.3d 668, 678 (9th Cir. 2005).

suggesting that decisions made by interested fiduciaries are subject to more exacting standards of prudence. "[T]hey should have realized that, since their judgment on this score could scarcely be unbiased, at the least they were bound to take every feasible precaution to see that they had carefully considered the other side, to free themselves, if indeed this was humanly possible, from any taint of the quick negative reaction characteristic of targets of hostile tender offers."[84]

Of course, review for prudence—even applying heightened scrutiny—does not ensure complete integrity of decision making. With adequate investigation, independent advice, and full deliberation, the well-advised fiduciary can avoid prudence violations, even as he pursues a mutually beneficial course of action. By going through the motions of reasoned decision making and reaching a determination that appears, in retrospect, to have been designed to best promote participants' interest in benefits, the fiduciary can ensure that his action will be upheld, even if that course was in fact chosen because of the advantages it offers to the fiduciary, the employer, or another interested party. In this situation, the practical impossibility of determining motivations gives the fiduciary freedom to select, from among the alternatives that would yield comparable benefits for participants, the course of action that also promotes another interest. In this limited sense, the subjective loyalty standard of the exclusive benefit rule sometimes permits the fiduciary to promote the joint welfare of the employer and employees.[85] In contrast, a prophylactic ban on conflicts of interest, such as trust law's objective duty of loyalty, would prevent such mutually beneficial decisions even where the employer's gains were not made at the employees' expense.

C. PROHIBITED TRANSACTIONS

Holding nonneutral fiduciaries to a standard of subjective loyalty has the advantage of permitting some actions that benefit the employer or fiduciary without injuring plan participants. But that occasional benefit could come at a formidable cost. If the exclusive benefit and prudence rules were the sole means of policing fiduciary conduct, the result would be frequent, fact-intensive inquiries into the decision maker's state of mind. Immense legal expenses and frequent mistakes would follow.[86] ERISA limits these costs by imposing a set of prohibited-transaction rules that outlaw certain conflict-of-interest transactions on the basis of readily identified objective criteria. "Congress enacted § 406 'to bar categorically a transaction that [is] likely to injure

---

84 *Bierwirth*, 680 F.2d at 276. "One way for the trustees to inform themselves would have been to solicit the advice of independent counsel." *Id*. at 272.

85 The maneuvering room inherent in the exclusive benefit rule is a much more limited freedom than Fischel and Langbein advocate (*supra* Chapter 4 notes 69–71 and accompanying text). On the employees' side, only the interest in plan benefits is cognizable (not employee welfare writ large), and the workers' interest in benefits cannot be materially sacrificed to advance employer objectives.

86 *See* S. Rep. No. 93-383, at 95 (1973), *reprinted in* 1 ERISA Legislative History, *supra* Chapter 1 note 56, at 1069, 1163–64 (noting that an arm's-length standard of dealing requires substantial enforcement efforts, "resulting in sporadic and uncertain effectiveness").

the . . . plan.'"[87] By cheaply screening out the cases where there is a strong likelihood that the participants' interest will be compromised, the prohibited-transaction rules narrow the operation of the exclusive benefit rule to a range of cases in which the latter rule's high costs may be justified.

Prohibited transactions are of three types: party-in-interest transactions, employer-investment transactions, and fiduciary conflicts. A fiduciary is prohibited from causing the plan to engage in a transaction with a "party in interest" if the fiduciary knows or should know that the transaction involves a direct or indirect sale, exchange, or leasing of property, lending of money or other extension of credit, or furnishing of goods, services, or facilities between the plan and the party in interest. Also prohibited is the transfer of plan assets to or use of plan assets by a party in interest.[88] A "party in interest," with whom such dealings are forbidden, means any plan fiduciary, regardless of the extent or nature of his fiduciary capacity; the plan's legal counsel; any plan employee or other person providing services to the plan (i.e., independent contractors); an employer of covered employees; a union, any of whose members are covered by the plan; any person who owns, directly or indirectly, a controlling interest in such an employer or union; and any corporation, partnership, trust, or estate that is controlled, directly or indirectly, by any of the foregoing persons (for example, a subsidiary of the employer, or a partnership in which the plan's accountant holds a 50 percent or greater interest in capital or profits).[89] Certain close relatives of an individual who is a party in interest (specifically, the spouse, ancestors, lineal descendants, and spouses of lineal descendants) are also included as parties in interest, as is any person who is an employee, officer, director, or 10 percent or greater shareholder or partner of a plan service provider, employer, union, or of any business, trust, or estate that controls or is controlled by the employer or union, or that is controlled by a plan fiduciary or service provider.[90] In short, Congress defined "party in interest" broadly, "to encompass those [individuals and] entities that a fiduciary might be inclined to favor at the expense of the plan's beneficiaries."[91]

Prohibited employer-investment transactions involve the fiduciary's acquiring or holding employer securities or employer real property if the fiduciary knows or should know that the property in question does not constitute "qualifying employer securities" or "qualifying employer real property," or if the plan's holdings of qualifying employer securities or real property exceed 10 percent of the fair market value of the plan's assets.[92] These prohibitions apply independently of the general fiduciary

---

87   Lockheed Corp. v. Spink, 517 U.S. 882, 888 (1996) (quoting Comm'r v. Keystone Consol. Indus., 508 U.S. 152, 160 (1993)). *Accord* Cutaiar v. Marshall, 590 F.2d 523, 528–30 (3d Cir. 1979) (prohibited-transaction rules apply without regard to good faith or fairness of the transaction; they establish a blanket prohibition, relief from which is available only by use of the statutory exemption procedure).

88   ERISA § 406(a)(1)(A)–(D), 29 U.S.C. § 1106(a)(1)(A)–(D) (2006).

89   ERISA § 3(14)(A)–(E), (G), 29 U.S.C. § 1002(14)(A)–(E), (G) (2006).

90   ERISA § 3(14)(F), (H), (I), 3(15), 29 U.S.C. § 1002(14)(F), (H), (I), 1002(15) (2006).

91   Harris Trust & Sav. Bank v. Salomon Smith Barney, Inc., 530 U.S. 238, 242 (2000).

92   ERISA §§ 406(a)(1)(E), (a)(2), 407(a), 29 U.S.C. §§ 1106(a)(1)(E), (a)(2), 1107(a) (2006). "Qualifying employer security" generally means stock or debt instruments issued by the

duty to diversify plan investments; but an exception is provided for certain defined contribution pension plans (including profit-sharing plans, stock bonus plans, and employee stock ownership plans) that explicitly provide for the acquisition and holding of larger amounts of qualifying employer securities or real property.[93]

The third type of prohibited transaction forbids a fiduciary from dealing with the assets of the plan for his own account (i.e., self-dealing), receiving consideration from any party dealing with the plan (i.e., kickbacks), or representing any party in a transaction involving the plan whose interests are adverse to the interests of the plan or the interests of its participants or beneficiaries.[94] Unlike party-in-interest and employer-investment prohibited transactions, fiduciary conflict transactions are barred without regard to whether the fiduciary knows or should know that the dealing in question is forbidden, and more stringent procedural safeguards apply to a request for an administrative exemption from the ban.[95]

Prohibited transactions (as so defined) are banned even if the fiduciary actually acted in good faith and regardless of whether the result of the transaction is fair to plan participants and beneficiaries. In effect, such dealings are conclusively presumed to be undertaken to promote a conflicting interest, and even if no loss ensues, participants can insist that the fiduciary disgorge any profits made through the use of plan assets.[96] This approach bears an obvious resemblance to trust law's handling of self-dealing,

---

employer or its affiliate, but in the case of indebtedness, special requirements apply to ensure that the price of the instrument is not excessive, that the plan doesn't have too large a stake in employer debt, and that at least half of the debt issue is held by persons independent of the issuing employer. ERISA § 407(d)(1), (d)(5), (e), 29 U.S.C. § 1107(d)(1), (d)(5), (e) (2006). "Qualifying employer real property" generally means realty leased to the employer or its affiliate, but only if there are multiple parcels (a substantial number of which are dispersed geographically), and each parcel and its improvements are suitable for more than one use. ERISA § 407(d)(2), (d)(4), 29 U.S.C. § 1107(d)(2), (d)(4) (2006).

93 ERISA §§ 404(a)(1)(C), 407(b), (c)(3), 29 U.S.C. §§ 1104(a)(1)(C), 1107(b), (c)(3) (2006). In plan years beginning after 2006, defined contribution plan participants must, in some cases, be allowed to direct the plan to switch their account investments from employer securities to diversified investment options. ERISA § 204(j), 29 U.S.C. § 1054(j) (2006); *see* I.R.C. § 401(a)(35) (2006).

94 ERISA § 406(b), 29 U.S.C. § 1106(b) (2006). For purposes of the ban on self-dealing, a fiduciary's "own interest" is "read broadly in light of Congress' concern with the welfare of plan beneficiaries." Leigh v. Engle, 727 F.2d 113, 126 (7th Cir. 1984) (fiduciary who is an officer of an acquiring corporation, who uses plan assets to purchase stock in a corporation that is the target of a takeover attempt by the acquiring corporation, has an interest in the outcome of the control contest).

95 *Compare* ERISA § 406(a)(1) (introductory clause) ("knows or should know"), 406(a)(2) (same), 29 U.S.C. § 1106(a)(1), (2) (2006), *with* ERISA § 406(b), 29 U.S.C. § 1106(b) (2006). Formal adjudication is required for the Labor Department to grant an exemption to the fiduciary conflict prohibitions, while informal notice-and-comment procedures are ordinarily all that is required to support a regulatory exemption from the party-in-interest or employer-investment prohibitions. Compare the last two sentences of ERISA § 408(a), 29 U.S.C. § 1108(a) (2006); in the case of fiduciary conflict transactions, the Secretary of Labor must afford opportunity for a hearing and make "a determination on the record." *See* 29 C.F.R. § 2570.46 (2009) (affording opportunity for hearing).

96 ERISA § 409(a), 29 U.S.C. § 1109(a) (2006).

according to which a trustee who deals with the trust in his personal capacity (e.g., buys trust assets for his own account, sells individually owned property to the trust, borrows from or loans money to the trust) is automatically liable for breach of the duty of loyalty, regardless of good faith or the objective fairness of the transaction (the "no-further-inquiry" rule).[97] In contrast, trust law treats certain less egregious conflicts of interests more leniently, in that the trustee is allowed to defend the breach of trust claim by proving that the transaction was fair to the trust's beneficiaries and was undertaken in good faith. ERISA's prohibited-transaction provision, like the trust law self-dealing rule, dispenses with such difficult context-specific factual determinations in favor of a blanket ban, but ERISA's ban is far more encompassing. While it includes fiduciary acts that constitute self-dealing under traditional trust law standards, ERISA also refuses to give individualized consideration to dealings with any other person who has a significant connection with the plan. The startling breadth of ERISA's automatic-breach rule is necessitated by the difficulty of administering the subjective loyalty standard (i.e., the exclusive benefit rule) as the primary safeguard of employees' interests.

Exemptions

Left unmodified, the statutory proscriptions would interdict many deals that are fair and commercially reasonable. Recognizing this overbreadth, Congress modulated the prohibitions with a series of narrow statutory exceptions and a procedure for granting regulatory relief. For example, a person providing services to the plan is a party in interest, and the furnishing of services between the plan and a party in interest is designated a prohibited transaction.[98] Consequently, ERISA would bar the provision of *any* services to a plan absent a statutory exception that allows a party in interest to provide "office space, or legal, accounting, or other services necessary for the establishment or operation of the plan, if no more than reasonable compensation is paid therefor."[99] Similarly, all employees of an employer, any of whose workers are covered by the plan, are parties in interest, and the list of prohibited transactions includes loans between a plan and a party in interest.[100] This lending ban would outlaw plan loans to participants but for a statutory exception for even-handed plan loans that are adequately secured and bear a reasonable rate of interest.[101] The proliferation of plans permitting individuals to direct the investment of their defined contribution

---

97   *See, e.g.*, Unif. Trust Code § 802(b) & cmt. (2000); Restatement (Third) of Trusts § 78 cmt. b (2007); Restatement (Second) of Trusts § 170 cmt. b (1959); Bogert & Bogert, *supra* Chapter 4 note 74, § 543, at 218–19, 248; John H. Langbein, *Questioning the Trust Law Duty of Loyalty: Sole Interest or Best Interest?*, 114 Yale L.J. 929 (2005) (explaining the origins, scope, and rationale of the rule in the private trust context, and recommending modification).

98   ERISA §§ 3(14)(B), 406(a)(1)(C), 29 U.S.C. §§ 1002(14)(B), 1106(a)(1)(C) (2006).

99   ERISA § 408(b)(2), 29 U.S.C. § 1108(b)(2) (2006).

100   ERISA §§ 3(14)(C), (H), 406(a)(1)(B), 29 U.S.C. §§ 1002(14)(C), (H), 1106(a)(1)(B) (2006).

101   ERISA § 408(b)(1), 29 U.S.C. § 1108(b)(1) (2006).

plan savings led Congress in 2006 to grant a statutory exemption from the prohibited-transaction rules for the provision of investment advice to participants and beneficiaries under such self-directed plans, if certain safeguards are met.[102]

The other statutory exceptions are quite specialized and limited; so, to provide flexibility, Congress included a mechanism for granting administrative exemptions from ERISA's prohibited-transaction rules. These exemptions may be either generic (so-called class exemptions) or transaction-specific, and may be subject to such conditions as the Secretary of Labor considers appropriate. An exemption may issue only if all interested persons are notified and given the opportunity to present their views, and only if the Labor Department finds that the exemption is "(1) administratively feasible, (2) in the interests of the plan and of its participants and beneficiaries, and (3) protective of the rights of participants and beneficiaries of such plan."[103] To date, more than 25 class exemptions have been granted, the terms of which must be carefully consulted to determine whether a particular insider transaction is actually prohibited.[104]

Remedies

The prohibited-transaction rules forbid a fiduciary from engaging in the designated transactions. A threatened transgression may be enjoined, and a fiduciary who commits a violation is personally liable to restore any losses to the plan.[105] In contrast, the conduct of a party in interest who deals with the fiduciary is not expressly outlawed.[106] That omission raised doubts as to whether a nonfiduciary party in interest may be held liable for participating in a prohibited transaction. The Supreme Court has held that ERISA § 502(a)(3) authorizes suit against a nonfiduciary party in interest to a prohibited transaction, provided that the defendant is not a bona fide purchaser of plan assets.[107] Where the plan received value, the party in interest must be shown to have had actual or constructive knowledge that the transaction violated the prohibited-transaction rules.[108] The Court indicated that "appropriate equitable relief" may include

---

102   ERISA § 408(b)(14), (g), 29 U.S.C. § 1108(b)(14), (g) (2006); *see* I.R.C. § 4975(d)(17), (f)(8) (2006).

103   ERISA § 408(a), 29 U.S.C. § 1108(a) (2006). Where an exemption to the fiduciary conflict prohibitions is sought, the Labor Department is required to provide opportunity for a hearing (formal adjudication procedures), but in other cases (involving party-in-interest or employer-investment transactions, that is), notice-and-comment procedures suffice. *Id.*

104   Notice of the grant of any administrative exemption is published in the Federal Register, 29 C.F.R. § 2570.48 (2009), and the full text of class exemptions can be obtained electronically or through topical reporters. *E.g.*, 6 PENS. & PROFIT SHARING 2D (RIA) ¶ 93,001.

105   ERISA §§ 409(a), 502(a)(2), (3), 29 U.S.C. §§ 1109(a), 1132(a)(2), (3) (2006).

106   H.R. REP. No. 93-1280, at 306 (1974) (Conf. Rep.), *reprinted in* 3 ERISA LEGISLATIVE HISTORY, *supra* Chapter 1 note 56, at 4277, 4573 ("Under the labor provisions (title I), the fiduciary is the main focus of the prohibited transaction rules.").

107   Harris Trust & Sav. Bank v. Salomon Smith Barney, Inc., 530 U.S. 238 (2000).

108   *Id.* at 251. The Court interpreted ERISA § 502(a)(3) to incorporate trust law remedial principles, including the trust pursuit rule. *Id.* at 249–52. *See* RESTATEMENT (SECOND) OF TRUSTS §§ 284, 291, 294 (1959).

rescission of the transaction, restitution of the plan assets, and disgorgement of profits that the party in interest made through use of those assets.

Excise Tax and Civil Penalties

Congress was not content to remedy prohibited transactions; it sought to deter them. To supplement the prohibited-transaction rules, Congress enacted an excise tax counterpart that imposes a nondeductible 15 percent penalty tax on any "disqualified person" who participates in certain prohibited transactions involving a qualified or formerly qualified pension plan.[109] The tax Code's definition of a "disqualified person" is essentially the same as ERISA's definition of a "party in interest."[110] While ERISA's prohibited-transaction rules focus on the fiduciary, the excise tax is directed at deterring the counterparty from entering into the transaction. It does so by making the disqualified person (party in interest) liable for the penalty without regard to intent, knowledge, or fault.[111]

The penalty tax is limited in scope to pension plans that have, at some point, qualified for preferential tax treatment. To deter insider abuse of other employee benefit plans, Congress authorized the Secretary of Labor to assess a corresponding 5 percent civil penalty on a party in interest who engages in a prohibited transaction with a plan that is not subject to the excise tax.[112]

An additional civil penalty is potentially applicable in cases of serious insider abuse of an employee benefit plan. The penalty can apply against a fiduciary who violates any of her responsibilities, or against another person who knowingly participates in the

---

109   I.R.C. § 4975 (2006) (excise tax), *id.* § 275(a)(6) (deduction disallowed). In addition to qualified or formerly qualified pension plans, the prohibited-transactions excise tax also applies to individual retirement accounts and certain medical and educational savings accounts, *id.* § 4975(e)(1), but does not apply to governmental or church plans, *id.* § 4975(g).

110   *Compare* ERISA § 3(14), (15), 29 U.S.C. § 1002(14), (15) (2006) (labor title definition of "party in interest"), *with* I.R.C. § 4975(e)(2)–(6) (2006) (excise tax definition of "disqualified person"). The category of disqualified persons subject to the excise tax is narrower than ERISA's definition of "party in interest" in one important respect: employees of the employer, the union, or various affiliated businesses are treated as parties in interest, but only highly compensated employees are classified as disqualified persons. *Compare* ERISA § 3(14)(A), (H), 29 U.S.C. § 1002(14)(A), (H) (2006), *with* I.R.C. § 4975(e)(2)(A), (H) (2006). In addition, a fiduciary acting solely in his fiduciary capacity is not subject to the excise tax. I.R.C. § 4975(a), (b) (2006) ("other than a fiduciary acting only as such").

111   H.R. REP. NO. 93-1280, at 306 (1974) (Conf. Rep.), *reprinted in* 3 ERISA LEGISLATIVE HISTORY, *supra* Chapter 1 note 56, at 4277, 4573. *Accord id.* at 321, *reprinted in* 3 ERISA LEGISLATIVE HISTORY, *supra* Chapter 1 note 56, at 4588 ("The first-level tax is imposed automatically without regard to whether the violation was inadvertent."). Under the labor provisions, a fiduciary will only be liable if he knew or should have known that he engaged in a prohibited transaction. Such a knowledge requirement is not included in the tax provisions. This distinction conforms to the distinction in present law in the private foundation provisions (where a foundation's manager generally is subject to a tax on self-dealing if he acted with knowledge, but a disqualified person is subject to tax without proof of knowledge).

112   ERISA § 502(a)(6), (i), 29 U.S.C. § 1132(a)(6), (i) (2006).

fiduciary's violation, whether the transgression involves a prohibited transaction or not.[113] The penalty is set at 20 percent of the "applicable recovery amount," which is the amount of damages recovered from the fiduciary or the knowing participant under a settlement agreement with the Labor Department, or by judgment in an enforcement action brought by the Labor Department. The Labor Department's involvement serves a screening function, preventing application of the penalty where the misdeeds are doubtful or inconsequential. Where the violation involves a prohibited transaction, setoff is allowed for any excise tax (or the cognate civil penalty) imposed on the fiduciary or knowing participant.[114]

D. PARTICIPANT-DIRECTED INVESTMENTS

In view of Congress's objective to stamp out mismanagement and abuse of employee benefit funds, one might expect that ERISA's fiduciary duties, reinforced by objective prohibited-transaction rules, would apply with special force to investment decision making. While intensive oversight is the norm for defined benefit pension plans and welfare benefit funds,[115] the fiduciaries of many defined contribution pension plans are largely absolved of investment responsibility. That absolution is granted where a plan permits a participant or beneficiary to exercise control over the investment of assets in his own account and the participant or beneficiary actually exercises such control.[116] If the sponsor washes its hands of investment management, ceding responsibility to plan participants and beneficiaries, then fiduciary obligations are relaxed on the theory that employer abuse of pension funds is no longer a concern. Instead, the focus in this situation should be on worker autonomy and promoting informed financial decision making.[117] The recent rise to dominance of defined contribution plans, and 401(k) plans in particular, has been accompanied by the proliferation of such participant-directed investments. A recent study reports that the proportion of defined contribution plan participants who manage the investment of some or all of their account assets increased from 15 to 86 percent between 1986 and 2005, and that participant direction

---

113   ERISA § 502(*l*), 29 U.S.C. § 1132(*l*) (2006). Under ERISA § 502(a)(6), the Secretary of Labor can sue to collect the penalty.

114   ERISA § 502(*l*)(4), 29 U.S.C. § 1132(*l*)(4) (2006).

115   ERISA § 403(b)(4), 29 U.S.C. § 1103(b)(4) (2006), allows the Secretary of Labor to exempt welfare plans from the requirement that plan assets be held in trust by a trustee with exclusive investment management authority, but no such exemption has been granted.

116   ERISA § 404(c)(1), 29 U.S.C. § 1104(c)(1) (2006).

117   *See generally supra* Chapter 1C. *But see* Susan J. Stabile, *Freedom to Choose Unwisely: Congress' Misguided Decision to Leave 401(k) Plan Participants to Their Own Devices*, 11 CORN. J.L. & PUB. POL'Y 361 (2002) (arguing from a behavioral economics perspective that plan sponsors retain substantial control over participant investment decisions through their ability to manipulate the framing or context of investment choices).

was particularly prevalent in 401(k) plans, where, by 2005, about 95 percent of participants had some say over the investment of their accounts.[118]

Not surprisingly, given the ubiquity of participant-directed defined contribution plans, the scope of fiduciary immunity in situations where selected investments perform poorly has been challenged. ERISA section 404(c) provides that if a participant or beneficiary is granted and exercises control over assets in his account in the manner provided by Labor Department regulations, then "no person who is otherwise a fiduciary shall be liable under this part for any loss, or by reason of any breach, which results from such participant's or beneficiary's exercise of control."[119] Accordingly, the "it's-his-own-damn-fault" defense applies if (1) regulatory conditions for the exercise of control are satisfied,[120] and (2) the loss "results from" such an exercise of control. A regulation issued in 1992 provides detailed guidance on the conditions that must be satisfied for a plan to be considered to give participants the opportunity to exercise independent control over the assets in their accounts, but recent litigation has called into question the meaning of the causation element (that the loss result from the participant's exercise of control).

The regulation defines an "ERISA section 404(c) plan" as a defined contribution plan that provides an opportunity for a participant or beneficiary to exercise control by choosing the manner in which some or all of the assets in his account will be invested from among a broad range of investment alternatives.[121] To constitute a broad range of investment alternatives, the plan must offer at least three core investments, each of which is diversified and has materially different risk and return characteristics, and which in various combinations allow the participant to adjust the aggregate risk and

---

118   William E. Even & David A. Macpherson, *The Growth of Participant Direction in Defined Contribution Plans*, 2, 23 (IZA (Institute for the Study of Labor) Disc. Paper No. 4088, 2009), *available at* http://papers.ssrn.com/sol3/papers.cfm?abstract_id=1369834#.

119   ERISA § 404(c)(1)(B), 29 U.S.C. § 1104(c)(1)(B) (2006). "[U]nder this part" refers to part 4 of ERISA title I, the fiduciary responsibility provisions, including both the general fiduciary duties and the prohibited-transaction rules. Notice that the liability shield does not extend to the Code's prohibited-transaction excise tax, I.R.C. § 4975. 29 C.F.R. § 2550.404c-1(d)(3) (2009).

120   The fiduciary of a plan that does not satisfy the conditions of the regulation is not entitled to the defense of § 404(c), but the regulation states that its standards do not speak to whether the fiduciary of a non-compliant plan has breached his obligations. 29 C.F.R. § 2550.404c-1(a)(2) (2009); Preamble to 29 C.F.R. § 2550.404c-1, 57 Fed. Reg. 46,906 (Oct. 13, 1992) ("[N]on-complying plans do not necessarily violate ERISA; non-compliance merely results in the plan not being accorded the statutory relief described in section 404(c)."). *Jenkins v. Yager*, 444 F.3d 916, 924 (7th Cir. 2006), relied on these provisions to find an "implied exception" to ERISA §§ 403 and 405 was available to a plan that allowed participants to select investments but that did not satisfy § 404(c). *Id.* at 923–24. Instead of finding that an automatic breach resulted from the delegation of investment choice, the court reviewed the selection and monitoring of investment alternatives and the provision of information to plan participants for prudence. *Id.* at 924–26. The interpretation of the relationship between § 404(c) and §§ 403 and 405 discussed below (*infra* text accompanying Chapter 4 notes 127–156) indicates the *Jenkins* was wrongly decided.

121   29 C.F.R. § 2550.404c-1(b)(1) (2009).

return characteristics of his portfolio over an appropriate range.[122] Participants must be allowed to give investment instructions as to these three core investment alternatives at least once within any three-month period.[123] The regulation demands that the plan enable informed autonomous decision making. The participant or beneficiary must be warned that plan fiduciaries may be relieved of liability for losses and be provided with or have the opportunity to obtain sufficient information to make informed decisions with respect to any available investment alternative (not just the three core alternatives that satisfy the broad range requirement).[124] Such information includes a description of available investment alternatives and their general risk and return characteristics; an explanation of transaction fees and the latest available information on annual operating expenses; a prospectus for investments in registered securities; and information concerning the value of shares or units of designated investment alternatives along with their past and current performance, net of expenses, presented in a reasonable and consistent basis.[125] Additional safeguards come into play if employer stock is offered as an investment alternative: the stock must be publicly traded in sufficient volume to permit prompt execution of transactions; voting and tender rights must be passed through to the account owner; and procedures must be established to maintain confidentiality of information relating to the purchase, holding, and sale of employer stock, and the exercise of voting and tender rights, including the appointment of an independent fiduciary in situations (such as a takeover battle) fraught with potential for undue employer influence over the exercise of shareholder rights.[126]

Purpose and Scope, In General

Where the conditions of the regulation are satisfied, and a participant or beneficiary exercises independent control over the assets in her account, "no other person who is a fiduciary with respect to such plan shall be liable for any loss . . . that is a direct and necessary result of that participant's or beneficiary's exercise of control."[127] The scope of this relief has become a matter of controversy in the courts. The question is whether immunity extends to a fiduciary who is alleged to have acted imprudently or disloyally in selecting a designated investment alternative, or in continuing to make it available, where a loss ensues to participants and beneficiaries who select that investment vehicle. Some appellate courts have concluded that section 404(c) must have been

---

122   29 C.F.R. § 2550.404c-1(b)(3) (2009).

123   29 C.F.R. § 2550.404c-1(b)(2)(ii)(C) (2009).

124   29 C.F.R. § 2550.404c-1(b)(2)(i)(B)(*1*)(*i*) (2009). To ensure autonomy the regulation defines "independent control" to bar improper influence by the plan sponsor or fiduciary and to prohibit concealment of material non-public facts regarding the investment (unless disclosure would constitute a violation of law). *Id.* § 2550.404c–1(c)(2).

125   29 C.F.R. § 2550.404c-1(b)(2)(i)(B) (2009). Some of these items must be provided directly by an identified plan fiduciary or his designee, while others need be provided only upon request.

126   29 C.F.R. § 2550.404c-1(d)(2)(ii)(E)(*4*) (2009). There is an affirmative duty to provide participants with an explanation of procedures established to preserve the confidentiality of information relating to investments in employer stock. *Id.* § 2550.404c-1(b)(2)(i)(B)(*1*)(*vii*).

127   29 C.F.R. § 2550.404c-1(d)(2)(i) (2009).

intended to apply in these circumstances, for absent a breach by the plan fiduciary there would be no liability in any case and therefore no need for an affirmative defense.[128] Other courts and judges reject this surplusage argument, concluding that plan fiduciaries remain on the hook for the faulty initial selection of an investment option and for the failure to adequately monitor its continuing propriety.[129]

This difference of opinion is largely attributable to the failure of the section 404(c) regulation to explicitly define which losses are "a direct and necessary result of [the] participant's or beneficiary's exercise of control." A simple, plain meaning interpretation would suggest that if the participant's investment choice was *one* causal factor ("necessary result of"), then the defense is available even if a plan fiduciary's *ex ante* breach of duty in making the investment option available was also a necessary condition for the loss (joint causation). One might argue that investment selection alone does not establish that a loss results from a participant's "exercise of control" because immunity requires informed choice by the account owner.[130] The regulation, however, defines an ERISA section 404(c) plan by reference to the *opportunity* to exercise control over assets, which requires that the participant or beneficiary "is provided *or has the opportunity to obtain* sufficient information to make informed decisions with regard to investment alternatives available under the plan." Consequently, if publicly available information indicates that a particular investment alternative is problematic (for example, excessively risky due to inadequate diversification, or yielding a low net return due to high management expenses), then it appears that the mere availability of that information absolves the plan fiduciary who selected or continued the investment alternative.[131]

---

128   Langbecker v. Elect. Data Sys. Corp., 476 F.3d 299, 311 (5th Cir. 2007) (participants' argument "would render the § 404(c) defense applicable only where plan managers breached no fiduciary duty, and thus only where it is unnecessary"); *id.* at 312 ("A plan fiduciary may have violated the duties of selection and monitoring of a plan investment, but § 404(c) recognizes that participants are not helpless victims of every error."); *see In re* Unisys Sav. Plan Litig., 74 F.3d 420, 445 (3d Cir. 1996) (plain language of ERISA § 404(c) suggests that fiduciary breach of duty of prudence and diversification in selecting investment alternative does not bar application of the defense so long as participant's or beneficiary's exercise of control is a substantial contributing factor in bringing about the loss). *See also* Hecker v. Deere & Co., 556 F.3d 575, 589, *supplemented by* 569 F.3d 708 (7th Cir. 2009) (declining to answer whether the § 404(c) safe harbor applies to the selection of investment options for a plan in all circumstances, but finding that it does apply where a broad range of investment options are offered that allowed participants to avoid allegedly excessive fees), *petition for cert. filed*, 78 U.S.L.W. 3239 (U.S. Oct. 14, 2009) (No. 09-447).

129   DiFelice v. U.S. Airways, Inc., 497 F.3d 410, 418 n.3, 423–24 (4th Cir. 2008) ("[A] fiduciary must initially determine, and continue to monitor, the prudence of *each* investment option available to plan participants."); Franklin v. First Union Corp., 84 F. Supp. 2d 720, 732 (E.D. Va. 2000); *see Langbecker*, 476 F.3d at 320–22 (Reavley, J., dissenting, citing commentators and courts).

130   *See In re Unisys Sav. Plan Litig.*, 74 F.3d at 447 (ERISA § 404(c) defense depends on the sponsor's provision of understandable information to participants, but events in the case preceded effective date of the section 404(c) regulation).

131   This, of course, ignores the reality that plan members, many of whom may be financially unsophisticated, are likely to interpret the listing of an option on the plan's menu of investment

In opposition to this plain meaning reading of the regulation, participants have pointed to the Labor Department's interpretation. A warning buried in a footnote to the preamble to the final regulation stated:

> [T]he Department points out that the act of limiting or designating investment options which are intended to constitute all or part of the investment universe of an ERISA 404(c) plan is a fiduciary function which, whether achieved through fiduciary designation or express plan language, is not a direct or necessary result of any participant direction of such plan.[132]

Although the Labor Department has followed that position in rulings[133] and litigation, courts have disagreed on the degree of deference (if any) such an interpretation of the agency's own regulation deserves.[134] Curiously, both the Labor Department and the courts seem to have overlooked the fact that this interpretation is not just buried in a footnote; it appears in the text of the preamble[135] and is also clearly implicated in an example contained in the regulation itself.[136]

Resort to a broader perspective—interpreting ERISA as a whole and in the context of its trust law origins—supports the Labor Department's position that "[a]ll of the fiduciary provisions of ERISA remain applicable to both the initial designation of investment alternatives and investment managers and the ongoing determination

---

alternatives as tantamount to the sponsor's endorsement of the propriety of the option. Such assumed expert prescreening of investment alternatives undercuts the worker's incentive to independently investigate. Accordingly, the mere opportunity to search out and obtain sufficient information would not actually translate into a fully informed decision. *See* Stabile, *supra* Chapter 4 note 117, at 378–86.

132 Preamble to 29 C.F.R. § 2550.404c-1, 57 Fed. Reg. 46,906, 46,924 n.27 (1992).

133 ERISA Advisory Op. 98-04A (May 28, 1998); Dep't of Labor Information Letter to Douglas O. Kant, 1997 ERISA LEXIS 59, at **4–5 (Nov. 26, 1997).

134 *Compare* Hecker v. Deere & Co., 569 F.3d 708, 710 (7th Cir. 2009) ("With respect, we cannot agree with the Secretary that the footnote in the preamble is entitled to full *Chevron* [467 U.S. 837 (1984)] deference."), *and Langbecker*, 476 F.3d at 310–11 & n.22 (footnote not reasonable interpretation of statute even if *Chevron* standard applies), *with DiFelice*, 497 F.3d at 418 n.3 (citing footnote as authority).

135 At another point, the preamble states:
> The Department emphasizes, however, that the act of designating investment alternatives (including look-through investment vehicles and investment managers) in an ERISA section 404(c) plan is a fiduciary function to which the limitation on liability provided by section 404(c) is not applicable. All of the fiduciary provisions of ERISA remain applicable to both the initial designation of investment alternatives and investment managers and the ongoing determination that such alternatives and managers remain suitable and prudent investment alternatives for the plan. Therefore, the particular plan fiduciaries responsible for performing these functions must do so in accordance with ERISA.

Preamble to 29 C.F.R. § 2550.404c-1, 57 Fed. Reg. 46,906, 46,922 (1992).

136 See 29 C.F.R. § 2550.404c-1(f) (2009), Example 8, which observes:
> F [the plan fiduciary] does have a duty to monitor M's [one of three designated investment managers whom participants may appoint to manage their account assets] performance to determine the suitability of continuing M as an investment manager, however, and M's imprudence would be a factor which F must consider in periodically reevaluating its decision to designate M.

that such alternatives and managers remain suitable and prudent investment alternatives for the plan."[137] The key to understanding section 404(c) lies in its relationship to sections 403 and 405, the mandatory trusteeship and cofiduciary liability provisions of ERISA.

Investment management, including the authority to acquire, hold, or dispose of plan assets, is a trustee function. ERISA section 403(a) makes investment management by the trustee(s) a mandatory, nondelegable duty: "the trustee or trustees shall have *exclusive* authority to manage and control the assets of the plan."[138] The only exceptions are for (1) plans that call for investment management to be under the direction of a named fiduciary and (2) plans that allow the named fiduciary to appoint one or more investment managers to whom the authority to manage, acquire, and dispose of assets is delegated.[139] That the duty to make investment decisions is personal and nondelegable is confirmed by ERISA's rules governing cofiduciary liability. Dovetailing with the exceptions to the trustee's exclusive responsibility for asset management, section 405 provides that a trustee is absolved from liability (1) for following the instructions of a named fiduciary where the plan provides for investment management by a named fiduciary,[140] and (2) for the acts or omissions of investment managers where the plan provides for delegation of the investment duties to one or more investment managers.[141] Most revealing is section 405(c), which generally allows a plan to specify procedures for the delegation of *any* fiduciary responsibility, and correspondingly limits the liability of other fiduciaries for the acts or omissions of a proper delegate. The statute expressly restricts that blanket delegation authority in one respect: delegation is forbidden for "trustee responsibilities," defined as any responsibility "to manage or control the assets of the plan."[142]

Because investment management is in general a nondelegable trustee function, in the absence of section 404(c), a trustee who permitted participants or beneficiaries to direct the investment of their accounts would commit an automatic breach of fiduciary duty.[143] Consequently, the trustee would be personally liable for any losses

---

137   *Supra* Chapter 4 note 135.

138   ERISA § 403(a), 29 U.S.C. § 1103(a) (2006) (emphasis added).

139   ERISA §§ 403(a)(1), (2), 402(c)(3), 29 U.S.C. § 1103(a)(1), (2), 1102(c)(3) (2006).

140   *Compare* ERISA § 403(a)(1), 29 U.S.C. § 1103(a)(1) (2006), *with* ERISA § 405(b)(3)(B), 29 U.S.C. § 1105(b)(3)(B) (2006).

141   *Compare* ERISA § 403(a)(2), 29 U.S.C. § 1103(a)(2) (2006), *with* ERISA § 405(d)(1), 29 U.S.C. § 1105(d)(1) (2006).

142   ERISA § 405(c)(1), (3), 29 U.S.C. § 1105(c)(1), (3) (2006).

143   Many participant-directed plans provide in the plan document that each participant is a "named fiduciary" with the power to direct the investment of own individual account. That formal designation renders the participant a cofiduciary with the trustee, and potentially subjects the trustee to cofiduciary liability under section 405(a)(3) based on knowledge of the participant's breach and failure to take remedial action. The directed trustee defense of section 405(b)(3)(B) expressly does not apply to section 405(a) violations. Accordingly, just as in the case where no such designation is made and the participants function as de facto fiduciaries (discussed immediately below, text accompanying Chapter 10 notes 144-50), the co-fiduciary liability analysis applies where the plan authorizes participant-directed investments by formally designating participants as named fiduciaries.

resulting from that breach, including losses flowing from imprudent investment decisions by made by the account owner.[144] Even if the plan expressly called for participant decision making, the trustee's exposure would not be limited.[145] Therefore, absent section 404(c), the trustee who allowed participants or beneficiaries to direct the investment of their own accounts would be liable as a cofiduciary for certain losses caused by their investment decisions. Specifically, the participants granted investment authority would, due to the improper delegation of trustee responsibilities, be acting as de facto or functional fiduciaries.[146] Therefore, if such a participant's investment selection is imprudent, or under-diversified, or involves a conflict of interest (e.g., investing in securities of a business that a participant or her spouse owns or controls), then the loss is caused by a breach of fiduciary responsibility, and the trustee would be personally liable for the loss as a cofiduciary.[147] Moreover, the trustee would be subject to suit by the very participant whose investment choice constituted a breach: the participant would have standing to bring a civil action to enforce fiduciary obligations against the trustee.[148]

The effect of section 404(c), where it applies, is to create a narrow exception to the foregoing rules, absolving the plan trustee from liability for losses caused by undiversified, imprudent, or conflicted investment decisions made by participants or beneficiaries. Observe that section 404(c)(1)(A), besides giving the trustee a defense, also provides that the participant or beneficiary who exercises control over her account "shall not be deemed to be a fiduciary by reason of such exercise." If the participant cannot be deemed a (de facto) fiduciary, then the trustee cannot be liable under section 405(a)(2) for enabling the participant's breach. In contrast, a delegation of investment decision making that does not comport with section 404(c) is itself a breach, even if there is no showing of independent fault by the fiduciary (e.g., imprudence) in initially selecting or continuing to make available designated investment alternatives. Because the trustee would be responsible for losses attributable to the account owner's mistakes where the menu of investment alternatives was properly constructed, the defense has a real immunizing effect. It follows that section 404(c) cannot be considered surplusage

---

144 ERISA § 409(a), 29 U.S.C. § 1109(a) (2006).

145 *See* ERISA § 404(a)(1)(D) 29 U.S.C. § 1104(a)(1)(D) (2006) (cannot follow plan terms if in conflict with ERISA), ERISA § 410(a), 29 U.S.C. § 1110(a) (2006) (exculpatory provisions void as against public policy).

146 *See supra* Chapter 4A.

147 The trustee would be liable for actions (impermissible delegation) that enabled the breach by another (de facto) fiduciary. ERISA § 405(a)(2), 29 U.S.C. § 1105(a)(2) (2006).

148 ERISA § 502(a)(2), 29 U.S.C. § 1132(a)(2) (2006). While such a suit by the participant might appear inequitable, under traditional trust law, a trustee could be held liable to a trust beneficiary even if the beneficiary consented to a breach of trust if, when he gave consent, the beneficiary did not know "the material facts which the trustee knew or should have known and which the trustee did not reasonably believe that the beneficiary knew." RESTATEMENT (SECOND) OF TRUSTS § 216(2)(b) & cmt. k (1959). Improper delegation of investment management when the trustee knows that plan participants lack sufficient expertise to avoid imprudent or under-diversified investments would seem to fall within this exception to the consent defense.

if its operation is limited to that situation.[149] Stated another way, ERISA section 404(c), in combination with section 403(a), provides a third exception to the ban on delegation of investment management, along with a corresponding limitation on trustee liability.[150]

This contextual and functional reading of section 404(c) is consistent with and lends support to the Labor Department's interpretation of the limited scope of the defense. Traditional trust law similarly provides that a trustee is under a duty not to delegate investment decision making.[151] Further, the trustee of a private trust is liable for the acts of an agent "which if done by the trustee would constitute a breach of trust, if the trustee . . . (b) delegates to the agent the performance of acts which he was under a duty not to delegate."[152] Recall that the Supreme Court has recognized that ERISA's fiduciary obligations "draw much of their content from the common law of trusts" and "reflect[] a special congressional concern about plan asset management. . . ."[153]

ERISA's legislative history also seems consistent with this interpretation of section 404(c). Reports on early versions of comprehensive pension reform bills in both the House and Senate indicate that the bills were intended to allow participant-directed investments in certain circumstances.[154] The Senate version of H.R. 2 did not expressly authorize participant-directed investments, apparently because it did not need to. Instead, it defined fiduciary broadly enough to include participants with power to control investments and also permitted agreements "allocating specific duties or responsibilities among fiduciaries."[155] In contrast, the House version of H.R. 2 provided that assets shall be held in trust by one or more trustees "who shall have exclusive authority and discretion to manage, and exclusive control of, the assets of the plan."[156] That *exclusive* authority was subject to exceptions for investment directions by named

---

149   *See supra* Chapter 4 note 128 and accompanying text.

150   In effect, then, the trustee is solely responsible for investment management except where: (1) the plan assigns that task to a named fiduciary; (2) the plan authorizes delegation to one or more investment managers; or (3) a defined contribution plan permits a participant or beneficiary to exercise control over the assets in his account, and such control is actually exercised in accordance with the standards of § 404(c). In addition, note that the trust instrument may permit multiple trustees to divvy up investment management tasks and in so doing limit their exposure for breaches by a cotrustee. ERISA § 405(b)(1)(B), 29 U.S.C. § 1105(b)(1)(b) (2006).

151   RESTATEMENT (SECOND) OF TRUSTS § 171 & cmt. h (1959).

152   RESTATEMENT (SECOND) OF TRUSTS § 225(2). *See also id.* § 224(2)(b) (liability for improper delegation to cotrustee).

153   Varity Corp. v. Howe, 516 U.S. 489, 496, 511 (1996); *see supra* text accompanying Chapter 4 note 57. *Accord* LaRue v. DeWolff, Boberg & Assocs., 128 S. Ct. 1020, 1024 n.4 (2008).

154   "It is not the intention of the Committee, however, that where the sole power of control, management or disposition with respect to plan funds rests with the participants themselves, as may be the case with respect to certain plans where the participant has the sole discretion over an individual account established in his name, that such participants shall be regarded as fiduciaries." S. REP. NO. 93-127, at 29 (Apr. 18, 1973). *Accord* H.R. REP. NO. 93-533, at 11 (Oct. 2, 1973) (same).

155   H.R. 2, 94th Cong. §§ 511, 502(a) (1974) (version passed by the Senate on Mar. 4, 1974) (adding §§ 15(f) and 3(25) to the Welfare and Pension Plans Disclosure Act).

156   H.R. 2, 94th Cong. § 111(e) (1974) (version passed by House on Feb. 28, 1974).

fiduciaries (called "administrators" in this bill) and investment managers, and permitted allocation of duties among multiple trustees, but it did not contain an exception for participant-directed investments. Accordingly, it appears that compliance with a plan provision allowing participant-directed investments would have subjected the trustee to liability. Against this background, section 404(c) was added in conference. Apparently, when the conference committee adopted the House's approach, making investment management a (generally) nondelegable trustee function, someone realized that the limited exceptions contained in the House version of the bill would, as a practical matter, rule out participant-directed investments.

Limited Menu and Open Access Plans

If one accepts that ERISA section 404(c) was intended only to shield the trustee from derivative liability for losses resulting from imprudent or conflicted investment decisions *by the participant* that were made possible by improper delegation (trustee enablement of the participant's breach, that is), then claims premised on imprudence or disloyalty *by the trustee* in the selection or continuance of investment alternatives should not be barred. Yet this reading hardly resolves all the incongruities and questions raised by section 404(c). From the standpoint of pension policy, the most glaring problem is the difference in treatment under the current section 404(c) regulation between limited menu and open access plans.[157] The Labor Department has stated that "the act of limiting or designating investment options which are intended to constitute all or part of the investment universe of an ERISA section 404(c) plan is a fiduciary function"[158] but the regulations also acknowledge that a section 404(c) plan could give participants and beneficiaries complete discretion by permitting them to invest any portion of their account in "any asset administratively feasible for the plan to hold."[159] If the plan provides a limited menu of investment choices, the Labor Department contends that plan fiduciaries remain subject to all of ERISA's fiduciary obligations "in both the initial designation of investment alternatives and investment managers and the ongoing determination that such alternatives and managers remain suitable and prudent."[160] In contrast, if the plan confers unbounded discretion to select any

---

157 The regulation does not refer to limited menu or open access plans in so many words, but it does carefully distinguish between "investment alternatives" generally and "designated investment alternatives." *E.g.*, 29 C.F.R. § 2550.404c-1(b)(2)(i)(B)(*1*)(*ii*) (2009). Designated investment alternative is defined as "a specific investment identified by a plan fiduciary as an available investment alternative under the plan." *Id.* § 2550.404c-1(e)(4). In general, designated investment alternatives bring with them greater duties to provide information in response to a participant's request, while for other investment alternatives, the plan fiduciary can simply rely on the participant's "opportunity to obtain sufficient information to make informed decisions." *See id.* § 2550.404c-1(b)(2)(B)(i)(2).

158 Preamble to 29 C.F.R. § 2550.404c-1, 57 Fed. Reg. 46,906, 46,924 n.27 (1992).

159 29 C.F.R. § 2550.404c-1(f), Example 1 (2009).

160 Preamble to 29 C.F.R. § 2550.404c-1, 57 Fed. Reg. 46,906, 46,922 (1992), *supra* Chapter 4 note 135.

administratively feasible investment (an open access plan), the regulation strongly implies that plan fiduciaries are absolved of all responsibility.[161] This distinction creates an incentive to leave participants completely on their own despite their typically limited (often nonexistent) knowledge and experience as investors. Participants in these circumstances may feel overwhelmed by choice and paralyzed by the volume of information pertinent to their task. The consequence is likely to be ill-considered choice (following the recommendation of a family member, coworker, or friend, for instance) or no choice at all.[162] Therefore, open access plans may produce poorer overall investment performance compared to employer-screened investment options. That unintended consequence of liability avoidance is clearly perverse. It also stands in opposition to Congress's recent efforts to increase retirement savings by authorizing 401(k) plans to include automatic enrollment and escalating contributions levels.[163] Such default rules are designed to harness employee inertia to promote greater retirement savings.

According to the Labor Department, fiduciary obligations attach to the selection and continuance of a designated investment alternative even if, instead of a limited menu of investment options, the plan generally allows participants to direct the trustee to invest in any other asset that is administratively feasible for the plan to hold (open access). That position, if followed by the courts, would protect employees who rely to their detriment on the employer's assumed screening and apparent endorsement of particular funds or investment options. The Seventh Circuit's decision in *Hecker v. Deere & Co.*[164] suggests that the courts might not adopt that approach, however. The plan in *Hecker* allowed participants to choose between 23 Fidelity mutual funds, two additional investment funds managed by Fidelity, and a fund devoted to Deere stock,

---

161   *Compare* 29 C.F.R. § 2550.404c-1(f), Example 8 (2009) (where fiduciary designates three investment managers whom participants may designate to manage their account assets, the fiduciary has an ongoing duty to monitor performance to determine continuing suitability of designated managers), *with id.* Example 9 (where plan gives participants total discretion in choosing an investment manager plan, fiduciary has no duty to determine suitability of manager selected). In addition to negative implications from the preamble explaining the final regulation, this result follows from ERISA's definition of fiduciary—if a trustee or other plan official has no discretionary authority and exercises no control over management of assets, then "to th[at] extent" he is not a fiduciary. ERISA § 3(21)(A), 29 U.S.C. § 1102(21)(A) (2006).

162   Under ERISA § 404(c)(1), a participant or beneficiary must make a decision—that is, affirmatively exercise control—for the defense to be available to plan fiduciaries. ERISA § 404(c)(5) and its implementing regulation absolve fiduciaries from liability if, in the absence of an election, the participant's account assets are invested in a qualified default investment alternative. 29 C.F.R. § 2550.404c-5 (2009).

163   I.R.C. §§ 401(k)(13), (m)(12), 416(g)(4)(H) (2006); ERISA § 514(e), 29 U.S.C. § 1144(e) (2006) (preemption of state laws that restrict automatic contribution arrangements); *see* STAFF OF THE JOINT COMM. ON TAXATION, GENERAL EXPLANATION OF TAX LEGISLATION ENACTED IN THE 109TH CONGRESS, at 527–34 (2007).

164   556 F.3d 575, 589, *supplemented by* 569 F.3d 708 (7th Cir. 2009) (declining to answer whether the § 404(c) safe harbor applies to the selection of investment options for a plan in all circumstances, but finding that it does apply where a broad range of investment options are offered that allowed participants to avoid allegedly excessive fees), *petition for cert. filed*, 78 U.S.L.W. 3239 (U.S. Oct. 14, 2009) (No. 09-447).

or they could use a Fidelity-operated brokerage facility to invest in any of about 2,500 other mutual funds managed by other companies.[165] In answer to plaintiffs' complaint that the Fidelity funds were imprudent because they charged excessive fees, the court pointed to the wide range of expense ratios available from other mutual fund companies through the brokerage feature.[166] In effect, open access to other mutual funds was relied upon to defeat the claim that plan fiduciaries should be held responsible for the poor yield of specific funds that were designated investment alternatives. In rejecting a petition for rehearing, the *Hecker* panel attempted to disavow that implication, which alarmed the Secretary of Labor, but the asserted factual distinction is not altogether convincing.[167]

Supposing that the courts ultimately adopt the Labor Department's position that open access does not negate claims for imprudent designation of specific investment alternatives, the victory might be only temporary. Sponsors could respond by amending their plans to provide open access without any designated investment alternative. With no particular funds or investment vehicles specified, participants would be entirely bereft of guidance. Absent any selection or ostensible screening, the current regulation seems to foreclose plan fiduciary liability. One might argue that a realistic opportunity to exercise control requires that participants who are not financial industry professionals be provided some basic guidance, but while the statute seems susceptible to that interpretation, the current regulation would have to be amended to implement it.[168]

Employer Stock Funds

Intractable prudence issues frequently arise where stock in the employer corporation is offered as an investment option. To be permissible under an ERISA section 404(c) plan, stock in the employer corporation must satisfy several criteria, including that it be publicly traded in sufficient volume to permit expeditious execution of directions to buy or sell.[169] Even if these conditions are satisfied, facilitating undiversified investment in the employer invites imprudent risk-taking. Fiduciaries of profit-sharing or stock bonus plans (including employee stock ownership plans, ESOPs) can be released from the duty to diversify and from their obligation of prudence "to the extent that it

---

165 556 F.3d at 578.
166 556 F.3d at 590 ("If particular participants lost money or did not earn as much as they would have liked, that disappointing outcome was attributable to their individual choices.").
167 569 F.3d at 711.
168 The existing regulation requires the "opportunity to obtain sufficient information to make informed decisions with regard to investment alternatives available under the plan" but does not demand the ability to process and evaluate that information. 29 C.F.R. § 2550.404c-1(b)(2)(i) (B) (2009). Nor does the regulation require any provision of investment advice. *Id.* -1(c)(4).
169 More precisely, the fiduciaries of an ERISA section 404(c) plan have a defense to claims arising out of the acquisition or sale of employer stock only if these criteria are satisfied. Failure to satisfy these criteria would not necessarily defeat status as a 404(c) plan or negate the availability of the defense as applied to the selection of other investment alternatives. 29 C.F.R. § 2550.404c-1(d)(2)(ii)(E)(*4*) (2009); *see id.* -1(b)(2)(ii)(B)(*1*)(*vii*) (disclosure of confidentiality protections).

requires diversification" when they invest in employer stock if the plan explicitly authorizes such investment.[170] Such an "eligible individual account plan" also exempts the fiduciary from the ban on acquiring or holding more than 10 percent of the fair market value of plan assets in employer securities or real property.[171] These eligible individual account plan diversification exceptions apply whether plan fiduciaries or participants make investment decisions.[172] Consequently, many publicly traded corporations offer an employer stock fund as a designated investment alternative in their 401(k) plan (in addition to investments that provide the required broad range of investment alternatives).

Predictably, participants invested in company stock sue when its value drops substantially, whether the decline is due to general economic conditions, industry downturns, or firm-specific reverses. Faced with the individual account plan diversification exception, complaints in such "stock drop cases" allege that the investment in employer stock (or, in the case of participant-directed investments, the continued availability of the employer stock fund as an investment alternative) was either imprudent apart from its concentration, or breached the duty of loyalty. If, however, the stock is publicly traded (as it will be under an ERISA section 404(c) plan), an asserted breach of the duty of care runs into a major stumbling block. While stock in the employer corporation may have a very high risk of loss compared to an equity stake in a more stable company, the market will have taken that risk into account in pricing so that the risk is compensated by the small chance of a very large gain compared to the safer investment. Assuming efficient capital markets, while individual stocks differ in their risk profiles (risk dispersion), for each the risk is fully compensated. Consequently, the stock of a single publicly traded company, even one on the verge of bankruptcy, has a net positive expected return. Hence with proper pricing, a single stock investment is always economically sensible, apart from loss aversion. Loss aversion, of course, is the point of diversification, but there is no duty to diversify under the eligible individual account plan exception. Absent an obligation to minimize the risk of large losses, then, a publicly traded stock would always seem to be a prudent investment. Prudence, in other words, arguably has no content apart from the duty to diversify. Nevertheless, Congress determined that the duty of care has some meaning and independent force as applied to a single investment viewed in isolation, because in the case of an eligible individual account plan, it withdrew the prudence requirement "only to the extent that it requires diversification."[173]

Litigants, Labor Department lawyers, and judges have struggled with this conundrum in stock drop cases. The law on this issue is unsettled and rapidly evolving, but two possible reconciliations might be emerging. For conceptual clarity, they can be called the "mispricing" and "administrative deviation" approaches.

---

170 ERISA §§ 404(a)(2), 407(d)(3), (4), (6), 29 U.S.C. §§ 1104(a)(2), 1107(d)(3), (4), (6) (2006).

171 ERISA §§ 406(a)(2), 407(a), (b)(1), 29 U.S.C. §§ 1106(a)(2), 1107(a), (b)(1) (2006).

172 In fact, a 401(k) plan that is not an ESOP ordinarily cannot require that participants' elective deferrals be invested in employer stock, but participant-directed investment of elective deferrals in employer stock is permitted. ERISA § 407(b)(2), 29 U.S.C. §§ 1107(b)(2) (2006).

173 ERISA § 404(a)(2), 29 U.S.C. § 1104(a)(2) (2006).

Recall that a single publicly traded stock, however risky, was assumed to have a net positive expected return based on the efficient capital market hypothesis. The mispricing approach, which has more theoretical force than judicial support, questions that assumption. In stock drop cases, the Labor Department takes the position that the presumption that employer stock is a prudent investment for an eligible individual account plan "can be overcome if plan fiduciaries knowingly allowed the plan to purchase stock that was overpriced."[174] Many stock drop cases include an allegation that the employer stock price was "artificially inflated" due to fraud or material non-public information known to plan fiduciaries;[175] such claims seem to invoke this ground for liability. Plan fiduciaries are typically corporate executives, and the courts have yet to work out how to reconcile mispricing claims with securities law restrictions on insider trading.[176]

The administrative deviation approach is drawn from long-standing trust law doctrine and is better grounded in ERISA case law. The analysis has its origin in *Moench v. Robertson*,[177] a suit for breach of fiduciary duties by former ESOP plan participants against members of the plan committee. The committee had continued to invest plan contributions in stock of the employer bank throughout a two-year period during which federal bank regulators repeatedly expressed concern about the financial condition of the bank, and the stock price plummeted from $18.25 to pennies per share. Defendants, who were corporate directors as well as members of the plan committee, argued that even in that situation, investing solely in employer stock was permissible due to the special nature of an ESOP. Because Congress intended the ESOP to be both an employee retirement benefit plan and a technique of corporate finance that would encourage employee ownership,[178] the Third Circuit concluded that neither goal should prevail to the exclusion of the other. In limited circumstances, therefore, "ESOP fiduciaries can be

---

174 Meredith Z. Maresca, *ERISA Practitioners Discuss Future Litigation Based on Past Year's Court Developments*, 35 Pens. & Ben. Rep. (BNA) 2604, 2605 (2008) (reporting comments of Labor Department attorney Timothy Hauser). *See In re* Ford Motor Co. ERISA Litig., 590 F. Supp. 2d 883, 890 (E.D. Mich. 2008) (defendant argues that "in the absence of a fraud on the market, fiduciaries cannot be expected to outguess the market as to how the publicly-known risks connected with a stock should be priced"); *id.* at 891 (Ford's position "would apparently mean that the only remaining duty of such a fiduciary would be to ensure that nothing is impeding market mechanisms from accurately pricing the stock").

175 *E.g.*, Urban v. Comcast Corp., No. 08-773, 2008 U.S. Dist. LEXIS 87445, at **19–23, **37–38 (E.D. Pa. Oct. 28, 2008); *In re* Bausch & Lomb Inc. ERISA Litig., No. 06-CV-6297, 2008 U.S. Dist. LEXIS 106269, at *14 (W.D.N.Y. Dec. 12, 2008).

176 For example, in *Kirschbaum v. Reliant Energy, Inc.*, 526 F.3d 243, 256 (5th Cir. 2008), the court observed:

A further objection to tempering the *Moench* [*v. Robertson*, 62 F.3d 553 (3d Cir. 1995)] presumption is that, in some cases, requiring a fiduciary to override the terms of a company stock purchase plan could suggest the necessity of trading on insider information. Such a course is prohibited by the securities laws. Fiduciaries may not trade for the benefit of plan participants based on material information to which the general shareholding public has been denied access. Moreover, from a practical standpoint, compelling fiduciaries to sell off a plan's holdings of company stock may bring about precisely the result plaintiffs seek to avoid: a drop in the stock price.

177 62 F.3d 553 (3d Cir. 1995).

178 *Id.* at 569.

liable under ERISA for continuing to invest in employer stock according to the plan's direction."[179] To accommodate the ESOP's competing purposes, the court held that an ESOP fiduciary who invests assets in employer stock is entitled to a presumption that it acted consistently with ERISA, but the plaintiff may overcome that presumption by introducing evidence that, owing to circumstances that the settlor did not know nor anticipate, continuing to invest in employer stock would defeat or substantially impair the accomplishment of the plan's purpose to provide workers retirement savings.[180]

The Third Circuit subsequently concluded that the *Moench* rationale is not limited to ESOPs, but applies as well to other types of eligible individual account plans, including plans that call for participant-directed investments. Specifically, *Edgar v. Avaya, Inc.* concerned a participant-directed 401(k) plan, the terms of which required that an employer stock fund be among the available investment alternatives.[181] The *Moench* presumption, as it is called, has garnered adherents in several other courts,[182] but thus far no consensus has developed on how dire the employer's prospects must become to render continued investment in employer stock imprudent.[183]

Moench attempts to resolve the conflict between multiple plan objectives when the goals of employee ownership and employee retirement security become incompatible. The standard announced by the Third Circuit was taken directly from the rule on administrative deviation in the Second Restatement of Trusts, which provides in part:

> The court will direct or permit the trustee to deviate from the terms of the trust if owing to circumstances not known to the settlor and not anticipated by him compliance would defeat or substantially impair the accomplishment of the purposes of the trust; and in such case, if necessary to carry out the purposes of the trust, the court may direct the trustee to do acts which are not authorized or are forbidden by the terms of the trust.[184]

---

179   *Id.* at 556.

180   *Id.* at 571.

181   503 F.3d 340, 343, 347 (3d Cir. 2007).

182   *E.g.*, Kirshbaum v. Reliant Energy, 526 F.3d 243, 254 (5th Cir. 2008); Pugh v. Tribune Co., 521 F.3d 686, 701 (7th Cir. 2008); Kuper v. Iovenko, 66 F.3d 1447, 1458 (6th Cir. 1995); *In re* Bausch & Lomb Inc. ERISA Litig., 2008 U.S. Dist. LEXIS 106269, at *17 (W.D.N.Y. Dec. 12, 2008).

183   *Edgar*, 503 F.3d at 349 n.13 ("We do not interpret *Moench* as requiring a company to be on the verge of bankruptcy before a fiduciary is required to divest a plan of employer securities."); Lalonde v. Textron, Inc., 369 F.3d 1, 6 (1st Cir. 2004) (because the "important and complex area of law implicated by plaintiffs' claims is neither mature nor uniform . . . we believe that we would run a very high risk of error were we to lay down a hard-and-fast rule"); Brieger v. Tellabs, Inc., No. 06 C 1882, 2009 U.S. Dist. LEXIS 49747, at *37 (N.D. Ill. June 1, 2009) (leaving open whether the standard is "impending collapse or something short of that"); *In re* Ford Motor Co. ERISA Litig., 590 F. Supp. 2d 883, 892–93 (E.D. Mich. 2008) (rejecting the "imminent collapse standard in favor of a rule requiring divestiture "at the point at which company stock becomes so risky that no prudent fiduciary, reasonably aware of the needs and risk tolerance of the plan's beneficiaries, would invest any plan assets in it, regardless of what other stocks were also held in the plan's portfolio").

184   Restatement (Second) of Trusts § 167(1) (1959). Further, section 167(2) states that where the trustee reasonably believes there is an emergency, he may deviate from the terms of the trust without first obtaining judicial authorization.

While a number of federal courts deciding ERISA cases have followed *Moench*, the opinions fail to address the premises and scope of the Restatement rule, perhaps because the Third Circuit provided an erroneous citation.[185] Some consideration of administrative deviation and the doctrine's recent evolution might illuminate the problem fiduciaries confront under plans that invest in employer stock.

Administrative deviation, as the term implies, allows a court to remove a restriction on the trustee's administrative powers or strike a specific direction by the settlor concerning the manner of trust administration, where due to a change in circumstances, continued compliance with the trust's terms would seriously undermine the ability to effectuate the goals of the trust. The settlor's instruction to invest in particular property, such as stock of a designated corporation, is normally such an administrative term that could be sacrificed in the interest of the trust beneficiaries. In the case of an eligible individual account plan, however, the instruction to invest in employer stock is not a managerial detail; it reflects a core purpose to promote employee ownership and so is arguably one of the "purposes of the trust" coexisting side-by-side with retirement saving. This suggests that divesting employer stock disregards a material purpose of the trust and so might be better analogized to distributive deviation, a change in trust terms governing the identity of beneficiaries or the nature of their interests.[186] Moreover, even if lifting the direction to invest in employer stock (or, in the case of an ERISA section 404(c) plan, to allow investment in an employer stock fund) is viewed as administrative deviation, the rule of the Restatement provides access to judicial relief because the settlor ordinarily cannot fix the problem. That is, the administrative deviation rule for private trusts exists because the settlor cannot amend the trust unless he expressly reserved the power to revoke or modify; and even if he did, the settlor has typically died by the time dramatically changed circumstances appear.

Under ERISA, of course, every plan must be subject to amendment,[187] and so the fiduciaries of an ESOP or other eligible individual account plan can always apply to the sponsor for relief from the instruction to invest in employer stock. The decision on such an amendment would be a settlor or plan design question, of course, and therefore not subject to fiduciary obligations. Assume that in response to such an amendment request the sponsor insists upon continued investment in employer stock despite the risks. That determination would effectively preclude the conclusion that employee ownership is a subsidiary goal that the settlor would sacrifice in favor of the primary purpose of providing for workers' retirement income needs. In such circumstances, administrative deviation would clearly be inappropriate under private trust law.

---

185   *Moench*, 62 F.3d at 571 & n.6 (citing Restatement (Second) of Trusts § 227 cmt. g); *Edgar*, 503 F.3d at 348 (repeating mistaken citation). Only a few provisions of the *Third Restatement*, those relating to the prudent investor rule, were available when *Moench* was decided. *See*, Restatement (Third) of Trusts § 228 cmt. e (1992), (paraphrasing the distributive deviation rule and citing section 167 of the Second Restatement).

186   For background on distributive deviation and the very different approaches to the issue taken by courts in the United States and the United Kingdom (along with other British Commonwealth countries), see Peter J. Wiedenbeck, *Missouri's Repeal of the Claflin Doctrine—New View of the Policy Against Perpetuities?*, 50 Mo. L. Rev. 806 (1985).

187   ERISA § 402(b)(3), 29 U.S.C. § 1102(b)(3) (2006).

This is not to say that the *Moench* approach is necessarily misguided. Rather, it merely demonstrates that the ERISA issue is not really concerned with the settlor's (plan sponsor's) purposes and priorities. Instead of trying to discern and carry out the intentions of the settlor when powers and purposes conflict, in the stock drop cases the courts are trying to discern and carry out the purposes of Congress when employee ownership and retirement security objectives become irreconcilable. The question is one of statutory interpretation, not plan interpretation. Because an eligible individual account plan must be a pension plan (by ERISA's definition), and is a specific type of profit-sharing or stock bonus plan, the courts seem clearly correct in their conclusion that, when push comes to shove, the retirement savings objective must prevail over employee ownership. Of course, the harder question is, when is that point reached?

The lesson here is that the *Moench* line of cases is simply drawing on a loosely related private trust law concept to fashion a federal common law rule under ERISA. In stock drop cases, the courts are construing ERISA in circumstances where the *statutory* purposes conflict; they are not obliged to follow private trust doctrines pertaining to administrative or distributive deviation. Moreover, even if they look to trust law for guidance, ERISA courts should recognize that the conditions for granting deviation from the terms of a private trust have evolved and now are much more capacious than the Second Restatement indicates. Consequently, the trust law analogy would support a much less restrictive approach to divestiture of employer stock than the opinions in *Moench* and its progeny imply.

Two points warrant brief mention. On permissible trust investments, the Third Restatement provides:

In investing the funds of a trust, the trustee

(a) has a duty to conform to any applicable statutory provisions governing investment by trustees; and

(b) has the powers expressly or impliedly granted by the terms of the trust, and, except as provided in §§ 66 and 76, has a duty to conform to the terms of the trust directing or restricting investments by the trustee.[188]

A comment to this section recognizes that investment directions imposed by the trust terms "are ordinarily binding on the trustee in managing trust assets, thus often displacing the normal duty of prudence."[189] That ordinary obligation, however, is subject to the exception in section 66, which states the modern rule on equitable deviation, both administrative and distributive.

The court may modify an administrative or distributive provision of a trust, or direct the trustee to deviate from an administrative or distributive provision, if because

---

188   RESTATEMENT (THIRD) OF TRUSTS § 91 (2007). *Accord id.* § 76(1) ("[The] duty to administer the trust diligently and in good faith, in accordance with the terms of the trust and applicable law."). A comment elaborates that the "normal duty of a trustee to obey the terms of the trust also does not apply to provisions that are invalid because they are unlawful or against public policy." *Id.* § 76(1) cmt. b(1).

189   *Id.* § 91 cmt. e.

of circumstances not anticipated by the settlor the modification or deviation will further the purposes of the trust.[190]

Under this approach it is not necessary "that the situation be so serious as to constitute an 'emergency' or to jeopardize the accomplishment of trust purposes."[191] This, of course, displaces the more restrictive "defeat or substantially impair" standard for administrative deviation under section 167 of the *Second Restatement*, the rule invoked by *Moench*.

Perhaps as important as the liberalized standard for deviation is the fact that a trustee faced with a conflict between trust terms is not placed in an impossible situation. *Moench* and other cases observe that the courts should not be quick to find that prudence requires divestiture of employer stock. "[T]he courts must recognize that if the fiduciary, in what it regards as an exercise of caution, does not maintain the investment in employer's securities, it may face liability for that caution, particularly if the employer's securities thrive."[192] Commentary in the *Third Restatement* confirms that a trustee who believes substantial harm will result to the trust or its beneficiaries if action is not taken quickly may deviate from the terms of the trust without prior court authorization. If such action is taken and "the court should subsequently determine that deviation was not justified under the principles of this Section, the trustee will not be liable in the absence of bad faith or unreasonable disregard of the terms of the trust."[193]

E. CONCLUSION

A robust voluntary system of employment-based pension and welfare benefits requires competence and integrity in benefit plan administration. Absent assurance of professionalism, workers will lose confidence in the plan; demand for benefit programs will suffer as participants discount employer promises by the anticipated probability of loss through managerial misconduct. Sponsors generally share the interest in faithful plan administration, but the employer's overriding goal is to get the most out of its investment, which sometimes requires changing the plan or adapting its application to unforeseen circumstances.

ERISA's fiduciary responsibility provisions mediate between employee protection and employer flexibility. While the central fiduciary duties were borrowed from state trust law, three modifications strengthen employee safeguards. First, a sweeping functional definition of fiduciary imposes stringent obligations on anyone with decision-making authority or access to plan assets. Second, ERISA's fiduciary duties are uniform and uncompromising—they cannot be relaxed by including exculpatory

---

190   RESTATEMENT (THIRD) OF TRUSTS § 66(1) (2003). Additional guidance on distributive deviation is provided in § 65(2), which conditions judicial approval of a modification inconsistent with a material purpose of the trust on a finding that the reasons for the modification outweigh the material purpose. This is a modern liberalized version of the "*Claflin* doctrine," analyzed in Wiedenbeck, *supra* Chapter 4 note 186.

191   RESTATEMENT (THIRD) OF TRUSTS § 66(1) cmt. a (2003).

192   Moensch v. Robertson, 62 F.3d 553, 571–72 (3d Cir. 1995).

193   RESTATEMENT (THIRD) OF TRUSTS § 66 cmt. e (2003).

provisions in the instrument. In contrast to traditional trust law, fiduciary duties under ERISA are not default rules that may be modified by agreement of the parties. Third, the prohibited-transaction rules, with the associated excise tax and civil penalty, deter insider transactions that are rife with potential for abuse.

These exacting employee protections have their limits, however. ERISA demands that every employee benefit plan contain a procedure for amendment, and the courts interpret the definition of fiduciary as excluding acts relating to amendment or termination. Consequently, amendments are not required to be for the exclusive benefit of participants and beneficiaries, leaving the employer free to cut back plan coverage or future benefit accruals as circumstances dictate. Limited flexibility is also provided by allowing employer representatives to serve as fiduciaries and holding them to a standard of subjective loyalty. These concessions permit the fiduciary to enter into a transaction that is advantageous to the employer so long as the employer's gain does not come at the employees' expense.

ERISA's fiduciary rules implicitly protect an interest that is distinct from the immediate concerns of the employer and employees. Only the provision of plan benefits is cognizable under the exclusive benefit rule; job security and other interests of participants and beneficiaries, however urgent, are beyond the pale. This uncompromising objective safeguards the societal interest in employee benefit plans (and taxpayers' investment in qualified retirement plans) by empowering the Labor Department and dissident participants to object to diversion of benefit funds to other purposes, providing another check on opportunistic behavior.

Despite these protections, society's overarching goal of retirement income security clashes with ERISA's tolerance of participant-directed investments and concentrated holdings of employer stock under defined contribution pension plans, including most 401(k) plans. ERISA section 404(c) grants participants freedom to select investments, and if the plan provides the requisite alternatives and information, it may absolve plan fiduciaries from liability for losses resulting from workers' choices. In addition, ERISA section 404(a)(2) permits certain profit-sharing and stock bonus plans to make undiversified investments in stock of the employer corporation, and if the stock is publicly traded, that decision can be left to employees by offering an employer stock fund as an investment alternative under a participant-directed plan. Few workers have investment expertise, however, and their freedom to choose unwisely frequently brings them to grief. What originated as a concession to practice in an era when defined benefit plans were the norm and defined contribution plans, where they existed, simply offered a supplemental savings opportunity, has become, in the age of 401(k) plan ascendency, a dominant design feature that imperils the prospect of comfortable retirement. Courts have begun to grapple with this conflict between statutory authorization of participant choice and concentrated holdings of employer stock on the one hand, and retirement security on the other. Case law to date reflects tentative steps to intervene in situations where continued investment in employer stock presents egregious risk, but the decisions thus far have failed to recognize that the source of the conflict lies not in the terms of the plan or the exigent circumstances facing plan fiduciaries, but rather in ERISA itself. Therefore the solution lies in the judicial power to compromise incongruous commands by developing federal common law.

Chapter 5

Enforcement

ERISA's enforcement mechanism has proven to be highly contentious. It has long been a major focus of litigation, and in recent years, it has become enmeshed in the highly charged political debate over health care reform. The source of all the controversy is a set of limitations on participants' ability to obtain complete relief for alleged violations of the plan or of ERISA. These limitations—on standing, the scope of judicial review of fiduciary decision making, causes of action, and remedies—are the focus of this chapter.

The rich law and economics literature on efficient breach of contract teaches that limitations on relief and the measure of damages are as important as the underlying substantive law in shaping the behavior of contracting parties. Similarly, ERISA's enforcement regime molds the conduct of employee benefit plan sponsors, participants, and administrators, affecting (consciously or not) the level of compliance with the statutory norms. Employers contend that limitations on relief are, like preemption, crucial to the maintenance of a voluntary system of employment-based pension and welfare benefit delivery. Without them, cost increases would curtail plan sponsorship and workforce coverage, and that change would have profound distributional implications. Disappointed workers, on the other hand, complain that enforcement limitations permit an unintended and unacceptably high level of fiduciary misconduct and systematic employer abuse of benefit programs.[1]

The main battleground on which this war is waged is ERISA § 502, the statute's civil enforcement provision.[2] While the statute authorizes criminal sanctions in three limited circumstances,[3] the sanctions are almost never invoked. Instead, the civil penalties and causes of action established by section 502 are the primary means of implementing ERISA. The civil penalties, which are directed against various disclosure violations and fiduciary breaches, have been briefly addressed in preceding chapters.[4] Here, the focus is on obtaining legal and equitable relief for a violation of the terms of the plan or the requirements of ERISA.

A. STANDING

Section 502(a) establishes three basic enforcement actions, apart from civil penalties. First, a plan participant or beneficiary may bring a claim to recover benefits due under the plan or to clarify his rights to future benefits under the plan.[5] Second, the Secretary of Labor or a participant, beneficiary, or fiduciary may bring an action for damages or for equitable relief to enforce ERISA's fiduciary obligations.[6] Third, a participant, beneficiary, or fiduciary may bring an action "(A) to enjoin any act or practice which violates any provision of this title or the terms of the plan, or (B) to obtain appropriate equitable relief (i) to redress such violations or (ii) to enforce any provision of this title or the terms of the plan."[7]

---

1   *See supra* Chapter 1C.
2   ERISA § 502, 29 U.S.C. § 1132 (2006).
3   Willful violation of ERISA's reporting and disclosure obligations subjects the offender to imprisonment for up to ten years and a fine of up to $100,000 ($500,000 if the defendant is a corporation or other entity) under ERISA § 501, 29 U.S.C. § 1131 (2006); coercive interference with protected rights is criminalized by ERISA § 511, 29 U.S.C. § 1139 (2006); and it is a crime for persons previously convicted of specified offenses to intentionally violate a ban on carrying out various functions for an employee benefit plan, ERISA § 411(b), 29 U.S.C. § 1111(b) (2006). In addition, three sections of the criminal code create ERISA-related crimes: 18 U.S.C. § 664 (2006) (theft or embezzlement from an employee benefit fund); *id.* § 1027 (false statements or concealment of facts concerning reports or records of employee benefit plans); *id.* § 1954 (offer, acceptance, or solicitation of anything of value to influence employee benefit plan operations).
4   Civil penalties for various disclosure violations are prescribed by ERISA § 502(a)(1)(A), (a)(6), (c), 29 U.S.C. § 1132(a)(1)(A), (a)(6), (c) (2006). *See supra* Chapter 3. In addition, the Secretary of Labor is authorized to assess civil penalties for certain breaches of fiduciary obligations, ERISA § 502(*l*), (m), 29 U.S.C. § 1132(*l*), (m) (2006). *See supra* Chapter 4.
5   ERISA § 502(a)(1)(B), 29 U.S.C. § 1132(a)(1)(B) (2006).
6   ERISA §§ 502(a)(2), 409, 29 U.S.C. §§ 1132(a)(2), 1109 (2006).
7   ERISA § 502(a)(3), 29 U.S.C. § 1132(a)(3) (2006). In certain circumstances, the Secretary of Labor is given corresponding authority to seek equitable enforcement of ERISA, but not to

Each entry on the list of civil enforcement actions in section 502(a) begins with a designation of the persons by whom the suit may be brought. Courts have generally interpreted the statutory specification of eligible plaintiffs as exhaustive—persons who do not fit within the designated categories lack standing.[8] For the most part, this approach works because Congress wisely placed primary responsibility for enforcing ERISA in the hands of the interested private parties, i.e., the plan participants, beneficiaries, and fiduciaries. In two respects, however, legislative limitations on standing have proven problematic.

First, participants and beneficiaries in a defined benefit pension plan may have little or no incentive to enforce ERISA's fiduciary obligations. Minimum funding standards and the Pension Benefit Guaranty Corporation (PBGC) termination insurance system largely insulate covered workers from loss of vested pension benefits.[9] This security blunts the incentive for fiduciary oversight and makes it unwise to rely on participant monitoring in the case of a defined benefit pension plan.[10] Instead, standing should be

---

enforce the terms of any particular plan. *Compare id., with* ERISA § 502(a)(5), 29 U.S.C. § 1132(a)(5) (2006). In the case of a tax-qualified pension, profit-sharing, stock bonus, or annuity plan, Labor Department enforcement is authorized only at the request of the Treasury Department, or suit may be brought in a representative capacity upon the written request of a participant, beneficiary, or fiduciary. ERISA § 502(b)(1), 29 U.S.C. § 1132(b)(1) (2006).

8   Leuthner v. Blue Cross & Blue Shield of Ne. Pa., 454 F.3d 120, 125 (3d Cir. 2006) (statutory standing requirement of § 502(a), that plaintiff be a plan participant or beneficiary, displaces prudential zone of interests test for standing in ERISA cases); Felix v. Lucent Techs., Inc., 387 F.3d 1146, 1160 n.14 (10th Cir. 2004) (§ 502(a) designation of plaintiffs limits subject-matter jurisdiction); Miller v. Rite Aid Corp., 334 F.3d 335, 340 (3d Cir. 2003) ("ERISA § 502(a)(1) . . . *restricts* civil actions brought against a plan administrator to actions brought by a 'participant or beneficiary.'" (emphasis added) (quoting Saporito v. Combustion Eng'g Inc., 843 F.2d 666, 670–71 (3d Cir. 1988), *vacated on other grounds by* Combustion Eng'g, Inc. v. Saporito, 489 U.S. 1049 (1989))). *But see* Vartanian v. Monsanto Co., 14 F.3d 697, 701–02 (1st Cir. 1994) (looking to whether plaintiff is within the zone of interests, ERISA was intended to protect, and citing *Association of Data Processing Service Organizations v. Camp*, 397 U.S. 150 (1970), the font of the modern prudential test for standing).

9   Most defined benefit plans are well funded, and unless the sponsor is in financial distress, an underfunded plan cannot be terminated, so that continued applicability of the minimum funding standards will eventually eliminate the shortfall. ERISA § 4041(b)(1)(D), 29 U.S.C. § 1341(b)(1)(D) (2006) (standard termination permitted only if plan assets sufficient to pay all benefit liabilities). Where termination of an underfunded plan is authorized, the PBGC steps in to pay guaranteed benefits. ERISA § 4022, 29 U.S.C. § 1322 (2006). *See generally infra* Chapter 9B.

10   In contrast, participants in a defined contribution pension plan are not guaranteed any particular level of benefits; they are entitled only to the balance in their accounts. ERISA § 3(34), 29 U.S.C. § 1002(34) (2006) (defined contribution plan defined as a pension plan that provides "benefits based solely on the amount contributed to the participant's account, and any income, expenses, gains and losses, and any forfeitures of accounts of other participants which may be allocated to such participant's account"). Because defined contribution plan participants are directly harmed by bad investments or theft, they have a strong interest in fiduciary oversight.
     Although welfare plans are usually defined benefit arrangements, this incentive problem does not ordinarily arise. Participants normally do not acquire vested rights to welfare benefits, and so losses from fiduciary misconduct jeopardize continuation of the plan. Multiemployer welfare benefit funds are found in some industries (trucking and construction, for example),

granted to the real party in interest—the defined benefit plan sponsor—because it is the sponsor who will be obliged to make up any losses that might be caused by fiduciary breach.[11] Standing might also be granted to the PBGC, which is secondarily liable for a funding shortfall, as it will have to pay guaranteed benefits if the sponsor cannot.

Second, the meaning of the term "participant" has caused difficulty in the standing context. The statute defines participant as "any employee or former employee . . . who is or may become eligible to receive a benefit of any type from an employee benefit plan."[12] Eligibility to receive a benefit is generally the central contested issue in a claim for benefits and normally defines the scope of informational rights and fiduciary obligations. Consequently, defining proper plaintiffs by reference to participant status would often force the courts to take a peek at the merits of the claim to resolve the standing question.

It is possible to imagine a sequence of events (e.g., hiring, satisfaction of plan membership conditions, fulfilling service requirements for vesting) that, however unlikely, would permit almost anyone "to become eligible to receive a benefit" from any particular plan. Such a literal reading would make surplus the statutory reference to eligibility, effectively equating participant status with the set of all current and former employees. But that cannot have been intended. In the case of a pension plan, it is clear that an employee does not become a participant unless and until he starts earning benefits under the plan,[13] and the subjunctive language, "may become eligible," was apparently intended to indicate that workers whose accrued benefits have not yet vested are nonetheless entitled to statutory protection. For a welfare plan, the subjunctive language indicates that participation begins as soon as "the individual becomes eligible . . . for a benefit subject only to occurrence of the contingency for which the benefit is provided."[14] For example, an employee who would be entitled to health care benefits if she or her dependents were injured or sick is a current plan participant. Similarly, an employee is a current life insurance plan participant if a death benefit would be due upon her demise.

---

but because employers are permitted to limit their liability to the amount contributed to the fund, and because welfare benefits are not guaranteed, participants and beneficiaries of funded welfare plans bear the risk of loss.

11   *See* Harley v. Minn. Mining & Mfg. Co., 284 F.3d 901, 905–07 (8th Cir. 2002) (defined benefit plan participants lacked standing to sue for fiduciary breach under ERISA § 502(a)(2) because they suffered no injury as a result of overfunding). In the case of an overfunded plan, the sponsor ordinarily takes the surplus (after paying a tax on the reversion) and so has an interest in preserving it. ERISA §§ 403(c)(1), 4044(d)(1), 29 U.S.C. §§ 1103(c)(1), 1344(d)(1) (2006). *Accord* I.R.C. § 401(a)(2) (2006). A 20 or 50 percent tax on reversions from a qualified defined benefit plan is imposed by I.R.C. § 4980 (2006).

12   ERISA § 3(7), 29 U.S.C. § 1002(7) (2006).

13   The statute imposes precise minimum standards on the commencement of pension plan participation in ERISA § 202(a)(4), 29 U.S.C. § 1052(a)(4) (2006). *Accord* I.R.C. § 410(a)(4) (2006); Treas. Reg. § 1.410(a)-4(b) (as amended in 1980). (Note that Treasury regulations prescribed under I.R.C. §§ 410 and 411 are authoritative interpretations of the corresponding provisions of ERISA's labor title. 29 C.F.R. § 2530.200a-2 (2009).)

14   29 C.F.R. § 2510.3-3(d)(1)(i)(B) (2009).

Dealing with outgoing employees has proven harder. A sponsor may assert that separation from service terminates the right to all benefits under the terms of a plan.[15] Can a former employee contest that reading? It would seem that the former worker has standing if and only if she will prevail on the merits. In *Firestone Tire & Rubber Co. v. Bruch*,[16] the Supreme Court majority refused to be quite so literal:

> In our view, the term "participant" is naturally read to mean either "employees in, or reasonably expected to be in, currently covered employment," *Saladino v. I.L.G.W.U. National Retirement Fund*, 754 F.2d 473, 476 (CA2 1985), or former employees who "have . . . a reasonable expectation of returning to covered employment" or who have "a colorable claim" to vested benefits, *Kuntz v. Reese*, 785 F.2d 1410, 1411 (CA9) (*per curiam*), cert. denied, 479 U.S. 916 (1986). In order to establish that he or she "may become eligible" for benefits, a claimant must have a colorable claim that (1) he or she will prevail in a suit for benefits, or that (2) eligibility requirements will be fulfilled in the future. "This view attributes conventional meanings to the statutory language since all employees in covered employment and former employees with a colorable claim to vested benefits 'may become eligible.' A former employee who has neither a reasonable expectation of returning to covered employment nor a colorable claim to vested benefits, however, simply does not fit within the [phrase] 'may become eligible.'" *Saladino v. I.L.G.W.U. National Retirement Fund, supra*, at 476.[17]

Firestone's "colorable claim" gloss allows the adjudication of bona fide eligibility disputes without unnecessary procedural complications, but it does not solve all the problems. Take the example of an employee who alleges that his decision to retire was based on employer misrepresentations constituting a breach of fiduciary duty and who shows that absent the misrepresentation, he would have continued working and so qualified for greater benefits. The First Circuit held that the "receipt of payment cannot be used to deprive him of 'participant' status and hence, standing to sue under ERISA" provided that the true facts were not available to the employee until after he received all of his vested benefits.[18]

In response to a similar fiduciary misrepresentation claim, the Third Circuit put the matter this way:

> A plan administrator's alleged ERISA violation should not be the means by which the plan is able to insulate itself from suits arising from the alleged violation. We will not read ERISA so myopically. As the Sixth Circuit observed, "ERISA should not be construed to permit the fiduciary to circumvent his ERISA-imposed fiduciary duty in this manner." Therefore, in the proper case, we may find that a plaintiff has statutory standing if the plaintiff can in good faith plead that she was

---

15   *See* 29 C.F.R. § 2510.3-3(d)(2)(i)(A) (2009) (welfare plan participation ends on the earliest date on which the individual is "ineligible to receive any benefit under the plan even if the contingency for which the benefit is provided should occur").

16   489 U.S. 101 (1989). For Justice Scalia's literal interpretation, see his concurring opinion, *id.* at 119.

17   489 U.S. at 117–18.

18   Vartanian v. Monsanto Co., 14 F.3d 697, 703 (1st Cir. 1994).

an ERISA plan participant or beneficiary and that she still would be but for the alleged malfeasance of a plan fiduciary.[19]

The circuits are split on the issue, but the majority have embraced this "but for" extension of participant status.[20]

The approach of testing participant status at the time of the alleged violation was adopted by the Ninth Circuit for retaliatory discharge claims. In *McBride v. PLM International, Inc.*,[21] the plaintiff alleged that he was discharged in violation of ERISA § 510 for his vociferous objections to the proposed termination of the employer's pension plans. After he was fired, McBride, along with all other participants, received a lump-sum distribution of his benefits, and the plan was terminated. Consequently, at the time McBride brought suit, he was a former employee who had received all benefits due under the plan and who, even if reinstated, had no "reasonable expectation of returning to covered employment" because the plans had been terminated. Relying on ERISA's protective policy, the court concluded that an "employer cannot be allowed to evade section [510] accountability simply by terminating the plan and distributing the benefits."[22] To prevent that injustice, the court held that standing to assert section 510 claims must be determined at the time of the alleged ERISA violation, rather than the usual approach of judging standing as of the time of filing suit.[23] An extended dissent charged that this special whistleblower exception was unfaithful to the statutory language as well as both Supreme Court (i.e., *Firestone*) and Ninth Circuit precedent.[24]

In the misrepresentation and retaliatory discharge contexts the "but for" test grants standing to a former employee who asserts that his separation from service was caused by an ERISA violation. Does a former employee have standing if separation from service was unrelated to the claimed violation of plan terms or ERISA? Suppose an individual takes distribution of her entire account balance in the company's defined contribution pension plan following separation from service, and then later discovers that the plan fiduciaries might have breached their duties of loyalty or care in making investments or selecting available investment options. May such a former employee bring suit for the additional amount that would have been in her account absent the breach, or does cashing out of a defined contribution plan extinguish participant status?

---

19   Leuthner v. Blue Cross & Blue Shield of Ne. Pa., 454 F.3d 120, 129 (3d Cir. 2006) (quoting Swinney v. GMC, 46 F.3d 512, 518–19 (6th Cir. 1995)).

20   The circuits' positions are cataloged in *Leuthner v. Blue Cross & Blue Shield of Northeastern Pennsylvania*, 454 F.3d 120, 128–29 (3d Cir. 2006), and *Felix v. Lucent Technologies, Inc.*, 387 F.3d 1146, 1159–61 (10th Cir. 2004). *Compare* Raymond v. Mobil Oil Co., 983 F.2d 1528, 1532–37 (10th Cir. 1993) (standing to bring a constructive discharge claim denied, relying on *Firestone*), *with* Christopher v. Mobil Oil Co., 950 F.2d 1209, 1219, 1220 (5th Cir. 1992) (standing to challenge the same actions granted).

21   179 F.3d 737 (9th Cir. 1999).

22   *Id.* at 743.

23   *Id.* at 744.

24   *Id.* at 746–53 (Beezer, J., dissenting).

Standing originally presented a barrier to such suits.[25] Since 2007, a series of appellate decisions have coalesced around the view that a former employee who seeks payment of the additional amount that her account would have contained if it were unimpaired by fiduciary misconduct is asserting a colorable claim to benefits, and is therefore a proper plaintiff.[26]

Welfare benefits are not required to vest under ERISA, and so the references in *Firestone* to a "colorable claim to vested benefits" might call into question the power to adjudicate welfare plan eligibility disputes. No policy consideration supports such a distinction, and the "vested" language has not proved a stumbling block to standing in claims involving welfare plans.[27] Whether the assignee of a welfare plan participant or beneficiary has standing to sue has been challenged, however. Unlike pension benefits, welfare benefits are assignable.[28] A health care provider, for example, may accept an assignment of the patient's plan benefits instead of insisting on payment when services are rendered. If the claim for benefits is denied, can the doctor or hospital bring suit? Although assignees are not specifically listed in the statute, the courts almost uniformly hold that an assignee has derivative standing to bring an action under section 502 in place of the assignor participant or beneficiary.[29] Moreover, a valid assignment amounts to the participant's designation of a person entitled to collect plan benefits, and therefore seems to fit the statutory definition of "beneficiary."[30]

B. SCOPE OF REVIEW

ERISA enforcement actions invariably challenge a plan official's decision making. When called to account, the decision maker may argue that his official status or

---

25   *See* 34 Pens. & Ben. Rep. (BNA) 115–17 (2007) (synopsis of conflicting district court decisions issued during 2006 involving former employee standing).

26   *E.g.*, Vaughn v. Bay Envtl. Mgmt. Inc., 544 F.3d 1008 (9th Cir. 2008); Lanfear v. Home Depot, Inc., 536 F.3d 1217 (11th Cir. 2008); Evans v. Akers, 534 F.3d 65 (1st Cir. 2008); Wangberger v. Janus Capital Group, Inc., 529 F.3d 207 (4th Cir. 2008); Bridges v. Am. Elec. Power Co., 498 F.3d 442 (6th Cir. 2007); Graden v. Conexant Sys. Inc., 496 F.3d 291 (3d Cir. 2007); Harzewski v. Guidant Corp., 489 F.3d 799 (7th Cir. 2007). The Supreme Court cited *Harzewski* with apparent approval in *LaRue v. DeWolff Boberg & Assocs.*, 552 U.S. 248, ___, 128 S. Ct. 1020, 1026 n.6 (2008), which may account for the rapid alignment of appellate court approaches. *See also* Bilello v. JPMorgan Chase Ret. Plan, 592 F. Supp. 2d 654, 662–67 (S.D.N.Y. 2009) (former employee cashed out of a cash balance defined benefit plan has standing to pursue claim for additional benefits based on theory that plan amendment reducing benefit accruals was ineffective due to lack of required prior notice).

27   *See* Andre v. Salem Tech. Servs. Corp., 797 F. Supp. 1416 (N.D. Ill. 1992) ("vested" in the context of welfare plans should be taken to mean "fixed in time during the employment relationship"; alternatively, former employee who incurred covered expenses is "eligible to receive a benefit" within the meaning of ERISA).

28   *See* ERISA § 206(d)(1), 29 U.S.C. § 1056(d)(1) (2006) (anti-alienation rule limited to pension plans).

29   *E.g.*, Misic v. Bldg. Serv. Employees Health & Welfare Trust, 789 F.2d 1374 (9th Cir. 1986).

30   ERISA § 3(8), 29 U.S.C. § 1002(8) (2006).

presumed expertise entitles the decision to a presumption of correctness, or to some special weight in court. The intensity of judicial scrutiny will often determine the outcome on judicial review, and yet the statute is silent on the question of the appropriate scope of review. Faced with this lacuna, courts have had to choose between de novo review and the abuse-of-discretion standard, the two principal candidates for scope of review.

Plan Interpretations

In ERISA's early years, most lower courts applied the abuse-of-discretion standard to fiduciary decision making, as that limited scope of review had been applied under the Taft-Hartley Act to suits for benefits brought against trustees of collectively bargained plans. In 1989, the Supreme Court rejected that approach in *Firestone Tire & Rubber Co. v. Bruch*.[31] Turning to the trust law origins of ERISA, the Court noted that a deferential standard of review is appropriate where a trustee is granted discretionary powers, but that a trustee's interpretation of the terms of the trust is ordinarily reviewed by the courts de novo.[32] De novo review of plan interpretations, the Court observed, is also consistent with the contract law basis of suits for benefits prior to ERISA.[33] Accordingly, the *Firestone* Court held that "a denial of benefits challenged under § 1132(a)(1)(B) [ERISA § 502(a)(1)(B)] is to be reviewed under a *de novo* standard unless the benefit plan gives the administrator or fiduciary discretionary authority to determine eligibility for benefits or to construe the terms of the plan."[34]

Employers retain the power to amend their benefit plans,[35] and if the plan does not cover unionized workers, they can typically do so unilaterally. Not surprisingly, sponsors responded to *Firestone* by inserting in their plans an express grant of fiduciary discretion to interpret plan terms and determine benefit eligibility, although some question remains as to how clear a grant of discretionary authority must be to work a relaxation of the scope of review.[36] Therefore, notwithstanding the Court's conclusion that de novo review is the general or default mode of judicial oversight for benefit claim denials, as a practical matter the abuse-of-discretion standard is now overwhelmingly dominant.[37]

---

31   489 U.S. 101, 109 (1989) (a comparison of the statutes "shows that the *wholesale* importation of the arbitrary and capricious standard into ERISA is unwarranted").

32   *Id.* at 111–12.

33   *Id.* at 112–13.

34   *Id.* at 115.

35   ERISA § 402(b)(3), 29 U.S.C. § 1102(b)(3) (2006).

36   *See infra* Chapter 5 note 40.

37   That development has been sharply criticized, but not on the policy ground on which it is most vulnerable. *See* Jay Conison, *Suits for Benefits Under ERISA*, 54 U. Pitt. L. Rev. 1 (1992). A limited scope of review works, in effect, a relaxation of fiduciary duties, and is therefore inconsistent with the command of ERISA § 410(a) that "any provision in an agreement or instrument that purports to relieve a fiduciary from responsibility or liability for any responsibility, obligation or duty imposed under this part shall be void as against public policy." 29 U.S.C. § 1110(a) (2006).

The *Firestone* opinion concerns the standard of review applicable to benefit claim denials based on plan interpretations, and the Court expressed "no view as to the appropriate standard of review" in other areas.[38] Two vitally important questions that have vexed the lower courts concern the proper scope of review to be applied to fiduciary findings of fact and to claims determinations made by a fiduciary who is allegedly acting under a conflict of interest.

Factfinding

Although *Firestone* involved a question of plan interpretation, the Court conditioned its approval of de novo review on the absence of an express grant of discretion to construe plan terms *or to determine eligibility for benefits*.[39] Since eligibility for benefits commonly turns upon disputed issues of fact, the implicit approval of discretionary power to determine eligibility suggests that the Court would adopt the same approach to review of factfinding (i.e., de novo review if the plan is silent, but only limited oversight if discretion is expressly conferred). After *Firestone*, of course, plan provisions expressly limiting judicial scrutiny—for example, by providing that the fiduciary's determination on eligibility questions shall be "final" or "unreviewable" or "conclusive"—are the norm.[40]

In the aftermath of *Firestone*, the circuits split on the proper scope of review to be applied to findings of fact. Hewing close to the line marked by the Supreme Court, in the absence of an explicit reservation of discretionary authority, most appellate courts undertake searching de novo review.[41] Nevertheless, important differences from

---

38   *Firestone*, 489 U.S. at 108.

39   *Id.* at 115.

40   See, for example, the model pension plans published in 2 Michael J. Canan, Qualified Retirement Plans 705 (West Group 2007) (profit-sharing plan administrator granted "sole discretion, to interpret or construe the Plan and to determine all questions that may arise hereunder"); *id.* at 862 (same, money purchase pension plan); *id.* at 1031 (same, defined benefit plan); *id.* at 1260 (same, 401(k) plan). *Accord* CCH Pension Plan Guide-Plans and Clauses ¶¶ 30,047 (model defined benefit plan, with an explanatory note on *Firestone*); *id.* at 30,133 (model money purchase pension plan); *id.* at 31,133 (model profit-sharing plan). Model group health plans also commonly include an express grant of discretion. *E.g.*, Michael J. Canan & William D. Mitchell, Employee Fringe and Welfare Benefit Plans 591 (1997) (discretion to interpret the plan, with instruction that the exercise of discretion is to be reviewed under the arbitrary and capricious standard).

41   *E.g.*, Kinstler v. First Reliance Std. Life Ins. Co., 181 F.3d 243, 249–51 (2d Cir. 2000) (discussing circuit split); Pierre v. Conn. Gen. Life Ins. Co., 502 U.S. 973 (1991) (White, J., dissenting from denial of certiorari).

      Those appellate courts that apply de novo review absent a grant of discretionary authority differ among themselves on how explicit the conferral of discretion must be to trigger the more deferential abuse-of-discretion standard. *E.g.*, *Kinstler*, 181 F.3d at 251–52 (submission of "satisfactory proof" insufficient to relax standard of review); Sandy v. Reliance Std. Life Ins. Co., 222 F.3d 1202 (9th Cir. 2000) (same; reviewing circuit split and noting "awkward position of construing the effect of identical language in plan documents of the same insurer differently from the Sixth Circuit"). Even if the fiduciary has clearly been given factfinding discretion,

plan interpretation may justify restricted oversight of factfinding even without explicit plan instructions. Factfinding, after all, whether by lower courts or administrative agencies, has traditionally been accorded substantial deference, and the weighing of competing versions of events, especially when credibility is an issue, may be thought to be an inherently discretionary function.[42] Concerns about caseload may also support restricted judicial scrutiny; second-guessing a multitude of routine fact determinations could swamp the courts. These factors led the Fifth Circuit to approve the abuse-of-discretion test for factfinding, even without a plan provision explicitly granting discretion.[43]

Expertise is another policy concern that may justify a limited scope of review. A decision maker possessed of specialized knowledge or experience is comparatively better qualified than a court to make decisions involving that specialized subject matter. Because a specialist will often evaluate information differently than a generalist judge, de novo review (i.e., substituted judgment) may forfeit the value of this expertise. Alternatively, the expert might seek to have the decision sustained by educating the reviewing court as to the validity of the expert's evaluation, effectively replicating any relevant specialized knowledge, but then de novo review entails duplication, delay, and inefficiency. By giving specialized decision makers some leeway, a limited scope of review (like the abuse-of-discretion test) promotes an efficient, expert resolution of the issue. Plan fiduciaries making eligibility determinations are repeatedly presented with similar fact patterns or types of evidence (e.g., medical records under a health plan, or wage and hour reports under a pension plan), so expertise may be an important value in fiduciary decision making.[44]

---

some circuits hold that de novo review applies if the claim denial is not actually based on an exercise of discretion. *E.g.*, Gilbertson v. Allied Signal, Inc., 328 F.3d 625 (10th Cir. 2003) (automatic denial under Labor Department regulations because of passage of time).

42 *Cf.* Black & Decker Disability Plan v. Nord, 538 U.S. 822 (2003) (ERISA disability plan administrators not obliged to accord special weight to opinions of claimant's treating physicians vis-à-vis views of plan consultants).

43 *E.g.*, Pierre v. Conn. Gen. Life Ins. Co., 932 F.2d 1552, 1559 (5th Cir. 1991) (factfinding inherently discretionary; moreover, de novo review of facts "is a difficult and uncertain exercise on a cold record" and the "courts simply cannot supplant plan administrators, through de novo review, as resolvers of mundane and routine fact disputes"); Meditrust Fin. Servs. Corp. v. Sterling Chems., Inc., 168 F.3d 211, 213–14 (5th Cir. 1999) (reaffirming *Pierre* despite its rejection by other circuits).

44 Expertise forms a primary justification for the limited scope of judicial review of factfinding in administrative law. *See generally*, Bernard Schwartz, Administrative Law §§ 10.1, 10.5–10.6 (3d ed. 1991) (limited judicial review of agency factfinding explained by considerations of relative expertise—i.e., comparative competence of the agency and reviewing court—and efficiency). Similar considerations apply to judicial review of a benefit plan administrator's factual determinations where the administrator has special knowledge or experience. *See Pierre*, 932 F.2d at 1562 ("The heart of this case is the weight to be given to certain 'hearsay' statements. Even in resolving this dispute, the plan administrator enjoys certain advantages that the courts do not have. He is much closer to the facts and the investigation. Acting through its agents, [the defendant] conducted the investigation and interviewed the declarant."). *Contra* Luby v. Teamsters Health, Welfare & Pension Trust Funds, 944 F.2d 1176, 1183 (3d Cir. 1991) ("Plan administrators are not governmental agencies who are frequently granted deferential review

Conflicted Decision Making

Where a plan specifically confers discretion in construing its terms or in determining eligibility for benefits, *Firestone* ordinarily demands deferential abuse-of-discretion review. But does that relaxed standard apply where the decision maker is subject to a conflict of interest? In its parting observation in *Firestone*, the Court noted that "[o]f course, if a benefit plan gives discretion to an administrator or fiduciary who is operating under a conflict of interest, that conflict must be weighed as a 'facto[r] in determining whether there is an abuse of discretion.'"[45]

Consider a plan that is funded by the purchase of insurance, with the insurer making final decisions on benefit eligibility. The insurer is acting as fiduciary, yet because claims are paid out of the insurer's own assets, benefit grants adversely impact the insurer's profitability. The same sort of direct financial impact is present where a welfare plan is self-insured and claims decisions are made by an employee of the sponsor. As a result of the multiple-hat problem,[46] such inherent or "structural" conflicts of interest are pervasive facts of life in benefit claims decisions.

Thanks to the absence of guidance in the *Firestone* dicta, the question of the impact of such structural conflicts on the intensity of judicial review of benefit claim denials long bedeviled and divided the lower courts.[47] Nearly two decades after *Firestone*, the Supreme Court took up the conflict of interest problem in *Metropolitan Life Insurance Company v. Glenn*.[48] *Glenn* holds that a conflict of interest necessarily exists when an entity both determines employee eligibility for benefits and pays those benefits out of its own pocket.[49] As suggested in *Firestone*, courts should consider this conflict of interest as a factor in determining whether a plan administrator's denial of benefits constitutes an abuse of discretion, but the existence of the conflict does not trigger a higher standard of review (such as *de novo* review).[50] The Court refused to specify a

---

because of their acknowledged expertise. Administrators may be laypersons appointed under the plan, sometimes without any legal, accounting, or other training preparing them for their responsible position, often without any experience in or understanding of the complex problems arising under ERISA, and, as this case demonstrates, little knowledge of the rules of evidence or legal procedures to assist them in factfinding."). Since these early post-*Firestone* cases, factfinding expertise has received little attention in the ERISA context, apparently because the ubiquitous adoption of plan amendments expressly conferring discretion has made the issue moot.

45   Firestone Tire & Rubber Co. v. Bruch, 489 U.S. 101, 115 (1989) (quoting Restatement (Second) of Trusts § 187 cmt. d (1959)).

46   *See supra* Chapter 4A.

47   *See generally*, Kathryn J. Kennedy, *Judicial Standard of Review in ERISA Benefit Claim Cases*, 50 Am. U. L. Rev. 1083, 1146–62 (2001); John H. Langbein, *Trust Law as Regulatory Law; The UNUM/Provident Scandal and Judicial Review of Benefit Denials Under ERISA*, 101 Nw. U. L. Rev. 1315 (2007).

48   128 S. Ct. 2343 (2008).

49   *Id.* at 2346.

50   *Id.* at 2350. Before *Glenn*, several circuits adopted a heightened or modified standard of review in conflict-of-interest cases, but once the *Glenn* decision was rendered, courts abandoned the heightened standard. Doyle v. Liberty Life Assurance Co. of Boston, 542 F.3d 1352 (11th Cir. 2008); Champion v. Black & Decker (U.S.) Inc., 550 F.3d 353 (4th Cir. 2008); Estate of Schwing v. Lilly Health Plan, 562 F.2d 522 (3d Cir. 2009).

detailed set of instructions on the impact of this factor, holding instead that the weight to be given the conflict should be based on the circumstances of the particular case.[51] *Glenn* also disavowed special procedural or evidentiary mechanisms—like shifting the burden of proof—that some circuits had imposed to smoke out whether a structural conflict actually affected the decision.[52]

While *Glenn* embraces an indefinite totality-of-the-circumstances approach, the Court's opinion offers a few clues on the influence of a conflict on the overall assessment of factors. First, the conflict should be given little weight if the there are mechanisms in place to promote fair and correct benefit determinations.

> [The conflict] should prove less important (perhaps to the vanishing point) where the administrator has taken active steps to reduce potential bias and to promote accuracy, for example, by walling off claims administrators from those interested in firm finances, or by imposing management check that penalize inaccurate decisionmaking irrespective of whom the inaccuracy benefits.[53]

This discount for structural safeguards seems likely to induce insurers and sponsors of large self-insured plans to institute such internal controls (as perhaps it was intended to do).[54]

Another question is whether, in the absence of internal safeguards, a conflict of interest may be discounted (or disregarded) based upon the existence of a reputational

---

Pre-*Glenn* the Second Circuit applied de novo review, empowering the reviewing court to substitute its judgment on eligibility for benefits, but only if the plaintiff produced evidence that a structural conflict actually infected decision making. Sullivan v. LTV Aerospace & Def. Co., 82 F.3d 1251, 1255-56 (2d Cir. 1996). *Glenn* prompted the Second Circuit to abandon its de novo review in favor of treating a conflict of interest as a distinct factor. McCauley v. First UNUM Life Ins. Co., 551 F.3d 126, 137 (2d Cir. 2008) (finding that the plan administrator abused its discretion in denying plaintiff's claim).

51   *Glenn*, 128 S. Ct. at 2346, 2351–52. The Court relied on trust law to support the conclusion that a conflict of interest does not trigger a higher standard of review: "Trust law continues to apply a deferential standard of review to the discretionary decisionmaking of a conflicted trustee, while at the same time requiring the reviewing judge to take account of the conflict when determining whether the trustee, substantively or procedurally, has abused his discretion." *Id.* at 2350. In dissent, Justices Scalia and Thomas took ERISA's trust law origins much further— they would look to trust law for concrete guidelines on the content of abuse of discretion review. Applying trust law, they would find that a conflict is relevant only to the question whether the trustee abused his discretion by acting with an improper motive, and that it is wholly irrelevant (not a factor to be considered) to the question whether the trustee's decision was reasonable. *Id.* at 2356–61 (Scalia, J. dissenting).

52   *Glenn* prompted the Eleventh Circuit to abandon its burden-shifting approach and consider a conflict of interest as an additional factor to be weighed. Doyle v. Liberty Life Assurance Co. of Boston, 542 F.3d 1352 (11th Cir. 2008).

53   *Glenn*, 128 S. Ct. at 2351.

54   Justice Kennedy agreed with the Court's legal analysis, including the combination-of-factors method of review, but concluded that the case should have been remanded because, "so far as one can tell, the Court of Appeals made no effort to assess whether MetLife employed structural safeguards to avoid conflicts of interest, safeguards the Court says can cause the importance of the conflict to vanish. *Id.* at 2356 (Kennedy, J., concurring in part and dissenting in part).

interest or some other market mechanism tending to discourage short-term, self-interested decision making. Before *Glenn*, some circuits had applied law and economic reasoning to disregard structural conflicts on the ground that market forces provide adequate countervailing incentives for fair decision making.[55] MetLife, the defendant in the *Glenn* case, deployed this reasoning to assert that there was no cognizable conflict of interest. The Court rejected that defense because "ERISA imposes higher-than-marketplace quality standards on insurers."[56] Yet the Court acknowledged that an approach that finds "the *existence* of a conflict can nonetheless take account of the circumstances to which MetLife points so far as it treats those, or similar, circumstances as diminishing the *significance* or *severity* of the conflict in individual cases."[57] Thus, under the totality-of-the-circumstances approach, countervailing market forces are relevant, but their strength depends upon case-specific facts.[58]

A final (and more speculative) clue to the handling of a structural conflict might lie in *Glenn*'s administrative law analogy. In addition to its reliance on ERISA's trust law origins,[59] the Court drew support from certain cases examining the lawfulness of bureaucratic action.[60] Abuse-of-discretion review is, of course, best known and most

---

55   *E.g.*, Mers v. Marriott Int'l Group Accidental Death & Dismemberment Plan, 144 F.3d 1014, 1020–21 (7th Cir. 1998) ("We presume that a fiduciary is acting neutrally unless a claimant shows by providing specific evidence of actual bias that there is a significant conflict. The existence of a potential conflict is not enough." (citations omitted)); Perlman v. Swiss Bank Corp. Comprehensive Disability Prot. Plan, 195 F.3d 975, 981 (7th Cir. 1999); Rud v. Liberty Life Assurance Co., 438 F.3d 772 (7th Cir. 2006); Wright v. R. R. Donnelley & Sons Co. Group Benefits Plan, 402 F.3d 67, 75 (1st Cir. 2005) (following the market forces rationale, while recognizing that other circuits are unpersuaded). The reasoning in this line of cases was that the amount involved in an individual benefit claim is too small to affect a large employer or insurer, and that the employer has an interest in maintaining a reputation for fair dealing with its employees. Similarly, Judge Easterbrook discounted an insurer–fiduciary's conflict on the ground that group insurance policies are experience-rated, with the employer agreeing to reimburse the insurer for benefit payments or pay higher premiums for future years' coverage, so that the insurer does not ultimately bear the cost of approved claims. *Perlman*, 195 F.3d at 981.

     After extensive analysis the Third Circuit rejected the market forces approach. Pinto v. Reliance Std. Life Ins. Co., 214 F.3d 377, 388 (3d Cir. 2000). A leading ERISA scholar extensively criticized the Seventh Circuit decisions in an article that the *Glenn* court cited to illustrate the principle that a conflict of interest takes on greater significance where an insurance company has a history of biased benefit claims administration. Langbein, *supra* Chapter 5 note 47, cited at 128 S. Ct. at 2350, 2351.

56   *Glenn*, 128 S. Ct. at 2350.

57   *Id.*; *see* Denmark v. Liberty Life Assur. Co., 566 F.3d 1, 9 (1st Cir. 2009) (in the wake of *Glenn*, "the market forces rationale no longer allows a reviewing court to disregard a structural conflict without further analysis").

58   *See Pinto*, 214 F.3d at 392 (Cases holding "that an employer fiduciary is not conflicted, generally assume that the company is stable and will act as a repeat player: The presumed desire to maintain employee satisfaction is based on this premise. When companies are breaking up, or laying off a significant percentage of their employees, or moving all their operations, these incentives diminish significantly.").

59   *See supra* Chapter 5 note 51.

60   *Glenn*, 128 S. Ct. at 2351, 2352.

fully developed in the context of judicial oversight of administrative decisions. It is a fundamental tenet of administrative law that reliance on an irrelevant or improper consideration is an abuse of discretion.[61] A fiduciary's consideration of his own or his employer's interest—or, for that matter, anything other than participants' interest in plan benefits—is unmistakably out-of-bounds under ERISA, and is therefore an abuse of discretion.[62] Yet supposing that the outcome in a close case is influenced in part by a desire to control the insurer's or plan sponsor's costs, the fiduciary's claim denial surely will not disclose that fact. Therefore, where a benefit claim is rejected by a conflicted administrator, the real issue is whether there is sufficient circumstantial evidence of a possible violation of the exclusive benefit rule to set the decision aside. As a practical matter, considering the conflict of interest as a factor when conducting abuse-of-discretion review might mean (as in administrative law) that the reviewing court should look to evidence that is outside the decision file compiled by the fiduciary (the usual "record" on review) to uncover improprieties, or draw adverse inferences from procedural irregularities.[63] The fiduciary's contemporaneous explanation of the claim denial, if incomplete or unconvincing in light of the record evidence (physicians' reports concerning disability, for example), would similarly raise or reinforce suspicions.[64] The administrative law analogy, while suggestive, opens up other nettlesome questions, like whether a reviewing court which finds a benefit denial to have been an abuse of discretion should simply remand the claim to the fiduciary under instructions to decide again, this time giving no weight to cost considerations.

---

61   *E.g.*, Motor Vehicle Mfrs. Ass'n v. State Farm Mut. Auto. Ins. Co., 463 U.S. 29, 43 (1983) ("Normally, an agency rule would be arbitrary and capricious if the agency has relied on factors which Congress has not intended it to consider, entirely failed to consider an important aspect of the problem, offered an explanation for its decision that runs counter to the evidence before the agency, or is so implausible that it could not be ascribed to a difference in view or the product of agency expertise."). The administrative law analogy to the problem discussed here is "hard look" review (also known as review for reasoned decision making) under the abuse-of-discretion standard. *See generally* 1 RICHARD J. PIERCE, JR., ADMINISTRATIVE LAW TREATISE § 7.4 (4th ed. 2002), 2 *id.* § 11.4; ERNEST GELLHORN & RONALD M. LEVIN, ADMINISTRATIVE LAW AND PROCESS IN A NUTSHELL 102–07, 116–19 (5th ed. 2006).

62   Recall that a potentially compromising position does not automatically transgress the fiduciary's duty, for ERISA's exclusive benefit rule demands only subjective loyalty. *See supra* Chapter 4B.

63   *E.g.*, Denmark v. Liberty Life Assur. Co., 566 F.3d 1, 10 (1st Cir. 2009) ("The majority opinion in *Glenn* fairly can be read as contemplating some discovery on the issue of whether a structural conflict has morphed into an actual conflict."); Burke v. Pitney Bowes Inc. Long-Term Disability Plan, 544 F.3d 1016, 1028 (9th Cir. 2008) (district court may "consider evidence outside the administrative record to decide the nature, extent, and effect on the decision-making process of any conflict of interest" (quoting Abatie v. Alta Health & Life Ins. Co., 458 F.3d 955, 970 (9th Cir. 2006))).

64   *E.g.*, Pinto v. Reliance Std. Life Ins. Co., 214 F.3d 377, 393–95 (3d Cir. 2000) (in case of structural conflict, court looks to process by which result was achieved, and may draw negative inference from unexplained inconsistent treatment of apparently similar facts, and unexplained selectivity in use of expert evidence; district court may take evidence regarding conflict of interest).

C. CAUSES OF ACTION

ERISA authorizes three private civil enforcement actions. First, a plan participant or beneficiary may bring a claim to recover benefits due under the plan or to clarify his rights to future benefits under the plan. Second, the Secretary of Labor or a participant, beneficiary, or fiduciary may bring an action for damages or for equitable relief to enforce ERISA's fiduciary obligations. Third, a participant, beneficiary, or fiduciary may bring an action "(A) to enjoin any act or practice which violates any provision of this title or the terms of the plan, or (B) to obtain appropriate equitable relief (i) to redress such violations or (ii) to enforce any provision of this title or the terms of the plan."[65]

The Supreme Court has stressed that ERISA's "carefully integrated civil enforcement provisions" form an "interlocking, interrelated and interdependent remedial scheme" that provides "strong evidence that Congress did *not* intend to authorize other remedies that it simply forgot to incorporate expressly."[66] Consequently, the Court has rejected arguments that the statutory enforcement scheme should be supplemented with implied private rights of action. "We are reluctant to tamper with an enforcement scheme crafted with such evident care as the one in ERISA."[67] Because it was intended to be comprehensive, ERISA's enforcement mechanism has exceptional preemptive force, superseding related state law causes of action.

> In sum, the detailed provisions of § 502(a) set forth a comprehensive civil enforcement scheme that represents a careful balancing of the need for prompt and fair claims settlement procedures against the public interest in encouraging the formation of employee benefit plans. The policy choices reflected in the inclusion of certain remedies and the exclusion of others under the federal scheme would be completely undermined if ERISA-plan participants and beneficiaries were free to obtain remedies under state law that Congress rejected in ERISA.[68]

Accordingly, the actions authorized by ERISA § 502(a) provide the *exclusive* means for vindicating private rights under employee benefit plans.

The scope of two of the three private enforcement actions is clear: the claim for benefits, ERISA § 502(a)(1), amounts to a federal law contract claim, while ERISA § 502(a)(2) authorizes plan-based relief for breach of fiduciary obligations.[69] The third claim, for equitable enforcement of ERISA or the terms of the plan, ERISA § 502(a)(3), is the most expansive, and has been the foundation for novel theories of liability.

---

65   ERISA § 502(a)(3), 29 U.S.C. § 1132(a)(3) (2006).
66   Mass. Mut. Life Ins. Co. v. Russell, 473 U.S. 134, 146 (1985).
67   *Id.* at 147.
68   Pilot Life Ins. Co. v. Dedeaux, 481 U.S. 41, 54 (1987). *Accord* Ingersoll-Rand Co. v. McClendon, 498 U.S. 133, 144 (1990).
69   *See infra* Chapter 5 note 103.

Fraud and Misrepresentation

Curiously, ERISA calls into question the existence and extent of fraud liability for misrepresentations involving employee benefit plans. The statute, by its terms, contains no federal antifraud rule; it limits the federal courts' authority to apply traditional legal remedies,[70] and it expressly preempts state law, including common-law actions for fraud and deceit.[71] Yet ERISA's disclosure provisions are designed to promote better career and financial planning by giving workers access to important information about plan terms and finances. To increase efficiency through improved decision making, the information disseminated must be correct. Participants who have been misled by inaccurate or incomplete SPDs have sought relief by bringing estoppel claims under section 502(a)(3).[72] That provision is also the authority for *individual* relief against a fiduciary who, whether through disloyalty or neglect, misrepresents material facts relating to an employee benefit plan.[73]

Participation in a Fiduciary Breach

Section 502(a)(2), by virtue of its cross-reference to section 409, allows enforcement of ERISA's fiduciary responsibility provisions against fiduciaries alone. In contrast, ERISA's equitable enforcement provision, section 502(a)(3), authorizes equitable relief to redress statutory violations without restricting permissible defendants. For a time, reliance on section 502(a)(3) as the source of nonfiduciary liability for knowing participation in a breach of fiduciary obligations was scotched by *Mertens v. Hewitt Associates*[74]

> [W]hile ERISA contains various provisions that can be read as imposing obligations upon nonfiduciaries, including actuaries, no provision explicitly requires them to avoid participation (knowing or unknowing) in a fiduciary's breach of fiduciary duty. It is unlikely, moreover, that this was an oversight, since ERISA does explicitly impose "knowing participation" liability on cofiduciaries. That limitation appears all the more deliberate in light of the fact that "knowing participation" liability on the part of *both* cotrustees *and* third persons was well established under the common law of trusts.[75]

Although these observations were dicta, after *Mertens*, the lower courts dutifully rejected claims against third parties allegedly involved in breach of fiduciary duties imposed by section 404.[76]

---

70   *See infra* Chapter 5D.
71   ERISA § 514(a), (c), 29 U.S.C. § 1144(a), (c) (2006) (preemption includes state decisional law).
72   *See supra* Chapter 3B.
73   *See supra* Chapter 3D.
74   508 U.S. 248, 254 (1993).
75   *Id.* at 253–54 (dictum) (citations and footnote omitted).
76   *E.g.*, Reich v. Rowe, 20 F.3d 25, 30–33 (1st Cir. 1994) ("[J]udicial remedies for nonfiduciary participation in a fiduciary breach fall within the line of cases where Congress deliberately omitted a potential cause of action rather than the cases where Congress has invited the courts

Claims against nonfiduciaries for participation in a prohibited transaction, however, continued to be treated by the courts of appeals as authorized by ERISA § 502(a)(3).[77] Inasmuch as the prohibited-transaction rules, like general fiduciary duties, impose obligations only on fiduciaries, the distinction is not very convincing.[78] In *Harris Trust & Savings Bank v. Salomon Smith Barney, Inc.*,[79] the Supreme Court held that a nonfiduciary party in interest who knowingly participates in a prohibited transaction can be called to account under section 502(a)(3). Although the duty to avoid prohibited transactions is imposed by section 406 on the fiduciary, and not on the party in interest with whom the fiduciary deals, the Court concluded that section 502(a)(3)—which does not restrict the range of possible defendants—itself imposes an obligation on persons dealing with a fiduciary to refrain from knowingly participating in a violation of ERISA.[80] The Court's reasoning, moreover, was not limited to parties in interest involved in prohibited transactions. The analysis seems to extend with equal force to any person who knows or should know that he is engaging in a transaction that is a breach of fiduciary duty or otherwise violates ERISA.[81]

Wrongful Discharge and Retaliation

Section 510[82] protects participants and beneficiaries from dismissal and other adverse employment actions taken to discourage or prevent them from gaining or asserting rights under an employee benefit plan. In many respects, it is the linchpin of the whole matrix of federal pension and welfare benefit protections. Most American workers are employees at-will. In this environment, assurances of benefit program integrity (conduct controls) and mandatory minimum standards (content controls) by themselves have little meaning, for the employer can dissuade workers from asserting

---

to engage in interstitial lawmaking."); Reich v. Cont'l Cas. Co., 33 F.3d 754, 757 (7th Cir. 1994); Reich v. Compton, 57 F.3d 270, 284 (3d Cir. 1995); Reich v. Stangl, 73 F.3d 1027, 1034 (10th Cir. 1996).

77   *E.g.*, Reich v. Compton, 57 F.3d at 287 (imposing liability on nonfiduciary involved in prohibited transaction even though he was *not* a party in interest); Landwehr v. DuPree, 72 F.3d 726, 734 (9th Cir. 1995); Reich v. Stangl, 73 F.3d at 1032; LeBlanc v. Cahill, 153 F.3d 134, 152–53 (4th Cir. 1998); Herman v. S.C. Nat'l Bank, 140 F.3d 1413, 1421–22 (11th Cir. 1998).

78   *Compare* ERISA § 406, 29 U.S.C. § 1106 (2006), *with* ERISA § 404(a)(1), 29 U.S.C. § 1104(a)(1) (2006).

79   530 U.S. 238 (2000).

80   *Id.* at 245–49.

81   *Id.* at 248–51. The *Harris Trust* rationale would apparently also allow suit to be brought under ERISA § 502(a)(3) to recover plan assets from a transferee who was *not* a purchaser for value, even if the transferee had no reason to know of the fiduciary's breach. The Supreme Court suggested that section 502(a)(3) would authorize recovery of a gratuitous transfer of plan assets from an innocent recipient. *Id.* at 251 & n.3. This position reflects the traditional trust pursuit rule, under which property transferred in breach of trust may be recovered from any recipient other than a bona fide purchaser. *See* RESTATEMENT (SECOND) OF TRUSTS §§ 289, 292 (1959); 4 SCOTT ON TRUSTS, *supra* Chapter 3 note 11, §§ 289, 292.

82   ERISA § 510, 29 U.S.C. § 1140 (2006).

benefit rights by holding the paycheck hostage.[83] The federal cause of action for wrongful discharge or retaliation, however, is not independently enforceable; wrongful discharge or retaliation can only be vindicated under section 502.[84] As a result, relief for a violation of section 510 is limited to equitable remedies under section 502(a)(3), such as an injunction ordering reinstatement.

Two elements are necessary to support an action under ERISA § 510. The worker must have suffered some type of adverse employment action, and that detriment must have been imposed for an improper purpose. Each component of the claim presents important interpretive issues. Section 510 makes it unlawful to "discharge, fine, suspend, expel, discipline, or discriminate against a participant or beneficiary." Clearly, "discriminate against" is a catchall provision, intended to outlaw unfavorable changes in the terms and conditions of employment not otherwise specifically enumerated, including, for example, demotion, transfer, or loss of seniority. Could a change in the employee benefit plan itself constitute such discrimination? If health care costs become too high, does an employer "discriminate against" participants for exercising their rights (overutilization, to the employer's way of thinking) when it amends the plan to reduce benefits? Several courts have held that section 510 does not extend to detrimental alterations of pension and welfare plans.[85]

A showing of specific intent to retaliate or interfere with protected rights is the second element of a cause of action under ERISA § 510. Direct evidence of an unlawful purpose (e.g., a supervisor's statement that the worker is being fired or demoted for claiming benefits) is rarely available. Accordingly, unlawful intent must be shown by circumstantial evidence, and courts applying section 510 have looked to cases under Title VII of the Civil Rights Act for guidance in allocating the burden of producing evidence of discriminatory intent. Using the Title VII approach, the plaintiff must make out a prima facie case of unlawful interference by showing that he has rights protected by ERISA, that he is qualified for his position, and that the circumstances of the adverse employment action give rise to an inference of discrimination. If the prima facie case is established, then the burden shifts to the defendant to articulate some legitimate, nondiscriminatory reason for the adverse action. If the employer offers such a reason, the plaintiff must be given an opportunity to prove that the asserted

---

83   ERISA § 510 is one of a number of statutes that make limited inroads on the employment-at-will doctrine in order to safeguard employees in the exercise of federal employment rights. Other examples include the noninterference provisions of the Fair Labor Standards Act, 29 U.S.C. § 215(a)(3) (2006), and the Occupational Safety and Health Act, 29 U.S.C. 660(c) (2006). Similarly, a variety of federal and state "whistleblary" statutes protect employees from retaliation for reporting certain illegal employer conduct.

84   ERISA § 510, 29 U.S.C. § 1140 (2006) (final sentence).

85   *E.g.*, McGath v. Auto-Body N. Shore, Inc., 7 F.3d 665, 668 (7th Cir. 1993); Haberern v. Kaupp Vascular Surgeons Ltd. Defined Benefit Pension Plan, 24 F.3d 1491, 1502–04 (3d Cir. 1994). *See also* McGann v. H & H Music Co., 946 F.2d 401, 407–08 (5th Cir. 1991) (questioning whether a change in plan terms can constitute illegal discrimination under section 510). *See infra* text accompanying Chapter 5 note 92.

reason was not the true basis for the adverse action, but was rather a pretext for unlawful interference.[86]

Section 510 bars both retaliation for "exercising any right to which [the participant or beneficiary] is entitled" and "interfering with the attainment of any right to which such participant *may become* entitled." The scope of the latter prohibition is unclear. At its core, it was intended to prohibit employee dismissals to avoid vesting, and many cases so hold. For example, in *Gavalik v. Continental Can Co.*,[87] the defendant was found to have systematically reduced its workforce by laying off employees whose pensions were close to vesting and ultimately paid $415 million to settle the class action.[88] Yet the indefinite and future-sounding language of section 510 is susceptible to an interpretation that would go far beyond vesting, to protect much more inchoate rights—for example, the right to accrue future benefits.

Inter-Modal Rail Employees Association v. Atchison, Topeka and Santa Fe Railway Co.[89] presented the question whether the subjunctive language of section 510 (i.e., "any right to which such participant may become entitled under the plan") refers only to rights capable of vesting. The case involved unionized employees of a Santa Fe Railway subsidiary who were terminated en masse when the railway decided to contract out the rail-to-truck cargo transfer work previously performed by the subsidiary. Many of the workers were kept on by the successful bidder, but that company provided less generous pension and welfare benefits than the Santa Fe subsidiary. The workers brought suit under section 510, claiming that their termination was motivated by the railway's desire to reduce benefit costs by preventing the workers from claiming the higher pension and welfare benefits provided under the subsidiary's benefit plans.

The Ninth Circuit held that section 510 prohibits acts intended to prevent a pension from vesting, but does not authorize a cause of action for interference with welfare benefits because ERISA does not require vesting under welfare plans. The Supreme Court reversed, holding that section 510 also protects certain rights under welfare plans even though they are not subject to vesting. The Court based its conclusion on the plain meaning of the statutory language, which applies to any "employee benefit plan," not just pension plans, and to "any right," not just nonforfeitable rights.[90] The employer argued that its acknowledged right to amend or terminate a welfare plan is incompatible with a broad reading of section 510—after all, there is no need to fire employees to control benefit costs if the sponsor remains free to fire (amend or terminate) the plan. The Court disagreed, noting that ERISA requires that a plan provide a procedure for amendment, and that "[t]he formal amendment process would be undermined if § 510 did not apply because employers could 'informally' amend their plans one participant at a time."[91] Accordingly, when the employer wants to reduce benefit

---

86   *E.g.*, Dister v. Cont'l Group, Inc., 859 F.2d 1108, 1111–15 (2d Cir. 1988).

87   812 F.2d 834 (3d Cir. 1987).

88   18 Pens. Rep. (BNA) 8 (1991).

89   520 U.S. 510 (1997).

90   *Id.* at 514–15.

91   *Id.* at 516.

costs, it must own up to the fact and do so explicitly by invoking the plan amendment process.

This process-oriented analysis supports the view that a detrimental plan amendment cannot constitute forbidden "discrimination" within the meaning of section 510. If the noninterference provision forces benefit cutbacks out in the open and ensures that appropriate safeguards apply, then an employer's use of the plan amendment process cannot be a violation.[92] This view of the role of section 510 is consistent with the "apparent authority" approach to determining the effectiveness of informal plan amendments that was proposed earlier in connection with disclosure claims.[93] In each case, worker understanding of the change would be the touchstone of validity: if the employer leads participants to reasonably understand that a change has been made, the company cannot later disavow it, nor can an actual change in employment practices work a secret amendment.

As a last resort, the employer in *Inter-Modal Rail* argued that if section 510 applies to welfare plans, it "only protects the employee's right to cross the 'threshold of eligibility,' for welfare benefits."[94] An employee who is eligible to receive benefits, the argument goes, has already attained her rights (i.e., "become entitled") under the plan, and section 510 has spent its force. The Supreme Court remanded the case for consideration of that question, leaving unresolved the scope of welfare plan rights protected by section 510. For two reasons, the proffered distinction between initial eligibility (plan membership) and the ongoing right to earn benefits (benefit accrual) does not sit well with the Court's focus on the plain meaning of the statute. First, section 510 protects "any right," not just plan membership and vesting. Second, section 510 never applies at all until a worker becomes a "participant," at which point the "threshold of eligibility" for a welfare plan has already been crossed.[95] More important, the proposition that section 510 protects the integrity of the plan amendment process, preventing covert cutbacks, compels the conclusion that its strictures extend beyond satisfaction of membership conditions.

D. REMEDIES

In addition to specifying the forms that civil enforcement actions must take and the persons with standing to institute them, section 502(a) also limits the relief available under ERISA. These limits have been a major focus of litigation since the statute's enactment. A series of Supreme Court decisions between 1985 and 1996 clarified ERISA's remedial restrictions. In effect, the Court announced that ERISA does not

---

92 Nor is there a violation of the duty of loyalty, because the amendment of an employee benefit plan is not a fiduciary act. Curtiss-Wright Corp. v. Schoonejongen, 514 U.S. 73, 98 (1995) (welfare plan); Lockheed Corp. v. Spink, 517 U.S. 882, 891 (1996) (pension plan). *See supra* text accompanying Chapter 4 notes 18–24.

93 *See supra* Chapter 3C.

94 *Inter-Modal Rail*, 520 U.S. at 516.

95 ERISA § 3(7), 29 U.S.C. § 1002(7) (2006); 29 C.F.R. § 2510.3-3(d)(1)(i)(B) (2009).

provide complete relief to injured workers and was never intended to do so, despite ERISA's declaration of policy to "protect . . . the interests of participants in employee benefit plans and their beneficiaries, by . . . providing for appropriate remedies, sanctions, and ready access to the Federal courts."[96] "Appropriate" remedies are defined by reference to ERISA's distributive norms and the reality that employers are not required to provide welfare or pension benefits to their workers.[97] Nevertheless, the balance struck in the 93rd Congress is open to revision and may be remade in the context of health care reform legislation.

Tort-Like Damages

In addition to financial hardship, wrongful delay or denial of benefits can cause emotional distress, and in the case of medical care, even permanent injury or death. Tort-like consequential damages (such as awards for pain and suffering, for lost earning capacity, or for wrongful death) are not recoverable in employee benefits cases, nor are punitive damages. The claim for benefits sounds in contract, and so has never been conceived as authorizing the imposition of tort-like "extracontractual" damages.[98] In *Massachusetts Mutual Life Insurance Co. v. Russell*[99] the Court refused to recognize an implied private right of action for emotional distress or punitive damages based on improper processing of benefit claims. The Court was "reluctant to tamper with an enforcement scheme crafted with such evident care as the one in ERISA" because, "[i]n contrast to the repeatedly emphasized purpose to protect contractually defined benefits, there is a stark absence—in the statute itself and in its legislative history—of any reference to an intention to authorize the recovery of extracontractual damages."[100]

The Court later extended this principle, holding that a state tort action for bad-faith insurance claims handling is incompatible with section 502's remedial scheme and therefore preempted, even though the case involved an insured plan and ERISA exempts state laws regulating insurance from preemption.[101] The Court set aside an award of emotional distress and punitive damages, finding that Congress clearly expressed an intent that the civil enforcement provisions of ERISA § 502(a) be exclusive.[102]

Accepting that section 502(a) establishes a civil enforcement mechanism that is not to be supplemented by either federal common law or state law, section 502(a) expressly authorizes suit in cases of fiduciary misconduct. A corrupt or incompetent denial of

---

96   ERISA § 2(b), 29 U.S.C. § 1001(b) (2006).

97   *See supra* Chapter 1C.

98   *See* Mass. Mut. Life Ins. Co. v. Russell, 473 U.S. 134, 144 (1985) (the claim for benefits, ERISA § 502(a)(1)(B), "says nothing about the recovery of extracontractual damages, or about the possible consequences of delay in the plan administrators' processing of a disputed claim").

99   473 U.S. at 145–48.

100 *Id.* at 147, 148.

101 Pilot Life Ins. Co. v. Dedeaux, 481 U.S. 41, 57 (1987).

102 *Id.* at 52, 57; *see supra* Chapter 5 notes 66–68 and accompanying text.

benefits (in contrast to a merely mistaken one) implicates fiduciary liability. (Eligibility decisions, or the factual determinations on which they depend, are fiduciary functions because they are discretionary.) For two reasons, a participant or beneficiary cannot recover tort-type damages where the denial of benefits is a breach of fiduciary duty. First, section 502(a)(2), by virtue of its reliance on section 409, safeguards plan assets. While it clearly authorizes monetary awards *to the plan*, it does not offer a remedy for collateral injuries sustained by individual participants and beneficiaries as a result of a fiduciary breach.[103] Second, remedies under section 502(a)(3), which can run in favor of particular individuals rather than to the plan as a whole,[104] are limited to "appropriate equitable relief," which means, according to the Court in *Mertens v. Hewitt Associates*, remedies "*typically* available in equity (such as injunction, mandamus and restitution, but not compensatory damages)."[105] Therefore, although wrongful denial of benefits may be a breach of fiduciary duty and may cause serious harm—including emotional distress, permanent physical impairment, disease, or even death—ERISA offers no redress for such injuries.

Equitable Relief

Still to be considered is the nature of "appropriate equitable relief" that is available to participants and beneficiaries under ERISA § 502(a)(3). The *Mertens* opinion explained that "'[e]quitable' relief must mean *something* less than *all* relief."[106] The distinction between money damages, "the classic form of *legal* relief," and "those categories of relief that were *typically* available in equity" formed the touchstone of the Court's decision.[107] To make that distinction meaningful, an injunction to compel the payment of money due under the plan, or an order for specific performance of a payment obligation, must be treated as money damages in substance. While an injunction is an equitable remedy in form, such monetary relief was not *typically* available in equity, and so it cannot be awarded under section 502(a)(3).[108]

Monetary recoveries could sometimes be had in equity via an order of restitution,[109] but restitution is a remedy with both legal and equitable antecedents. *Great-West Life & Annuity Insurance Co. v. Knudson*[110] presented the question whether restitution is

---

103   LaRue v. DeWolff, Boberg & Assocs., 552 U.S. 248, ___, 128 S. Ct. 1020, 1026 (2008) (holding that "although § 502(a)(2) does not provide a remedy for individual injuries distinct from plan injuries, that provision does authorize recovery for fiduciary breaches that impair the value of plan assets in a participant's individual account"); *Russell*, 473 U.S. at 142, 144.

104   Varity Corp. v. Howe, 516 U.S. 489, 507–15 (1996) (rejecting the argument, based on *Russell*, that fiduciary obligations are enforceable only under ERISA §§ 502(a)(2) and 409).

105   508 U.S. 248, 256 (1993).

106   *Id.* at 258 n.8.

107   *Id.* at 255, 256.

108   Great-West Life & Annuity Ins. Co. v. Knudson, 534 U.S. 204, 210–11 (2002).

109   *Mertens*, 508 U.S. at 256; Harris Trust and Sav. Bank v. Salomon Smith Barney, Inc., 530 U.S. 238, 253 (2000).

110   534 U.S. 204 (2002).

"appropriate equitable relief" under section 502(a)(3). The case involved a suit to enforce the reimbursement provision of a health care plan, which gave the plan the right to receive the amount of any medical benefits paid by the plan that the beneficiary recovers from a third party. The plan covered about $41,000 of the medical expenses of the respondent, who became a quadriplegic as a result of an automobile accident. The negotiated settlement of her tort suit allocated almost the entire $650,000 settlement to a trust for future medical expenses and to attorneys' fees. Less than $14,000 was designated as attributable to past medical expenses subject to the plan's reimbursement rights.[111] The petitioner, the plan's stop-loss insurer and assignee of the plan's reimbursement rights, brought suit in federal court under ERISA § 502(a)(3) seeking reimbursement of the full amount of covered medical expenses.[112] The Supreme Court held that section 502(a)(3) authorizes restitution only if the relief sought corresponds to the form of restitution traditionally available in equity.[113] Such equitable restitution transfers (via a constructive trust or equitable lien) particular property or identifiable proceeds in the defendant's possession to a plaintiff who is judged the equitable owner of those specific funds. Legal restitution, in contrast, imposes personal liability to pay for benefits conferred by the plaintiff, benefits that cannot be traced to identifiable funds in the defendant's hands (for example, where the benefit was services performed by plaintiff, or where money or property obtained from plaintiff has been dissipated).[114] Because the proceeds of the tort settlement in *Knudson* were not paid to the plan beneficiary, the suit did not seek the recovery of specific property, and as a claim for legal restitution, it was not authorized by ERISA's equitable relief provision.[115]

In 2006, the Court revisited the issue whether a suit to enforce the reimbursement provision of a health care plan seeks "appropriate equitable relief" under section 502(a)(3). *Sereboff v. Mid Atlantic Medical Services, Inc.*[116] involved facts very similar to *Knudson*, except that the proceeds of the tort settlement from which the fiduciary sought reimbursement were distributed to the plan beneficiaries on whom the plan imposed the reimbursement obligation. Consequently, the administrator's action sought recovery via the imposition of "a constructive trust or equitable lien on a specifically identified fund, not from the Sereboffs' assets generally, as would be the case with a contract action at law."[117] The settlement fund, however, was created after Sereboff became a participant subject to the reimbursement provision, and the Sereboffs argued that equitable restitution required that the funds sought be traceable to an asset in existence at the time the contract was made.[118] The Court distinguished equitable restitution from an equitable lien by agreement and relied on prior case law to hold that "the fund over which a lien is asserted need not be in existence when the contract

---

111   *Id.* at 207–08.
112   *Id.* at 208.
113   *Id.* at 218.
114   *Id.* at 213–14.
115   *Id.* at 214.
116   547 U.S. 356 (2006).
117   *Id.* at 363.
118   *Id.* at 364–65.

containing the lien provision is executed."[119] Accordingly, the plan administrator's action sought equitable relief under section 502(a)(3), the enforcement of an equitable lien by agreement, even if that relief would not be classified as equitable restitution.

The line between legal and equitable restitution has tremendous practical importance for claims based upon interference with ERISA-protected rights under section 510. Clearly, a court can order reinstatement of an unlawfully terminated employee. But can an award of back pay accompany reinstatement? Payment of lost wages does not return a specific item in which plaintiff owned an interest. Instead, back pay looks more like ordinary contract damages, classic legal relief. Viewed in that light, back pay awards are apparently beyond the remedial power of the federal courts in ERISA § 510 cases.[120]

A group life insurance plan participant in *Callery v. U.S. Life Insurance Co.*[121] continued to pay premiums for $100,000 of insurance on the life of her husband after their divorce. Upon the husband's death, the plan insurer denied liability and refunded the premiums because the policy excluded divorced spouses from eligibility for coverage. The participant brought suit against her employer for failure to provide an SPD and for breach of fiduciary duty in failing to notify her of the coverage exclusion, and she sought $100,000 as equitable relief under section 502(a)(3).[122] Relying on *Mertens* and *Knudson*, the Tenth Circuit concluded that an award of the face amount of the life insurance was not equitable restitution and so was not available under section 502(a)(3).[123] The court declined the invitation of the Secretary of Labor, as amicus curiae, to distinguish *Mertens* and *Knudson* as cases seeking compensation from a nonfiduciary, and refused to hold that broader monetary remedies are "appropriate equitable relief" against a breaching fiduciary.[124]

Policy—ERISA's Remedial Balance

LaRue v. DeWolff, Boberg & Associates[125] illustrates the interaction of ERISA's remedial mechanisms. There, a 401(k) plan participant sued the fiduciary under section 502(a)(3) for failure to follow his investment directions, seeking compensation for the additional value his account would have had if his instructions had been properly executed. As the additional value had never been realized by the fiduciary, there was no misappropriated fund to serve as a basis for equitable restitution. In pre-merger equity courts, profits that a trust beneficiary would have made but for a breach of trust

---

119   *Id.* at 366.
120   *See Knudson*, 534 U.S. at 218 n.4 (disputing dissenting opinion's assertion that Congress treated back pay in employment discrimination cases as a form of equitable relief); Dana M. Muir, *ERISA Remedies: Chimera or Congressional Compromise*, 81 Iowa L. Rev. 1, 37–38 (1995).
121   392 F.3d 401 (10th Cir. 2004).
122   ERISA § 502(a)(3), 29 U.S.C. § 1132(a)(3) (2006).
123   *Callery*, 392 F.3d at 406.
124   *Id.* at 409.
125   552 U.S. 248, 128 S. Ct. 1020 (2008).

were recoverable (a remedy known as surcharge).[126] The Fourth Circuit "rejected the notion that whether a particular form of relief is 'equitable' depends on the identity of the parties" (i.e., whether the defendant is a breaching fiduciary) and dismissed the claim as seeking money damages.[127] Under a defined benefit plan, lost profits attributable to a fiduciary breach affect funding, potentially impacting all participants, and therefore a claim for plan-based relief lies under sections 502(a)(2) and 409. In contrast, fiduciary mistakes under participant-directed defined contribution plans often impact only one individual, which presents the question whether restoring a single participant's account to the balance it should have attained is authorized by sections 502(a)(2) and 409 as make-whole relief "to the plan." In *LaRue*, the Fourth Circuit also concluded that such particularized recovery is not within the ambit of section 502(a)(2).[128]

The Supreme Court unanimously reversed the Fourth Circuit's decision in *LaRue*, holding that "although § 502(a)(2) does not provide a remedy for individual injuries distinct from plan injuries, that provision does authorize recovery for fiduciary breaches that impair the value of plan assets in a participant's individual account."[129] The Court declined to address the question of the availability of the surcharge remedy as "appropriate equitable relief" under section 502(a)(3) despite having granted certiorari on the issue.[130] A concurring opinion explored a third possibility: that LaRue might have framed his complaint as a claim for benefits under section 502(a)(1)(B), in which case the remedy sought (lost profits) would conform nicely to a cause of action that corresponds to breach of contract. If such a claim for benefits is cognizable, the concurring justices suggested that it might preclude a claim for breach of fiduciary duty under sections 502(a)(2) and 409. Otherwise, artful drafting might circumvent important limitations on a claim for benefits, including the requirement of exhaustion of administrative remedies and a limited scope of review.[131]

---

126   RESTATEMENT (SECOND) OF TRUSTS §§ 205(c) & cmt. i, 211 (1959).

127   LaRue v. DeWolff Boberg & Assocs., 450 F.3d 570 (4th Cir. 2006), *rev'd*, 552 U.S. 248, 128 S. Ct. 1020 (2008).

128   450 F.3d at 574.

129   *LaRue*, 128 S. Ct. at 1026 (2008).

130   *Id.* at 1023.

131   *Id.* at 1027 (Roberts, C.J., concurring). Whether redress for a fiduciary breach like that alleged in *LaRue* could actually be obtained via a suit for benefits under section 502(a)(1)(B) is an open question (as Chief Justice Roberts conceded). Typically, an action to recover benefits due is brought against the plan or the person who controls administration of the plan. ABA SECTION OF LABOR AND EMPLOYMENT LAW, EMPLOYEE BENEFITS LAW 746–49 (2d ed. Supp. 2007). A defined contribution plan, however, ordinarily has no assets that are not allocated to individual accounts, which makes enforcement of a money judgment against the plan problematic, as it threatens to deprive other participants of their benefits. This obstacle might be avoided by holding that a fiduciary who is alleged to have caused a shortfall in a defined contribution plan account is a proper defendant and may be held personally liable for breach of fiduciary duty in a suit brought by the participant under section 502(a)(1)(B) to "enforce his rights under the terms of the plan." *See* ERISA § 502(d)(2), 29 U.S.C. § 1132(d)(2) (2006) (money judgment against a plan enforceable only against the plan as an entity or a person held liable in his individual capacity).

ERISA's civil enforcement section has been interpreted to provide a comprehensive specification of the persons entitled to bring suit, the causes of action that are available to them, and the relief that can be granted. The statute's broad preemption of state law ensures that injured claimants have nowhere else to turn.[132] Yet the conclusion that section 502(a) is the exclusive means of vindicating workers' benefit rights means that many glaring injuries go uncompensated: participants and beneficiaries can recover benefits wrongly withheld, but not consequential damages. An erroneous denial of health care benefits can cause permanent injury or death, attended by mental anguish, pain, suffering, and loss of income, for both the patient and dependent family members, but none of these injuries are redressable under ERISA. As currently interpreted, only two monetary remedies are authorized: the suit for benefits (section 502(a)(1)(B)) and plan-based relief for breach of fiduciary duty (sections 502(a)(2) and 409).[133] The catchall enforcement provision, section 502(a)(3), authorizes only "appropriate equitable relief," not money damages.[134]

The Supreme Court asserts that this result is the product of a deliberate congressional compromise between competing objectives. As noted above, the Court says section 502(a) "represents a careful balancing of the need for prompt and fair claims settlement procedures against the public interest in encouraging the formation of employee benefit plans."[135] The fear is that the large and unpredictable damage awards characteristic of tort-type relief might discourage employer sponsorship, with the result that full compensation would come at the cost of restricted coverage. Congress, in short, decided to promote widespread worker access to benefits at the expense of the

---

132 ERISA § 514, 29 U.S.C. § 1144 (2006), discussed *infra* Chapter 6. The preemptive force of ERISA is at its greatest under section 502(a)—it so completely displaces state law actions to enforce rights under employee benefit plans that any such action is removable to federal court, even if the complaint makes no reference to federal law. Metro. Life Ins. Co. v. Taylor, 481 U.S. 58 (1987) (complete preemption exception to well-pleaded complaint rule applies to actions to enforce employee benefit plans because ERISA § 502(a) was modeled on section 301 of the Labor-Management Relations Act of 1947).

133 Plan-based relief under section 502(a)(2) need not inure to the benefit of all plan participants and beneficiaries. That provision also "authorize[s] recovery for fiduciary breaches that impair the value of plan assets in participant's individual account" under a defined contribution plan. *LaRue*, 552 U.S. at ___, 128 S. Ct. at 1026.

134 Varity Corp. v. Howe, 516 U.S. 489, 511–12 (1996) (ERISA § 502(a)(2) reflects special congressional concern with asset management, but that is not inconsistent with an intent to make individual relief for breach of fiduciary duty available under section 502(a)(3), which was designed to serve as a catchall safety net); *see* Great-West Life & Annuity Ins. Co. v. Knudson, 534 U.S. 204, 221 (2002) ("We will not attempt to adjust the 'carefully crafted and detailed enforcement scheme' embodied in the text that Congress has adopted." (quoting Mertens v. Hewitt Assocs., 508 U.S. 248, 254 (1993)). *But see* Great-West Life & Annuity Ins. Co. v. Knudson, 534 U.S. 204, 234 (2002) (Ginsburg, J., dissenting) ("[I]n my view Congress cannot plausibly be said to have 'carefully crafted' such confusion."); Aetna Health Inc. v. Davila, 542 U.S. 200, 223 (2004) (Ginsburg, J., concurring) ("[F]resh consideration of the availability of consequential damages under § 502(a)(3) is plainly in order.") (citing with approval John Langbein, *What ERISA Means by "Equitable": The Supreme Court's Trail of Error in Russell, Mertens, and Great West*, 103 Colum. L. Rev. 1317 (2003)).

135 Pilot Life Ins. Co. v. Dedeaux, 481 U.S. 41, 54 (1987).

ERISA: PRINCIPLES OF EMPLOYEE BENEFIT LAW

injured few. In recent years, however, ERISA's enforcement scheme has become entangled in the public policy debate over health care reform, which may force Congress to reappraise the remedial balance that it struck in 1974.

E. CONCLUSION

In the main, courts have applied ERISA's enforcement apparatus narrowly, insisting on strict adherence to the statutory wording. That interpretive approach is premised on the assumption that Congress supplied a meticulously crafted, comprehensive response to statutory and plan transgressions. Wish as one might for a studied balance between competing interests, the reality is that ERISA's compliance kit is haphazard and incomplete. The defects become apparent upon examination of the primary limitations on participants' ability to obtain complete relief for violations of the plan or ERISA.

Congress wisely placed primary enforcement responsibility in the hands of interested private parties, relying most importantly on plan participants. While generally sound, that decision is marred by two defects. First, defined benefit plan participants have little incentive to monitor and enforce fiduciary obligations because the sponsor's liability to correct underfunding, backstopped by the PBGC insurance system, largely insulates workers from losses resulting from fiduciary misconduct. Neither the plan sponsor nor the PBGC—the real stakeholders—were given standing to sue, however. Second, the statute's definition of participant, "any employee or former employee . . . who is or may become eligible to receive a benefit," provides little guidance with respect to former employees who lose coverage upon separation from service. Where an outgoing employee alleges that his departure was occasioned by a violation of ERISA, or that the defined contribution account balance distributed to him was insufficient due to a fiduciary breach, the courts now generally allow the suit to go forward.

Every employee benefit plan must have a claims procedure, including a mechanism for review of benefit denials by the appropriate fiduciary (plan-level appeal). A disappointed claimant can seek relief in court, yet the statute is silent on the intensity of judicial scrutiny of the fiduciary's decision. Where the plan gives the fiduciary discretion to determine benefit eligibility or interpret the plan, those questions are decided using a deferential scope of review. Even where the claim is denied by a fiduciary acting under a conflict of interest, divided loyalty does not trigger de novo or some other heightened standard of review. The Supreme Court insists that the conflict is merely to be weighed as one factor in an overall abuse-of-discretion calculus, without recourse to special procedural, evidentiary, or burden-of-proof rules. While the presence of a conflict is only one factor, it may cast many others in a different light; in the presence of a conflict, slipshod investigation by the fiduciary or selectively crediting some types of evidence over others may take on a new meaning, supporting an inference of improper purpose. The lower courts have been assigned the task of ferreting out the effects of a conflict (if any). It seems safe to predict that the admissibility on judicial review of evidence outside the decision file submitted by a fiduciary is likely to become a focus of litigation, and that courts will place great weight on the persuasiveness of the fiduciary's written explanation of the adverse decision.

There are a couple of curious omissions from the private civil enforcement actions authorized by section 502(a) of ERISA. Despite the centrality of disclosure and fiduciary duties, the statute does not expressly authorize fraud claims, nor does it clearly allow claims against a nonfiduciary who knowingly participates in a breach. Civil penalties that may be imposed for specified disclosure violations are not an adequate substitute for fraud liability (*see* Chapter 3). Nor can fiduciary liability offer complete relief if a nonfiduciary who knowingly participates in the breach escapes with plan assets. Judicial decisions have largely mended these holes, but they reinforce skepticism as to ERISA's "carefully integrated civil enforcement provisions."

Remedial limitations are the final piece of the enforcement puzzle. Despite the serious physical, emotional, and financial harm that may ensue from an improper denial of benefits, tort-like damages (such as awards for pain and suffering, lost earning capacity, or wrongful death) are not recoverable in employee benefits cases, nor are punitive damages. While this resolution of the tension between protecting workers and promoting widespread voluntary plan sponsorship predates the tort reform movement, it can still be fairly characterized as reflecting a deliberate congressional compromise. Of less certain provenance is section 502(a)(3), which authorizes "appropriate equitable relief" to redress violations of ERISA or the terms of the plan. ERISA's origins lie in law of trusts; trusts are a creature of equity, and equity offered ample measures of monetary relief to redress fiduciary misconduct. The Supreme Court construes appropriate equitable relief as limited to remedies "*typically* available in equity," which rules out most monetary recompense unless it can be cast in the form of equitable restitution (return of a misappropriated fund). In particular, this reading may rule out back pay awards in wrongful discharge or retaliation suits, as well as recovery of profits that an individual participant would have made but for a fiduciary's breach (equitable surcharge).

Chapter 6

Preemption

"[Many consider] the crowning achievement of this legislation [to be] the reservation to Federal authority the sole power to regulate the field of employee benefits. With the preemption of the field we round out the protection afforded participants by eliminating the threat of conflicting and inconsistent State and local regulation."[1]

ERISA's uncertain impact on state law has "generated an avalanche of litigation in the lower courts."[2] Hundreds of ERISA preemption issues are presented annually to the federal courts, with the Supreme Court deciding on average almost one such case each term.[3] After three decades of elucidation, the flood shows little sign of abating.

---

1   120 Cong. Rec. 29,197 (1974), *reprinted in* 3 ERISA Legislative History, *supra* Chapter 1 note 56, at 4656, 4670 (remarks of Rep. Dent). *Accord* 120 Cong. Rec. 29,933 (1974), *reprinted in* 3 ERISA Legislative History, *supra* Chapter 1 note 56, at 4746 (remarks of Sen. Williams) (Congress "intended to preempt the field for Federal regulations, thus eliminating the threat of conflicting or inconsistent State and local regulation of employee benefit plans").

2   De Buono v. NYSA-ILA Med. & Clinical Serv. Fund, 520 U.S. 806, 808 n.1 (1997).

3   Justice Stevens noted that by 1992 there were over 2,800 judicial opinions addressing ERISA preemption. D.C. v. Greater Wash. Bd. of Trade, 506 U.S. 125, 135 n.3 (1992)

The culprit lies in section 514(a), ERISA's express preemption clause that, while "conspicuous for its breadth,"[4] is also notorious for its indeterminacy. The Supreme Court has said

> Section 514(a) marks for pre-emption "all state laws insofar as they . . . relate to any employee benefit plan" covered by ERISA, and one might be excused for wondering, at first blush, whether the words of limitation ("insofar as they . . . relate") do much limiting. If "relate to" were taken to extend to the furthest stretch of its indeterminacy, then for all practical purposes pre-emption would never run its course, for "really, universally, relations stop nowhere."[5]

The result has been a search for extra-textual limits on preemption.

It is not the ambition of this chapter to make sense of the welter of lower court ERISA preemption decisions. Instead, this chapter outlines the general framework of preemption analysis, describes the evolution of the Supreme Court's approach in ERISA cases, and distinguishes areas that are settled from those that are in flux.

There are four generally recognized categories of statutory preemption: express, conflict, obstacle, and field. Congress may, by explicit statutory language, reserve exclusive federal control over a specified subject (express preemption). Where the federal statute is silent as to its preemptive force, any state law that directly conflicts with a provision of the national legislation must fall (conflict preemption). Absent direct conflict between state law and federal statutory language, compliance with the commands of both sovereigns is technically possible, yet additional state-imposed requirements, either substantive or procedural, might impair the accomplishment of national goals. Attention to the structure and purposes of the federal statute may indicate that a more burdensome or nonuniform rule, while not contradicting Congress's language, would nonetheless undercut its objectives. This implied preemption is of two types, although the division is not a sharp one. Where uniformity or cost concerns loom large, a specific state law requirement may pose an obstacle to the federal goal, and so it is displaced by implication (obstacle preemption). Alternatively, the subject matter or comprehensiveness of the federal statute may support the inference that Congress intended it to stand alone, without supplementation by complementary state laws (field preemption).[6]

The Supreme Court succinctly summarized the relationships between these four categories of statutory preemption in an early ERISA case:

> Where the pre-emptive effect of federal enactments is not explicit, "courts sustain a local regulation 'unless it conflicts with federal law or would frustrate the federal

---

(Stevens, J., dissenting). The Supreme Court itself issued about twenty ERISA preemption opinions between 1981 and 2007.

4   FMC Corp. v. Holliday, 498 U.S. 52, 58 (1990).

5   N.Y. State Conference of Blue Cross & Blue Shield Plans v. Travelers Ins. Co., 514 U.S. 645, 655 (1995) (citations omitted).

6   *See generally* Viet D. Dinh, *Reassessing the Law of Preemption*, 88 GEO. L.J. 2085, 2105–06 (2000).

scheme, or unless the courts discern from the totality of the circumstances that Congress sought to occupy the field to the exclusion of the States.'"[7]

A. DELIBERATE STATE REGULATION OF BENEFIT PLANS: FIELD PREEMPTION

"[W]e have virtually taken it for granted that state laws which are 'specifically designed to affect employee benefit plans' are pre-empted under § 514(a)."[8]

Section 514(a) states that ERISA supersedes "any and all state laws insofar as they may now or hereafter relate to any employee benefit plan" that is subject to federal regulation.[9] ERISA's exceptionally broad express preemption provision may seem to make the other three grounds for setting aside state law (conflict, obstacle, and field preemption) irrelevant. Yet the full reach of section 514(a), depending as it does on whether a state law "relate[s] to" an employee benefit plan, remains unresolved. Given this ambiguity in the scope of express preemption, other grounds for setting aside state law become important. This is because the various bases of preemption can operate independently,[10] and because section 514(a) was clearly intended to expand upon the preemption that would result without the express congressional directive.

It is instructive to begin with the question, what would be the extent of federal preemption in the absence of section 514? The answer, it seems, is that the scope of implied preemption under ERISA would be different for welfare and pension plans. Recall that all employee benefit plans, both welfare and pension, are subject to various conduct controls (including reporting and disclosure obligations, fiduciary responsibility rules, and the federal enforcement mechanism), while pension plans are also subject to detailed content regulation (including minimum standards governing participation, benefit accrual, vesting and spousal protection, and, in the case of defined benefit plans, advance funding and termination insurance requirements). Pension content regulation is limited to specified subjects, but the limits were intended to promote sponsorship by maintaining flexibility. In unregulated areas, such as setting coverage and benefit levels, employers can tailor the plan to fit their own budget and personnel priorities, and even in highly regulated areas like vesting, employers are allowed to exceed the statutory minimum standards. State laws that would encroach on employers' freedom

---

7   Metro. Life Ins. Co. v. Massachusetts, 471 U.S. 724, 747–48 (1985) (quoting Allis-Chalmers Corp. v. Lueck, 471 U.S. 202, 209 (1985), and Malone v. White Motor Corp., 435 U.S. 497, 504 (1978)).

8   Mackey v. Lanier Collection Agency & Serv., Inc., 486 U.S. 825, 829 (1988); Ingersoll-Rand Co. v. McClendon, 498 U.S. 133, 140 (1990).

9   ERISA § 514(a), 29 U.S.C. § 1144(a) (2006).

10 Writing separately in *Cipollone v. Liggett Group, Inc.*, 505 U.S. 504, 532 (1992), Justice Blackmun asserted that where there is an express statutory preemption provision, the courts do not apply conflict analysis. That statement was later disavowed by the Court in *Freightliner Corp. v. Myrick*, 514 U.S. 280, 289 (1995), and is conceptually unsound. *See* Dinh, *supra* Chapter 6 note 6, at 2101–03.

in plan design would increase costs and curtail coverage. Consequently, limited federal subject-matter regulation is not compatible with state controls in other areas, for Congress was not simply concerned with preventing specified abuses; it also sought to expand the availability of private pensions. The combination of detailed regulation of some subjects and the deliberate preservation of employer control over others shows that pension plan regulation is a delicate balance that would be upset by state intervention. In short, pension plan regulation is "so pervasive as to make reasonable the inference that Congress left no room for the States to supplement it."[11] As the Supreme Court observed in one of its first forays into ERISA, Congress "meant to establish pension plan regulation as exclusively a federal concern."[12]

Field preemption would not be inferred in the case of welfare plans, however. ERISA is nearly silent about the content of welfare benefit programs, and in the absence of express preemption, it is not obvious that that forbearance betokens a preference for laissez-faire. Far from promoting welfare plans, history shows that Congress included them to achieve the limited objective of stamping out fiduciary abuse of welfare benefit funds, especially looting by union officials. The bill's fiduciary responsibility rules were the hook that brought in welfare plans, with reporting and disclosure and the federal enforcement regime conceived as means to that end. Disclosure was expected to deter abuses, but should they occur, it would alert workers and arm them with the information they would need to enforce their rights. Mandated benefit laws and state regulation of welfare plan content are not inconsistent with this focus on effective fiduciary monitoring. In light of Congress's limited objective, in the absence of express preemption, state supplementation of ERISA's conduct controls might even have been acceptable. For instance, a state might enact more detailed disclosure rules, or forbid agents, employees, or persons related to the sponsor from serving as plan fiduciaries, or authorize punitive damages as a remedy for willful breach. Not only do such more exacting requirements not contradict ERISA, but they positively promote Congress's goal of eradicating welfare fund abuses. Laws of this sort present no obstacle to attaining the national objective, and so there seems to be no call for implied preemption (either obstacle or field) of state welfare plan regulation. Had Congress kept silent on ERISA's preemptive effect, it appears that the slender federal interest in welfare plans would have supported conflict preemption alone.

Congress, of course, did not keep silent on ERISA's preemptive effect; it ordered that ERISA shall supersede "any and all state laws insofar as they may now or hereafter relate to any employee benefit plan."[13] While the uncertain scope of the "relate to [a] plan" standard has bedeviled the courts, this much is clear: Congress can only have meant to expand upon the preemption that would otherwise be inferred. That would be field preemption in the case of pension plans, but probably only conflict preemption in the case of welfare plans.

---

11   Rice v. Santa Fe Elevator Corp., 331 U.S. 218, 230 (1947), *quoted in* Pennsylvania v. Nelson, 350 U.S. 497, 502 (1956).

12   Alessi v. Raybestos-Manhattan, Inc., 451 U.S. 504, 523 (1981) (quoted language actually refers to section 514(a), ERISA's express preemption provision).

13   ERISA § 514(a), 29 U.S.C. § 1144(a) (2006).

While the legislative history of ERISA's preemption provision is sparse, it does have something to say about the scope of express preemption. At a minimum, section 514 was meant to exclude state regulation directed to the operation or content of both welfare and pension plans. That Congress meant at least to legislate field preemption is shown by the change from prior versions of the bill, which would have set aside those state laws that "relate to the reporting and disclosure responsibilities, and fiduciary responsibilities" or "to subject matters regulated by this Act or the Welfare and Pension Plans Disclosure Act."[14] Under these approaches, states would not have been allowed to impose more burdensome conduct controls, nor regulate pension plan content in areas that ERISA addresses, but nothing would stop mandated benefits or other content regulation of welfare plans. Given this history, the Supreme Court concluded early on that "§ 514(a) [cannot] be interpreted to pre-empt only state law dealing with the subject matters covered by ERISA—reporting, disclosure, fiduciary responsibility, and the like."[15] By dispensing with limitations on regulatory subject matter, Congress took over "sole power to regulate the field of employee benefits."[16] In the absence of federal action, such field preemption protects from state interference "conduct that Congress intended to be unregulated."[17] That is, Congress reserved to private decision making all aspects of employee benefit plans not addressed by federal regulation.

B. GENERAL STATE LAWS: CONFLICT AND OBSTACLE PREEMPTION

"That phrase [superseding state laws that 'relate to' a plan] gives rise to some confusion where . . . it is asserted to apply to a state law ostensibly regulating a matter quite different from pension plans."[18]

---

14   H.R. 2, 93d Cong. § 514(a) (as passed by the House, Mar. 6, 1974), *reprinted in* 3 ERISA LEGISLATIVE HISTORY, *supra* Chapter 1 note 56, at 3898, 4057–58; H.R. 2, 93d Cong. § 699(a) (as passed by the Senate, Mar. 4, 1974), *reprinted in* 3 ERISA LEGISLATIVE HISTORY, *supra* Chapter 1 note 56, at 3599, 3820. Jacob Javits, the Senate cosponsor and longtime Republican advocate of comprehensive pension reform legislation, observed that earlier versions of the bill "defined the perimeters of preemption in relation to the areas regulated by the bill." In contrast, he explained that the broad preemption language of the conference bill would close the door to state laws that "deal with some particular aspect of private welfare or pension benefit plans not clearly connected to the Federal regulatory scheme." 120 CONG. REC. 29,942 (1974) (remarks of Sen. Javits), *reprinted in* 3 ERISA LEGISLATIVE HISTORY, *supra* Chapter 1 note 56, at 4770–71.

15   Shaw v. Delta Air Lines, Inc., 463 U.S. 85, 98 (1983).

16   *See supra* text accompanying Chapter 6 note 1 (remarks of Rep. Dent). *Accord* Alessi v. Raybestos-Manhattan, Inc., 451 U.S. 504, 523 (1981) (Congress "meant to establish pension plan regulation as exclusively a federal concern"); N.Y. State Conference of Blue Cross & Blue Shield Plans v. Travelers Ins. Co., 514 U.S. 645, 656 (1995) (same for welfare plans).

17   Metro. Life Ins. Co. v. Massachusetts, 471 U.S. 724, 749 (1985) (referring to field preemption implied under the National Labor Relations Act).

18   *Alessi*, 451 U.S. at 523–24.

The hard question is whether, or to what extent, Congress intended ERISA's express preemption provision to extend beyond field preemption. Some evidence suggests that it expected a longer reach. ERISA contains a savings clause that excepts from preemption "any generally applicable criminal law of a state."[19] Presumably, this stipulation was included to ensure that criminal sanctions would apply to larceny or embezzlement from an employee benefit fund. But "generally applicable criminal laws" like larceny and embezzlement are not laws directed at regulating pension or welfare plans, and so would not be displaced if Congress meant only to occupy the field. The Supreme Court said in 1983:

> To interpret § 514(a) to pre-empt only state law specifically designed to affect employee benefit plans would be to ignore the remainder of § 514. It would have been unnecessary to exempt generally applicable state criminal statutes from pre-emption in § 514(b), for example, if § 514(a) applied only to state law dealing specifically with ERISA plans.[20]

Despite its allure, this negative inference proves too much. If a statutory savings clause is necessary to preserve generally applicable state criminal laws from express preemption, then it would seem that generally applicable state laws in other areas must fall (on the principle that *expressio unis est exclusio alterius*). Besides general criminal laws, ERISA § 514, as originally enacted, expressly saved only state laws regulating insurance, banking, and securities. Nevertheless, the Supreme Court has repeatedly found that some generally applicable state laws in other fields escape preemption, including garnishment, health care regulation, prevailing wage laws, and hospital gross receipts taxes.[21]

The Court has also held that other sorts of generally applicable state laws are preempted.[22] Sometimes the result is presented as an application of express preemption, but that is difficult to reconcile with the decisions that allowed other general state laws to stand. The discussion that follows explores this perplexing state of affairs. Viewed through the lens of the Court's early approach to ERISA preemption, the division between acceptable and superseded state laws is indistinct and unfocused. Attention to case outcomes, however, shows that the state laws that the Supreme Court has set aside fall into three well-defined categories. That pattern of preemption supports the following two propositions: (1) section 514(a), ERISA's express preemption clause, works only field preemption; and (2) general state laws are ousted only if they run afoul of traditional conflict or obstacle preemption analysis.

---

19   ERISA § 514(b)(4), 29 U.S.C. § 1144(b)(4) (2006).

20   Shaw v. Delta Air Lines, Inc., 463 U.S. 85, 98 (1983).

21   Mackey v. Lanier Collection Agency & Serv., Inc., 486 U.S. 825 (1988) (garnishment); N.Y. State Conference of Blue Cross & Blue Shield Plans v. Travelers Ins. Co., 514 U.S. 645 (1995) (health care regulation); Cal. Div. of Labor Standards Enforcement v. Dillingham Constr., N.A., Inc., 519 U.S. 316 (1997) (prevailing wage law); De Buono v. NYSA-ILA Med. & Clinical Servs. Fund, 520 U.S. 806, 814–15 (1997) (hospital gross receipts tax).

22   *E.g.*, *Shaw*, 463 U.S. 85 (antidiscrimination law); Boggs v. Boggs, 520 U.S. 833 (1997) (community property law).

Early Approach to Preemption

Working from the "deliberately expansive" language of section 514(a),[23] the Supreme Court, in its first 15 years of ERISA preemption jurisprudence, emphasized that Congress had enacted an express preemption clause that was "conspicuous for its breadth"[24] and concluded that a state law must give way "even if the law is not specifically designed to affect such plans, or the effect is only indirect, and even if the law is consistent with ERISA's substantive requirements."[25] With one important exception, in those early years the Court held preempted *every* state law it encountered that had an impact on pension or welfare plans.[26]

"A law 'relates to' an employee benefit plan, in the normal sense of the phrase, if it has a connection with or reference to such a plan."[27] This early interpretation of ERISA's preemption clause became a mantra in subsequent decisions, and one that is still repeated today. Taken to require a two-part inquiry,[28] experience has shown that the first part is indeterminate and the second is overbroad. The Court has not disavowed this formulation, but the trend of recent decisions is to downplay express preemption.

In the first prong of the query, "connection with" is merely a synonym for "relate to," and is equally unbounded. "For the same reasons that infinite relations cannot be the measure of pre-emption, neither can infinite connections."[29] Congress could not have meant to suspend every state law that has any effect, however minimal or indirect, on an employee benefit plan or its constituents (i.e., sponsors, fiduciaries, participants, and beneficiaries). Yet while a line between acceptable and unacceptable effects must be drawn, formulations like "relate to" and "connection with" offer no principled basis on which to draw it. From the start, the Court noted that "[s]ome state actions may affect employee benefit plans in too tenuous, remote, or peripheral a manner to warrant finding that the law 'relates to' the plan."[30] But "too tenuous, remote,

---

23 Pilot Life Ins. Co. v. Dedeaux, 481 U.S. 41, 46 (1987).

24 FMC Corp. v. Holliday, 498 U.S. 52, 58 (1990).

25 District of Columbia v. Greater Wash. Bd. of Trade, 506 U.S. 125, 130 (1992) (internal citations and quotation marks omitted).

26 The exception was Georgia's general garnishment law as applied to a participant's interests in a vacation pay plan. *Mackey*, 486 U.S. 825. In addition, in two other cases the Court found that state laws relating to employee benefits survived preemption because they did not affect an employee benefit "plan." Fort Halifax Packing Co. v. Coyne, 482 U.S. 1 (1987) (state may require nondiscretionary lump-sum severance payments in the event of plant closing because one-time contingent obligation does not entail the establishment or maintenance of a plan); Massachusetts v. Morash, 490 U.S. 107 (1989) (practice of compensating discharged employees for unused vacation time subject to state's wage-payment statute because not a welfare plan).

27 Shaw v. Delta Air Lines, Inc., 463 U.S. 85, 96–97 (1983).

28 Cal. Div. of Labor Standards Enforcement v. Dillingham Constr., N.A., 519 U.S. 316, 324 (1997).

29 N.Y. State Conference of Blue Cross & Blue Shield Plans v. Travelers Ins. Co., 514 U.S. 645, 656 (1995).

30 *Shaw*, 463 U.S. at 100 n.21. After announcing this limitation, the Court immediately observed that "[t]he present litigation plainly does not present a borderline question, and we express no views about where it would be appropriate to draw the line." *Id.*

or peripheral" is merely a characterization—a conclusory label, not a standard for decision—and subsequent cases do little to give it content.[31]

Under the second (the "reference to a plan") prong of the inquiry, the Court held preempted three laws: "a law that 'impos[ed] requirements by reference to [ERISA] covered programs,' a law that specifically exempted ERISA plans from an otherwise generally applicable garnishment provision, and a common-law cause of action premised on the existence of an ERISA plan."[32] The first of these three cases shows that the "reference" standard, although easily applied, sometimes yields outcomes that seem impossible to justify. The law at issue in *District of Columbia v. Greater Washington Board of Trade* was a District of Columbia statute requiring employers who provide health insurance to their employees to provide equivalent health insurance coverage to injured employees receiving workers' compensation benefits.[33] Because the statute "specifically refers to welfare benefit plans regulated by ERISA," the Court found it preempted "on that basis alone."[34] The precedent provided by two prior "reference" cases was the only support offered for the result. In dissent, Justice Stevens emphasized that the purpose of the District's law was to compute "workers' compensation benefits on the basis of the entire remuneration of injured employees when a portion of the remuneration is provided by an employee benefit plan."[35] "Nothing in ERISA," he explained, "suggests an intent to supersede the State's efforts to enact fair and complete remedies for work-related injuries; it is difficult to imagine how a State could measure an injured worker's health benefits without referring to the specific health benefit that the worker receives."[36] Attending to the policies of the state and federal laws led Justice Stevens to conclude that "a state law's mere reference to an ERISA plan is an insufficient reason for concluding that it is pre-empted."[37] In striking down state laws that do not interfere with federal objectives, mechanistic application of the "reference" standard sometimes causes overbroad preemption.

By resting its early decisions on the interpretation of section 514(a), the Supreme Court indicated that express preemption bars some, but not all, general state laws that affect a plan. Under this approach, however, the statutory text offers no clear-cut stopping point. Consequently, the Court is forced to grapple with the uncertain extent

---

31 *See* District of Columbia v. Greater Wash. Bd. of Trade, 506 U.S. 125, 130 n.1 (1992) (suggesting that "many laws of general applicability," such as general garnishment laws, are too tenuous, remote, or peripheral to warrant preemption); *N.Y. State Conference*, 514 U.S. at 661 (health care quality control and hospital workplace regulation too tenuous for preemption); *Dillingham*, 519 U.S. at 330 (apprenticeship training standards and wages paid on public works projects "quite remote from the areas with which ERISA is expressly concerned"). *But see Mackey*, 486 U.S. at 842 (Kennedy, J., dissenting) (general garnishment laws not tenuous, remote, or peripheral).

32 *Dillingham*, 519 U.S. at 324 (citation omitted).

33 District of Columbia v. Greater Wash. Bd. of Trade, 506 U.S. at 126–27, 128. From a long-term perspective, this case can be seen as the high-water mark of the Court's expansive interpretation of ERISA preemption.

34 *Id.* at 130.

35 *Id.* at 133.

36 *Id.* at 137–38.

37 *Id.* at 137.

of laws that "relate to [a] plan" on a case-by-case basis. In its first preemption case, the Court observed, "That phrase gives rise to some confusion where . . . it is asserted to apply to a state law ostensibly regulating a matter quite different from pension plans."[38] More recently, it has admitted that "our prior attempt to construe the phrase 'relate to' does not give us much help drawing the line here."[39] None of the opinions posit a determinate test for whether a generally applicable state law has a sufficiently close relationship to an employee benefit plan to trigger preemption. Instead, results are often justified by analogy to the few prior data points offered by earlier decisions.

Categories of Preempted Laws

Putting aside *Greater Washington Board of Trade*, all of the state laws that the Court has held superseded fall into three categories. First, state laws that affect the type or amount of benefits provided under a pension or welfare plan are uniformly set aside.[40] Second, laws that affect the identification of plan beneficiaries likewise fall.[41] Third, laws that provide additional remedies for conduct violating ERISA are also preempted.[42]

In the first category, laws mandating that a plan provide benefits of a certain type or amount interfere with a central design feature that Congress intended to reserve to the plan sponsor to promote flexibility and maximize voluntary plan sponsorship. The policy of laissez-faire is strongest in matters touching upon workforce coverage (participation rules) and the type and amount of benefits to be provided by the plan. Consequently, mandated benefit rules (and, likely, mandated coverage rules) cannot stand.[43] This, of

---

38 Alessi v. Raybestos-Manhattan, Inc., 451 U.S. 504, 523–24 (1981).

39 N.Y. State Conference of Blue Cross & Blue Shield Plans v. Travelers Ins. Co., 514 U.S. 645, 655 (1995).

40 *Alessi*, 451 U.S. 504 (law prohibiting integration of workers compensation and pension benefits); Shaw v. Delta Air Lines, Inc., 463 U.S. 85 (1983) (state antidiscrimination law requiring provision of pregnancy benefits); FMC Corp. v. Holliday, 498 U.S. 52 (1990) (law prohibiting subrogation of health care plan from recovery based on motor vehicle tort claim). *See also* Metro. Life Ins. Co. v. Massachusetts, 471 U.S. 724 (1985) (law mandating inclusion of minimum mental health benefits in heath insurance policies purchased by employee health care plans relates to a plan within the meaning of section 514(a), but preemption avoided by insurance savings clause).

41 Boggs v. Boggs, 520 U.S. 833 (1997) (community property law permitting deceased nonparticipant spouse to devise an interest in the survivor's pension); Egelhoff v. Egelhoff, 532 U.S. 141 (2001) (nonprobate transfer law providing automatic revocation on divorce of spousal beneficiary designation).

42 Pilot Life Ins. Co. v. Dedeaux, 481 U.S. 41, 46 (1987) (common-law action seeking emotional distress and punitive damages for bad-faith insurance claims processing); Ingersoll-Rand Co. v. McClendon, 498 U.S. 133 (1990) (common-law wrongful discharge claim seeking compensation for mental anguish and punitive damages based on firing to prevent pension vesting).

43 In holding that a gross receipts tax on hospitals could be applied without preemption to facilities run by an ERISA health care plan, the Supreme Court emphasized that "[t]his is not a case in which New York has forbidden a method of calculating pension benefits that federal law permits, or required employers to provide certain benefits." De Buono v. NYSA-ILA Med. & Clinical Servs. Fund, 520 U.S. 806, 814–15 (1997) (footnotes omitted).

course, is a result that follows automatically from field preemption, which would be inferred in the case of pension plans, and which is confirmed and extended to the case of welfare plans by ERISA's express preemption provision. As the Court has repeatedly observed, "we have virtually taken it for granted that state laws which are 'specifically designed to affect employee benefit plans' are pre-empted under § 514(a)."[44]

Preemption of the second category, laws affecting the identification of plan beneficiaries, is almost as clear-cut. Here, however, the state laws at issue were not "specifically designed to affect employee benefit plans"; instead, they were laws of general application. *Boggs v. Boggs*[45] held Louisiana community property law preempted insofar as it allowed a nonparticipant spouse to make a testamentary transfer of an interest in the undistributed pension benefits of the surviving participant spouse. Louisiana's community property regime did not deal with subject matters regulated by ERISA (e.g., funding, vesting, fiduciary obligations), nor was it directed at welfare or pension plans, so it hardly seemed a candidate for field preemption.[46] In its prospects for withstanding preemption, community property seemed to have everything going for it. The Court acknowledged that it "is more than a property regime[; it] is a commitment to the equality of husband and wife" that "implement[s] policies and values lying within the traditional domain of the States."[47] Yet when applied to confer a devisable interest on a nonparticipant spouse, it frustrates ERISA's purposes because it diverts funds destined to provide retirement income for the participant and any later spouse.[48] Moreover, the transfer of an interest by will or intestacy fails to satisfy the requirements of a qualified domestic relations order (QDRO), the sole ERISA-endorsed mechanism for granting a nonbeneficiary access to accumulated pension savings.[49] Accordingly, *Boggs* represents a straightforward application of obstacle preemption.[50]

Another instance of preemption of state laws affecting identification of plan beneficiaries involved the state of Washington's nonprobate transfer law. *Egelhoff v. Egelhoff*[51] held preempted a statute providing for automatic revocation on divorce of a spousal beneficiary designation. Although the statute explicitly referred to employee benefit plans, it needn't have, as it applied generally to a wide range of will substitutes (such as contractual payable-on-death clauses and revocable inter vivos trusts). The Supreme Court found the law to be expressly preempted by ERISA, not because it

---

44   Mackey v. Lanier Collection Agency & Serv., Inc., 486 U.S. 825, 829 (1988); Ingersoll-Rand Co. v. McClendon, 498 U.S. 133, 140 (1990). *See supra* text accompanying Chapter 6 notes 8–17.

45   520 U.S. 833 (1997).

46   The Court found it unnecessary to consider the applicability of field preemption. *Id.* at 841.

47   *Id.* at 840.

48   *Id.* at 852 ("[I]t would be inimical to ERISA's purposes to permit testamentary recipients to acquire a competing interest in undistributed pension benefits, which are intended to provide a stream of income to participants and their beneficiaries."). *Accord* Ablamis v. Roper, 937 F.2d 1450 (9th Cir. 1991).

49   *Boggs*, 520 U.S. at 843–44, 848–51.

50   The *Boggs* Court referred to its decision as an application of conflict preemption, but it used the term "conflict" broadly, to include not only contradictory commands, but also state laws that frustrate ERISA's objects. *Id.* at 841.

51   532 U.S. 141 (2001).

made reference to employee benefit plans, but because it had an "impermissible connection with ERISA plans."[52]

> The statute binds ERISA plan administrators to a particular choice of rules for determining beneficiary status. The administrators must pay benefits to the beneficiaries chosen by state law, rather than to those identified in the plan documents. The statute thus implicates an area of core ERISA concern. In particular, it runs counter to ERISA's commands that a plan shall "specify the basis on which payments are made to and from the plan," and that the fiduciary shall administer the plan "in accordance with the documents and instruments governing the plan," making payments to a "beneficiary" who is "designated by a participant, or by the terms of [the] plan." In other words, unlike generally applicable laws regulating "areas where ERISA has nothing to say," which we have upheld notwithstanding their incidental effect on ERISA plans, this statute governs the payment of benefits, a central matter of plan administration.[53]

While resting its decision on express preemption, this analysis suggests that laws affecting beneficiary designation actually contradict ERISA, so that conflict preemption is also called for. Alternatively, the identification of plan beneficiaries may be such a "core ERISA concern" that it (like the type and amount of benefits or the extent of workforce coverage) must yield to field preemption.

The third category of state laws that the Supreme Court has found superseded consists of laws providing additional remedies for conduct violating ERISA. Common-law tort actions for bad-faith breach of contract in insurance claims processing, and for wrongful discharge to prevent pension vesting, fall under this ban.[54] Such state law claims support awards of compensatory damages for nonpecuniary injuries (such as emotional distress) or even punitive damages, remedies that are not authorized by ERISA's civil enforcement provision. In several cases, the Court has held that that omission was quite deliberate: "The policy choices reflected in the inclusion of certain remedies and the exclusion of others under the federal scheme would be completely undermined if ERISA-plan participants and beneficiaries were free to obtain remedies under state law that Congress rejected in ERISA."[55] In other words, under ERISA, as elsewhere, the nature of the remedy defines the extent of the right. Such supplemental remedies would upset the balance of considerations employers face in deciding whether to sponsor a plan.[56] ERISA's legislative history also persuaded the Court that

---

52 *Id.*, 532 U.S. at 147.

53 *Id.*, 532 U.S. at 147–48 (footnotes and citations omitted).

54 Pilot Life Ins. Co. v. Dedeaux, 481 U.S. 41, 46 (1987); Ingersoll-Rand Co. v. McClendon, 498 U.S. 133 (1990).

55 *Ingersoll-Rand*, 498 U.S. at 144 (quoting Mass. Mut. Life Ins. Co. v. Russell, 473 U.S. 134, 146 (1985), discussed *supra* Chapter 5D).

Conversely, the existence of long-standing state law remedies for medical malpractice was one factor that persuaded the Court that mixed eligibility and treatment decisions by HMO physicians are not fiduciary acts subject to ERISA's fiduciary duty and enforcement provisions. Pegram v. Herdrich, 530 U.S. 211, 235-36 (2000); *see supra* Chapter 4 notes 25-34 and accompanying text.

56 "Any such provision [allowing additional state law remedies] patently violates ERISA's policy of inducing employers to offer benefits by assuring a predictable set of liabilities,

Congress intended section 502(a), the civil enforcement provision, to have uniquely "powerful preemptive force."[57] Supplemental state remedies, therefore, would present an obstacle to the full accomplishment of ERISA's policies. In *Ingersoll-Rand*, as in *Boggs*, the Supreme Court referred to its decision as an application of conflict preemption. But here too, the conflict is with ERISA's underlying objectives; it does not entail a direct contradiction of commands.[58]

The Purposive Approach

Each of the three categories of state laws that the Supreme Court has held preempted— laws affecting the type or amount of benefits, laws affecting the identification of beneficiaries, and laws supplementing ERISA's remedies—offends ERISA's fundamental policies. Notwithstanding the Court's asserted reliance on express preemption, application of conventional principles of field preemption and obstacle preemption is sufficient to explain these decisions. Perhaps despairing of its efforts to capture the elusive plain meaning of "relate to," in 1997 the Court announced a new context-sensitive and policy-oriented interpretation of section 514(a):

> [T]o determine whether a state law has the forbidden connection, we look both to "the objectives of the ERISA statute as a guide to the scope of the state law that Congress understood would survive," as well as to the nature of the effect of the state law on ERISA plans.[59]

This standard makes express preemption turn on a purposive inquiry that seems to embody the approach of field and obstacle preemption. Even more forthrightly, Justice Scalia observed:

> I think it would greatly assist our function of clarifying the law if we simply acknowledged that our first take on this statute was wrong; that the "relate to" clause of the pre-emption provision is meant, not to set forth a *test* for pre-emption,

---

under uniform standards of primary conduct and a uniform regime of ultimate remedial orders and awards when a violation has occurred." Rush Prudential HMO, Inc. v. Moran, 536 U.S. 355, 379 (2002).

57   *Ingersoll-Rand*, 498 U.S. at 144. Aetna Health Inc. v. Davila, 542 U.S. 200, 209 (2004) ("[A]ny state law cause of action that duplicates, supplements, or supplants the ERISA civil enforcement remedy conflicts with the clear congressional intent to make the ERISA remedy exclusive and is therefore preempted."). The Court has gone so far as to hold that a law, arguably saved from express preemption because it regulates insurance, nevertheless falls to implied preemption where it would supplement ERISA's remedial scheme. *Davila*, 542 U.S. at 217–18. *See Pilot Life*, 481 U.S. at 56–57. *But see* UNUM Life Ins. Co. of Am. v. Ward, 526 U.S. 358, 386 n.7 (1999) (noting Solicitor General's disavowal of the argument that remedial conflict requires preemption of a law that would otherwise be protected by the insurance saving clause).

58   *Ingersoll-Rand*, 498 U.S. at 145; Boggs v. Boggs, 520 U.S. 833, 843–44 (1997).

59   Cal. Div. of Labor Standards Enforcement v. Dillingham Constr., N.A., Inc., 519 U.S. 316, 325 (1997) (quoting N.Y. State Conference of Blue Cross & Blue Shield Plans v. Travelers Ins. Co., 514 U.S. 645, 656 (1995)). *Accord* Egelhoff v. Egelhoff, 532 U.S. 141, 147 (2001).

but rather to identify the field in which ordinary *field pre-emption* applies—namely, the field of laws regulating "employee benefit plan[s]. . . ." I think it accurately describes our current ERISA jurisprudence to say that we apply ordinary field pre-emption, and, of course, ordinary conflict pre-emption. Nothing more mysterious than that; and except as establishing that, "relates to" is irrelevant.[60]

Here, the term "conflict preemption" is used to include conflict with the underlying policy of the federal statute (i.e., it subsumes obstacle preemption). Accordingly, Justice Scalia is prepared to construe ERISA's preemption clause to legislate field preemption only; outside the field of laws regulating employee benefit plans, he would uphold general state laws, except insofar as they actually conflict with federal regulation or create an obstacle to the accomplishment of ERISA's policies.

There is great explanatory force in the proposition that generally applicable state laws are superseded only if they conflict with ERISA or present an obstacle to the achievement of its goals, not because they run afoul of express preemption. Under this view, all generally applicable state laws survive express preemption without needing the protection of a savings clause (express or implied) because they simply fail to "relate to" a plan. If their application would undermine ERISA's purposes, however, the federal interest must prevail. This approach cannot reduce preemption issues to a simple algorithm because ERISA's purposes sometimes conflict. Yet by focusing debate on the right question—the proper balance of ERISA's competing policies—it should yield more coherent results.

This analysis of what the Court has done leaves a much more modest role for express preemption than the Court's pronouncements assert. The limited function of ERISA § 514(a) is confirmed by a series of cases in which the Court has refused to set aside general state laws that impose substantial costs on employee benefit plans. The case that led the retreat from the extremist implications of express preemption is *New York State Conference of Blue Cross & Blue Shield Plans v. Travelers Insurance Company.*[61] That case challenged the enforceability of statutory surcharges on inpatient hospital care imposed on patients whose bills were paid by a variety of providers other than Blue Cross/Blue Shield (the "Blues"), including commercial insurers and HMOs. The object of the New York law was to make insuring with the Blues relatively more attractive, in order to offset cost disadvantages stemming from the Blues' practice of open enrollment. Despite this deliberate effort to influence the choices of health plan administrators, the Court upheld the charges.

> An indirect economic influence . . . does not bind plan administrators to any particular choice and thus function as a regulation of an ERISA plan itself; commercial insurers and HMO's may still offer more attractive packages than the Blues.

---

60 *Dillingham,* 519 U.S. at 336 (citations omitted) (concurring opinion of Justice Scalia). Concurring in a subsequent decision, Justice Scalia, joined by Justice Ginsburg, observed, "if [section 514(a)] is interpreted to be anything other than a reference to our established jurisprudence concerning conflict and field pre-emption [it] has no discernible content that would not pick up every ripple in the pond, producing a result 'that no sensible person could have intended.'" *Egelhoff,* 532 U.S. at 153.

61 514 U.S. 645 (1995).

Nor does the indirect influence of the surcharges preclude uniform administrative practice or the provision of a uniform interstate benefit package if a plan wishes to provide one. It simply bears on the costs of benefits and the relative costs of competing insurance to provide them.[62]

Pointing to hospitals' long-standing practice of providing indigent care through cross-subsidies imposed by means of charge differentials for commercial insurers, the Court saw nothing about ERISA that suggested a purpose to bar such practices when imposed by state law.[63] If state laws having indirect effects on plan costs were preempted, quality standards for hospital services and basic regulation of workplace conditions would fall, but the Court found no indication that Congress intended to displace general health care regulation.[64] Therefore, the Court concluded that indirect economic effects flowing from the application of general state laws do not call for preemption, at least if the effects are not so acute "as to force an ERISA plan to adopt a certain scheme of substantive coverage or effectively restrict its choice of insurers."[65]

Subsequent cases reaffirm that indirect influences, in the form of economic incentives created to serve legitimate state ends, don't trigger preemption.[66] Qualitatively, such influences may, by virtue of their indirectness, have only a "tenuous, remote, or peripheral connection with covered plans,"[67] but quantitatively their impact can be substantial. Tension exists between the Court's acceptance of such influences and the notion that Congress intended to give sponsors wide latitude in structuring benefit programs to maximize their advantage.[68] Costs figure prominently in plan design, so substantial cost increases, even if indirect, will sway an employer's decisions. The following section investigates this apparent contradiction.

---

62   *Id.* at 659–60.

63   *Id.* at 660.

64   *Id.* at 660–61, 664–65.

65   *Id.* at 668.

66   Cal. Div. of Labor Standards Enforcement v. Dillingham Constr., N.A., 519 U.S. 316, 332, 333 (1997) (prevailing wage law's economic incentive for ERISA apprenticeship program to comply with state qualification requirements acceptable absent showing that inducement is "tantamount to a compulsion"); *De Buono*, 520 U.S. at 814–15 (state gross receipts tax on medical centers applicable to facilities operated directly by ERISA health care plans). The tax in *De Buono* fell on the plan directly, but nonetheless represented an indirect economic influence because, like the quality control standards and workplace safety regulation discussed in *New York State Conference*, 514 U.S. at 658–62, it was a general law that increased the costs of covered services, whether provided by an ERISA plan or otherwise.

67   *N.Y. State Conference*, 514 U.S. at 661; *Dillingham*, 519 U.S. at 330. The "tenuous, remote, or peripheral" limitation on express preemption was announced in dicta in *Shaw v. Delta Air Lines, Inc.*, 463 U.S. 85, 100 n.21 (1983), and repeated in subsequent cases. *See supra* Chapter 6 notes 30–31 and accompany-ing text.

68   *See supra* Chapter 1C.

C. COSTS AND PREEMPTION POLICY

"Congress pre-empted state laws relating to *plans*, rather than simply to *benefits*."[69]

"In sum, cost uniformity was almost certainly not an object of pre-emption."[70]

Federal preemption obviously achieves uniformity in the regulation of employee benefit plans. The Supreme Court has suggested that interstate administrative uniformity, with its tendency to minimize costs, was *the* central object of preemption.[71] Nevertheless, an exclusive focus on uniformity is misleadingly incomplete; ERISA, after all, does not except uniform state laws from preemption. Freedom of contract (laissez-faire) more accurately captures the central objective of preemption. Freedom of contract preserves a system of voluntary plan sponsorship and prevents the states from upsetting the balance Congress struck between the quantity and quality of employer-provided welfare and pension benefits. That balance is cost-driven, of course, but not all costs are created equal. Since its retreat from the "uncritical literalism" of its early approach to preemption,[72] the Court has indicated that state laws that affect the cost of certain goods or services generally are not displaced when those goods or services are financed or provided through an employee benefit plan. Employee benefit plans are not immune from indirect costs imposed generally in the legitimate exercise of a state's police power, even if interstate differentials in the cost of plan benefits are the result.

Uniformity Versus Laissez-Faire

An employer-initiated severance pay arrangement generally constitutes a welfare plan (or, under some circumstances, a pension plan). Nevertheless, in *Fort Halifax Packing Co. v. Coyne*,[73] the Supreme Court found that a Maine law requiring one-time severance payments in the event of a plant closing was not preempted by ERISA because the statute "neither establishes, nor requires an employer to maintain, an employee welfare benefit 'plan. . . . '"[74] The Court equated an ERISA plan with an "ongoing administrative program for processing claims and paying benefits."[75] That criterion, the Court explained, is supported by the policy of preemption. Conforming a benefit program to a patchwork of state regulation would forfeit the advantages of uniform administrative practice, and the resulting cost increases "might lead those employers

---

69   Fort Halifax Packing Co. v. Coyne, 482 U.S. 1, 11 (1987).

70   *N.Y. State Conference*, 514 U.S. at 662.

71   *See Fort Halifax*, 482 U.S. at 11.

72   *N.Y. State Conference*, 514 U.S. at 656.

73   482 U.S. 1 (1987).

74   *Id*. at 6.

75   *Id*. at 12.

with existing plans to reduce benefits, and those without such plans to refrain from adopting them."[76] In contrast, a contingent, one-time obligation to make nondiscretionary, lump-sum payments of the sort imposed by the Maine law entails no such inefficiency.[77]

State conduct controls (such as additional reporting requirements, higher fiduciary standards, or specified procedures for claim processing) may interfere with uniform administration, and so must be set aside.[78] "Pre-emption ensures that the administrative practices of a benefit plan will be governed by only a single set of regulations."[79] But the *Fort Halifax* Court used the term "administrative practices" capaciously, to include the funding, computation, and payment of benefits, and so state laws that mandate certain types or levels of benefits likewise disrupt uniform administrative practices. The Justices worried that differing state laws would force a plan "to make certain benefits available in some States but not in others."[80] For that reason, the Court explained, ERISA preempted a Hawaii law mandating employer provision of specified health insurance benefits.[81] Similarly, the Court noted that it struck down a New Jersey statute that prohibited offsetting worker compensation payments against pension benefits (in *Alessi v. Raybestos-Manhattan, Inc.*[82]) because the statute "force[d] the employer either to structure all its benefit payments in accordance with New Jersey law, or to adopt different payment formulae for employees inside and outside the State."[83] Thus, from this view of preemption policy, state content controls are just as pernicious as conduct controls.

Uniformity, however, is only part of the concern underlying ERISA preemption, and perhaps not the most important part. As the Court noted, benefits mandated by one state could be extended to participants in other states to achieve uniformity.

---

76 *Id.* at 11.

77 *Id.* at 12. The Court also observed that the Maine plant-closing law "not only fails to implicate the concerns of ERISA's pre-emption provision, it fails to implicate the regulatory concerns of ERISA itself." *Id.* at 15. Looking to the legislative history of ERISA's fiduciary-responsibility rules, the Court concluded that "[t]he focus of the statute thus is on the administrative integrity of benefit plans—which presumes that some type of administrative activity is taking place." *Id. Fort Halifax* was examined earlier (Chapter 2A), where it was seen that discretionary decision making and asset handling have emerged as criteria for the kinds of administrative activity it takes to make a plan. Close attention to the definition of fiduciary (Chapter 4A) reveals that those two functions (i.e., managerial discretion and custody of assets) invariably trigger fiduciary obligations, and so it seems that the essence of a plan is the presence of a fiduciary.

78 *Id.* at 9 ("A plan would be required to keep certain records in some States but not in others; . . . to process claims in a certain way in some States but not in others; and to comply with certain fiduciary standards in some States but not in others.").

79 *Id.* at 11.

80 *Id.* at 9.

81 *Id.* at 12–13 (discussing Standard Oil Co. v. Agsalud, 633 F.2d 760 (9th Cir. 1980), *summarily aff'd*, 454 U.S. 801 (1981)). By later amendment, Congress saved the Hawaii law. ERISA § 514(b)(5), 29 U.S.C. § 1144(b)(5) (2006).

82 451 U.S. 504 (1981).

83 *Fort Halifax*, 482 U.S. at 10.

Similarly, a plan could comply with the most restrictive state procedural standards (conduct controls). If states impose conflicting procedural protections, the problem could be sidestepped by including a choice-of-law provision in the plan document. Approaches such as these would ensure nationwide operational uniformity, but it would come at the price of increased expense and reduced employer flexibility.[84]

Increased cost and reduced flexibility "might lead those employers with existing plans to reduce benefits, and those without such plans to refrain from adopting them."[85] State imposition of more demanding standards, while ensuring first-rate coverage for some workers, would cause a larger proportion of the U.S. labor force to receive smaller benefits, or none at all. Federal preemption prevents the states from upsetting the balance Congress struck between the quantity and quality of employee benefit plan coverage.[86] ERISA leaves unregulated some subjects, such as workforce coverage and benefit levels, and imposes only minimum standards even in fields that are intensively controlled, such as pension funding and vesting. Thus, federal law preserves an important residue of freedom of contract. Under a system of voluntary plan sponsorship, additional state regulation would shift the equilibrium, reducing the availability of employee benefits. By prohibiting state intrusion, preemption reserves that policy decision for Congress.

The Relevance of Costs

A commitment to freedom of contract bars the states from imposing more onerous and costly requirements. But how far does this cost-containment principle extend? A plan may incur higher costs because of state regulatory action that is not directed at employee

---

84   In addition, the choice-of-law solution would only eliminate conflicts for plan employers, not employees.

      Although selection of one state's law meets the employer's cost-based need for uniform administrative procedures, it is not enough from the worker's perspective. Even though any one plan could be interpreted and administered in accordance with the law of a single state, one worker may need to evaluate numerous alternative plans associated with different employment opportunities. Those plans may select different governing laws (corresponding to the differing locations of corporate headquarters, for example), making the precise contours of competing benefit offers dependent on the idiosyncrasies of several states' contract and trust law. Under these circumstances, fully informed evaluation of competing job offers is probably uneconomic—the cost of identifying the vagaries of alternative legal regimes would likely exceed the benefit of a marginally more valuable compensation package. A single set of interstitial rules (contract and trust) governing all plans would limit information costs and increase the efficiency of the labor market.

      Wiedenbeck, *supra* Chapter 1 note 57, at 569–70 (footnote omitted).

85   *Fort Halifax*, 482 U.S. at 11.

86   Referring to the cost consequences of restricting the integration of pension plans with Social Security, the House Ways and Means Committee observed: "Employees, as a whole, might be injured rather than aided if such cost increases resulted in slowing down the growth or perhaps even eliminated private retirement plans." H.R. REP. NO. 93-807, at 69 (1974), *reprinted in* 2 ERISA LEGISLATIVE HISTORY, *supra* Chapter 1 note 56, at 3189.

benefit plans as such. Is state public health legislation preempted because increased life expectancy triggers higher costs for defined benefit pension plans? Employee benefit plans are designed to provide insurance or financing for morbidity (health and disability plans) and mortality (pension and life insurance plans) losses. It cannot be the case that states are barred from addressing public health and safety concerns because of their laws' incidental effects on benefit costs under ERISA plans. Cognizance of this implication seems to be what put the brakes on the Supreme Court's early expansive interpretation of section 514(a).[87]

Perhaps cost control is the fundamental objective of ERISA preemption, but the objective is limited to containing *plan* costs—that is, barring state coverage and benefit mandates, and containing the cost of benefit delivery (i.e., plan administration). Employment and health laws, which vary from state to state, also lead to interstate differentials in costs faced by a large employer providing a uniform nationwide package of benefits. Such "cost uniformity was almost certainly not an object of preemption," says the Supreme Court.[88] That is, laws affecting the cost of freely contracted benefits, whether by altering insured risks or changing the cost of covered services, were not expected to fall to ERISA preemption. A natural calamity like a serious flu epidemic can substantially affect costs incurred by a health care plan (or even a defined benefit pension plan), but so can local health and welfare regulation, like a state immunization program, hospital quality-of-care standards, or wage and hour legislation. Possible cost effects should not undermine such unremarkable exercises of state police power. Instead, state action of these sorts should, like the possibility of an epidemic, be treated as just another component of the financial risk that the plan sponsor assumes when promising to provide benefits dependent on health or longevity. The indirect cost consequences of general laws designed to serve legitimate state ends are both ubiquitous and indistinguishable from other risks that normally inhere in plan sponsorship. General state laws speak to a wider audience than employers and plan participants, and that broader constituency offers some assurance that those laws are supported by public policy justifications independent of ERISA's concerns and are not designed to alter the congressional balance between benefit plan quantity and quality.

A pair of preemption decisions provides vivid confirmation that the distinction between acceptable and unacceptable costs is not a matter of magnitude. *Mackey v. Lanier Collection Agency & Services, Inc.*[89] held that Georgia's general garnishment statute could be applied to collect money owed by a welfare plan participant from

---

87   *See* N.Y. State Conference of Blue Cross & Blue Shield Plans v. Travelers Ins. Co., 514 U.S. 645, 661 (1995) (noting that hospital quality standards and basic employment regulation increase costs, but "to read the pre-emption provision as displacing all state laws affecting costs and charges on the theory that they indirectly relate to ERISA plans that . . . cover such services would effectively read the limiting language in § 514(a) out of the statute"). *See supra* Chapter 6B.

88   *N.Y. State Conference*, 514 U.S. at 662.

89   486 U.S. 825 (1988).

benefits due the participant under the plan, even though application of the law would subject the plan to substantial legal and administrative costs.

> Petitioners are required to confirm the identity of each of the 23 plan participants who owe money to respondent, calculate the participant's maximum entitlement from the fund for the period between the service date and the reply date of the summons of garnishment, determine the amount that each participant owes to respondent, and make payments into state court of the lesser of the amount owed to respondent and the participant's entitlement. Petitioners must also make decisions concerning the validity and priority of garnishments and, if necessary, bear the costs of litigating these issues. Further, as trustees of a multiemployer plan covering participants in several States, petitioners are potentially subject to multiple garnishment orders under varying or conflicting state laws.[90]

On the other hand, in *Egelhoff v. Egelhoff*,[91] the Court concluded that ERISA preempts a Washington statute calling for automatic revocation of a spousal beneficiary designation upon divorce, even though the statute functioned only as a default rule that could be overridden by including specific language in the plan. Consequently, the statute's interference with nationally uniform plan administration (i.e., making the administrator pay benefits to the person specified by state law instead of the beneficiary identified in accordance with plan documents) could be avoided at minimal cost.

Thus, while high administrative costs did not trigger preemption in *Mackey*, a law that imposed very little cost was preempted in *Egelhoff*. The difference, of course, is that *Mackey* involved a general state law that could stand because garnishment of welfare benefits does not undermine ERISA's objectives, while the divorce revocation statute in *Egelhoff* was directed at plan beneficiary designation and so fell to field preemption, and arguably conflict preemption as well. Put differently, high costs do not necessarily determine the fate of a general state law, while low costs cannot save a state law that regulates plan content or operations.

D. THE ROLE OF FEDERAL COMMON LAW

> "It is also intended that a body of Federal substantive law will be developed by the courts to deal with issues involving rights and obligations under private welfare and pension plans."[92]

Express preemption clears the field of employee benefit plan regulation, leaving matters not addressed by ERISA open to private ordering (freedom of contract). Occasionally, however, preemption sweeps away state laws that actually facilitate private ordering. Consider state killer laws, which revoke beneficiary designations naming a person who murders the property owner. Such laws are designed to carry out

---

90   *Id.* at 842 (Kennedy, J., dissenting).
91   532 U.S. 141 (2001).
92   120 Cong. Rec. 29,942 (remarks of Sen. Javits), *reprinted in* 3 ERISA Legislative History, *supra* Chapter 1 note 56, at 4771.

the owner's probable intent in a situation that was not foreseen, and presumably killer laws do so in the overwhelming majority of cases. Yet under *Egelhoff*, the revocation of a participant's beneficiary designation by operation of such a state law, and the designation by law of a substitute taker, would be preempted. This scenario was presented to the Supreme Court as an argument weighing against preemption of the divorce revocation law sub judice. Avoiding the problem, the Court responded that such slayer "statutes are not before us, so we do not decide the issue."[93] The Court noted, however, that the principle underlying such statutes has a long history and has been adopted almost everywhere, and that near uniformity may mitigate such statutes' interference with ERISA.[94]

The intimation that a sufficiently broad consensus among the states may save from preemption a law regulating plan terms is misguided. Perhaps such a near universal principle should apply to employee benefit plans, but not as a matter of state law. To apply a state killer statute would violate the "reservation to Federal authority [of] the sole power to regulate the field of employee benefits."[95] That reservation was not to *congressional* authority specifically, but to federal authority generally, and Congress contemplated that the federal courts would exercise interstitial lawmaking power under ERISA. Accordingly, the proper approach might be for the courts to adopt a nationally uniform killer disqualification rule as a matter of the federal common law of employee benefit plans.

The appropriate scope of judicial lawmaking under ERISA is an important and still unresolved question. Clearly, congressional silence is not enough to justify judicial intervention, for the absence of legislative standards was often, by conscious forbearance, intended to preserve a large area of freedom of contract. That flexibility, in turn, was designed to promote broad sponsorship. That goal may offer the best guideline for the federal courts' exercise of their common-law powers. If the proposed rule could adversely affect sponsorship by increasing plan costs or reducing employer flexibility, then it should be left to the free play of economic forces—off limits, that is, for the courts. If, instead, the rule responds to unforeseen circumstances by filling a gap in the plan contract, then common-law development may be warranted.[96]

Kennedy v. Plan Administrator for DuPont Savings and Investment Plan[97] illustrates these competing concerns. The case presented the question whether to enforce an ex-spouse's waiver of pension benefits where the participant died without having changed a pre-divorce beneficiary designation naming the former spouse as successor.

---

93   *Egelhoff*, 532 U.S. at 152.

94   *Id.*

95   120 CONG. REC. 29,197 (1974), *reprinted in* 3 ERISA LEGISLATIVE HISTORY, *supra* Chapter 1 note 56, at 4656, 4670. *See supra* Chapter 6 note 1 and accompanying text.

96   A good example of the creation of common-law rules under ERISA is *PM Group Life Insurance Co. v. Western Growers Assurance Trust*, 953 F.2d 543 (9th Cir. 1992) (self-insured health care plan of each parent covered infant's hospital expenses, but plans contained incompatible coordination-of-benefits provisions; rule adopted to determine which plan bears primary liability).

97   555 U.S. ___, 129 S. Ct. 865 (2009), discussed *infra* Chapter 8B.

The Court suggested that such a waiver might in certain circumstances be given effect as a matter of federal common law,[98] but it held that where the plan required distribution to the beneficiary designated in accordance with the method specified by the plan, the waiver must be disregarded. The interest in simple, low-cost plan administration dissuaded the Court from looking beyond the plan's beneficiary designation rules.[99] Noting that *Boggs* and *Egelhoff* held state laws affecting the identification of plan beneficiaries preempted, the unanimous Court declared: "What goes for inconsistent state laws goes for a federal common law of waiver that might obscure a plan administrator's duty to act 'in accordance with the documents and instruments.'"[100]

E. THE INSURANCE SAVINGS CLAUSE

Additional considerations come into play when ERISA collides with a state law regulating insurance, banking, or securities. Section 514(b)(2), ERISA's insurance savings clause, provides in part that "nothing in this title shall be construed to exempt or relieve any person from any law of any State which regulates insurance, banking, or securities."[101] This reservation of state authority is not an "unqualified deferral to state law"; rather, the savings clause "leaves room for complementary or dual federal and state regulation" in these fields.[102]

Complementary state regulation, however, is permissible only insofar as it applies to independent insurance companies and insurance contracts. Although a self-funded pension or welfare plan functions as an insurer, in the sense that the plan pools and underwrites risk, ERISA's "deemer clause" provides that "[n]either an employee benefit plan . . . nor any trust established under such a plan, shall be deemed to be an insurance company or other insurer, . . . or to be engaged in the business of insurance" for purposes of state laws regulating insurance.[103] Consequently, pension and welfare plans that provide benefits through the purchase of insurance are subject to indirect state insurance regulation (by operation of the savings clause), while self-insured

---

98   129 S. Ct. at 874, 875 n.10. The waiver had been incorporated in a divorce decree, but that was "only happenstance"—"recognizing a waiver in a divorce decree would not be giving effect to state law." In principle, a court could apply "federal [common] law to a document that might also have independent significance under state law." *Id*. at 874.

99   *Id*. at 876. Despite countervailing equitable considerations, ERISA's policy of promoting voluntary sponsorship supports carrying out the plan's directive to pay the person whose name is on file. The prospect of increased cost, uncertainty, and delay "are good and sufficient reasons for holding the line, just as we have done in cases of state laws that might blur the bright-line requirements to follow plan documents in distributing benefits." *Id*.

100   *Id*. at 877.

101   ERISA § 514(b)(2)(A), 29 U.S.C. § 1144(b)(2)(A) (2006).

102   John Hancock Mut. Life Ins. Co. v. Harris Trust & Sav. Bank, 510 U.S. 86, 98 (1993).

103   ERISA § 514(b)(2)(B), 29 U.S.C. § 1144(b)(2)(B) (2006).

benefit plans are not (by operation of the deemer clause).[104] The Supreme Court explained:

> We read the deemer clause to exempt self-funded ERISA plans from state laws that "regulat[e] insurance" within the meaning of the saving clause. By forbidding States to deem employee benefit plans "to be an insurance company or other insurer . . . or to be engaged in the business of insurance," the deemer clause relieves plans from state laws "purporting to regulate insurance." As a result, self-funded ERISA plans are exempt from state regulation insofar as that regulation "relate[s] to" the plans. State laws directed toward the plans are pre-empted because they relate to an employee benefit plan but are not "saved" because they do not regulate insurance. State laws that directly regulate insurance are "saved" but do not reach self-funded employee benefit plans because the plans may not be deemed to be insurance companies, other insurers, or engaged in the business of insurance for purposes of such state laws. On the other hand, employee benefit plans that are insured are subject to indirect state insurance regulation. An insurance company that insures a plan remains an insurer for purposes of state laws "purporting to regulate insurance" after application of the deemer clause. The insurance company is therefore not relieved from state insurance regulation. The ERISA plan is consequently bound by state insurance regulations insofar as they apply to the plan's insurer.[105]

The distinction between insured and self-insured plans leads to dramatic differences in the applicability of state law. Express (read field) preemption ordinarily bars deliberate state regulation of employee benefit plans, including laws requiring that a plan provide specified benefits or cover certain workers (content regulation) and laws regulating the administration of an employee benefit plan (conduct regulation). But where the plan provides benefits through the purchase of insurance, the savings clause lets stand state laws requiring that certain benefits be included in the policy,[106] as well as laws regulating the insurance claims process.[107]

---

104 Metro. Life Ins. Co. v. Massachusetts, 471 U.S. 724, 747 (1985) ("We are aware that our decision results in a distinction between insured and uninsured plans, leaving the former open to indirect regulation while the latter are not. By so doing we merely give life to a distinction created by Congress in the 'deemer clause,' a distinction Congress is aware of and one it has chosen not to alter."). A benefit plan is treated as self-insured and exempt from state regulation even if it limits its risk by purchasing stop-loss insurance, although the stop-loss policy would be subject to state regulation. *See* Russell Korobkin, *The Battle Over Self-Insured Health Plans, or "One Good Loophole Deserves Another,"* 5 YALE J. HEALTH POL'Y L. & ETHICS 89, 117–18 (2005) ("If states are unhappy that [health plans] use stop-loss insurance to make self-insuring a relatively more attractive option than purchasing state-regulated third-party insurance, their best response is to regulate stop-loss insurers in a way that undermines that advantage.").

105 FMC Corp. v. Holliday, 498 U.S. 52, 61 (1990).

106 *Metro. Life*, 471 U.S. 724 (mandatory minimum mental health coverage); *see Holliday*, 498 U.S. at 60–61 (anti-subrogation law preempted as applied to self-funded plan, but would be saved if benefits were insured).

107 UNUM Life Ins. Co. of Am. v. Ward, 526 U.S. 358 (1999) (California decisional law prohibiting an insurer from denying claim as untimely unless the insurer was prejudiced by delay applied to claims under disability insurance policy purchased to provide welfare plan benefits);

Notwithstanding the savings clause, some state laws that regulate insurance may still be preempted. The savings clause "leaves room for complementary or dual federal and state regulation," but ERISA still "calls for federal supremacy when the two regimes cannot be harmonized or accommodated."[108] The Court "discern[ed] no solid basis for believing that Congress, when it designed ERISA, intended fundamentally to alter traditional preemption analysis. State law governing insurance generally is not displaced, but 'where [that] law stands as an obstacle to the accomplishment of the full purposes and objectives of Congress,' federal preemption occurs."[109] The Court has suggested that a state insurance law cause of action or remedy might present such an obstacle, because Congress intended ERISA's civil enforcement scheme to provide the exclusive means of relief.[110] Moreover, in recent decisions involving state laws regulating insurance claims handling, after finding the laws in question to be protected by the savings clause, the Court proceeded to consider (and reject) arguments that the laws undermined ERISA's objectives.[111]

The scope of the savings clause turns upon the meaning of a "law . . . which regulates insurance," a phrase Congress left undefined. In its initial encounters with the savings clause, the Court looked for guidance to criteria identified by case law interpreting the McCarran-Ferguson Act's reference to the "business of insurance."[112] In 2003, the Court disavowed that approach and made a "clean break from the McCarran-Ferguson factors," holding that "for a state law to be deemed a 'law . . . which regulates insurance' under [the savings clause], it must satisfy two requirements. First, the state law must be specifically directed toward entities engaged in insurance. Second, . . . the state law must substantially affect the risk pooling arrangement between the insurer and the insured."[113] To satisfy the latter factor, the law need not control the terms of the insurance policy so long as it affects risk.[114]

Rush Prudential HMO Inc. v. Moran, 536 U.S. 355 (2002) (required opportunity for independent review of medical necessity under Illinois HMO Act applies to benefits provided by HMO under contract with health care plan); Ky. Ass'n of Health Plans, Inc. v. Miller, 538 U.S. 329 (2003) (Kentucky's "any willing provider" statute, by limiting HMOs' ability to restrict physician access, is a law that regulates insurance).

108 John Hancock Mut. Life Ins. Co. v. Harris Trust & Sav. Bank, 510 U.S. 86, 98 (1993).

109 *Id.* at 99 (quoting Silkwood v. Kerr-McGee Corp., 464 U.S. 238, 248 (1984)).

110 Aetna Health Inc. v. Davila, 542 U.S. 200, 217–18 (2004); Pilot Life Ins. Co. v. Dedeaux, 481 U.S. 41, 51–57 (1987) (arguably dicta, in that the Court had concluded that the Mississippi cause of action for bad-faith breach of contract is not a law that regulates insurance). *But see UNUM Life*, 526 U.S. at 377 n.7 (noting, but not addressing, Solicitor General's argument questioning *Pilot Life*'s obstacle preemption analysis).

111 *UNUM Life*, 526 U.S. at 377 ("notice prejudice rule complements rather than contradicts" ERISA's claims-handling rules); *Rush*, 536 U.S. at 375–80, 384–86.

112 *Metro. Life*, 471 U.S. at 742–44; *Pilot Life*, 481 U.S. at 48–51; *UNUM Life*, 526 U.S. at 373–75; *Rush*, 536 U.S. at 373–75.

113 Ky. Ass'n of Health Plans, Inc. v. Miller, 538 U.S. 329, 341–42 (2003).

114 *Id.* at 338.

F. CONCLUSION

ERISA's express preemption clause, section 514(a), is "conspicuous for its breadth,"[115] and for many years the Supreme Court approached preemption questions by construing section 514(a) in such a way as to distinguish between those state laws that bear too closely on employee benefit plans and those that have only a "tenuous, remote or peripheral" connection, with the former being preempted because they "relate to [a] plan," and the latter not. But attributing everything to the reach of express preemption runs into the difficulty that the Court's metric of relatedness is at best difficult to discern, and at worst indeterminate. Since 1995, the Justices have struggled to rein in ERISA preemption, yet the Court has not repudiated its earlier holdings, nor yet disavowed its earlier reasoning.

Attention to case outcomes and the conceptual underpinnings of preemption leads to a much more coherent explanation. ERISA's express preemption clause can be construed to mandate field preemption not only for pension plans, which the statute intensively regulates, but for welfare plans as well, even though the federal law leaves them largely unregulated. As such, any state law designed to regulate the content or conduct of any employee benefit plan, whether pension or welfare, falls prey to express preemption, even if it concerns an issue on which ERISA is silent. In legislating field preemption, Congress intended to promote sponsorship by preserving freedom of contract on matters that it did not address.

The validity of general state laws that incidentally affect an employee benefit plan is best understood without reference to express preemption. Laws aimed at achieving state goals in areas such as health care regulation, employment training, taxation, and the like, clearly lie outside the field of benefit plan regulation. Therefore, if section 514(a) is interpreted as legislating field preemption, express preemption leaves such laws untouched.

Although express preemption can be construed to leave general state laws undisturbed, in some situations the application of those laws to employee benefit plans may undermine the accomplishment of ERISA's purposes. Accordingly, legitimate state regulation in other fields may be superseded by the application of general principles of conflict and obstacle preemption. Proper application of obstacle preemption, of course, demands close attention to ERISA's policies. Cost-containment promotes plan sponsorship and forms the principal justification for express (field) preemption. Nevertheless, the indirect cost that a general state law may impose on an employee benefit plan or its sponsor is *not* a factor that can be taken into account in applying *obstacle* preemption. For the simple reason that regulation always imposes costs, financial impact alone is not enough to invalidate an otherwise legitimate general state law.

Simply stated, the conclusion is that ERISA's express preemption clause accomplishes only field preemption, and decisions holding generally applicable state laws superseded are best understood as applications of conflict or obstacle preemption. This methodology cannot reduce preemption issues to a simple algorithm, because obstacle preemption requires careful attention to statutory objectives and ERISA's purposes

---

115   FMC Corp. v. Holliday, 498 U.S. 52, 58 (1990).

sometimes conflict. Yet by focusing debate on the right question—the impact of the state law in question on the proper balance of ERISA's competing policies—this approach should yield more coherent results. Attention to those policies should have the added advantage of revealing when an offending state law is symptomatic of a real need that should be met by the interstitial elaboration of federal common law. Congress intended to preserve wide latitude for private ordering (laissez-faire) within the domain of employee benefits, and so judicial lawmaking that facilitates rather than restricts private ordering is fully justified.

PART III

Content Controls
Pension Plans

We have seen that ERISA incorporates two very different approaches to the regulation of employee benefits. As discussed in Part II, the administration of all employee benefit plans is subject to federal oversight to promote informed participation and ensure compliance with plan terms. The specification of welfare plan terms is generally left to market forces;[1] in contrast, the substance of a pension promise is regulated in several important respects. Thus, ERISA monitors only the administration or *conduct* of most welfare plans, while pension plans are subject to both *conduct* and *content* regulation.

ERISA's pension plan content controls constrain the terms of most deferred compensation programs in three broad areas. First, the accumulation of pension savings is influenced by rules governing eligibility for plan participation, the rate at which benefits accrue under defined benefit plans, and when benefits vest (Chapter 7). Second, the distribution of pension benefits can be made only to certain persons and at certain times (Chapter 8). Third, pension claims are converted from unsecured contract rights (that are implicitly contingent on the long-term financial health of the sponsor) into property rights by the requirement that defined benefit plans be funded

---

1 Congress has made inroads on this general principle of laissez-faire in recent years by imposing limited standards for the content of certain group health care plans. The Consolidated Omnibus Budget Reconciliation Act of 1986 (COBRA) added Part 6 to ERISA Title I, which requires that a group health plan of an employer with more than twenty employees offer participants and beneficiaries who would lose health insurance coverage as a result of certain changes in employment or family status the opportunity to purchase continuation coverage at group rates for a period of 18 or 36 months. ERISA §§ 601–609, 29 U.S.C. §§ 1161–1169 (2006). In 1996, Part 7 of ERISA Title I was enacted, which seeks to increase health insurance portability by prohibiting group health plans from imposing certain health-status-based eligibility rules and strictly limiting preexisting condition coverage exclusions. ERISA §§ 701–707, 29 U.S.C. §§ 1181–1191c (2006); *see* I.R.C. §§ 4980B, 4980D, 9801–9833 (2006) (excise taxes imposed for failure to satisfy corresponding continuation coverage and portability requirements).

and insured (Chapter 9). These pension plan content controls are generally applicable, but an exception to all of them is made for top-hat plans.[2]

The pattern of substantive pension regulation deserves special notice. To preserve a system of voluntary plan sponsorship, Congress trod lightly. Most matters were left unregulated, including the central design issues of a pension plan, namely, the extent of workforce coverage and the level of benefits. Where it chose to regulate, Congress restricted but did not eliminate freedom of contract. Instead of mandating particular plan features, it set minimum standards for certain key terms, leaving sponsors the flexibility to exceed the baseline.[3] Legislative intervention was not directed to ensuring a particular level of retirement income. Instead, reliability is the principle that animates ERISA's pension content controls. The employer may craft the program to cover as many or as few workers as desired, at any benefit level it chooses,[4] but once a pension promise is made, the statute backs it up by restricting plan terms that would undercut the commitment. Traditionally, those restrictions have been understood as paternalistic protection of the interests of plan participants and beneficiaries. But it isn't necessarily so. By limiting the variability of the more arcane plan terms, ERISA standardizes ancillary features of the pension contract. Standardization reduces information costs, and so may actually improve worker career and financial planning.[5]

---

2 ERISA §§ 201(2), 4021(b)(6), 29 U.S.C. §§ 1051(2), 1321(b)(6) (2006). *See supra* Chapter 2D.

3 *See supra* Chapter 1C.

4 Tax law nondiscrimination standards, however, deny preferential tax treatment for deferred compensation if, in actual operation, either the membership of the plan or the contributions or benefits that it provides unduly favor highly compensated employees. I.R.C. §§ 401(a)(3), (a)(4), (a)(5), (*l*), 410(b), 414(q) (2006). Qualified defined benefit plans are also required to cover at least fifty employees or, if fewer, 40 percent of all employees (but never fewer than two employees, except in cases where the employer has only one employee). *Id.* § 401(a)(26). All employees of certain commonly controlled or functionally related businesses are taken into account in applying these tax law nondiscrimination and minimum coverage rules. *Id.* § 414(b), (c), (m), (n). These tax rules are examined in depth in Chapter 10B.

5 *See supra* Chapter 1C.

Chapter 7

Accumulation

Three sets of rules bear on an employee's accumulation of pension rights. ERISA imposes minimum standards governing (1) participation (also known as plan membership or coverage), (2) benefit accrual (the earning of benefits by the performance of services), and (3) vesting (the attainment of a nonforfeitable right to future benefits). A worker must be a plan member to earn pension rights, but that alone is not enough to ensure that benefits will ultimately be paid. Pension plans may (and commonly do) make the payment of earned benefits contingent upon the satisfaction of prescribed conditions, like working a specified minimum number of years for the employer, failing which the pension is forfeited (i.e., accrued benefits may be subject to defeasance by conditions subsequent). Once all such conditions are satisfied, the pension is said to "vest," or become nonforfeitable. At that point, the participant is entitled to the *eventual* distribution of her accrued benefit (not immediately, but at the time and in the manner specified by the distribution rules of the plan and ERISA).[1] Accordingly, participation, accrual, and vesting are all necessary to establish a worker's right to pension benefits.

---

1   *See infra* Chapter 8.

Imposing vesting standards was a principal means to achieving ERISA's central goal of increasing retirement income security. Previously, pre-retirement vesting was not generally required. A plan could lawfully hold a worker's pension hostage until the moment the worker reached retirement age, so that an employee who quit or was fired on the brink of retirement could lose pension savings accumulated over many years of faithful service. Finding that unconscionable, Congress determined to limit the duration of forfeiture conditions. ERISA provides that once a participant completes a reasonable period of service (today, seven years or less), the participant's pension rights become irrevocable. We shall see that ERISA's participation and benefit accrual rules are a byproduct of the central decision to limit forfeitures, in that the rules function in part to prevent evasion of the vesting standards.

A. PARTICIPATION

Pension plan coverage, like sponsorship itself, is voluntary. The decision to offer a plan does not obligate the employer to cover all employees or any particular group of employees. ERISA's regulation of pension plan participation is limited to banning the use of certain age and service conditions on plan membership. In general, a plan cannot impose minimum age and service requirements that are more demanding than reaching age 21 and completing one year of service; alternatively, two years of service can be required, but only if participants are at all times fully vested.[2] ERISA also outlaws all maximum age conditions (that is, provisions excluding from membership workers who are older than a specified age).[3] Even when an employee who is older than 21 completes a year of service, she can still be excluded from participation on other grounds (such as pay rate, work situs, or job classification) because ERISA leaves all other eligibility criteria unregulated.[4]

A year of service, for purposes of the prohibited eligibility conditions, means a 12-month period in which the employee has at least 1,000 hours of service, with the first such period beginning on the date of initial employment.[5] All years of service

---

2   ERISA § 202(a)(1), 29 U.S.C. § 1052(a)(1) (2006); *see* I.R.C. § 410(a)(1) (2006). Tax-exempt educational institutions may impose a minimum age condition of 26 rather than 21 if participants are immediately fully vested, but this extended age condition cannot be combined with the two-year service condition. ERISA § 202(a)(1)(B)(ii), 29 U.S.C. § 1052(a)(1)(B)(ii) (2006); *see* I.R.C. § 410(a)(1)(B)(ii) (2006).

3   ERISA § 202(a)(2), 29 U.S.C. § 1052(a)(2) (2006); *see* I.R.C. § 410(a)(2) (2006).

4   For example, the First Circuit found:

> Despite Plaintiffs' attempt to hitch their claim to ERISA's minimum participation standards limiting the use of age- or length-of-service-related conditions of participation, their true complaint remains that the GTE ERISA plans use arbitrary criteria to establish an employee's threshold eligibility for plan participation—a complaint that has nothing to do with ERISA's minimum participation standards. Indeed, Plaintiffs identify no statutory provision that prohibits the use of such arbitrary eligibility criteria.

> Edes v. Verizon Comms., Inc., 417 F.3d 133, 143 (1st Cir. 2005).

5   ERISA § 202(a)(3), 29 U.S.C. § 1052(a)(3) (2006); *see* I.R.C. § 410(a)(3) (2006). An "hour of service" was left for regulatory definition. Service may be credited by counting actual hours of

must be counted for purposes of determining eligibility to participate unless the employee incurs a "break in service," defined as a 12-month period during which the employee has 500 or fewer hours of service.[6] A plan that uses the two-year, 100 percent vested entry rule may provide that an employee who has a break in service loses credit for service before the break, thereby delaying participation until two years of service are completed *after* the break.[7] In addition, any plan may provide that an employee who incurs a break in service after becoming a participant loses credit for his pre-break service *until* completing a year of service after the break.[8] Under this rule, pre-break service is only temporarily disregarded; upon completing a year of post-break service, all pre-break service must again be taken into account, with the result that the employee is retroactively entitled to plan membership as of the start of the first year of service after the break. The impact of these service-break rules is softened where absence from work is occasioned by the birth or adoption of a child. In that case, the period of the maternity or paternity leave is counted as hours of service, up to a maximum of 501 hours, but solely for purposes of avoiding a break in service (*not* for purposes of determining contributions or benefits earned under the plan).[9]

ERISA does not demand immediate admission to the plan once all permissible eligibility requirements have been satisfied. Instead, participation must commence no later than the beginning of the next plan year or, if earlier, a date that is six months after satisfying the age and service requirements. This rule accords sponsors the administrative advantage of bringing all new members into the plan on fixed semiannual entry dates (such as January 1 and July 1), while limiting the maximum waiting period to six months.[10]

---

work and paid leave, where employment records are adequate to support the determination. Alternatively, hours of service may be credited using various hour equivalencies (based on working time, employment period, or earnings) or the elapsed-time method. 29 C.F.R. § 2530.200b-2, -3 (2009); Treas. Reg. § 1.410(a)-7 (1980).

6   ERISA § 202(b)(1), 29 U.S.C. § 1052(b)(1) (2006); *see* I.R.C. § 410(a)(5)(A) (2006).

7   ERISA § 202(b)(2), 29 U.S.C. § 1052(b)(2) (2006); *see* I.R.C. § 410(a)(5)(B) (2006).

8   ERISA § 202(b)(3), 29 U.S.C. § 1052(b)(3) (2006); *see* I.R.C. § 410(a)(5)(C) (2006). As originally enacted, ERISA authorized a third break-in-service rule, known as the "rule of parity," which permitted a plan to permanently disregard all years of service before a break for an employee who is not vested and who incurs a number of consecutive one-year breaks in service that equals or exceeds the number of his pre-break years of service. Recognizing the disparate impact of the rule of parity on women who leave work for a period of child-rearing, the Retirement Equity Act of 1984 tightened this rule by making it applicable only if the service break was at least five years long. When ERISA was later amended to shorten permissible vesting periods to five years, the rule of parity—which can only apply to totally nonvested participants—became irrelevant (though it survives as a statutory artifact. ERISA § 202(b)(4), 29 U.S.C. § 1052(b)(4) (2006); *see* I.R.C. § 410(a)(5)(D) (2006)).

9   ERISA § 202(b)(5), 29 U.S.C. § 1052(b)(5) (2006); *see* I.R.C. § 410(a)(5)(E) (2006). *Cf.* ERISA § 204(b)(4)(A), 29 U.S.C. § 1054(b)(4)(A) (2006); *see* I.R.C. § 411(b)(4)(A) (2006) (parenthetical clause excludes maternity/paternity leave period for purposes of determining accrued benefits).

10   ERISA § 202(a)(4), 29 U.S.C. § 1052(a)(4) (2006); Treas. Reg. § 1.410(a)-4(b) (as amended in 1980); Rev. Rul. 80-360, 1980-2 C.B. 142; *see* I.R.C. § 410(a)(4) (2006). Observe, however, that a participant who has a break in service may be entitled to reenter the plan retroactively as

All the prohibited age and service conditions rules (including the rules governing service credit, breaks in service, and time of entry) prescribe minimum standards. The plan sponsor is free to specify more liberal membership criteria by not imposing any age or service criteria, by imposing lower requirements, or by declining to utilize the break-in-service rules. Indeed, the minimum standard (age 21 with one year of service) is so exacting, and the record-keeping necessary to implement service conditions so burdensome, that one might wonder if employers would be better off simply dropping service conditions on plan membership. Because three years of service can be required for vesting, benefits won't have to be paid to short-term employees even if they are allowed to participate, and the resulting forfeitures can be used to reduce future employer contributions.

Nevertheless, pension plans still overwhelmingly contain minimum age and service conditions, highly restricted though they are. There are several advantages in doing so. First, service conditions avoid the plan-administration costs (record-keeping and accounting) that would be entailed in keeping track, for a prolonged period, of small accrued benefits earned by numerous short-term employees. Second, some benefit costs are saved for those employees who do stay long enough to vest because they will not have earned any deferred compensation for work performed in the year or two it took them to become participants. Third (and most important), employees excluded from participation by minimum age or service conditions do not have to be taken into account in applying the tax law's tests for discrimination in plan coverage, making it more likely that the plan will qualify for preferential tax treatment.[11]

ERISA's prohibited age and service condition rules are a compromise. They are based on the belief that "it is desirable to have as many employees as possible covered by private pension plans and to begin such coverage as early as possible, since an employee's ultimate pension benefits usually depend to a considerable extent on the number of his years of participation in the plan."[12] But that preference for early coverage was tempered by a concern for employer costs, especially the administrative burden of covering transient employees.[13] In attempting to induce early coverage of

---

of the date he returns to work, provided he completes a year of service after returning to work. An additional waiting period is *not* permissible. Treas. Reg. § 1.410(a)-4(b)(2), Example (3) (as amended in 1980); Rev. Rul. 80-360, Plan 4, *supra.*

11   *See* I.R.C. § 410(b)(4)(A) (2006). Because pay rates typically rise as age and experience increase, a smaller proportion of employees who are young or recently hired will be highly compensated, compared to the workforce as a whole. If employees who are under age 21 or who have less than a year of service had to be taken into account in testing for coverage non-discrimination, many plans that exclude such workers from membership would find that they are in jeopardy of disqualification. Therefore, as a practical matter, ERISA's permission to impose limited age and service conditions would be largely illusory without a corresponding concession in coverage nondiscrimination testing.

12   H.R. Rep. No. 93-807, at 43–44 (1974), *reprinted in* 2 ERISA Legislative History, *supra* Chapter 1 note 56, at 3115, 3163–64; H.R. Rep. No. 93-779, at 42–43 (1974), *reprinted in* 2 ERISA Legislative History, *supra* Chapter 1 note 56, at 2584, 2631–32.

13   H.R. Rep. No. 93-807, at 44 (1974), *reprinted in* 2 ERISA Legislative History, *supra* Chapter 1 note 56, at 3115, 3164; H.R. Rep. No. 93-779, at 43 (1974), *reprinted in* 2 ERISA Legislative History, *supra* Chapter 1 note 56, at 2584, 2632.

workers who would prefer additional cash compensation, ERISA's participation standards betray an element of a forced savings program.[14]

The ban on extended service conditions also functions to prevent evasion of the vesting rules. Vesting is tied to years of service; currently, a participant will have a nonforfeitable right to his entire accrued benefit after at most seven years of service. If minimum service conditions on plan membership were not controlled, a sponsor wanting to avoid paying benefits to short-service workers could do so by simply holding them out of the plan for an extended period, rather than by admitting them and forfeiting benefits in the event of early departure. Being fully vested under a plan that delays entry for 15 years is little different from being a participant whose nominal accrued benefit remains forfeitable for 15 years.

B. BENEFIT ACCRUAL

Pension plan participation is significant primarily because it brings with it the opportunity to earn (or "accrue") benefits under the plan.[15] Participation is a necessary condition for accruing pension benefits, and most participants in active service earn increased retirement savings; but participant status alone is not sufficient to ensure current benefit accrual. In addition to participation, plans may, and commonly do, condition benefit increases on some sort of current-year service requirement. A defined benefit plan is not required to take a participant's service into account for purposes of determining accrued benefits if the employee has less than 1,000 hours of service during the accrual computation period (a calendar year, plan year, or other consecutive 12-month period designated by the plan).[16] An employee who has at least 1,000 hours of service during the accrual computation period must receive some credit for benefit accrual purposes, but if the employee's service is less than that required by the plan to qualify as a full year of participation, then the plan may grant only a fractional year of participation (the fraction being at least equal to the ratio of the employee's service to that required for full credit).[17] A defined contribution plan may go even further and provide that a participant whose employment terminates before the last day of the plan year will not share in the allocation of employer contributions or forfeitures for the year, even if she has more than 1,000 hours of service.[18]

---

14   Wiedenbeck, *supra* Chapter 1 note 57, at 574 (footnotes omitted). The anti-alienation requirement (discussed *infra* Chapter 8B) is the other principal forced savings component of ERISA.

15   *See* 29 C.F.R. § 2530.204-1(b)(1) (2009) (service before an employee first becomes a participant need not be taken into account in determining accrued benefits under a defined benefit plan).

16   ERISA § 204(b)(4)(C), 29 U.S.C. § 1054(b)(4)(C) (2006); 29 C.F.R. § 2530.204-2(c)(1), -1(b)(1) (2009); *see* I.R.C. § 411(b)(4)(C) (2006).

17   ERISA § 204(b)(4)(B), 29 U.S.C. § 1054(b)(4)(B) (2006); 29 C.F.R. §§ 2530.204-2(c)(1), 2530.200b-1(a) (2009); *see* I.R.C. § 411(b)(4)(B) (2006).

18   29 C.F.R. § 2530.200b-1(b) (2009) (final four sentences). *But cf.* Treas. Reg. § 1.410(b)-6(f) (as amended in 1994) (outgoing employee who fails to accrue a benefit because of such a last-day requirement must be taken into account in coverage nondiscrimination testing if she has more than 500 hours of service).

A participant's accrued benefit is the total amount of deferred compensation that has been earned to date. Under a defined contribution plan, the accrued benefit at any time is simply the current balance in the participant's individual account and therefore reflects contributions and forfeitures allocated to the account as well as an appropriate share of plan income, expenses, gains, and losses.[19] Under a defined benefit plan, the accrued benefit must be specified by the plan and is expressed in the form of an annual benefit (annuity payment) commencing at normal retirement age.[20] Consistent with the policy of maintaining a voluntary pension system, ERISA does not specify the amount of contributions or benefits to be provided under a plan. But while the employer is free to set the level of pension contributions or benefits, ERISA regulates the *rate* at which contributions or benefits are earned from year to year. Limitations on the rate of accrual serve two purposes: preventing age discrimination and preventing evasion of the vesting requirements by backloading benefits under a defined benefit plan.

Age Discrimination

In 1986, Congress amended ERISA, the Age Discrimination in Employment Act (ADEA), and the qualified plan provisions of the tax Code, to outlaw age discrimination in the accrual of pension benefits. In the case of a defined contribution plan, allocations of contributions or forfeitures to an employee's account may not be cut off, nor may the rate of allocation be reduced, on account of the attainment of any age.[21] Similarly, a defined benefit plan cannot cease benefit accrual or reduce the rate of accrual based on the employee's age.[22] Benefit accrual can be stopped on grounds that are not age-based, such as an overall limitation on the amount of accrued benefits or a limitation on the number of years of service or years of participation that the plan takes into account in determining accrued benefits.[23] But while service-based limitations on *additional* accrual are permissible, a defined benefit plan cannot reduce previously accrued benefits on account of increasing service.[24]

There has been a trend since the 1990s of large employers substituting cash balance plans for their traditional defined benefit pension plans. A cash balance plan is a defined

---

19   ERISA § 3(23), (34), 29 U.S.C. § 1002(23), (34) (2006); *see* I.R.C. §§ 411(a)(7)(A)(ii), 414(i) (2006).

20   ERISA § 3(23), (24), (35), 29 U.S.C. § 1002(23), (24), (35) (2006); *see* I.R.C. §§ 411(a)(7)(A)(i), (a)(8), 414(j) (2006).

21   ERISA § 204(b)(2), 29 U.S.C. § 1054(b)(2) (2006); ADEA § 4(i)(1), 29 U.S.C. § 623(i)(1) (2006); *see* I.R.C. § 411(b)(2) (2006).

22   ERISA § 204(b)(1)(H), 29 U.S.C. § 1054(b)(1)(H) (2006); ADEA § 4(i)(1), 29 U.S.C. § 623(i) (1) (2006); *see* I.R.C. § 411(b)(1)(H) (2006).

23   ERISA § 204(b)(1)(H)(ii), 29 U.S.C. § 1054(b)(1)(H)(ii) (2006); ADEA § 4(i)(2), 29 U.S.C. § 623(i)(2) (2006); *see* I.R.C. § 411(b)(1)(H)(ii) (2006). Despite the absence of a corresponding statutory authorization, the same principle apparently applies to defined contribution plans. That is, contributions may be cut off because the participant's account balance exceeds a specified level or because of a limitation on the number of years for which contributions will be made (i.e., where the plan specifies a maximum number years of active participation).

24   ERISA § 204(b)(1)(G), 29 U.S.C. § 1054(b)(1)(G) (2006); *see* I.R.C. § 411(b)(1)(G) (2006).

benefit plan that mimics a defined contribution plan—specifically, a money-purchase pension plan. Active plan participants earn annual pay credits (for example, 5 percent of compensation) and interest credits according to a specified rate or index (for example, prime plus 1 percent); at retirement, each participant is entitled to a benefit defined as the cumulative total of her prior pay and interest credits.[25] Younger workers have more time before retirement during which they accrue interest credits under a cash balance plan, while the traditional defined benefit plans that the new cash balance plans replaced typically favored older workers with a higher rate of benefit accrual.[26] This difference has triggered a spate of ERISA age discrimination litigation. The Seventh Circuit, in an opinion by Judge Easterbrook, ruled that the age discrimination rule for defined benefit plans, including the cash balance plan at issue, has the same meaning as the rule for defined contribution plans, and that differences attributable to the time value of money are not age discrimination. "[R]emoving a feature that gave extra benefits to the old does not discriminate against them. Replacing a plan that discriminates against the young with one that is age-neutral does not discriminate against the old."[27] Despite the Seventh Circuit's pronouncement, district courts in other circuits differ on whether cash balance plans violate ERISA's age discrimination ban.[28]

---

25 Cash balance plan benefits are defined without reference to actual trust fund investment results, so that benefits are not based solely on contributions to an individual account, with adjustment for income, gain, losses, and expenses allocated to that account. Because participants are insulated from the risks and rewards of investment performance, technically the arrangement is not an individual account (i.e., defined contribution) plan. Instead, cash balance plans are defined benefit plans. ERISA § 3(34), (35), 29 U.S.C. § 1002(34), (35) (2006); see I.R.C. § 414(i), (j) (2006). As such, they are subject to ERISA's minimum standards on benefit accrual and actuarial funding, as well as the PBGC insurance program and restrictions on termination.

26 The benefit formula under a traditional defined benefit plan is typically tied to final average or highest average compensation. For example, under a unit credit plan, the annuity at normal retirement age might be specified as 1.5 percent of final average compensation multiplied by the participant's years of service. Because compensation levels in most occupations systematically increase with increasing job tenure, under such a formula, a larger proportion of the final retirement benefit is earned in the later years of service, as the compensation factor increases each year. This "backloading" of the rate at which a defined benefit pension is earned is permissible under ERISA's minimum standards on benefit accrual (discussed immediately below), because in testing for excessive backloading, those standards ignore future compensation increases.

27 Cooper v. IBM Pers. Pension Plan, 457 F.3d 636, 642 (7th Cir. 2006), cert. denied, 549 U.S. 1175 (2007). In reaching its decision, the court concluded that the term "benefit accrual," used in the defined benefit plan age discrimination rule, ERISA § 204(b)(1)(H)(i), refers to the annual addition to pension rights, and so has a meaning different from "accrued benefit," as defined in ERISA § 3(23), which refers to the participant's accumulated pension entitlement. Cooper, 457 F.3d at 641. Accord Register v. PNC Fin. Servs. Group, Inc., 477 F.3d 56 (3d Cir. 2007).

28 Compare Hirt v. Equitable Ret. Plan, 441 F. Supp. 2d 516 (S.D.N.Y. 2006) (no age discrimination), and Laurent v. PriceWaterhouseCoopers LLP, 448 F. Supp. 2d 537, 553–54 (S.D.N.Y. 2006) (same), and Drutis v. Quebecor World (USA) Inc., 459 F. Supp. 2d 580 (E.D. Ky. 2006) (same), with Richards v. FleetBoston Fin. Corp., 427 F. Supp. 2d 150 (D. Conn. 2006) (refusing to dismiss age discrimination claims), and In re J.P. Morgan Chase Cash Balance Litig., 460 F. Supp. 2d 479 (S.D.N.Y. 2006) (same), and In re Citigroup Pension Plan ERISA Litig., 470 F. Supp. 2d 323 (S.D.N.Y. 2006) (same).

Prospectively, however, the Pension Protection Act of 2006 amended ERISA to ensure that new cash balance plans providing age-neutral pay and interest credits are not discriminatory and to grant a safe harbor for conversions of traditional defined benefit plans into cash balance plans.[29]

Voluntary early retirement incentives remain lawful, and Congress provided a safe harbor for subsidized early retirement benefits and Social Security bridge payments under defined benefit plans.[30] Therefore, an employer may use increased benefits to induce early retirement (the carrot), but an age-based cutback in the ability to earn additional retirement income (the stick) is not an acceptable tool of personnel management. These rules presumably increase total labor costs for older workers, and are an instance of ERISA's incorporation of covert distributive norms.[31]

Backloaded Accrual Under Defined Benefit Plans

The age discrimination rules prevent *decreases* in the rate of pension accrual as a worker gets older. For defined benefit plans, ERISA also bars excessive *increases* in the rate that benefits are earned over the course of a worker's career. Functionally, patrolling increases in the rate of benefit accrual backstops the vesting rules. Vesting requires that a participant's right to deferred compensation become irrevocable once she completes a reasonable period of service, often five years. Vesting applies to a participant's accrued benefit, which is the total pension accumulation *earned to date*. Left unregulated, a defined benefit plan could defeat the vesting rules by defining a participant's accrued benefit to require prolonged service before significant pension obligations arise. For instance, a plan might promise (and the employer might tout) a generous retirement annuity but stipulate in fine print that the promised benefit is

---

29   ERISA § 204(b)(5), 29 U.S.C. § 1054(b)(5) (2006); *see* I.R.C. § 411(b)(5) (2006). The new rules are effective for periods beginning after June 29, 2005, but the statute provides that the amendments are not to be construed to create an inference as to the meaning of the age discrimination rules as in effect before that date. Pension Protection Act of 2006, Pub. L. No. 109-280, § 706(d), (e)(1), 120 Stat. 780, 991 (2006).

30   ADEA § 4(f)(2)(B)(ii), (*l*)(1)(A)(ii), 29 U.S.C. § 623(f)(2)(B)(ii), (*l*)(1)(A)(ii) (2006); ERISA § 204(b)(1)(G), (b)(1)(H)(v), 29 U.S.C. § 1054(b)(1)(G), (b)(1)(H)(v) (2006); *see* I.R.C. § 411(b)(1)(G), (b)(1)(H)(iv) (2006). Subsidized early retirement occurs where benefit payments commence before the normal retirement age (NRA) specified in the plan (hence, early retirement) and the amount of benefits is not reduced to the level (i.e., actuarial equivalence to the pension payable at NRA) that would fully offset the longer payment period (the subsidy). Social Security bridge payments are additional pension benefits paid temporarily to early retirees to substitute for Social Security benefits until the retirees are old enough to receive either reduced or unreduced old-age benefits. (The earliest that individuals may claim reduced Social Security old-age benefits is age 62; unreduced benefits are payable at full retirement age, which is increasing gradually from 65, for persons born in 1937 or earlier, to 67, for those born in 1960 or later.) The Older Workers Benefit Protection Act of 1990 amended the cited ADEA provisions to counteract a restrictive interpretation announced by the Supreme Court in *Public Employees Retirement System v. Betts*, 492 U.S. 158 (1989).

31   The termination insurance program of ERISA Title IV is also rife with distributional implications. *See infra* Chapter 9B.

earned at the rate of one dollar per year for each of the first 29 years of service, with the balance earned in the thirtieth year of service. Such delay or "backloading" of benefit accrual, if allowed, would cause a long-term employee who separates from service prior to normal retirement age (NRA) to have a fully vested right to a trivial amount of benefits. The minimum standards on benefit accrual do not allow it.

The anti-backloading rules apply only to defined benefit plans; age-based or service-based increases in contributions under defined contribution plans are permissible. (The policy implications of this distinction will be explored shortly.) Backloading has no impact on participants whose employment continues until the plan's NRA, hence the concern of the accrual rules is with the benefit entitlement of participants who separate from service before that time. ERISA does not require that a participant's accrued benefit at any time be given by applying the plan's formula for the normal retirement benefit to the participant's years of participation at the time in question. Instead, ERISA allows the accrued benefit of a participant who separates from service before retirement age to be defined by the terms of the plan, subject only to the anti-backloading rules. The rules prohibit substantial increases in the rate at which the promised retirement benefit is earned over a member's years of participation.

To provide flexibility, a plan need only satisfy one of three alternative anti-backloading tests. The tests establish a floor on the portion of the normal retirement benefit that must be earned with each year of plan participation. That floor (like so many of ERISA's pension content controls) sets a *minimum* standard: any amount of frontloading is permissible.[32]

ERISA's alternative accrual rate standards are known as the 3 percent rule, the $133^1/_3$ percent rule, and the fractional rule. Under the 3 percent rule, a participant's accrued benefit on separation from service must be no less than the product of (1) the number of years of plan participation (up to a maximum of $33^1/_3$), and (2) 3 percent of the normal retirement benefit to which the participant would have been entitled if participation had begun at the plan's earliest possible entry date and continued to the earlier of age 65 or the plan's NRA.[33] An important feature of the 3 percent rule is that all plan participants accrue benefits (expressed as a percentage of compensation) at a uniform annual rate, regardless of when their membership began.

The $133^1/_3$ percent rule is satisfied if no participant (actual or hypothetical) can experience a greater than one-third increase in the annual rate of benefit accrual between a given year of plan participation and any later year.[34] That is, the rate of accrual for any future year of participation cannot exceed $133^1/_3$ percent of the rate for

---

32   Where benefits are frontloaded, the rate of accrual eventually decreases. The decrease will not violate the age discrimination rules if it is based on increasing years of service rather than age.

33   ERISA § 204(b)(1)(A), 29 U.S.C. § 1054(b)(1)(A) (2006); *see* I.R.C. § 411(b)(1)(A) (2006). If plan benefits depend on compensation, the compensation taken into account under the 3 percent rule is the highest average computation over a period of at most ten consecutive years (even if the promised retirement benefit is a function of compensation over some longer period, such as career average compensation). Treas. Reg. § 1.411(b)-1(b)(1)(ii)(A) (1977).

34   ERISA § 204(b)(1)(B), 29 U.S.C. § 1054(b)(1)(B) (2006); *see* I.R.C. § 411(b)(1)(B) (2006).

any prior year. This approach permits some upward variation in accrual rates over a particular worker's career, and so sanctions a modest amount of backloading.

The fractional rule requires that the accrued benefit of a participant who separates from service before normal retirement age must be at least equal to the product of (1) the normal retirement benefit to which the participant would be entitled under the terms of the plan had he continued to work for the employer until NRA, assuming that such employment would not change the amount of compensation taken into account under the plan's benefit formula, and (2) the ratio of the departing employee's actual number of years of plan participation on separation from service to the total number of years he would have participated in the plan had he continued working to NRA.[35]

Carollo v. Cement & Concrete Workers District Council Pension Plan[36] illustrates the impact of the benefit accrual rules. The plan in *Carollo* provided for pension accrual at the rate of 2 percent of career average compensation for the first 24 years of service, but participants who worked for 25 years without an extended break in service had their pension benefits recalculated for all previous years of service at 2 percent of final average compensation. For each year of service beyond 25, however, the benefit accrued at the rate of 1.66 percent of final average compensation. The defendant argued that the plan complied with the anti-backloading rules because the rate of accrual actually *decreased* with increasing service. Taking its cue from a Treasury Regulation, the court ruled that a plan may not circumvent the prohibition on benefit accrual rate increases by changing the base used in the calculation.[37] The retroactive switch from career average to final average compensation caused an immediate large jump in total accrued benefits in the twenty-fifth year of service that exceeded the limited backloading permitted by the $133^1/_3$ percent rule. Therefore, the plan failed to satisfy ERISA's benefit accrual minimum standards.[38]

Amendments Affecting Accrual Provisions

The final component of ERISA's regulation of benefit accrual prohibits certain amendments that would alter a pension plan's accrual provisions. First, a participant's accrued

---

35 ERISA § 204(b)(1)(C), 29 U.S.C. § 1054(b)(1)(C) (2006); *see* I.R.C. § 411(b)(1)(C) (2006). If plan benefits are based on average compensation, no more than the last ten consecutive years may be taken into account when determining the projected normal retirement benefit under the fractional accrual rule. Treas. Reg. § 1.411(b)-1(b)(3)(ii)(A), -1(b)(3)(iii), Example (2) (1977).

36 964 F. Supp. 677 (E.D.N.Y. 1997).

37 *Id.* at 681–82. Treas. Reg. § 1.411(b)-1(b)(2)(ii)(F) (1977).

38 Revenue Ruling 78-252 provides an excellent concrete example of the application of the anti-backloading rules. The ruling involves a defined benefit plan that promises a normal retirement benefit at age 65 of 2.4 percent of the participant's average compensation for each year of participation, offset by 2 percent of the participant's Social Security primary insurance benefit for each of the first 25 years of participation. The ruling shows that *if the plan defines the accrued benefit at any time as the amount given by applying the benefit formula to the participant's years of participation at that time*, none of the three alternative benefit accrual rules is satisfied.

benefit may not be decreased by plan amendment.[39] This rule, known as the accrued benefit anti-cutback rule, applies to both defined benefit and defined contribution plans. It functions as an adjunct to the vesting rules by protecting an employee's previously earned pension rights from forfeiture. Retroactive reductions in accrued benefits would often violate ERISA's vesting rules, but the accrued benefit anti-cutback rule is broader, as it protects even nonvested participants from pension cutbacks.[40] Only retirement-type benefits are protected; medical benefits, life insurance, and other ancillary benefits that are provided under some pension plans are not.[41] Retirement benefits, however, are strongly protected. *Central Laborers' Pension Fund v. Heinz*[42] presented the question whether a plan amendment expanding the categories of post-retirement employment that trigger a plan provision requiring suspension of payment of previously accrued early retirement benefits violates the anti-cutback rule. A unanimous Supreme Court held that it does, noting that "an amendment placing materially greater restrictions on the receipt of the benefit 'reduces' the benefit just as surely as a decrease in the size of the monthly benefit payment."[43]

> [The participant] was being reasonable if he relied on [plan terms that allowed him to supplement retirement income with certain permissible employment] in planning his retirement. The 1998 amendment undercut any such reliance, paying retirement income only if he accepted a substantial curtailment of his opportunity to do the kind of work he knew. We simply do not see how, in any practical sense, this change of terms could not be viewed as shrinking the value of Heinz's pension rights and reducing his promised benefits.[44]

Most important, the overall amount cannot be reduced.[45] In addition, in most instances, optional forms of distribution cannot be eliminated with respect to benefits

---

39   ERISA § 204(g)(1), 29 U.S.C. § 1054(g)(1) (2006); *see* I.R.C. § 411(d)(6)(A) (2006).

40   *See* ERISA §§ 203(a)(3)(C), 204(g)(1), 302(d)(2), 29 U.S.C. §§ 1053(a)(3)(C), 1054(g)(1), 1082(d)(2) (2006) (permitted funding-based reductions in accrued benefits expressly excepted from vesting rules); I.R.C. §§ 411(a)(3)(C), (d)(6)(A), 412(d)(2) (2006) (same).

41   Treas. Reg. §§ 1.411(a)-7(a)(1), 1.411(d)-4, Q&A-1(d) (as amended in 2000); Arndt v. Sec. Bank S.S.B. Employees' Pension Plan, 182 F.3d 538 (3d Cir. 1999) (increases in pension benefits payable at NRA based on grant of imputed service credit for period of disability is a disability benefit rather than an early retirement benefit or retirement-type subsidy, and so may be eliminated by plan amendment).
      There is a circuit split over whether plant shutdown benefits (early retirement pensions contingent on plant closure) are protected by the anti-cutback rule. *See, e.g.,* Bellas v. CBS, Inc., 221 F.3d 517 (3d Cir. 2000); Ameri R. Giannotti, Comment, *ERISA's Anticutback Rule and Contingent Early Retirement Benefits,* 68 U. Chi. L. Rev. 1342 (2001).

42   541 U.S. 739 (2004).

43   *Id.* at 744 (quoting from the lower court opinion, 303 F.3d 802, 805 (7th Cir. 2002)). *Accord* Frommert v. Conkright, 433 F.3d 254, 268 (2d Cir. 2006).

44   *Heinz,* 541 U.S. at 744–45. Treas. Reg. § 1.411(d)-3(a)(3)(i) (as amended in 2006). The regulation was amended to incorporate the holding in *Heinz.* T.D. 9280, 2006-38 I.R.B. 450.

45   Protecting the amount of previously earned retirement benefits is clearly fundamental to retirement security, but in exigent circumstances, this principle is subject to one narrow exception. Deferred compensation earned in the immediately preceding plan year may be reduced if funding the additional accrued benefits would impose substantial business hardship, provided that

already accrued.[46] (Of course, prospective plan amendments can decrease future accruals or eliminate distribution options for benefits not yet earned.)

Consequently, a defined benefit plan early retirement option, whether subsidized or not, must continue to be made available with respect to benefits previously accrued,[47] and a lump-sum distribution alternative (under either a defined contribution or a defined benefit plan) must likewise abide. Distribution timing options are important to participants because of the pension anti-alienation rule.[48] Because accrued benefits are nontransferable, a worker who doesn't like the normal form of distribution provided by the plan ordinarily cannot sell his interest and use the proceeds to arrange a payment stream better suited to his circumstances. Defined contribution plans, however, commonly permit a single-sum distribution of all or a portion of the participant's account balance. If such a plan is qualified, a participant can arrange a tax-free rollover of a single-sum distribution into an individual retirement account (IRA), and as owner of the IRA, she can thereafter largely control the timing of distributions.[49]

---

several stringent conditions are satisfied. ERISA §§ 204(g)(1), 302(d)(2), 29 U.S.C. §§ 1054(g)(1), 1082(d)(2) (2006); *see* I.R.C. §§ 411(d)(6)(A), 412(d)(2) (2006). In the case of a multiemployer plan, such funding-related benefit cutbacks may be retroactive as far back as two years.

The alteration of a defined benefit plan's method of determining actuarial equivalence, such as changing the plan's interest rate assumption, can have a dramatic impact on the amounts payable under different timing options, so retroactive changes in actuarial assumptions have long been understood to be impermissible. Rev. Rul. 81-12, 1981-1 C.B. 228. *See* I.R.C. § 430(h)(5) (2006).

46 Regulations implementing the anti-cutback rule go even further, outlawing plan terms that grant the employer discretion to approve payment of benefits in a particular form, presumably because such discretion could be exercised to de facto eliminate the option. Treas. Reg. § 1.411(d)-4, Q&A-4 (as amended in 2005). Discretionary distribution alternatives had previously been quite common, and their wholesale elimination posed transition problems for some plans. *E.g.*, Auwarter v. Donohue Paper Sales Corp. Defined Benefit Pension Plan, 802 F. Supp. 830 (E.D.N.Y. 1992) (following change in corporate control, new management denied former executives generous lump-sum distribution; denial was ineffective because plan failed to comply with transition rules for elimination of discretion). In strictly limited situations, the regulations permit elimination of optional benefit forms that are redundant or are burdensome to plan administration and of de minimis value to participants. Treas. Reg. § 1.411(d)-3(c) to -3(g) (as amended in 2006), issued under the authority of ERISA § 204(g)(2), 29 U.S.C. § 1054(g)(2) (2006) (final two sentences), and I.R.C. § 411(d)(6)(B) (2006) (final two sentences).

47 If early retirement is subsidized, a special, more stringent limitation comes into play. Where, at the time of the plan amendment, a participant has not satisfied special eligibility conditions attached to a retirement-type subsidy (e.g., early retirement benefits available without actuarial reduction to an employee who is at least age sixty and has thirty years of service), but the participant thereafter does satisfy those conditions, she must be entitled to a benefit that is not less than the amount of her subsidized pre-amendment accrued benefits. ERISA § 204(g)(2), 29 U.S.C. § 1054(g)(2) (2006) (second sentence); *see* I.R.C. § 411(d)(6)(B) (2006) (second sentence).

48 ERISA § 206(d)(1), 29 U.S.C. § 1056(d)(1) (2006); *see* I.R.C. § 401(a)(13)(A) (2006). *See generally infra* Chapter 8B.

49 I.R.C. §§ 402(c), 408(a)(6), (d) (2006).

In recognition of this flexibility, defined contribution plans may be amended to eliminate a particular form of distribution if affected participants have ready access to a single-sum distribution.[50]

Nothing in the accrual rules explored thus far prevents an employer from *prospectively* amending a plan to reduce future contributions or benefits. ERISA § 204(h), however, provides that an amendment that significantly reduces the rate of future benefit accrual under a defined benefit or money purchase pension plan cannot take effect unless each participant is given reasonable advance written notice of the amendment.[51] Under ERISA's generally applicable reporting and disclosure rules, the plan administrator is required to provide participants notice of material modifications in a plan within 210 days after the close of the plan year in which the change is adopted.[52] Not only is earlier notice demanded of accrual rate reductions, but the sanction for failure to give timely notice is much more serious: the amendment does not take effect. The *advance* notice required of accrual rate reductions gives affected employees a chance to object to their employer, seek alternative employment, or take other steps to protect their interests.[53] Consistent with a focus on information costs, the rule was apparently designed to promote better retirement planning.[54]

---

50   ERISA § 204(g)(5), 29 U.S.C. § 1054(g)(5) (2006); *see* I.R.C. § 411(d)(6)(E) (2006); *see also* Treas. Reg. § 1.411(d)-4, Q&A-2(e) (as amended in 2005). A similar rule allows the transfer in a plan merger of a participant's account balance from one defined contribution plan to another, even though the transferee plan doesn't provide all the same forms of distribution, provided that the participant consents to the transfer after receiving notice of its consequences, and the transferee plan allows single-sum distributions. (The single-sum distribution does not have to be accessible at the same time that a distribution could have been obtained under the transferor plan.) ERISA § 204(g)(4), 29 U.S.C. § 1054(g)(4) (2006); *see* I.R.C. § 411(d)(6)(D) (2006); *see also* Treas. Reg. § 1.411(d)-4, Q&A-3(b) (as amended in 2005). *See* STAFF OF THE JOINT COMM. ON TAXATION, 108TH CONG., GENERAL EXPLANATION OF TAX LEGISLATION ENACTED IN THE 107TH CONGRESS, at 130–33 (Comm. Print 2003).

51   ERISA § 204(h), 29 U.S.C. § 1054(h) (2006). Alternate payees (family law creditors entitled to plan payment under a qualified domestic relations order) and unions representing plan participants must also be provided advance notice of the change. The plan amendment can be ignored only in cases of egregious failure to give the required advance notice, ERISA § 204(h)(6), 29 U.S.C. § 1054(h)(6) (2006). I.R.C. § 4980F (2006) imposes an excise tax penalty for late notice. *See* Treas. Reg. § 54.4980F-1 (2003).

52   ERISA § 104(b)(1), 29 U.S.C. § 1024(b)(1) (2006). *See supra* Chapter 3A.

53   *See* Frommert v. Conkright, 433 F.3d 254, 268, 269 (2d Cir. 2006); Davidson v. Canteen Corp., 957 F.2d 1404 (5th Cir. 1992).

54   Reductions in the rate that future contributions will be allocated to a participant's account under a profit-sharing or stock bonus plan are not subject to the section 204(h) advance notice requirement. In contrast to a money pension plan (a defined contribution plan that is subject to section 204(h) and ERISA's funding rules), the amount contributed from year to year under a profit-sharing or stock bonus plan need not be specified in the plan; it can be left to the discretion of the employer. Where contributions are wholly discretionary, the possibility of an allocation rate reduction does not undercut a participant's ability to plan for retirement, because the participant could not prudently count on getting anything more anyway.

C. VESTING

"Primarily, [ERISA] was a consumer protection bill. Vesting was its main focus."[55]

Statutory Standards

ERISA's vesting rules draw a fundamental distinction between employee- and employer-financed pension rights. The accrued benefit derived from employee contributions must be nonforfeitable (fully vested) at all times; to the extent that a pension is paid for with the employee's money, the employer is not permitted to hold it hostage.[56] The accrued benefit derived from employer contributions, however, can be made subject to forfeiture for violation of any conditions the employer chooses to impose, but only for a limited period of time.[57] Once the participant completes a reasonable period of service, his pension saving must be secure, regardless of whether he continues to work for the plan sponsor, although distribution of the vested benefit may be deferred until retirement age.

ERISA prescribes alternative generally applicable minimum vesting schedules for accrued benefits derived from employer contributions.[58] A defined benefit plan may comply with either the five-year cliff or the three-to-seven-year graded vesting schedule. Under the five-year cliff schedule, the entire employer-financed accrued benefit of a participant with less than five years of service may be subject to forfeiture, but once the participant completes five years of service, her pension rights must be fully vested at all times thereafter. Under the three-to-seven-year graded schedule, a participant with three years of service must have a nonforfeitable right to at least 20 percent of the accrued benefit derived from employer contributions, and her vested percentage must

---

55   Cummings, *supra* Chapter 1 note 54, at 881.
56   ERISA § 203(a)(1), 29 U.S.C. § 1053(a)(1) (2006); *see* I.R.C. § 411(a)(1) (2006). Although intuitively appealing, this distinction between employee- and employer-financed benefits is in fact highly artificial because the definition of employee contributions is largely formalistic. *See* I.R.C. § 414(h)(1) (2006). While common at the time ERISA was enacted, plans calling for after-tax employee contributions have become less prevalent as a result of subsequent tax law developments, particularly the advent of section 401(k) plans. In the unusual case where a plan is funded by both employer and employee contributions, the distinct status of the two types of contributions under the vesting rules requires a method for distinguishing the portions of a participant's accrued benefit that are derived from employee and employer contributions. These tracing or allocation rules are supplied by ERISA § 204(c), 29 U.S.C. § 1054(c) (2006). *See* I.R.C. § 411(c) (2006).
57   A forfeiture of accrued benefits derived from employer contributions, when that forfeiture is triggered by the withdrawal of employee contributions, is subject to special restrictions so as not to undercut the protection afforded employee contributions. ERISA § 206(c), 29 U.S.C. § 1056(c) (2006); *see* I.R.C. § 401(a)(19) (2006).
58   ERISA originally authorized another schedule, the "Rule of 45," which called for incremental vesting under a schedule that took into account both age and years of service. That alternative was repealed by the Tax Reform Act of 1986, which greatly accelerated vesting under the remaining schedules.

increase by 20 percent with each succeeding year of service, so that a participant with seven or more years of service is fully vested.[59] For contributions made in plan years beginning after 2006, defined contribution plans must provide more rapid vesting, satisfying either a three-year cliff or a two-to-six-year graded schedule (again, at 20 percent per year).[60]

The vesting schedules apply to the participant's entire accrued benefit derived from employer contributions, regardless of when it was earned. Once a participant satisfies the cliff schedule, for example, all prior employer contributions (in the case of a defined contribution plan) or accruals (in the case of a defined benefit plan) become vested—even increases occurring within the last three or five years, respectively—and all subsequent contributions or benefits are secure from the moment they are earned.[61]

As is typical of ERISA's pension content controls, these alternative statutory vesting schedules are just minimum standards: a plan may call for more rapid vesting, or even provide that all accrued benefits are immediately nonforfeitable.[62] In addition, upon reaching normal retirement age, a participant must be fully vested, even if at that time he does not have sufficient service to vest under the applicable schedule.[63]

Vesting turns upon years of service. Service counting and break-in-service rules are used that closely correspond to those used to specify permissible minimum-service conditions.[64] For vesting purposes, however, years of service before age 18 or before the employer established the plan may be disregarded.[65] Service before a particular

---

[59]   ERISA § 203(a)(2)(A), 29 U.S.C. § 1053(a)(2)(A) (2006); see I.R.C. § 411(a)(2)(A) (2006). ERISA originally permitted ten-year cliff vesting and graded vesting over a five- to fifteen-year period. The five-year cliff and three-to-seven-year graded schedules became effective for plan years beginning after 1988.

[60]   ERISA § 203(a)(2)(B), 29 U.S.C. § 1053(a)(2)(B) (2006); see I.R.C. § 411(a)(2)(B) (2006).

[61]   This once-and-for-all aspect of vesting is subject to one minor exception: a defined contribution plan that is a profit-sharing, stock bonus, or money purchase pension plan may call for class-year vesting, under which an employee's right to employer contributions made in a particular plan year become nonforfeitable only if the employee is still performing services for the employer for five plan years thereafter. ERISA § 203(c)(3), 29 U.S.C. § 1053(c)(3) (2006). Under this rolling vesting schedule, a worker employed for decades still would lose employer contributions made over the last five years should he separate from service before normal retirement age. Although it remains legal, class-year vesting is now rarely encountered because such plans no longer qualify for preferential tax treatment. I.R.C. § 411(d)(4) (2006), which formerly authorized class-year vesting for certain qualified plans, was repealed in 1986. See Treas. Reg. § 1.411(d)-5 (1988).

[62]   ERISA § 203(d), 29 U.S.C. § 1053(d) (2006). The tax law qualification requirements do not contain a parallel declaration, but the tax Code's vesting requirements are interpreted as minimum standards despite that oversight. Treas. Reg. § 1.411(a)-4(a) (as amended in 2005).
       Immediate vesting is encouraged by the rule allowing plans to impose a two-year service condition on membership, provided that accrued benefits are at all times fully vested. ERISA § 202(a)(1)(B)(i), 29 U.S.C. § 1052(a)(1)(B)(i) (2006); see I.R.C. § 410(a)(1)(B)(i) (2006). See *supra* Chapter 7A.

[63]   ERISA § 203(a), 29 U.S.C. § 1053(a) (2006) (first sentence); see I.R.C. § 411(a) (2006) (first sentence).

[64]   ERISA § 203(b)(2)–(4), 29 U.S.C. § 1053(b)(2)–(4) (2006); see I.R.C. § 411(a)(5), (6) (2006). See *supra* Chapter 7 notes 5–9.

[65]   ERISA § 203(b)(1), 29 U.S.C. § 1053(b)(1) (2006); see I.R.C. § 411(a)(4) (2006).

employee became a participant cannot be ignored, however, so a plan that imposes a one-year minimum-service condition on membership must count that pre-participation service toward vesting.

ERISA bars certain changes in a pension plan's vesting schedule. A plan amendment is not permitted to reduce any employee's vested percentage, even if the employee would not have to be vested under the statutory minimum standards.[66] For example, a plan that provides full vesting after two years of service might be amended to substitute five-year cliff vesting, but that amendment cannot be applied to the previously accrued benefits of participants who have between two and five years of service, because that would subject to a risk of loss benefits that had become nonforfeitable under the prior terms of the plan. Amendments that delay vesting without reducing current nonforfeitable rights are permitted, but any participant having at least three years of service (counting all years, and disregarding the break-in-service rules) must be given sixty days to elect to continue to have the old vesting schedule apply.[67] So, for example, if a plan is amended to switch from a five-year cliff to three-to-seven-year graded vesting, each participant with at least three years of service must be given the choice to remain on the cliff schedule, which employees who expect to leave with between five and seven years of service would wish to do.

In a few tightly circumscribed situations, forfeiture of employer-financed pension benefits is permitted in spite of the vesting rules.[68] Most important, rights may be made contingent upon survival to retirement age, because pensions are designed to provide a source of income to meet retirement living expenses. Accordingly, a plan may call for forfeiture on death of the participant—even a fully vested participant—provided that the deceased leaves no spouse entitled to a survivor annuity under ERISA's spousal protection rules.[69]

Apart from the few very limited statutory exceptions, all contingencies must vanish within a time frame that satisfies ERISA's minimum vesting rules. The term "nonforfeitable," as used in ERISA, means nonforfeitable for *any* reason, other than

---

66 ERISA § 203(c)(1)(A), 29 U.S.C. § 1053(c)(1)(A) (2006); *see* I.R.C. § 411(a)(10)(A) (2006); Treas. Reg. § 1.411(a)-8(a) (1977). This vesting anti-cutback rule complements the accrued benefit anti-cutback rule, ERISA § 204(g), 29 U.S.C. § 1054(g) (2006), discussed *supra* text accompanying Chapter 7 notes 39–50. Section 204(g) outlaws plan amendments that reduce previously earned pension rights, while section 203(c)(1)(A) prohibits amendments that do not directly reduce previously earned rights but expose those rights to increased risk of loss.

67 ERISA § 203(c)(1)(B), 29 U.S.C. § 1053(c)(1)(B) (2006); *see* I.R.C. § 411(a)(10)(B) (2006); Treas. Reg. § 1.411(a)-8T(b) (1988). The election period must begin no later than the date the vesting amendment is adopted and continue for at least sixty days after the later of (1) the date the amendment is adopted, (2) the date the amendment becomes effective, or (3) the date the participant is given written notice of the amendment. Treas. Reg. § 1.411(a)-8T(b)(2) (1988).

68 Accrued benefits financed by employee contributions cannot be forfeited in these circumstances. The exceptions listed in each of subparagraphs (A) through (E) of ERISA § 203(a)(3), 29 U.S.C. § 1053(a)(3) (2006), apply only to a "right to an accrued benefit derived from employer contributions." *See* I.R.C. § 411(a)(3)(A)–(G) (2006).

69 ERISA § 203(a)(3)(A), 29 U.S.C. § 1053(a)(3)(A) (2006); *see* I.R.C. § 411(a)(3)(A) (2006). On the spousal protection rules generally, see *infra* Chapter 8C.

the express statutory exceptions (like death without a spouse entitled to survivor benefits).[70] Even if a plan calls for forfeiture in circumstances that are unrelated to length of service—such as forfeiture in the event of dismissal for cause, or forfeiture upon violation of a noncompetition agreement—pension rights cannot be revoked once a participant has accumulated enough years of service to be fully vested. Prior to ERISA, many plans granted benefits to participants whose employment terminated before retirement age, provided they had completed a specified (often lengthy) period of service. Some of these plans also provided that a participant who committed various sorts of malfeasance would lose all benefits regardless of length of service (so-called "bad boy" forfeiture). Different forfeiture conditions, that is, would operate over different periods; commonly, forfeiture for inadequate service was time limited, while "bad boy" forfeiture was not. In response to ERISA, some of these plans were amended to bring forfeiture for inadequate service within one statutory vesting schedule, while forfeiture for malfeasance was subject to another.

Participants challenged this situation, arguing that the same statutory vesting schedule must apply to *all* causes of forfeiture.[71] On one hand, the statutory minimum standards are expressed as alternatives, and the inclusive "or" would support multiple vesting schedules. On the other hand, because "nonforfeitable" means unconditional, a participant has a "nonforfeitable right" only when *all* contingencies terminate, which suggests that the *combined* preclusive effect of all contingencies must fit within *one* of ERISA's alternative minimum standards. The cases conform to the latter view: a pension plan may specify multiple causes of forfeiture and may even provide that those conditions operate over different periods, but all such contingencies must terminate within a time frame that satisfies the same statutory schedule.[72] For example, a defined benefit plan could vest benefits at the rate of 25 percent per year of service beginning with the participant's second year of service, but also require forfeiture of all employer-derived accrued benefits if a participant is dismissed for cause before completing five years of service. Here, both forfeiture conditions—inadequate tenure and dismissal for

---

70 ERISA § 3(19), 29 U.S.C. § 1002(19) (2006), provides:

The term "nonforfeitable" when used with respect to a pension benefit or right means a claim obtained by a participant or his beneficiary to that part of an immediate or deferred benefit under a pension plan which arises from the participant's service, which is unconditional, and which is legally enforceable against the plan. For purposes of this paragraph, a right to an accrued benefit derived from employer contributions shall not be treated as forfeitable merely because the plan contains a provision described in section 203(a)(3).

Accord Treas. Reg. §§ 1.411(a)-4(a) (as amended in 2005) & 1.411(a)-4T(a) (1988).

71 A regulation first issued in 1975 expressly permits the forfeiture of accrued benefits in excess of the minimum amount that ERISA requires to be nonforfeitable. The regulation includes an example showing that a plan may contain multiple vesting schedules applicable to different causes of forfeiture, but in the example, each of the plan's forfeiture conditions complies with the *same* statutory vesting schedule (cliff vesting). Treas. Reg. § 1.411(a)-4(a), -4(c) Example (1) (as amended in 2005). *Accord* Lojek v. Thomas, 716 F.2d 675, 680 (9th Cir. 1983).

72 *E.g.*, Hummell v. S. E. Rykoff & Co., 634 F.2d 446, 450–51 (9th Cir. 1980); Nedrow v. McFarlane & Hays Co. Profit Sharing Plan & Trust, 476 F. Supp. 934, 937 (E.D. Mich. 1979). *See* Rev. Rul. 85-31, 1985-1 C.B. 153, 154.

cause—fit within the five-year cliff standard. (Of course, vesting at 25 percent per year starting with the second year of service is more generous than necessary, and also satisfies the three-to-seven-year graded schedule.) In contrast, the plan would violate ERISA if its general schedule vested benefits at the rate of 20 percent per year of service (again starting with the second year) and, in addition, called for complete forfeiture on dismissal for cause within five years. In this case, service-based vesting would only satisfy the three-to-seven-year graded schedule (the vested percentage does not reach 100 percent until the sixth year of service, beyond the five-year cliff), while the bad boy forfeiture would only satisfy the five-year cliff schedule (complete forfeiture after three or four years of service contravenes the partial vesting requirement of the three-to-seven-year graded schedule).

Where a plan imposes multiple forfeiture conditions that do not all comply with the same statutory schedule, a court must revise the plan to conform to ERISA's requirements. But what principles apply to determine whether cliff or graded vesting should be made generally applicable? The cases seem to take the statutory standard to which the plan's general vesting provision (that is, forfeiture for inadequate service) conforms and apply it to the bad boy clause, but the opinions offer no persuasive reason for doing so.[73] The policy of promoting sponsorship by maintaining employer flexibility suggests an inquiry into the relative importance to a particular employer of discouraging malfeasance (indicating that the plan's bad boy clause should not be cribbed) versus encouraging longer job tenure. In contrast, an emphasis on employee expectations and the goal of promoting retirement planning counsels review of the SPD to determine whether one or the other vesting schedule was given prominence. If each is adequately disclosed, preference should be given to the schedule used by the plan's general vesting provision, as many workers will have taken the plan's length-of-service requirements into account in making decisions about changing jobs and saving for retirement.

Enforcement

A plan failing to comply with the vesting standards can be brought into line by participant action. Participants and beneficiaries have standing to sue for equitable relief to redress violations of ERISA, and that relief could include an injunction ordering the payment of benefits improperly forfeited (restitution).[74]

Suppose that the plan's terms comply with the minimum vesting standards, but workers are laid off shortly before they would vest. Section 510 prohibits intentional interference with vesting, making it unlawful for an employer to discharge or otherwise penalize a participant "for the purpose of interfering with the attainment of any

---

73   *E.g., Hummell*, 634 F.2d at 452; *Nedrow*, 476 F. Supp. at 937–38.

74   *See generally supra* Chapter 5D. A former employee whose benefits are forfeited in violation of ERISA has a colorable claim to vested benefits and thus has standing to sue under the Supreme Court's interpretation of "participant." Firestone Tire & Rubber Co. v. Bruch, 489 U.S. 101, 117–18 (1989), discussed *supra* Chapter 5A.

right to which such participant may become entitled under the plan" or ERISA.[75] While the full reach of this protection has yet to be resolved, dismissals to prevent vesting were a core concern.[76] Section 510 liability requires proof of specific intent to interfere with the attainment of vested rights, but that intent need not be directed against specific individuals; ERISA is violated if an employer acts to minimize pension claims in deciding which plants to close.[77]

Instead of terminating employees to prevent vesting, suppose that the employer terminates the plan. Does ERISA provide relief if a plan is amended or terminated to prevent participants from vesting? Several courts have concluded that section 510 was only meant to bar adverse employment actions (to "discharge, fine, suspend, expel, discipline" a worker), and that its catchall ban on "discriminat[ion] against a participant" does not embrace detrimental alteration of plan terms.[78] Nor does ERISA demand early vesting upon plan termination. The tax Code, however, expressly requires that *qualified* plans provide for the immediate vesting of the accrued benefits of all affected employees in the event of a partial or complete termination of the plan, and a partial termination may include "the exclusion, by reason of a plan amendment, of a group of employees who have previously been covered by the plan."[79]

---

75 ERISA § 510, 29 U.S.C. § 1140 (2006). Section 510 is enforced via section 502, generally by a suit for injunction or other appropriate equitable relief. *See generally supra* Chapter 5C.

76 "A further protection for employees is the prohibition against discharge, or other discriminatory conduct toward participants and beneficiaries which is designed to interfere with attainment of vested benefits or other rights under the bill, or to discourage the exercise of any rights afforded by the legislation." 120 Cong. Rec. 29,933 (1974) (remarks by Sen. Williams, a cosponsor of ERISA, explaining the conference report), *reprinted in* 3 ERISA Legislative History, *supra* Chapter 1 note 56, at 4745. Whether section 510 extends beyond vesting, barring actions intended to prevent welfare plan participants or vested pension plan participants from earning additional benefits, remains unclear. See the discussion of *Inter-Modal Rail Employees Ass'n v. Atchison, Topeka & Santa Fe Railway*, 520 U.S. 510 (1997), *supra* text accompanying Chapter 5 notes 89–95.

77 *See generally* Dana M. Muir, *Plant Closings and ERISA's Noninterference Provision*, 36 B.C. L. Rev. 201 (1995). *But see* Nemeth v. Clark Equip. Co., 677 F. Supp. 899, 909 (W.D. Mich. 1987) (section 510 not violated where pensions accounted for only 20 percent of higher costs of plant selected for closing because it would have been shut down even if pension costs had been ignored); Lorraine Schmall & Nathan Ihnes, *Failure of Equity: Discriminatory Plant Closing as an Irremediable Injury Under ERISA*, 55 Cath. U. L. Rev. 81 (2005) (back pay remedy may be unavailable).

78 *See supra* Chapter 5 note 84 and accompanying text. The Supreme Court has observed that section 510 reinforces the formal amendment process by ensuring that employers cannot "'informally' amend their plans one participant at a time." *Inter-Modal Rail*, 520 U.S. at 516, discussed *supra* text accompanying Chapter 5 notes 89–95. However, the Court did not go so far as to say that a plan amendment motivated by the purpose of preventing vesting would be valid.

79 I.R.C. § 411(d)(3) (2006); Treas. Reg. § 1.411(d)-2(b)(1) (1975). The tax Code's vesting-on-termination rule predates ERISA. (Its predecessor was enacted in 1962 as I.R.C. § 401(a)(7) (repealed 1974).) It was enacted to prevent abuse of the tax subsidy and, presumably for that reason, the rule was not extended to nonqualified plans under ERISA. The anti-abuse policy is suggested by the fact that benefits are required to vest only "to the extent funded." On plan termination, a sponsor is generally permitted to claim a reversion of any excess funds

Nearly all retirement savings programs are intended to qualify for preferential tax treatment, so pension plans generally contain a clause calling for vesting on complete or partial termination. Even though such a clause has its genesis in the tax law, ERISA gives participants and beneficiaries a private right of action to enforce their rights under the terms of the plan,[80] and many of the disputes over whether a partial termination has occurred have triggered litigation between excluded participants and the plan. The IRS has offered no authoritative guidance on how large the group of excluded workers must be to support a finding of partial termination. The courts have repeatedly struggled with the issue and with whether all excluded employees should be considered for this purpose, or only those who are not fully vested and so would lose benefits absent the partial termination finding. An illuminating 2004 opinion by Judge Posner collects the authorities and concludes, first, that a 20 percent reduction in plan participation is the appropriate rule of thumb for determining whether a partial termination occurred; second, that in computing the fraction of participants excluded by plan amendment, both vested and nonvested participants should be taken into account in both the numerator and the denominator; third, that a 20 percent exclusion establishes only a rebuttable presumption of partial termination; and fourth, that the purpose of I.R.C. § 411(d)(3) is to prevent the employer from obtaining a windfall at the expense of participants who are not fully vested, and so deviations from the 20 percent guideline should be based on the presence or absence of such a predatory motive.[81]

Vesting Policy

ERISA's vesting rules have been notably successful, but the security they offer has come at a price. Because pension sponsorship is voluntary, employers can make a trade-off between coverage and vesting, and they will do so if the reduction of forfeitures makes pension coverage too costly.[82] That response would have clear-cut distributional effects. Long-term employees in high-turnover jobs—the loyal or lucky few who would have qualified for pensions under plans with prolonged forfeiture periods—will lose out because their employers cannot afford to pay benefits to their many transient coworkers.[83] Instead of cutting back coverage, employers could accommodate vesting cost increases by reducing benefits (prospectively) or limiting benefit increases. In that event, the pensions of vested shorter-term workers would come out

---

in the pension trust. *See infra* Chapter 9C. Insofar as the overfunding is caused by the forfeiture of nonvested benefits on termination (reducing plan liabilities), Congress decided that the employer has no legitimate claim to the tax-subsidized reversion.

80   ERISA § 502(a)(1)(B), (a)(3), 29 U.S.C. § 1132(a)(1)(B), (a)(3) (2006).

81   Matz v. Household Int'l Tax Reduction Inv. Plan, 388 F.3d 570 (7th Cir. 2004). *See* Rev. Rul. 2007-43, 2007-2 C.B. 45 (IRS follows 20 percent presumption of *Matz*).

82   *See supra* Chapter 1C.

83   *See* Daniel I. Halperin, *Special Tax Treatment for Employer-Based Retirement Programs: Is It "Still" Viable as a Means of Increasing Retirement Income?*, 49 TAX L. REV. 1, 16–21 (1993).

of the savings of their long-tenure colleagues.[84] ERISA, in other words, favors smaller pensions for many short-term workers over larger pensions for the few who make a career-long commitment.

Limiting employers' ability to use contingent deferred compensation to encourage loyalty and longevity of service seems to have reduced average job tenures.[85] Labor mobility increases the economy's responsiveness to changes, both in production technology and demand for goods and services.[86] But labor mobility may also decrease firms' willingness to invest in training, for it reduces their ability to recoup their investment, as workers shop their new skills for higher pay elsewhere.

By restricting forfeitures, ERISA limits freedom of contract. In assessing the wisdom of that infringement of private autonomy, it is good to remember that mandatory vesting has both distributional and efficiency implications (as outlined above). Clearly, favoring the many over the few was the politically astute course of action once forfeitures became a subject of widespread public concern. Broader pension recipiency, however, is not necessarily inconsistent with collective welfare maximization.

ERISA's minimum vesting standards, like the anti-backloading benefit accrual rules, mask a major policy ambiguity between worker protection and worker empowerment. The often-expressed concern over workers' loss of "anticipated retirement benefits owing to the lack of vesting" is equivocal on this point.[87] Absent vesting, pension receipt could be mistakenly anticipated either because workers underestimate their risk of forfeiture or because they base their expectations on affordable but incomplete information.

---

84 Congress was acutely aware of the cost implications of mandatory vesting. To reduce the risk that employers would resort to undesirable cost containment strategies, ERISA § 207, 29 U.S.C. § 1057 (2006) (repealed 2006), authorized the Secretary of Labor to grant variances, for periods of up to seven years, from ERISA's benefit accrual and/or vesting rules. Such variances could only be granted to plans in effect on January 1, 1974, and only if the Labor Department found that ERISA's accrual or vesting rules would increase costs to such an extent that it created a substantial risk of discontinuance of the plan or of a substantial reduction in benefit levels or other compensation.

Concerns about the cost of vesting were expressed early and often during the development of pension reform proposals. *See, e.g.*, S. REP. No. 93-127, at 12–13, 73–79, *reprinted in* 1 ERISA LEGISLATIVE HISTORY, *supra* Chapter 1 note 56, at 598–99, 659–65 (actuarial study of likely cost of mandatory vesting); 118 CONG. REC. 16,919–20 (1972) (remarks of Sen. Taft asserting that immediate vesting would trigger a 50 percent reduction in benefit levels); Richard M. Nixon, Private Pension Plans, H.R. DOC. No. 92-182, at 3 (1971) (if "set at too early a point, so that too many younger workers were vested, [required vesting] could create a considerable burden for employers and reduce the level of benefits for retiring workers"); PRESIDENT'S COMM. ON CORPORATE PENSION FUNDS AND OTHER PRIVATE RETIREMENT AND WELFARE PROGRAMS, PUBLIC POLICY AND PRIVATE PENSION PROGRAMS 44–46 (1965) [hereinafter PRESIDENT'S COMMITTEE REPORT].

85 Douglas A. Wolf & Frank Levy, *Pension Coverage, Pension Vesting, and the Distribution of Job Tenures*, *in* RETIREMENT & ECONOMIC BEHAVIOR 23, 25–28 (H. Aaron & G. Burtless eds., Brookings Inst., Washington, D.C.) (1984).

86 *See* S. REP. No. 93-383, at 14 (1973), *reprinted in* 1 ERISA LEGISLATIVE HISTORY, *supra* Chapter 1 note 56, at 1063, 1082 (Finance Committee report observes that "failure to vest more rapidly is charged with interfering with the mobility of labor, to the detriment of the economy").

87 ERISA § 2(a), 29 U.S.C. § 1001(a) (2006).

Most of the vesting rules are, in fact, consonant with both the protective and the information cost rationales.[88]

Conceptually, ERISA's accrual and vesting rules may draw support from either a worker protective policy or information cost concerns, but politically, these interventions in the market for deferred compensation originate in a preference for broader distribution of pension benefits. Much of the public pressure for vesting requirements grew out of the fact that contingencies were often downplayed, with the result that workers came to understand their pension coverage as representing a right to deferred wages, as opposed to *conditional* deferred wages (or a lottery ticket). As such, forfeitures were seen as an unfair refusal to pay earned compensation.[89] Effective disclosure might have eradicated this misapprehension,[90] but Congress chose instead to ratify it. Its goal was to promote greater access to private pensions to supplement Social Security.

Under a regime of voluntary plan sponsorship, mandatory vesting may not achieve broader distribution because higher costs may trigger terminations. But employers do not bear the full cost of employee pensions. Most pension plans, both before ERISA's enactment and since, have been designed to satisfy the Internal Revenue Code's definition of a qualified pension, profit-sharing, stock bonus, or annuity plan, in order to

---

88   The vesting amendment rules may be an illuminating exception. Recall that a plan cannot be amended to reduce any participant's current nonforfeitable accrued benefit (even a participant who would not yet have vested under ERISA's minimum standards); and that any participant with at least three years of service must be allowed to continue on the plan's former vesting schedule if she chooses, even if the new schedule conforms to ERISA and does not curtail her vested rights. Since the difference in timing between one acceptable vesting schedule and another is slight, these rules do not seem necessary to protect workers from misjudging the long-term risk of forfeiture. The rules do, however, make it safe to rely on near-term decisions founded on the plan's existing provisions, thereby facilitating career and financial planning.

89   *See* Michael S. Gordon, *Overview: Why Was ERISA Enacted?*, *in* S. Spec. Comm. on Aging, 98th Cong., The Employee Retirement Income Security Act of 1974: The First Decade 8, 15–17 (Comm. Print 1984) (1958 disclosure legislation unleashed torrent of mail from constituents complaining of failure to qualify for pension, and 1971 Senate Labor Subcommittee hearings publicized series of late-career forfeiture horror stories); H.R. Rep. No. 93-533, at 6 (1973), *reprinted in* 2 ERISA Legislative History, *supra* Chapter 1 note 56, at 2348, 2353 ("In its final analysis, the issue basically resolves itself into whether workers, after many years of labor, whose jobs terminate voluntarily or otherwise, should be denied benefits that have been placed for them in a fund for retirement purposes."); S. Rep. No. 99-313, at 590 (1986) ("[I]t is arguable that an employee who . . . accepts a reduced current compensation package in exchange for qualified plan benefits should not have receipt of plan benefits made contingent on an overly lengthy deferred vesting schedule.").

90   During debate on ERISA, Representative Erlenborn, Republican House manager of the bill, observed:

> [I]f people do have this sort of meaningful information made available to them, I think some of the unwarranted expectations that gave rise to the horror stories that people were not getting what they anticipated will be a thing of the past, because many of them are based on what people anticipated getting that they never were entitled to, because they did not honestly know what was in their pension plan; they did not honestly know what their rights would be.

120 Cong. Rec. 4284 (1974), *reprinted in* 2 ERISA Legislative History, *supra* Chapter 1 note 56, at 3386–87.

obtain preferential tax treatment (tax-deferred accumulation, that is). The result is a large public subsidy for pension savings. With a net revenue loss now on the order of $100 billion annually, there is a strong societal stake in employment-based retirement savings programs.[91] In enacting ERISA, Congress declared that pension plans "substantially affect the revenue of the United States because they are afforded preferential Federal tax treatment," and that it is "desirable in the interests of employees and their beneficiaries [and] for the protection of the revenue of the United States . . . that minimum standards be provided assuring the *equitable character* of such plans."[92] Public money comes with strings attached, and the accrual and vesting rules insist that short-service employees get a reasonable share of subsidized retirement savings.[93]

D. CONCLUSION

Entitlement to a pension requires that a worker become a plan member, earn deferred compensation by performing service under the plan, and satisfy any conditions necessary to avoid forfeiture of benefits. These three components of pension accumulation—participation, benefit accrual, and vesting—share a close functional and policy relationship.

Functionally, the decision to restrict the duration of forfeiture conditions necessitated legal intervention with respect to participation and benefit accrual as well. Banning forfeiture after ten years of service would be illusory if plans could require fifteen years of service to qualify for membership, for example. Alternatively, consider a defined benefit plan that grants prompt membership and immediate vesting, but under which the promised retirement annuity is earned disproportionately in the final year or two before normal retirement age. Left unregulated, such "backloading" of benefit accrual would give a long-term employee who separates from service before normal retirement age vested rights in a trivial amount of benefits. Either of these stratagems

---

91   *See supra* Chapter 1D and Chapter 1 notes 83–84.

92   ERISA § 2(a), 29 U.S.C. § 1001(a) (2006) (emphasis added).

93   PRESIDENT'S COMMITTEE REPORT, *supra* Chapter 7 note 84, at 39, 42 (vesting required as "a matter of equity and fair treatment"; vesting recommended as condition of favorable tax treatment because "[t]he Committee is convinced that a vesting requirement is necessary if private pension plans are to serve the broad social purpose justifying their favored status"). Vesting was proposed as a condition of receiving favorable tax treatment along with the original version of the tax law nondiscrimination rules in 1942, but it was not enacted at that time. *Revenue Revision of 1942: Hearings Before the H. Comm. on Ways and Means*, 77th Cong. 2405–09 (1942) (statement of Randolph Paul, special tax adviser to the Secretary of the Treasury).

Using public money to induce broader pension distribution is, of course, the motif of the qualified retirement plan provisions of the Internal Revenue Code. A new variation on that theme was adopted with the tremendous acceleration of vesting required by the 1986 amendments. The goal of this faster vesting was to increase the retirement security of women, minorities, and lower-income workers. These historically disadvantaged groups had shorter average job tenures and were therefore more likely to lose their retirement benefits under ERISA's original lengthy vesting schedules. S. REP. NO. 99-313, at 590 (1986).

would defeat the pension expectation that ERISA's vesting rules were intended to protect.

Policy-wise, ERISA's accumulation rules shape both the distribution and quality of pensions. Tight limits on age and service conditions encourage early plan entry of otherwise eligible workers. Early membership, combined with fairly even year-by-year benefit accrual and rapid vesting, provides a longer accumulation period and potentially higher benefits, but may also force the employer to provide more contributions or benefits to employees who work for the firm for only a few years (albeit long enough to vest). Instead of bestowing pensions on those few workers who make a career-long commitment to the firm, ERISA's accumulation rules incorporate a preference for broader distribution of retirement savings. This covert distributive norm comes at a price: young and recently hired workers generally value retirement savings less than their senior coworkers, while on the employer side, the utility of a pension plan as a workforce bonding mechanism (an inducement to long and loyal service) is restricted. Given our system of voluntary employment-based pension plans, where these cost increases prove material, the employer is free to respond by terminating the plan, decreasing future benefit accruals, or restricting coverage (i.e., limiting eligibility based on criteria other than age or service). Yet because our pension system is tax subsidized (and so only semi-private), in many instances, increased costs will be met by the public subsidy (i.e., the preferential tax treatment of qualified retirement savings, discussed in Chapter 9).

The benefit accrual and vesting rules assure that any employer's pension promise meets a baseline standard of quality. This limited regulation of pension plan content may be seen as either paternalistic worker protection or efficiency-enhancing worker empowerment. Restrictions on backloading and forfeitures protect workers who casually rely on the employer's pension promise without attending to the details. By outlawing pension limitations that are often overlooked or misunderstood, participants are given the right to receive what they consider their due.

Instead of aligning the content of the pension promise with workers' mistaken (over-) estimation of its value, effective disclosure of accrual rates and forfeiture risks could, in principle, alter workers' assessment of the promise (by downward adjustment) to make it congruent with their pension's actual expected value. Whether disclosure can be "effective" is another matter, however. The time and expense involved in understanding plan terms and assessing individual risks (determining expected value) would often exceed the advantage that could be gained by comparing pension plans associated with alternative employment opportunities. Reining in abstruse outlier plan terms could be used as a mechanism to limit information costs and thereby allow workers to inexpensively assess salient differences that remain. From this information cost perspective, reducing variation in accrual rates and forfeiture risks empowers workers to compare retirement plan alternatives and make better career and financial planning decisions.

Chapter 8

Distribution

Once an employee has become a participant, has earned benefits, and has worked long enough to vest, the employer cannot cancel that employee's pension (see *supra* Chapter 7 on the rules governing accumulation). A vested participant does not normally have an immediate right to the money, however, nor can she direct its payment to someone else. Pension plans are designed to provide workers with a secure source of retirement income, not to facilitate general purpose savings. Therefore, access to pension savings is restricted, either by the terms of the plan or by ERISA itself.

ERISA's rules governing pension plan distributions are a curious mix of not-altogether-coherent policies. The rules address three issues. First, the timing of distributions is restricted. Second, the anti-alienation rule generally limits the recipients of distributions to the participant and her beneficiaries. And third, the participant's spouse is, in effect, designated primary beneficiary.

A. TIMING

Despite its central goal of increasing the security of *retirement* income, ERISA has little to say about the timing of plan distributions. Instead, the task of discouraging pre-retirement (in-service) distributions, as well as excessive deferral (intergenerational transfers), is left almost entirely to the tax law.

Early Distributions

Private pensions supplement Social Security old-age benefits to help maintain workers' standard of living after retirement. To replace lost wage or salary income, pensions must be available upon retirement. Defined benefit plans have traditionally provided distribution in the form of a life annuity commencing at a specified retirement age. Defined contribution plans, in contrast, commonly permit distribution in the form of a lump-sum payment upon separation from service. Separation from service may occur long before permanent withdrawal from the labor force. Such pre-retirement distributions create a risk that pension benefits, instead of being saved to provide support in retirement, will be devoted to more immediate goals, like increasing current consumption or sending children to college. Nevertheless, ERISA does not restrict pre-retirement pension plan distributions.

The task of restricting early distributions is left entirely to the tax law. Qualified pension plans have always been directed to retirement savings and generally are prohibited from allowing in-service distributions or providing nonretirement benefits.[1] Profit-sharing and stock bonus plans, in contrast, need not be devoted exclusively to retirement saving, but may provide short-term deferred compensation by making available in-service distributions after as little as two years of participation, or in the event of the employee's financial hardship.[2] Such liberal access to distributions creates the risk that qualified plan savings will be dissipated before retirement. Congress has tried to avoid that result by imposing an additional 10 percent income tax on early distributions from qualified plans that are not preserved as retirement savings by

---

[1] Treas. Reg. § 1.401-1(b)(1)(i) (as amended in 1976). Statutory amendments were enacted in 2006 to facilitate phased retirement programs, under which employees are allowed to reduce their work schedules and receive a portion of their accrued pension benefits during a period of transition between full-time employment and complete retirement. I.R.C. § 401(a)(36) (2006) (qualified pension plan may permit in-service distributions to employees aged 62 or older); ERISA § 3(2)(A), 29 U.S.C. § 1002(2)(A) (2006) (final sentence) (in-service distributions to employees aged 62 or older satisfy ERISA's definition of pension plan). *See* Prop. Treas. Reg. § 1.401(a)-3, 69 Fed. Reg. 65108, 65112 (Dec. 28, 2004) (proposed rule would allow qualified pension plan to distribute phased retirement benefits to an employee who, being at least 59½ years old, voluntarily reduces his customary work schedule by at least 20 percent).

[2] A profit-sharing plan is "primarily a plan of deferred compensation," Treas. Reg. § 1.401-1(b) (1)(ii) (as amended in 1976), while a pension plan, in the tax Code's parlance, must be meant "to provide for the livelihood of the employees or their beneficiaries after the retirement of such employees," *id.* § 1.401-1(a)(2)(i). Rev. Rul. 54-231, 1954-1 C.B. 150 ("fixed number of years" means two or more); Rev. Rul. 68-24, 1968-1 C.B. 150 (same); Rev. Rul. 71-224, 1971-1 C.B. 124 (financial hardship, if objectively defined, is permissible grounds for distribution of vested interest in an employee's profit-sharing account).

being promptly contributed to another qualified plan or an individual retirement account (IRA).[3]

Late Distributions

To ensure that pension plan savings are available to finance retirement, ERISA requires that the plan provide that, *absent the participant's consent*, distributions must commence within sixty days after the close of the plan year in which either (1) the participant attains the earlier of age 65 or the plan's normal retirement age (NRA), or, if later, (2) the participant separates from service. If plan participation commenced within ten years of the relevant date (whichever applies), further delay is permissible; distributions need not begin earlier than sixty days after the close of the plan year in which the tenth anniversary of initial participation falls.[4] This rule is meant to grant access to benefits as soon as the participant is likely to need retirement income, upon separation from service at an advanced age. Where separation from service occurs earlier, payment can generally be deferred until the plan's normal retirement age (but not later than age 65), which is the time when the participant was led to expect his pension would be available. If the plan allows for payment of early retirement benefits, however, a vested participant who has enough service to qualify for early retirement benefits, but who separates from service before the earliest age for payment, must be permitted to start taking distribution once he satisfies the age requirement.[5] The amount payable to such a former employee is the benefit to which he would be entitled at NRA (i.e., his accrued benefit), actuarially reduced for early commencement.[6] A former employee is not entitled to any early retirement subsidy that the plan may offer because the purpose of such a subsidy is to induce separation from service.

---

3   I.R.C. §§ 72(t), 402(c) (2006). The early distribution penalty tax generally applies to distributions made before the employee attains age 59½, but does not apply to distributions made following separation from service after age 55, to distributions on account of disability, to distributions to a beneficiary after the death of the employee, or to annuity-type distributions, regardless of when they commence, paid over the life or life expectancy of the employee (or over the joint lives or life expectancies of the employee and his designated beneficiary). Distributions to cover extraordinary medical expenses are also exempt. An early distribution that would otherwise trigger the tax becomes nontaxable if contributed to another qualified plan or IRA within sixty days of receipt because the tax applies only to the amount of a distribution that is *includible* in gross income, and such a "rollover" renders a distribution *excludible* from gross income. *Compare* I.R.C. § 72(t)(1) (2006), *with id.* § 402(c)(1).

4   ERISA § 206(a), 29 U.S.C. § 1056(a) (2006); *see* I.R.C. § 401(a)(14) (2006).

5   ERISA § 206(a), 29 U.S.C. § 1056(a) (2006) (final sentence); *see* I.R.C. § 401(a)(14) (2006) (final sentence).

6   ERISA § 206(a), 29 U.S.C. § 1056(a) (2006) (final sentence); *see* I.R.C. § 401(a)(14) (2006) (final sentence); Treas. Reg. § 1.401(a)-14(c) (1976).

B. ANTI-ALIENATION

Standing alone, constraints on early distributions are insufficient to prevent premature dissipation of retirement savings. Instead of waiting for distributions to commence, a participant determined to use his pension for other purposes could sell his interest immediately. Similarly, the short-sighted participant could run up his personal debts, leaving his creditors to collect from his pension accumulation. To prevent such indirect plundering of retirement savings, ERISA generally requires that pension benefits be nontransferable.[7]

According to the Supreme Court, ERISA's "anti-alienation provision can 'be seen to bespeak a pension law protective policy of special intensity: Retirement funds shall remain inviolate until retirement.'"[8] The goal is to "safeguard a stream of [retirement] income for pensioners" and their dependents by putting it beyond their own reach, and beyond the reach of their creditors.[9] By making retirement savings inaccessible, ERISA's spendthrift clause works as a precommitment device that tends to bind the worker to a particular use of the fund.[10] In so limiting participants' freedom of choice, the value of pension accruals is impaired for many workers, relative to cash, because they have more immediate and higher-priority uses for their compensation.[11] Mandatory spendthrift protection, of course, reflects a congressional judgment that those priorities are often misguided.

Inalienability serves the employer's interest as well, by ensuring that pension savings will be available to provide an incentive for retirement. Consequently, pension trusts commonly included spendthrift restraints long before ERISA demanded it. Uncertainty and variation in state spendthrift trust law, however, made it difficult for workers to gauge the accessibility of pension savings offered under plans of different employers. ERISA's anti-alienation requirement, by mandating uniform efficacious spendthrift protection for all pensions, reduces those information costs. Hence the anti-alienation rule promotes improved worker career and financial planning. Thus, while it is central to the protective policy, anti-alienation also serves ERISA's goal of increasing efficiency through better-informed decision making.[12]

Congress has authorized a few narrow exceptions to the anti-alienation requirement. Once distributions have begun, a voluntary revocable assignment of not more than

---

7 ERISA § 206(d)(1), 29 U.S.C. § 1056(d)(1) (2006); *see* I.R.C. § 401(a)(13)(A) (2006).

8 Boggs v. Boggs, 520 U.S. 833, 851 (1997) (quoting JOHN LANGBEIN & BRUCE WOLK, PENSION AND EMPLOYEE BENEFIT LAW 547 (2d ed. 1995)). Or, as the committee reports explained, the anti-alienation rule is meant to "ensure that the employee's accrued benefits are actually available for retirement purposes." H.R. REP. NO. 93-779, at 66 (1974); H.R. REP. NO. 93-807, at 66 (1974).

9 Guidry v. Sheet Metal Workers Nat'l Pension Fund, 493 U.S. 365, 376 (1990).

10 *See generally* Richard H. Thaler & H.M. Shefrin, *An Economic Theory of Self Control*, *in* QUASI RATIONAL ECONOMICS 77, 81–84 (Richard H. Thaler ed., 1991); Hersh M. Shefrin & Richard H. Thaler, *The Behavioral Life-Cycle Hypothesis*, *in id.* at 91, 95–96, 103–07.

11 This impairment of value, in turn, increases the need to subsidize pensions, which is accomplished via the preferential tax treatment accorded qualified pension, profit-sharing, and stock bonus plans. *See infra* Chapter 10B.

12 Wiedenbeck, *supra* Chapter 1 note 57, at 575. *See supra* Chapter 1C.

10 percent of any benefit payment is permissible.[13] The grant of an interest in benefits to secure repayment of a loan from the plan, provided that the loan meets certain tests to prevent favoritism, is also allowed.[14] The plan loan exception undercuts the policy of the anti-alienation rule: if loan proceeds are used for nonretirement purposes and are not repaid, enforcement of the security interest will extinguish the participant's pension. For that reason, the tax Code discourages most plan loans other than small, short-term loans.[15]

Involuntary assignments (i.e., enforcement of creditors' claims against a participant's or beneficiary's interest in the pension plan) are generally barred as well.[16] And ERISA's restraint on alienation is even effective in bankruptcy proceedings. A debtor's interest in an ERISA-regulated pension plan is excluded from the bankruptcy code's definition of property of the estate, so that retirement savings continue to be shielded from creditors, even as all other property interests are marshaled for creditors' benefit.[17]

---

13 Curiously, the tax Code's qualification criteria permit limited, voluntary revocable assignments only if the participant or beneficiary is already receiving benefits under the plan, while ERISA's corresponding exception is not restricted to benefits that are already in pay status. *Compare* ERISA § 206(d)(2), 29 U.S.C. § 1056(d)(2) (2006), *with* I.R.C. § 401(a)(13)(A) (2006). *See* Treas. Reg. § 1.401(a)-13(d)(1) (as amended in 1988) (exception extends to assignments by beneficiaries, although the tax Code mentions only participants; 10 percent limit applies to the total of all assignments, multiple assignments of 10 percent each impermissible).

14 ERISA § 206(d)(2), 29 U.S.C. § 1056(d)(2) (2006); *see* I.R.C. § 401(a)(13)(A) (2006). A security interest in plan benefits is valid only if it backs a plan loan that is made in accordance with specific provisions in the plan, that is available to all participants or beneficiaries on a reasonably equivalent basis in amounts that do not favor highly compensated employees, and that is adequately secured and bears a reasonable rate of interest. I.R.C. § 4975(d)(1) (2006). These anti-favoritism criteria apply whether the plan loan is made to a "disqualified person" or not (designated insiders and related parties who are subject to the penalty tax on prohibited transactions). Treas. Reg. § 1.401(a)-13(d)(2)(iii) (as amended in 1988).

15 I.R.C. § 72(p) (2006). The discouragement takes the form of taxing the proceeds of plan loans as distributions (under general tax principles, ordinary loan proceeds are not income). As deemed distributions, the loan proceeds might also trigger the additional 10 percent tax on early withdrawals, I.R.C. § 72(t) (2006). To avoid taxation, the total amount of plan loans must not exceed the *lesser* of (1) $50,000 (but with amounts repaid within the prior year treated as outstanding and counted against this limit) or (2) one-half of the present value of the participant's vested accrued benefit (or $10,000, if greater). In addition, the loan must be subject to level amortization with payments at least quarterly, and, except in the case of a loan to purchase a principal residence, must be for a term of not more than five years. I.R.C. § 72(p)(2) (2006).

16 The IRS takes the position that federal tax levies and judgments can be enforced against pension plan benefits notwithstanding the anti-alienation rule, Treas. Reg. § 1.401(a)-13(b)(2) (as amended in 1988), presumably on the authority of ERISA's federal law savings clause, ERISA § 514(d), 29 U.S.C. § 1144(d) (2006). *See* I.R.C. § 72(t)(2)(A)(vii) (2006) (levy excepted from additional tax on early distributions). *But see* Guidry v. Sheet Metal Workers Nat'l Pension Fund, 493 U.S. 365, 375–76 (1990) (Taft-Hartley Act's remedial provisions do not override ERISA's anti-alienation rule despite the federal law savings clause), discussed *infra* text accompanying Chapter 8 notes 18–20.

17 11 U.S.C. § 541(c)(2) (2006); Patterson v. Shumate, 504 U.S. 753 (1992).

The startling force of the anti-alienation rule is illustrated by *Guidry v. Sheet Metal Workers National Pension Fund*.[18] Guidry, who was both the chief executive officer of a union local and a trustee of the local's pension fund, pleaded guilty to embezzling more than $377,000 from the union and later stipulated to the entry of a judgment of $275,000 in favor of the union. While serving his prison sentence, Guidry brought suit against two union pension plans in which he was a participant, claiming that they were wrongfully refusing to pay benefits. The plans countered that Guidry's accrued benefits should be paid to the union under a constructive trust. The Supreme Court held that the Taft-Hartley Act's general authorization of "appropriate equitable relief" to remedy violations of an officer's duties to the union does not override ERISA's anti-alienation provision. The Court refused to approve any generalized equitable exception to the anti-alienation rule based on employee wrongdoing, observing:

> Section 206(d) reflects a considered congressional policy choice, a decision to safeguard a stream of income for pensioners (and their dependents, who may be, and perhaps usually are, blameless), even if that decision prevents others from securing relief for the wrongs done them. If exceptions to this policy are to be made, it is for Congress to undertake that task.[19]

Guidry was found not to have violated any duty owed *to the pension plans*, and so the case did not present an internal conflict between ERISA's remedies for fiduciary breach and its anti-alienation provision. The Court declined to resolve that conflict,[20] and a circuit split quickly developed on this issue.[21] In 1997, Congress accepted the Court's invitation to legislate exceptions to the anti-alienation policy, declaring that an order offsetting a participant's pension benefits against an amount the participant owes the plan is enforceable if the liability arises from conviction of a crime involving the plan, a judgment for breach of an ERISA fiduciary obligation, or a settlement agreement with the Labor Department or the Pension Benefit Guaranty Corporation (PBGC) involving alleged violations of fiduciary obligations. But where the pension being offset is subject to the spousal survivor annuity rules, Congress protected the spouse's interest. If the spouse is not also liable for the harm done to the plan and has not voluntarily consented to the setoff, then a portion of the wrongdoer's accrued benefits sufficient to provide the spouse with ERISA's minimum required survivor annuity protection must be preserved.[22]

In contrast to ERISA's laissez-faire attitude toward distribution timing, the statute takes a remarkably hard line on indirect access to pensions. The anti-alienation rule prevents participants and beneficiaries from transferring undistributed pension accumulations, and so bars anticipation by sale or execution by creditors. Taken together,

---

18   493 U.S. 365 (1990).
19   *Id.* at 376 (footnote omitted).
20   *Id.* at 373.
21   *Compare* Herberger v. Shanbaum, 897 F.2d 801 (5th Cir. 1990) (offset of breaching fiduciary's pension barred), *with* Coar v. Kamizir, 990 F.2d 1413 (3d Cir. 1993) (offset permitted).
22   ERISA § 206(d)(4), (d)(5), 29 U.S.C. § 1056(d)(4), (d)(5) (2006); *see* I.R.C. § 401(a)(13)(C), (a)(13)(D) (2006). ERISA's spousal survivor annuity requirements are discussed *infra* Chapter 8C.

these rules prohibit participants and their beneficiaries from doing indirectly what the plan could lawfully have allowed them to do directly (i.e., by authorizing in-service or early distributions). Still, where a plan does not, in fact, permit pre-retirement distributions (defined benefit plans commonly forbid them), the anti-alienation rule reinforces the employer's design control, increasing the utility of the plan as an instrument of personnel policy, perhaps thereby encouraging sponsorship. In backstopping the plan's distribution rules, the stringent national anti-alienation rule is commonly viewed as another of ERISA's worker protection devices. This protection, however, is of an unusual sort. Anti-alienation doesn't safeguard against *employer* abuses, such as misrepresentation, forfeiture, or insolvency (compare ERISA's disclosure, vesting, and funding rules). Instead, anti-alienation protects workers from their *own* improvidence.[23]

Qualified Domestic Relations Orders

The anti-alienation rule makes pension plans a sort of federal law spendthrift trust.[24] State spendthrift trust law recognizes a number of public policy exceptions: certain categories of creditors' claims may be enforced against a protected beneficial interest, notwithstanding a restraint on alienation.[25] Foremost among these favored claims are claims for support by the spouse or children of the beneficiary.[26] Whether federal courts would adopt a comparable family law creditor exception to ERISA's anti-alienation rule was a hotly contested issue during ERISA's first decade. In the Retirement Equity Act of 1984, Congress stepped in to resolve the controversy, creating an express statutory exception for family law creditors whose claims satisfied certain requirements.[27] The conditions that must be met to make family law claims enforceable against a pension plan are set forth in the definition of a "qualified domestic relations order," or QDRO. At the same time, however, Congress amended ERISA's preemption provision to make clear that support claims not meeting the strict definition of a QDRO are unenforceable against pension plans.[28]

---

23 It also simplifies planning by clarifying exactly where a worker stands in terms of access to her pension savings—like it or not, wherever you live and whatever the plan has to say about transferability, you can't get the money until all distribution conditions are satisfied. *See supra* Chapter 8 note 12 and accompanying text.

24 RESTATEMENT (SECOND) OF TRUSTS § 152(2) (1959) provides: "A trust in which by the terms of the trust or by statute a valid restraint on the voluntary and involuntary transfer of the interest of the beneficiary is imposed is a spendthrift trust."

25 RESTATEMENT (SECOND) OF TRUSTS § 157 (1959); 2A SCOTT ON TRUSTS, *supra* Chapter 3 note 11, § 157.

26 RESTATEMENT (SECOND) OF TRUSTS § 157(a) (1959); 2A SCOTT ON TRUSTS, *supra* Chapter 3 note 11, § 157.1.

27 ERISA § 206(d)(3), 29 U.S.C. § 1056(d)(3) (2006), enacted by Pub. L. No. 98-397, § 104 (1984). The corresponding tax law qualification requirements appear as I.R.C. §§ 401(a)(13)(B), 414(p) (2006).

28 ERISA § 514(b)(7), 29 U.S.C. § 1144(b)(7) (2006). *See* S. REP. NO. 98-575, at 19 (1984) ("conforming changes to the ERISA preemption provision are necessary to ensure that only

To be "qualified," a domestic relations order must recognize the participant's liability to a spouse, former spouse, child, or other dependent of a participant for the payment of child support, alimony, or marital property, and it must also authorize such an "alternate payee" to collect from the plan.[29] In addition, the order must meet a number of statutory criteria that are designed to protect pension plans from increased costs, so that enforcing one participant's family support obligations will not impair the interests of other participants and their beneficiaries. There are two components to this endeavor. First, ERISA demands a certain degree of specificity and clarity in order to minimize compliance costs and avoid having the plan become enmeshed in litigation. Second, family law creditors' claims must not increase the plan's liability to pay benefits.

To be a QDRO, the order must "clearly specif[y]" (1) the name and address of the participant and each payee covered by the order, (2) the amount or percentage of the participant's benefits to be paid to each alternate payee, or the manner for determining the amount or percentage, (3) the number of payments or periods to which the order applies, and (4) the plans to which the order applies.[30] The purpose is to enable the plan administrator to act on the order alone, without having to look behind the document to resolve ambiguities or supply missing information, and without being sued by rival claimants. Where an order lacks the necessary information, but the plan administrator has independent knowledge of the missing facts, the courts disagree on whether the order is a QDRO. Some adopt a lenient attitude suggested by the legislative history, while others, fearing that controversies over the existence and extent of such subjective knowledge would embroil the plan in litigation, are more strict.[31]

---

those orders that are excepted [by the QDRO rules] from the spendthrift provisions are not preempted by ERISA"; domestic relations order not a prohibited alienation of benefits "if and only if" it is a QDRO). *Accord* I.R.C. § 401(a)(13)(B) (2006) (anti-alienation rule "shall apply" to a domestic relations order unless it is determined to be a QDRO). *See* Ablamis v. Roper, 937 F.2d 1450, 1458 (9th Cir. 1991) (rejecting argument that ERISA's anti-alienation provision is simply inapplicable to allocations or transfers between spouses); Boggs v. Boggs, 520 U.S. 833, 851 (1997).

29   ERISA § 206(d)(3)(B), (K), 29 U.S.C. § 1056(d)(3)(B), (K) (2006); *see* I.R.C. § 414(p)(1), (8) (2006). *See* Hawkins v. Comm'r, 86 F.3d 982, 989–91 (10th Cir. 1996) (where marital property settlement agreement incorporated in divorce decree stated that wife was to receive $1 million from husband's pension plan, order was sufficient to recognize right to receive plan benefits, even though wife not referred to as alternate payee and agreement did not mimic statutory language).

30   ERISA § 206(d)(3)(C), 29 U.S.C. § 1056(d)(3)(C) (2006); *see* I.R.C. § 414(p)(2) (2006).

31   *Compare Hawkins*, 86 F.3d at 991–93 (QDRO specificity requirement must be enforced because required by plain meaning and to avoid embroiling plan in costly litigation), *with* Metro. Life Ins. Co. v. Wheaton, 42 F.3d 1080, 1085 (7th Cir. 1994) (strict compliance with QDRO specificity requirements not necessary). This difference of opinion is reviewed in *Stewart v. Thorpe Holding Co. Profit Sharing Plan*, 207 F.3d 1143 (9th Cir. 2000). *See* S. Rep. No. 98-575, at 20 (1984) (order with incorrect address should be treated as QDRO if administrator has independent knowledge of current address); Pension and Welfare Benefits Administration, U.S. Department of Labor, *QDROs*: The Division of Pensions Through Qualified Domestic Relations Orders 17 (1997) (if incomplete information is "easily obtainable," administrator should not reject order as defective).

ERISA forbids plan compliance with a domestic relations order that would force the plan to pay increased benefits or that would require the plan to provide any type or form of benefit or any option not otherwise available under the plan.[32] Nor may effect be given to an order that would require the payment of benefits to a family law claimant if the benefits are required to be paid under a prior QDRO to another alternate payee (a first-in-time rule).[33] These rules shield the plan from any obligation to provide different or increased benefits to family law creditors. So, for example, the divorced spouse of a 40-year-old participant cannot immediately collect all or a portion of the participant's accrued benefits if the plan does not permit lump-sum distributions at that time. If the plan does allow such distributions, a QDRO may call for immediate payment to the spouse, even if the participant elects payment in the form of an annuity. That is, a QDRO may be drafted to award the alternate payee a separate interest in a specified portion of the participant's benefits, with the alternate payee treated like a participant with respect to that interest, including having the right to select among alternative investments and having the right to choose the form and timing of distributions from among the options (if any) available to participants under the plan. (This is known as the separate interest approach.) Alternatively, a QDRO may be drafted to give the alternate payee a specified share of payments made under the form of distribution applicable to the debtor-participant, with the alternate payee receiving benefit

---

32   The prospect of increased benefit liabilities is presented where an otherwise proper QDRO is not presented to the plan until after the retirement or death of the participant. If a divorced participant remarries and later retires, for example, the pension would normally be payable in the form of a qualified joint and survivor annuity (QJSA) with the new spouse (*see infra* Chapter 8C). If the former spouse presents a domestic relations order after retirement, it could not be honored without either decreasing payments from a QJSA that is already in the distribution phase (a type of benefit not otherwise provided by the plan) or increasing plan benefits. Consequently, several appellate decisions hold that an order presented after the participant's retirement or death is not a QDRO. Hopkins v. AT&T Global Info. Solutions Co., 105 F.3d 153 (4th Cir. 1997) (state court order to collect alimony and granting former wife survivor benefits not QDRO because not entered until after participant's retirement, at which time surviving spouse benefits vested in second wife); Rivers v. Cent. & S.W. Corp., 186 F.3d 681 (5th Cir. 1999) (first wife's community property claim, presented years after participant retired with QJSA and died, not QDRO because benefits vested in second wife on date of retirement); Samaroo v. Samaroo, 193 F.3d 185 (3d Cir. 1999) (divorced participant's defined benefit pension forfeited on death without surviving spouse; divorce decree did not give former wife survivor benefits, and post-death amendment purporting to confer survivorship rights not QDRO because it would increase plan benefits). *But see* Trs. of the Dir. Guild of Am.-Producer Pension Benefits Plans v. Tise, 255 F.3d 661 (9th Cir. 2000) (if, before participant's death, plan has notice of state court order requiring payment of child support from pension, order may be modified after death to fulfill QDRO requirements, despite impact on nonspouse death beneficiary).

33   ERISA § 206(d)(3)(D), 29 U.S.C. § 1056(d)(3)(D) (2006); *see* I.R.C. § 414(p)(3) (2006). Similarly, procedural rules protect the plan from inconsistent liability. Payments to the participant are suspended during the period in which the status of a domestic relations order as a QDRO is being determined; if the matter cannot be resolved within 18 months, the withheld amounts are then paid to the participant, and any later determination that the order is a QDRO is given only prospective effect. ERISA § 206(d)(3)(H), 29 U.S.C. § 1056(d)(3)(H) (2006); *see* I.R.C. § 414(p)(7) (2006).

payments only when the participant receives payments. (This method of division is known as the shared payment approach.)

The prohibition on departures from the plan's ordinary distribution rules is subject to one important exception involving the time for commencement of distributions. Where a plan makes no provision for in-service distributions, the continued employment of the debtor–participant would normally bar distribution to alternate payees, even if a spouse or child has a pressing need for immediate support payments. To prevent this hardship, a special rule permits access by alternate payees on the later of (1) the date the participant attains age fifty, or (2) the earliest date on which the participant could begin receiving benefits if the participant separated from service.[34]

The QDRO rules reflect an accommodation between family law and pension policy. A homemaker who expects retirement support from an employee-spouse's pension may be impoverished by a late-life divorce. In such situations, giving the ex-spouse access to the participant's pension is a logical extension of Congress's recognition that two people may be relying on the participant's retirement income. ERISA gives a spouse the right to receive a survivor annuity in the event of the participant's death;[35] similar protections would be appropriate where the marriage ends in divorce. Yet this retirement security concern is obviously not the principal impetus for the QDRO rules. Children and other nonspouse dependents can be granted an interest in pension benefits as alternate payees. For a spouse, pension access may provide the wherewithal to finance a marital property settlement rather than providing support, much less retirement support. And we have just seen that where distributions are conditioned on separation from service, access may be granted as early as the participant's attainment of age fifty, even if the participant is still employed. In this field, pension policy takes a back seat to enforcement of family law obligations. That is apparent, as well, from the fact that retirement income protection is available under a QDRO, but is neither required nor automatically included as a default rule. A former spouse can be granted survivorship rights in the participant's pension (with the consequence that any subsequent spouse of the participant will be denied that protection), but only "to the extent provided" in the QDRO.[36]

Overriding a Beneficiary Designation

Upon the death of the participant, any remaining benefits go to her beneficiaries.[37] The beneficiary is "the person designated by a participant, or by the terms of an

---

34   ERISA § 206(d)(3)(E), 29 U.S.C. § 1056(d)(3)(E) (2006); *see* I.R.C. § 414(p)(4) (2006). For illustrations of the operation of this special timing rule, see PENSION AND WELFARE BENEFITS ADMINISTRATION, U.S. DEPARTMENT OF LABOR, QDROS: THE DIVISION OF PENSIONS THROUGH QUALIFIED DOMESTIC RELATIONS ORDERS 42–43 (1997).

35   *See infra* Chapter 8C on the spousal protection rules.

36   ERISA § 206(d)(3)(F), 29 U.S.C. § 1056(d)(3)(F) (2006); *see* I.R.C. § 414(p)(5) (2006). To be qualified, however, the domestic relations order granting survivorship rights must be entered before the participant dies. *See supra* Chapter 8 note 32.

37   Recall, however, that a plan may call for forfeiture on the death of the participant if the spousal protection rules do not apply. ERISA § 203(a)(3)(A), 29 U.S.C. § 1053(a)(3)(A) (2006);

employee benefit plan," as entitled to plan benefits.[38] Pension plan survivor benefits amount to a death-time donative transfer from the participant. Under state wills and succession laws, a property owner's beneficiary designation is revoked by operation of law in some circumstances. Typically, divorce cuts off all gifts under a will in favor of a spouse,[39] and an intentional killer is barred from taking the victim's property as heir or devisee.[40] Similar beneficiary disqualification issues can arise with respect to pensions, but they are complicated by ERISA's anti-alienation and preemption provisions.

Divorce is the most common issue. Almost invariably, pension plan beneficiary designations can be changed by the participant, and while spousal consent to the change is often required, that is not an obstacle following divorce.[41] Where the participant designates a spouse as beneficiary, the parties are later divorced, and the participant subsequently dies without having changed the beneficiary designation, what inference should be drawn from the participant's inaction? Was the failure to change the beneficiary designation an oversight, or does it evidence a continuing desire to benefit the former spouse? State laws calling for revocation of bequests to a former spouse proceed from the view that in this situation, failure to change the will was probably inadvertent, so that a default rule of revocation on divorce is most likely to effectuate the owner's desires. The same considerations apply to pension plan beneficiary designations, but ERISA makes no provision for revocation on divorce. Nor is there any indication that the omission of any provision was deliberate; Congress simply never considered the issue.

The states have, however. Nonprobate transfer laws in some jurisdictions call for revocation on divorce of spousal beneficiary designations made pursuant to succession provisions in a wide variety of contracts, including life insurance, annuity contracts, bank accounts, payable-on-death instructions, and employee benefit plans.[42] Application of such a state law to a pension plan beneficiary designation effects a transfer of succession rights from the former spouse, working an involuntary alienation of benefits in contravention of the literal terms of ERISA's spendthrift clause. Beyond their specific conflict with the anti-alienation rule, state divorce revocation laws seem

---

see I.R.C. § 411(a)(3)(A) (2006). Defined benefit plans often call for forfeiture in the event the participant dies without a surviving spouse, but defined contribution plans rarely contain such a provision.

38   ERISA § 3(8), 29 U.S.C. § 1002(8) (2006). *See also* Treas. Reg. § 1.401-1(b)(4) (as amended in 1976) (for purposes of the definition of qualified pension, profit-sharing, and stock bonus plans, the beneficiaries of the employee include "the estate of the employee, dependents of the employee, persons who are the natural objects of the employee's bounty, and any persons designated by the employee to share in the benefits of the plan after the death of the employee").

39   *See, e.g.,* Unif. Probate Code §§ 1-201(19), 2-804 (1990); Mo. Rev. Stat. § 474.420 (2000).

40   *See, e.g.,* Unif. Probate Code §§ 1-201(19), 2-803 (1990).

41   *See* ERISA § 205(c)(2), 29 U.S.C. § 1055(c)(2) (2006); I.R.C. § 417(a)(2) (2006). *See generally infra* Chapter 8C.

42   *See, e.g.,* Unif. Probate Code § 1-201(19) (1990) (instrument subject to divorce revocation rules includes "deed, will, trust, insurance or annuity policy, account with POD designation, security registered in beneficiary form (TOD), pension, profit-sharing, retirement, or similar benefit plan"); Mo. Rev. Stat. § 461.051, .048, .062.3(5), (9) (2000).

to run afoul of ERISA's statutory preemption provision, for by altering the plan beneficiary, they apparently "relate to [an] employee benefit plan."[43]

The Supreme Court faced this issue in *Egelhoff v. Egelhoff*.[44] There, the decedent had named his wife as beneficiary under both his employer-provided life insurance and pension plans. The participant died as a result of an automobile accident less than three months after the couple divorced, not having changed his beneficiary designation under either plan. The decedent's children from a prior marriage challenged the former wife's entitlement to benefits, relying on a Washington statute that revokes transfers to a former spouse under a "payable on death provision of a life insurance policy, employee benefit plan, annuity or similar contract, or individual retirement account." Nonprobate transfers to which the statute applies are redirected as though the former spouse died on the date of divorce.[45] Applying that rule, the children claimed the life insurance proceeds as heirs and asserted survivors' rights in the pension under a plan provision appointing default beneficiaries in the absence of an effective beneficiary designation by the participant.[46] The former wife, of course, argued that ERISA prevents application of the state divorce revocation statute, and that, as the participant's designated beneficiary, she was entitled to benefits under the terms of the plans.

The Court held that Washington's nonprobate transfer law ran afoul of ERISA. The divorce revocation rule was preempted because it "directly conflicts with ERISA's requirements that plans be administered, and benefits paid, in accordance with plan documents."[47] Here, the plan documents included the deceased participant's written beneficiary designation. The Washington statute prevented uniform plan administration because administrators could not simply make payment to the beneficiary whose name was on file. Instead, they would have to familiarize themselves with state law and investigate the marital status of beneficiaries to determine whether a beneficiary designation remained valid. In cases where the participant worked in one state and

---

43 ERISA § 514(a), 29 U.S.C. § 1144(a) (2006).

44 532 U.S. 141 (2001).

45 WASH. REV. CODE § 11.07.010 (1994).

46 *Egelhoff*, 532 U.S. at 145. In the court below, the children also argued that they were entitled to pension benefits apart from the divorce revocation statute, because the participant's ex-wife had voluntarily waived her right to pension benefits in a property settlement incorporated in the divorce decree. Egelhoff v. Egelhoff, 989 P.2d 80, 83–84 (Wash. 1999). The Supreme Court did not take up this question. The enforceability of such a waiver is discussed *infra*, text accompanying notes 55–61.

47 *Egelhoff*, 532 U.S. at 150. *See* ERISA §§ 402(b)(4), 404(a)(1)(D), 29 U.S.C. §§ 1102(b)(4), 1104(a)(1)(D) (2006). The Court did not address whether Washington's divorce revocation law conflicts with ERISA's anti-alienation rule, perhaps because that ground of decision was only relevant to the pension plan. Benefits under the life insurance program (a welfare plan) were not subject to transfer restrictions. ERISA §§ 201(1), 206(d)(1), 29 U.S.C. §§ 1051(1), 1056(d) (1) (2006). Moreover, even though application of the divorce revocation statute would work a transfer of pension benefits, it is far from clear that this is the sort of transfer against which ERISA's anti-alienation rule was directed. The transfer is not a voluntary disposition (sale or gift, for example) of the participant's interest, nor does it give creditors access to the fund. Consequently, the divorce revocation law does not undercut the goal of ensuring that pensions will be available to provide retirement income to participants and their beneficiaries. Instead, it simply supplies an answer to the question, who is the participant's intended beneficiary?

resided in another, with the former spouse perhaps living in a third, reliance on state law would present choice-of-law issues and potentially conflicting legal obligations.[48] This sort of nonuniformity is unacceptable because increased plan-administration costs ultimately reduce net benefits to employees, thereby imposing "precisely the burden that ERISA preemption was intended to avoid."[49]

Preemption of state divorce revocation laws clears the way for uniform plan administration. Yet from the standpoint of effectuating the average participant's intent, the Washington statute seems to achieve the preferable result. The Court could have secured the benefits of uniformity *and* better served participants' interests by holding the Washington statute preempted and simultaneously adopting the same approach as a matter of federal common law. Congress expected the judiciary to develop interstitial rules to implement ERISA,[50] and the effectiveness of spousal beneficiary designations following divorce seems to call for just that sort of limited lawmaking. None of the opinions in *Egelhoff* consider the possibility that preemption could go hand-in-hand with creation of a federal common-law rule. That oversight is unfortunate, for it offers the solution to a conundrum that troubled both the majority and the dissent, namely, that state slayer laws might also be preempted. The prospect of federal courts ordering an award of survivor benefits to a named beneficiary who murdered the plan participant is clearly unpalatable. In dissent, Justice Breyer asserted that state killer laws are virtually indistinguishable from the Washington divorce revocation statute, so that they too would fall prey to the Court's ERISA preemption analysis.[51] The Court majority

---

48 *Egelhoff*, 532 U.S. at 148–49. State law is actually highly uniform in calling for automatic revocation of gifts under a will in favor of a spouse upon divorce and in providing for disposition of the property as if the ex-spouse had died on the date of divorce. But while wills law is consistent on this point, the same cannot be said for the treatment of nonprobate transfers. Many states have not legislated with respect to nonprobate transfers, leaving the status of spousal beneficiary designations following divorce up in the air. In those jurisdictions, uncertainty will reign until the question receives a definitive judicial resolution, for the courts may not follow the wills law analogy, looking instead to the handling of former spouse beneficiaries under life insurance policies or revocable trusts.

49 *Egelhoff*, 532 U.S. at 150 (quoting Fort Halifax Packing Co. v. Coyne, 482 U.S. 1, 29 (1987)). In addition to cost containment, preemption preserves employer flexibility in setting plan terms (freedom of contract). *See supra* Chapter 6C. An employee benefit plan could be drafted to provide a specific default taker in the event of divorce. A plan might specify, for example, that in the event of divorce, benefits will be paid to secondary beneficiaries designated by the participant. Looking to state law takes the matter of divorce revocation out of the hands of the plan sponsor (or, in the case of a collectively bargained plan, the sponsor and the union). The *Egelhoff* opinion did not address this concern, which (unlike uniformity) weighs against creation of a federal common-law rule of divorce revocation.

50 120 CONG. REC. 29,942 (1974) (remarks of Sen. Javits) ("A body of Federal substantive law will be developed by the courts to deal with issues involving rights and obligations under private welfare and pension plans."). *See* Pilot Life Ins. Co. v. Dedeaux, 481 U.S. 41, 56 (1987); Firestone Tire & Rubber Co. v. Bruch, 489 U.S. 101, 110–11 (1989).

51 *Egelhoff*, 532 U.S. at 159–60 (Breyer, J., dissenting). As with divorce revocation, killer laws work an automatic substitution of beneficiaries by operation of law, and they may be rationalized as an attempt to identify the individuals who would have been the intended beneficiaries had the circumstances been foreseen.

sidestepped the issue, but suggested that the longer history and greater uniformity of state killer laws might save them from preemption.[52] A better solution would vindicate ERISA's uniformity interest by holding state killer laws preempted, while announcing a federal common-law rule barring an intentional killer from taking his victim's welfare or pension plan benefits.[53]

Egelhoff holds that ERISA supersedes state divorce revocation laws, and the Court did not announce a federal common-law rule of automatic revocation on divorce. That still leaves one important question unanswered. Where an ex-spouse renounces her claim to the pension as part of a property settlement, and the participant later dies without having changed his beneficiary designation, should such a voluntary waiver (as distinguished from revocation by operation of law) be given effect? Such a waiver, even if incorporated in the divorce decree, is not a QDRO because it does not give the former spouse a right to benefits; instead it disclaims any such right.[54]

The divorce waiver problem arises when a participant who named his or her spouse as plan beneficiary fails to change that designation after divorce. The divorce revocation issue presented in *Egelhoff* arose in the same way. In a waiver case, however, the court is not faced with mere inaction. Instead of uncertainty as to the intended beneficiary, the inference that the participant's failure to name a substitute taker was inadvertent seems unmistakable. The participant, after all, negotiated the waiver of rights in plan benefits as part of the divorce settlement, and the ex-spouse agreed to the waiver in return for other concessions, presumably a larger share of the participant's other assets.[55] In these circumstances, declining to enforce a divorce waiver that is voluntary and sufficiently specific seems unjust. Yet there is a downside to doing the right thing. Resort to extrinsic documents and the application of context-dependent standards to

---

52   *Egelhoff,* 532 U.S. at 152. Disqualification of an intentional killer under state law is almost universal, either by statute or judicial decision (typically by the application of constructive trust principles to prevent unjust enrichment), although there is some variation in the procedural details.

53   *See* Guardian Life Ins. Co. v. Finch, 395 F.3d 238 (5th Cir. 2004) (after *Egelhoff,* courts may still rely on federal common law to identify welfare plan beneficiary). The frequency of homicide is quite low compared to divorce, so the additional administrative burden imposed by such a federal common-law rule (compared to simply paying the beneficiary whose name is on file) would be insignificant. Moreover, general equitable principles (unclean hands defense), together with a concern for public respect for the courts and the legal system, would seem to compel this result. *See* New Orleans Elec. Pension Fund v. Newman, 784 F. Supp. 1233, 1236 (E.D. La. 1992) (Louisiana killer statute not preempted; alternatively, killer not entitled to benefits under federal law); I.R.S. Priv. Ltr. Rul. 90-08-079 (Nov. 30, 1989) (principles embodied in state killer statute constitute an implied exception to anti-alienation and spousal survivor annuity rules). *Guidry v. Sheet Metal Workers National Pension Fund,* 493 U.S. 365 (1990) (discussed *supra* text accompanying Chapter 8 notes 18–20), in which the Supreme Court refused to create an equitable exception to the anti-alienation rule, is distinguishable in this respect, for there, the Court based its decision on concern for the needs of the participant's "blameless" beneficiaries. *Guidry,* 493 U.S. at 376.

54   ERISA § 206(d)(3)(B)(i)(I), 29 U.S.C. § 1056(d)(3)(B)(i)(I) (2006); *see* I.R.C. § 414(p)(1)(A) (i) (2006); Kennedy v. Plan Adm'r for DuPont Sav. & Inv. Plan, 129 S. Ct. 865, 873 (2009).

55   *See* McGowan v. NJR Serv. Corp., 423 F.3d 241, 253 (3d Cir. 2005) (Becker, J., concurring), *cert. denied,* 549 U.S. 1174 (2007).

determine their validity (such as a federal common law rule on enforceable waivers) muddies the water. By complicating the task of determining the appropriate payee, distributions would be delayed and plan-administration expenses would escalate. Those costs could be avoided by ignoring the equities and emphasizing instead the fiduciary obligation to follow plan documents, namely, the unchanged pre-divorce beneficiary designation. Given this value-laden tradeoff, it's hardly surprising that a circuit split developed on the question whether a waiver of beneficiary status in the context of a divorce settlement can be given effect under ERISA.[56]

The Supreme Court opted for certainty in *Kennedy v. Plan Administrator for DuPont Savings and Investment Plan.*[57] William Kennedy, a pension plan participant, had properly designated his wife Liv as beneficiary. When they divorced, the decree provided that Liv relinquished all rights under any retirement, pension, or similar benefit plan associated with William's employment, but William failed to change his beneficiary designation after the divorce. The Court concluded that a waiver which does not attempt to direct pension plan benefits to another taker is not an assignment or alienation and so "escape[s] . . . inevitable nullity under the express terms of the anti-alienation clause."[58] Nevertheless, the Court unanimously held that the administrator properly paid plan benefits to the participant's ex-wife because, even though Liv had apparently agreed to the waiver incorporated in the divorce decree, the plan documents provided for payment to the designated beneficiary. The fiduciary duty to act in accordance with the documents and instruments governing the plan overrides a waiver that might otherwise be effective under federal common law, allowing the plan administrator "to look at the plan documents and records conforming to them to get clear distribution instructions, without going to court."[59]

> The point is that by giving a plan participant a clear set of instructions for making his own instructions clear, ERISA forecloses any justification for enquiries into nice expressions of intent, in favor of the virtues of adhering to an uncomplicated rule: "simple administration, avoid[ing] double liability, and ensur[ing] that beneficiaries get what's coming quickly, without the folderol essential under less-certain rules."[60]

Still, there are equities to consider, and so prompt payment of the designated beneficiary might not be the end of the matter. *Kennedy* left open the issue whether *after distribution* the participant's estate could bring an action in state or federal court to

---

56 *E.g.*, Manning v. Hayes, 212 F.3d 866 (5th Cir. 2000) (enforcing divorce waiver); Hill v. AT&T Corp., 125 F.3d 646, 648 (8th Cir. 1997) (same); Estate of Altobelli v. IBM, 77 F.3d 78 (4th Cir. 1996) (same); Metro. Life Ins. Co. v. Hanslip, 939 F.2d 904 (10th Cir. 1991) (same); Fox Valley & Vicinity Const. Workers Pension Fund v. Brown, 897 F.2d 275, 279–80 (7th Cir. 1990) (same). *Contra* McGowan v. NJR Serv. Corp., 423 F.3d 241 (3d Cir. 2005) (waiver ineffective), *cert. denied*, 549 U.S. 1174 (2007); Krishna v. Colgate Palmolive Co., 7 F.3d 11 (2d Cir. 1993) (same); McMillan v. Parrott, 913 F.2d 310 (6th Cir. 1990) (same).

57 129 S. Ct. 865 (2009); *see supra* Chapter 6D.

58 *Kennedy*, 129 S. Ct. at 870 (waiver not assignment), 874 (quotation).

59 *Id.* at 876.

60 *Id.* at 875–76 (quoting Fox Valley & Vicinity Const. Workers Pension Fund v. Brown, 897 F.2d 275, 283 (7th Cir. 1990) (Easterbrook, J., dissenting)).

recover benefits paid to the ex-spouse.[61] Because the plan and its fiduciaries would not be parties, such a suit might vindicate the waiver without embroiling the plan in litigation that would inflate plan-administration expenses to the long-run disadvantage of other participants.

C. SPOUSAL RIGHTS

Survivor Protection

To prevent the impoverishment of surviving spouses, ERISA requires that most plans provide (as a default) that distributions be made in the form of a qualified joint and survivor annuity (QJSA), under which distributions are made during the joint lives of the participant and his or her spouse, and continue for the life of the survivor. The surviving spouse's annuity must be equal to at least half of (and cannot exceed) the amount paid periodically while both are living, and the combined value of the joint and survivor annuity must be actuarially equivalent to the participant's accrued benefit.[62] ERISA also provides the participant's spouse with qualified pre-retirement survivor annuity (QPSA) protection.[63] The surviving spouse must be entitled to receive QPSA distributions for the period beginning on the participant's death, if the participant dies after having attained the earliest retirement age permitted under the plan, or for the period beginning with the month in which the participant would have reached the plan's earliest retirement age, if the participant dies earlier.[64] The amount of the surviving spouse's annuity is set by QJSA rules and depends on whether the participant died before or after attaining the earliest retirement age.[65]

The spousal survivor annuity protections have a very broad scope. They apply to all defined benefit plans and to defined contribution plans that are subject to ERISA's minimum funding standards (meaning money purchase pension plans, in general). Profit-sharing and stock bonus plans, which are the types of defined contribution plans that are not subject to the minimum funding standards, must also provide QJSA and

---

61   129 S. Ct. at 875 n.10.
62   ERISA §§ 205(a)(1), (d), 3(23), 29 U.S.C. §§ 1055(a)(1), (d), 1002(23) (2006); see I.R.C. §§ 401(a)(11)(A)(i), 417(b), 411(a)(7) (2006).
63   ERISA § 205(a)(2), (e), 29 U.S.C. § 1055(a)(2), (e) (2006); see I.R.C. §§ 401(a)(11)(A)(ii), 417(c) (2006); Treas. Reg. § 1.401(a)-20, Q&A-13 (as amended in 2006) (forfeiture on death not permissible with respect to QPSA or spousal survivor rights under profit-sharing or stock bonus plan).
64   ERISA § 205(e)(1)(A)(i), (e)(1)(B), 29 U.S.C. § 1055(e)(1)(A)(i), (e)(1)(B) (2006); see I.R.C. § 417(c)(1)(A)(i), (c)(1)(B) (2006).
65   ERISA § 205(e)(1)(A), 29 U.S.C. § 1055(e)(1)(A) (2006); see I.R.C. § 417(c)(1)(A) (2006). In the case of a defined contribution plan participant who dies before distributions commence, the surviving spouse need only be provided with a life annuity, the value of which is equal to at least half of the participant's vested account balance, with the result that it is still permissible for a defined contribution plan to require forfeiture on death of up to half of a married participant's account. ERISA § 205(e)(2), 29 U.S.C. § 1055(e)(2) (2006); see I.R.C. § 417(c)(2) (2006).

QPSA protection unless the plan provides that the participant's vested account balance is payable in full on the death of the participant to the surviving spouse. This spousal right of survivorship in the entire account balance obviously substitutes for life annuity protection. Even if the normal form of distribution under a profit-sharing or stock bonus plan is a lump-sum payout to the surviving spouse, any participant who elects distribution in the form of a life annuity must get a QPSA or QJSA unless the survivor protections are waived, with spousal consent, under the rules described below.[66] Moreover, the survivor annuity distribution requirements apply to all vested benefits, whether they are derived from employer or employee contributions.[67] Consequently, even in-service withdrawals of prior voluntary employee contributions to a money purchase pension plan must be paid as a QJSA unless the survivor protections are properly waived with spousal consent.[68]

Plans are permitted to impose a one-year marriage requirement as a precondition to spousal protections (including both the survivor annuities and the substitute right of survivorship, whichever applies), and a marriage after the annuity starting date does not entitle the spouse to QJSA protection.[69] On the other hand, divorce after the QJSA starting date does not cut off the former spouse's right to receive the survivor annuity, unless a QDRO provides otherwise.[70] Nor may a plan terminate annuity payments (whether QJSA or QPSA) to a surviving spouse because the spouse remarries after the participant's death.[71]

Recognizing that workers should not be forced to pay the price of unnecessary spousal protection, Congress requires that participants be permitted to waive the QJSA and QPSA forms of distribution.[72] In addition, for plan years beginning after 2007, a participant who waives the plan's QJSA or QPSA protections must be allowed to elect a qualified optional survivor annuity (QOSA) to provide a choice in the level of the survivor annuity. A QOSA is defined as a joint and survivor annuity that is actuarially equivalent to a single life annuity for the life of the participant, but if the plan's QJSA survivor annuity is 75 percent or more of the annuity during the participant's life (remember that it must be at least 50 percent and not more than 100 percent), then the survivor annuity payment under the QOSA is set lower, at 50 percent of annual payment during the participant's life. Alternatively, if the survivor payment level under the plan's QJSA is less than 75 percent, then the survivor annuity payment under the

---

66 ERISA § 205(b)(1), 29 U.S.C. § 1055(b)(1) (2006); *see* I.R.C. § 401(a)(11)(B) (2006).

67 Treas. Reg. § 1.401(a)-20, Q&A-11, Q&A-12 (as amended in 2006).

68 Treas. Reg. § 1.401(a)-20, Q&A-9, Example (as amended in 2006). A participant could, however, without spousal consent, rifle a profit-sharing or stock bonus account via in-service distributions, leaving very little in the account that is subject to the spouse's right of survivorship. *See* ERISA § 205(b)(1)(C), 29 U.S.C. § 1055(b)(1)(C) (2006); *see also* I.R.C. § 401(a)(11)(B)(iii) (2006).

69 ERISA § 205(b)(3), (f), 29 U.S.C. § 1055(b)(3), (f) (2006); *see* I.R.C. §§ 401(a)(11)(D), 417(d) (2006).

70 Treas. Reg. § 1.401(a)-20, Q&A-25(b)(3) (as amended in 2006); S. REP. No. 98-575, at 15–16 (1984).

71 Treas. Reg. § 1.401(a)-20, Q&A-25(b)(1) (as amended in 2006); *id.* § 1.401(a)-11(b)(2), -11(g)(2)(ii) (as amended in 2003).

72 ERISA § 205(c), 29 U.S.C. § 1055(c) (2006); *see* I.R.C. § 417(a) (2006).

QOSA is set higher, at 75 percent of annual payment during the participant's life.[73] ERISA requires that participants be given a written explanation of the effect of a waiver, and of the substitution of a QOSA, and conditions the validity of the waiver on spousal consent.[74] The explanation facilitates retirement planning, as does the choice of an alternative survivor annuity level (i.e., the QOSA), while the consent requirement protects the nonparticipant spouse—from the participant.

To promote careful consideration, the required explanation of the consequences of waiving QJSA distribution must be provided within a reasonable time before the annuity starting date, and any election to waive the survivor annuity must generally be made within the 180-day period preceding the annuity starting date.[75] That is, the explanation and waiver must come once distributions (including lump-sum and in-service distributions[76]) are about to commence—when the mind is focused on retirement support needs, rather than years earlier when retirement may be only a dim and unreal prospect. Moreover, the election must remain revocable throughout that 180-day period.[77]

Aligning information with receptivity is more difficult in the case of the QPSA, for there is no single identifiable time at which workers and their spouses are likely to focus on the financial consequences of an unexpected death. In this case, Congress requires that an explanation of the QPSA, and the method and consequences of waiving it, must generally be supplied within the period between the start of the plan year in which the participant attains age 32 and the close of the plan year before the participant turns 35, or, if later, within a reasonable period after the worker becomes a participant.[78] The period for waiving the QPSA, or revoking a prior waiver,

---

73 ERISA § 205(c)(1)(A), (d)(2), 29 U.S.C. § 1055(c)(1)(A), (d)(2) (2006); *see* I.R.C. § 417(a)(1) (A), (g) (2006).

74 ERISA § 205(c), 29 U.S.C. § 1055(c) (2006); *see* I.R.C. § 417(a) (2006). A waiver contained in a prenuptial agreement is ineffective because the consent is not given by a "spouse." Treas. Reg. § 1.401(a)-20, Q&A-28 (as amended in 2006); *e.g.*, Hagwood v. Newton, 282 F.3d 285 (4th Cir. 2002). Where the participant bears no cost from survivor protection, there is nothing to be gained by waiver, and so the sponsor is allowed to dispense with the explanation and waiver requirements, provided that the plan does not allow participants to either waive the spousal survivor annuities or substitute a nonspouse beneficiary. ERISA § 205(c)(5), 29 U.S.C. § 1055(c)(5) (2006); *see* I.R.C. § 417(a)(5) (2006); Treas. Reg. § 1.401(a)-20, Q&A-37, -38 (as amended in 2006).

75 ERISA § 205(c)(1)(A)(i), (c)(3)(A), (c)(7)(A), 29 U.S.C. § 1055(c)(1)(A)(i), (c)(3)(A), (c)(7) (A) (2006); *see* I.R.C. § 417(a)(1)(A)(i), (a)(3)(A), (a)(6)(A) (2006). An exception allows the explanation to be provided after the annuity starting date, but in this event, the period for waiving the QJSA is extended until thirty days after the explanation is provided. ERISA § 205(c)(8)(A), 29 U.S.C. § 1055(c)(8)(A) (2006); *see* I.R.C. § 417(a)(7)(A) (2006).

76 ERISA § 205(h)(2), 29 U.S.C. § 1055(h)(2) (2006); *see* I.R.C. § 417(f)(2) (2006); Treas. Reg. § 1.401(a)-20, Q&A-9 (as amended in 2006).

77 ERISA § 205(c)(1)(A)(iii), (c)(7)(A), 29 U.S.C. § 1055(c)(1)(A)(iii), (c)(7)(A) (2006); *see* I.R.C. § 417(a)(1)(A)(i), (a)(6)(A) (2006).

78 ERISA § 205(c)(3)(B), 29 U.S.C. § 1055(c)(3)(B) (2006); *see* I.R.C. § 417(a)(3)(B) (2006). The regulations specify that in the case of an employee who becomes a participant at age 35 or older, a "reasonable period" for providing the explanation means a period of one year before and after becoming a participant. Treas. Reg. § 1.401(a)-20, Q&A-35(c) (as amended in 2006).

must ordinarily commence the first day of the plan year in which the participant attains age 35 and continue to the date of the participant's death.[79]

A participant's waiver of QJSA or QPSA protection is ineffective unless accompanied by the spouse's consent. That consent must be in writing, acknowledge the effect of the waiver, and be witnessed by a plan administrator or notary. In addition, the spouse's consent must specify the specific nonspouse beneficiary and, in the case of a QJSA waiver, specify the particular optional form of benefit payment (such as an annuity for the life of the participant only). Unless the consent expressly permits future changes without further consent of the spouse, the participant cannot later designate another beneficiary or form of distribution.[80] Any such spousal consent binds only the spouse who gives it, not any later husband or wife of the participant,[81] but a plan may provide that consent, once given, is irrevocable.[82] As the consent is necessary to validate the participant's waiver, it must apparently be obtained within the permitted waiver period and at a time when the parties are married.[83] Comparable spousal consent is required to use the participant's accrued benefit as security for plan loans because repayment of a loan by setoff would deplete spousal survival benefits.[84] These consent requirements empower the spouse with a veto over the participant's decision

---

If a participant separates from service before age 35, the QPSA waiver explanation must be provided within the period of one year before and after separation from service. ERISA § 205(c)(3)(B)(ii), 29 U.S.C. § 1055(c)(3)(B)(ii) (2006) (final sentence); *see* I.R.C. § 417(a)(3)(B)(ii) (2006) (final sentence); Treas. Reg. § 1.401(a)-20, Q&A-35(b) (as amended in 2006).

79   ERISA § 205(c)(7)(B), 29 U.S.C. § 1055(c)(7)(B) (2006); *see* I.R.C. § 417(a)(6)(B) (2006). If a participant separates from service before the QPSA waiver period would ordinarily begin (i.e., the first day of the plan year in which the participant attains age 35), the period must start earlier, on separation from service. ERISA § 205(c)(7), 29 U.S.C. § 1055(c)(7) (2006) (final sentence); *see* I.R.C. § 417(a)(6) (2006) (final sentence). These statutory rules suggest that the QPSA is not waivable before the year in which the participant turns 35, with the result that the survivor annuity is automatically provided to spouses of workers who die before their mid-thirties. However, the regulations authorize pre-age-35 waivers, provided that the participant is given a written explanation, the spouse consents, and the early waiver becomes ineffective upon the beginning of the plan year in which the participant's 35th birthday occurs. If there is no new waiver after the statutory election period commences, the spouse must receive a QPSA upon the participant's death. Treas. Reg. § 1.401(a)-20, Q&A-33(b) (as amended in 2006). *But see* S. REP. NO. 98-575, at 15 (1984) ("Of course, the preretirement survivor benefit coverage may become automatic prior to the time that the participant is entitled to decline such coverage.").

80   ERISA § 205(c)(2)(A), 29 U.S.C. § 1055(c)(2)(A) (2006); *see* I.R.C. § 417(a)(2)(A) (2006); Treas. Reg. § 1.401(a)-20, Q&A-31 (as amended in 2006).

81   ERISA § 205(c)(2), 29 U.S.C. § 1055(c)(2) (2006) (final sentence); *see* I.R.C. § 417(a)(2) (2006) (final sentence).

82   Treas. Reg. § 1.401(a)-20, Q&A-30 (as amended in 2006).

83   Treas. Reg. § 1.401(a)-20, Q&A-28 (as amended in 2006) (consent contained in premarital agreement ineffective even if within the applicable election period for waiver); Hurwitz v. Sher, 982 F.2d 778 (2d Cir. 1992).

84   ERISA § 205(c)(4), 29 U.S.C. § 1055(c)(4) (2006); *see* I.R.C. § 417(a)(4) (2006); Treas. Reg. § 1.401(a)-20, Q&A-24 (as amended in 2006).

to waive ERISA's survivor protections so that retirement planning takes into account the support needs of *both* parties.[85]

ERISA's distribution requirements ensure that the participant's decision making takes into account the retirement income needs of his or her spouse. In effect, a spouse automatically becomes the participant's primary beneficiary with a prescribed minimum interest in the pension. (Apart from the spouse, ERISA does not insist that anyone be granted an interest in the participant's pension, nor does it require that a beneficiary be given an interest of any particular value.) This statutory spousal beneficiary designation can be changed only with the spouse's consent, which empowers the spouse to look out for himself or herself.

Community Property

If instead of surviving, the worker's spouse is the first to die, what becomes of the spouse's priority? Can a nonparticipant spouse obtain property rights in a pension that are transferable on death by bequest or inheritance? In *Boggs v. Boggs*,[86] the Supreme Court determined that ERISA's spousal protection scheme is exclusive, and that greater rights afforded by state community property laws present an obstacle to the accomplishment of ERISA's objectives and so must give way under conflict preemption analysis.

In *Boggs*, the participant and his first wife were longtime residents of Louisiana, a community property state. The wife died in 1979, before her husband retired, and left a will transferring ownership of most of her property to the couple's three sons. The participant husband soon remarried, and when he retired in 1985, he began receiving monthly annuity distributions under his employer's defined benefit pension plan, as well as a large lump-sum distribution from a defined contribution plan. Upon the participant's death in 1989, his second wife began receiving QJSA spousal survivor annuity payments. After their father's death, however, the sons asserted claims based on their mother's will to a portion of the annuity payments (including undistributed amounts and payments already made, both before and after the participant's death) and

---

85   As originally enacted, ERISA made the QJSA the default form of distribution for married participants, but permitted the participant acting alone to select another mode of payment. The danger this unilateral decision making posed for dependent spouses (impoverishment caused by the participant's neglect, selfishness, or malice) was noted by some congresswomen during the 1974 legislative debates, but it was another ten years before the fix was made. *See* 120 CONG. REC. (Feb. 26, 1974), 4445 (Feb. 27, 1974) (remarks of Rep. Schroeder) ("While the legislation under consideration does mandate survivorship benefits to be automatic unless they are explicitly waived, I would support a plan whereby both the worker and spouse are required to waive their rights to these benefits. Since it is the spouse who is directly affected, he or she should participate directly in the process of waiver."), *reprinted in* 2 ERISA LEGISLATIVE HISTORY, *supra* Chapter 1 note 56, at 3475, 3497; 120 CONG. REC. 4773 (Feb. 28, 1974) (remarks of Rep. Chisholm), *reprinted in* 3 ERISA LEGISLATIVE HISTORY, *supra* Chapter 1 note 56, at 3572.

86   520 U.S. 833 (1997). *See supra* Chapter 6 notes 45–50 and accompanying text.

to part of the lump-sum distribution (which had been rolled over into an individual retirement account from which no withdrawals had been made).[87]

The Court explained that the sons' claim to a share of the survivor annuity conflicted with the spousal protections accorded by ERISA § 205:

> ERISA's solicitude for the economic security of surviving spouses would be undermined by allowing a predeceasing spouse's heirs and legatees to have a community property interest in the survivor's annuity. Even a plan participant cannot defeat a nonparticipant surviving spouse's statutory entitlement to an annuity. It would be odd, to say the least, if Congress permitted a predeceasing nonparticipant spouse to do so. Nothing in the language of ERISA supports concluding that Congress made such an inexplicable decision. Testamentary transfers could reduce a surviving spouse's guaranteed annuity below the minimum set by ERISA (defined as 50% of the annuity payable during the joint lives of the participant and spouse).[88]

Accordingly, ERISA preempts state law rights to a share of the spousal survivor annuity.

More important, the Court also held that ERISA precludes a testamentary transfer by a nonparticipant spouse of a community property interest in undistributed pension plan benefits, even if there is no subsequent spouse entitled to survivor protection. Recognizing such a transfer would reduce pension distributions to the participant or beneficiaries. Such a bequest would violate ERISA in two ways. First, ERISA is designed to protect the interests of plan participants and beneficiaries, but the legatee of a predeceased nonparticipant spouse is neither a participant nor a beneficiary, because "beneficiary" is defined as a person designated either by the participant or by the terms of the plan.[89] Second, the testamentary transfer of the predeceased spouse's community property interest is prohibited by the anti-alienation rule.[90] The Court observed that it would be "inimical to ERISA's purposes to permit testamentary recipients to acquire a competing interest in undistributed pension benefits."[91] The Court majority concluded that Congress meant to favor the retirement support needs of the living participant over the property rights of the deceased spouse.[92] In sum, spousal

---

87   *Boggs*, 520 U.S. at 836–37.

88   *Id.* at 843–44. The Court also noted that under state wills law, the recipient of a bequest that would deprive the surviving spouse of the support required by ERISA might not even be a family member.

89   *Id.* at 848–51. *See* ERISA § 3(8), 29 U.S.C. § 1002(8) (2006).

90   *Boggs*, 520 U.S. at 851–52. *See* ERISA § 206(d)(1), 29 U.S.C. § 1056(d)(1) (2006).

91   *Boggs*, 520 U.S. at 852.

92   *Id.* at 854 ("Congress has decided to favor the living over the dead and we must respect its policy."). In a questionable extension of this reasoning, the Ninth Circuit ruled that where a former spouse, who is entitled under a divorce decree to a portion of the participant's pension as community property, dies before pension payments commence, her interest is extinguished. Instead of finding that the ex-spouse's judicially confirmed community property interest passes to her heirs, the court concluded that *Boggs* and *Egelhoff* require that the participant be reinstated in the entire pension. Branco v. UFCW-N. Cal. Employers Joint Pension Plan, 279 F.3d 1154 (9th Cir. 2002).

pension rights under ERISA are not about mandating gender equity, but about promoting retirement support.

D. CONCLUSION

When it comes to pension plan distributions, ERISA's anti-abuse and worker-protective impulses have less force than on matters involving fiduciary conduct and pension accumulation (Chapters 4 and 7). In this area, Congress legislated against the background of long-standing tax law rules, adding as a new motif the imposition of restraints on the participant.

Generally, pension distributions must commence promptly once the participant reaches the plan's normal retirement age (or age 65, if earlier), unless the participant is still working for the plan sponsor, in which case the start date can be delayed until separation from service. Additional delay is possible if the participant consents, which necessitated tax law intervention to discourage excessive deferral (publicly subsidized intergenerational wealth transfers). Similarly, the task of restricting early distributions has been left to the tax law, which provides carrots and sticks (tax-deferred rollover treatment and early distribution penalties) in an effort to prevent pension savings from being dissipated before retirement. The historic flexibility of the qualified retirement plan distribution rules is the source of many of the continuing challenges of pension policy, such as whether rollovers should be mandatory for distributions made before age 55, and whether distributions should be required to made as life annuities rather than lump-sum payouts. These questions are explored in Chapter 10.

In contrast to its acquiescence in the tax law's distribution timing rules, ERISA now has much to say about permissible pension plan distributees. The basic commands are two: retirement savings are nontransferable, and the participant's spouse is granted (in effect) a co-ownership interest.

Pensions receive automatic spendthrift protection by federal law. ERISA's anti-alienation rule prevents the participant from gaining access to his retirement savings by sale or encumbrance. This barrier is necessary to give effect to plan terms governing the timing and form or distributions, for without it, a participant could accomplish indirectly what the plan attempts to forbid. If pension rights were transferable, a defined benefit plan requiring distribution in the form of a life annuity commencing at age 65 could, for example, be converted by sale into a lump sum of cash at age 47. Anti-alienation in this context is generally understood as paternalism (forced saving), but it may also serve the employer's interest in assuring that financial arrangements made to induce older workers to exit the workforce are not undermined. The pension anti-alienation rule is remarkably robust; it routinely withstands bankruptcy and most crime victims' restitution claims. The statute yields, however, to family law creditors who may obtain access to a participant's pension under a qualified domestic relations order, even if their claim relates to current support needs (as opposed to retirement income) or adjusts property rights. To shield other participants from adverse effects, a qualified domestic relations order must not increase the plan's benefit liability, and ERISA establishes a process to minimize administrative costs.

Beyond restraining the participant (and his creditors) from obtaining access to retirement savings during working years, ERISA also restricts the participant's ability to unilaterally determine succession to his pension. Originally, plans were allowed to forfeit all employer-financed benefits upon death of the participant, regardless of length of service. The Retirement Equity Act of 1984 generally limited forfeiture on death to instances where the participant leaves no surviving spouse, granted the spouse an interest in the participant's pension, and protected that interest by giving the spouse a say over changes in the participant's successor. Defined benefit and money purchase pension plans must provide minimum survivor annuity protection to the participant's spouse as the default form of distribution, while profit-sharing and stock bonus plans must either provide such spousal survivor annuities or give the spouse the right to take the participant's entire vested account balance on death. The participant acting alone cannot designate a nonspouse beneficiary or otherwise dispense with these spousal protections. Such changes are effective only if the spouse gives written consent after full disclosure. Recognizing that married individuals without pension savings of their own frequently count on their husband's or wife's plan for retirement support, ERISA protects the nonparticipant spouse from short-sighted or malevolent decisions by the participant.

Succession questions frequently arise for unmarried participants, particularly because defined contribution plans typically do not call for forfeiture on death. Apart from a qualified domestic relations order, ERISA supersedes any state law that would identify takers or work a substitution of pension plan beneficiaries, including state inheritance, wills, and community property regimes. Preemption even applies to laws that would correct a divorced participant's inadvertent failure to change a beneficiary designation in favor of the former spouse. Despite sometimes inequitable results, preemption in such circumstances at least yields an easily administered rule (i.e., pay the person whose name is on file) which avoids the complication and expense that state law variation could inject. Yet sometimes there is no need to economize on justice in determining a successor. Federal courts could effectuate prevalent preferences uniformly and at minimal cost by coupling preemption of state law with announcement of interstitial federal common-law rules governing succession to welfare and pension plan benefits. But, as the Supreme Court warned in 2009, federal common law will not be allowed to displace *plan* rules that serve the goal of uniform, low-cost administration.

Chapter 9

Security

"The Congress finds . . . that owing to the inadequacy of current minimum standards, the soundness and stability of plans with respect to adequate funds to pay promised benefits may be endangered; that owing to the termination of plans before requisite funds have been accumulated, employees and their beneficiaries have been deprived of anticipated benefits; and that it is therefore desirable in the interests of employees and their beneficiaries, for the protection of the revenue of the United States, and to provide for the free flow of commerce, that minimum standards be provided assuring the equitable character of such plans and their financial soundness.

* * *

It is hereby further declared to be the policy of this Act to protect interstate commerce, the Federal taxing power, and the interests of participants in private pension plans and their beneficiaries by improving the equitable character and the soundness of such plans by requiring them to vest the accrued benefits of employees with significant periods of service, to meet minimum standards of funding, and by requiring plan termination insurance."[1]

---

[1]   ERISA § 2(a), (c), 29 U.S.C. § 1001(a), (c) (2006).

To increase the security of the pension promise, ERISA requires systematic advance funding of future benefits.[2] Instead of mandating a particular funding schedule, however, Congress imposed only a minimum funding obligation, leaving employers the flexibility to contribute larger amounts, subject to certain upper limits set by tax law deductibility rules.[3] Moreover, until 2008, ERISA tolerated considerable flexibility in the determination of the annual minimum funding obligation.

Congress chose not to insist upon immediate full funding of all accrued benefits under defined benefit plans, and so employees are exposed to the risk that the plan may be terminated before sufficient assets have been accumulated to pay all promised benefits. The termination insurance system of ERISA Title IV, administered by the Pension Benefit Guaranty Corporation (PBGC), was instituted to limit, but not eliminate, this risk. Because participants in defined benefit plans bear a residual risk of loss to the extent that unfunded uninsured benefits prove uncollectible (i.e., in cases of employer insolvency), information concerning the funded status of the plan is pertinent to their situation, as it is also to the PBGC and firm creditors. To facilitate planning and self-protection, ERISA requires that certain disclosures be made to these interested parties.

During the 1980s and 1990s, many plans became substantially overfunded. This embarrassment of riches raised the question whether (or to what extent) the employer, who is obligated to correct underfunding, should be granted a reciprocal right of access to excess assets. Under ERISA, plan assets must generally be held in trust and cannot revert to the employer prior to plan termination, although the reclamation of erroneous contributions is permitted in limited circumstances. An unintended consequence of those benefit security rules was to create pressure to terminate overfunded plans to obtain the surplus. That incentive, together with the complexity and cost of compliance with the funding rules, may have contributed to the recent pronounced trend away from defined benefit plan sponsorship. This phenomenon illustrates once again that there is a delicate balance between quality-control regulation and voluntary plan sponsorship.

A. MINIMUM FUNDING STANDARDS[4]

As a practical matter, a full funding requirement would have largely halted the practice of granting past-service credit. Past-service credit refers to benefits created retroactively for service before the plan was instituted, or subsequent retroactive benefit enhancements. Immediate funding of the large liability created by such retroactive

---

2   This chapter is limited to explaining the law governing single-employer defined benefit plans. The funding, insurance, and withdrawal liability rules governing multiemployer plans are beyond the scope of this book.

3   *See* I.R.C. §§ 404(a)(1), (a)(7), (o), 412, 430 (2006). Contributions in excess of the maximum deductible amount may be carried forward for deduction in subsequent years. *Id.* § 404(a)(1)(E). But concerns about excessive prefunding led Congress in 1987 to strongly discourage excess contributions by imposing an excise tax of 10 percent of the amount of nondeductible contributions to a qualified plan. *Id.* § 4972.

4   Portions of the discussion in this section are adapted from PETER J. WIEDENBECK & RUSSELL K. OSGOOD, CASES AND MATERIALS ON EMPLOYEE BENEFITS 389–96, 443–46 (1996), and is reprinted with permission of West, a Thomson Reuters business.

benefit grants would often impose a crushing cash flow burden. And because defined benefit plans are commonly instituted once a business has achieved the stability and profitability necessary to provide for its founders' retirement, discouraging past-service credits might curtail the growth of private plan coverage. Apparently, Congress thought it wiser public policy to allocate and control the risk of loss associated with unfunded past-service liabilities than to prohibit such benefit commitments.

Congress acted to limit the risk of plan default by strengthening minimum funding standards. Naturally, the key element of the new regime was the requirement that unfunded past-service liabilities be systematically retired. ERISA originally required that outstanding past-service liabilities be amortized over a forty-year period, while past-service liabilities created or increased after the law took effect were to be funded over at most thirty years. Since enactment, ERISA has been repeatedly amended to tighten the minimum funding rules. Underfunding caused by grants of past-service credit in plan years beginning after 2007 must generally be eliminated by level annual installment payments over seven years.[5]

The minimum funding standards only *limit* the risk of plan default. Long-term amortization of past-service benefits concedes an extended period during which plan assets will, in the event of termination, be insufficient to pay promised benefits. Congress enacted the termination insurance system of ERISA Title IV and associated employer liability rules to *allocate* the remaining risk of underfunding (*see infra* Chapter 9B).

Funding Overview

ERISA's minimum funding standards apply to most pension plans other than profit-sharing and stock bonus plans. Governmental and church plans are exempt, as are plans that do not call for employer contributions and certain plans funded exclusively with the purchase of individual or group insurance or annuity contracts.[6] It is important to note that there is an exception for wholly unfunded plans promising deferred compensation to "a select group of management or highly-compensated employees" (commonly called "top-hat" plans).[7]

---

5   ERISA §§ 302(a), 303(a)(1)(B), (c), (d), 29 U.S.C. §§ 1082(a), 1083(a)(1)(B), (c), (d) (2006); *see* I.R.C. §§ 412(a), 430(a)(1)(B), (c), (d) (2006).

6   ERISA § 301(a), 29 U.S.C. § 1081(a) (2006). ERISA's funding rules apply only to pension plans, *see* ERISA § 301(a)(1), 29 U.S.C. § 1081(a)(1) (2006) (welfare plans exempt), and are primarily concerned with the actuarial problems involved in the advance funding of defined benefit pensions. One type of defined contribution plan, the money purchase pension plan, is covered to ensure that promised contributions are made when due. ERISA § 302(a)(2)(B), 29 U.S.C. § 1082(a)(2)(B) (2006); *see* I.R.C. § 412(a)(2)(B) (2006). Profit-sharing and stock bonus plans are not subject to the funding rules, ERISA § 301(a)(8), 29 U.S.C. § 1081(a)(8) (2006), apparently because contributions under such plans may be discretionary, in which case there is no contribution obligation to enforce.

7   ERISA § 301(a)(3), 29 U.S.C. § 1081(a)(3) (2006). *See supra* Chapter 2D. Excess benefit plans (whether funded or not) are also exempt from the minimum funding rules, but by definition, such plans cover only highly compensated employees. ERISA §§ 3(36), 4(b)(5), 301(a)(9), 29 U.S.C. §§ 1002(36), 1003(b)(5), 1081(a)(9) (2006).

For plan years beginning before 2008, the employer's funding obligation is determined with reference to the plan's actuarial funding method. Actuarial funding methods are akin to depreciation methods, which estimate a cost of producing income (the decline in value of structures or of equipment that wears out) and allocate the cost over the multiple taxable years that compose the expected life of the property. Advance funding of a defined benefit pension presents a similar problem. One must *estimate* both the *total cost* and *total period* over which benefits will be earned. The annual funding obligation follows from a rule for allocating that total cost among taxable years within that total period. The plan's actuarial funding method supplies the allocation rule. For example, assume that a plan provides each participant a benefit of $X per year at age 65. The cost of an immediate single life annuity of $X is readily determinable; call this cost $Y. For funding purposes, the question is, what savings pattern should the plan follow to generate the $Y through yearly contributions during the participant's period of service? The savings pattern is the plan's actuarial cost method. As with any timing rule, consistency is critical, so a change in the plan's actuarial method requires consent, just as change in a taxpayer's method of accounting (or method of depreciation) does.[8]

Most defined benefit plans do not promise a fixed-dollar benefit. Instead, they determine retirement benefits by a formula that takes into account each participant's compensation, years of service, and retirement age. Accordingly, each participant's pension can only be estimated, and to do this, the sponsor must make some assumptions as to duration of service, future compensation increases, retirement age (especially if the plan provides subsidized early retirement benefits), and, if the plan calls for forfeiture on death, mortality rates. If the plan provides ancillary benefits, such as disability income or life insurance, probability estimates for these eventualities are needed as well. The probability estimates for such contingencies are called actuarial assumptions. Actuarial assumptions must be reasonable and periodically revised in light of actual experience[9] (just as the useful life and salvage value estimates used to compute traditional depreciation allowances were required to be reasonable).

There is one major conceptual difference between actuarial funding and depreciation: depreciation allocates a past expenditure, while actuarial funding accumulates for a future expenditure. Returning to the earlier example, the cost of an $X single life annuity may be $Y *at age 65*, but the employer does not need to contribute $Y. Instead, it must save enough so that the combination of contributions and fund earnings will total $Y. That is, to determine required contributions, the $Y future cost must be discounted by the anticipated rate of fund earnings. This "interest rate" actuarial assumption has a major impact on funding obligations.

---

8   *Compare* ERISA § 302(c)(5)(A), 29 U.S.C. § 1082(c)(5)(A) (2000) (repealed 2006), *and* I.R.C. § 412(c)(5)(A) (2000) (repealed 2006), *with* I.R.C. § 446(e) (2006).

9   ERISA § 303(h)(1), 29 U.S.C. § 1083(h)(1) (2006) (effective for plan years beginning after 2007; prior years correspond to ERISA § 302(c)(3), 29 U.S.C. § 1082(c)(3) (2000) (repealed 2006)); *see* I.R.C. § 430(h)(1) (2006) (effective for plan years beginning after 2007; prior years correspond to I.R.C. § 412(c)(3) (2000) (repealed 2006)).

Prior to 2008, ERISA allowed plan sponsors to compute their minimum funding obligation according to the actuarial funding method selected by the plan, and the statute expressly authorized six acceptable actuarial methods.[10] The acceptable methods can yield very different cost calculations. Under some methods, the plan's annual benefit cost depends on the plan's liability for benefits actually earned during the year, while other methods compute projected total benefits and allocate that career aggregate cost in level amounts or as a level percentage of pay over the participant's period of service. Past-service benefits are also financed differently under the various actuarial methods, with some breaking out the cost of retroactive benefits as a distinct supplemental liability that is amortized over a fixed period of up to thirty years, while other methods fund the liability over the projected future period of service of the participants who are granted past-service benefits.[11] In addition, under any given actuarial method, the sponsor's funding obligation could vary dramatically according to the actuary's assumptions concerning the fund's investment performance (the interest rate assumption), the likelihood of forfeiture as a result of death (mortality assumption), the probability of lump-sum distributions or early retirement benefits, and other factors. While ERISA required that actuarial methods be consistently applied, with actuarial assumptions reasonable and subject to revision in light of actual experience,[12] ERISA's original approach to advance funding gave actuaries (and so, indirectly, plan sponsors) very wide latitude.

The Pension Protection Act of 2006 adopts a much stricter approach to defined benefit plan funding. In support of the new legislation, the Treasury explained:

> One reason for this problem [widespread underfunding and a rash of plan terminations causing large claims against the PBGC] is the byzantine and often ineffectual set of funding rules under current law. They are needlessly complex and often fail to ensure that many pension plans become and remain adequately funded. Current rules give employers too much discretion in setting their funding targets and provide insufficient opportunity for plans to become well funded. Current rules also do not provide enough incentive to be well funded because there are few significant consequences that arise from a plan being poorly funded, especially for a plan sponsor in poor financial health.[13]

---

10   ERISA § 3(31), 29 U.S.C. § 1002(31) (2006); ERISA § 302(a), (b), (c)(1), 29 U.S.C. § 1082(a), (b), (c)(1) (2000) (repealed 2006); *see* I.R.C. § 412(a), (b), (c)(1) (2000) (repealed 2006). ERISA § 3(31) declares that "[t]he terminal funding cost method and the current funding (pay-as-you-go) cost method are not acceptable actuarial cost methods." Pay-as-you-go involves no advance funding, while terminal funding merely sets aside the cost of promised benefits when the worker retires. These techniques expose workers to a prolonged risk of employer default and are therefore incompatible with the goal of increasing the security of the pension promise.

11   *See generally*, PETER J. WIEDENBECK & RUSSELL K. OSGOOD, CASES AND MATERIALS ON EMPLOYEE BENEFITS 389–437 (1996); DAN M. MCGILL & DONALD S. GRUBBS JR., FUNDAMENTALS OF PRIVATE PENSIONS 239–327 (6th ed. 1989).

12   ERISA § 302(c)(3), (c)(5), 29 U.S.C. § 1082(c)(3), (c)(5) (2000) (repealed 2006); *see* I.R.C. § 412(c)(3), (c)(5) (2000) (repealed 2006).

13   U.S. DEPARTMENT OF THE TREASURY, GENERAL EXPLANATIONS OF THE ADMINISTRATION'S FISCAL YEAR 2007 REVENUE PROPOSALS 76 (Feb. 2006) [hereinafter TREASURY GENERAL EXPLANATIONS].

Responding to these concerns, the new law makes sweeping changes in pension funding. As explained below, freedom of choice in actuarial methods is gone; underfunding triggered by grants of past-service benefits must be rapidly retired; interest rate and mortality assumptions are henceforth prescribed. In return for stricter minimum funding obligations, the 2006 legislation encourages plan sponsors to exceed the minimum by relaxing the tax Code's limits on the deductibility of advance funding contributions.[14]

Starting in 2008, defined benefit pension plans must compute their minimum funding obligation with reference to two components: the funding target and the target normal cost.[15] The funding target is "the present value of all benefits accrued or earned under the plan as of the beginning of the plan year," and the target normal cost is "the present value of all benefits which are expected to accrue or to be earned under the plan during the plan year."[16] Consequently, the new funding rules are geared to the plan's legal liability for benefits actually earned through the current year, rather than being tied to a share of the plan's projected future benefit obligation. Moreover, where the plan's benefit formula is based on compensation (e.g., a unit credit formula using a highest average or final average compensation multiplier), "if any benefit attributable to services performed in a preceding year is increased by reason of any increase in compensation during the current plan year, the increase in such benefit shall be treated as having accrued during the current plan year," thereby increasing the target normal cost and the minimum required contribution.[17]

Where, as of the start of the plan year, the value of plan assets is less than the funding target (the present value of all previously accrued benefits), the resulting funding shortfall must be amortized in level annual installments over the next seven years.[18] This rule applies regardless of whether the shortfall is traceable to a drop in the value of plan assets or an increase in plan liabilities. Accordingly, retroactive benefit enhancements (past-service benefits) must be funded over seven years, not the thirty-year amortization period ERISA originally authorized.[19]

---

14   I.R.C. § 404(a)(1)(A), (o) (2006). The "cushion amount" allows sponsors to deduct contributions that render a plan substantially overfunded relative to existing benefit liabilities (determined on a plan termination basis). In order to control the cost of the qualified plan tax subsidy, prior law strongly discouraged such overfunding by means of a full funding limit on deductions and the excise (penalty) tax on nondeductible contributions. *Id.* §§ 404(a)(1)(A) (final sentence), 412(c)(7), 4972 (2000) (amended 2006). TREASURY GENERAL EXPLANATIONS, *supra* Chapter 9 note 13, at 78–79.

15   ERISA §§ 302(a), 303(a), 29 U.S.C. §§ 1082(a), 1083(a) (2006); *see* I.R.C. §§ 412(a), 430(a) (2006).

16   ERISA § 303(d)(1), (b), 29 U.S.C. § 1083(d)(1), (b) (2006); *see* I.R.C. § 430(d)(1), (b) (2006).

17   ERISA § 303(b), 29 U.S.C. § 1083(b) (2006); *see* I.R.C. § 430(b) (2006).

18   ERISA § 303(a)(1)(B), (c), 29 U.S.C. § 1083(a)(1)(B), (c) (2006); *see* I.R.C. § 430(a)(1)(B), (c) (2006).

19   Prior to 2008, the minimum funding standard only required that new grants of past-service benefits be funded over either thirty years or the future career of affected participants. ERISA § 302(b)(2)(B)(iii), 29 U.S.C. § 1082(b)(2)(B)(iii) (2000) (repealed 2006); *see* I.R.C. § 412(b)(2)(B)(iii) (2000) (repealed 2006). Accordingly, retroactive liberalization of the plan's benefit

Actuarial Assumptions

Experience showed that plan sponsors in financial difficulty often minimized their minimum funding obligation by adopting overly optimistic assumptions regarding investment performance (i.e., interest rate assumptions based on returns to equity, causing a high discount rate to be used in determining the present value of liabilities), while downplaying the magnitude of expected benefits. The Pension Protection Act of 2006 requires that the interest rate used in determining the funding target be based on the yield of investment-grade corporate bonds having periods of maturity that correspond to the timing of expected benefit payments under the plan. The mortality tables used by the plan are similarly prescribed.[20] In line with prior law, other actuarial assumptions must each be reasonable, "taking into account the experience of the plan and reasonable expectations," and such assumptions must, "in combination, offer the actuary's best estimate of anticipated experience under the plan."[21]

The reasonableness of actuarial assumptions is ordinarily based upon the experience under the plan "unless it is established that past experience is not likely to recur and thus is not a good indication of future experience."[22] Assumptions that are mutually inconsistent or that conflict with the benefit structure of the plan are unreasonable.[23] For a new plan, where experience is no guide, actuarial assumptions must be based on "reasonable expectations." The IRS has suggested that assumptions would be evaluated in light of experience "[a]fter a plan has been in effect for a period of five years or so."[24]

---

formula could cause a plan that is terminated within a few years after the grant of past-service benefits to have far greater benefit liabilities than it has accumulated assets with which to pay them. Because of the extended period allowed for funding past-service benefits, such a plan might have complied with ERISA's minimum funding rules at all times. ERISA's original funding rules tolerated this situation so as not to discourage the grant of past-service benefits. The 2006 amendments strike a new balance between promoting and securing retroactive benefit grants. TREASURY GENERAL EXPLANATIONS, *supra* Chapter 9 note 13, at 78.

20 ERISA § 303(h)(2), (h)(3), 29 U.S.C.A. § 1083(h)(2), (h)(3) (2006); *see* I.R.C. § 430(h)(2), (h)(3) (2006).

21 ERISA § 303(h)(1), 29 U.S.C. § 1083(h)(1) (2006) (effective for plan years beginning after 2007; prior years correspond to ERISA § 302(c)(3), 29 U.S.C. § 1082(c)(3) (2000) (repealed 2006)); *see* I.R.C. § 430(h)(1) (2006) (effective for plan years beginning after 2007; prior years correspond to I.R.C. § 412(c)(3) (2000) (repealed 2006)).

22 Prop. Treas. Reg. § 1.412(b)-1(h)(1), 47 Fed. Reg. 54,093, 54,098 (Dec. 1, 1982).

23 *See* Prop. Treas. Reg. § 1.412(b)-1(h)(3), (4). In *Rhoades, McKee & Boer v. United States*, 43 F.3d 1071 (6th Cir. 1995), the court found unreasonable (1) an assumption of retirement at age 60 where the participant would have to work until age 63 to qualify for an increase in plan benefits, and (2) the use of a female mortality table for a male participant where "'the only explanation . . . seems to be an effort to increase contribution levels.'" *Rhoades, McKee*, 43 F.3d at 1076 (quoting from the district court's opinion).

24 Rev. Rul. 63-11, 1963-1 C.B. 94, 96. In *Wachtell, Lipton, Rosen & Katz v. Comm'r*, 26 F.3d 291 (2d Cir. 1994), the IRS argued that the actuary should have based the interest rate assumption more on the first two years of plan experience than on long-term statistical averages. The Second Circuit disagreed. There was expert actuarial testimony that experience in the early years of a plan is not given much weight, and the IRS had previously announced that a change

Actuarial assumptions must not only be reasonable, in combination they must also "offer the actuary's best estimate of anticipated experience under the plan." The IRS has argued that this condition obligates the plan's actuary to "neutrally pick the most likely result" from within the range of reasonable actuarial assumptions.[25] The courts of appeals have generally rejected this substantive interpretation of the best-estimate test on the ground that it is inconsistent with the latitude in professional judgment that Congress intended to give actuaries, and because it would render the reasonableness test superfluous.[26] Instead, several appellate courts have concluded that the best-estimate test imposes only a procedural hurdle: the plan must show that the assumptions selected reflect the independent professional judgment of the actuary.[27] The weakness of the procedural approach lies in the fact that the absence of overt pressure does not guarantee independence; the actuary is not likely to be ignorant of the sponsor's financial needs, and there is nothing to prevent a sponsor from "shopping around" for a complaisant actuary.

Starting in 2008, additional constraints on actuarial assumptions come into play if a plan with more than 500 participants is significantly underfunded. To account for the greater likelihood that a plan maintained by a financially weak sponsor will be called upon to pay benefits on an accelerated schedule, for such at-risk plans, all employees who will be eligible to elect benefits during the current and ten succeeding plan years must be assumed to retire at the earliest possible retirement date under the plan and to elect the retirement benefit that would result in the highest present value of benefits.[28] If the plan has been in at-risk status for two of the four preceding years, the plan's funding target and target normal cost are also increased by a "loading factor" to "reflect the additional administrative cost of purchasing a group annuity if the plan were to terminate."[29]

---

would not be required "unless there has been a consistent pattern of substantial gains over a period of years from sources which would be likely to recur in the future." *Wachtell, Lipton,* 26 F.3d at 296 (quoting Rev. Rul. 63-11). *But see* Jerome Mirza & Assocs. v. United States, 882 F.2d 229 (7th Cir. 1989) (actuary's use of 5 percent interest rate based on long-term returns on large pension fund equity investments unreasonable where newly established plan that invested in certificates of deposit would quickly be fully funded, at a time when long-term certificates of deposit paid about 12 percent interest).

25   Vinson & Elkins v. Comm'r, 7 F.3d 1235, 1238 (5th Cir. 1993).

26   *Id.* at 1238; *Wachtell, Lipton,* 26 F.3d at 296; Citrus Valley Estates v. Comm'r, 49 F.3d 1410, 1414–15 (9th Cir. 1995); *Rhoades, McKee,* 43 F.3d at 1075.

27   *Vinson & Elkins,* 7 F.3d at 1238 ("One goal of such an inquiry would be to determine whether assumptions truly came from the plan actuary or whether they were instead chosen by plan management for tax planning or cash flow purposes."). *Accord Wachtell, Lipton,* 26 F.3d 291; *Citrus Valley,* 49 F.3d 1410; *Rhoades, McKee,* 43 F.3d 1071.

28   ERISA § 303(i), 29 U.S.C.A. § 1083(i) (2006); *see* I.R.C. § 430(i) (2006).

29   ERISA § 303(i), 29 U.S.C. § 1083(i) (2006); *see* I.R.C. § 430(i) (2006). *See also* TREASURY GENERAL EXPLANATIONS, *supra* Chapter 9 note 13, at 77, 83.

Relief Provisions

The Treasury is allowed to waive (that is defer, not excuse) compliance with the minimum funding standard if the employer is unable to satisfy it without *temporary* substantial business hardship (substantial business hardship, in the case of a multiemployer plan) and if enforcement would be adverse to the interests of plan participants in the aggregate.[30] Waiver offers the possibility of deferral of the entire minimum contribution for the year, excepting only the amount required to amortize previously waived minimum funding obligations. The employer must notify each affected labor organization, participant, and beneficiary (and any alternate payee under a qualified domestic relations order) of the waiver application, and the IRS must consider any relevant information submitted by these affected parties.[31] If the requested waiver would cause the plan's funding shortfall to reach $1 million or more, certain PBGC protective measures come into play, including the right to comment on the request and the possible grant of a security interest.[32]

Another relief mechanism is available in certain extraordinary cases, where the minimum funding standards would cause temporary substantial business hardship and a waiver is unavailable or inadequate. If the IRS is notified and finds that these

---

30 ERISA § 302(c), 29 U.S.C. § 1082(c) (2006) (effective for plan years beginning after 2007; prior years correspond to ERISA § 303, 29 U.S.C. § 1083 (2000) (repealed 2006)); *see* I.R.C. § 412(c) (2006) (effective for plan years beginning after 2007; prior years correspond to I.R.C. § 412(d) (2000) (repealed 2006)). In determining whether the substantial business hardship condition is satisfied, the IRS considers (among other factors) (1) whether the employer is operating at a loss; (2) whether there is substantial unemployment or underemployment in the business and industry concerned; (3) whether profits and sales in the industry are depressed or declining; and (4) whether it is reasonable to expect that the plan will be continued only if the waiver is granted. *See* Rev. Proc. 2004-15, § 2.03(2), (4), 2004-1 C.B. 490 (specified facts concerning the employer's financial condition and the nature and extent of business hardship must be submitted with request for waiver). All members of the employer's controlled group (under the commonly controlled business and affiliated service group rules) are treated as a single employer in making this hardship evaluation. ERISA § 302(c)(5)(B), 29 U.S.C. § 1082(c)(5)(B) (2006); *see* I.R.C. § 412(c)(5)(B) (2006).

31 ERISA § 302(c)(6), 29 U.S.C. § 1082(c)(6) (2006) (effective for plan years beginning after 2007; prior years correspond to ERISA § 303(e), 29 U.S.C. § 1083(e) (2000) (repealed 2006)); *see* I.R.C. § 412(c)(6) (2006) (effective for plan years beginning after 2007; prior years correspond to I.R.C. § 412(f)(4) (2000) (repealed 2006)). Although these parties have a right to comment, their ability to comment effectively is seriously hampered by the fact that the waiver application is treated as confidential return information. ERISA § 302(c)(4)(B), 29 U.S.C. § 1082(c)(4)(B) (2006) (effective for plan years beginning after 2007; prior years correspond to ERISA § 306(b), 29 U.S.C. § 1086(b) (2000) (repealed 2006)); *see* I.R.C. § 412(c)(4)(B) (2006) (effective for plan years beginning after 2007; prior years correspond to I.R.C. § 412(f)(3)(B) (2000) (repealed 2006)); McGarry v. Sec'y of the Treasury, 853 F.2d 981 (D.C. Cir. 1988).

32 ERISA § 302(c)(4), 29 U.S.C. § 1082(c)(4) (2006) (effective for plan years beginning after 2007; prior years correspond to ERISA § 306, 29 U.S.C. § 1086 (2000) (repealed 2006)); *see* I.R.C. § 412(c)(4) (2006) (effective for plan years beginning after 2007; prior years correspond to I.R.C. § 412(f)(3) (2000) (repealed 2006)).

conditions are satisfied, it may approve a plan amendment that retroactively reduces participants' accrued benefits, notwithstanding ERISA's anti-cutback rule.[33] An amendment adopted within two and one-half months after the close of a plan year may reduce benefits that have accrued since the start of that year, but only to the extent required by the circumstances.[34]

If either of these relief methods has been employed, the plan generally cannot be amended to increase plan liabilities, whether by increasing benefits, changing benefit accrual, or accelerating benefit vesting, for as long as the waiver is in effect, or for 12 months after adoption of an amendment that reduces accrued benefits.[35] A comparable ban on liability-increasing amendments applies to any underfunded plan insured by the PBGC for as long as the sponsor is subject to bankruptcy administration.[36] Beginning in 2006, significantly underfunded plans became subject to additional restrictions. Plans that are less than 80 percent funded generally may not be amended to increase benefit liabilities, and if funding falls below 60 percent, further benefit accruals must cease (i.e., benefits are frozen). Lump-sum and other accelerated distribution options, which deplete funds and increase risks for other participants, may also be restricted for plans that are less than 80 percent funded or whose sponsor is subject to bankruptcy or insolvency proceedings.[37]

Enforcement

Minimum funding contributions are due eight and one-half months after the close of the plan year.[38] Underfunded single-employer plans must make quarterly installments of 25 percent of the lesser of 90 percent of the required minimum contribution for the

---

33   *See supra* Chapter 7 notes 39–45 and accompanying text.

34   ERISA §§ 204(g)(1), 302(d)(2), 29 U.S.C. §§ 1054(g)(1), 1082(d)(2) (2006) (effective for plan years beginning after 2007; for prior years, latter provision corresponds to ERISA § 302(c)(8), 29 U.S.C. § 1082(c)(8) (2000) (repealed 2006)); *see* I.R.C. §§ 411(d)(6)(A), 412(d)(2) (2006) (effective for plan years beginning after 2007; for prior years, latter provision corresponds to I.R.C. § 412(c)(8) (2000) (repealed 2006)).

35   ERISA § 302(c)(7), 29 U.S.C. § 1082(c)(7) (2006) (effective for plan years beginning after 2007; prior years correspond to ERISA § 304(b), 29 U.S.C. § 1084(b) (2000) (repealed 2006)); *see* I.R.C. § 412(c)(7) (2006) (effective for plan years beginning after 2007; prior years correspond to I.R.C. § 412(f)(1) (2000) (repealed 2006)). Such a liability-increasing amendment is nevertheless allowed if it is required for qualification, if it merely repeals a prior benefit cutback, or if the IRS finds that it is reasonable and provides only a de minimis increase in plan liabilities.

36   ERISA § 204(i), 29 U.S.C. § 1054(i) (2006); *see* I.R.C. § 401(a)(33) (2006).

37   ERISA § 206(g), 29 U.S.C. § 1056(g) (2006); *see* I.R.C. §§ 401(a)(29), 436 (2006). *See also* TREASURY GENERAL EXPLANATIONS, *supra* Chapter 9 note 13, at 79–80.

38   ERISA § 303(j), 29 U.S.C. § 1083(j) (2006) (effective for plan years beginning after 2007; prior years correspond to ERISA § 302(c)(10), 29 U.S.C. § 1082(c)(10) (2000) (repealed 2006)); *see* I.R.C. § 430(j) (2006) (effective for plan years beginning after 2007; prior years correspond to I.R.C. § 412(c)(10) (2000) (repealed 2006)).

year or 100 percent of the required minimum contribution for the prior year. Interest is also due on such contributions or installments, computed from the valuation date of the plan (generally the first day of the plan year to which the contribution relates), and the interest rate is increased by five percentage points on past-due installments.[39] For a single-employer plan, the sponsor and all members of its controlled group bear joint and several liability for the annual minimum contribution and any required installments.[40] Moreover, if the aggregate amount of past-due minimum contributions (including required installments and interest) exceeds $1 million, then an underfunded insured single-employer plan is given a lien against all property rights of the sponsor and all members of its controlled group.[41] The lien, which is perfected and enforced by the PBGC, continues until the close of the first plan year in which the unpaid balance of required payments falls below $1 million.

Although the IRS generally interprets and administers the minimum funding requirements, any plan participant, beneficiary, or fiduciary may seek an injunction enforcing ERISA's minimum funding standards.[42] The Secretary of Labor may also seek enforcement, but if the plan is qualified, the Labor Department can sue only if requested to do so by the Treasury or by the written request of one or more participants, beneficiaries, or fiduciaries.[43] In addition, if the amount of missed contributions exceeds $1 million, the PBGC may bring suit.[44]

To put extra teeth in the rules, ERISA's funding requirements are replicated in the qualified plan provisions of the Internal Revenue Code.[45] Noncompliance with the tax law version triggers a nondeductible annual tax on the employer equal to 10 percent of the amount of unpaid required minimum contributions, which rises to 100 percent if the shortfall is not timely corrected.[46]

---

39 ERISA § 303(j), 29 U.S.C. § 1083(j) (2006) (effective for plan years beginning after 2007; prior years correspond to ERISA § 302(e), 29 U.S.C. § 1082(e) (2000) (repealed 2006)); *see* I.R.C. § 430(j) (2006) (effective for plan years beginning after 2007; prior years correspond to I.R.C. § 412(m) (2000) (repealed 2006)).

40 ERISA § 302(b)(2), (d)(3), 29 U.S.C. § 1082(b)(2), (d)(3) (2006) (effective for plan years beginning after 2007; prior years correspond to ERISA § 302(c)(11)(B), 29 U.S.C. § 1082(c) (11)(B) (2000) (repealed 2006)); *see* I.R.C. § 412(b)(2), (d)(3) (2006) (effective for plan years beginning after 2007; prior years correspond to I.R.C. § 412(c)(11)(B) (2000) (repealed 2006)). For this purpose, "controlled group" means the composite employer used by the tax law to test for discrimination under the qualified retirement plans.

41 ERISA § 303(k), 29 U.S.C. § 1083(k) (2006) (effective for plan years beginning after 2007; prior years correspond to ERISA § 302(f), 29 U.S.C. § 1082(f) (2000) (repealed 2006)); *see* I.R.C. § 430(k) (2006) (effective for plan years beginning after 2007; prior years correspond to I.R.C. § 412(n) (2000) (repealed 2006)).

42 ERISA § 502(a)(3), 29 U.S.C. § 1132(a)(3) (2006).

43 ERISA § 502(a)(5), (b), 29 U.S.C. § 1132(a)(5), (b) (2006).

44 ERISA § 4003(e), 29 U.S.C. § 1303(e) (2006).

45 I.R.C. §§ 412, 430, 436 (2006).

46 I.R.C. § 4971 (2006).

Disclosure of Funded Status

Participants in a defined benefit pension plan bear a residual risk of loss to the extent that their benefits are unfunded and uninsured. In the four largest underfunded plan terminations that had occurred as of 2005, only two-thirds of the shortfall was covered by PBGC, with the remainder, some $6 billion, representing a loss to plan participants.[47] Information concerning the funded status of the plan could facilitate financial planning and self-protection. ERISA sets forth requirements concerning disclosure of funding information to participants and beneficiaries. As originally written, the requirements were rudimentary, but they were substantially strengthened in 2006.[48]

B. PBGC TERMINATION INSURANCE[49]

ERISA's minimum funding rules have been repeatedly tightened since 1974, but they still concede an extended period during which plan assets will, in the event of termination, be insufficient to pay promised benefits. Without intervention, participants would bear that risk of loss because plan sponsors have traditionally disclaimed liability for unfunded benefits. Congress intervened by instituting a mandatory termination insurance system for defined benefit plans under ERISA Title IV. That system shifts the risk of loss from participants to defined benefit plan sponsors generally, including financially healthy sponsors of fully funded plans. ERISA's *reallocation* of the risk of underfunding works a wholesale conversion of workers' expectancies into entitlements.

The termination insurance system of ERISA Title IV applies only to defined benefit pension plans, and it contains the familiar exceptions for governmental and church plans, plans that do not provide for post-ERISA employer contributions, and plans established and maintained outside the United States for nonresident aliens.[50] Also excepted from termination insurance coverage are unfunded plans providing deferred compensation to a select group of management or highly compensated employees (i.e., top-hat plans), excess benefit plans (whether funded or not), and plans established

---

47   PBGC, The Impact of Pension Reform Proposals on Claims Against the Pension Insurance Program, Losses to Participants, and Contributions 6 (2005), http://www.pbgc.gov/docs/impact_of_reform_proposals_1005.pdf.

48   ERISA § 101(a)(2), (f), 29 U.S.C. § 1021(a)(2), (f) (2006) (effective for plan years beginning after 2007; for prior years, ERISA § 4011, 29 U.S.C. § 1311 (2000) (repealed 2006) imposed less stringent notice requirements). *See supra* Chapter 3A. Participants and beneficiaries must also be promptly notified if, as a result of severe underfunding, benefit accruals are frozen or the plan becomes subject to restrictions on plant shutdown benefits or lump-sum distributions. ERISA §§ 101(j), 502(a)(6), (c)(4), 29 U.S.C. §§ 1021(j), 1132(a)(6), (c)(4) (2006).

49   The discussion in this section is adapted from Peter J. Wiedenbeck & Russell K. Osgood, Cases and Materials on Employee Benefits 787–832 (1996), and is reprinted with permission of West, a Thomson Reuters business. This section addresses the termination insurance program for single-employer plans only. The rules governing insurance of multiemployer pension plan benefits and the withdrawal liability imposed upon an employer's dissociation from a multiemployer plan are beyond the scope of this monograph.

50   ERISA § 4021(a), (b)(1)–(5), (7), 29 U.S.C. § 1321(a), (b)(1)–(5), (7) (2006).

and maintained exclusively for substantial owners.[51] In terms of both access to information and bargaining power, substantial owners and highly paid employees are in a better position than the rank-and-file to protect themselves from the risk of underfunding, and Congress left them to their own devices. Lastly, Title IV contains an unusual exception for a plan of a "professional service employer," which has not at any time since the date of enactment of ERISA had more than 25 active participants.[52]

The termination insurance program is administered by the Pension Benefit Guaranty Corporation (PBGC), a government corporation within the Department of Labor.[53] To accomplish its mission of ensuring uninterrupted payment of benefits, the PBGC charges plan sponsors annual premiums[54] and may borrow up to $100 million from the U.S. Treasury,[55] but its obligations are *not* backed by the full faith and credit of the United States.[56]

Guaranteed Benefits

With certain exceptions, the PBGC guarantees the payment "of all nonforfeitable benefits (other than benefits becoming nonforfeitable solely on account of the termination of a plan) under a single-employer plan which terminates at a time when this title applies to it."[57] For purposes of Title IV, a "nonforfeitable benefit" means

> a benefit for which a participant has satisfied the conditions for entitlement under the plan or the requirements of this Act (other than submission of a formal application, retirement, completion of a required waiting period, or death in the case of a benefit which returns all or a portion of a participant's accumulated mandatory employee contribution upon the participant's death), whether or not the benefit may subsequently be reduced or suspended by a plan amendment, an occurrence of any condition, or operation of this Act or the Internal Revenue Code of 1986. . . . [58]

Under this definition, added in response to the Supreme Court's first decision involving ERISA,[59] the right to a disability pension is not guaranteed unless the injury or

---

51   ERISA §§ 4021(b)(6), (8), (9), 4022(b)(5)(A), 29 U.S.C. §§ 1321(b)(6), (8), (9), 1322(b)(5)(A) (2006). "Substantial owner" is defined to mean sole proprietors, partners who own a greater than 10 percent stake in capital or profits, and shareholders who own greater than 10 percent in value of either the voting stock or all stock of the corporation. ERISA § 4021(d), 29 U.S.C. § 1321(d) (2006).

52   ERISA § 4021(b)(13), (c)(2), (c)(3), 29 U.S.C. § 1321(b)(13), (c)(2), (c)(3) (2006).

53   ERISA § 4002(a), 29 U.S.C. § 1302(a) (2006).

54   ERISA §§ 4005(b)(1), 4007(a), (e), 29 U.S.C. §§ 1305(b)(1), 1307(a), (e) (2006).

55   ERISA § 4005(c), 29 U.S.C. § 1305(c) (2006).

56   ERISA § 4002(g)(2), 29 U.S.C. § 1302(g)(2) (2006).

57   ERISA § 4022(a), 29 U.S.C. § 1322(a) (2006).

58   ERISA § 4001(a)(8), 29 U.S.C. § 1301(a)(8) (2006).

59   Nachman Corp. v. PBGC, 446 U.S. 359 (1980) (rejecting sponsor's argument that Title I definition of "nonforfeitable," ERISA § 3(19), 29 U.S.C. § 1002(19) (2006), controls scope of PBGC's guarantee).

other disability occurred before the date of plan termination.[60] Moreover, the PBGC imposes the condition that only *pension* benefits are guaranteed, meaning:

> a benefit payable as an annuity, or one or more payments related thereto, to a participant who permanently leaves or has permanently left covered employment, or to a surviving beneficiary, which payments by themselves or in combination with Social Security, Railroad Retirement, or workmen's compensation benefits provide a substantially level income to the recipient.[61]

Although single-sum payments are generally excluded, if the plan provides a life annuity alternative, the PBGC guarantees that alternative, and it will also pay out *as an annuity* the value of a single-sum benefit provided under the plan on the death of a participant.[62]

Early retirement benefits are guaranteed to participants who have satisfied any applicable age or service conditions, even if not yet retired.[63] If the plan offers subsidized early retirement, the full benefit is guaranteed, even though the employer subsidy might be viewed as financing a holiday (early exit from the labor force) rather than old age support. Similarly, plant shutdown benefits that are in pay status when a plan terminates are guaranteed, even though the pension may commence many years before the plan's normal retirement age.[64]

Benefits that vest on termination (under I.R.C. § 411(d)(3)) are *not* guaranteed, nor are benefits that accrue after a plan becomes disqualified.[65] There are two other important limits on the guarantee. First, there is a maximum guaranteed amount (a policy limit, if you will). The actuarial value of guaranteed benefits cannot exceed the value of a life annuity, commencing at age 65, paying $750 per month in 1974 dollars, indexed for inflation ($4,312.50 monthly in 2008).[66] The guaranteed benefit also cannot exceed the participant's average monthly gross income from the employer during her highest-paid five consecutive calendar-year period.[67] Second, for benefits that have been in effect less than five years (either because the plan was instituted or benefits were increased within that period), the guarantee is not fully effective; instead, it is

---

60   29 C.F.R. §§ 4022.3(c), 4022.4(a)(1), (3), 4022.6(a) (2009). The latter regulation also requires that, to be insured, a disability pension must be payable "on account of the total and permanent disability of a participant which is expected to last for the life of the participant."

61   29 C.F.R. §§ 4022.2, 4022.3(b) (2009).

62   29 C.F.R. § 4022.7(a), (c)(1) (2009).

63   An early retirement pension is paid as an annuity, and only formal application and retirement stand in the way of entitlement for an active participant who has satisfied all applicable age and service conditions. Consequently, in this situation the early retirement pension satisfies the definition of "nonforfeitable benefit" quoted earlier. *See supra* text accompanying Chapter 9 note 58.

64   29 C.F.R. §§ 4022.2, 4022.3, 4022.4(a)(1), (3) (2009). *See* RICHARD A. IPPOLITO, THE ECONOMICS OF PENSION INSURANCE 75–80 (1989) (special early benefits accounted for nearly 25 percent of the claims in a sample of large plan terminations).

65   ERISA § 4022(a) (parenthetical clause), (b)(6), 29 U.S.C. § 1322(a), (b)(6) (2006).

66   ERISA § 4022(b)(3)(B), 29 U.S.C. § 1322(b)(3)(B) (2006); 29 C.F.R. § 4022.22(b) (2009); 72 Fed. Reg. 67,644–45 (2007) (to be codified at 29 C.F.R. Part 4022 Appendix D).

67   ERISA § 4022(b)(3)(A), 29 U.S.C. § 1322(b)(3)(A) (2006); 29 C.F.R. § 4022.22(a) (2009).

phased in at the rate of 20 percent per year.[68] But in the case of a majority owner (determined using the tax Code's constructive ownership rules), the amount of new benefits that would otherwise be guaranteed (taking into account the general five-year phase-in, if applicable) is further limited by a ten-year pro rata phase-in.[69]

The allocation of the assets of a terminating insured single-employer plan is governed by ERISA. Following the technique of bankruptcy law, benefit claims are assigned to six different priority categories. Plan assets are used to pay all accrued benefits assigned to priority Category 1 in full before any payment is made toward Category 2 benefits, and so on down the ladder (with a reversion possible if all six categories are paid in full).[70] Within a category, assets are generally allocated in proportion to the present value of each participant's accrued benefits assigned that priority.[71] Thus, if an underfunded plan runs out of assets in priority Category 3, all accrued benefits assigned to the top two categories will be paid in full, no payment will be made to satisfy benefits in Categories 4, 5, and 6, and Category 3 claims will generally be paid pro rata.

ERISA's asset allocation priority schedule is drawn more with a view to protecting participants' expectations than for the purpose of reducing moral hazard and protecting the PBGC. Available funding is devoted first to certain favored categories of benefits, whether guaranteed or not. The top three categories clearly evidence the anxiety to preserve reliance interests; they cover (1) voluntary employee contributions; (2) mandatory employee contributions; and (3) benefits that were in pay status—or, in the event of retirement, could have been in pay status—three years before the date of plan termination. The fourth category covers all other guaranteed benefits, but includes, in addition, benefits payable to majority owners that are not guaranteed because of the ten-year phase-in. Amounts that exceed the dollar cap on guaranteed benefits can be funded under Category 3 (as benefits that were or could have been in pay status three years before termination)' before any allocation is made toward Category 4, which includes the guaranteed benefits of most active workers.[72] To that extent, more guaranteed benefits are left unfunded, resulting in higher insured losses. Category 5 covers all other nonforfeitable benefits under the plan (e.g., benefits that are not guaranteed because they vest on termination); any other benefits fall in Category 6 (e.g., disability benefits where the disability occurs after termination).

---

68   ERISA § 4022(b)(1), (7), 29 U.S.C. § 1322(b)(1), (7) (2006); 29 C.F.R. § 4022.25 (2009).

69   ERISA § 4022(b)(5), 29 U.S.C.A. § 1322(b)(5) (2006) (generally effective for terminations initiated after 2005).

70   ERISA § 4044(a), (d), 29 U.S.C. § 1344(a), (d) (2006). The possibility of a reversion is discussed more fully *infra* Chapter 9C, concerning overfunded defined benefit plan termination.

71   ERISA § 4044(b)(2), (b)(3), 29 U.S.C. § 1344(b)(2), (b)(3) (2006). If plan assets run out in Category 5, a special rule provides for allocation first to the amount of Category 5 benefits the participants would be entitled to under the plan as in effect five years before termination, with any remaining assets allocated according to successive plan amendments within that five-year period. ERISA § 4044(b)(4), 29 U.S.C. § 1344(b)(4) (2006). In addition, the plan is permitted to establish priority subcategories based on age, service, or disability, or a combination thereof. ERISA § 4044(b)(7), 29 U.S.C. § 1344(b)(7) (2006); 29 C.F.R. § 4044.17(a) (2009).

72   29 C.F.R. § 4044.13(a) (2009) (final sentence).

The right to terminate an underfunded plan is severely restricted so that the sponsor remains subject to ongoing funding obligations. Underfunded plans may be terminated in a "distress termination," which requires that the sponsor and each member of its controlled group be (1) in liquidation proceedings under bankruptcy or insolvency law; (2) unable to pay its debts and continue in business if the plan continues; or (3) subject to unreasonably burdensome pension costs solely as a result of a decline in the covered workforce.[73] In addition, the PBGC may initiate termination when necessary to protect the interests of plan participants or the insurance program, and must terminate any plan that has insufficient assets to pay current benefits.[74] Accordingly, a sponsor can shed its funding obligation only if it and all related businesses are in dire financial straits.

If an underfunded plan is terminated, whether by the PBGC or in a distress termination, the sponsor is liable to the PBGC for "the total amount of the unfunded benefit liabilities (as of the termination date) to all participants and beneficiaries under the plan" together with interest from the termination date.[75] Accordingly, the sponsor's liability extends to all benefits, even those not guaranteed by the PBGC. As originally enacted, ERISA made the sponsor of an underfunded plan liable to the PBGC for the amount of unfunded guaranteed benefits,[76] but until 1986 that reimbursement liability was capped at 30 percent of the sponsor's net worth.[77] To prevent evasion, liability to the PBGC extends beyond the contributing sponsor; all businesses under common control with the plan sponsor bear joint and several liability for the funding shortfall.[78]

---

73   ERISA § 4041(a)(1), (c)(1)(C), (c)(2)(B), 29 U.S.C. § 1341(a)(1), (c)(1)(C), (c)(2)(B) (2006). *See In re* Kaiser Aluminum Corp., 456 F.3d 328 (3d Cir. 2006) (where a sponsor seeks distress termination of multiple plans, determination whether sponsor will be unable to pay its debts and continue in business is made considering the aggregate financial burden of all plans sought to be terminated, not on a plan-by-plan basis).

74   ERISA § 4042(a), 29 U.S.C. § 1342(a) (2006).

75   ERISA § 4062(b)(1)(A), 29 U.S.C. § 1362(b)(1)(A) (2006). *See* United Steelworkers of Am. v. United Eng'g, Inc., 52 F.3d 1386 (6th Cir. 1995) (ERISA preempts suit brought by employees and union directly against the employer for nonguaranteed benefits; workers must look to PBGC enforcement of PBGC's claim as the sole source of recovery).

76   Note that the PBGC is designated a "guarantor," not an insurer. Under the law of suretyship, a guarantor who is called upon to pay a debt is subrogated to all the creditor's rights and remedies against the principal debtor. The PBGC's claim for reimbursement of unfunded guaranteed benefits corresponds to the surety's right of subrogation.

77   ERISA § 4062(b), Pub. L. No. 93–406, § 4062, 88 Stat. 829, 1029 (1974) (amended 1986).

78   ERISA § 4062(a), 29 U.S.C. § 1362(a) (2006). Common control is currently defined by reference to the commonly controlled business rules in the Internal Revenue Code's qualified plan provisions. ERISA § 4001(a)(13), (14), 29 U.S.C. § 1301(a)(13), (14) (2006); *see* I.R.C. § 414(b), (c) (2006). The control group liability principle was established early in the administration of the termination insurance program. The original version of ERISA § 4062 made "the employer who maintained a plan" liable to reimburse the PBGC for payment of guaranteed benefits, but Title IV's expansive definition of employer, ERISA § 4001(b)(1), 29 U.S.C. § 1301(b)(1) (2006), was held to impose joint and several liability on all commonly controlled businesses. PBGC v. Ouimet Corp., 630 F.2d 4, 12 (1st Cir. 1980), *appeal after remand*, 711 F.2d 1085 (1st Cir. 1983) (applying family attribution rules to determine group membership and allocating entire liability to solvent affiliates of bankrupt sponsor).

Nor can the financially healthy members of a controlled group shed their liability by arranging a strategic pre-termination disaffiliation. If, for example, the cash-strapped sponsor of an underfunded plan is sold off with the expectation that the plan will later have to be terminated, the seller (and related businesses) may remain liable for the underfunding. ERISA was amended in 1986 to provide such continuing liability if a principal purpose behind the disaffiliation was to evade liability and the plan is ultimately terminated within five years after the sale.[79] Even without statutory authority, some courts reached the same result by ruling that the circumstance of the transaction, analyzed under substance-over-form principles, showed that disaffiliation amounted to constructive termination.[80]

To reduce pre-termination funding erosion, Congress tightened requirements for obtaining a waiver of the minimum funding obligation and barred benefit increases for as long as a waiver is in effect.[81] Plant shutdown and other unpredictable contingent event benefits still do not need to be advance funded, but once the contingency that triggers entitlement occurs, the benefits must be rapidly funded (using a seven-year amortization schedule).[82] Distributions that commence within three years before plan

---

79   ERISA § 4069(a), 29 U.S.C. § 1369(a) (2006). In *PBGC v. White Consolidated Industries*, 998 F.2d 1192 (3d Cir. 1993), *appeal after remand*, 215 F.3d 407 (3d Cir. 2000), the seller agreed to make substantial contributions to several underfunded pension plans for five years after sale of the sponsoring unprofitable subsidiaries, allegedly to avoid predecessor liability by preventing termination of the plans within five years. The Third Circuit held that the five-year limit on predecessor liability does not begin to run until the company that transferred the pension plan stops making substantial post-transfer contributions. *White Consol. Indus.*, 998 F.2d at 1198–2000; Blaw Knox Retirement Plan v. White Consol. Indus., 998 F.2d 1185, 1192 (3d Cir. 1993) (same facts). *See also* Raytech Corp. v. PBGC, 241 B.R. 790 (Bankr. D. Conn. 1999) (successor liability for minimum funding contributions imposed on recipient of fraudulent conveyance).

80   *E.g., In re* Consol. Litig. Concerning Int'l Harvester's Disposition of Wis. Steel, 681 F. Supp. 512 (N.D. Ill. 1988) (disaffiliation a constructive termination where the buyer does not have a reasonable chance of paying for unfunded pension benefits and seller intended to evade pension funding obligations). *But see White Consol. Indus.*, 998 F.2d at 1201 (constructive termination theory of *International Harvester* does not apply to transactions after January 1, 1986, to which predecessor liability rule of ERISA § 4069 applies); *White Consol. Indus.*, 215 F.3d at 419 n.15 (dicta expressing uncertainty whether "the tax policy considerations at the heart of the sham transfer doctrine translate neatly when used to disregard a sale transaction for purposes of imposing pension liability").

81   ERISA § 302(c), 29 U.S.C. § 1082(c) (2006) (effective for plan years beginning after 2007; prior years correspond to ERISA §§ 303, 304(b), 306, 29 U.S.C. §§ 1083, 1084(b), 1086 (2000) (repealed 2006)); *see* I.R.C. § 412(c) (2006) (effective for plan years beginning after 2007; prior years correspond to I.R.C. § 412(d), (f)(3) (2000) (repealed 2006)). Waivers can be granted to a single-employer plan in no more than three of any fifteen years; the waived funding deficiency must be amortized over five years; to qualify for a waiver the employer and all members of its controlled group must be experiencing temporary substantial business hardship; the IRS must consult the PBGC on the waiver application; and the grant of a waiver may be conditioned on the employer's granting security for repayment.

82   For plan years beginning after 2007, underfunding triggered by a plant closing or other unpredictable contingent event must be amortized over seven years, along with funding shortfalls attributable to all other events. ERISA § 303(a), (c), (d)(1), 29 U.S.C. § 1083(a), (c), (d)(1) (2006); *see* I.R.C. § 430(a), (c), (d)(1) (2006). In addition, however, qualified plans are

termination can be recovered from the recipient to the extent that pre-termination distributions exceed, by more than a specified amount, the present value of the benefits that would have been guaranteed had payments been made as a life annuity.

PBGC Monitoring and Enforcement

ERISA grants the PBGC three major types of liens against the property of the sponsor of an underfunded plan. First, a lien arises for the amount that plan assets at termination prove insufficient to pay all benefit liabilities, whether guaranteed or not. The PBGC's lien, however, is limited to 30 percent of the collective net worth of all members of the contributing sponsor's controlled group.[83] Second, the PBGC is given a lien for the amount of delinquent minimum funding contributions as soon as they exceed $1 million.[84] The third type of PBGC lien comes into play when the IRS requires security as a condition of granting a minimum funding waiver.[85]

For a number of reasons, the PBGC's liens often fail to work in bankruptcy. The liens for plan asset insufficiency and delinquent minimum funding contributions must be perfected in the same manner as a federal tax lien in order to be effective against later judgment or secured creditors or against the bankruptcy trustee. But once the sponsor files for bankruptcy, the automatic stay prevents the PBGC from taking the steps necessary to perfect the liens. Moreover, if bankruptcy proceedings result in liquidation rather than reorganization of the sponsor, the PBGC's liens are denied secured status even if perfected pre-petition; instead, the PBGC's claims must settle for the seventh priority status accorded tax claims.[86]

Typically, the PBGC's liens are not perfected in time to be effective in bankruptcy. Lacking secured status, the PBGC has asserted that the claims underlying its liens are entitled to one or another priority in bankruptcy. In general, however, the courts have held that claims for benefits that accrued prior to bankruptcy filing are not entitled to priority.[87]

---

required to include a provision that bars the payment of unpredictable contingent event benefits if such benefits would cause the plan's funding level to fall below 60 percent in the year in which the triggering event occurs. I.R.C. §§ 401(a)(29), 436(a), (b) (2006). Recognizing that plant closings within a few years of plan termination can dramatically inflate underfunding, Congress first imposed accelerated funding requirements on unpredictable contingent event benefits in 1994. ERISA § 302(d)(1)(B), (d)(5)(A), 29 U.S.C. § 1082(d)(1)(B), (d)(5)(A) (2000) (repealed 2006); *see* I.R.C. § 412(*l*)(1)(B), (*l*)(5)(A) (2000) (repealed 2006).

83 ERISA § 4068, 29 U.S.C. § 1368 (2006).

84 ERISA § 303(k), 29 U.S.C. § 1083(k) (2006) (effective for plan years beginning after 2007; prior years correspond to ERISA § 302(f), 29 U.S.C. § 1082(f) (2000) (repealed 2006)); *see* I.R.C. § 430(k) (2006) (effective for plan years beginning after 2007; prior years correspond to I.R.C. § 412(n) (2000) (repealed 2006)).

85 ERISA § 302(c)(4), 29 U.S.C. § 1082(c)(4) (2006); *see* I.R.C. § 412(c)(4) (2006).

86 *See generally* Daniel L. Keating, *Chapter 11's New Ten-Ton Monster: The PBGC and Bankruptcy*, 77 MINN. L. REV. 803, 825–40 (1993); DANIEL L. KEATING, BANKRUPTCY AND EMPLOYMENT LAW §§ 4.3–4.8 (1995).

87 KEATING, BANKRUPTCY AND EMPLOYMENT LAW, *supra* Chapter 9 note 86, § 4.4; PBGC v. CF & I Fabricators of Utah, Inc., 150 F.3d 1293 (10th Cir. 1998) (lien for delinquent minimum

Proposals have been advanced to grant the PBGC super-priority in bankruptcy or to completely prohibit underfunded plan termination except in cases where the sponsor will be liquidated (rather than reorganized in bankruptcy).[88] But current law is clear: to be able to enforce employer liability, the PBGC must perfect its liens prior to bankruptcy filing. The lien for plan asset insufficiency does not even arise until plan termination, so to protect its interest, the PBGC would first have to terminate the plan prior to bankruptcy filing. (Recall that ERISA allows the PBGC to initiate termination if the plan has failed to meet its minimum funding standard or if plan continuation is expected to unreasonably increase the possible long-run loss to the PBGC.)

Both pre-petition plan termination and lien perfection call for vigilant monitoring, which requires access to information. ERISA requires the plan administrator or contributing sponsor to notify the PBGC of the occurrence of certain situations, called reportable events, that may indicate possible risk to the financial status of the plan or a threat to the PBGC insurance program.[89] Such notification is due within thirty days after the administrator or contributing sponsor knows or has reason to know that a reportable event has occurred. This reporting requirement is designed to give the PBGC the opportunity to act promptly to protect participants and the insurance system by (for example) perfecting or enforcing liens or involuntarily terminating plans. In addition, if the aggregate unfunded vested benefits liabilities of a privately held sponsor and the other members of its controlled group exceed $50 million, then thirty-day *advance* notification is required of certain reportable events.[90]

C. OVERFUNDED PLAN TERMINATION

The sponsor of an overfunded single-employer plan may voluntarily discontinue the program at any time, provided that certain procedures are followed. Where plan assets will be sufficient to pay all benefit liabilities, the transaction is known as a standard termination, which is accomplished in several steps.[91] First, the plan administrator must provide each affected party with a written "notice of intent to terminate" not less

---

funding contributions not entitled to tax priority; administrative priority available only to the extent unpaid contributions attributable to post-petition services). Section 507(a)(4) of the Bankruptcy Code gives fourth priority to up to $10,000 per employee of unsecured claims for employee benefits based on services rendered within 180 days before bankruptcy filing, but the amount is reduced by the priority for unpaid wages and payments on behalf of employees to other benefit plans. 11 U.S.C. § 507(a)(4) (2006).

88   Daniel L. Keating, *Pension Insurance, Bankruptcy and Moral Hazard*, 1991 Wisc. L. Rev. 65, 100; Keating, Bankruptcy and Employment Law, *supra* Chapter 9 note 86, §§ 4.9–4.10.

89   ERISA § 4043, 29 U.S.C. § 1343 (2006).

90   ERISA § 4043(b), 29 U.S.C. § 1343(b) (2006).

91   ERISA § 4041(a), (b), 29 U.S.C. § 1341(a), (b) (2006); 29 C.F.R. § 4041.21 (2009). The PBGC publication, *Standard Termination Filing Instructions*, *available at* http://www.pbgc.gov/docs/500_instructions.pdf (last visited Feb. 21, 2008), contains a complete explanation of the steps involved in a standard termination.

than sixty nor more than ninety days before the proposed termination date.[92] The affected parties entitled to receive notice are each participant, each beneficiary of a deceased participant, each alternate payee under a qualified domestic relations order (QDRO), and every union representing participants.[93] Second, within 180 days after the proposed termination date, the administrator must send a "notice of plan benefits" to each participant, to the beneficiaries of each deceased participant, and to alternate payees under any QDRO. The notice of plan benefits reports the amount and form of benefits to which the specific participant or beneficiary is entitled and the personal data (e.g., age, years of service, compensation history) and actuarial data (e.g., mortality table and interest rate if benefits will or may be paid in a lump sum) on which those benefits are based.[94] Third, after providing the notice of plan benefits, and within 180 days after the proposed termination date, the administrator must send the PBGC a completed PBGC Form 500, the "standard termination notice," which includes the certification of an enrolled actuary showing that the projected amount of plan assets, as of the proposed date of final distribution, will be sufficient to cover the actuarial present value at that date of all benefit liabilities accrued to the proposed termination date.[95] Fourth, a "notice of annuity information," reporting the names and addresses of insurers from whom the plan administrator will purchase annuity contracts, must be provided no later than 45 days before the distribution date to affected parties (other than those who will be forced to take a lump sum because of the small value of their benefits).[96] The PBGC has sixty days after receiving the standard termination notice (Form 500) to review the information provided for completeness, to ascertain that proper notices were issued to all persons entitled thereto, and, most important, to ensure that the plan assets will be sufficient to satisfy all benefit liabilities.[97] If the PBGC finds a problem, it issues a notice of noncompliance, which calls a halt to the termination.

If no notice of noncompliance is received, the plan administrator proceeds to make a final distribution of plan assets.[98] Satisfaction of benefit liabilities is accomplished in

---

92   ERISA § 4041(a)(2), (b)(1)(A), 29 U.S.C. § 1341(a)(2), (b)(1)(A) (2006); 29 C.F.R. § 4041.23 (2009).

93   ERISA § 4001(a)(21), 29 U.S.C. § 1301(a)(21) (2006). If an affected party has designated in writing someone else to receive notice, the administrator must follow that instruction. *Id.* The notice of intent to terminate need not be provided to the PBGC in the case of a standard termination, ERISA § 4041(a)(2), 29 U.S.C. § 1341(a)(2) (2006).

94   ERISA § 4041(b)(1)(B), (b)(2)(B), 29 U.S.C. § 1341(b)(1)(B), (b)(2)(B) (2006); 29 C.F.R. §§ 4041.24, 4041.25(a) (2009).

95   ERISA § 4041(b)(1)(B), (b)(2)(A), 29 U.S.C. § 1341(b)(1)(B), (b)(2)(A) (2006); 29 C.F.R. §§ 4021.24(a), 4041.25(a) (2009); PBGC Form 500, Standard Termination Notice.

96   29 C.F.R. §§ 4041.23(b)(5), 4041.27 (2009); ERISA § 4041(a)(2), 29 U.S.C. § 1341(a)(2) (2006).

97   ERISA § 4041(a)(2)(C), (d)(1), 29 U.S.C. § 1341(a)(2)(C) (d)(1) (2006); 29 C.F.R. § 4041.31(a) (2009). The sixty-day review period may be extended with the consent of the plan administrator. ERISA § 4041(a)(2)(C)(ii), 29 U.S.C. § 1341(a)(2)(C)(ii) (2006); 29 C.F.R. § 4041.26(a) (2) (2009).

98   ERISA § 4041(a)(2)(D), 29 U.S.C. § 1341(a)(2)(D) (2006); 29 C.F.R. § 4041.28 (2009).

three ways. The plan administrator provides for most participants and beneficiaries by purchasing irrevocable commitments from an insurance company to pay all promised benefits, with the insurer issuing nontransferable group or individual annuity contracts to participants. This purchase of annuity contracts allows the plan to go out of existence while assuring retirees uninterrupted pension payment and providing a source of payment for the accrued benefits of workers who haven't yet qualified (by satisfying age, retirement, or other conditions) for the commencement of distributions according to the terms of the plan. The annuities so provided, however, are not guaranteed by the PBGC, and the notice of intent to terminate must warn participants and beneficiaries of this fact.[99] To provide for participants who cannot be located, ERISA permits the plan administrator to transfer the participant's benefit to the PBGC, which runs a clearinghouse to search for missing participants.[100] Alternatively, if the plan so provides, the administrator can simply pay a participant the actuarial present value of his accrued benefit in cash, provided that it is worth less than $5,000.[101] The deadline for making these distributions is the later of (1) 180 days after expiration of the PBGC's 60-day review period or (2) 120 days after receipt of a favorable IRS determination letter, provided that the plan administrator submits a valid request for an IRS determination letter by the time she files the Form 500 with the PBGC.[102] The administrator has thirty days after finishing benefit distributions to certify to the PBGC that the close-out process has been properly completed.[103]

An overfunded plan will have assets left after making arrangements for the payment of all benefit liabilities. In the unusual case of a contributory defined benefit plan,

---

99   29 C.F.R. § 4041.23(b)(9) (2009). The selection of the annuity provider is, however, a fiduciary act that must be carried out prudently and "solely in the interest of the participants and beneficiaries." ERISA § 404(a)(1), 29 U.S.C. § 1104(a)(1) (2006). ERISA's civil enforcement provision expressly provides that participants and beneficiaries who receive annuities in satisfaction of their interests under a plan retain standing to enforce fiduciary duties involved in the selection of the annuity provider. ERISA § 502(a)(9), 29 U.S.C. § 1132(a)(9) (2006).

100   ERISA §§ 4041(b)(3)(A)(ii), 4050, 29 U.S.C. §§ 1341(b)(3)(A)(ii), 1350 (2006). The PBGC's missing participant pension search program is now an online resource, https://search.pbgc.gov/mp/ (last visited Feb. 21, 2008).

101   The immediate cash-out can be involuntary (i.e., made without consent of the participant and his spouse) and is permissible even if, under the terms of the plan, the participant's benefits would not otherwise be distributable for many years. ERISA § 205(g), 29 U.S.C. § 1055(g) (2006); see I.R.C. §§ 417(e), 411(a)(11) (2006). Such cash-outs undermine retirement income security because the money is likely to be spent, rather than saved for retirement, but Congress compromised security in favor of avoiding the administrative cost of preserving de minimis benefits.

102   29 C.F.R. § 4041.28(a)(1) (2009). The employer will ordinarily request an IRS determination that the plan is qualified at the time of termination to ensure that participants will receive favorable tax treatment (continued tax deferral) of distributions. If the plan is qualified, no tax is due on receipt of an annuity contract (later distributions under the contract are taxed under the annuity rules), and a cash-out distribution may be eligible for tax-free rollover to an IRA. I.R.C. § 402(a), (c)(1) (2006); Treas. Reg. § 1.402(a)-1(a)(2) (as amended in 2005).

103   ERISA § 4041(b)(3)(B), 29 U.S.C. § 1341(b)(3)(B) (2006); 29 C.F.R. § 4041.29 (2009), PBGC Form 501, Post-Distribution Certification.

a share of the overfunding must be distributed to participants, with the share determined by the percentage of the participants' accrued benefits that were financed by mandatory employee contributions.[104] Overfunding that is not so attributed to mandatory employee contributions may be distributed to the employer, but only if the plan provides for such a reversion and it does not violate any provision of law.[105] Moreover, plan amendments that would authorize or increase such a reversion cannot be made on the eve of termination; they are effective only if they have been in effect for at least five full calendar years.[106]

ERISA's anti-inurement, exclusive benefit, and prohibited-transaction rules (and their tax law counterparts) prevent an employer from withdrawing excess assets from an ongoing pension plan.[107] That prohibition led overfunded plan sponsors to devise techniques by which they could formally terminate the plan to reclaim its excess assets, yet continue the accrual of benefits for active participants without interruption. In a termination/reestablishment transaction, the employer establishes a new defined benefit plan covering the same group of employees as the terminated plan under the same benefit formula. In a spin-off termination, the employer splits an overfunded plan into two, one covering active employees and another covering retirees. The plan covering active employees satisfies the minimum funding standards and continues in operation, but all excess assets are assigned to the plan for retirees, which is terminated to claim the reversion. When these techniques were approved in the early 1980s by the agencies charged with ERISA enforcement,[108] there was a rapid and dramatic increase in overfunded plan terminations.[109]

---

104   ERISA § 4044(d)(3), 29 U.S.C. § 1344(d)(3) (2006). Voluntary employee contributions are not taken into account in this computation because, pursuant to ERISA § 204(c)(4), 29 U.S.C. § 1054(c)(4) (2006), and I.R.C. § 411(d)(5) (2006), voluntary employee contributions made under a defined benefit plan are treated as constituting a separate defined contribution plan.

105   ERISA §§ 403(c)(1) (exception to anti-inurement rule), 4044(d)(1), 29 U.S.C. §§ 1103(c)(1), 1344(d)(1) (2006). These provisions were derived from the qualified plan exclusive benefit rule, which dates from 1938. The tax Code conditions qualification on proof that

> it is impossible, at any time prior to the satisfaction of all liabilities with respect to employees and their beneficiaries under the trust, for any part of the [trust] corpus or income to be (within the taxable year or thereafter) used for, or diverted to, purposes other than for the exclusive benefit of his employees or their beneficiaries. . . .

I.R.C. § 401(a)(2) (2006).

106   ERISA § 4044(d)(2), 29 U.S.C. § 1344(d)(2) (2006).

107   The exclusive benefit rule, the anti-inurement rule, and the prohibited-transaction rule all expressly except transfers on plan termination that are authorized by section 4044, which permits reversions under the conditions described above. ERISA §§ 403(c)(1), 404(a)(1), 408(b)(9), 29 U.S.C.A. §§ 1103(c)(1), 1104(a)(1), 1108(b)(9) (2006); see I.R.C. §§ 401(a)(2), 4975(d)(12) (2006).

108   Rev. Rul. 83-52, 1983-1 C.B. 156; U.S. Department of Treasury, U.S. Department of Labor, Pension Benefit Guaranty Corporation, *Joint Implementation Guidelines for Terminations of Defined Benefit Pension Plans*, reprinted in 23 Tax Notes 1088 (1984) [hereinafter *Joint Implementation Guidelines*].

109   For a full account of the history of these developments and the policy issues involved, see the outstanding article by Norman P. Stein, *Reversions from Pension Plans: History, Policies and Prospects*, 44 Tax L. Rev. 259 (1989).

To quell the rash of overfunded plan terminations, Congress took two steps. First, all plans involved in a spin-off termination are disqualified unless a proportionate part of the excess assets is allocated to each resulting plan; the entire surplus can no longer be allocated to the plan covering retirees (a plan destined for termination).[110] Second, to recapture tax benefits, a special 20 percent excise tax is imposed on employer reversions from qualified plans.[111] To discourage employers from simply terminating an overfunded defined benefit plan without making any provision for workers to obtain additional pension benefits, the excise tax is raised from 20 percent to 50 percent of the reversion unless the employer establishes a qualified replacement plan (which may be either defined benefit or defined contribution) covering at least 95 percent of the active participants in the terminated plan who continue as employees, and transfers 25 percent of the excess assets (reduced by certain benefit increases made under the terminating plan) to the replacement plan. Alternatively, the additional 30 percent exaction can be avoided without establishing a new plan, provided that 20 percent of the excess assets are used to provide a pro rata increase in accrued benefits under the terminating plan.[112] ERISA expressly obligates the fiduciary of the terminating plan and the fiduciary of the qualified replacement plan (if any) to follow the excise tax requirements, thereby subjecting the fiduciary's conduct to ERISA's civil enforcement mechanism.[113]

The rule that there can be no reversion prior to plan termination still stands. On a temporary basis, however, Congress has authorized one inroad on this principle: excess assets from an overfunded defined benefit plan may be transferred to a special account that is used to pay retiree health benefits.[114] Such a diversion of overfunding amounts to a prohibited reversion from an ongoing pension plan followed by a contribution of the reversion to a retiree health benefit (i.e., welfare) plan. Nevertheless, the pension plan is not disqualified, and the employer is excused from paying taxes on the transferred amounts. This flexibility to redirect excess pension savings to meet retiree health care needs illustrates once again the delicate balance between ERISA's promotional and protective urges, this time in the context of a trade-off between welfare and pension benefits.

---

110 I.R.C. § 414(*l*)(2) (2006). *See* S. Rep. No. 100-445, at 443–45 (1988). In addition, the *Joint Implementation Guidelines, supra* Chapter 9 note 108, required advance notice to all employees covered under a plan that will be split in two under a spin-off termination. These special notice requirements are now prescribed by 29 C.F.R. §§ 4041.23(c), 4041.24(f), 4041.27(a)(2) (2009).

111 I.R.C. § 4980(a) (2006).

112 I.R.C. § 4980(d) (2006).

113 ERISA § 404(d), 29 U.S.C. § 1104(d) (2006).

114 I.R.C. § 420(a), (b), (e)(2) (2006) (expires Dec. 31, 2013). *See* ERISA § 408(b)(13), 29 U.S.C. § 1108(b)(13) (2006) (exception to prohibited-transaction rule). Transfers made after August 17, 2006, may be used to finance estimated retiree health benefits for a period of up to ten years. I.R.C. § 420(f) (2006). Any assets so transferred are not counted toward satisfaction of the pension plan's minimum funding obligation. ERISA § 303(*l*), 29 U.S.C. § 1083(*l*) (2006); *see* I.R.C. § 430(*l*) (2006). Administrators must give advance notice of such transfers of excess pension assets to retiree health benefits accounts. *See* ERISA §§ 101(e), 502(a)(1)(A), (c)(1), 29 U.S.C. §§ 1021(e), 1132(a)(1)(A), (c)(1) (2006).

D. CONCLUSION

The defined benefit plan funding, insurance, and termination rules dramatically illustrate the tensions and trade-offs between ERISA's principal policies (*supra* Chapter 1C), particularly the delicate balance between the statute's worker protection and pension promotion impulses. Faced with public outcry over defeated worker expectations from terminated underfunded plans,[115] Congress might have simply mandated periodic, simplified disclosure of the plan's funded status and the sponsor's financial condition, leaving it to workers to determine how much risk they were willing to bear and to take steps to protect themselves (e.g., by seeking alternative employment or bargaining for better funding). Instead, Congress required systematic advance funding of accrued benefits, insisted that employers stand behind their pension promises by outlawing disclaimer of liability for unfunded benefits, and instituted a mandatory government-run insurance program to guarantee most pensions in the event that an underfunded plan is terminated and the sponsor is unable to make good the shortfall.

Those substantive defined benefit plan quality controls were tempered by the recognition of cost constraints inherent in a system of voluntary plan sponsorship. Immediate full funding was not required, for that would have deterred employers from granting past-service benefits and discouraged the formation or expansion of defined benefit plans. The compromise, long-term amortization of past-service benefits, concedes an extended period of underfunding, during which the PBGC termination insurance program protects participants. To contain insurance costs and limit moral hazard, not all benefits are guaranteed, which leaves participants exposed to a residual risk of loss from underfunding, and leaves a role for disclosure rules (notice of underfunding and of limits on the PBGC insurance) so workers can respond.

Since ERISA's enactment, PBGC losses have led Congress to repeatedly tighten the funding and insurance rules. Over time, PBGC insurance premiums have been made more risk-based (reducing the cross-subsidy from health sponsors to workers in failing industries), and financially healthy sponsors have been barred from terminating underfunded plans. To reduce the risk of insured losses, past-service liability amortization periods have been reduced from 40 to 30, to 18, and now 7 years, discretion in setting actuarial assumptions has been restricted, and the flexibility ERISA originally preserved in the selection of the plan's actuarial funding method was eliminated by the 2006 amendments.

These restrictions on employer autonomy have started to pinch—since the 1990s there has been an accelerating trend away from defined benefit plans, as sponsors prohibit new entrants or freeze benefit accrual under existing plans, convert their defined benefit plans to cash balance or other hybrid plans, or terminate their defined benefit

---

115   *See* James A. Wooten, *"The Most Glorious Story of Failure in the Business"*: *The Studebaker-Packard Corporation and the Origins of ERISA*, 49 Buff. L. Rev. 683 (2001); Michael S. Gordon, *Overview: Why Was ERISA Enacted?*, *in* S. Spec. Comm. on Aging, 98th Cong., The Employee Retirement Income Security Act of 1974: The First Decade 1, 8, 11 (Comm. Print 1984).

plans and substitute 401(k) or other less costly defined contributions programs. As the walls close in, employers are voting with their feet, fleeing the defined benefit pension system. But that exodus carries with it a fundamental realignment of risks and responsibilities: in a defined contribution universe, workers typically have to make savings and investment decisions for themselves, conserve their resources in retirement, suffer the consequences of their own mistakes, and bear the burden of financial and economic calamities over which they have no control. Retirement is a whole new world out there, and it's not for the fainthearted.[116]

---

116   *See generally* EDWARD A. ZELINSKY, THE ORIGINS OF THE OWNERSHIP SOCIETY (2007).

PART IV

Tax Controls
Retirement Savings and Health Care

Chapter 10

Taxes and Retirement Saving

ERISA erected a "comprehensive and reticulated"[1] structure of pension regulation, including both conduct and content controls, upon a foundation laid by the Internal Revenue Code's preexisting (albeit embryonic) criteria for granting favorable tax treatment to qualified pension, profit-sharing, stock bonus, and annuity plans.[2] Indeed, that favorable tax treatment was largely responsible for the rapid growth of the private pension system in the latter half of the twentieth century, and many of the problems that ERISA addressed had emerged because of the rudimentary nature of prior tax law requirements. Aside from the PBGC termination insurance system, Congress replicated all of ERISA's pension content controls in the Internal Revenue Code, imposing them as additional conditions on attaining qualified plan status.[3] This duplication supplements ERISA's enforcement regime, bolstering it with a powerful tax-based incentive to comply that is backed by regular expert monitoring (IRS audits).[4]

The special tax treatment accorded qualified deferred compensation implicates traditional tax policy concerns about equity, efficiency, and administrability, and those norms have far-reaching implications that extend well beyond ERISA's principal policies (*see* Chapter 1C). Consequently, the Code imposes tax controls on qualified plans that are distinct from and apply in addition to those qualification criteria that reiterate ERISA's pension content controls. The favorable tax treatment of qualified plans

---

1 Nachman Corp. v. PBGC, 446 U.S. 359, 361 (1980).

2 With respect to conduct controls, ERISA's fiduciary duties have antecedents in the requirement that the assets of a qualified pension, profit-sharing, or stock bonus plan be held "for the exclusive benefit of [the employer's] employees or their beneficiaries," I.R.C. § 401(a)(2) (2006), and the long-standing requirement that a qualified plan must be a "definite written program or arrangement which is communicated to employees," Treas. Reg. § 1.401-2(a)(2) (as amended in 1976), created the prospect that participants might have enforceable contract rights. With respect to content controls, before ERISA the IRS sometimes insisted that qualified plans provide pre-retirement vesting to prevent a higher rate of turnover among rank-and-file employees from causing forfeitures that would skew the amount of deferred compensation actually paid so as to discriminate in favor of highly compensated employees. S. Rep. No. 93-383, at 44–45 (1973), *reprinted in* 1 ERISA Legislative History, *supra* Chapter 1 note 56, at 1069, 1112–13; Rev. Rul. 71-263, 1971-1 C.B. 125; *see* Rev. Rul. 68-302, 1968-1 C.B. 163; Rev. Rul. 73-299, 1973-2 C.B. 137.

3 Specifically, the pension content controls imposed by parts 2 and 3 of ERISA Title I (including the participation, benefit accrual, vesting, anti-alienation, spousal protection, and minimum funding standards) were also incorporated in the qualified plan provisions by ERISA Title II. In addition, the prohibited-transaction rules of ERISA §§ 406–408, 29 U.S.C. §§ 1104–1108 (2006), were reproduced in I.R.C. § 4975 (2006). With a few exceptions (including the prohibited-transaction rules), the pension conduct controls were assigned to the exclusive domain of labor law.

4 Historically, overlapping labor and tax law jurisdictions are more accurately ascribed to political considerations than to the functional advantage of increased compliance through tax enforcement. In a colossal political miscalculation, the Senate Finance Committee derailed comprehensive pension legislation in 1972 at the behest of business groups and the Nixon Administration. The resulting public outcry gave momentum to the reform movement and assured the cooperation of the tax-writing committees in the Ninety-Third Congress. Michael S. Gordon, *Overview: Why Was ERISA Enacted? in* S. Spec. Comm. on Aging, 98th Cong., The Employee Retirement Income Security Act of 1974: The First Decade 1, 23–25 (Comm. Print 1984).

provides an inducement to saving, and the tax controls seek to structure the incentive so that it induces retirement savings that would not otherwise occur. The tax controls, in other words, are an effort to properly target and control the tax subsidy.

This chapter begins with an examination of the standard treatment of deferred compensation (so-called "nonqualified" deferred compensation) under the federal income tax, and compares that approach with the taxation of amounts deferred under qualified pension, profit-sharing, stock bonus, and annuity plans ("qualified" deferred compensation). Section A also explores the relationship between such qualified retirement plans and other tax-favored savings arrangements, including traditional and Roth Individual Retirement Accounts (IRAs). The study then takes up the qualified plan rules that have no ERISA counterparts—in the terminology used here, these are the "tax controls." Section B is devoted to the nondiscrimination rules, which are the central mechanism for channeling public assistance into additional savings, but their efficacy is highly sensitive to workforce composition, income tax rates, and the availability of other tax-sheltered savings opportunities. Section C turns to a set of tax controls that limit the amount of the tax subsidy: caps on qualified plan savings, advance funding limits, and distribution timing constraints. Section D considers a number of proposals that would reform or replace the nondiscrimination rules, including some observations on the future of the (semi-) private pension system.

A. TAXATION OF DEFERRED COMPENSATION

Nonqualified Deferred Compensation

General tax timing principles provide that income is taxable in the year to which it is properly attributable under the taxpayer's method of accounting.[5] Except for the owners of some unincorporated businesses, nearly all individuals use the cash receipts and disbursements method of accounting (also know as the *cash method* or *cash-basis accounting*), according to which items of income are reported for the taxable year in which they are actually or constructively received.[6] Constructive receipt occurs when income, although not actually reduced to the taxpayer's possession,

> is credited to his account, set apart for him, or otherwise made available so that he may draw upon it at any time, or so that he could have drawn upon it during the taxable year if notice of intention to withdraw had been given. However, income is not constructively received if the taxpayer's control of its receipt is subject to substantial limitations or restrictions.[7]

So under the cash method, *unfunded* deferred compensation is *ordinarily* not taxable until the amount is actually paid, even though a legal right to payment has been earned by the performance of services. The qualifications—"unfunded" and "ordinarily"—are hugely important, however.

---

5   I.R.C. §§ 446(a), 451(a) (2006).
6   Treas. Reg. § 1.451-1(a) (as amended in 1993).
7   Treas. Reg. § 1.451-2(a) (as amended in 1979).

Other rules come into play if a deferred compensation obligation is advance-funded rather than simply being left to payment out of the employer's general assets when the time comes. If property is transferred as compensation for services, such in-kind compensation is taxable to the person who performed the services (whether employee or independent contractor) in the first taxable year in which the transferee's rights in the property first become transferable or not subject to a substantial risk of forfeiture.[8] Where in-kind compensation comes with significant strings attached, this rule takes a wait-and-see approach to taxation, deferring inclusion in gross income until it becomes reasonably clear that contingencies will be resolved in the worker's favor (so that the recipient will get to keep the property). The amount included in gross income is the unrestricted fair market value of the property at the time the property first becomes transferable or not subject to a substantial risk of forfeiture (whichever occurs earlier) reduced by any amount paid for the property.[9] A condition that requires the future performance of substantial services constitutes a substantial risk of forfeiture.[10]

---

8   I.R.C. § 83(a) (2006). "Transferable" in this context has a special meaning and does not refer to the mere existence of the power of alienation. Instead, property is transferable only if a transferee's rights in such property are not subject to a substantial risk of forfeiture. *Id.* § 83(c)(2). Hence "transferable" refers to the ability to transfer free of the risk of loss, and the critical event under section 83(a)—the moment when the property first becomes transferable or not subject to a substantial risk of forfeiture—is the earliest time when the risk of loss is actually eliminated or could be lifted simply by transferring the property. Thus everything comes down to the actual or constructive elimination of the substantial risk of forfeiture. Accordingly, the two conditions under section 83(a) will sometimes be referred to simply as not subject to a substantial risk of forfeiture.

    Even if the property is received by a spouse, child, or another beneficiary, the income is taxed of the person who performed the services. *Id.* In this context, section 83 merely codifies the assignment-of-income doctrine, the general principle that income from services is taxable to the person who earns it, regardless of who actually receives it. Lucas v. Earl, 281 U.S. 111 (1930); Helvering v. Eubank, 311 U.S. 122 (1940) (labor income is taxed to the service provider whether the right to collect the income is assigned before or after services are performed).

9   I.R.C. § 83(a) (2006). Temporary restrictions on transfer, such as prohibitions on assignment or the imposition of a formula price (so-called lapse restrictions), are ignored in determining the amount of income from in-kind compensation. *Id.* § 83(a)(1) (parenthetical clause); Treas. Reg. § 1.83-1(a)(1)(i) (as amended in 2003), *id.* § 1.83-3(h), -3(i) (as amended in 2005). In order to prevent abuse, this rule deliberately disregards the fact that such restrictions may depress value and so, in principle, limit the extent of enrichment. Prior to the enactment of section 83, cooperatively imposed formal restrictions had been used to obtain unjustified tax deferral. *See* Sakol v. Comm'r, 574 F.2d 694 (2d Cir. 1978) (rejecting constitutional challenge to temporary overtaxation mandated by inclusion of unrestricted fair market value). Permanent formula price constraints (so-called nonlapse restrictions) are taken into account in determining the amount included in gross income. Treas. Reg. § 1.83-3(h) (as amended in 2005), *id.* § 1.83-5(a) (1978).

10   I.R.C. § 83(c)(1) (2006). Contingencies that do not depend upon the future performance of substantial services may or may not constitute a substantial risk of forfeiture. In general, a risk of forfeiture is substantial if there is a significant likelihood that the forfeiture condition will be triggered and enforced, as determined by a realistic evaluation of all the facts and circumstances. *See* Treas. Reg. § 1.83-3(c) (as amended in 2005). A requirement that property be retransferred to the employer if the employee is discharged for cause or for committing a crime

If employer stock or other property is transferred to an employee outright (i.e., unconditionally) as current in-kind compensation, then there is no risk of loss that would defer taxation, and the worker must include in gross income the value of the property on receipt (less the amount paid for it, if any). On the other hand, if company stock is transferred to an employee subject to the condition that the shares be returned to the employer if the employee separates from service within 12 years after receiving the stock, then the value of the shares would never be taxed to an employee who fails to satisfy the employment condition, while a worker who stays on long enough would not include the stock in income until 12 years after receipt and would then report its current value.[11]

"Property," for purposes of I.R.C. § 83, consists of real and personal property of all sorts "other than either money or an unfunded and unsecured promise to pay money or property in the future," and it specifically includes "a beneficial interest in assets (including money) which are transferred or set aside from the claims of creditors of the transferor, for example, in a trust or escrow account."[12] This definition determines

---

is not a substantial risk of forfeiture, while loss upon accepting employment with a competitor is not "ordinarily" considered to represent a substantial risk, but may do so if the particular facts (such as the age and skill level of the employee and his or her alternative employment opportunities) indicate that there is a realistic possibility that the eventuality will come to pass. *Id.* -3(c)(2).

11 Dividends paid while the stock remains subject to the substantial risk of forfeiture would be taxed to the employee, but as additional compensation (ordinary income), rather than as dividends (eligible for reduced tax rates under section 1(h) at the time of this writing). Treas. Reg. § 1.83-1(a)(1) (as amended in 2003) (penultimate sentence).

It should also be noted that the conclusion in the text assumes that the employee(s) awarded the contingent stock are not disproportionately older workers who would be close to retirement age upon satisfaction of the 12-year service condition. If that assumption is incorrect, then the arrangement arguably constitutes a pension plan under ERISA § 3(2)(A), 29 U.S.C. § 1002(2)(A) (2006), because, it would operate to provide retirement income to employees as a result of surrounding circumstances. Due to the risk of forfeiture, an employee receiving such a stock award could not prudently consume its value during the interim, resulting in preservation of the asset throughout the forfeiture period, at the close of which the stock's value is available to finance retirement needs. *See supra* Chapter 2C. If the contingent stock awards are a pension plan, then the 12-year employment condition is unlawful because ERISA mandates faster vesting (presumably either 3-year cliff or 2-to-6-year graded vesting for defined contribution plans under ERISA § 203(a)(2)(B), 29 U.S.C. § 1053(a)(2)(B) (2006), *see supra* Chapter 7C), and that earlier elimination of the risk of loss would correspondingly trigger taxation sooner under I.R.C. § 83 (2006). Query whether earlier vesting by operation of law eliminates the incentive for long-term saving such that the arrangement would no longer satisfy ERISA's definition of pension plan? (That is, this situation presents a potential circularity problem.)

12 Treas. Reg. § 1.83-3(e) (as amended in 2005). The exclusion from the definition of property of a legally binding but unsecured promise to pay ("an unfunded and unsecured promise to pay money or property in the future") preserves cash-basis accounting. A contractual right to future payment is income under the accrual method as soon as it has been earned by performance; not so under the cash method because there is no constructive receipt until the time for payment falls due. If a general creditor's contractual right to future payment were deemed property so as to trigger inclusion as in-kind compensation, section 83 would in effect require accrual method accounting for deferred payment obligations, swallowing up the cash method.

the scope of the rules governing taxation of in-kind compensation and is the source of a fundamental distinction in tax treatment between "funded" and "unfunded" deferred compensation. Because a mere "unsecured promise to pay money or property in the future" is not subject to section 83, the general rules of cash-basis accounting apply, with the result that such earned but unsecured deferred compensation is not income until it is received. In contrast, if the promise to pay in the future is backed by a transfer of money or property in trust, the beneficiary's interest in the trust (which constitutes an equitable ownership interest in the underlying assets) is subject to section 83, and the person who performed the services will be taxed as soon as the beneficiary's interest is substantially vested. That could be immediately on contribution to the trust if the interest is unconditional, or at some later time when conditions are satisfied and the risk of loss is eliminated. Significantly, section 83 can trigger taxation of such "funded" deferred compensation far in advance of actual distribution. If, however, the employee's interest in deferred compensation remains forfeitable until the time specified for payment—for example, if payment at age 65 is conditioned on continued employment until that time—then section 83(a) delays taxation until distribution (just as cash-basis accounting would if the promise of future payment were unfunded).

Section 83 may call for the taxation of funded deferred compensation in advance of receipt, but "funded" and "unfunded" must be understood as loose references to the key classification, "an unfunded and unsecured promise to pay money or property in the future"—as references, that is, to whether a payment obligation is property within the meaning of section 83. In fact, use of the terms *funded* and *unfunded* to differentiate the respective spheres in which the in-kind compensation regime and cash-basis accounting hold sway is something of a misnomer because security for payment has proven to be the critical consideration. An advance funding vehicle known as a "rabbi trust" was developed in the 1980s to provide a source of funds to pay promised deferred compensation without triggering taxation in advance of receipt.[13] Under a rabbi trust, the employer makes contributions to the trust as services are performed, and the trustee invests the assets and distributes deferred compensation at the times specified in the plan (typically upon a participant's retirement, death or disability); but the trust instrument expressly provides that if the employer becomes insolvent, the trustee shall cease making distributions and all trust assets will thenceforth be held for the benefit of the employer's general creditors.[14] The IRS ruled that neither the creation of the trust nor

---

13   The arrangement is so named because the first IRS letter ruling analyzing the tax consequences of such a funding vehicle involved a trust established by a congregation for the benefit of its rabbi. I.R.S. Priv. Ltr. Rul. 81-13-107 (Dec. 31, 1980). The rabbi trust device quickly became very popular (for the reason explained *infra* note 14), and the IRS was inundated with requests for private rulings. Eventually the IRS responded by issuing model rabbi trust language that taxpayers may adopt with assurance that employees will not be taxed prior to distribution of the deferred compensation. Rev. Proc. 92-64, 1992-2 C.B. 422.

14   As the insolvency contingency indicates, a rabbi trust does not protect plan participants from the employer's creditors. Instead of security from creditors, the advantage of a rabbi trust lies in the security it provides in the event of a change of control of the sponsoring employer. Participating employees are typically incumbent management whose positions may be in jeopardy following a hostile takeover or other change in control. A hostile new management team

the employer's contribution of assets constituted a transfer of property subject to section 83. Because there was no constructive receipt, the IRS further concluded that taxation would be deferred until distribution. The rabbi trust rulings demonstrated that insulation from the payor's creditors is the key element of "property" for purposes of section 83, and that absent such protection, the time for taxation of deferred compensation is given by the principles of cash-method accounting.[15]

A remarkable feature of the rabbi trust rulings is that the IRS expressly conditioned its conclusions concerning the tax consequences of the arrangement on the labor law status of the program under ERISA Title I.[16] Specifically, the tax results (inapplicability of section 83 and delayed inclusion under the cash method) are contingent on the deferred compensation program qualifying as a "top-hat" plan: an unfunded plan "maintained by an employer primarily for the purpose of providing deferred compensation to a select group of management or highly compensated employees." While never fully elaborated, the IRS apparently reasons that (1) ERISA creates

---

may be reluctant to give full effect to deferred compensation programs designed by and for ousted executives, possibly at the expense of shareholders. A rabbi trust may provide that following a change of control, the trust instrument cannot be amended, nor can the trustee be removed without the consent of the plan participants, and may provide for court appointment or participant involvement in the selection of any successor trustee. By triggering more robust insulation from new management, plan participants may avoid the expense and delay of litigation to enforce their rights to deferred compensation. A rabbi trust, in other words, protects incumbent management from a change of heart following a shift in employer ownership or control.

15   The section 83 regulations state that an "unfunded and unsecured promise to pay money or property in the future" is not property, and clearly indicate that a promise to pay that is both funded *and* secured is to be classified as property. Treas. Reg. § 1.83-3(e) (as amended in 2005). The regulatory definition is silent (perhaps deliberately noncommittal) about the status of a promise that is funded but unsecured, as in the case of a rabbi trust, where, as a practical matter, the promise of future payment is advance funded (assets are segregated and invested to provide means of payment), but the assets remain at risk in the event of insolvency (unsecured). As a matter of interpretation, the rabbi trust rulings resolve this ambiguous case, and in concluding that section 83 does not apply, the IRS implicitly rules that "property" status turns only upon security from the employer's general creditors.

The rabbi trust rulings are also conditioned upon the fact that participants' rights to deferred compensation under the plan and trust were expressly declared to be nontransferable. *See, e.g.,* I.R.S. Priv. Ltr. Rul. 92-28-026 (Apr. 13, 1992) (participant's interest under plan and trust may not be anticipated, assigned, mortgaged, pledged, or encumbered); Rev. Proc. 92-64, § 5.02, text Section 13(b), 1992-2 C.B. 422, 427 (required anti-alienation language of model rabbi trust). Presumably this anti-alienation condition is imposed to avoid application of the cash equivalence doctrine, under which receipt of a promissory note or other transferable promise to pay is treated in certain cases as the receipt of cash and taxed immediately. *Compare* Cowden v. Comm'r, 289 F.2d 20, 24 (5th Cir. 1961) (conditions for application of cash equivalence doctrine), *with* Williams v. Comm'r, 28 T.C. 1000 (1957), *acq.*, 1958-1 C.B. 6 (no income on receipt of note where maker was without funds and repeated attempts to sell note were unsuccessful).

16   *E.g.,* I.R.S. Priv. Ltr. Rul. 92-28-026 (Apr. 13, 1992) (conclusions introduced with proviso "that the creation of the Trust does not cause the Plan to be other than 'unfunded' for purposes of Title I of ERISA"); Rev. Proc. 92-65, § 3.01(d), 1992-2 C.B. 428 (to obtain favorable letter ruling on constructive receipt "the plan must state that it is the intention of the parties that the arrangements be unfunded for tax purposes and for purposes of Title I of ERISA").

property for purposes of I.R.C. § 83 because it insulates employee benefit plan assets from the employer's creditors, and (2) application of section 83 demands taxation in advance of distribution because mandatory pension vesting extinguishes any substantial risk of forfeiture.[17] Top-hat plans are excused from ERISA's general asset protection rules, however.[18] Therefore, in the case of a top-hat plan, federal law would not override the rabbi trust provision, and the exposure of top-hat plan assets to general creditors sidesteps section 83. Top-hat plan treatment requires both that the deferred compensation arrangement be "unfunded" and limited to a "select group of management or highly compensated employees." Taking its lead from the IRS, the Labor Department interprets unfunded to mean unsecured from the employer's creditors, so the advance segregation of assets does not cause a rabbi trust to be funded.[19] If the program's coverage extends beyond a select group of management or highly compensated employees, however, then the top-hat plan exemption is unavailing, [20] and ERISA's protections would trigger taxation in advance of receipt. For this reason the coverage of nonqualified deferred compensation programs is strictly limited.[21]

The rules governing the timing of the employee's inclusion of nonqualified deferred compensation also control the timing of the employer's deduction. Regardless of the employer's usual method of accounting, I.R.C. § 404(a)(5) suspends the employer's deduction until the employee includes the deferred compensation in gross income. This matching principle is necessary to achieve approximate tax neutrality between current and deferred compensation.[22] That is, if the employer and the employee have

---

17   *See* ERISA § 403(c)(1), 29 U.S.C. § 1103(c)(1) (2006) ("[T]he assets of a plan shall never inure to the benefit of any employer and shall be held for the exclusive purpose of providing benefits to participants in the plan and their beneficiaries and defraying reasonable expenses of administering the plan."); ERISA § 203(a), 29 U.S.C. § 1053(a) (2006) (mandatory pension plan vesting).

18   ERISA § 401(a)(1), 29 U.S.C. § 1101(a)(1) (2006). *See generally supra* Chapter 2D.

19   ERISA Advisory Op. 90-14A (U.S. Dep't of Labor 1990).

20   ERISA Advisory Op. 90-14A, n.1 (U.S. Dep't of Labor 1990). The Labor Department defines management or highly compensated employees functionally, as those individuals who "by virtue of their position or compensation level, have the ability to affect or substantially influence, through negotiation or otherwise, the design and operation of their deferred compensation plan, taking into consideration any risks attendant thereto, and, therefore, would not need the substantive rights and protections of Title I." *Id.*

21   This observation is not limited to rabbi trust arrangements. It also applies to a naked promise of deferred compensation that is not limited to a select group. In many instances, a broader promise of specified future benefits would trigger ERISA's pension plan funding obligations, ERISA §§ 301(a)(3), 302(a), 29 U.S.C. §§ 1081(a)(3), 1082(a) (2006). Such advance funding, combined with insulation from the employer's creditors, would cause the transfer of property necessary to bring I.R.C. § 83 into play. If instead, the promise of future payments is in the nature of a profit-sharing plan, with amounts credited for future payment (together with interest or earnings thereon) on a contingent or discretionary basis, then ERISA's advance funding rules would not apply. ERISA § 301(a)(8), 29 U.S.C. § 1081(a)(8) (2006).

22   Judge Halpern, concurring in *Albertson's Inc. v. Commissioner*, 95 T.C. 415 (1990), *aff'd*, 42 F.3d 537 (9th Cir. 1994), explained:

    To allow an accrual method employer to deduct interest [credited to executive deferred compensation accounts] in advance of inclusion by employees would frustrate the matching principle apparent in the statute. It can be said that the effect of that matching principle is that

access to the same investment opportunities and are subject to the same tax rate, then, under the matching rule, the employee will have the same amount available after taxes whether he receives $X in current compensation and invests the after-tax amount for some period, or instead leaves the $X in the employers' hands under an agreement that the employer will invest the deferred compensation on behalf of the employee and pay the full amount accumulated to the employee at the end of the period.[23]

In 2004, Congress revisited constructive receipt and its relation to section 83 and concluded that aggressive tax planners had gone too far. The result, section 409A, imposes new limits on nonqualified deferred compensation plans. The limits are of two sorts. First, the participant's control over distribution timing is cabined: (1) the election to defer must generally be made before the start of the taxable year in which the services are performed, (2) the plan must provide that deferred amounts cannot be distributed earlier than six specified times (separation from service, disability, death, a time specified when the compensation is deferred, change of ownership or control of the corporate payor, or an unforeseeable emergency), and (3) subsequent elections to further delay payment must generally be made at least 12 months before the payment is due and in some cases (distributions tied to separation from service, change of control, or a date fixed by the plan) must call for at least five years of additional deferral.[24] Second, certain rabbi trusts that offer de facto creditor protection, including offshore trusts and trusts that restrict assets to payment of benefits if the employer's financial health deteriorates, are treated as funded. Failure to comply with these requirements triggers taxation of the deferred compensation as soon as it is not subject to a substantial risk of forfeiture, regardless of whether any assets have been set aside to finance future payment. This will often require deferred amounts to be included in gross income far in advance of actual payment.[25] Moreover, if the plan fails to comply with the new distribution timing rules, then interest is charged from the time the compensation is earned, and a 20 percent penalty tax is imposed.[26] Where they apply, the section 409A interest and penalty exaction biases the tax system against

---

the employer is being taxed in substitution for not currently taxing the employee. If the employer were allowed an interest deduction, then the present discounted value of the tax burden on the employer would not be equivalent (i.e., would be less than) an immediate tax on the employee (assuming, of course, equal tax rates).

97 T.C. at 432 (footnotes omitted).

23   If the employer's tax rate is lower than the employee's, there will be an advantage in deferred compensation, while tax considerations favor current compensation if the employee's tax rate is lower. The tax-exempt employer (zero tax rate) presents a particularly common and acute case favoring deferral, which led to special rules governing nonqualified deferred compensation programs sponsored by state and local governments, charitable organizations, and other tax-exempt employers. *See* I.R.C. § 457 (2006). Deferred compensation arrangements of foreign corporations and of partnerships having foreign persons or tax-exempt organizations as partners also present considerable potential for abuse (deferral by the employee without surrogate taxation of the employer), which led Congress in 2008 to restrict deferral in such instances. I.R.C § 457A (West Supp. 2009).

24   I.R.C. § 409A(a)(2)-(4) (2006).

25   I.R.C. § 409A(a)(1)(A), (b)(1) (2006).

26   I.R.C. § 409A(a)(1)(B) (2006).

deferred compensation.[27] Thus, Congress has constructed a tax regime that distinguishes between "good" nonqualified deferred compensation, meaning arrangements that comply with section 409A and therefore get the benefit of the tax neutrality (with deferred amounts taxed to the employee only upon distribution), and "bad" nonqualified deferred compensation, meaning arrangements that run afoul of section 409A and so are taxed more heavily than current compensation (with deferred amounts taxed upon substantial vesting, which might be long before distribution).

Qualified Retirement Plans

While slightly infringed by section 409A, the long-standing goal of tax neutrality between current and nonqualified deferred compensation remains the norm. In contrast, markedly favorable tax treatment is accorded compensation deferred through a qualified pension, profit-sharing, stock bonus, or annuity plan (qualified retirement plans).[28] There are three major components of the preferential income tax treatment of such qualified deferred compensation.[29] First, the employer receives a current deduction (subject to certain limits) for amounts actually contributed to the plan.[30] Second, the trust that holds the plan assets is generally exempt from taxation on its investment income.[31] Third, any amount contributed on behalf of an individual employee is not included in gross income until actually distributed by the plan; upon distribution, trust

---

27 Michael Doran, *Executive Compensation Reform and the Limits of Tax Policy*, Tax Policy Center Discussion Paper No. 18 (Nov. 2004), *available at* http://www.taxpolicycenter.org/ UploadedPDF/311113_TPC_dp18.pdf.

28 Because qualified deferred compensation must be advance funded and protected from the employer's creditors, it entails a transfer of property within the meaning of section 83, but a special exception removes qualified retirement plans from the operation of that provision. I.R.C. § 83(e)(2) (2006).

29 In addition to favorable income tax treatment, contributions to and distributions from qualified retirement plans are generally exempt from the federal payroll taxes, including Social Security and unemployment taxes. I.R.C. § 3121(a)(5) (2006) (exclusion from taxable wages under FICA, the Federal Insurance Contributions Act, which finances Social Security and Medicare Hospital Insurance program), *id.* § 3306(b)(5) (exclusion from taxable wages under FUTA, the Federal Unemployment Tax Act). These exemptions confer a substantial benefit, as the combined employer and employee shares of the FICA tax amount to 15.3 percent of wages, while the employer's FUTA tax rate is 6 percent of wages (but only on the first $7,000 of annual wages). These payroll tax exemptions do *not* apply to elective or salary reduction contributions made under a 401(k) plan or a 403(b) tax-sheltered annuity, however. *Id.* §§ 3121(a)(5)(D), (v)(1), 3306(b)(5)(D), (r)(1). Note that the payroll tax exemptions have the greatest value with respect to qualified deferred compensation earned by moderately paid workers; due to the limit on wages subject to Social Security taxes (the contribution and benefit base, $106,800 in 2009), and the $7,000 wage limit under FUTA, additional compensation earned by highly paid employees is subject only to the Medicare Hospital Insurance tax (1.45 percent each on the employer and the employee).

30 I.R.C. § 404(a)(1)-(3) (2006).

31 I.R.C. § 501(a) (2006).

ERISA: PRINCIPLES OF EMPLOYEE BENEFIT LAW

or annuity earnings are taxable to the recipient as well.[32] In some circumstances, distributions may be eligible for further tax deferral if they are directly transferred to or promptly reinvested in another qualified plan or an individual retirement account (so-called rollovers).[33] Even absent a rollover, if securities of the employer corporation are distributed, the net appreciation in the value of the securities that accrued during the plan's ownership may not be taxable until the employee later sells the stock or other securities.[34] Observe that these rules grant the employer a deduction upon contribution even though the employee does not simultaneously report income, nor is the investment income taxed until distributed to the employee. The resulting deferred taxation of both compensation and earnings thereon is the source of the qualified plan tax preference. Because the deferral may extend over decades, its value is immense. Assuming constant tax rates, deferral is equivalent to exempting from tax the investment's yield during the period of deferral.[35] In 2005, the value of assets held in qualified trusts was $5,082 billion[36]; assuming an average 10 percent return and 25 percent tax rate, the tax subsidy for qualified plan savings is worth about $130 billion *annually*.

The operational tax rules applied to qualified deferred compensation are straightforward (as the description in the preceding paragraph suggests), but they come into play only if the deferred compensation is paid under a program that satisfies the definition of a qualified plan. The general definition of a qualified plan is extraordinarily long and complex; it imposes hundreds of conditions that must be satisfied to obtain favorable tax treatment. Some of this length and complexity is attributable to the fact that

---

32   I.R.C. §§ 83(e)(2), 402(a), 403(a)(1) (2006). Distributions are subject to state or local income taxation (if any) only by the state in which the recipient resides, not by the state where the deferred compensation was earned. 4 U.S.C. § 114 (2006); *see* H.R. Rep No. 104-389 (1995). Thus, a pension earned over a 30-year career of work in New York, for example, would be subject to no state income tax burden if the employee retires and moves to Florida or another state that does not impose a personal income tax. The federal ban on source-state taxation of pension income applies not only to qualified retirement savings programs, but also to non-qualified deferred compensation arrangements if the distributions are to be made in substantially equal installments over the life (or life expectancy) of the recipient or over a period of not less than ten years. 4 U.S.C. § 114(b)(1)(H)(i) (2006).
33   I.R.C. §§ 402(c), 401(a)(31), 403(a)(4), (5) (2006).
34   I.R.C. § 402(e)(4) (2006). Continued tax deferral is granted to net appreciation of employer securities attributable to employee after-tax contributions, presumably on the theory that the transition from indirect employee ownership (through a qualified plan) and direct ownership (post-distribution) is not a sufficient change to warrant gain recognition. In addition, however, appreciation on employer securities is also excluded if the securities are attributable to pre-tax employer contributions, but only if the securities are distributed as part of a lump-sum distribution. The deferral accorded appreciation in securities bought with employer contributions is not a product of general tax principles, but apparently persists as a residue of the favorable tax treatment formerly accorded lump-sum distributions from qualified plans.
35   See *infra* Chapter 10 note 43 and accompanying text for proof of this assertion. The equivalence between deferred taxation and tax exemption of the investment return means that the qualified plan tax preference may alternatively be viewed as having its source in section 501, the tax exemption of the qualified trust.
36   Employee Benefit Research Institute, EBRI Databook on Employee Benefits, Table 11.3(c) (Feb. 2007), http://www.ebri.org/pdf/publications/books/databook/DB.Chapter%2011.pdf.

Congress reproduced most of ERISA's pension plan content controls (specifically, the rules governing pension accumulation and distribution) in the tax definition of a qualified retirement plan.[37] But the definition also contains many conditions not found in ERISA. These independent tax law criteria (examined in Chapter 10B and 10C, below) attempt to properly target and contain the retirement savings tax subsidy.

Individual Retirement Accounts

Just under half of the U.S. labor force is covered under any form of employer-sponsored retirement savings program, and that number has remained essentially unchanged since the early 1970s. Is tax-subsidized retirement saving out of reach for people who happen to work for companies that do not sponsor any sort of qualified plan? In enacting ERISA. Congress sought to make the opportunity for tax-favored retirement savings available to all workers by creating a new savings vehicle, the individual retirement account (IRA).[38] Under the current version of the IRA rules, an individual with earned income is allowed to make tax-deductible contributions of up to $5,000 annually ($6,000 if the taxpayer is 50 years of age or older) to an individual retirement account.[39] If the taxpayer or the taxpayer's spouse is an active participant in an employer plan at any time during the taxable year, and if the taxpayer's adjusted gross income (computed with certain modifications) exceeds a specified threshold, then the maximum allowable contribution deduction is reduced.[40] This income phase-out permits low- and moderate-income workers to make tax-deductible IRA contributions even if they participate in a qualified plan, but high-income plan participants cannot supplement their qualified retirement plan savings in this manner. In addition to the contribution deduction, the IRA itself is exempt from tax, so that contributions and investment earnings are not subject to income tax until distributed.[41] Consequently, amounts saved in an IRA receive the same sort of long-term tax deferral as employer contributions to a qualified retirement plan.

---

37 See supra Chapters 7–8. The prospect of losing favorable tax treatment provides a powerful incentive for sponsors to keep their plans in compliance with the pension accumulation and distribution rules, including restrictions on age and service conditions and the minimum standards governing benefit accrual, vesting, anti-alienation, and spousal protection. While private parties lack standing to enforce the tax law, the duplication of these rules in the Code and ERISA assures that violations can still be redressed via ERISA's civil enforcement regime. See Chapter 5.

38 An IRA proposal was first advanced by the Nixon Administration, apparently as part of an unsuccessful effort to head off more comprehensive pension reform legislation. See Richard Nixon, Message from the President Concerning Private Pension Plans (Dec. 8, 1971), reprinted in PUBLIC PAPERS OF THE PRESIDENTS OF THE UNITED STATES: RICHARD NIXON, 1971, entry 384, at 1168 (1972); Michael S. Gordon, Overview: Why Was ERISA Enacted?, in S. SPEC. COMM. ON AGING, 98TH CONG., THE EMPLOYEE RETIREMENT INCOME SECURITY ACT OF 1974: THE FIRST DECADE, at 18.

39 I.R.C. § 219(a), (b) (2006).

40 I.R.C. § 219(g) (2006).

41 I.R.C. § 408(e)(1), (d)(1) (2006).

Effective in 1998, Congress sanctioned an alternative form of IRA, the "Roth IRA." Contributions to a Roth IRA are not deductible, but the account is tax-exempt, and qualified distributions are entirely excluded from gross income.[42] Thus, the principal difference between the traditional and the Roth IRA lies in the income tax treatment of contributions and distributions, which are reversed. Under a traditional IRA, both contributions and investment earnings go untaxed until distribution, while under a Roth IRA, contributions are tax-paid, but investment earnings get tax forgiveness. If certain conditions are satisfied, these two regimes are financially equivalent: tax deferral until distribution (the result of deductible contributions to a traditional IRA) has the same yield as immediate taxation of the amount invested (no deduction for Roth IRA contributions) combined with exempting the income from the investment from tax.[43] For example, assume that a taxpayer, whose marginal income tax rate is 35 percent, contributes $1,000 to a traditional IRA, where it earns 6 percent (compounded annually) for 12 years, at which time the entire balance of the account is distributed. The $1,000 IRA account balance will grow to $2,012.20 in that time $(= \$1,000 \times (1.06)^{12})$, and the 35 percent tax on the full amount distributed (contribution plus earnings) will leave $1,307.93 $(= 65$ percent of $2,012.20)$ after tax. Alternatively, if the contribution is not deductible, the taxpayer will have only $650 to invest after tax, which, at a 6 percent annual rate of return, will grow to $1,307.93 in 12 years $(= \$650 \times (1.06)^{12})$, and no further tax would be due on a qualified distribution from a Roth IRA. In contrast, outside of an IRA the $1,000 would be taxed initially, as would the annual 6 percent return, so that the $650 invested would grow at an after-tax rate of only 3.9 percent $(= 65\% \times 6\%)$ producing at the end of 12 years a total of only $1,028.73 $(= \$650 \times (1.039)^{12})$.

Immediate deduction and yield exemption are equivalent only if: (1) the taxpayer's marginal tax rate remains constant over the life of the account; (2) the contribution deduction produces immediate tax savings at that marginal rate (i.e., the deduction is neither limited nor deferred, and does not push the taxpayer into a lower rate bracket); and (3) investment opportunities at the assumed rate of return are not limited. The graduated rate structure of the federal income tax can cause an individual's tax rate to change due to a change in annual income. Consequently, the traditional IRA is the better choice for a taxpayer who expects to have a substantially lower annual income

---

42   I.R.C. § 408A(a), (c)(1), (d)(1) (2006).

43   Assume t is the taxpayer's marginal income tax rate and r is the annual rate of investment return, and let n represent the period (number of years) of the investment. Then a $1 contribution to a traditional IRA will grow to $(1 + r)^n$, and the entire balance will be taxed on distribution, yielding $(1 - t)(1 + r)^n$ after taxes. For a Roth IRA, because the contribution is nondeductible, the initial after-tax investment would be only $(1 - t)$; this amount would grow by a factor of $(1 + r)^n$, and no further taxes would be due upon distribution, which again yields $(1 - t)(1 + r)^n$ after taxes. Emil M. Sunley, Jr., *Employee Benefits and Transfer Payments*, *in* COMPREHENSIVE INCOME TAXATION 75, 77 n.5 (Joseph A. Pechman ed. 1977); Michael J. Graetz, *Implementing a Progressive Consumption Tax*, 92 HARV. L. REV. 1575, 1597–1623 (1979); DAVID F. BRADFORD & U.S. TREASURY TAX POLICY STAFF, BLUEPRINTS FOR BASIC TAX REFORM 107-11, 115–17 (2d ed. 1984).

during retirement. In contrast, taxpayers who expect Congress to hike income tax rates are better served by paying tax sooner under a Roth IRA.

Other technical differences can have an important bearing on the choice between traditional and Roth IRAs. The contribution limits for each form of account are coordinated,[44] and each has an income phase-out. Because the dollar amount of the maximum annual contribution is the same for traditional and Roth IRAs (generally, $5,000, inflation adjusted), but Roth accounts are funded with after-tax dollars, a taxpayer who can afford to make the maximum contribution to a Roth IRA despite the current tax burden can accumulate a larger amount.[45] The phase-out applies to a traditional IRA only if the taxpayer or his spouse is an active participant in a qualified plan, while the phase-out on allowable contributions to a Roth IRA applies generally. The income threshold that triggers the phase-out is substantially higher for Roth than for traditional IRAs, so middle-income taxpayers covered by an employer plan can contribute $5,000 to a Roth IRA even though they cannot make any deductible contributions to a traditional IRA.[46] In addition, Roth IRAs are not subject to the rules applicable to traditional IRAs prohibiting contributions after the account owner reaches age 70½, and requiring distributions to commence in the calendar year following the year in which the taxpayer reaches age 70½ (or the year she retires, if later).[47]

Curiously, the choice between a traditional and a Roth IRA is not irrevocable. A taxpayer who qualifies under both sets of rules may contribute to either or both a traditional and a Roth IRA in a given tax year, subject to a combined annual contribution limit.[48] Moreover, the owner of a traditional IRA can generally make a qualified rollover contribution to a Roth IRA regardless of the annual contribution limit simply by paying tax on the amount distributed from the traditional IRA and contributing the distribution (or any desired portion thereof) to a Roth IRA within 60 days.[49] Indeed, a traditional IRA may simply be converted to a Roth IRA, and if such rollovers or

---

44   I.R.C. §§ 219(b), 408A(c)(2) (2006).
45   Assuming, as in the preceding example, that the taxpayer is subject to a 35 percent marginal rate and that invested IRA funds will yield a 6 percent compound annual return for 12 years, then a $5,000 contribution to a traditional IRA will produce $6,940 after taxes (= $5,000 × $(1.06)^{12}$ × 65%), while a $5,000 Roth IRA contribution will produce $10,061 (= $5,000 × $(1.06)^{12}$). Of course, this is because a $5,000 pre-tax traditional IRA contribution is equivalent to an after-tax Roth IRA contribution of only $3,250 (= $5,000 × 65%) for a taxpayer subject to the 35 percent marginal rate; or, stated differently, a $5,000 Roth contribution is equivalent to a traditional IRA contribution of $7,692 (= $5,000/65%).
46   I.R.C. §§ 219(g)(3)(B), 408A(c)(3)(C) (2006).
47   I.R.C. § 408A(c)(4), (5) (2006).
48   I.R.C. § 408A(c)(2) (2006).
49   I.R.C. § 408A(c)(6) (2006) (qualified rollover contribution exempt from annual contribution limit), id. § 408A(d)(3)(A), (B) (rollover to Roth IRA conditioned on taxation of traditional IRA distribution), id. § 408A(e) (definition of qualified rollover contribution), id. § 408(d)(3) (60-day time limit). Prior to 2010, rollovers or conversions from a traditional to a Roth IRA were permitted only if the taxpayer's adjusted gross income did not exceed $100,000 and the taxpayer was not a married individual filing a separate return. I.R.C. § 408A(c)(3)(B) (2006) (in effect for taxable years beginning before January 1, 2010).

conversions occur in 2010, the taxpayer is allowed to report the income attributable to the traditional IRA distribution half in 2011 and half in 2012.[50]

The general equivalence between deferred inclusion (à la qualified plans and traditional IRAs) and yield exemption (à la Roth IRAs) is illustrated by recently-enacted permission to engraft Roth-style accounts on certain qualified plans. Some types of defined contribution plans are funded in whole or in part by employees, who make elective salary reduction contributions to their individual accounts. Under a 401(k) plan, for example, each eligible employee may choose whether to receive a portion of his compensation in cash or direct that it be contributed to his retirement savings account, and if the plan satisfies the definition of a qualified cash-or-deferred arrangement (CODA), the employee's elective deferral is generally treated as an excludible (i.e., pre-tax) employer contribution.[51] Similar elective deferrals are authorized under so-called tax-sheltered annuities (also known as 403(b) plans), a special qualified retirement savings program that can be provided for employees of tax-exempt charitable organizations and public schools.[52] Elective deferrals under 401(k) and 403(b) plans, together with any matching or nonelective employer contributions, historically received the same tax deferral treatment accorded other qualified retirement plans: contributions are excluded from the employee's gross income (even though currently deductible by a taxable employer), fund earnings accumulate tax-free, and contributions and earnings are taxed only when actually distributed to the employee.[53] Starting in 2006, however, 401(k) and 403(b) plans are allowed to offer employees the option to direct their elective deferrals into a separate "designated Roth account."[54] Contributions to such an account are includible in the employee's income (after-tax), but just as under a Roth IRA, qualified distributions are entirely tax-free, so that instead of tax deferral, the designated Roth account exempts the yield on elective

---

50   I.R.C. § 408A(d)(3)(C) (2006) (account conversion treated as rollover), I.R.C. § 408A(d)(3) (A)(iii) (2006) (amendment notes) (deferred inclusion in succeeding two taxable years of qualified rollover contributions occurring in 2010); Treas. Reg. § 1.408A-4 (as amended in 2008). The special rule for traditional-to-Roth rollovers or conversions occurring in 2010 is a budget gimmick enacted as part of the Tax Increase Prevention and Reconciliation Act of 2005 as a "revenue offset." Pub. L. No. 109-222, § 512, 120 Stat. 345, 365 (2006); H.R. Rep. No. 109-455, at 314 (2006) (Conf. Rep.) (liberalizing rules for traditional-to-Roth IRA rollovers and conversions projected to generate large revenue increases in 2001–2013, and second largest aggregate revenue offset over the ten-year budget window 2006–2015). Although Roth IRAs are projected to lose revenue in the long run relative to traditional IRAs, rollovers and conversions from traditional IRAs accelerate taxable distributions and therefore increase tax revenues during the limited ten-year forecasting period Congress uses for budget purposes.

51   I.R.C. §§ 401(k), 402(e)(3) (2006).

52   I.R.C. §§ 403(b)(1), 402(e)(3) (2006). TIAA-CREF (Teachers Insurance and Annuity Association—College Retirement Equities Fund), which administers retirement plans for more than 15,000 colleges, universities, schools, research centers, and other nonprofit institutions, is the premier 403(b) plan provider.

53   *See supra* Chapter 10 notes 28–34 and accompanying text.

54   I.R.C. § 402A (2006).

contributions.[55] Because designated Roth accounts are tax prepaid, participants who anticipate a tax increase can hedge that portion of their retirement savings.[56]

Other Tax-Favored Savings Vehicles

Congress has replicated the Roth IRA mechanism (nondeductible contributions and tax-exempt earnings) in the context of savings for education. Both a Coverdell education savings account (ESA) and a qualified tuition program (often known as a "529 plan") allow after-tax contributions to earn a tax-exempt investment return provided that distributions from the account are dedicated to the payment of qualified educational expenses.[57] Coverdell ESAs and 529 plans differ in their specification of qualified educational expenses.[58] Coverdell ESAs are subject to a contribution limit with an income phase-out,[59] but 529 plans are not so restricted,[60] which goes far to account for their popularity as college savings vehicles for high-income families.

The Bush Administration repeatedly proposed two more general Roth-IRA-like tax-favored savings devices, the "Retirement Savings Account" (RSA) and the

---

55   I.R.C. §§ 402A(a)(1), (d), 408A(d)(2)(A) (2006); Treas. Reg. § 1.402A-1 (as amended in 2007). To be a qualified distribution, the designated Roth account must, in general, have been held for a minimum of five taxable years. I.R.C. § 402A(d)(2)(B) (2006).

56   Rollover or conversion of prior accumulated elective contributions into a designated Roth account is not authorized, but distributions from such an account may be rolled over into another designated Roth account or Roth IRA. I.R.C. § 402A(c)(3) (2006). As part of a qualified plan, designated Roth accounts are subject to the minimum distribution rule which requires that distributions commence no later than the attainment of age 70½ or separation from service. I.R.C. § 401(a)(9) (West Supp. 2009). Roth IRAs are exempt from the minimum distribution rule. I.R.C. § 408A(c)(5) (2006). It appears that elective contributions and earnings accumulated in a designated Roth account could be rolled over into a Roth IRA in order to sidestep the minimum distribution rule.

57   I.R.C. § 530(a), (d)(2)(A) (2006) (Coverdell ESA earnings and distributions), id. § 529(a), (c)(1), (c)(3)(B)(ii) (529 plan earnings and distributions). Distributions not devoted to eligible educational expenses are taxed to the recipient to the extent of earnings, and a penalty is imposed by increasing the rate of tax on the includible amount by 10 percent unless an exception applies. Penalty exceptions are provided for distributions made on account of the death, disability, or receipt of a scholarship by the beneficiary. Id. §§ 530(d)(4), 529(c)(6).

58   Qualified education expenses under a 529 plan are generally limited to tuition and mandatory fees for higher education, plus room and board costs for students studying at least half-time. I.R.C. § 529(e)(3) (2006). In contrast, eligible education costs under a Coverdell ESA are broadly defined to include tuition and fees, books, supplies and equipment, and room and board, whether these expenses are for higher education or elementary or secondary school. Hence a Coverdell ESA distribution used to pay room and board at a private prep school would be tax-free. Id. § 530(d)(2), (3).

59   I.R.C. § 530(b)(1)(A) (2006) ($2,000 annual maximum and beneficiary must be under age 18), id. § 530(c) (income phase-out).

60   See I.R.C. §§ 529(b)(6) (2006), which requires only that a qualified tuition program must provide "adequate safeguards to prevent contributions on behalf of a designated beneficiary in excess of those necessary to provide for the qualified higher education expenses of the beneficiary."

"Lifetime Savings Account" (LSA). The scope and implications of these initiatives are discussed in Chapter 10D below.

B. TARGETING THE TAX SUBSIDY

The favorable tax treatment of qualified plans provides an inducement to saving. That favorable tax treatment is granted only if the plan satisfies certain tax law conditions designed to structure the incentive so that it induces retirement savings that would not otherwise occur. These tax controls, in other words, are an effort to properly target the tax subsidy and confine its magnitude. The tax controls fall into four broad categories: nondiscrimination rules, caps on qualified plan savings, advance funding limits, and distribution timing constraints. This section explores nondiscrimination in depth. Chapter 10C offers an overview of the remaining tax controls, which operate in combination to limit the amount of the tax subsidy.

Before doing so, however, it is useful to examine overall objectives with some care. Why do we want to encourage savings? Savings for what purpose(s)? Savings by whom? Answers to these questions will illuminate the function of the tax controls, and disagreement on these matters goes far to explaining the contradictions and instability of the pension tax rules.

The overall personal savings rate in the United States, as a percentage of disposable income, has undergone a fairly steady decline from about 10 percent in the early 1980s to less than 2 percent in 2007.[61] Because savings are the source of investment capital which fuels higher productivity and real wages, this decline signals danger for long-term economic growth. For that reason, many analysts and politicians now advocate measures to encourage savings generally, particularly measures that would move the federal tax system from a realized income tax toward a consumption tax. This macroeconomic concern has seen expression in recent years in a relaxation of various limits on tax-subsidized retirement savings, in the emergence of tax-favored educational savings (such as 529 plans), and in repeated calls for all-purpose Roth-IRA-like tax-advantaged savings accounts (discussed in Chapter 10D below).

Instead of encouraging savings generally, the traditional and still dominant justification for the special tax treatment accorded qualified plans is to induce greater *retirement* savings. Social Security old-age benefits provide a baseline level of retirement income, but for a large majority of retirees, Social Security alone is inadequate to maintain their pre-retirement standard of living. Most workers need to supplement Social Security with pensions or private savings to avoid painful cutbacks in their personal budgets and cramped lifestyles in retirement. Without another source of support, even low-wage workers, who receive Social Security benefits that constitute a larger share of their pre-retirement wages than other workers, will experience a significant drop in their standard of living upon retirement. Most experts estimate that retirees

---

61 Bureau of Economic Analysis, U.S. Department of Commerce, National Income and Product Accounts Table 2.1: Personal Income and Its Disposition, http://www.bea.gov/national/nipaweb/SelectTable.asp?selected=N#52 (last revised Oct. 29, 2009).

typically need to replace about 70 to 80 percent of their pre-retirement earnings to maintain their standard of living.[62]

As Figure 10-1 illustrates, Social Security alone cannot fill the bill. The "Low" earnings level depicted in the figure is roughly comparable to a career of full-time minimum wage work; the "Very Low" earnings level corresponds to a low-paid worker with substantial gaps in labor force participation. These workers get relatively more from Social Security because the program contains a redistributive component (the benefit schedule is progressive or bottom-weighted), but the low earner still falls far short of the 80 percent benchmark. Moreover, the replacement rates shown are computed as a proportion of career average compensation, which arguably overstates Social Security's importance to workers in the upper half of the earnings distribution.

Figure 10-1
Social Security Replacement Rates
(Retirement at Age 65 in 2007)

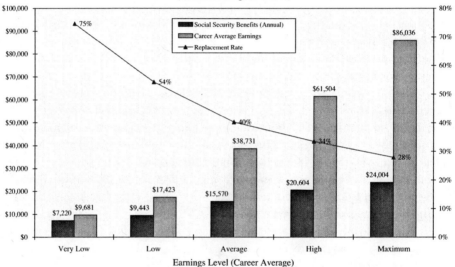

Earnings Level (Career Average)

Earnings levels represent 25%, 45%, 100%, and 160% of average wage; maximum reflects annual earnings equal to taxable wage base.
Source: Data from SSA, 2007 Board of Trustees' Report, Table VI.F10, and author's correspondence with SSA actuaries.

---

62   The measure of pre-retirement earnings used to compute replacement rates (the denominator of the fraction) is not standardized. Depending on the purpose of the computation, some measure of final pre-retirement earnings or of career average earnings may be used, and such differences can yield dramatic variations in numerical results. *See* Andrew G. Biggs & Glenn R. Stringstead, *Alternate Measures of Replacement Rates for Social Security Benefits and Retirement Income*, 68 Soc. Sec. Bull. 1 (2008), *available at* http://www.socialsecurity.gov/policy/docs/ssb/v68n2/v68n2p1.pdf; Johannes Binswanger & Daniel Schunk, *What is an Adequate Standard of Living During Retirement?* (CentER Disc. Paper Series No. 2008-82), *available at* http://papers.ssrn.com/sol3/papers.cfm?abstract_id=1275702 (survey of prospective preferred levels of old-age spending finds that adequate levels of retirement spending exceed 80 percent of working life spending for a majority of respondents and that minimum acceptable replacement rates depend strongly on income).

Because real wages of skilled workers tend to increase with age and experience, Social Security replacement rates would be lower if computed with reference to immediate pre-retirement earnings (such as average compensation over the final five years of work), which is the point of comparison retirees presumably use in considering whether they have experienced a drop in their living standards.

Retirees at virtually every income level need to supplement Social Security to preserve their accustomed lifestyles, but why do they need public assistance (the tax subsidy) to do so? Rather than relying on individuals to supplement Social Security with private savings (or suffer the consequences of their failure to do so), the tax law encourages accumulation through qualified plans which, by virtue of their preferential tax treatment, represent public-private hybrid saving. This elaborate hybrid (or semi-private) retirement savings system is an effort to counteract an assumed bias in favor of current consumption (an assumption that seems well founded in light of the long-term dismal trend in overall personal savings).

As an incentive, the qualified plan tax subsidy is justified only insofar as it induces retirement savings that would not otherwise occur. To the extent that public monies benefit people who would save adequately on their own, the subsidy is so much wasted revenue. Low- and moderate-income workers are less able to save on their own (lower disposable income). In addition, they are less likely to prioritize retirement saving because restricted access makes the funds unavailable for more urgent objectives, like saving for education, home ownership, or to build a reserve against illness or unemployment (so-called precautionary saving). Rank-and-file workers are not only less able to save and less focused on retirement, they are less likely to be induced to save by the prospect of tax relief. Recall that the qualified plan subsidy is cast in the form of tax deferral (or equivalently, tax exemption of the investment return). At present, however, the lowest-income 40 percent of households pay almost no federal income tax.[63] In contrast, high-income individuals have the ability to save on their own, and because they are subject to high marginal tax rates, they would receive the greatest benefit from a tax allowance that grants deferral (or exemption of investment returns) based on individual savings decisions. This is the challenge to which the tax controls, and particularly the nondiscrimination rules, are addressed: granting tax deferral for retirement savings on an individual basis would do very little to increase saving by low- and middle-income workers, while it would give a windfall to the highly paid, who would simply shift their other savings into the tax-advantaged form. Giving all taxpayers, regardless of income, access to IRAs, for example, is likely to induce: (1) no additional savings by low-income taxpayers; (2) portfolio rearrangement by high-income savers to take advantage of the tax reduction (such behavior is known as

---

63   In 2006, just over 40 percent of all individual income tax returns reported a positive adjusted gross income (AGI) of less than $25,000. The total income tax liability of those taxpayers, as a proportion of their total AGI, was 2.3 percent. (Moreover, half of the total tax was paid by the 8 percent of filers with AGI between $20,000 and $25,000.) Justin Bryan, *Individual Income Tax Returns, 2006*, Table 1, 2008 SOI BULLETIN 5, 21, 45, *available at* http://www.irs.gov/pub/irs-soi/08fallbulintax.pdf.

tax arbitrage); and (3) some new savings by moderate-income individuals for whom the tax benefit increases their return enough to make saving more attractive than otherwise-preferred consumption alternatives.

Nondiscrimination and Redistribution

These considerations indicate that deferred taxation of amounts devoted to retirement saving, if extended on the basis of individual savings decisions, would generate a wasteful—even perverse—distribution of public assistance. The qualified plan non-discrimination rules, first enacted in 1942, seek to avoid that result by conditioning favorable tax treatment of deferred compensation on the dual requirements that (1) the program's coverage does not unduly favor highly compensated employees, and (2) the "contributions or benefits provided under the plan [expressed as a proportion of compensation] do not discriminate in favor of highly compensated employees."[64] A leading Treasury tax policy official told Congress that the qualified plan nondiscrimination rules mean that the "reduction in taxes is designed to induce high-income taxpayers to save for retirement in such a manner that there will also be benefits for rank-and-file employees who are not only less able to save, but also less likely to be induced to do so by reason of tax relief."[65] Professors Fischel and Langbein explained:

> Despite the strongly voluntary or consensual basis of the private pension system, various features of pension regulation are designed to interfere with individual autonomy in pension saving. For example, the anti-discrimination norm—the bed-rock principle of pension taxation—conditions access to tax advantaged pension saving for a firm's better paid workers upon extensive participation of the firm's lower paid workers. The rationale is to create incentives for management to induce lower paid workers to engage in higher levels of pension saving than they would if allowed unfettered choice. Whether this strategy is very successful is open to question, but it exemplifies the idea that some employees should be protected against their inclination to save too little for retirement.[66]

To understand the operation and assess the effectiveness of the nondiscrimination rules, it is helpful to illustrate their application to a simple fact pattern. Assume that a hypothetical employer's workforce is composed of three employees, X, Y, and Z, and that each is 45 years old. X, an executive, is a highly compensated employee (HCE) who earns a salary of $120,000 and is subject to the 28 percent marginal income tax

---

64   I.R.C. §§ 401(a)(3)-(5), 410(b) (quotation from § 401(a)(4)).

65   *National Pension Policies: Private Pension Plans: Hearings Before the Subcomm. on Retirement Income and Employment of the House Select Comm. on Aging*, 95th Cong. 228, 230 (1978) (statement of Daniel I. Halperin, Tax Legislative Counsel, U.S. Department of the Treasury).

66   Daniel Fischel & John H. Langbein, *ERISA's Fundamental Contradiction: The Exclusive Benefit Rule*, 55 U. CHI. L. REV. 1105, 1122–23 (1988) (footnotes omitted).

rate; Y and Z are nonhighly compensated employees (NHCEs), and each earns $60,000 and is taxed at the 15 percent rate. Suppose that instead of a raise, the employer allows each employee to independently elect whether the employer will contribute an amount equal to 5 percent of the employee's salary to a retirement account (to be invested and the accumulated balance distributed to the employee at age 65), or pay the 5 percent to the employee currently as additional cash compensation. Finally, assume that X, the executive, already saves a substantial portion of her after-tax income for retirement, but Y and Z do not: Y would save if he could get a somewhat higher return on his money than the market now offers, while Z confronts urgent immediate consumption needs (such as family medical and educational expenses) and so strongly disprefers saving. Figure 10-2 illustrates how these workers are likely to exercise their choice between retirement saving and additional salary.

Figure 10-2*
Nondiscrimination and Redistribution

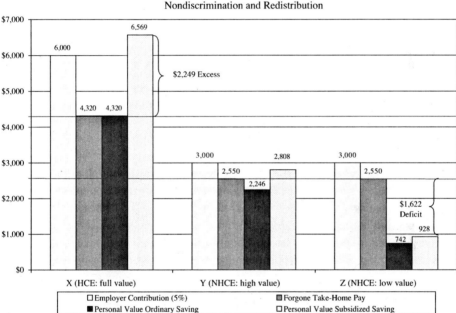

* Assumptions: (1) all amounts saved, whether personally or in an employer-sponsored retirement fund, earn 8 percent compound annual return for 20 years; (2) each employee's tax rate remains constant for the 20-year duration of the retirement account; (3) Y values deferred compensation by applying a personal (internal) discount rate that is 10 percent greater than the 6.8 percent (= 85% of 8%) after-tax rate of return his savings would earn; (4) Z values deferred compensation by applying a personal (internal) discount rate that is double his 6.8% after-tax rate of return on savings.

For each worker, the first column represents the employer's current outlay (5 percent of salary), whether contributed to a retirement account or paid in cash. The second column is the after-tax value of the employer's payment, and so reflects the amount of consumption the worker would forgo (lesser take-home pay) in selecting a retirement account contribution. The third column, labeled "Personal Value Ordinary Saving," shows each employee's individual assessment (personal valuation) of the saving alternative under the normal income tax rules. By assumption, X would save at least this amount of her after-tax income on her own, and so for X, the present value of the savings option is equal to her forgone take-home pay (in other words, X's personal discount rate is just equal to her after-tax rate of return, 72 percent of 8 percent, or 5.76 percent). By comparison, Y slightly prefers current consumption, and Z strongly favors immediate needs, as reflected in their lower personal valuations of saving compared to additional take-home pay. The final column, labeled "Personal Value Subsidized Saving," displays the value of tax-deferred saving (as under traditional IRA treatment) for each employee, which is higher than for ordinary saving because of the additional accumulation tax deferral facilitates.[67]

The results shown in Figure 10-2 confirm the qualitative predictions made earlier. If the tax-advantaged savings opportunity is made available on an individual basis, then the highly compensated employee, who would have saved anyway, obtains a large benefit by deferring a substantial tax obligation (high marginal rate) for an extended period. X can get $2,249 more just by rearranging her investments to make use of the tax-deferred savings vehicle. Rather than increasing savings, that arbitrage opportunity might actually *reduce* savings by X and other high-income individuals who have the wherewithal to save because, thanks to the tax concession, they need to put less aside to meet future goals. Z, the middle-income worker with pressing obligations, will not be persuaded to save by tax deferral alone because at his low tax rate, the incremental return to saving is just too small to make a difference. Y, however, would be moved to save by the tax allowance because it increases his return enough to counteract his impatience and make it worthwhile to postpone consumption.

Figure 10-2 also demonstrates the logic of the nondiscrimination rules. Instead of granting tax deferral on an individual basis, consider a system that conditions the benefit for the highly compensated employee on proportional saving by the rank-and-file workers. Z's personal circumstances are such that he will not consent to reducing his current consumption by $2,550 in favor of savings that are worth only $928 to him. But observe that the tax advantage to X is large enough that it would be worthwhile for X to bribe Z to participate in order to satisfy the nondiscrimination condition. Moreover, because qualified retirement plans are employer-mediated programs, X does not have to take the step of personally making a side payment to induce Z's acquiescence. Instead, the employer can accomplish the transfer by reducing X's current compensation by more than the $6,000 retirement contribution made on behalf of X, while at the same time contributing $3,000 for Z without reducing Z's current compensation by the full amount. On the facts illustrated, Z will accept the $3,000 retirement contribution if his salary is reduced by no more than $1,092 (equivalent to $928 of foregone consumption at Z's 15 percent rate), which means that the employer would

---

67   The amount shown is each employee's individual assessment of the present after-tax value of tax-preferred saving. It is computed by taking the future value of the account (using a compound 8 percent tax-free rate of return), reducing that amount by the tax due on distribution, and discounting that after-tax accumulation by the employee's personal discount rate. For X that discount rate is simply her after-tax rate of return on savings, 5.76 percent; for Y and Z the personal discount rate is their after-tax rate of return, 6.8 percent, adjusted to reflect impatience (increased by 10 percent or 100 percent, respectively).

have to increase Z's total compensation by $1,908 ($1,622 after tax) to satisfy the nondiscrimination requirement. The employer recoups this added cost from X, who should be willing to trade any amount less than $9,124 of her (pre-tax) salary for the $6,000 retirement contribution. The $3,124 compensation savings that can be extracted from X (equivalent to $2,249 after tax at X's 28 percent rate) is of course more than sufficient to fund the $1,908 compensation increase necessary to bribe Z to participate. The exact disposition of this extra tax subsidy, together with a small amount of compensation that could be extracted from Y (who would trade $3,304 in salary for the $3,000 qualified plan contribution), is indeterminate. Presumably, relative bargaining power will determine its division between the employer and the employees (X, in particular), and some amount will have to be captured by the employer to compensate it for the additional costs it will incur in administering the plan.

By conditioning favorable tax treatment on broad participation, the nondiscrimination rules can, in the right circumstances, effect a hidden transfer (or covert redistribution, if you will) of the tax subsidy from high-income, high-preference employees to lower-paid workers who are reluctant savers. Nondiscrimination tends to redirect public monies from windfall tax savings by highly paid workers into retirement savings that would not otherwise occur, and so operates to better target the tax subsidy. Yet the complex system that has evolved is riddled with defects and limitations. For although the nondiscrimination rules are the central mechanism for channeling public assistance into additional retirement savings, their efficacy is highly sensitive to employee preferences, workforce composition, income tax rates, and the availability of other tax-sheltered savings opportunities. Many of these limitations are apparent upon further consideration of the example in Figure 10-2. First consider employee preferences: if Y were in financial straits almost as tight as Z (high personal discount rate due to current consumption needs), then the compensation savings that could be extracted from X ($3,124 maximum) would be insufficient to fund the compensation increases necessary to persuade both Y and Z to participate. Therefore, the nondiscrimination condition could not be satisfied without increasing employer costs. Assuming that the employer operates in a competitive industry where that is not feasible, it will not sponsor a plan, and the rank-and-file workers will not have retirement savings.

Workforce composition—meaning the number, pay levels, and ages of employees—is another crucial set of factors. Hiring a third person at a $60,000 salary would sink the plan if that new worker's propensity to save were closer to Z's than Y's. On the other hand, the addition of a second HCE-saver like X would generate a great deal of additional tax savings that would not have to be redistributed to satisfy the nondiscrimination rules if Y and Z remain the only NHCEs; and in that case, the tax subsidy would entail a lot of wasted revenue (shared, in some fashion, between the HCEs and the company). Similarly, the original three-person workforce would be awash in wasted subsidy if X were instead paid $240,000 and taxed in the 33 percent bracket.[68]

---

68   Assuming the same facts on which Figure 10-2 is based, except for X's higher salary and tax rate, then the $12,000 contribution (5 percent of $240,000) would be worth $19,685 in salary to X, $7,685 more than the employer contribution. Of that excess, only $1,908 is needed to buy Z's cooperation.

Tax savings available for redistribution depend not only on the HCE-saver's contribution and tax rate, but also on the duration of saving. The facts on which Figure 10-2 is based assume that the amount contributed for each employee would remain in the account for 20 years until distribution. If, instead, X is only eight years away from retirement, the tax advantage in qualified plan savings would not be sufficient to cover the additional compensation cost required to secure Z's participation.

Because the amount of subsidy is based on the value of tax deferral, legislative income tax rate changes can dramatically affect the attractiveness of qualified plan saving. This underappreciated link can sometimes cause tax and pension policies to work at cross purposes. Consider the Tax Reform Act of 1986, which broadened the base of the individual income tax and in return drastically lowered income tax rates, with the top bracket rate falling from 50 to 28 percent. That statute made the coverage and amount nondiscrimination rules more demanding and tightened the vesting rules, which changes generally increase the cost of maintaining a qualified plan by forcing more benefits to be provided to low-paid, low-preference employees. Yet at the same time that Congress insisted on greater redistribution, it drastically reduced the tax rate and the value of deferral for high-income savers, thereby cutting the subsidy available to meet those increased costs! The unforeseen but predictable result was a marked decline in the attractiveness of instituting or expanding qualified retirement savings programs. For any particular employer, the exact impact of tax rate reductions depends, of course, on the factors described above, namely individual savings preferences and workforce composition (number, pay levels, and ages of employees). As seen above, a workforce that includes a lot of highly paid savers can generate much more tax subsidy than needed to satisfy the nondiscrimination rules; any subsidy in excess of the amount that must be shifted to low-paid, reluctant savers either benefits high-paid workers who would save on their own or is captured by the employer (through reduced compensation). From the perspective of nondiscrimination policy, this excess subsidy is wasted revenue, and in this instance, lowering tax rates reduces waste and improves the effectiveness of redistribution. Another employer whose workforce includes few highly paid savers and is composed predominately of low-paid workers with urgent consumption needs (non-savers), may find that a tax rate reduction makes qualified plan sponsorship uneconomic, because the reduced subsidy means that the potential compensation cost savings that might be extracted from high-paid workers is now insufficient to induce enough participation from low-paid workers to satisfy the nondiscrimination rules. In this case, the post-tax-cut subsidy may simply be too small to pay the compensation increases needed to bribe enough low-paid workers into the plan.[69]

---

69 *See generally* Daniel I. Halperin, *Special Tax Treatment for Employer-Based Retirement Programs: Is It "Still" Viable as a Means of Increasing Retirement Income?*, 49 Tax L. Rev. 1 (1993). See Peter J. Brady, *Pension Nondiscrimination Rules and the Incentive to Cross Subsidize Employees*, 6 J. Pen. Econ. & Fin. 127 (2007), which uses a simulation analysis to model the impact of nondiscrimination rules on 401(k) plans, and finds that only firms with a relatively low ratio of NHCEs to HCEs (less than about 4 to 6) would have an economic incentive to sponsor a plan.

The upshot of all this is that enriching the subsidy by increasing tax rates, while it will make plan sponsorship more attractive across-the-board and induce some employers to institute a plan who previously could not afford to offer one, will not necessarily trigger additional redistribution under preexisting plans. Instead of being shifted to low-income non-savers, the additional subsidy associated with established programs—programs that met nondiscrimination standards under the stingier prior regime—might just be pocketed by the employer or its highly paid workers. Conversely, curtailing the subsidy by reducing tax rates might reduce wasted revenue and increase the efficiency of redistribution in some cases, but under a system of voluntary sponsorship, that step might cause some employers to discontinue existing programs and deter other employers from instituting new plans. Despite their maddening complexity, the nondiscrimination rules accomplish only haphazard and imperfect redistribution. Nor do they apply universally: governmental plans are now entirely exempt from the antidiscrimination imperative, and the coverage nondiscrimination standard is relaxed for church plans.[70]

Discrimination in Coverage

The central coverage nondiscrimination rule, known as the ratio percentage test, requires that the percentage of nonhighly compensated employees (NHCEs) who benefit under a qualified plan must be at least 70 percent of the percentage of highly compensated employees (HCEs) benefitting under the plan.[71] (The regulations rephrase this test by requiring that the plan's "ratio percentage," defined as the percentage of NHCEs who benefit divided by the percentage of HCEs who benefit, must equal or exceed 70 percent, rounded to the nearest hundredth of a percentage point.[72]) Generally speaking, an employee is treated as "benefitting" under the plan for a given year if she

---

70   I.R.C. §§ 401(1)(5)(G), 414(d) (2006). The nondiscrimination exemption covers plans of federal, state, and local governments and their agencies and instrumentalities. It also covers plans maintained by an Indian tribal government or an agency or instrumentality thereof for employees performing noncommercial essential governmental functions. The complete exemption of state and local governmental plans from nondiscrimination obligations was enacted in 1997 (previously, governmental plans were subject to the relaxed pre-ERISA requirements applied to church plans), and the legislation also retroactively excused prior discrimination by such plans. Taxpayer Relief Act of 1997, Pub. L. No. 105-34, § 1505(a)(1), (d)(2), 111 Stat. 788, 1063–64. The only explanation Congress offered was an unelaborated nod to "the unique circumstances of governmental plans and the complexity of compliance." STAFF OF THE JOINT COMM. ON TAXATION, 105TH CONG., GENERAL EXPLANATION OF TAX LEGISLATION ENACTED IN 1997, at 436 (Comm. Print 1997). Church plans are allowed to use pre-ERISA coverage standards by I.R.C. § 410(c)(1)(B) (2006) and Treas. Reg. § 1.410(b)-2(e) (as amended in 1994). These reduced qualification standards for government and church plans are, of course, related to the complete exemption of such plans from ERISA's labor law requirements. *See supra* Chapter 2D; I.R.C. § 411(e) (2006), *id.* § 401(a) '(final sentence) (governmental and church plans exempt from cognate tax qualification rules).

71   I.R.C. §§ 401(a)(3), 410(b)(1)(B) (2006).

72   Treas. Reg. §§ 1.410(b)-2(b)(2), 1.410(b)-9 (as amended in 1994).

receives an allocation of employer contributions or forfeitures to her account under a defined contribution plan for the year, or she receives an increase in the dollar amount of her accrued benefit under a defined benefit plan.[73] Thus, an employee benefits (and is counted in the numerator of either the HCE or NHCE fraction) if she earns an increase in retirement savings based upon current service. Such workers are sometimes referred to as "active participants." If a firm has 10 HCEs and 50 NHCEs, for example, and 8 of the HCEs receive an employer contribution under a profit-sharing plan for the year, then the ratio percentage test is satisfied if at least 28 NHCEs also get a contribution (28 of 50 NHCEs, or 56%, divided by 8 of 10 HCEs, or 80%, gives a plan ratio percentage of 70.00%).

A plan that fails the ratio percentage test standing alone still has two alternatives for establishing coverage nondiscrimination.[74] First, under a technique known as plan aggregation, the employer may designate two or more pension, profit-sharing, stock bonus, or annuity plans that use the same plan year as being part of a larger program for nondiscrimination testing. If the combined coverage of the two plans is adequate *and* the contributions or benefits provided under the composite program do not discriminate in favor of highly compensated employees, then each of the plans is treated as satisfying the nondiscrimination tests.[75] Returning to the example of a firm with 10 HCEs and 50 NHCEs, assume that 8 of the HCEs and none of the NHCEs receive an employer contribution under a profit-sharing plan, while 28 of the NHCEs are active participants in a money purchase pension plan under which they receive annual contributions of 5 percent of compensation. Clearly, the coverage of the money purchase pension plan for the rank-and-file is nondiscriminatory (as is any plan that covers no HCE), but the profit-sharing plan tested alone is just as clearly discriminatory, as it covers no NHCE and has a ratio percentage of zero. If the plans' combined coverage is tested, however, the ratio percentage is satisfactory. If the money purchase and profit-sharing plans use the same plan year, the plan aggregation rule permits such composite testing provided that the contribution rate under the profit-sharing plan does not exceed 5 percent of compensation. That is so because composite coverage testing is authorized only if the plans are also tested together for amount nondiscrimination,

---

73   Treas. Reg. § 1.410(b)-3(a)(1) (as amended in 2004), § 1.401(a)(4)-2(c)(2)(ii) (as amended in 2007).

74   A special rule provides that a plan of an employer that has no NHCEs at any time during the plan year is treated as satisfying the coverage nondiscrimination test even though it benefits only one or more HCEs. I.R.C. § 410(b)(6)(F) (2006); Treas. Reg. 1.410(b)-2(b)(5) (as amended in 1994). The tax subsidy is obviously wasted in this unusual situation. The concession does, however, forestall an unseemly but predictable response in such circumstances—the employer might otherwise create a make-work job for one half-time minimum wage employee and grant that superfluous worker plan membership in order to satisfy the ratio percentage test.

75   I.R.C. § 410(b)(6)(B) (2006); Treas. Reg. 1.410(b)-7(d) (as amended in 2004). This plan aggregation permission is an exception to the general rule that each pension, profit-sharing, stock bonus, or annuity plan must independently satisfy all components of the definition of a qualified plan (hundreds of conditions) to be eligible for favorable tax treatment.

and a higher rate of contribution under the profit-sharing plan would cause contributions under the combined program to favor HCEs.[76]

The second alternative to separate application of the ratio percentage test is the average benefit test, which has two components: (1) the nondiscriminatory classification test; and (2) a numerical group-average benefit comparison.[77] The first element, the nondiscriminatory classification test, demands that the employees who benefit must be identified categorically (not by name or similar enumeration) under a reasonable classification based on objective business criteria, such as job category, geographic location, salaried versus hourly pay, etc. In addition, the group of employees so identified must yield a ratio percentage that falls within a specified acceptable range. A ratio percentage of at least 50 percent is always acceptable. (Recall that there is no need to resort to the average benefit test if the plan's ratio percentage is 70 percent or greater.) The safe harbor is expanded to permit a ratio percentage below 50 percent if the proportion of rank-and-file employees in the workforce (known as the nonhighly compensated employee concentration percentage) exceeds 60 percent of all employees. In addition, a somewhat lower ratio percentage (but never more than 10 points below the safe harbor) is permissible if, based on a discretionary assessment of all the facts and circumstances, including the nature and importance of the underlying business reason for the classification, the IRS finds that the classification is not discriminatory. Figure 10-3 displays the acceptable ratio percentages under the nondiscriminatory classification test as a function of the employer's NHCE concentration percentage.[78]

The nondiscriminatory classification test is only a gateway to the second and distinctive component of the average benefit test, which is a numerical group-average benefit comparison, generally known as the average benefit percentage test. The average benefit percentage test requires that "the average benefit percentage for employees who are not highly compensated employees is at least 70 percent of the average benefit percentage for highly compensated employees."[79] The benefit percentage for each employee is the total employer-provided contribution or benefit under *all* qualified plans for the year, expressed as a percentage of the employee's compensation.[80] The average benefit percentage of each group (HCEs and NHCEs) is the average of the benefit percentages of each member of the group; in computing these group averages *employees are included whether or not they participate in any plan.*[81] Thus an employee

---

76   If contributions under the profit-sharing plan are based in whole or part on factors other than current compensation (for example, age or length of service), then the eight covered HCEs would have different contribution rates as a percentage of pay.

77   I.R.C. § 410(b)(1)(C), (b)(2) (2006); Treas. Reg. §§ 1.410(b)-2(b)(3) (as amended in 1994). Somewhat confusingly, both the overall test and the second component thereof (the numerical group average benefit comparison) are commonly known as the average benefit percentage test.

78   The ratio percentage ranges falling within the safe harbor and discretionary zones are prescribed by formulae and a table in Treas. Reg. § 1.410(b)-4(c)(4) (1991). Figure 10-3 presents those data in graphical form.

79   I.R.C. § 410(b)(2)(A)(ii) (2006).

80   I.R.C. § 410(b)(2)(C) (2006). Instead of computing benefit percentages on the basis of contributions or benefits for the plan year, the employer may elect to use a period composed of the plan year and the one or two preceding years. *Id.*

81   I.R.C. § 410(b)(2)(B) (2006).

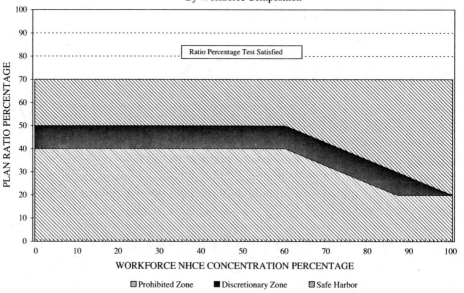

Figure 10-3
Nondiscriminatory Classification Test Results
By Workforce Composition

Ratio Percentage Test Satisfied

PLAN RATIO PERCENTAGE

WORKFORCE NHCE CONCENTRATION PERCENTAGE

▧ Prohibited Zone   ■ Discretionary Zone   ▧ Safe Harbor

who does not benefit from any qualified plan has a benefit percentage of zero, which reduces the average benefit percentage of the group to which he belongs.

The average benefit percentage test substitutes an intergroup benefit rate comparison for the coverage rate comparison of the ratio percentage test. The benefit rates compared are *global* rates—amounts earned under all qualified pension and profit-sharing plans (whether of the defined contribution or defined benefit sort) are aggregated to compute the per-employee total amount of employer-funded deferred compensation. By looking beyond the amounts earned under the plan in question, the test recognizes that the tax subsidy associated with savings by the highly compensated can be shifted to rank-and-file employees as effectively by establishing another plan for their benefit as by including them in the plan that covers and is tailored to the preferences of managerial and professional personnel. This broader comparison implements the central policy of the antidiscrimination norm while increasing employer flexibility.[82]

The employer's increased flexibility can be observed by noting the options available when a plan fails the ratio percentage test. The eligibility rules of the plan could be modified to increase the coverage rate for nonhighly compensated employees, or they could be changed to restrict the coverage of highly compensated employees. These are the obvious means of compliance with the ratio percentage test. The average benefits test offers two additional alternatives: (1) the plan could be amended to provide nonhighly compensated participants a higher rate of contributions or benefits than highly compensated members receive; or (2) the employer could establish (or increase contributions or

---

82   Recall that preserving employer autonomy (maintaining a voluntary employment-based pension system) is a central policy of ERISA. *See supra* Chapter 1C.

benefits under) another plan with coverage favoring the rank-and-file. These options involve no adjustment in the coverage of the plan that fails the ratio percentage test.

The average benefit test also increases employer flexibility by allowing a trade-off between coverage and benefits. The employer is permitted to cover a proportion of rank-and-file employees that is less than 70 percent of the highly compensated coverage rate on the condition that the amount of contributions or benefits flowing to the rank-and-file does not fall below the amount that would be allowed by the ratio percentage test (assuming a plan that grants each active participant an amount of contributions or benefits that is a fixed proportion of compensation). But observe that the trade-off works both ways: an employer that covers an overall proportion (under all qualified plans, that is) of NHCEs that is greater than 70 percent of the HCE coverage rate may give the rank-and-file workers a lower rate of contributions or benefits (as a proportion of compensation) because broader coverage at a lower amount can still satisfy the group-average benefit comparison. This insight suggests that the average benefit test functions as a liberalized version of plan aggregation: the employer is permitted to validate the coverage of a plan with membership tilted in favor of HCEs by taking into account NHCEs covered under other plans, and if specified conditions are met, it may do so even if the plans tested as a single program would not satisfy the amount nondiscrimination test.[83]

In one important respect, however, the average benefit test is not as tolerant as plan aggregation. The nondiscriminatory classification test imposes a threshold condition tied to the ratio percentage of a single plan: coverage may be skewed in favor of the HCEs (a ratio percentage of at least 50 percent always satisfies the nondiscriminatory classification test), but if the disparity between coverage rates of the highly paid and the rank-and-file is too great (a ratio percentage below 20 percent is always disqualifying), then the group-average benefit comparison is unavailable. Consequently, a management plan that does not have some substantial coverage of rank-and-file employees cannot pass the average benefit test even if all NHCEs are covered under another plan that is almost as generous. For example, consider a company that covers all HCEs under a defined contribution plan with the employer contributing 10 percent of compensation. That HCE-only plan could qualify via plan aggregation if the company also maintains a plan that covers 70 percent of its NHCEs and also provides at least a 10 percent contribution rate (and uses the same plan year). Yet the HCE-only plan is disqualified if the company sponsors another plan that covers *all* NHCEs at a 7 percent contribution rate, even though the amount of retirement savings on behalf of the rank-and-file workers may be at least as great as in the preceding case! Plan aggregation is

---

83   Recall that if plan aggregation is elected for purposes of coverage testing, the programs must also be treated as a single plan for purposes of testing for discrimination in contributions or benefits. I.R.C. §§ 410(b)(6)(B), 401(a)(4) (2006). *See supra* Chapter 10 notes 75–76 and accompanying text. Not so under the average benefit test—while coverage testing is conducted on a consolidated basis, each plan is tested separately under Code section 401(a)(4). The average benefit test is more expansive than plan aggregation in a second way as well: multiple plans can be tested under the average benefit test even if they do not share the same plan year. *Compare* Treas. Reg. § 1.410(b)-5(d)(3) (as amended in 1993), and § 1.410(b)-7(e)(1) (as amended in 2004), *with* § 1.410(b)-7(d)(5).

not allowed because contributions under the combined program favor HCEs (as a proportion of compensation), and although the average benefit percentage of the group of NHCEs (7 percent) is at least 70 percent of the average benefit percentage of the group of HCEs (10 percent), the HCE-only plan cannot resort to the average benefit percentage test because the nondiscriminatory classification test blocks entrance (the ratio percentage of the HCE-only plan is zero). Suppose instead that the company covers all HCEs and half of its NHCEs under the plan with a 10 percent contribution rate, and that the rest of the NHCEs are covered by another plan with only a 4 percent contribution rate. Now the 10 percent plan passes the nondiscriminatory classification test (a ratio percentage of 50 percent always falls within the safe harbor), and the average contribution percentage of the group of NHCEs (i.e., (10%+4%)/2) is 70 percent of the average contribution percentage for the group of HCEs. This curiously inconsistent result seems to be an anomaly.[84]

The traditional approach to identifying discrimination entails a two-step process applied separately to each plan, first checking plan coverage and then making sure that the percentage of pay saved under that particular plan does not favor the highly paid. The central insight of the average benefit percentage test is that the traditional approach is unnecessarily restrictive. The objective of the antidiscrimination principle is to shift the tax subsidy into additional retirement saving for low-paid workers. That goal can be achieved under one plan, but it might be achieved as well or better under multiple plans tailored to the needs and preferences of different segments of the workforce. By computing employee benefit percentages with reference to the employer-provided contribution or benefit under all qualified plans maintained by the employer, the average benefit percentage test allows consolidated nondiscrimination testing (to a point). Consolidated testing enables the employer to take the subsidy captured from highly paid savers under one plan and pay it out under another plan geared to rank-and-file employees. The nondiscriminatory classification test, however, limits the consolidated approach to situations where the workforce segmentation in plan coverage is not too closely correlated with compensation level. A second perplexing feature of the average benefit percentage test is its limited role as an alternative coverage standard (substituting for the ratio percentage test): although it represents an amalgam of the traditional coverage and amount nondiscrimination tests, the average benefit percentage test is not allowed to substitute for both. Instead, if a plan's coverage is accepted under the average benefit test even though its membership favors HCEs, the plan must still independently pass the amount nondiscrimination test, notwithstanding the fact that the average benefit percentage test functions as a consolidated workforce-wide amount nondiscrimination test.[85] The average benefit percentage test was an innovation that first

---

84   The statutory language imposing the nondiscriminatory classification test came with historical baggage that apparently convinced the Treasury that substantial NHCE participation in the HCE-dominated plan must be required. Other justifications have been suggested, but they do not seem compelling. The best explanation appears to be simply that the average benefit test was not very clearly thought through. *See* WIEDENBECK & OSGOOD, *supra* Chapter 3 note 39, at 206–07, 213–15, 219.

85   As currently implemented by regulations, the general approach to testing for discrimination in the amount of contributions or benefits (the rate group testing methodology, *infra* text accompanying

appeared in the conference committee report to the Tax Reform Act of 1986, and so these mysterious limitations on the scope of the test might be artifacts of its hasty and not-fully-thought-through origins.[86]

Definitions: Employee, Highly Compensated Employee

Nondiscrimination testing is a game of numbers. Computation of coverage rates or average benefit percentages demands clear answers to the questions whether an individual must be taken into account as an employee, and if so, whether she is to be categorized as a highly compensated employee (HCE) or a nonhighly compensated employee (NHCE). The scope of the term employee is crucial to accomplishing redistribution: if the coverage nondiscrimination requirement were applied only to the employees of a single legal entity, it could be evaded simply by segregating the workforce between two commonly controlled businesses, one of which employs the highly paid executive and professional staff and sponsors a generous retirement plan, while the other hires the rank-and-file and makes no provision for retirement savings. Such a loophole would render the coverage rules a nullity. To prevent this, ERISA amended the Code's qualified plan rules to provide that all employees of a controlled group of

---

Chapter 10 notes 131-41) is somewhat more demanding than the group-average approach of the average benefit percentage test. It should be noted that if the nondiscriminatory classification test were repealed so that a plan limited to HCEs could avail itself of the average benefit percentage test, then there would be no point in applying a separate amount nondiscrimination test to the HCE-only plan. The two average benefit percentage test anomalies are linked.

Applying the nondiscriminatory classification test as an adjunct to the average benefit percentage test prevents qualification of a plan that provides a very high level of benefits (as a percentage of compensation) to one or a few favored NHCEs while the rest of the rank-and-file get nothing. Correspondingly, applying the general amount nondiscrimination test (rate group testing) to a plan that relies on the nondiscriminatory classification test and the average benefit percentage test to validate coverage prevents a single HCE from earning benefits that are significantly greater than the benefits provided to any NHCE. In each instance, the limited role that current law accords the average benefit percentage test (looking behind group averages) prevents a situation from developing that might seem unfair. From a redistribution standpoint, however, only the first scenario is troublesome—while broad distribution of retirement savings among NHCEs who wouldn't save on their own is desirable, it shouldn't matter that the source of the redistributed funds is concentrated among a few HCE-savers.

86 H.R. Rep. No. 99-841, at II-412 to II-417 (1986) (Conf. Rep.). There is some circumstantial evidence of the source of the average benefits percentage test. In an article published in 1985, the author explicitly suggested that separate coverage and amount testing could be dispensed with by treating nonparticipants as receiving zero contributions or benefits and computing the average amount of contributions or benefits provided for the group of highly compensated employees with similar averages computed for one or more lower compensation ranges. Peter J. Wiedenbeck, *Nondiscrimination in Employee Benefits: False Starts and Future Trends*, 52 Tenn. L. Rev. 167, 256–57 (1985). That academic insight was not developed into a detailed proposal, but a copy of the article was sent to the Joint Committee on Taxation during the gestation of the 1986 Act. It should be noted, however, that combined coverage and amount testing was foreshadowed by the special nondiscrimination standard applicable to 401(k) plans, the actual deferral percentage test (discussed below).

businesses (regardless of whether the firms are incorporated) must be treated as employed by a single employer.[87] A controlled group means a parent-subsidiary group, a brother-sister group, or a combined group (brother-sister firms having one or more subsidiaries). In general, a parent-subsidiary group consists of firms linked by 80 percent ownership ties.[88] A brother-sister group consists of two or more firms if at least 80 percent of each is owned by a group of five or fewer individuals, estates, or trusts, but only if their common ownership exceeds 50 percent, determined by adding each owner's smallest percentage interest in either company (the common ownership or overlap percentage).[89] Constructive ownership (attribution) rules are applied in determining whether these ownership tests are met.[90]

In the 1970s, individual members of some professional service firms began to incorporate, substituting their newly formed professional corporations as partners in the partnership. Each separate professional corporation could then sponsor a plan covering its own workforce (typically consisting of its sole owner-employee), while the professional partnership, which employed the associates and support staff, provided little if any qualified plan savings. Ordinarily none of the separately incorporated professionals held a controlling stake in partnership (greater than 50 percent share of capital or profits), so the controlled group rule did not apply. Congress responded by demanding that all employees of an "affiliated service group" be treated as employed by a single employer, where affiliated service group means two or more business organizations that are functionally integrated and share ties of ownership (even if common control is lacking).[91] Finally, a company that pays another organization (such as a temporary staffing firm) for the use of its employees must treat such workers as its own employees if they perform services on a substantially full-time basis for a year or longer under the primary direction of the company that hires them out.[92] This "leased employee" rule, in combination with the workforce aggregation required for affiliated service groups and commonly controlled businesses, creates a broad functional definition of employee for purposes of nondiscrimination testing, which is largely immune from manipulation.

Sometimes, however, the workforce aggregation rules sweep too broadly. Consider a conglomerate or holding company that controls businesses in two or more industries that produce different goods or services. If generous pension coverage is typical in one industry but not in the other, then application of the coverage nondiscrimination rules on an enterprise-wide basis would competitively disadvantage one line of business or the other. Management would be put to the choice of either sponsoring no plan, which

---

87   I.R.C. §§ 414(b), (c), 1563(a), (f)(5) (2006).

88   I.R.C. § 1563(a)(1) (2006).

89   I.R.C. § 1563(f)(5)(A) (2006); Treas. Reg. § 1.414(c)-2(c) (as amended in 1994).

90   I.R.C. § 1563(d), (f) (2006). For example, in applying the definition of brother-sister corporations, stock actually owned by the spouse or minor child of an individual may be treated as owned by the individual.

91   I.R.C. § 414(m) (2006). *See* Lloyd M. Garland, M.D., F.A.C.S., P.A. v. Comm'r, 73 T.C. 5 (1979); H.R. Rep. No. 96-1278, at 34–35 (1980) (affiliated service group rule enacted to require workforce aggregation in situations like *Garland*).

92   I.R.C. § 414(n) (2006).

would handicap them in recruiting and retaining talent in the industry in which pension coverage is the norm, or covering everyone, which would raise labor costs in the industry that does not typically offer retirement savings (pension costs could not be recouped from workers who strongly prefer current cash compensation). While the nondiscrimination rules are intended to work redistribution, no such cross-subsidy is required between independently-owned firms operating in different industries. To alleviate this competitive disadvantage and reduce the influence of the qualified plan rules on ownership structure (thereby promoting economic neutrality), in certain situations an aggregated workforce can be disaggregated along industry lines. If the employer operates two or more qualified separate lines of business (QSLOBs), the nondiscrimination rules can sometimes be applied independently to the workforce of each line of business.[93] Treasury regulations implementing the QSLOB rules are unusually complex and burdensome, even by tax law standards, no doubt in an effort to guard against the reemergence of coverage abuses.[94] In any event, from the standpoint of economic substance, QSLOB workforce disaggregation is seriously under-inclusive, as many functionally distinct businesses cannot qualify.[95]

The controlled group, affiliated service group, and leased employee workforce aggregation rules mark the outer boundary of the set of workers that must be taken into account in nondiscrimination testing. The coverage rules, however, allow certain limited categories of employees to be excluded from consideration (treated as not employed). Consequently, exclusion of these workers from plan membership will not weigh against qualification even if the excluded workers disproportionately fall into the category of nonhighly compensated employees.

There are several important categories of excludible employees. First, as noted in the discussion of workforce disaggregation, in testing the coverage of a plan that benefits employees of a qualified separate line of business (QSLOB) the employees of all other QSLOBs can be ignored.[96] Second, nonresident alien employees are excludible

---

93   I.R.C. §§ 410(b)(5), 414(r) (2006). A workforce that is combined under the affiliated service group rule cannot be broken apart under the QSLOB provision. *Id.* § 414(r)(8); Treas. Reg. § 1.414(r)-2(b)(3)(iv) (as amended in 1994).

94   To keep matters straight, the Treasury took the unusual and extremely helpful step of issuing a flowchart to clarify relationships between the components of the section 414(r) regulations, which span some 46 pages in the Code of Federal Regulations. Treas. Reg. § 1.414(r)-0(c) (as amended in 1994).

95   The two most serious limitations on the availability of QSLOB testing are both statutory. Workforce disaggregation is not available if a line of business has fewer than fifty nonexcludible employees, however functionally distinct it may be. I.R.C. § 414(r)(2) (2006). Still more problematic, the coverage of a plan may be tested separately with respect to the employees of a QSLOB only if the plan also satisfies a modified version of the nondiscriminatory classification test as applied to the aggregated workforce. I.R.C. § 410(b)(5)(B) (2006); Treas. Reg. § 1.414(r)-8(b) (as amended in 1994). Consequently, an enterprise with operations in two different industries may not be able to rely on QSLOB testing to validate the coverage of a plan that is limited to workers in one line of business if the ratio of NHCEs to HCEs working in the other line of business is much larger.

96   I.R.C. §§ 410(b)(5), 414(r) (2006); Treas. Reg. § 1.410(b)-6(e) (as amended in 2006). The QSLOB exclusion does not apply for purposes of the threshold requirement of I.R.C.

if they receive no earned income from the employer that constitutes income from sources within the United States, or if a treaty exempts their U.S.-source compensation from the taxation by the United States.[97] Third, employees covered under a bona fide collective bargaining agreement are excludible in testing plans covering other segments of the workforce provided there is evidence that retirement benefits were the subject of good faith bargaining.[98] Consequently, unionized workers are allowed to trade off retirement savings for higher pay despite the overall aim of discrimination testing, which is to counteract just such a preference for current consumption.[99]

If a plan imposes permissible minimum age and service eligibility conditions and excludes all employees who have not satisfied those conditions from benefitting under the plan, then employees who fail to meet those entry conditions can also be ignored in applying the coverage nondiscrimination tests.[100] Because young and recently hired workers typically fall in the NHCE category, plan qualification frequently turns upon the license to treat these employees as excludible. Where two or more plans that use different minimum age and service conditions are considered together in testing coverage—as with elective plan aggregation or in computing employee benefit percentages under the average benefit percentage test—only those employees who fail to satisfy all of the different sets of age and service conditions are excludible.[101] Just as

---

§ 410(b)(5)(B) (2006), that the plan must satisfy a relaxed, nondiscriminatory classification test on an employer-wide basis.

97   I.R.C. § 410(b)(3)(C) (2006); Treas. Reg. § 1.410(b)-6(c) (as amended in 2006). The treaty rule applies only if all employees so situated are actually excluded from membership. *Id.* Protection would be lost, for example, if a highly paid, nonresident alien employee were covered by the plan but low-paid foreign workers were not.

98   I.R.C. §§ 410(b)(3)(A), 7701(a)(46) (2006); Treas. Reg. § 1.410(b)-6(d) (as amended in 2006). The requirement that the collective bargaining agreement be bona fide prevents an employer from setting up a company union to "represent" low-paid workers who decline retirement plan coverage in order to make those NHCEs excludible in testing the coverage of a plan that is limited to managerial and professional personnel. In addition, the exclusion of employees covered by collective bargaining vanishes if more than 2 percent of the employees covered by the agreement are highly compensated employees who perform any of various designated professional services. Treas. Reg. § 1.410(b)-6(d)(2)(iii)(B) (as amended in 2006), § 1.410(b)-9 (as amended in 2004).

99   Data reveal that the overall pension plan coverage rate for unionized workers is actually higher than for the nonunionized segment of the labor force, which might suggest that collective decision making offsets any individual propensity to over-discount the value of retirement savings. Bureau of Labor Statistics, U.S. Department of Labor, Employee Benefits in the United States, March 2009, Table 1 (July 28, 2009), *available at* http://www.bls.gov/news.release/pdf/ebs2.t01.pdf (in 2009, 80 percent of union workers in private industry participated in a retirement plan compared to 48 percent of nonunion workers; overall participation rate was 51 percent). The aggregate data, however, are not adjusted to correct for selection issues (e.g., that unions are concentrated in large firms, in particular industries, nor for differences in pay or skill levels between union members and other workers).

100 I.R.C. § 410(b)(4) (2006); Treas. Reg. § 1.410(b)-6(b) (as amended in 2006). For ERISA's rules concerning permissible age and service conditions, see *supra* Chapter 7A.

101 I.R.C. § 410(b)(2)(D) (2006) (average benefits percentage test); Treas. Reg. § 1.410(b)-6(b)(2) (as amended in 2006). If a plan applies age and service conditions that are less restrictive than ERISA would allow (typically, age 21 and one year of service), then the employer is allowed

incoming employees (those who have not yet satisfied minimum age and service conditions) may be excluded, a limited category of outgoing workers is also excludible. If an employee terminates employment during the year with no more than 500 hours of service and does not receive a benefit for that final year solely because the plan requires that a participant be employed on the last day of the plan year or complete a minimum period of service within the year, then such departing workers can be ignored provided that the exclusion is applied to all employees so situated.[102]

Once the workforce aggregation and excludible employee rules are applied, all the individuals who must be taken into account in testing for coverage discrimination have been identified. Each member of that universe of employees must then be assigned to one of two mutually exclusive categories, highly compensated employee (HCE), or nonhighly compensated employee (NHCE). The qualified plan rules generally classify an employee as highly compensated if she was a 5 percent owner at any time during the current or preceding year or her compensation from the employer for the preceding year exceeded $80,000, indexed for inflation ($110,000 in 2009).[103] A company with many workers earning more than that compensation threshold may elect to limit the compensation-based HCE category to the group composed of the highest-paid 20 percent of all employees.[104] The 5 percent owner category includes any employee who owns, directly or via application of constructive ownership rules, 5 percent or more of the outstanding stock of a corporation or stock possessing 5 percent or more of the total combined voting power of all stock of the corporation, or any person who owns more than 5 percent of the capital or profits interest in an unincorporated employer (sole proprietor or partner).[105]

The 5 percent owner category applies regardless of pay level. Owners can decline current compensation and shift their remuneration into the form of dividends or retained earnings (i.e., appreciation in the value of their ownership interest in the business), but they are still the high-income workers who are the source of the subsidy and present the greatest risk of abuse. Assume, for example, that the HCE definition did not include the 5 percent owner rule, and the business owners set their stated compensation at $109,000 in 2009. In that event, the plan could cover *only* the owners and it would be treated as nondiscriminatory, because by definition, any plan that covers no HCE satisfies the ratio percentage test. In applying the HCE definition to employees of

---

to treat the arrangement as two plans, one covering employees who have attained age 21 and completed one year of service, and the other covering those employees who have not. These deemed separate plans are tested independently for coverage discrimination. In testing the plan covering employees who satisfy the age 21 and one year of service condition, all employees who do not meet that age and service standard are excludible even if they are actually covered by the plan. In testing the plan covering workers who have not attained age 21 or completed a year of service, all employees who have met that standard are excludible, as are all employees who have not met any less exacting age and service conditions imposed by the plan. Treas. Reg. § 1.410(b)-6(b)(3) (as amended in 2006), § 1.410(b)-7(c)(3) (as amended in 2004).

102 Treas. Reg. § 1.410(b)-6(f) (as amended in 2006).
103 I.R.C. § 414(q)(1) (2006); Notice 2008-102, 2008-2 C.B. 1106.
104 I.R.C. § 414(q)(1)(b)(ii), (q)(3), (q)(5) (2006).
105 I.R.C. §§ 414(q)(2), 416(i)(1)(B), 318 (2006).

a controlled group or an affiliated service group, the 5 percent owner category applies to any employee who has that status with respect to any component member of the group of businesses. So, for example, an individual who is a 5 percent owner of the stock of a subsidiary corporation is tagged as an HCE along with any employees having a 5 percent or greater stake in the parent.[106]

Minimum Coverage Requirement

The ban on favoritism imposed by the coverage nondiscrimination tests is a relative standard, meaning that the proportion of NHCEs who must benefit under the plan is fixed by reference to the rate of coverage of HCEs. In addition, a defined benefit plan is required to cover an absolute minimum number of workers, regardless of their compensation level. To be qualified, a defined benefit plan must benefit the lesser of 50 employees or 40 percent of all employees, except that if the company employs only two, three, or four employees, then the required minimum coverage is two.[107] On its face, this minimum body count requirement does not seem related to the antidiscrimination norm, but it is. The core purpose of the rule is to put a stop to small defined benefit plans, especially single-member plans. By relying on plan aggregation to satisfy the nondiscrimination standards, businesses could establish individual defined benefit plans for each executive or professional employee with features that were distinct from the program covering the rank-and-file (such as different funding levels or distribution options, for example). Although combined coverage testing under the plan aggregation rule is conditioned on combined testing for amount nondiscrimination,[108] Congress was concerned that discrimination could escape detection due to the complexity and flexibility inherent in combined testing, and that the IRS did not have the resources to strictly scrutinize many plans covering a very small number of employees.[109] To stop to this abuse, elective plan aggregation cannot be used to satisfy the minimum coverage requirement, and the Treasury is authorized to treat separate benefit structures included under one plan as separate plans, each of which must independently satisfy the minimum coverage rule.[110]

The minimum coverage requirement applies to a defined benefit plan even if it is the only qualified plan of the employer and even if it contains only a single benefit structure.[111] Given its antidiscrimination origin, this seems curiously over-inclusive. Where there is only one plan, there can be no problem with discrimination eluding detection because of the complexity of comparability analysis. Yet in this instance, there may be an independent justification for the minimum coverage requirement.

---

106   Treas. Reg. § 1.414(q)-1T, Q&A-8. (as amended in 1994)
107   I.R.C. § 401(a)(26) (2006).
108   I.R.C. § 410(b)(6)(B) (2006).
109   S. Rep. No. 99-313, at 586–88 (1986).
110   I.R.C. § 401(a)(26)(H) (2006); Treas. Reg. §§ 1.401(a)(26)-2(d)(1)(iii), -3 (1991).
111   A plan that benefits no HCE and which is not aggregated with any other plan of the employer in order to satisfy nondiscrimination standards is exempted by rule from the minimum coverage requirement. Treas. Reg. § 1.401(a)(26)-1(b)(1) (as amended in 1993).

The administrative cost of issuing determination letters, plan audits, and enforcement is largely independent of the number of participants, and such high fixed costs suggest that there may be a governmental interest in discouraging the proliferation of small plans. The social advantage of increased retirement savings for a handful of low-paid workers might be more than offset by the public burden of administering the system, which burden is not taken into account in the employer's decision whether to sponsor a plan. Under an expanded cost-benefit analysis, in other words, the redistribution achieved by small-membership qualified plans may be insufficient to justify the governmental costs of administering the system. While plausible, this administrative cost justification for a minimum participation rule seems never to have been presented to or relied upon by Congress, and several features of the existing rule do not mesh well with this explanation.[112]

Sanctions for Deficient Coverage

As definitional criteria for qualified retirement plan status, failure to satisfy the coverage nondiscrimination rule or the minimum coverage requirement brings with them unfavorable tax consequences. Disqualification renders trust earnings taxable[113] and ordinarily entails taxation of employees in advance of distribution because general tax timing rules require inclusion by the person performing services as soon as her compensation is freed of any substantial risk of forfeiture.[114] Generally, the amount taxable is the amount attributable to contributions made in years in which the plan is not qualified, not the full value of the employee's interest under the plan.[115] Accordingly, a participant whose interest is substantially vested pays tax on his share of contributions made in the employer's taxable year that ends with or within the plan year of disqualification, while a substantially nonvested participant pays no tax at that time (if she becomes substantially vested in a subsequent year, she will then be liable for tax on the

---

112 Most notably, the administrative cost justification standing alone would not support the exemption of defined contribution plans. Administrative costs are generally much lower for defined contribution plans because actuarial computations are not required for purposes of funding and discrimination testing; but this consideration indicates that a lower minimum coverage requirement might be justified for defined contribution plans, not that they should be exempt. (Prior to its amendment in 1996, section 401(a)(26) applied to both defined contribution and defined benefit plans.) Nor do administrative cost concerns support the 40 percent alternative to the 50-employee minimum. The 40 percent alternative not only permits a small employer to have a low-membership plan, but it also tolerates concurrent sponsorship of multiple low-membership plans.

113 Upon disqualification, the trust loses its status as a tax-exempt organization under I.R.C. § 501(a) (2006).

114 I.R.C. § 83(a), (e)(2) (2006); *see supra* text accompanying Chapter 10 notes 8–21. *See* I.R.C. §§ 402(a), 403(a)(1) (2006) (tax deferral until distribution conditioned upon meeting definition of qualified trust or qualified annuity plan).

115 I.R.C. §§ 402(b)(1), 403(c) (2006); Treas. Reg. §§ 1.402(b)-1(a), (b), 1.403(c)-1 (as amended in 2007).

portion of her interest in the trust attributable to contributions made in disqualified years).[116]

The timing of the employer's deduction for contributions made in a year in which the plan is disqualified is controlled by the time at which amounts become includible in the employees' income.[117] ERISA requires rapid vesting, and the Code demands immediate vesting for most 401(k) plan contributions, and so most participants are likely to be substantially vested in their interests and immediately taxable on contributions made when the plan is disqualified. Under the matching rule, this means that the employer's deduction would not be deferred, and to that extent, the employer suffers no direct adverse tax effects from disqualification.

These observations show that the immediate adverse tax consequences of disqualification typically fall on employees, not on the employer, nor are they limited to the executives whose actions or inattention caused the problem. The usual tax consequences of disqualification , in other words, are not focused on the parties responsible. To better target the sanction, the usual impact of disqualification is modified where the fault lies in a violation of the coverage nondiscrimination rule or the minimum coverage requirement. In such cases, HCEs are required to include as income their entire vested accrued benefit under the plan, even if it is largely or entirely attributable to contributions made in years when the plan was qualified![118] On the other hand, workers who have always been nonhighly compensated are not taxed *at all* if the *sole* reason for disqualification is a violation of the coverage rules.[119] Thus, innocent NHCEs are sometimes exempted from immediate adverse tax consequences, while HCEs are in for a load of tax hurt. In this instance, Congress armed the IRS with a big stick to focus the minds of the actors who are in the best position to influence compensation policy.

Discrimination in Contributions or Benefits

To be qualified, every plan that satisfies the coverage nondiscrimination test must also show that "the contributions or benefits provided under the plan do not discriminate in

---

116   The amount of contributions made on behalf of a participant is easily determined under a defined contribution plan, but the absence of separate accounts presents a formidable obstacle to implementing contribution-based taxation in the case of a disqualified defined benefit plan. To alleviate this difficulty, the employer is given a strong incentive to amend the plan to set up separate accounts: failing to do so results in complete disallowance of any deduction for the contribution. I.R.C. § 404(a)(5) (2006); Treas. Reg. § 1.404(a)-12(b)(3) (as amended in 1978). If the employer fails to establish separate accounts, an allocation of contributions must somehow still be made in order to tax the employees. The regulations provide for allocation of a defined benefit plan contribution under a specified formula "or under any other method utilizing recognized actuarial principles which are consistent with the provisions of the plan under which such contributions are made and the method adopted by the employer for funding benefits under the plan." Treas. Reg. § 1.402(b)-1(a)(2) (as amended in 2007).

117   I.R.C. § 404(a)(5) (2006), discussed *supra* text accompanying Chapter 10 notes 22–23.

118   I.R.C. § 402(b)(4)(A), (C) (2006).

119   I.R.C. § 402(b)(4)(B) (2006).

favor of highly compensated employees."[120] That standard contains both qualitative and quantitative elements.[121]

The qualitative component demands that each significant benefit, right, or feature provided under the plan be made available in a nondiscriminatory fashion. The objective here is equal access or opportunity; disparity between actual utilization rates of HCEs and NHCEs is not per se disqualifying. A principal concern is with optional forms of distribution. Assume that a plan provides that a participant's accrued benefit will ordinarily be distributed as a life annuity commencing at normal retirement age, but allows participants who meet certain eligibility conditions to elect an actuarially equivalent lump-sum distribution instead. Here, there is no favoritism in the value conferred (due to the actuarial equivalence of the two payment methods), but if the eligibility conditions imposed on the lump-sum alternative are correlated with compensation level, then access to the optional form of distribution might unduly favor HCEs. For instance, if lump-sum distribution can be selected only by employees who have a specified minimum net worth, or who work in certain job categories, occupations, or geographic locations (e.g., head office personnel only), then in operation the condition, although neutral on its face, might restrict eligibility in a way that affords greater choice to HCEs.[122] The IRS has consistently interpreted the nondiscrimination rules to forbid such qualitative favoritism and has consistently applied the rules by assessing the impact of specified eligibility conditions in operation, based on the facts and circumstances of the particular workforce.[123]

The quantitative component, often referred to as the amount nondiscrimination test, is satisfied if the amount of contributions or benefits provided under the plan, expressed as a share of each employee's compensation, does not favor HCEs. Hence, a qualified plan may provide retirement savings that represent a fixed or uniform proportion of

---

120   I.R.C. § 401(a)(4) (2006).

121   A third element adds a temporal component to review for discrimination in contributions or benefits. The tests for qualitative and quantitative favoritism, although performed annually on the basis of the actual operation of the plan, take into account only the impact of the terms of the plan as currently in effect. That is, the tests for qualitative and quantitative favoritism are static and would not capture favoritism accomplished by means of changes in plan terms over time. Therefore, a temporal or dynamic element is required to prevent abuse. Treas. Reg. § 1.401(a)(4)-5 (as amended in 1993), *see infra* Chapter 10 note 126.

122   *E.g.*, Rev. Rul. 85-59, 1985-1 C.B. 135, declared obsolete, Rev. Rul. 93-87, 1993-2C.B. 124 (because ruling position now specifically covered by regulations).

123   Treas. Reg. § 1.401(a)(4)-4 (as amended in 2004) now governs the determination whether plan benefits, rights, or features are made available in a nondiscriminatory manner. The regulation applies to all optional forms of benefit (distribution alternatives), ancillary benefits (nonretirement benefits such as life or health insurance, or plant shutdown benefits), and any other right or feature that can reasonably be expected to have meaningful value to employees, such as plan loans or the right to direct investments. *Id.* -4(e). The regulation provides that each benefit, right, or feature must satisfy both a current availability and an effective availability requirement. The current availability test is largely mechanical and seems intended to function as an objective filter. In contrast, effective availability calls for an overall judgment that in actual operation "[b]ased on all the relevant facts and circumstances the group of employees to whom the benefit, right, or feature is effectively available must not substantially favor HCEs." *Id.* -4(c)(1).

each employee's compensation (up to a specified compensation cap[124]) even if the dollar amount saved for highly paid workers is ten times larger than for some low-paid employees.

Regulations adopted in 1993 implement the amount nondiscrimination requirement. After fifty years, the Treasury elaborated the pithy statutory command that contributions or benefits not discriminate with detailed regulations under section 401(a)(4) (filling 100 pages of the Code of Federal Regulations). Most of this frightful complexity can be safely left to experts and actuaries, but the resolution of two central interpretive problems deserves notice.

Clearly, a defined contribution plan is most readily tested for discrimination in the amount of contributions, while it is natural to test a defined benefit plan for disparities in the amount of benefits. Now consider a plan that provides benefits that are a larger proportion of compensation for HCEs than for other employees. For example, the normal retirement benefit for an HCE might be 40 percent of final average compensation, while the NHCE benefit is only 35 percent. If the HCEs are younger than the NHCEs, however, their benefits will be funded over a longer period, and therefore the contributions necessary to fund benefits for the HCEs might not be disproportionate to compensation. Does such a plan violate the amount nondiscrimination requirement? Must a defined benefit plan be tested only for discrimination in benefits, and a defined contribution plan tested only for discrimination in contributions, or can benefits be converted into equivalent contributions (and vice versa) for purposes of the amount nondiscrimination requirement? The statute refers to "contributions or benefits," but whether logical disjunction or implied parallelism was intended is far from clear. In drafting the regulations, the Treasury followed its prior ruling position and opted for flexibility: a cross-testing rule allows defined benefit plans to be tested on a contributions basis, and defined contribution plans on a benefits basis.[125]

The second conundrum that the regulation-drafters had to resolve concerns the meaning of discrimination, where some but not all rank-and-file employees receive contributions or benefits that represent a smaller proportion of pay than the amount granted one or more HCEs. Contributions or benefits might be based on age or length of service (in whole or in part), and under profit-sharing or stock bonus plans, contributions can be tied to objective measures of profitability or productivity.[126]

---

124   I.R.C. § 401(a)(17) (2006). The $200,000 cap on compensation that may be taken into account under a qualified plan is adjusted for inflation and stands at $245,000 in 2009. As explained later, the compensation cap is the link between the amount nondiscrimination rule and limits on the maximum amount of contributions or benefits that may be provided under a qualified plan. *See infra* Chapter 10 note 184 and accompanying text.

125   Treas. Reg. § 1.401(a)(4)-8 (as amended in 2001).

126   A qualified plan must be "a definite written program or arrangement which is communicated to employees," Treas. Reg. § 1.401-1(a)(2) (as amended in 1976). A pension plan, as the term is used for tax purposes, means a plan designed to provide benefits to employees or their beneficiaries on retirement or for a period of years thereafter, and may be either a defined benefit or a defined contribution arrangement. In either case, discretion in amount is barred because the arrangement will "be considered a pension plan if the employer contribution under the plan can be determined actuarially on the basis of definitely determinable benefits, or, as in the case of money purchase pension plans, such contribution are fixed without being geared to profits."

Formulae that take into account such factors can yield a wide range of contribution or benefit accrual rates for both highly compensated and rank-and-file employees. Does the plan "discriminate" if *any* NHCE earns lesser benefits (as a proportion of compensation) than any HCE? The Treasury first proposed just such an extremist or hard-line definition of prohibited favoritism.[127] Plan sponsors, of course, lobbied for a more forgiving standard. Ultimately, the Treasury settled upon a testing approach that accommodates plans that generate a variety of allocation or accrual rates for HCEs and NHCEs, so long as the range of rates for the two groups largely overlaps.[128]

Id. -1(b)(1)(i). The employer may retain discretion as to the overall amount contributed to a profit-sharing or stock bonus plan from year to year, but the plan must nevertheless "provide a definite predetermined formula for allocating the contribution made to the plan among the participants." *Id.* -1(b)(1)(ii). The core concept of a "defined benefit" or "defined contribution" plan, in other words, has always been interpreted to bar discretion in setting the amounts earned by individual employees, even though a central tenet of our voluntary employment-based retirement savings system is that the sponsor remains free to set or amend the plan's provisions governing the amount of deferred compensation (the formula governing benefit accrual or contribution allocation). *See supra* Chapter 1C.

It should be noted that the employer's general freedom to change the amount of retirement savings could be abused. Some oversight of the timing of plan amendments is necessary to prevent the employer from taking advantage of changes in workforce composition to accomplish favoritism by means of plan provisions that, viewed in isolation, appear even-handed. An across-the-board increase in benefits taking effect after most NHCEs have left the plan, and the elimination of an ancillary benefit after most HCEs have already taken advantage of it, are examples of the problem. Therefore, in addition to the requirement that all benefits, rights and features under the plan be made available on a nondiscriminatory basis (qualitative scrutiny) and the amount nondiscrimination test (quantitative scrutiny), the regulations provide that section 401(a)(4) is violated if the timing of a plan amendment or series of amendments has the effect of discriminating significantly in favor of HCEs or former HCEs. Treas. Reg. § 1.401(a)(4)-5 (as amended in 1993). The timing of the initial establishment or termination of the plan is also subject to review under this rule, but the determination whether the institution, amendment or termination of the plan has the effect of "discriminating significantly" is "based on all the relevant facts and circumstances." *Id.* -5(a)(2). Of particular concern are grants of past service benefits to current employees under a defined benefit plan (whether accomplished by initial establishment or subsequent amendment) where there has been significantly higher turnover among NHCEs than HCEs during the period for which credit is retroactively granted. Under a special safe harbor, however, uniform grants of up to five years of past-service credit under the plan's current benefit formula are deemed nondiscriminatory. *Id.* -5(a)(3).

127 With respect to contributions, Prop. Treas. Reg. § 1.401(a)(4)-2(c)(1) provided: "A plan satisfies the requirements of this section if no highly compensated employee in the plan has an allocation rate that exceeds that of any nonhighly compensated employee in the plan." 55 Fed. Reg. 19,897, 19,911 (May 14, 1990). The same approach was proposed for testing benefits. Prop. Treas. Reg. § 1.401(a)(4)-3(c)(1)(i), 55 Fed. Reg. at 19,914.

128 It is noteworthy that the final regulations did not adopt the position advocated by plan sponsors and practitioners, that the amount nondiscrimination test should be limited to a simple comparison of the average rate of contribution or benefits received by the two groups (HCEs and NHCEs). Presumably, the Treasury's concern was that the distribution of rates for the two groups might be distributed in a manner that provided systematically higher benefits to some HCEs. This could happen, for example, if the standard deviation of allocation or accrual rates was larger for HCEs than NHCEs, or if the two distributions were disparately skewed about the means.

A program that provides retirement savings proportionate to compensation is just what many employers want. By promising a uniform allocation or accrual rate, such a plan is assured of satisfying the amount nondiscrimination test, provided that each participant's contribution or benefit is based on a measure of compensation that does not itself discriminate. That can be accomplished either by using the statute's comprehensive definition of compensation or by consistently excluding certain items of irregular or additional compensation and showing that the resulting narrower measure does not systematically favor HCEs.[129] A plan that does so is assured of satisfying the amount nondiscrimination standard. Accordingly, the regulations dispense with annual operational testing for plans that meet stringent uniformity requirements.[130] These design-based safe harbors are often attractive because they reduce plan-administration costs and provide assurance of continuing qualification.

Annual amount nondiscrimination testing is required for plans that do not tie contributions or benefits to a fixed proportion of compensation. In developing a general test for discrimination, the Treasury hit upon a clever insight: the objective mechanical tests for coverage discrimination could be pressed into service to identify systematic favoritism in the amount of qualified retirement saving. That insight was implemented by requiring that each "rate group" under the plan must satisfy either the ratio percentage test or a modified version of the average benefits test, with those tests applied as if the rate group were a separate plan that benefits only the employees included in the rate group.[131] A rate group for a defined contribution plan is defined as the group of employees who receive allocations of employer contributions or forfeitures under the plan that equal or exceed (either as an absolute dollar amount or as a percentage of plan year compensation) the allocation received by a specific HCE plan member. There is a separate rate group for each HCE in the plan, which is composed of that particular HCE and all other plan members (both HCEs and NHCEs) who have an allocation rate greater than or equal to that HCE. "Thus, an employee is in the rate group for each HCE who has an allocation rate less than or equal to the employee's allocation rate."[132] The general test for nondiscrimination in contributions uses the technique of successive rate group coverage testing to prevent favoritism in the amounts of employer contributions and forfeitures added to participants' accounts during the year.

Rate group testing is best explained by reference to a simple illustration. Assume that Beta Corporation maintains a service-weighted profit-sharing plan.[133] Beta's workforce

---

129   I.R.C. § 401(a)(5)(B) (2006) (authorizing uniform relationship to compensation "within the meaning of section 414(s)"), *id.* §§ 414(s), 415(c)(3); Treas. Reg. § 1.414(s)-1 (as amended in 2007).

130   Treas. Reg. § 1.401(a)(4)-2(b)(2) (as amended 2007) (uniform allocation formula safe harbor for defined contribution plans), § 1.401(a)(4)-3(b) (as amended in 1993) (uniformity-based safe harbors for certain defined benefit plans).

131   Treas. Reg. § 1.401(a)(4)-2(c)(1), -2(c)(3)(i) (as amended in 2007).

132   Treas. Reg. § 1.401(a)(4)-2(c)(1) (as amended in 2007).

133   The defined contribution plan amount nondiscrimination regulations provide a simplified operational test for certain plans that base contributions in whole or in part on each employee's age or service. This special rule is available only if age or service is taken into account in the manner specified by the definition of a uniform points allocation formula, Treas. Reg.

consists of 12 nonexcludible employees, two of whom are highly compensated. Plan B covers both of the company's HCEs and 8 of the 10 NHCEs. Assume that Plan B's contribution formula produces the following allocation rates for the year, expressed as a percentage of each employee's plan year compensation, where H1 and H2 are Beta's HCEs and N1–N10 are the NHCEs:

Employee	Allocation Rate (%)
H1	9
H2	6
N1	9
N2	9
N3	8
N4	7
N5	6
N6	6
N7	6
N8	5
N9	0
N10	0

Plan B's ratio percentage (80 percent) easily satisfies the coverage nondiscrimination test, but Plan B plainly does not provide a uniform allocation rate. It will nevertheless pass the amount nondiscrimination test if *each* rate group under the plan satisfies either the ratio percentage test or a modified version of the average benefits test. Plan B has two rate groups, one corresponding to each HCE. Call them rate group 1 (RG1) defined by H1, and rate group 2 (RG2) defined by H2. Each rate group consists of all employees who have an allocation rate at least equal to the allocation rate of the HCE who defines the group. Therefore, RG1 is composed of H1, N1, and N2, and RG2 is composed of H1, H2, N1, N2, N3, N4, N5, N6, and N7 (i.e., all employees, whether highly compensated or not, with an allocation rate equal to or greater than the 6 percent received by H2). Treated as if it were a separate plan, the membership of RG2 satisfies the ratio percentage test (both HCEs are included and RG2 also includes 7 of 10 NHCEs). RG1, however, has a ratio percentage of only 40 percent (= 20% of NHCEs divided by 50% of HCEs). Consequently, in order for Plan B to pass the general test for nondiscrimination in contributions, RG1 must satisfy a modified version of the average benefits test.

---

§ 1.401(a)(4)-2(b)(3)(i)(A) (as amended in 2007). The general test is applied in this example, because insufficient facts are presented to know whether Plan B uses a uniform points allocation formula, and because, even if it did, the allocation rates assumed here (see the following table) would not satisfy the simplified operational test for a uniform points plan. That test requires that for the plan year in question, "the average of the allocation rates for the HCEs in the plan must not exceed the average of the allocation rates for the NHCEs in the plan." *Id*. -2(b)(3)(i)(B). The average HCE allocation rate for Plan B is 7.5 percent, while the average allocation rate for "NHCEs *in the plan*" (N1 through N8 only) is only 6.875 percent.

Recall that there are two components to the average benefits test: the nondiscriminatory classification test and the average benefits percentage test. For purposes of rate group coverage testing under the section 401(a)(4) regulations, each of these components is adjusted somewhat. The reasonable classification requirement is not applied in testing rate group coverage, and the nondiscriminatory classification test is deemed satisfied if the ratio percentage of the rate group equals or exceeds the midpoint between the safe harbor and prohibited zone ratio percentages for the plan in question (see Figure 10-3), or, if smaller, the ratio percentage of the plan.[134] (Observe that these alterations of the nondiscriminatory classification test eliminate any need for discretionary determinations.) Beta Corporation's NHCE concentration percentage is 83 percent (= 10 NHCEs/12 total nonexcludible employees). At that workforce composition, the midpoint between the safe harbor (32.75%) and prohibited zone (22.75%) boundaries is 27.75%,[135] so RG1's ratio percentage of 40 percent easily passes the nondiscriminatory classification test. For purposes of rate group coverage testing, the average benefits percentage test is automatically deemed satisfied by every rate group if it is satisfied by the plan as a whole.[136] Assuming that Plan B is the only qualified plan offered by Beta Corporation, the average benefit percentage of the HCEs is 7.5 percent (= 9% + 6%, divided by 2 HCEs), and the average benefit percentage for NHCEs is 5.6 percent (= 9% + 9% + 8% + 7% + 6% + 6% +6% + 5%, divided by 10 total NHCEs). The average benefit percentage of the NHCEs (5.6%) exceeds 70 percent of the average benefit percentage for the HCEs (70% × 7.5% = 5.25%), so the plan as a whole satisfies the average benefits percentage test, hence RG1 passes the modified average benefits test, and Plan B survives the amount nondiscrimination test. Notice that if N8 were not an active participant (zero contribution, like N9 and N10), Plan B's rate groups would not change (N8 is not included in either RG1 or RG2), but the plan as a whole would fail the average benefits percentage test (5.1% average NHCE allocation divided by 7.5% average HCE allocation is 68%), the coverage of RG1 would not pass muster, and Plan B would face disqualification on the ground that the amounts contributed favor HCEs.[137]

Abstracting from the technical detail and computational gymnastics, a logical pattern emerges. The technique of successive rate group coverage testing to identify amount discrimination is akin to the following protocol: (1) list all plan participants in descending order by rate of employer contribution; (2) identify all the HCEs on the list (by highlighting those names, for example); and (3) check to be sure that the HCEs are not heavily concentrated toward the top of the list. If the HCEs are either dispersed reasonably evenly throughout the list, or disproportionately represented toward the

---

134   Treas. Reg. § 1.401(a)(4)-2(c)(3)(ii) (as amended in 2007).

135   Treas. Reg. § 1.410(b)-4(c)(4) (1991), or consult Figure 10-3 *supra*.

136   Treas. Reg. § 1.401(a)(4)-2(c)(3)(iii) (as amended in 2007).

137   Two avenues might still be available to Beta Corporation to avoid disqualification. First, the rules governing integration with Social Security (specifically, operational integration via imputation of permitted disparity in testing for amount nondiscrimination) might justify the limited favoritism present here. *See infra* Chapter 10 notes 154–157 and accompanying text. Second, Beta could take advantage of a retroactive correction mechanism to avoid disqualification. *See infra* Chapter 10 notes 162–64 and accompanying text.

bottom, then the plan does not exhibit prohibited favoritism in the amount of retirement savings.

Despite its elegance, from a policy perspective, the technique of successive rate group testing has a couple of shortcomings. As an indicator of discrimination in the amount of qualified plan savings, it is arguably both over- and under-inclusive. First, suppose that H1 in the preceding example had gotten an allocation rate of 10 percent. Observe that if the highest allocation rate for the plan year happens to be received by an HCE, the plan is likely to be disqualified. The rate group defined by that HCE will have a ratio percentage of zero, given that no NHCE gets that much savings, and a ratio percentage below 20 percent is never acceptable under the nondiscriminatory classification test. In some circumstances, the regulation allows actual allocation rates to be grouped within ranges when determining rate group membership, with all rates falling within a given range treated as equal, and that allowance might sometimes be used to bring one or more NHCEs into the top rate group. Yet because the acceptable ranges are quite narrow, in many cases this expedient will prove unavailing.[138]

A second limitation of rate group coverage testing inheres in the fact that no attention is paid to the compensation of the employees within the rate groups. Consequently, the top rate group (meaning the rate group defined by the HCE with the highest allocation rate, which therefore has the smallest membership) might include the most highly paid HCE, and its coverage could pass muster even if the NHCEs included in that rate group were the lowest-paid plan members. The result would be substantial retirement savings by the HCE (highest allocation rate among HCEs applied to highest compensation), while the high allocation rates of the NHCEs in that rate group would not translate into large savings due to their meager compensation levels. Given the redistribution objective, some might view a systematic inverse relationship between NHCE plan members' compensation levels and allocation rates as troubling, if not indicative of abuse. The counterargument, of course, is that the problem is inherent in the mechanical two-group (i.e., HCE versus NHCE) coverage comparison, and a more exacting standard would be too complex and burdensome.

The amount nondiscrimination tests for defined benefit plans are structured like the rules for defined contribution plans described above. There are a number of safe harbors for plans that provide uniform benefits.[139] There is also a general test for benefit nondiscrimination that operates by applying the coverage nondiscrimination rules to successive rate groups.[140] But instead of testing allocation rates, the safe harbors and general test for defined benefit plans are applied with reference to *accrual rates*—the

---

138   Treas. Reg. § 1.401(a)(4)-2(c)(2)(v) (as amended in 2007). The lowest and highest allocation rates within the range must be within 5 percent (not 5 percentage points) above or below a midpoint allocation rate selected by the employer. Alternatively, if allocation rates are computed as a percentage of plan year compensation, a range of one-quarter of a percentage point above or below the selective midpoint is acceptable. *Id.* Besides the narrowness of the permitted range of allocation rate grouping, this strategy faces another ill-defined obstacle. The regulation prohibits grouping "if the allocation rates of the HCEs within the range generally are significantly higher than the allocation rates of the NHCEs within the range." *Id.* -2(c)(2)(v)(A).

139   Treas. Reg. § 1.401(a)(4)-3(b) (as amended in 1993).

140   *Id.* § 1.401(a)(4)-3(c).

increase in each employee's accrued benefit over a selected measurement period.[141] This dependence on accrual rates makes the benefit nondiscrimination regulation considerably more complex, and typically dependent upon actuarial calculations.

Integration with Social Security

Qualified plans encourage the accumulation of savings that will supplement Social Security old-age benefits, so that retired workers will have an adequate standard of living after they leave the labor force. (Recall that Social Security, the mandatory and near-universal public retirement program, provides only a baseline level of retirement income. For a large majority of retirees, Social Security alone is inadequate to maintain their pre-retirement standard of living.[142]) Social Security benefits, however, are not proportionate to pay; they are progressive (or bottom-weighted), meaning that Social Security replaces a larger proportion of low-income workers' pre-retirement earnings than for high-income workers. (See Figure 10-1 above.) Moreover, compensation in excess of the Social Security contribution and benefit base (also know as the taxable wage base; $106,800 in 2009) generates no additional benefits under the public retirement program. Hence highly paid workers need to save a larger proportion of their earnings in order to maintain their standard of living in retirement. This presents a fundamental policy question: should qualified plans, the semi-private retirement savings system, be allowed (or required) to take into account the structure of Social Security in setting the amount of contributions or benefits provided plan members? Arguably, the combination of qualified plan and Social Security benefits should form an integrated support system that delivers adequate retirement resources to all workers, regardless of compensation level. To do so, however, qualified plan coverage or benefits would have to be wrapped around Social Security in a way that *favors* higher-paid workers.

Since 1942, when nondiscrimination requirements were first imposed, Congress has, in one form or another, permitted plan sponsors to take account of Social Security benefits, which necessitates some loosening of the nondiscrimination rules. In the early years, qualified plans were allowed to entirely exclude from coverage any worker whose compensation was less than the Social Security taxable wage base, provided that the plan's contributions or benefits were (1) based solely on that portion of each participant's compensation that exceeded the wage base, and (2) not greater than the amount determined by applying a prescribed maximum contribution or benefit rate to that excess compensation. The maximum rates were loosely based on the rate of Social Security contributions and benefits with respect to compensation below the taxable wage base. If those conditions were satisfied, the excluded low-paid workers could be treated as active participants in testing for discriminatory coverage.[143] As Senator

---

141   *Id.* § 1.401(a)(4)-3(d) (including permission to group accrual rates within narrow ranges).

142   *See supra* text accompanying Figure 10-1.

143   Prior to its amendment in 1986, I.R.C. § 401(a)(5) provided in part:

   A classification shall not be considered discriminatory within the meaning of paragraph (4) [the amount nondiscrimination test] or section 410(b) [the prior law coverage nondiscrimination test] merely because it excludes employees the whole of whose remuneration constitutes

Gaylord Nelson complained during the debate on ERISA, "[p]ension benefits given to low-paid employees as an abstraction are taken away in the fine print of the income tax Code."[144]

Hikes in the taxable wage base during the 1970s and 1980s, combined with annual indexing since then, greatly exacerbated this problem. Indeed, the cutoff on Social Security taxes ($106,800 in 2009) is now very close to the compensation threshold for HCE classification ($110,000 in 2009). By way of comparison, in 2007 some 80 percent of U.S. households received income from all sources totaling less than $100,000.[145] Under these circumstances, a rule allowing complete exclusion of employees earning less than the taxable wage base would effectively eviscerate redistribution.

At the Treasury's urging, Congress revised the qualified plan integration rules in 1986 with the enactment of Code section 401(l).[146] Social Security integration no longer provides an excuse for the complete exclusion of lower-paid workers from plan membership—the revised approach to integration relaxes the amount nondiscrimination standard (specifically, the uniformity rule) but not the coverage requirement.[147] The integration rules ("permitted disparity") for defined contribution and defined benefit plans necessarily differ due to the different focus of those plan types (money going into the plan versus money paid out), but they share a common theme. An integrated plan must provide some contributions or benefits with respect to employee

---

"wages" under section 3121(a)(1) (relating to the Federal Insurance Contributions Act [FICA, the tax side of social security]) or merely because it is limited to salaried or clerical employees.

That prior law integration rule is elaborated by Treas. Reg. § 1.401-4(b) (as amended in 1993), and illustrated in Rev. Rul. 79-348, 1979-2 C.B. 161 (declared obsolete, Rev. Rul. 93-87, 1993-2 C.B. 124).

144   119 CONG. REC. 30,133 (Sept. 18, 1973).

145   U.S. CENSUS BUREAU, INCOME, POVERTY AND HEALTH INSURANCE COVERAGE IN THE UNITED STATES: 2008, Table A-1 at 29 (2009), *available at* http://www.census.gov/prod/2009pubs/p60-235.pdf.

146   During the Carter Administration, top Treasury tax policy officials foresaw this problem and urged prompt legislative action. *National Pension Policies: Private Pension Plans: Hearings Before the Subcomm. on Retirement Income and Employment of the House Select Comm. on Aging*, 95th Cong. 228–50 (1978) (statement of Daniel I. Halperin, Tax Legislative Counsel, U.S. Department of the Treasury). The current integration rules largely follow the solution recommended by the Treasury in 1978, but the fix was not adopted until 1986. The top-heavy plan rules enacted in 1982 require that each participant in a top-heavy plan who is not a key employee must get a specified minimum employer contribution or benefit from the plan without regard to Social Security integration. I.R.C. § 416(c), (e) (2006). In large measure, the section 416 top-heavy plan rules were a response to abuses resulting from the laxity of the traditional approach to integration. (Indeed, the top-heavy plan provision can be viewed as a stopgap that ought to have been repealed once integration standards were tightened.)

147   I.R.C. § 401(a)(5)(C) (2006) now provides: "A plan shall not be considered discriminatory within the meaning of paragraph (4) [requiring that contributions or benefits provided under the plan do not discriminate in favor of HCEs] merely because the contributions or benefits of, or on behalf of, the employees under the plan favor highly compensated employees (as defined in section 414(q)) in the manner permitted under subsection (l)." Observe that the prior reference to the section 410(b) coverage rules was dropped. *See supra* Chapter 10 note 143.

compensation that is less than the plan's integration level,[148] and the rate at which contributions or benefits are earned on compensation above the plan's integration level cannot exceed the rate applicable to compensation below the integration level by more than (1) 100 percent, or, if smaller, (2) an amount that approximates one-half of the average rate of contributions (i.e., taxes) or benefits under the Social Security retirement system.[149] The latter amount is set at 5.7 percent for defined contribution plans (which equals the portion of the employer's 6.2 percent Social Security tax rate that is used to finance old-age benefits), and three-quarters of a percentage point for any year of service taken into account under a defined benefit plan.[150]

A plan containing a contribution or benefit formula that complies with I.R.C. § 401(*l*) can automatically satisfy the amount nondiscrimination test. The uniform allocation formula safe harbor (the design-based safe harbor for defined contribution plans) may apply where "a plan satisfies section 401(*l*) in form."[151] So, for example, annual amount nondiscrimination testing would not be required of a money purchase pension plan that promised employer contributions equal to 7 percent of each participant's compensation up to the Social Security wage base plus 12.7 percent of any compensation in excess of the wage base (a formula that takes advantage of the maximum permitted disparity). If instead the plan promised employer contributions of only 5 percent of compensation up to the Social Security wage base, then it could not

---

148 The integration level is an amount of compensation specified in the plan (by dollar amount or formula), not greater than the Social Security taxable wage base, at or below which the rate at which contributions or benefits are provided is less than the rate applied above such amount. I.R.C. § 401(*l*)(5)(A) (2006). Typically, defined contribution plans use the taxable wage base as the integration level, while defined benefit plans use covered compensation, which is the average of the Social Security wage base in effect for each of the 35 years preceding the year in which the employee attains the Social Security retirement age (computed as if the wage base remains constant in future years). *See id.* § 401(*l*)(4)(C), (*l*)(5)(E). If a plan adopts a different integration level, the maximum permitted disparity (5.7 percent for defined contribution plans or 0.75 percent per year of service for defined benefit plans) might have to be reduced. *See* Treas. Reg. §§ 1.401(*l*)-2(d)(4), -3(d)(9) (as amended in 1993).

149 I.R.C. § 401(*l*)(2), (*l*)(3)(A), (*l*)(4)(A) (2006). The Federal Insurance Contributions Act (FICA) nominally imposes the payroll taxes that finance the Social Security system, half on the employer and half on the employee (collected by wage withholding). Starting from the premise that the employer can properly claim credit for only the employer-funded portion of the public retirement program, the maximum permitted disparity for defined contribution plans under section 401(*l*) (i.e., 5.7 percent) is based on one-half of the taxes that finance Social Security old-age benefits, and the maximum permitted disparity for defined benefit plans (0.75 percent per year) is one-half of the approximate average accrual rate of Social Security benefits. Unfortunately, this halfway consideration of Social Security is half-baked. Legal liability has no bearing on the economic incidence of the tax, meaning who suffers its real impact in reduced resources. In a competitive market, the division of the real burden of the payroll tax depends only on the price elasticities of labor supply and demand, regardless of how the tax is collected (whether solely from the employer, solely from the employee, or split between them in some way). For example, in many occupations, employment opportunities are sensitive to labor costs, but the number of hours worked is fairly insensitive to pay rate, and in those circumstances, the burden of the FICA tax would fall largely on labor, despite its 50/50 collection.

150 I.R.C. § 401(*l*)(2)(A)(ii), (*l*)(4)(A) (2006).

151 Treas. Reg. § 1.401(a)(4)-2(b)(2)(ii) (as amended in 2007).

provide more than 10 percent of any compensation in excess of the wage base (the maximum permitted disparity is the lesser of 5.7 percent or the base contribution percentage). Similarly, the defined benefit safe harbors may be availed of by a plan that "takes permitted disparity into account in a manner that satisfies section 401(*l*) in form."[152] Hence, a unit credit plan could avoid operational testing if it promised a normal retirement benefit of 1.25 percent of each participant's average annual compensation up to covered compensation, plus 2.0 percent of average annual compensation in excess of covered compensation, multiplied by the participant's years of service up to a maximum of 35 years.[153]

Suppose that a plan says nothing about integration, and its contribution or benefit formula produces higher allocation or accrual rates for HCEs. Can the employer defend this favoritism on the ground that the higher savings rate for HCEs is no more than the disparity that would have been tolerated if the plan had been properly integrated with Social Security? The amount nondiscrimination regulations say "yes." In computing allocation or accrual rates for purposes of the general tests for discrimination in contributions or benefits, the "disparity permitted under section 401(*l*) may be imputed in accordance with the rules of § 1.401(a)(4)-7."[154] The regulation permitting such operational integration calls for a lot of computation, but the concept is straightforward. "In general, [the regulation] allows permitted disparity to be arithmetically imputed with respect to employer provided contributions or benefits by determining an adjusted allocation or accrual rate that appropriately accounts for the permitted disparity with respect to each employee."[155] In the case of a defined contribution plan, adjusted allocation rates are derived by assuming that the plan takes full advantage of the maximum disparity permitted defined contribution plans and uses the Social Security taxable wage base as the integration level.[156] For a defined benefit plan, adjusted accrual rates are derived by assuming that the plan takes full advantage of the maximum disparity permitted defined benefit plans for the first 35 years of credited service and uses covered compensation as the integration level.[157] The adjusted (or deemed) allocation or accrual rates so determined for each employee are then evaluated under the general test for discrimination in the amount of contributions or benefits (the successive rate group coverage testing approach). This operational or de facto integration technique is called, appropriately enough, imputation of permitted disparity.

By requiring that an integrated plan provide significant savings for rank-and-file employees, section 401(*l*) increases the likelihood that the nondiscrimination rules will actually achieve some level of redistribution. The current integration regime is still

---

152 Treas. Reg. § 1.401(a)(4)-3(b)(6)(ii) (as amended in 1993).

153 To satisfy the uniform benefit safe harbor for unit credit plans, this plan would also have to define each employee's accrued benefit at any time as the amount determined by applying the plan's formula for the normal retirement benefit to the employee's years of service and average annual compensation determined at the time in question. Treas. Reg. § 1.401(a)(4)-3(b)(3) (as amended in 1993).

154 Treas. Reg. § 1.401(a)(4)-2(c)(2)(iv) (as amended in 2007), *id.* § 1.401(a)(4)-3(d)(3)(i) (as amended in 1993).

155 Treas. Reg. § 1.401(a)(4)-7(a) (as amended in 1993).

156 *Id.* -7(b)(1).

157 *Id.* -7(c)(1).

subject to criticism, however. The integration rules force less redistribution than would be required in their absence. That could be good or bad. If the tax subsidy associated with savings by highly paid employees is not large enough to fund proportionate savings by the rank-and-file, then relaxing the amount nondiscrimination test so that lower-paid workers get some retirement savings is clearly preferable to discontinuance of the plan. But if an unmitigated application of the uniformity test for favoritism would not trigger plan termination, then integration allows plan sponsors or their HCEs to retain a large share of the tax savings, and to that extent, the qualified plan tax preference is wasted. Which situation obtains, of course, depends on tax rates and work-force composition. Whether on balance integration preserves or inhibits redistribution is an unanswered empirical question. In any event, it is far from clear that integration fits with nondiscrimination, notwithstanding their historical codependence.

Some would object that the real purpose of integration is to prevent over-pensioning low-paid workers who receive a higher replacement rate due to the redistributive component of Social Security, and that such over-pensioning would likewise be wasteful. So it would, but the risk of such over-pensioning is slight, and integration is an ill-conceived remedy. Even very low-paid workers need to supplement Social Security to maintain an adequate standard of living in retirement. (Recall that the "Low" earnings level depicted in Figure 10-1 is roughly comparable to a career of full-time minimum wage work, and that produces a Social Security replacement rate of only 54 percent.) Rank-and-file workers actually covered by qualified plans get even lower Social Security replacement rates. Data reveal that qualified plan participation is strongly correlated with compensation level—coverage is skewed toward workers who earn average wages or higher. In particular, plan membership among the lowest-paid 40 percent of the labor force (those who receive the highest replacement rates under Social Security) is quite rare. Most important, the integration rules are simply not designed to prevent over-pensioning, as another glance at Figure 10-1 will show. Social Security replacement rates vary widely: from 54 percent for "Low" career earnings to 28 percent for "Maximum" earnings (which represents a worker who is paid an amount equal to the taxable wage base each year during her career). Both these workers need more retirement income than Social Security alone will provide to continue their accustomed lifestyles, and the "Low" earner clearly needs proportionately much less. An integrated qualified plan will make no such differentiation between these workers, however. Neither of them was paid more than the taxable wage base at any point in their careers, and so each of them would earn retirement savings according to the plan's base contribution percentage or base benefit percentage. Consequently, in proportion to pay, the "Maximum" earner gets no more savings than the "Low" earner. The integration rules, in other words, only allow a higher contribution or benefit rate to be applied to compensation beyond the reach of Social Security; they make no attempt to assure that the combination of Social Security and qualified plan benefits produces a uniform replacement rate over all compensation ranges.[158]

---

158   For a proposal that would coordinate Social Security and qualified plan benefits over all compensation levels, see Nancy J. Altman, *Rethinking Retirement Income Policies: Nondiscrimination, Integration, and the Quest for Worker Security*, 42 TAX L. REV. 433, 484 (1987).

In 1986, Congress enacted a limited over-pensioning rule. Notwithstanding the amount nondiscrimination precept, a defined benefit plan is allowed to provide that a participant's accrued benefit shall not exceed the participant's final pay from the employer reduced by half of the Social Security retirement benefits attributable to service with the employer.[159] Presumably, such a final pay limitation would be triggered only by a very low-paid employee (hence, high Social Security replacement rate) who is covered under a generous non-integrated defined benefit plan. In its current form, the limit does no more than allow the plan to cap benefits to avoid an outlandish work disincentive.

If it were determined that integration could be repealed without causing a net decrease in retirement savings for low-income workers, then an argument could be made that repeal should be accompanied by the enactment of a generally applicable limit on qualified plan savings to prevent over-pensioning. The precise limit should be set after consideration of the appropriate target replacement rate. For a defined benefit plan, the limit might look something like 80 percent of final pay reduced by 100 percent of the participant's Social Security primary insurance amount,[160] and an employer might be allowed to discontinue contributions under a defined contribution plan when the participant's account balance attained a level adequate to purchase an annuity contract that would pay such a benefit. Such a reformed version of the final pay limit would prevent waste from over-pensioning the lowest-paid plan members, but it would do so by simply allowing the employer or its HCEs to benefit from the waste (i.e., retain rather than redistribute the tax subsidy). In light of nondiscrimination policy, a better approach might prohibit both forms of waste by requiring the employer to take any amount of contributions or benefits that would represent excessive savings for the company's lowest-paid workers (who will have the highest Social Security replacement rates) and redistribute it among other NHCEs.

Correction Mechanisms

The primary focus of the nondiscrimination requirements is operational, and so plan sponsors will often be confronted with the situation where changes in workforce composition and compensation levels occurring throughout the year cause the plan to fail the nondiscrimination rules. Sometimes such operational violations may not even be detectable until after the close of the plan year, when complete data become available.[161]

---

159   I.R.C. § 401(a)(5)(D) (2006); Treas. Reg. 1.401(a)(5)-1(e) (as amended in 1993). Final pay is defined as the highest annual compensation received during the employee's last five years of service with the employer. Note that the final pay limitation takes into account only half of the Social Security primary insurance amount, on the view that the employer can properly claim credit for only the employer-funded portion of the public retirement program. The maximum permitted disparity under section 401(*l*) similarly takes into account only half of Social Security. *See supra* Chapter 10 note 149.

160   *See* Altman, *supra* Chapter 10 note 158, at 494–98.

161   Only a plan that grants membership to every nonexcludible NHCE and provides uniform allocations or benefits (i.e., takes advantage of the design-based amount safe harbor) is assured of ongoing compliance with the nondiscrimination standards, come what may.

The nondiscrimination regulations provide a retroactive correction mechanism to alleviate this difficulty. If certain conditions are satisfied, the coverage and amount nondiscrimination tests may be satisfied by a retroactive plan amendment that increases the allocations or accruals of employees who benefitted under the plan in during the plan year being corrected or that grants allocations or accruals to employees who did not benefit during the year being corrected.[162] In general, four conditions must be met for the corrective amendment to be taken into account in meeting prior year nondiscrimination obligations: (1) the amendment may not reduce any employee's benefits or options under the plan; (2) the amendment must be given effect for all purposes from the first day of the plan year being corrected; (3) the amendment must be adopted and implemented no later than the 15th day of the 10th month after the close of the plan year being corrected (the period is extended further if a determination letter relating to the amendment is requested by that date); and (4) the additional allocations or accruals resulting from the amendment must, when considered alone, benefit a group of employees that satisfies the section 410(b) coverage standards and satisfy section 401(a)(4).[163] The last requirement prevents an employer from retroactively maximizing the coverage rate of HCEs (taking full advantage of the favoritism inherent in the ratio percentage test, for example), or the HCE allocation or accrual rates. (An exception is made for a corrective amendment designed to conform the plan to one of the amount nondiscrimination regulatory safe harbors; such amendments are permitted even if they disproportionately advantage HCEs.) In addition, such corrective amendments must have substance—increasing contributions or benefits of nonvested NHCEs whose employment terminated before the end of the year being corrected will not pass muster because they could not receive any economic benefit from the amendment.[164]

The requirement that each significant benefit, right, and feature provided under the plan be made available in an evenhanded manner (the qualitative component of the ban on discrimination in contributions or benefits) presents a challenge for retroactive correction. After all, if during a particular year a participant was ineligible to elect a lump-sum distribution or obtain a plan loan, amending the plan documents to remove the restriction on access is not going to give her the money when she needed it last year. Nevertheless, prompt plan amendment to correct access problems will sometimes prevent disqualification if the amendment remains in effect for a minimum period going forward.[165]

In recent years, the IRS has come to appreciate that plan disqualification is often an overly harsh and poorly targeted sanction,[166] regardless of whether the fault lies in a violation of the nondiscrimination rules or some other qualification condition. To encourage continuing compliance and prompt correction of problems that occur, the IRS instituted a general administrative process, called the Employee Plans

---

162 Treas. Reg. § 1.401(a)(4)-11(g)(2) (as amended in 2004).
163 *Id.* § 1.401(a)(4)-11(g)(3)(ii)-(v).
164 *Id.* § 1.401(a)(4)-11(g)(4).
165 *Id.* § 1.401(a)(4)-11(g)(3)(iii), (vi).
166 *See supra* Chapter 10 notes 113–119 and accompanying text.

Compliance Resolution System (EPCRS), that allows plan sponsors to self-correct certain operational failures without payment of any fee or sanction, to voluntarily correct all qualification failures and obtain the Service's approval by paying a limited fee, and even to fix a qualification defect identified on audit by paying a reasonable sanction.[167] EPCRS maintains strong incentives for the plan sponsor to monitor compliance and intervene when necessary, while avoiding the often catastrophic and unproductive consequences of plan disqualification.

Discrimination Tests for 401(k) Plans

Special coverage and amount nondiscrimination tests, including a prohibition on integration with Social Security, are prescribed for cash-or-deferred arrangements, so-called 401(k) plans. The reason is that 401(k) plans are elective contribution programs that allow each employee to choose between taking a portion of her compensation as current cash or directing the employer to contribute it (on a pre-tax basis) to the employee's account under a profit-sharing or stock bonus plan. Contributions therefore depend on individual employee elections, and the employer has no direct control over how much, if any, each employee decides to contribute.

The general coverage nondiscrimination tests look to the relative proportions of HCEs and NHCEs who "benefit" under the plan, which in the case of a defined contribution plan means that an employee receives an allocation of employer contributions or forfeitures for the year. Elective contributions under a 401(k) plan are treated as pre-tax employer contributions, so under the usual approach, satisfaction of the coverage tests would be fortuitous, depending as it would on the outcome of individual employee elections that are largely beyond the employer's control. In deference to this state of affairs, Congress prescribed a special coverage nondiscrimination test for 401(k) plans that treats each employee who is eligible to elect to have a contribution made on his behalf as an employee who benefits under the plan.[168] This relaxed standard only demands that the opportunity to defer must not unduly favor HCEs (satisfy either the ratio percentage test or the average benefits test). Nondiscriminatory access, of course, does not assure nondiscriminatory utilization of the retirement savings opportunity, much less nondiscrimination in the actual amounts deferred. Because lower-paid employees often cannot afford any reduction in their current cash compensation, broad eligibility provides no assurance that there will be comparable utilization of such elective contribution arrangements by the highly compensated and nonhighly compensated segments of the workforce. As demonstrated earlier, granting tax deferral for retirement savings on an individual basis would do very little to increase saving by low- and middle-income workers, while it would give a windfall to the

---

167   Rev. Proc. 2008-50, 2008-2 C.B. 464.
168   I.R.C. §§ 410(b)(6)(E), 401(k)(3)(A)(i) (2006); Treas. Reg. § 1.410(b)-3(a)(2)(i) (as amended in 2004), § 1.401(k)-6 (as amended in 2009) (definition of eligible employee).

highly paid, who would simply shift their other savings into the tax advantaged form.[169] Without something more, a 401(k) plan would just be an employer-mediated IRA,[170] and the tax subsidy to high-income savers would not be shifted into retirement savings for rank-and-file workers who cannot afford to save. To implement antidiscrimination policy, therefore, the actual results of employee decision making must somehow be taken into account. That is accomplished via a special amount nondiscrimination standard for 401(k) plans, the actual deferral percentage (ADP) test.[171]

The ADP test limits the actual deferral percentage for the group of eligible HCEs for the current plan year by reference to the actual deferral percentage for the group of eligible NHCEs. For administrative convenience, the actual deferral percentage for the group of eligible NHCEs is ordinarily based on data from the preceding plan year, but at the election of the employer, current year data may be used for NHCEs as well.[172] These actual deferral percentages are defined as the group average (for the groups composed of eligible HCEs and eligible NHCEs) of the ratios, computed separately for each group member for the relevant year, of: (a) elective contributions *plus* qualified matching contributions and qualified nonelective contributions made by the employer; to (b) employee compensation.[173] A qualified matching contribution is an employer contribution made on account of the employee's elective deferral, which is at all times fully vested and subject to certain early distribution restrictions that are applicable to elective deferrals. Similarly, a qualified nonelective contribution is an employer contribution that is neither an elective deferral nor a matching contribution and that is subject to the same vesting and distribution rules.[174] An eligible employee who chooses not to make any elective contribution and for whom the employer makes no qualified nonelective contribution for the year is included in the computation of the group average with a deferral rate of zero, which reduces the ADP of the group to which he belongs.[175] In this fashion, the ADP test functions as a kind of combined coverage and

---

169 *See supra* text accompanying Chapter 10 notes 63–68.

170 Interestingly, the Treasury Department study that initiated the Reagan Administration's tax reform proposals (an effort that culminated in the 1986 Act) recommended repeal of section 401(k) on the ground that "IRAs . . . are the appropriate vehicle for receipt of deductible retirement plan contributions by individuals." 2 U.S. Department of the Treasury, Tax Reform for Fairness, Simplicity, and Economic Growth 357 (1984).

171 I.R.C. § 401(k)(3)(C) (2006) (contributions under cash-or-deferred arrangement do not discriminate in favor of HCEs if ADP test satisfied).

172 I.R.C. § 401(k)(3)(A) (2006) (final sentence). The election to use current year data, while not irrevocable, is generally binding for five years. Treas. Reg. § 1.401(k)-2(c)(1) (as amended in 2009). Consequently, the sponsor cannot switch back and forth in computing the NHCE deferral rate baseline, according to which year offers the most favorable number.

173 I.R.C. § 401(k)(3)(B), (D) (2006); Treas. Reg. § 1.401(k)-2(a)(2), -2(a)(3) (as amended in 2009). Observe that Social Security taxes are not taken into consideration, and so the ADP test is applied without integration with Social Security.

174 I.R.C. § 401(k)(3)(D)(ii), (m)(4)(C) (2006).

175 Treas. Reg. § 1.401(k)-2(a)(3)(i) (as amended in 2009).

amount nondiscrimination test. The ADP limit (or maximum disparity in deferral rates) is as follows[176]:

NHCE ADP	Maximum HCE ADP
0–2%	(NHCE ADP) × 200%
2–8%	(NHCE ADP) + 2 percentage points
8% or more	(NHCE ADP) × 125%

The function defined in the preceding table implies that the ratio of the average contribution rate of eligible NHCEs to the average contribution rate for HCEs under a 401(k) plan is sometimes permitted to be as low as 50 percent (if the NHCE does not exceed 2 percent), but may be required to be as high as 80 percent (if the NHCE ADP is 8 percent or more). If all nonexcludible employees are eligible to choose to defer a portion of their pay, then this ratio of average contribution rates is the same ratio that is computed for purposes of the average benefits percentage test of Code section 410(b)(2)(ii), which requires a relative contribution rate for NHCEs of at least 70 percent.

The inclusion of qualified matching contributions and qualified nonelective contributions in the computation of actual deferral percentages is critical, both to the employer's ability to satisfy the ADP test, and to the accomplishment of the test's purpose (viz., targeting the tax subsidy). If only elective contributions were taken into account, the NHCE actual deferral percentage would be depressed by the many low-paid employees who cannot afford a reduction in their current compensation. (Recall that all eligible employees are included under the ADP test, whether they choose to defer or not; if no contributions are made with respect to an employee, a deferral percentage of zero goes into the corresponding group average.) By offering to match elective deferrals (either dollar-for-dollar or at a specified percentage), the employer can increase the attractiveness of deferral. This should not only induce greater elective deferrals, but the matching contribution, if qualified, will also raise the deferral rate. Unfortunately, however, employee responsiveness to matching contributions cannot be predicted with certainty. For example, workers with pressing current consumption needs (who strongly disprefer deferred compensation, that is) may be unwilling to forego part of their pay even if the employer offers to double the value of their savings. But the employer can also increase the NHCE actual deferral percentage by making qualified nonelective contributions on behalf of NHCEs, even if the employees refuse to make any elective contributions. Thus, qualified matching and qualified nonelective contributions give the employer considerable influence over group deferral rates, and such employer contributions are the mechanism by which the tax subsidy associated

---

[176] *See* I.R.C. § 401(k)(3)(A)(ii) (2006). In the first year of a 401(k) plan's operation, there will be no preceding year NHCE deferrals against which to measure HCE deferrals. In this case, the ADP test is applied by assuming a prior year NHCE average deferral rate of 3 percent, or the employer may elect to use as the baseline for comparison the actual NHCE ADP for the first year. *Id.* § 401(k)(3)(E).

with savings by the highly paid may be redistributed to those who would not save on their own.

As a special amount nondiscrimination standard, the ADP test has its own fail safe mechanisms. In lieu of the general retroactive correction method described earlier, a violation of the ADP test may be promptly remedied by distributing excess contributions (along with earnings thereon) to the appropriate HCEs or, if the employee elects, by recharacterizing his share of the excess contributions as an after-tax employee contribution to the plan.[177]

Notwithstanding the broad array of mechanisms sponsors have at their fingertips to assure compliance with the ADP test (i.e., qualified matching contributions, qualified nonelective contributions, distribution or recharacterization of excess contributions), employers clamored for design-based safe harbors, and Congress has acquiesced. Instead of complying with the ADP test, a 401(k) plan is treated as nondiscriminatory if each employee eligible to participate is given reasonable advance notice each year of his rights under the plan (including the right to make elective deferrals and to receive matching or nonelective contributions, if applicable), and the plan satisfies one of two alternative employer contribution alternatives. The employer contribution alternatives are: (1) the employer matches NHCE deferrals dollar-for-dollar up to 3 percent of compensation and matches NHCE deferrals between 3 and 5 percent of compensation at a rate of 50 percent, and at any level of elective contribution the HCE matching rate is no higher than the rate applicable to NHCEs; or (2) the employer makes a nonelective contribution for each eligible NHCE of at least 3 percent of compensation.[178] If the plan provides eligible NHCEs with this minimum match or nonelective contribution, then elective deferrals by HCEs are constrained only by the contribution limits imposed by the maximum amount rules. Thus, safe harbor contributions (matching or nonelective) operate as a toll charge for permission to favor highly paid workers in the amount saved for retirement to a degree that would otherwise be wholly unacceptable. Selling indulgences has no doubt increased the popularity of 401(k) plans precisely because

---

177   I.R.C. § 401(k)(8) (2006); Treas. Reg. § 1.401(k)-2(b) (as amended in 2009). The total amount of excess contribution is determined by reducing contributions made on behalf of the HCEs having the highest deferral rates by the amounts necessary to bring the highest HCE deferral rate down to the level that will satisfy the ADP test. The total amount of excess contributions so determined, however, is distributed (or recharacterized as after-tax employee contributions) to those HCEs who deferred the highest dollar amounts, not (as was the case prior to 1997) to those with the highest deferral rates. *Compare* I.R.C. § 401(k)(8)(B)(ii) (2006), *with id.* (k)(8)(C).

Observe that the 401(k) correction devices work by *reducing* qualified plan savings for HCEs, rather than by *increasing* savings for rank-and-file employees, which is the technique applicable to other qualified plans.

178   I.R.C. § 401(k)(12) (2006). Even smaller employer contributions are required in the case of a SIMPLE 401(k) plan—the matching contribution need be only 100 percent on the first 3 percent of NHCE elective deferrals with no required match at higher contribution rates, while 2 percent nonelective contributions suffice. *Id.* § 401(k)(11). A SIMPLE 401(k) plan, however, can be offered only by a small employer (meaning fewer than 100 employees in the previous plan year) and then only if it is the only qualified plan of the employer. *Id.* §§ 401(k)(11)(A), (k)(11)(C), (k)(11)(D)(i), 408(p)(2)(C)(i).

it so seriously undermines the redistributive objective of the qualified plan system. While the nondiscrimination rules are admittedly a crude device for targeting the tax subsidy, decoupling the level of obligatory savings on behalf of rank-and-file workers from the amount that executives and highly paid professionals want to save guarantees that much of the subsidy will be wasted rather than redirected to low-paid employees who would not save on their own.

Starting in 2008, a 401(k) plan may include an automatic contribution arrangement under which eligible employees defer by default at least 3 percent of pay (initially, the default minimum deferral rate increases in one percent annual increments until it reaches 6 percent), and must elect out of participation to receive their full compensation in cash or contribute a lesser amount. Special notice and election out requirements apply to such an automatic enrollment feature. In addition, such automatic contribution arrangements are granted a safe harbor that exempts them from the ADP test.[179] The employer need only make either nonelective contributions of 3 percent of compensation or match employee deferrals at the rate of 100 percent for the first 1 percent of pay and 50 percent for deferrals between 1 and 6 percent of pay.[180]

C. LIMITING THE TAX SUBSIDY

In addition to nondiscrimination, which attempts to direct the tax subsidy into additional retirement savings for low income workers, other tax controls operate to limit the amount of the tax subsidy. These limitations fall into three broad categories: the maximum amount rule, advance funding limits, and distribution timing constraints.

Maximum Amount Rule

The Code caps the amount of tax-subsidized retirement savings that an employer can provide to an employee. To be qualified, the annual benefit of each participant under all defined benefit plans of the employer cannot exceed the smaller of $160,000 indexed for inflation ($195,000 in 2009) or 100 percent of the participant's average compensation for his high three years, where "annual benefit" is defined as the amount of a straight-life annuity commencing between ages 62 and 65 under a plan that provides no ancillary benefits and that is solely employer-funded (no employee contributions).[181] For a defined contribution plan, the annual addition to a participant's account in any year under all defined contribution plans of the employer is limited to the smaller of

---

179   I.R.C. § 401(k)(13)(A) (West Supp. 2009). Some companies introduced automatic enrollment features before the enactment of the statutory safe harbor. The number of 401(k) plans with automatic enrollment increased rapidly between 2004 and 2007. Alicia H. Munnell et al., *An Update on 401(k) Plans: Insights from the 2007 SCF*, at 3 (2009), http://crr.bc.edu/images/ stories/Briefs/ib_9_5.pdf.

180   I.R.C. § 401(k)(13)(D) (West Supp. 2009).

181   I.R.C. §§ 401(a)(16), 415(a), (b), (f) (2006); I.R.S. Notice 2008-102, 2008-2 C.B. 1106 (inflation adjustment).

$40,000 indexed for inflation ($49,000 in 2009) or 100 percent of the participant's compensation, where "annual addition" is defined as the sum of employer contributions, forfeitures, and (after-tax) employee contributions allocated to the account for the year.[182] The maximum amount rule proceeds from the intuitively appealing principle that "it is appropriate to provide some limitation of corporate pensions out of tax-sheltered dollars which are swollen completely out of proportion to the reasonable needs of individuals for a dignified level of retirement income."[183]

The maximum amount rule is closely related to nondiscrimination. The clearest connection is the compensation cap of Code section 401(a)(17), which provides that the maximum annual compensation that can be taken into account under a qualified plan is $200,000, indexed for inflation ($245,000 in 2009).[184] The compensation cap functions as the link between amount nondiscrimination and the maximum amount of contributions or benefits that may be provided under a qualified plan. Without such a cap, employers could offer their very highly paid executives the maximum amount of tax-subsidized savings while providing only trivial amounts to low- and middle-income workers. For example, the maximum permissible annual addition to an employee's account under a defined contribution plan is $49,000 in 2009. Absent the compensation cap, an executive earning $5 million would receive the maximum permissible employer contribution under a plan calling for uniform contributions at a rate of less than one percent (specifically, 0.98%) of compensation, but such a plan would generate a contribution of only $294 for a rank-and-file employee earning $30,000. In the face of such gigantic disparities in compensation, the proportional amount rule would require only a trivial level of redistribution. With the compensation cap, in contrast, an employer must be willing to offer a 20 percent contribution rate to maximize the executive's savings, which would yield a $6,000 contribution for the rank-and-file employee.

In combination, the maximum amount rule and the compensation cap put some teeth in amount nondiscrimination. Yet from another perspective, the maximum amount rule is founded on a fallacy, and in some circumstances may be deeply discordant with nondiscrimination policy. The fallacy is the premise that generous pensions for corporate executives are necessarily paid "out of tax-sheltered dollars." If the nondiscrimination rules are operating as intended, then executives do not get the tax subsidy, and it is instead shifted to pensions for lower-paid workers. Far from being tax-sheltered, in that event, qualified retirement savings for highly paid workers bear an implicit tax that largely captures the benefit of tax deferral and transforms it into

---

182   I.R.C. § 415(a), (c), (f)(1)(B) (2006); I.R.S. Notice 2008-102, 2008-2 C.B. 1106 (inflation adjustment). *See generally* Martin Fireproofing Profit-Sharing Plan and Trust v. Comm'r, 92 T.C. 1173 (1989).

183   H.R. REP. NO. 93-807, at 112 (1974), *reprinted in* 2 ERISA LEGISLATIVE HISTORY, *supra* Chapter 1 note 56, at 3115, 3232. The maximum amount rules proved to be the most contentious element of comprehensive pension reform legislation in the Senate. The political controversy surrounded where to draw the line between dignified and excessive levels of tax-subsidized retirement income. William M. Lieber, *An IRS Insider's View of ERISA*, 65 TAX NOTES 751 (1994).

184   I.R.C. § 401(a)(17) (2006); I.R.S. Notice 2008-102, 2008-2 C.B. 1106 (inflation adjustment).

higher compensation for rank-and-file employees. Indeed, if the nondiscrimination rules worked optimally, a CEO's $2.5 million pension would not be tax preferred because he would have paid for the full value of tax deferral during his working years through a reduction in other forms of compensation. If we limit the CEO's pension to $245,000 (the 2009 defined benefit plan dollar limit), then we reduce by a factor of ten the tax benefits available for redistribution to low-paid workers who cannot afford to save on their own.[185] The extent of tax deferral available to high-income savers, in other words, fixes the scope of possible redistribution. We have seen that the efficacy of the nondiscrimination rules depends upon tax rates and workforce composition,[186] and so we should be concerned that capping executives' qualified plan savings will make it uneconomic for some companies to sponsor a plan. In a workforce containing a high proportion of low-paid non-savers, the cost of securing sufficient participation by NHCEs to meet nondiscrimination standards may far exceed the compensation cost saving that can be extracted under current law from the few HCEs, and so the employer will make no provision for retirement savings for the rank-and-file. In contrast, if tax-deferred retirement savings by the few HCEs were not confined within the limits set by the maximum amount rule, the tax subsidy associated with increased saving by the HCEs might be sufficient to fund broad coverage. In such situations the maximum amount rule works at cross purposes with nondiscrimination, and actually prevents the establishment of a qualified plan that would benefit low- and middle-income workers. Tax savings at the top supply the fuel that drives the redistributive pump, and by constricting the fuel supply, Code section 415 sometimes shuts down the flow.

Is the maximum amount rule so misguided that it ought to be repealed? That response would be too simplistic. Despite prevailing constraints, many companies sponsor qualified plans (particularly large and mid-sized employers), and at any given time, almost half of the American labor force is covered. The current tax subsidy is adequate to fund these existing programs. Because they now satisfy nondiscrimination requirements, uncapping tax-deferred savings by HCEs would not by itself force any additional redistribution—instead of being shifted to employees who would not otherwise save for retirement, the increased subsidy would simply benefit the employer or its HCE-savers. In other words, for plans currently in place, the maximum amount rule at least limits the extent of wasted revenue, even though it may block all redistribution within other firms that employ a different mix of personnel. When an intuitively appealing but inflexible anti-abuse rule operates in tandem with a crude redistribution regime, the results are bound to be imperfect.

---

185   During debate on ERISA, Senator Gaylord Nelson asserted that "it is absurd to maintain that only by allowing highly paid corporate executives such lavish annual pensions will large corporations be willing to establish plans covering most of their workers. I believe that even the highest paid corporate executive would find some value in a much more modest annual pension." 119 Cong. Rec. 30,132 (Sept. 18, 1973), *reprinted in* 2 ERISA Legislative History, *supra* Chapter 1 note 56, at 1712. The defect in this reasoning is that, while the executive would find some value in a modest pension, the value so limited might not be large enough to make it worthwhile for the corporation to sponsor a plan due to the high costs imposed by the nondiscrimination requirements.

186   *See supra* text accompanying Figure 10-2.

Even if it were justified in principle, in execution the maximum amount rule is deeply flawed. Two defects are especially pernicious. First, the defined benefit and defined contribution plan limits are incomparable and therefore uncoordinated. The defined benefit plan limit is quite logically tied to the life annuity value of retirement savings, but instead of being similarly distribution-based, the defined contribution plan limit restricts the money going into the participant's account rather than the money going out. While simpler to apply, an annual contribution-based limit has no necessary connection to the eventual level of retirement support. A highly paid employee can accumulate far greater qualified retirement savings if she is covered under a defined contribution plan for most of her career than would be permissible if she were under a defined benefit plan for a prolonged period.[187] To be consistent, the defined contribution plan limit should be tied to the projected benefits that the participant's account balance would yield, or if a simpler approach that avoids actuarial computation is desired, the limit should at least be geared to the cumulative *total* additions (contributions and forfeitures) allocated to the participant's account to date, rather than to the annual addition for the current year. Second, an employee may now receive both the maximum annual addition under a defined contribution plan and the maximum annual benefit under a defined benefit plan if he is covered under plans of both types. ERISA originally prevented such double-dipping by imposing a combined limit,[188] but Congress repealed the combined limit in 1996, ostensibly as a simplification measure.[189]

---

187 Using the dollar limits applicable in 2009, for example, a defined contribution plan participant who received annual employer contributions to her account of $49,000 for 30 years beginning at age 35 would have an account balance of more than $3.8 million at age 65, assuming an annual rate of return of 6 percent. That accumulation is roughly equivalent to the value of a single life annuity of $260,000 (assuming that the annuity credits an internal rate of interest of 3 percent). In contrast, the defined benefit plan limit for 2009 is only $195,000. The disparity increases if the yield on the defined contribution plan is higher; at a growth rate of 8 percent, the contributions would accumulate to $5.66 million at age 65, roughly equal to the value of a single life annuity of $380,000.

188 I.R.C. § 415(e) (1994) (repealed 1996). For an account of the curious origins of the combined limit, see Lieber, *supra* Chapter 10 note 183.

189 H.R. REP. No. 104-280, pt. 2, at 417–19 (1995) (combined limit called "one of the most significant sources of complexity relating to qualified pension plans" and an unnecessary deterrent to plan sponsorship). The Clinton Administration went along with the repeal of the combined limit, apparently because it felt that the separate limits were adequately backstopped by I.R.C. § 4980A, which imposed a 15 percent excise tax on the amount by which aggregate annual distributions from all tax-favored retirement savings programs exceeded $155,000 (in 1996 dollars). In 1997, however, Congress proceeded to repeal the section 4980A excise tax. *See* Norman P. Stein, *Simplification and IRC § 415*, 2 FLA. TAX REV. 69 (1994). For background on the former excise tax, see Bruce Wolk, *The New Excise and Estate Taxes on Excess Retirement Plan Distributions and Accumulations*, 9 U. FLA. L. REV. 987 (1987).

Besides the former combined limit on contributions and benefits, I.R.C. § 415(e) (1994) (repealed 1996), a combined limit on deductible contributions may apply to an employer that sponsors one or more defined benefit pension plans and one or more defined contribution plans if at least one employee is covered under both types of plans. I.R.C. § 404(a)(7)(A), (a)(7)(C) (i) (2006). Despite its long history, that final brake on double dipping was largely removed by the Pension Protection Act of 2006, which exempted PBGC-insured defined benefit plans from the combined limit. *Id.* § 404(a)(7)(C)(iv). If the defined benefit plan is not insured (as in the

A second maximum amount rule applies to 401(k) plans and 403(b) tax-sheltered annuities (available to employees of public schools and tax-exempt educational organizations). While the section 415(c) overall limit on annual additions to defined contribution plans (i.e., the smaller of 100 percent of compensation or $40,000, indexed for inflation) applies to these programs, elective deferrals under such plans are subject to an independent limit of $15,000 (indexed to $16,500 for 2009).[190] An employee making the maximum elective deferral who is age 50 or older is allowed to defer up to an additional $5,000 per year (indexed to $5,500 for 2009), and these so-called catch-up contributions are permitted even if they would otherwise exceed the annual addition limit of section 415(c).[191] Before 2002, the general limit on elective deferrals was set much lower, at $7,000, and catch-up contributions were not permitted. That historically lower elective deferral limit reflected the view that cash-or-deferred arrangements should serve as supplementary programs offering workers the option to save more than the amount provided under a nonelective employer-funded qualified retirement plan (traditionally a defined benefit plan). The recent dramatic increase in the elective deferral limit reflects a trend toward 401(k) plans becoming the primary or sole retirement savings programs for many employers. Rather than supplementing other programs, today, 401(k) plans frequently substitute for other qualified retirement plans.[192]

Advance Funding Limits

The maximum amount rule, insofar as it is justified, prevents wasted revenue by limiting the amount of tax subsidy associated with savings by HCEs in situations where the nondiscrimination rules would not force redistribution of the subsidy. Tax deferral is the basis of the qualified plan subsidy, and the value of deferral is a function of three factors: the amount of income (here compensation) that escapes current taxation, the tax rate that would apply to that income, and the duration of deferral. The maximum amount rule cabins the subsidy (rightly or wrongly) by limiting the amount of compensation eligible for deferral. Alternatively, the extent of the tax subsidy can be controlled by adjusting the duration of deferral. The period of deferral is the time between the employer's deduction of deferred compensation and inclusion of distributions in the recipient's income. The tax Code (perhaps not surprisingly) contains rules that restrict both the beginning and the end of the deferral period. Limits on advance funding prevent the employer from deducting qualified deferred compensation too

---

case of a plan maintained by a professional service employer that has never had more than 25 active participants, see ERISA § 4021(b)(13), 29 U.S.C. § 1321(b)(13) (2006)), the employer can still deduct contributions of up to 6 percent of compensation under a defined contribution plan regardless of combined limit. I.R.C. § 404(a)(7)(C)(iii) (2006).

190   I.R.C. §§ 401(a)(3), 402(e)(3), (g)(1) (2006).
191   I.R.C. §§ 402(g)(1)(C), 414(v)(2), (v)(3)(A) (2006). The combination of other elective deferrals and catch-up contributions cannot exceed the participant's compensation, *id.* § 414(v) (2)(A), and so the exemption of catch-up contributions from the limit on annual additions under defined contribution plans has the effect of raising only the section 415(c) dollar limit ($49,000 for 2009). It is the dollar limit that affects middle- and upper-income employees.
192   *See infra* Figure 10-4 and Chapter 10 note 202.

early, while certain distribution timing rules prohibit employees from delaying distributions for too long.

Subject to certain limits, the employer receives a current deduction for amounts actually contributed to a qualified retirement the plan.[193] Prompt payment is required, according to the Supreme Court, because "an objective outlay-of-assets test" ensures "the integrity of the employees' plan and insure[s] the full advantage of any contribution which entitles the employer to a tax benefit."[194] If payment in cash or in-kind were all that was needed to secure the deduction, however, employers could greatly inflate the tax subsidy and shift most of the cost of deferred compensation onto the taxpaying public simply by contributing to a qualified trust sooner, thereby providing a longer accumulation period so that a larger share of future distributions will consist of exempt earnings. Egregious abuses are prevented by the requirement that qualified plan contributions must be "otherwise . . . deductible" under the tax Code, which typically means that they must qualify as an ordinary and necessary business expense.[195] Because the business expense deduction is limited to reasonable compensation for services actually rendered, the employer cannot deduct contributions to a qualified trust made before the employee earns the deferred compensation.[196] But what of a plan that heavily frontloads contributions or benefits? Suppose that a profit-sharing plan provides contributions equal to 100 percent of current compensation for each of an employee's first five years of service, and nothing thereafter? Such contributions are earned by contemporaneous service and would not exceed the current limit set by the maximum amount rule for lower-paid employees. Yet if such frontloaded contributions are invested for twenty or thirty years or longer, an exorbitant share (easily three-quarters or more) of the eventual retirement income distributions would be composed of trust earnings.[197] To prevent such raids on the fisc, Code section 404 imposes limits on the amount allowable as a deduction for contributions to a qualified trust. Contributions in excess of the deduction limit can theoretically be carried forward and deducted in a subsequent year, but practically, they are strongly discouraged by a 10 percent penalty tax on nondeductible contributions.[198]

---

193   I.R.C. § 404(a)(1)–(3) (2006).

194   Don E. Williams Co. v. Comm'r, 429 U.S. 569, 579 (1977) (footnote omitted) (accrual basis taxpayer's delivery of fully secured interest-bearing promissory notes to a qualified profit-sharing trust did not constitute payment and so did not qualify for deduction under Code section 404(a)). Payment before the due date (including extensions) of the employer's tax return is treated as payment on the last day of the taxable year, I.R.C. § 404(a)(6) (2006), and this grace period gives the employer time to gather the data necessary to determine the maximum deductible contribution for the year. *Don E. Williams*, 429 U.S. at 575.

195   I.R.C. § 404(a)(1) (2006) (introductory clause).

196   I.R.C. § 162(a)(1) (2006). Under general tax timing rules, prepaid compensation is a nondeductible capital expenditure, *id.* § 263, even absent language limiting the business expense deduction to reasonable compensation for services actually rendered.

197   Invested at a compound annual rate of return of 6 percent, a contribution would quadruple in value in less than 24 years. Of course, trust earnings might be higher or the accumulation period longer, and either factor would magnify the effect.

198   I.R.C. § 404(a)(1)(E), (a)(3)(A)(ii) (2006) (carry forward of excess contributions to pension trusts, and profit-sharing or stock bonus trusts, respectively), *id.* § 4972 (excise tax).

For profit-sharing and stock bonus plans, the limit on contributions paid by the employer (under all such plans) is now 25 percent of the compensation otherwise paid or accrued during the taxable year to beneficiaries under such plans.[199] Before 2002, the deduction limit for profit-sharing and stock bonus plans had been set at 15 percent of covered compensation, but if the employer also sponsored a money purchase pension plan (which is a type of defined contribution plan), a combined limit of 25 percent applied.[200] Consequently, deductible contributions of up to 15 percent of covered compensation could be made under the profit-sharing plan (which could be a 401(k) plan) along with deductible annual contributions of 10 percent of pay under the money purchase plan. Once the deduction limit for profit-sharing and stock bonus plans was raised to 25 percent, employers could make the maximum deductible contribution under a profit-sharing plan standing alone; no greater tax benefit could be secured by also sponsoring a money purchase pension plan covering the same workers. In a dramatic demonstration of the force of tax deferral, between 2001 and 2006, the number of money purchase plans declined by 72 percent, as shown in Figure 10-4. This amendment, along with the contemporaneous increase in the elective deferral limit discussed earlier,[201] has no doubt contributed to the recent widespread transformation of 401(k) plans from their former limited role as supplementary savings arrangements to their current exalted status as the exclusive qualified retirement savings program provided by many employers.[202]

---

199   I.R.C. § 404(a)(3)(A) (2006). The compensation cap imposed by section 410(a)(17) ($245,000 for 2009) and the maximum amount rule are applied in computing the deduction limit. *Id.* § 404(j), (*l*).

200   I.R.C. § 404(a)(3)(A)(i)(I) (2000) (amended 2001), § 404(a)(7)(A)(i) (2006). The 25 percent limit applied to the combination of a money purchase pension plan and a profit-sharing or stock bonus plan because, although it is a defined contribution program, for tax purposes a money purchase plan is classified as a pension plan. Consequently, before 2002, contributions to a money purchase plan were deductible under the pension plan limit of Code section 404(a)(1), rather than under the profit-sharing and stock bonus plan limit of section 404(a)(3). (Recall that money purchase pension plans, unlike profit-sharing and stock bonus plans, are subject to ERISA's minimum funding standards (*supra* Chapter 9A), and so a deduction for the amount of contributions necessary to satisfy the minimum funding standard was allowed by section 404(a)(1)(A)(i).) The 2001 legislation that increased the limit on deductible contributions from 15 to 25 percent for profit-sharing and stock bonus plans also added I.R.C. § 404(a)(3)(v) (2006) and the parenthetical clause in section 404(a)(1)(A), which make contributions to a money purchase plan subject to the deduction limit applicable to profit-sharing and stock bonus plans rather than the limit for defined benefit pension plans.

201   I.R.C. § 402(g)(1) (2006). *See supra* text accompanying Chapter 10 notes 190–192.

202   Craig Copeland, *Retirement Plan Participation*: *Survey of Income and Program Participation (SIPP) Data, 2006*, 30 EBRI NOTES 6-7 (2009) (in 2006 more than 30 percent of nonagricultural wage and salary workers over age 16 had a 401(k) plan as their primary retirement savings program, up from 7.5 percent in 1988 and 17.4 percent in 1993). From the standpoint of retirement income adequacy, many experts are troubled by this development. *E.g., supra* Chapter 10 note 179, at 10 (2009) ("The time may have come to consider returning 401(k) plans to their original position as a third tier on top of Social Security and employer-sponsored pensions.").

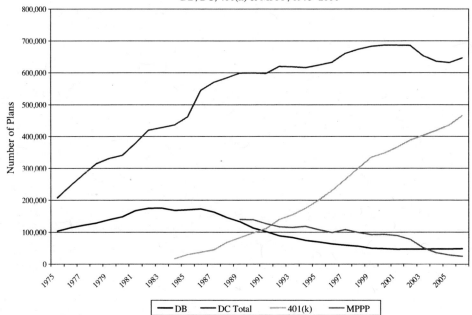

Figure 10-4

Number of Private Pension Plans:
DB, DC, 401(k) & MPPP, 1975–2006

DB = defined benefit plans; DC Total = defined contribution plans of all types; 401(k) = plans containing cash-or-deferred arrangement; MPPP = money purchase pension plans. DC Total includes the number of 401(k) plans and MPPPs each year (graphed separately) as well as other varieties of DC plans.

Source: Employee Benefit Security Administration (EBSA), U.S. Department of Labor, Private Pension Plan Bulletin Historical Tables and Graphs, Tables E1, E8 & E20 (Feb. 2009) (DB, DC Total and 401(k) data); EBSA, Private Pension Plan Bulletin: Abstract of Form 5500 Annual Reports, Table A1 (annually, 1989-2006) (MPPP data).

From the standpoint of retirement income security, the recent rapid decline in prevalence of money purchase pension plans seems undesirable. To reduce administrative costs, an employer wishing to make the maximum deductible retirement saving contribution would understandably prefer to do so under one plan rather than two. But a money purchase pension plan is the simplest qualified plan and hence the cheapest to maintain (lowest administrative cost). The virtual demise of money purchase plans following the increase in the deduction limit for profit-sharing and stock bonus plans indicates a strong sponsor preference for the latter program types. That preference stems from two factors: benefit cost and funding flexibility. Profit-sharing and stock bonus plans may include a qualified cash-or-deferred arrangement allowing partial funding via elective salary reduction contributions. The special nondiscrimination rules applicable to 401(k) plans (the actual deferral percentage test and the safe harbors for minimum matching or nonelective contributions) may in some instances require less redistribution and so entail lower benefit cost than the rules applicable to money purchase pension plans.[203] Moreover, annual contributions to a profit-sharing or stock bonus plan are not required—they can be tied to profits or left to the discretion of the

---

203   *See supra* text accompanying Chapter 10 notes 168–180.

employer, which permits reductions in the event the sponsor encounters cash flow problems.[204] A money purchase pension plan, in contrast, entails a contractual commitment to make specified annual contributions (usually a stated percentage of each participant's current compensation). That commitment can be enforced by a suit brought by one or more participants (or, in certain circumstances, by the Labor Department) to remedy a breach of ERISA's minimum funding standards, and so is relatively inflexible.[205] Thus, the lower deduction limit formerly applicable to profit-sharing and stock bonus plans encouraged employers to provide a portion of each worker's retirement savings in a form (i.e., a money purchase pension) that was less susceptible to cutbacks in difficult economic times. Removing the incentive to provide nondiscretionary baseline savings under a money purchase plan increases the risk that rank-and-file employees will not accumulate sufficient resources for retirement.

The deduction limit applicable to contributions to defined benefit pension plans has similarly been shaped by efforts to control the amount of the qualified retirement plan tax subsidy by limiting excessive prefunding. Consider a unit credit plan that promises an annuity commencing at age 65 equal to 1 percent of final average compensation per year of service. Upon hiring a 35-year-old, can the employer deduct an immediate contribution to the plan equal to the present value of 30 percent of the employee's projected final compensation, or must the pension be funded by annual contributions over the new employee's career? Lump-sum advance funding would allow employer contributions to accumulate trust earnings over a longer period, thereby increasing tax deferral and shifting more of the cost of the pension to other taxpayers. Immediate deduction of the present value of the total projected pension cost is obviously inappropriate under a unit credit plan because most of the pension is still unearned, and prepayments or reserves for future expenses are not ordinarily deductible. But what about a flat benefit plan that promises each participant an annuity at age 65 of 30 percent of final average compensation without regard to length of service? In this case, a legal obligation accrues upon admission to plan membership, and so an immediate contribution funding the total projected pension cost is arguably deductible.[206] Even in the case of a unit credit plan, substantial (albeit not complete) prefunding of unearned

---

204   *See supra* Chapter 1A.

205   ERISA §§ 301(a)(8) (minimum funding rules apply to money purchase pension plans but not other individual account plans), 302(a)(2)(B) (minimum funding standard for single-employer money purchase pension plan is satisfied if the employer makes the contributions required under the terms of the plan), 502(a)(3), (5) (civil action may be brought to redress violations of ERISA or enforce terms of plan), 29 U.S.C. §§ 1081(a)(8), 1082(a)(2)(B), 1132(a)(3), (5) (2006); *see* I.R.C. § 412(a)(2)(B), (e)(2) (2006) (tax law funding rules do not apply to profit-sharing or stock bonus plans). As discussed in Chapter 9A, the minimum funding rules do contain several relief provisions (e.g., waiver in cases of temporary substantial business hardship) that might relax the obligation to contribute to a money purchase plan in exigent circumstances.

206   *Compare* Jerome Mirza & Assocs. v. United States, 882 F.2d 229 (7th Cir. 1989) (deduction for full cost of immediate prefunding under flat benefit plan disallowed), *with* Citrus Valley Estates, Inc. v. Comm'r, 49 F.3d 1410 (9th Cir. 1995) (immediate deduction of full cost allowed). Under I.R.C. § 415(b)(5) (2006), the dollar limit on defined benefit pensions is now phased in over ten years of *plan participation* (prior to 1986, the phase-in was based on years

benefits was formerly possible due to the flexibility ERISA originally allowed in the plan's choice of actuarial funding method. Under certain actuarial funding methods (known as cost allocation actuarial methods), the projected total future benefit cost could be allocated between years of service as either a level dollar amount or a fixed percentage of pay, regardless of the rate at which benefits are actually earned each year under the plan's definition of accrued benefit. Compared to the cost of funding the benefits actually earned each year (known as the benefit allocation actuarial method), level funding required by the cost allocation methods calls for larger contributions in the early years of an employee's plan participation, which has the effect of partially prefunding benefits to be earned in later years of service.[207] That partial prefunding led to concerns about excessive subsidy, to which Congress responded in 1987 by tightening the full funding limit on the employer's contribution deduction.[208]

The Pension Protection Act of 2006 revamped the funding rules and eliminated choice in actuarial funding methods for single-employer defined benefit plans. The new minimum funding obligation for single-employer plans is specified by reference to the funding target and target normal cost for the plan year, and those quantities are determined by the present value of all benefits earned under the plan as of the beginning of the plan year, or expected to be earned during the plan year (respectively).[209] This approach rules out cost allocation actuarial funding methods, which are the level funding methods that permitted substantial prefunding of benefits not yet earned. The maximum deductible contribution is linked to the minimum funding obligation and therefore is also tied to benefits earned to date, which largely precludes excessive subsidization.[210] Congress recognized, however, that there is a trade-off between benefit security, which militates in favor of permitting or even encouraging a certain amount of overfunding, and cost-containment, which supports strict limits on prefunding unearned benefits. To accommodate these competing objectives, under the new deduction limit the employer is allowed to deduct, in addition to the amount necessary to fully fund all benefits earned during the current and previous plan years, an extra "cushion amount."[211] The cushion amount is defined as (1) one-half of the funding

---

of service with the employer), which prevents colossal upfront funding of the sort achieved in *Citrus Valley.*

207 WIEDENBECK & OSGOOD, *supra* Chapter 3 note 39, 396–99.

208 I.R.C. § 404(a)(1)(A) (2006) (final sentence as in effect for taxable years beginning before 2008), *id.* § 412(c)(7) (as in effect for taxable years beginning before 2008). H.R. REP. NO. 100-391, pt. II, at 1117–18 (1987) explained:

> The committee does not believe . . . that an employer should be entitled to make excessive contributions to a defined benefit pension plan to fund liabilities that it has not yet incurred. Such use of a defined benefit plan is equivalent to a tax-free savings account for future liabilities and is inconsistent generally with the treatment of unaccrued liabilities under the Code.

See U.S. DEPARTMENT OF THE TREASURY, REPORT TO THE CONGRESS ON THE EFFECT OF THE FULL FUNDING LIMIT ON PENSION BENEFIT SECURITY 4–5 (1991) (study of the impact of the 1987 restrictions on prefunding).

209 I.R.C. § 412(a)(2)(A) (2006) (as in effect for taxable years beginning after 2007), *id.* § 430(a), (b), (c)(1)-(4), (d)(1). *See supra* Chapter 9A.

210 I.R.C. § 404(o) (2006).

211 *Id.* § 404(o)(2)(A).

ERISA: PRINCIPLES OF EMPLOYEE BENEFIT LAW

target (i.e., the present value of benefits earned under the plan as of the start of the plan year) plus (2) the amount by which the funding target would increase if the benefits already earned were determined with reference to expected future increases in employee compensation (as where plan benefits are based on final average compensation, for example).[212]

Distribution Timing

It was noted earlier that ERISA has little to say about the timing of pension plan distributions. Instead, the tasks of discouraging pre-retirement distributions and preventing excessive deferral were left almost entirely to the tax law (see *supra* Chapter 8A). The qualified plan rules have much to say about distribution timing, and with respect to both early and late distributions, two distinct though related policies are in play. First, Congress has sought to target the tax subsidy so as to encourage *retirement* savings, as opposed to savings for other objectives, whether for precautionary purposes, education, home ownership, or bequests. Second, the distribution timing rules also function to influence the *amount* of the tax subsidy.

Late Distributions These dual objectives—controlling the purpose and amount of the tax subsidy—are readily apparent upon a review of the minimum distribution rule of Code section 401(a)(9). The minimum distribution rule forces qualified plans to pay out benefits, regardless of the participant's wishes, over a period that is roughly congruent with the time when most individuals need retirement income. Consequently, distributions cannot be delayed too long, ostensibly to avoid subsidizing intergenerational wealth transfers (bequests or inheritances). Of course, by establishing the maximum duration of accumulation, the minimum distribution rule also limits the duration of tax deferral and fixes the maximum amount of the tax subsidy. As such, it is the counterpart to the advance funding limits explored in the preceding section: the deduction limits set the earliest starting point for tax deferral, while the minimum distribution rule sets the latest endpoint.

In general, distributions must begin by April 1 of the year following the calendar year the employee attains age 70½ or (if later) retires. If the employee's entire interest in the plan is not paid out by that time, then it must be distributed in fairly even annual amounts over a period that does not exceed the life (or life expectancy) of the participant,

---

212 *Id.* § 404(o)(3). Ordinarily, compensation increases are not anticipated regardless of how reliably they can be projected. Instead, they are taken into account as an increase in target normal cost each year as they occur. *Id.* § 430(b)(2). Thus, the funding target and target normal cost under section 430 reflect termination-based legal liability (as did "current liability" used in the full funding limit of former section 412(c)(7)), rather than liability for accrued benefits determined on an ongoing or plan continuation basis. In the event of termination, accrued benefits would be determined based upon compensation history to the date of termination, *see* 29 C.F.R. § 4022.62(b)(2) (2009) (benefits not already in pay status computed according to participant's service and compensation on proposed termination date), while for an ongoing plan, future compensation increases may increase the value of benefits previously earned.

or the joint lives (or joint life expectancies) of the participant and designated beneficiary.[213] Yet if an elderly participant designates as beneficiary his infant granddaughter, payment over their joint lives or life expectancies could accomplish a large tax-subsidized intergenerational wealth transfer. To prevent this, Congress directed the Treasury to develop rules that, instead of cutting short the allowable distribution period, force more of the total amount to be distributed in the earlier part of that period, during the participant's lifetime.[214] The minimum distribution rule is prescribed as a qualification requirement, but its reach extends to most other forms of tax-preferred retirement savings, including tax-sheltered annuities for employees of public schools and tax-exempt organizations, eligible deferred compensation plans of state and local governments and tax-exempt organizations, and traditional IRAs.[215] In addition to possible disqualification, the minimum distribution rule is enforced by imposing on the payee a 50 percent penalty tax on the amount of any distribution shortfall.[216]

The minimum distribution rule is significantly relaxed as applied to Roth IRAs. No distributions are required from a Roth IRA while the owner is alive. The entire interest in the Roth IRA must be distributed by the end of the fifth calendar year following the owner's death unless the interest is payable to a designated beneficiary over (at most) his life expectancy, and distributions commence before the end of the calendar year following the owner's death. If, however, the sole beneficiary is the deceased owner's spouse, the spouse may treat the Roth IRA as his or her own, or may delay the

---

213   I.R.C. § 401(a)(9)(A) (2006).

214   I.R.C. § 401(a)(9)(A)(ii) (2006) provides that required distributions shall be made "in accordance with regulations." The regulations impose the "minimum distribution incidental benefit" (a/k/a MDIB) requirement. The MDIB rules provide that the required minimum distribution for a defined contribution plan is generally determined by dividing the account balance by a distribution period that is based on the joint life and last survivor expectancy of the employee and a hypothetical beneficiary who is ten years younger than the participant (or the joint life and last survivor expectancy of the employee and the employee's spouse, if the employee's spouse is the sole beneficiary). For years following the employee's death, the required distribution period is generally the remaining life expectancy of the employee's designated beneficiary as of the year following the employee's death (or the spouse's single life expectancy if the spouse is the employee's sole beneficiary). Treas. Reg. § 1.401(a)(9)-5 Q&A-4, Q&A-5 (as amended in 2007), § 1.401(a)(9)-9 Q&A-2 (2002). See T.D. 9887, 2002-1 C.B. 852, 854 (explanation of uniform lifetime distribution period); T.D. 9130, 2004-1 C.B. 1082, 1084. These rules have the effect of imposing a payout rate that forces most of the total distributions into the early years of the permissible distribution period, which is the time when the participant and his or her spouse are alive and can use retirement income. Similar rules apply to annuity distributions from defined benefit plans, and if the employee elects to take distribution in the form of a joint and survivor annuity with a nonspouse beneficiary who is more than ten years younger, the amount payable under the survivor annuity is reduced below the level of the employee's benefit in order to prevent excessive deferral. Treas. Reg. § 1.401(a)(9)-6 Q&A-2(c) (as amended in 2004).

215   I.R.C. § 403(b)(10) (2006) (tax-sheltered annuities), id. §§ 457(b)(5), (d)(2) (government and exempt-organization plans), 408(a)(6), (b)(3) (individual retirement accounts and annuities).

216   I.R.C. § 4974 (2006).

beginning of distributions until the time when the decedent would have attained age 70½.[217]

Common wisdom holds that the minimum distribution rule targets the tax subsidy on retirement saving, but there is cause for skepticism. A large majority of Americans have no significant assets apart from some home equity and their qualified retirement savings (including IRAs). Low- and moderate-income workers do not need to be required to take retirement distributions—they simply couldn't get along without the money. Realistically, only the top 5 percent of households, ranked by income distribution, have substantial savings besides their interests in a home and qualified retirement programs. Accordingly, the problem of excessive deferral is limited to the very affluent, and this elite group has plenty of other resources from which to make bequests (e.g., life insurance, investments). We can require them to take distributions in old age from their tax-preferred savings, but we cannot force them to use it for consumption. Even if they choose to consume it, any financial advantage they derive from qualified retirement savings just makes other resources available for transfer by gift, bequest, or inheritance. Forcing distributions to be contemporaneous with retirement does not prevent the tax subsidy from being passed on to the next generation, it only prevents that disposition from being readily apparent. From this perspective, the minimum distribution feint gives the tax subsidy political cover from popular opposition. Ironically, that misdirection is needed primarily to protect rank-and-file employees, who do not understand that the covert redistribution system embedded in the nondiscrimination rules makes their own retirement income dependent upon the tax benefits accorded the highest-paid participants.

This line of analysis indicates that the principal function of the minimum distribution rule is quantitative rather than qualitative. While we can't control the use to which high-income participants put any financial advantage they derive from qualified retirement savings, limiting the duration of tax deferral surely restricts the amount of the subsidy. The wisdom of that restriction is another matter. As with the maximum amount rule,[218] limiting tax benefits associated with savings by HCEs (in this case, by limiting the duration rather than the amount of HCE savings) limits the employer's potential compensation cost savings and necessarily caps the extent of potential redistribution. Given the imperfections of the nondiscrimination regime, relaxing or repealing the minimum distribution rule presumably would merely increase wasted revenue (i.e., would force no additional redistribution) associated with existing plans. But some companies do not currently sponsor a plan because their workforce composition is such that the tax savings that could be captured from high-paid participants is insufficient to induce enough rank-and-file participation to satisfy the nondiscrimination tests. As to these enterprises, a richer tax subsidy might support sufficient compensation cost savings to satisfy the nondiscrimination rules and make plan sponsorship feasible. Relaxing the minimum distribution rule is one way to enrich the subsidy, but there are other available alternatives (for example, permitting greater tax deferral by relaxing the maximum amount rule).

---

217   I.R.C. §§ 408A(c)(5), 401(a)(9)(B)(ii)-(iv) (2006); Treas. Reg. § 1.408A-6 Q&A-14 (1999).
218   *See supra* text accompanying Chapter 10 notes 185–186.

Early Distributions Pre-retirement distributions raise a different set of policy concerns. Unlike late distributions, which present the prospect of excessive deferral by a few very highly compensated employees, the availability of early distributions is particularly important to lower-paid workers. These are the employees who do not save adequately for retirement when left to their own devices and who are therefore the intended beneficiaries of redistribution. The maddeningly intricate system of nondiscrimination rules exists to induce greater retirement savings for rank-and-file employees, and so it would seem that pre-retirement distributions which dissipate those savings are simply anathema and ought to be banned outright. Doesn't proper targeting of the tax subsidy require locking up qualified plan accumulations until retirement? Perhaps, but history and politics have conspired against such a straightforward approach. Moreover, limited pre-retirement access to qualified plan accumulations may be essential to the success of the system, because a flat prohibition on early distributions might cause low-paid workers to place such a low value on qualified plan savings that the available tax subsidy (compensation savings extracted from HCE-savers) would be insufficient to persuade them to cooperate. Barring all early access to plan savings, in other words, would increase the rate at which low-paid workers discount the benefit, thereby necessitating a larger bribe (compensation increase) to induce their plan participation. Increasing the bribes needed to satisfy the nondiscrimination rules requires greater redistribution; perhaps more than HCE demand for tax-favored retirement savings could finance.[219] There is a trade-off between cost and quality, that is: iron-clad dedication of qualified plan savings to the provision of retirement income might require more redistribution than the system can support, triggering plan terminations. Thus, limiting late distributions affects high-income savers and reduces the amount of the available tax subsidy, while limiting early distributions impacts cash-strapped rank-and-file workers and increases the amount of subsidy that is required to satisfy nondiscrimination standards.

As mentioned, history and politics (perhaps more than redistribution theory and practice) have shaped the circumstances in which early distributions are permitted. Traditionally, pre-retirement distributions were far more readily available under a profit-sharing or stock bonus plan than under a pension plan. That difference derived from the fact that, by definition, a pension plan is a program "established and maintained by an employer primarily to provide systematically for the payment of definitely determinable benefits to his employees over a period of years, usually for life, *after retirement.*"[220] Pension plans may pay a disability pension or provide incidental death benefits, and may permit distribution on severance of employment or upon termination of the plan, but in-service distributions are disqualifying.[221] (To facilitate phased retirement programs, this rule was relaxed in 2006 to permit in-service distributions after

---

219   *See supra* Figure 10-2 and accompanying text.
220   Treas. Reg. § 1.401-1(b)(1)(i) (as amended in 1976) (emphasis added).
221   Treas. Reg. § 1.401-1(b)(1)(i) (as amended in 1976) (disability pension or incidental death benefits); *see* Rev. Rul. 56-693, 1956-2 C.B. 282 (distribution on severance of employment or termination of plan); Rev. Rul. 74-254, 1974-1 C.B. 91 (same).

the employee has attained age 62.[222]) Profit-sharing and stock bonus plans, in contrast, were originally conceived simply as programs providing *deferred* compensation, not necessarily *retirement* savings, and so in-service distributions were routinely permitted.[223] Specifically, in addition to the circumstances justifying distribution from a pension plan, distributions under a profit-sharing or stock bonus plan are allowed after a fixed number of years (meaning at least two), attainment of a specified age, or in the event of layoff, illness, or hardship.[224] These conditions are so capacious it is a wonder that any balance survived in a profit-sharing or stock bonus account until retirement, and frequently only good fortune or unusual self discipline preserved it.[225]

To discourage early distributions from qualified plans, an additional 10 percent tax is imposed on the taxable portion of distributions made before the date the employee attains age 59½ unless certain exceptions apply.[226] The exceptions allow early withdrawal without penalty if the distribution is made to the employee upon separation from service after age 55, is made to a beneficiary or the estate of the employee after death, is due to disability, or is paid in the form of a life or joint-life annuity commencing after separation from service.[227] Distributions to an alternate payee under a qualified domestic relations order and distributions that do not exceed the amount that would be allowed as a medical expense deduction to the employee (regardless of whether the employee itemizes deductions) are also exempt from the 10 percent levy.[228]

The early withdrawal tax applies not only to distributions from a qualified pension, profit-sharing, stock bonus, or annuity plan; it also reaches distributions from a tax-sheltered annuity or an individual retirement account or annuity (IRA).[229] In recent years, however, Congress has enacted a raft of additional exceptions that permit early withdrawals from IRAs for various worthy uses, including to pay health insurance premiums while unemployed, to pay higher education expenses of the taxpayer or his

---

222   I.R.C. § 401(a)(36) (2006); *see* ERISA § 3(2)(A) (final sentence), 29 U.S.C. § 1002(2)(A) (2006).

223   Treas. Reg. § 1.401-1(b)(1)(ii), (iii) (as amended in 1976).

224   *Id.*; Rev. Rul. 71-224, 1971-1 C.B. 124 (hardship distributions allowed); Rev. Rul. 54-231, 1954-1 C.B. 150 (fixed number of years means at least two); Rev. Rul. 68-24, 1968-1 C.B. 150 (profit-sharing plan that allows employees with at least sixty months of participation to withdraw all employer contributions, including those made within the preceding two years, is qualified).

225   Elective contributions under a 401(k) plan (which is ordinarily part of a profit-sharing or stock bonus plan), together with any qualified matching contributions or qualified nonelective contributions (i.e., contributions used to satisfy the special nondiscrimination standard applicable to 401(k) plans), are subject to more restrictive distribution rules. Distribution after a fixed number of years is not acceptable; instead, such amounts may be distributed only upon severance of employment, death, disability, plan termination, attainment of age 59½, hardship of the employee, or upon a reservist's call-up to active duty. I.R.C. § 401(k)(2)(B), (k)(3)(D), (k)(12) (E)(i), (k)(13)(D)(iii), (m)(4) (2006).

226   I.R.C. § 72(t)(1), (t)(2)(A)(i) (2006). This early withdrawal tax was enacted in 1986 and effectively marks the conversion of profit-sharing and stock bonus plans into *retirement* savings programs.

227   I.R.C. § 72(t)(2)(A), (t)(3)(B), (t)(4) (2006).

228   I.R.C. § 72(t)(2)(B), (C) (2006).

229   I.R.C. §§ 72(t)(1), 4974(c) (2006).

spouse, child, or grandchild (or of a child or grandchild of the spouse), to pay certain acquisition costs of first-time homebuyers, and distributions made to a reservist called to active duty.[230] Moreover, temporary relief was enacted to aid victims of Hurricane Katrina.[231] The upshot of all these exceptions is that "individual *retirement* account" has become a misnomer; IRAs are no longer dedicated retirement savings vehicles; they have morphed into tax-preferred savings accounts that may be used to fund a wide range of expenditures that Congress deems laudable. The IRA exceptions have a far broader reach than may at first appear, for they apply to early distributions from a roll-over IRA that houses assets accumulated under a qualified plan![232] Indeed, due to the ubiquity of rollovers of qualified plan account balances when workers change jobs, IRAs now hold the largest share of qualified retirement savings,[233] all of which is subject to leakage for various nonretirement purposes. Far from depressing the value of savings by locking them away for decades, after a job change and transfer to an IRA, qualified plan assets, while not quite up for grabs, are at least readily accessible to finance a number of common needs.

Plan Loans Like early distributions, plan loans present similar threats to retirement income security: if the loan is not repaid, the outstanding balance will be set off against the participant's accrued benefit, depleting resources available for support in retirement.[234] On the other hand, a ban on all plan loans might so impair the value of qualified plan savings for young, low-income employees as to make it impossible to satisfy the nondiscrimination rules—the bribes necessary to garner sufficient NHCE participation could become too pricey. Remember that a credit-constrained participant has nowhere else to turn—thanks to ERISA's anti-alienation rule, she cannot use her interest in the plan (frequently the only significant asset owned by a low-income worker) as security to obtain a loan from another lender.

Not surprisingly, in view of this state of affairs, qualified retirement plans may permit plan loans, but only under circumstances that make it likely that the funds will be available in retirement. There are two distinct requirements. First, to avoid

---

230   I.R.C. §§ 72(t)(2)(D)-(G), (t)(7), (t)(8), 7701(a)(37) (2006) (definition of individual retirement plan).

231   Katrina Emergency Tax Relief Act of 2005, Pub. L. No. 109-73, § 101, 119 Stat. 2016, 2017–19 (allowing penalty-free withdrawal of up to $100,000).

232   *See* McGovern v. Comm'r, T.C. Summary Op. 2003-137 (2003) (payment of qualified higher education expenses with amounts distributed from a qualified plan is subject to 10 percent early withdrawal tax even though additional tax would not have applied if the education expenses had been paid from an IRA, despite the fact that taxpayer had actually transferred the remainder of the qualified plan distribution into a rollover IRA).

233   At year-end 2007, IRAs held $4.75 trillion in assets, private sector defined contribution plans held $3.49 trillion, and private sector defined benefit plans held $2.33 trillion; in 2004, roll-overs to traditional IRAs amounted to $215 billion, compared to total contributions of $12.6 billion to traditional IRAs and another $14.7 billion to Roth IRAs. Craig Copeland, *IRA Assets and Contributions, 2007*, 29 EBRI Notes 2, 3, 8 (2008).

234   Recall that an exception to the anti-alienation rule permits plan loans to be secured by the participant's vested accrued benefit. ERISA § 206(d)(2), 29 U.S.C. § 1056(d)(2) (2006); I.R.C. § 401(a)(13)(A) (2006). *See generally supra* Chapter 8 notes 14–15 and accompanying text.

disqualification, plan loans must be available to employees on a nondiscriminatory basis under specific plan provisions calling for reasonable interest and adequate security.[235] Second, the maximum amount of all outstanding plan loans to the employee under all plans of the employer (as defined using the commonly controlled business and affiliated service group workforce aggregation rules) is the smaller of $50,000 or one-half of the present value of the employee's vested accrued benefit (but not less than $10,000).[236] In addition to limiting plan loans to a relatively small amount, they are generally required to be repaid by level amortization over five years. (An exception to the five-year term is allowed for loans used to purchase a principal residence, but in that case, the housing value will presumably be available in retirement even if the loan is not repaid.)[237] To the extent that a loan to a participant exceeds the limit set by section 72(p), or if the loan does not comply with the term or level amortization requirements, the plan is not disqualified, but receipt of the loan proceeds is treated as a plan distribution. Usually this means that the loan proceeds are taxable, and the 10 percent penalty tax on early withdrawals might also apply.[238]

A recent study of loan activity under 401(k) plans shows that loan features are common in large plans and that 90 percent of 401(k) plan participants were in plans that permitted loans. Nevertheless, relatively few participants make use of the feature; only 18 percent of those eligible to borrow had loans outstanding at the close of 2007. Moreover, the outstanding loan amount for participants who borrow from the plan tends to be small, averaging only 12 percent of the 2007 year-end account balance (net of loans).[239]

Rollovers Retirement savings may be dissipated if they are distributed during the participant's working years. Americans change jobs frequently, especially younger workers, and qualified plans (as we have seen, even including pension plans) may permit distribution of the participant's entire interest upon separation from service. If the present value of a participant's vested accrued benefit exceeds $5,000, it cannot

---

235   I.R.C. §§ 401(a)(13)(A), 4975(d)(1) (2006); Treas. Reg. § 1.401(a)-13(d)(2) (as amended in 1988); Rev. Rul. 89-14, 1989-1 C.B. 111 (reasonable interest rate required even if loan is to an employee who is not a disqualified person).

236   I.R.C. § 72(p) (2006). Permissible loan amounts are actually specified with reference to the highest outstanding balance of plan loans to the employee within the preceding one-year period. This rule prevents evasion of the five-year term limit via routine extensions or relending.

237   I.R.C. § 72(p)(2)(B), (C) (2006).

238   I.R.C. § 72(p)(1)(A), (t) (2006); Treas. Reg. § 1.72(p)-1, Q&A-11 (as amended in 2006). The repayment requirements (five-year level amortization) must be satisfied in both form and operation, and so an employee-borrower's failure to pay a required installment, if not promptly cured, can trigger a deemed taxable distribution after the loan is made. *Id.* Q&A-4, -10.

239   Jack VanDerhei et al., *401(k) Plan Asset Allocation, Account Balances, and Loan Activity in 2007*, EBRI ISSUE BRIEF No. 324, Dec. 2008, at 29, 40–41, *available at* http://www.ebri.org/pdf/briefspdf/EBRI_IB_12a-2008.pdf; Geng Li & Paul A. Smith, *New Evidence on 401(k) Borrowing and Household Balance Sheets* (Mar. 26, 2009) working paper posted on Social Science Research Network, *available at* http://ssrn.com/abstract=1369208 (share of eligible households with 401(k) loan balances about 15 percent, and many loan-eligible households carry much more expensive credit card and other consumer debt).

---

be distributed without the consent of the participant (and his or her spouse if married),[240] and in that case, the 10 percent additional tax on early withdrawals may discourage distribution and pre-retirement consumption. But if the present value is less than or equal to $5,000, a qualified plan can require distribution on separation from service, and such mandatory cash-outs are routinely used to avoid the administrative costs associated with maintaining small balances for long periods on behalf of departed former employees. For a number of reasons, even a participant with a larger balance who wants to continue saving for retirement may take distribution in spite of the additional tax. She may want access to the funds as a precaution, as in the situation where an undetermined portion may be needed for support during a period of unemployment. Or a former employee may take distribution because she is not comfortable with the plan's management or investment policies or options and fears her money will not be safe if left there for the long haul. In all of these cases, once the money comes into the hands of the employee, there is a serious risk that it will not actually be preserved for retirement, however responsible one's intentions may be when less flush with cash.

Rather than relying exclusively on the deterrent effect of the early withdrawal penalty tax to safeguard retirement savings, the Code also offers the inducement of continued post-distribution tax deferral through the rollover mechanism. Any distribution from a qualified plan other than a required minimum distribution, a hardship-based distribution, or an annuity distribution, if contributed within 60 days after receipt to an IRA, another qualified plan, a tax-sheltered annuity contract, or an eligible deferred compensation plan of a state or local government, is excluded from gross income under the tax-free rollover rules.[241] The rollover contribution need not be of the entire amount

---

240   I.R.C. §§ 411(a)(11), 417(e) (2006); ERISA §§ 203(e), 205(g), 29 U.S.C. §§ 1053(e), 1055(g) (2006).

241   I.R.C. § 402(c) (2006) (rollovers from qualified pension, profit-sharing or stock bonus plan), id. § 403(a)(4) (rollovers from qualified annuity plan). To be eligible for rollover treatment, the disbursing plan must be qualified at the time of the distribution, not simply when the employer made contributions. Treas. Reg. § 1.402(a)-1(a)(1)(ii) (as amended in 2005); Baetens v. Comm'r, 777 F.2d 1160 (6th Cir. 1985); Benbow v. Comm'r, 774 F.2d 740 (7th Cir. 1985).

Distributions under a term-certain annuity that has a period of less than ten years are also eligible for rollover treatment. I.R.C. § 402(c)(4)(A) (2006). Rollovers of distributions under tax-sheltered annuity contracts or eligible deferred compensation plans of state or local governments are also permitted under corresponding rules. Id. §§ 403(b)(8), 457(e)(16). Such liberal general rollover rules do not apply to eligible deferred compensation plans of nongovernmental tax-exempt employers, but a tax-free transfer from one eligible deferred compensation plan to another 457 plan (not to an IRA, a qualified plan, or a tax-sheltered annuity) is permitted. Id. § 457(e)(10).

Distributions from a traditional IRA can be rolled over to another traditional IRA, or to a qualified plan, tax-sheltered annuity, or eligible governmental deferred compensation plan, provided that the distribution is not from an inherited IRA. I.R.C. § 408(d)(3) (2006); see id. § 402(c)(11) (inherited IRA includes IRA that receives direct trustee-to-trustee transfer of qualified plan assets on behalf of nonspouse designated beneficiary of deceased employee). Rollovers to a Roth IRA are subject to special rules because contributions to a Roth IRA must be made out of after-tax income. Distributions from qualified plans and traditional IRAs ordinarily have not been subject to tax and therefore cannot be transferred to a Roth IRA without first being included in income. Id. § 408A(c)(3)(B) (AGI limit on rollovers to Roth IRA from

distributed—continued tax deferral is granted to any portion of the distribution that is timely transferred to an eligible receptacle.[242] Such a rollover contribution also excuses the amount so contributed from the early distribution penalty tax of section 72(t).[243] Even a distribution of property (e.g., employer stock distributed from a stock bonus plan) is eligible for tax-free rollover if the property received is transferred in-kind to the IRA, qualified plan, or other eligible receptacle,[244] or the property may be sold and the proceeds contributed.[245]

Instead of distribution to the participant followed by contribution to another plan or IRA within 60 days, rollovers may be accomplished by a direct trustee-to-trustee transfer. In lieu of taking distribution of an amount that would be eligible for tax-free rollover, the plan participant or IRA owner may instruct the trustee to transfer the amount directly to an IRA or qualified plan designated by the participant. Such direct transfers keep retirement savings out of the worker's hands for even the brief period (at most, 60 days) allowed by the rollover rules. By reducing temptation, direct transfers (also known as direct rollovers) might reduce asset leakage out of the retirement savings system. With that goal in mind, Congress promotes direct rollovers in two ways. First, all qualified pension, profit-sharing, stock bonus, and annuity plans (as well as tax-sheltered annuities and eligible deferred compensation plans of state or local government employers) are required to accept and execute proper direct rollover instructions, and the transfers are expressly excluded from gross income.[246]

---

a traditional IRA or qualified plan), (d)(3) (rollover contributions to Roth IRA must be included in income but additional 10-percent early withdrawal tax does not apply).

242   I.R.C. § 402(c)(1)(A) (2006) ("any portion of the balance"), *id.* §§ 402(c)(1) (parenthetical clause), 403(a)(4), (b)(8)(A), 408(d)(3)(D), 457(e)(16)(A). Where a distribution from a qualified plan includes amounts that would be received tax-free (e.g., after-tax employee contributions), then the maximum amount that may be rolled over is the otherwise-taxable portion of the distribution, except in cases where separate accounting for the after-tax portion of a contribution is feasible. *Id.* §§ 402(c)(2), 403(a)(4)(B); *see id.* § 401(a)(31)(C) (direct transfer qualification condition). Where a distribution from a traditional IRA includes amounts that are not subject to tax (i.e., after-tax or nondeductible contributions), the maximum permissible rollover to a qualified plan, tax-sheltered annuity, or eligible governmental deferred compensation plan is the amount of the IRA distribution that would otherwise be includible in gross income. In contrast, if the rollover is made to another IRA, then the contribution can include the nontaxable amount of the distribution. *Compare id.* § 408(d)(3)(A)(i), *with* (d)(3)(A)(ii).

243   I.R.C. § 72(t)(1) (2006) (additional tax applies to amount included in gross income, while portion of distribution rolled over is excluded from gross income).

244   I.R.C. §§ 402(c)(1)(C), 403(a)(4)(A)(iii), 403(b)(8)(A)(iii), 408(d)(3)(A), 457(e)(16)(A)(iii) (2006).

245   I.R.C. §§ 402(c)(6), 403(a)(4)(B), (b)(8)(B), 457(e)(16)(B) (2006). Special allocation or tracing rules come into play to assure appropriate partial taxation if distributed property is sold and the amount of the rollover contribution is less than the total value of money and property distributed.

246   I.R.C. §§ 401(a)(31), 402(e)(6), 403(a)(5), (b)(10), 404(a)(2), 457(d)(1)(C) and (d)(1) (final sentence) (2006). The instructions must specify the IRA or plan to which the direct rollover is to be made, and if the transfer is to a qualified plan, it must be a defined contribution plan, which, by its terms, permits such rollovers. Hence, while all qualified plans (along with 403(b) plans and governmental 457 plans) are required to make direct trustee-to-trustee transfers, they are *not* required to accept them. *Id.* § 401(a)(31)(E). Direct transfer to the participant's IRA is always an available alternative.

Second, direct rollovers are encouraged because they avoid the temporary imposition of the 20 percent withholding tax that is otherwise applied to eligible rollover distributions from tax-favored retirement savings programs.[247] The withholding tax is refundable, of course, but a participant who wishes to roll over the entire distribution will have to contribute within 60 days not only the net amount actually received (80 percent of the distribution), but also an additional amount from his or her own resources to make up for the 20 percent withheld. If the distribution is substantial, many workers would find it difficult to finance the additional contribution. If only the amount actually paid to the participant is rolled over, then only 80 percent of the distribution is excludible; the 20 percent that was withheld thus becomes a taxable distribution which (depending on timing) might also be subject to the additional tax on early distributions. Due to the cash flow burden imposed, one might predict that this withholding regime would actually discourage rollover of the full amount distributed, but the freedom from withholding of direct rollovers creates a countervailing incentive that encourages precommitment to the preservation of retirement savings. To promote such precommitment, the plan administrator is required to provide a participant who is scheduled to receive a distribution that is eligible for tax-free rollover with a written explanation of the direct rollover option and the withholding tax that will apply if a direct rollover is not elected.[248]

Experience shows that the likelihood and the amount of a rollover increase with the size of the distribution.[249] Distribution of the participant's full accrued benefit can be required without the participant's consent (mandatory cash-out) if the present value of the accrued benefit is not more than $5,000. Such small accumulations are likely to be spent on current consumption, particularly if the distribution is occasioned by the separation from service of a young employee. In an effort to increase the odds that

---

247 I.R.C. § 3405(c), (e)(1), (e)(5) (2006).

248 I.R.C. § 402(f) (West Supp. 2009). The explanation must be provided within a reasonable time before making the distribution, meaning not more than 180 days nor less than 30 days. Treas. Reg. § 1.402(f)-1, Q&A-2 (as amended in 2007); Prop. Treas. Reg. § 1.402(f)-1, Q&A-2(a) (expanding permissible period from 90 to 180 days), 2008-2 C.B. 1131, 1134. The IRS has published a model notice that plan administrators may use to satisfy their advance explanation obligations. I.R.S. Notice 2000-11, 2000-1 C.B. 572. The advance explanation requirement applies not only to eligible rollover distributions from qualified pension, profit-sharing, stock bonus plans, but also to distributions from qualified annuity plans, tax-sheltered annuities, and eligible governmental deferred compensation plans. I.R.C. §§ 403(a)(4)(B), 403(b)(8)(B), 457(e)(16)(B) (2006).

A recent empirical study found that the withholding tax and required explanation have led to substantial increases in rollovers, and that the effect was most pronounced for small lump-sum distributions. These findings, the authors conclude, are more consistent with a behavioral than a rational expectations model of decision making. Leonard E. Burman et al., *Effects of Public Policies on the Disposition of Pre-Retirement Lump-Sum Distributions: Rational and Behavioral Influences* at 22–26 Center Disc. Paper No. 2008-94, 2008, *available at* http://papers.ssrn.com/sol3/papers.cfm?abstract_id=1303982.

249 Craig Copeland, *Lump-Sum Distributions at Job Change*, 30 EBRI NOTES 2, 8-9 (2009) (analysis of Census Bureau data from the 2004 Survey of Income and Program Participation the shows that "the larger the distribution the more likely it was kept entirely in tax-qualified savings").

small retirement savings will be preserved, mandatory distributions in excess of $1,000 are required to be transferred directly into an IRA unless the distributee either designates some other qualified savings program or affirmatively elects to take the distribution herself.[250] This changes the default mode of distribution for mandatory cash outs exceeding $1,000 from distribution to the outgoing participant (who may be tempted to spend a small windfall) to direct rollover to an IRA.

D. REORIENTING PRIVATE PENSIONS

Thirty-five years after ERISA's enactment, the indictment against the contemporary private pension system sounds devastating. The project of supplementing Social Security via employer-mediated tax-subsidized deferred compensation programs has become monumentally complex, inordinately expensive, and largely ineffective in generating additional retirement saving. There is surely evidence to back each count. But is the case against qualified plans compelling?

The preceding review of the tax controls—the qualified plan rules that influence the amount and destination of the tax subsidy—offers convincing proof that the rules have indeed become monumentally complex *for plan sponsors and professionals*. That formidable complexity is largely invisible and irrelevant to plan participants and beneficiaries, the intended objects of the assistance. As has often been noted, the complexity with which tax policy makers should be concerned is the complexity faced by individual taxpayers, who typically navigate the system without professional guidance. The chief decisions presented to the average worker are how much to defer under a 401(k) plan, which investment options to select, and when to take distributions, none of which require a participant to contend with nondiscrimination rules or other daunting qualification conditions.[251] Experts who structure and administer the rules are adept

---

250 I.R.C. §§ 401(a)(31)(B), 403(b)(10), 404(a)(2), 457(d)(1)(C) (2006). While enacted in 2001, the effective date of the default rule requiring automatic direct rollover of mandatory cash-outs of amounts greater than $1,000 was delayed until the Labor Department issued regulations providing a safe harbor from ERISA's fiduciary duties for the selection of the rollover IRA provider and the investments products purchased with the funds. Economic Growth and Tax Relief Reconciliation Act of 2001, Pub. L. No. 107-16 § 657(a)(1), (c)(2)(A), (d), 115 Stat. 38, 135–37. Those regulations were issued in 2004 and became effective in 2005. 29 C.F.R. § 2550.404a-2 (2009). Even if the automatic rollover does not comply with the safe harbor, the fiduciary of the distributing plan is insulated from liability for losses occurring more than one year after the transfer into the IRA. ERISA § 404(c)(3), 29 U.S.C. § 1104(c)(3) (2006).

251 Note that the first two questions, contribution levels and investment choice, are not issues for defined benefit plan participants. These crucial matters have been shifted to individual decision making with the increasing dominance of elective contribution programs (such as 401(k) and 403(b) plans) that give participants control over the selection of investment options under ERISA § 404(c), 29 U.S.C. §1104(c) (2006). *See supra* Chapter 4D. Still, these saving and investment decisions primarily implicate financial planning skills (and may call for increased attention to providing workers with basic financial education), not knowledge of pension law. The matter of when to take distributions entails more tax and pension law complications, but the Code demands some advance written explanation of considerations pertinent to this issue. I.R.C. § 402(f) (2006); *see supra* Chapter 10 note 248.

at dealing with complexity and get paid for it, and so we need be concerned with the difficulties faced by specialists only insofar as the resulting transaction costs drag down the system, or the rules are so intricate that results become indeterminate.[252] Complexity, in other words, is primarily relevant to cost, and cost must be evaluated in light of benefit.

Turning to the charge that the retirement savings system is inordinately expensive, it is true that the preferential treatment accorded qualified retirement savings represents the first or second largest tax expenditure, with a net revenue loss in fiscal year 2009 estimated at $127 billion.[253] The preferential tax treatment of retirement savings is assuredly costly. Yet this "cost" is mislabeled insofar as the nondiscrimination rules actually redirect the tax subsidy into additional retirement savings for rank-and-file workers. The purpose of the tax allowance is redistribution, and the cost of accomplishing that goal is only the portion of the subsidy that is *not* shifted (whether retained by HCE-savers, captured by the employer, or used to defray administrative costs).[254]

Thus the case against the private pension system comes down to the question of efficacy. How much additional retirement saving (saving that would not otherwise occur) does the tax allowance actually generate, and is it enough? It is difficult to know how efficient our covert redistribution mechanism is in operation.[255] Lacking information on individual propensity to save, the existence of a plan with broad participation does not tell us how much (if any) new saving has been induced. Perhaps plans mostly operate as tax shelters for workers who would have saved anyway. Or perhaps the system is highly efficient, in the sense that foregone tax revenue is transmuted into

---

252 Some experts believe that high transaction costs have been an important driver of the migration away from defined benefit plans by small and medium-sized employers.

253 This figure includes the cost of traditional and Roth IRAs ($18.7 billion, total), as well as qualified plans ($107.8 billion, including defined contribution, defined benefit, and Keogh plans). By way of comparison, the single largest tax expenditure by the Joint Committee's reckoning is the exclusion of employer-provided health care and health insurance, estimated as $127.4 billion in fiscal 2009. Staff of the Joint Comm. on Taxation, Estimates of Federal Tax Expenditures for Fiscal Years 2008–2012, at 56, 57 (Comm. Print 2008), *available at* http://www.jct.gov/s-2-08.pdf. According to the Treasury Department's estimates, the revenue loss associated with all such qualified retirement savings arrangements in 2009 is $121.5 billion, while the exclusion of employer-provided health care costs $168.5 billion. Executive Office of the President, Office of Management and Budget, Analytical Perspectives, Budget of the U.S. Government, Fiscal Year 2009, at 287, 290, 291 (2008), *available at* http://www.gpoaccess.gov/usbudget/fy09/pdf/spec.pdf.

254 Redistribution ordinarily entails adverse effects on productivity incentives, of course. When it comes to qualified retirement savings, however, favorable tax treatment mitigates the income tax system's deterrent effect on saving to the extent that HCEs actually benefit.

255 It is safe to say that the costs associated with the administration of private plans are many times higher than the expense of running the Social Security system, which is about 1 percent of benefits paid. One estimate puts the expense of maintaining a defined benefit plan at 11 percent of benefits paid, and 6 percent on average for defined contribution plans. David M. Cutler, *Reexamining the Three-Legged Stool, in* Social Security: What Role for the Future? 125, 140 (Peter A. Diamond et al. eds., 1996). Of course, if Social Security included a system of private accounts, then program administration expenses would be far higher.

additional saving with minimal waste. Supposing the latter optimistic assumption were true, still the current system is inadequate. The active participation rate stubbornly hovers just under 50 percent of wage and salary workers aged 21 to 64,[256] and that number has been basically stagnant since the late 1970s. Yet almost all workers need to supplement Social Security to avoid a sharp drop in their standard of living in retirement.[257] Even for covered workers, many observers fear that the trend away from defined benefit plans to elective contribution programs that leave investment decisions to employees threatens benefit adequacy. Wasteful or not, much is amiss with the modern pension system.

Most experts believe that far-reaching reforms or fundamental overhaul is required to help Americans achieve an adequate level of retirement resources. This section reviews the major components of a number of proposals, ranging from incremental reforms, like adjusting the nondiscrimination regime or sweetening the subsidy to expand coverage, to schemes that would jettison nondiscrimination and substitute a structure designed to attain near-universal coverage.

Calibrating Nondiscrimination

The current nondiscrimination regime, for all its complexity, is a crude device for accomplishing redistribution because both the amount of available subsidy and the aggregate bribes required to satisfy the tests depend upon workforce composition, including factors such as age, compensation level, tax rate, and individual propensity to save. Simply making the nondiscrimination rules stricter, as by raising the acceptable ratio percentage from 70 to 80 percent, for example, would not necessarily increase qualified plan coverage overall. Firms with workforces containing a large proportion of high-income savers (so currently a lot of wasted subsidy) would expand NHCE coverage to meet the new standard, while other companies would terminate existing plans because the enhanced NHCE participation rate would be too costly. While there is no easy adjustment that will optimize redistribution, a number of modifications seem likely to improve the performance of the nondiscrimination rules. Four candidates are suggested here.

First, plan-by-plan testing for both coverage and amount discrimination accomplishes little beyond inflating compliance costs. Instead, all qualified plans of the employer (as defined under the workforce aggregation rules) could be subjected to a single consolidated application of the average benefits percentage test, with each plan deemed nondiscriminatory if the average benefit percentage of the group of all nonexcludible NHCEs is at least 70 percent of the average benefit percentage for the group

---

256   *E.g.*, Craig Copeland, *Employment-Based Retirement Plan Participation: Geographic Differences and Trends, 2007*, EBRI Issue Brief No. 322, Oct. 2008, at 7 (47.4% overall; 42.0% private sector; 75.4% public sector; 55.3% for full-time full-year workers), *available at* http://www.ebri.org/pdf/briefspdf/EBRI_IB_10-2008.pdf.

257   *See supra* Figure 10-1 and accompanying text.

of HCEs.[258] (Each nonexcludible employee's individual benefit percentage would be computed by summing the contributions and benefits earned by that employee under all plans, and a zero would be included in the group average for each nonexcludible employee who is not an active participant in any plan.) Such a global average benefits test would permit the employer to completely segregate HCEs and NHCEs into different plans having different features (including an HCE contribution or benefit rate that is somewhat higher than is available to any NHCE), and that increased flexibility should yield plans of greater value to their members.[259]

Second, nondiscrimination "safe harbors" of the sort allowed for 401(k) plans should be repealed (except perhaps for small employers). Recall that the ADP test is deemed satisfied if the employer is required to make a qualified nonelective contribution on behalf of each eligible NHCE equal to at least 3 percent of compensation, or if the employer is required to make qualified matching contributions on behalf of each eligible NHCE, dollar-for-dollar on elective contributions up to the first 3 percent of compensation with a 50 percent match of elective contributions between 3 and 5 percent of pay.[260] These safe harbors amount to selling indulgences for discrimination. If an employer makes 3 percent qualified nonelective contributions for all eligible employees, the firm's HCEs may each make the maximum elective deferral ($16,500 in 2009), even if no NHCE elects to defer any portion of her pay. The amendment of existing 401(k) plans to take advantage of the safe harbor is a strong indicator that the toll charge for favoritism is attractively priced, or in other words, that it wastes more subsidy (forces less redistribution) than the ADP test.

Third, the stringency of the nondiscrimination standard might be adjusted to reflect the proportion of the workforce that consists of NHCEs. In general, a workforce containing a high proportion of NHCEs generates little subsidy that could be redistributed (few HCE-savers that is) but contains a large number of low-paid workers who need help saving for retirement. Conversely, a workforce with relatively few NHCEs may be assumed to have a lot of subsidy that could be shifted, but fewer low-paid workers among whom to distribute it. Wasted subsidy might be reduced and qualified plan coverage expanded by calibrating the numerical nondiscrimination standard with the composition of the workforce. Assuming a single consolidated application of the average benefits percentage test (as suggested above), an employer with a workforce that has a low proportion of NHCEs might be required to show that its average benefit percentage for NHCEs is 90 percent (or 110 percent) of the benefit rate for HCEs, for example. In contrast, a firm with a workforce containing few HCEs might be allowed to pass the nondiscrimination standard with an NHCE average benefit percentage that is substantially lower than the 70 percent required by current law. Indeed, as the share

---

258 *See supra* text accompanying Chapter 10 notes 85–86. An additional anti-abuse rule might be required to assure that retirement savings are broadly distributed among NHCEs, rather than being concentrated in the hands of a favored few. *See supra* Chapter 10 note 85.

259 This flexibility would be obtained only if testing for qualitative discrimination (testing the availability of benefits, rights, and features; *see* Treas. Reg. § 1.401(a)(4)-5 (as amended in 1993)) were not conducted on a consolidated basis.

260 I.R.C. § 401(k)(12) (2006); Treas. Reg. § 1.401(k)-3 (as amended in 2009).

of workers who are HCEs gets smaller, the acceptable NHCE average benefit percentage might be decreased to a level that the available compensation cost savings could support—to 40, 30, or 20 percent, for example. Something akin to this is allowed under the nondiscriminatory classification test, where the acceptable plan ratio percentage is reduced (down to as low as 20 percent) as the proportion of NHCEs in the workforce increases, but that test serves only as a gateway to the average benefits percentage test which (under current law) imposes a 70 percent standard regardless of workforce composition.[261] A study of the relationship between plan sponsorship and workforce composition would need to be conducted to estimate how the required NHCE average benefit percentage should vary with NHCE workforce composition, and so set the proposed sliding-scale nondiscrimination standard.[262]

Finally, rather than prescribing a sliding-scale nondiscrimination standard, a fixed numerical benchmark could be imposed, as under current law, but the amount of the subsidy available to employers could be adjusted up or down with variations in workforce composition. While the value of the tax subsidy could be altered in a number of ways, perhaps the most straightforward approach would be to adjust the permissible maximum amount levels under Code section 415. Where a company's workforce is disproportionately composed of HCEs, the caps on the maximum dollar amount of annual benefits and annual additions (for defined benefit and defined contribution plans, respectively) for any participant could be reduced to limit the amount of tax-subsidized savings by highly paid workers, thereby reducing waste (i.e., subsidy in excess of the amount that must be redistributed to satisfy the nondiscrimination standard). Conversely, a firm that employs an unusually low percentage of HCEs could be allowed to give those executives a larger amount of qualified plan savings by raising the dollar caps under the maximum amount rule, so that higher savings levels would still generate enough subsidy to meet the nondiscrimination standard despite the smaller number of HCEs.

Sweetening the Subsidy

The preceding discussion shows that the traditional fixed and invariant nondiscrimination standard can sometimes be satisfied by a plan that accomplishes little redistribution (much wasted revenue), while in other situations, it cannot be satisfied at all because the compensation cost savings that can be extracted from highly paid workers is insufficient to pay all the bribes that would be needed to induce the requisite level of rank-and-file employee participation. The difference between the two situations (Company A sponsors a qualified plan, Company B does not), as has been shown, is usually attributable to difference in workforce composition (Company A employs predominately HCEs who want to save, Company B overwhelmingly employs

---

261 *See supra* Figure 10-3 and accompanying text.

262 It might be discovered that the simple binary HCE-NHCE classification is too crude to reveal a clear functional relationship to plan sponsorship. If so, a more sophisticated measure of compensation inequality within the workforce, such as the Gini coefficient, might be needed.

low-wage workers who cannot afford to save). Studies confirm that access to a retirement plan at work is not randomly distributed throughout the labor force. Instead, older, higher-paid workers are more likely to be employed by a company that sponsors a plan. Few small firms (meaning those with fewer than 100 employees) sponsor a plan, apparently due to differences in workforce composition. On average, small firm employees have lower earnings, less formal education, and are more likely to work part-time or part year than their counterparts at large firms. The characteristics of workers at small firms that sponsor retirement plans, however, are quite similar to workers at large firms that sponsor plans.[263]

> Although both administrative costs and workforce composition are likely to influence the employer's decision to sponsor a retirement plan, these facts support the explanation that, as of 2006, the low sponsorship rate at small firms was due more to differences in demand for retirement benefits by the firms' employees than to the fixed costs associated with starting up and administering a plan.[264]

Reduced demand, of course, increases the costs of complying with the nondiscrimination rules (higher bribes required) and so translates into a low qualified plan sponsorship rate. Inducing retirement savings in such circumstances is going to require more public money.

The saver's credit, enacted in 2001, is an effort to provide a larger savings incentive directly to low-income individuals (rather than by boosting the indirect subsidy available through a qualified plan).[265] The saver's credit can be up to 50 percent of the amount of qualified retirement savings contributions for the taxable year not in excess of $2,000. The 50 percent credit rate is available to taxpayers filing a joint return whose adjusted gross income (AGI) does not exceed $33,000 in 2009 ($16,500 for an unmarried individual). At higher incomes, the credit rate is smaller, and no credit is available at all if the AGI on a joint return is over $55,500 in 2009 ($27,750 for single taxpayers). A contribution to a traditional or Roth IRA, or an elective deferral under a 401(k) plan or 403(b) annuity, can qualify for the credit. The saver's credit is nonrefundable, and as of 2009 it has been little utilized because individuals with incomes low enough to qualify for the credit typically have little or no income tax liability to offset. The Obama Administration's fiscal year 2010 budget proposal would expand the saver's credit by increasing the income limit and making the credit refundable.[266]

---

263 Peter Brady & Stephen Sigrist, *Who Gets Retirement Plans and Why*, 14 ICI Research Perspective No. 2, 25–28 (2008), *available at* http://www.ici.org/pdf/per14-02.pdf.

264 *Id*. at 29

265 I.R.C. § 25B (2006).

266 Florence Olsen, *Budget Would Use Saver's Credit to Increase Retirement Security of Low-Income Workers*, 36 Pen. & Benef. Rep. (BNA) 451 (Mar. 3, 2009). A similar proposal is the "America's IRA," which would offer dollar-for-dollar government matching (capped at $2,000 per year) of IRA contributions by low-income workers who are not covered by an employer plan. Aspen Institute Initiative on Financial Security, Savings for Life: A Pathway to Financial Security for All Americans 24–27 (2007), *available at* http://www.aspeninstitute.org/sites/default/files/content/docs/initiative%20on%20financial%20security/Savings_for_Life.pdf. *See also* Gene Sperling, The Pro-Growth Progressive 193–201 (2005) (Universal 401(k) proposal with matching tax credits for low- and middle-income workers).

The Obama plan also seeks to boost saving by requiring employers that don't offer a plan to enroll workers in direct deposit IRAs and make default contributions to the IRAs through wage withholding unless the worker opts out.[267]

Another measure to increase the subsidy is a credit for pension plan start-up costs of small employers. A 50 percent credit for the costs of establishing and administering a new qualified retirement plan and expenses of providing retirement-related education to employees is granted to employers with no more than 100 workers for the plan's first three years, subject to a maximum credit amount of $500 per year.[268]

Bush Administration Proposals

A different approach to stimulating additional saving is exemplified by the tax recommendations repeatedly put forward by President George W. Bush, which would have expanded Roth-style tax-free savings opportunities in individual accounts of two types. The Retirement Savings Account (RSA) would allow contributions of up to $5,000 per year regardless of income or coverage under a qualified retirement plan.[269] As with a Roth IRA, contributions would be nondeductible (after-tax), but earnings would accumulate tax-free, and qualified distributions would be excluded from gross income. To dedicate RSAs solely to retirement saving, qualified distributions would be available only after attaining age 58 or in the event of death or disability. (The earnings portion of earlier distributions would be subject to tax, including a 10 percent additional tax.) The RSA would substitute for all current forms of IRAs, other than rollover IRAs created solely to receive qualified plan distributions.

Individuals would also be allowed to contribute up to $2,000 annually to a Lifetime Savings Account (LSA), another Roth-style personal account that could be used to save for any purpose. Hence the LSA would not be limited to saving for retirement, health care, or education (for which tax-favored accounts are currently available),

---

267 Office of Management and Budget, *Jumpstarting the Economy and Investing for the Future*, in A New EERA of Responsibility, Renewing America's Promise 17, 37 (2009), *available at* http://www.whitehouse.gov/omb/assets/fy2010_new_era/a_new_era_of_responsibility2.pdf; Michael W. Wyland, *Fiscal 2010 Budget 'Lays the Groundwork' for Workplace Automatic Direct-Deposit IRAs*, 36 Pen. & Benef. Rep. (BNA) 450 (Mar. 3, 2009). *See* Gary Burtless, *Expanding Participation in America's Workplace Retirement System*, in Pensions, Social Security, and the Privatization of Risk 40, 67–69 (Mitchell A. Orenstein ed., 2009); J. Mark Iwry & David C. John, Pursuing Universal Retirement Security Through Automatic IRAs, *available at* http://www.retirementsecurityproject.org/pubs/File/RSPAutoIRALongpaperFIN AL7.10.2007.pdf.

268 I.R.C. § 45E (2006).

269 U.S. Department of the Treasury, General Explanations of the Administration's Fiscal Year 2009 Revenue Proposals 9 (2008) [hereinafter Bush Administration's FY 2009 Revenue Proposals], *available at* http://www.treas.gov/offices/tax-policy/library/bluebk08.pdf. In contrast, deductible contributions to a traditional IRA are subject to a phase-out for workers whose income exceeds specified levels and who are covered by an employer-sponsored retirement plan. I.R.C. § 219(g) (2006). Roth IRA contributions are also subject to an income phase-out, but the income range is higher than for deductible contributions to a traditional IRA. *Id.* § 408A(c)(3).

but could also be used to save for the purchase of a car or a home or for precautionary purposes. LSA contributions would be allowed whether or not the contributor has earned income and regardless of his total income. The annual contribution limit would apply to all accounts held in a particular individual's name, rather than to the contributor, so that an affluent middle-aged couple could put $4,000 (total) into their own LSAs and also contribute $2,000 to accounts for each of their children (or grandchildren, etc.).[270]

The RSA-LSA combination was designed to both encourage and simplify savings.

> The current list of non-retirement exceptions within IRAs weakens the focus on retirement saving, and the IRA exceptions and special purpose savings vehicles place a burden on taxpayers to document that withdrawals are used for certain purposes that Congress has deemed qualified. In addition, the restrictions on withdrawals and additional tax on early distributions discourage many taxpayers from making contributions because they are concerned about the inability to access the funds should they need them. Consolidating the . . . types of IRAs under current law into one account dedicated solely to retirement, and creating a new account that could be used to save for any reason would simplify the taxpayer's decision-making process while further encouraging saving.[271]

From one perspective, the RSA-LSA proposal can be seen as a logical evolutionary step toward rationalizing current savings incentives. Yet the Bush Administration initiative carried with it two indirect effects that some analysts viewed as revolutionary and deeply troubling. First, the new Roth-style accounts would encourage *individual* savings, thereby rendering qualified plan savings relatively less attractive and undermining the nondiscrimination regime. Second, the Bush Administration's savings proposals would also have worked a fundamental transformation of the federal tax system.

The individual tax-favored savings opportunity presented by RSAs and LSAs would weaken interest in qualified retirement plans at all income levels. Low-paid workers, we have seen, derive little benefit from tax deferral and often have little ability to save. To induce their participation in a qualified retirement plan so as to satisfy the nondiscrimination rules, the employer must sweeten the deal by increasing their total compensation. This is done by making a contribution toward retirement savings that is larger than the amount of wages or salary low-paid employees are willing to forgo, which compensation increase (in effect, a bribe to entice participation) is financed by the tax subsidy extracted from highly paid employees who want to save. Limited access to qualified plan savings, particularly the additional tax on early distributions, presents a barrier to participation by low-income workers that the employer must pay

---

270   Unlike the RSA, which would replace traditional and Roth IRAs, the LSA apparently would not replace existing nonretirement tax-advantaged savings vehicles. Hence, health savings accounts, Coverdell educational savings accounts, and section 529 qualified tuition programs would apparently continue to exist alongside LSAs, considerably expanding tax-free savings opportunities.

271   BUSH ADMINISTRATION'S FY 2009 REVENUE PROPOSALS, *supra* Chapter 10 note 269, at 8.

to overcome.[272] The LSA, however, offers a vehicle for penalty-free short-term precautionary saving, and for many young or low-paid employees, that alternative might be more attractive than subsidized but restricted qualified plan savings.[273] Middle-income employees who want to save for retirement might conclude that they can save enough individually via the RSA-LSA combination that there is no advantage to be gained from participation in a qualified plan.[274] Moreover, the absence of income limits on RSA and LSA contributions would reduce somewhat demand for more generous employer-sponsored qualified retirement plan benefits among high-income savers— these HCEs, who are the source of the tax subsidy, do not have to share to the extent that they can save through tax-exempt individual accounts.[275]

---

272 The ban on in-service distributions under pension plans is also a significant barrier (and deterrent to NHCE participation), but profit-sharing and stock bonus plans can allow distribution after as little as two years of participation. In contrast, 401(k) plans cannot permit access to elective deferrals (nor to qualified matching and qualified nonelective contributions) after a stated period of participation or the lapse of a fixed number of years, but that restriction is ameliorated by the authorization of distributions of elective deferrals in the event of the employee's hardship. I.R.C. § 401(k)(2)(B), (k)(3)(D), (m)(4)(C) (2006); Treas. Reg. 1.401(k)-1(d)(3) (as amended in 2009) (definition of allowable hardship distributions). Hardship distributions are not exempted from the 10 percent additional tax on early distributions, however. I.R.C. § 72(t)(2) (2006).

273 This comparison holds only for employees who have some federal income tax liability. A worker can always save on his own outside of a qualified plan, IRA, or Roth-style account and retain complete access to his funds, and if his income is low enough, then any pay saved would bear no tax, and the interest or other investment earnings also would not be taxed. For such a worker, the LSA offers no more benefit than "taxable" personal savings.

274 Under current law, such workers could use an IRA (traditional or Roth) to accumulate $5,000 per year (inflation-indexed) of tax-favored retirement savings outside of a qualified plan, but with an LSA they could increase the amount of their tax-advantaged individual retirement saving. As described above, the annual LSA contribution limit most recently proposed was only $2,000, but earlier versions of the Administration's LSA proposal would have allowed much higher LSA contributions ($5,000 or $7,500 per year), and if the Bush plan were enacted, there would be continuing political pressure to raise the LSA contribution limit. U.S. DEPARTMENT OF THE TREASURY, GENERAL EXPLANATIONS OF THE ADMINISTRATION'S FISCAL YEAR 2007 REVENUE PROPOSALS 9 (2006) ($5,000 LSA limit), *available at* http://www.treas.gov/offices/tax-policy/library/bluebk06.pdf; U.S. DEPARTMENT OF THE TREASURY, GENERAL EXPLANATIONS OF THE ADMINISTRATION'S FISCAL YEAR 2004 REVENUE PROPOSALS 119 (2003) ($7,500 LSA limit), *available at* http://www.treas.gov/offices/tax-policy/library/bluebk03.pdf. Similarly, the 2005 recommendations of the President's Advisory Panel on Federal Tax Reform included a Roth-style "Save for Family" account to which a taxpayer could contribute up to $10,000 annually in addition to putting $10,000 into a "Save for Retirement" account, and the Save for Family account could be used for retirement (as well as for health care, education, or a down payment on a home). PRESIDENT'S ADVISORY PANEL ON FEDERAL TAX REFORM, SIMPLE, FAIR, AND PRO-GROWTH 120 (2005), *available at* http://permanent.access.gpo.gov/lps64969/TaxReformwholedoc.pdf.

275 Under current law, a high-income individual who is an active participant in a qualified plan cannot contribute to either a traditional or a Roth IRA due to the income-based limits on contributions to those accounts. I.R.C. §§ 219(g), 408A(c)(3) (2006). Under the Bush Administration proposal, such a high-income active participant could take advantage of the RSA and LSA, which would diminish interest in higher levels of plan contributions or benefits. Apparently, a high-income individual not covered by a qualified plan could contribute $5,000 to an RSA.

Beyond these individual tax-favored savings accounts, the Bush Administration also advocated consolidation and simplification of the rules governing all types of tax-favored defined contribution savings programs that permit elective or salary-reduction contributions (including, among others, 401(k) plans, 403(b) annuities, and eligible deferred compensation plans maintained by state or local governments or tax-exempt organizations). A new vehicle, called Employer Retirement Savings Accounts (ERSAs), would be available to all employers and be subject to relaxed nondiscrimination testing. In place of the ADP test applicable to 401(k) plans,[276] the average HCE contribution percentage could be 200 percent of the average NHCE contribution percentage if the average NHCE contribution percentage were 6 percent or less, but if the average NHCE contribution percentage exceeded 6 percent, no limit would apply to HCE contribution rates (other than the Code section 415 maximum annual addition). Under an alternative design-based safe harbor, if each NHCE were eligible to receive fully-vested employer contributions (either matching or nonelective) of at least 3 percent of compensation, no further nondiscrimination standards would apply.[277] In stark contrast to the proposal to repeal the 401(k) nondiscrimination safe harbors described earlier,[278] the expansion and relaxation of 401(k) rules proposed for ERSAs would say that once certain minimum[279] contributions are provided to NHCEs, no further redistribution is required. Regardless of how much the HCEs saved, they (or their employer) could retain the full value of their favorable tax treatment; none of the tax benefit would have to be shared with rank-and-file employees. Employer-sponsored ERSAs, in common with the proposed RSA and LSA Roth-style individual savings accounts, would achieve simplification by gutting redistribution, allowing tax relief to inure to the benefit of high-income workers and their employers.

From a broader perspective, the Bush Administration's saving proposals also would have pushed the federal tax system farther along the path to a consumption tax base. The $7,000 that anyone could put away in her RSA and LSA each year (more if contributions are made to LSAs for children or others) is more than most Americans save. Consequently, all investment returns—dividends, interest, capital gains, and so forth— would be tax-exempt for a large majority of taxpayers, for whom the federal tax system would become simply a tax on labor income.[280] Many economists and some tax policy

---

In comparison, under current law, that amount could be contributed to a traditional IRA (but not to a Roth IRA) because the income-based contribution limit for traditional IRAs applies only to active participants. *See* SPERLING, *supra* Chapter 10 note 266, at 190–91 (quoting Al Martin, president of the Small Business Council of America, saying that the Bush Administration's savings proposals "would gut the small business retirement plan system").

276   *See supra* Chapter 10 notes 171–177 and accompanying text.

277   BUSH ADMINISTRATION'S FY 2009 REVENUE PROPOSALS, *supra* Chapter 10 note 269, at 15–16.

278   *See supra* text accompanying Chapter 10 note 260.

279   Some would say token.

280   Many consumption-tax features have been engrafted onto the realization-based federal income tax over the years, among the most important being the treatment of qualified retirement savings. The current system is generally understood as a hybrid between an income and a consumption tax. The RSA-LSA proposal, if adopted, would have shifted the balance far closer to a pure consumption tax, but because the accounts would get Roth-style treatment, the resulting consumption tax would be of the prepaid sort. That is, instead of taxing consumption when it

experts favor consumption over income as the base for personal taxation on efficiency grounds. As a practical matter, the Bush Administration's savings proposals would have largely accomplished a covert conversion of the federal revenue system to a consumption tax.[281]

Toward Universal Coverage

Each of the reform proposals examined thus far—calibrating the nondiscrimination rules, sweetening the subsidy, and the Bush Administration's individual account proposals—recommends incremental change to the existing retirement savings system. While some of these approaches are designed to significantly increase the number of American workers accumulating tax-favored retirement savings, none of them aim at universal coverage. A comprehensive savings program to supplement Social Security has been thought to require a mandatory system. The 1981 report of the President's Commission on Pension Policy, for example, proposed:

> The Commission recommends that a Minimum Universal Pension System (MUPS) be established for all workers. The system should be funded by employer contributions. The Commission further recommends that a 3 percent of payroll contribution be established as a minimum benefit standard. All employees over the age of 25, with one year of service and 1,000 hours of employment with their employer would be participants in the system. Vesting of benefits would be immediate.

> Under a MUPS, current pension plans would be amended to provide the equivalent of what a MUPS would provide. The MUPS benefit would be a supplement to social security benefits and could not be integrated with social security.

> * * *

> Employers should be encouraged to maintain the accumulated funds in pension trusts or through arrangements with insurance companies and other financial institutions. However, those employers who do not wish to administer an employee pension plan could send their contributions to . . . a central MUPS portability fund which would be established to invest the funds in the economy. The fund should be administered by an independent Board of Trustees appointed by the President.[282]

---

occurs (by deducting savings and investments and later taxing the full proceeds when applied to consumption), current taxation of labor income deposited in Roth-type accounts amounts to taxing the present value of future consumption.

281 *See* Theodore R. Groom & John B. Shoven, *Deregulating the Private Pension System, in* THE EVOLVING PENSION SYSTEM 123–53 (William G. Gale et al. eds., 2005) ("[E]xpansion of qualified plans can serve as a practical substitute for fundamental tax reform based on a consumption model because pensions are already taxed on that basis and can therefore be expanded without addressing the difficult transitional issues that are involved in converting the entire system to a consumption *Id*. at 140.)"

282 PRESIDENT'S COMMISSION ON PENSION POLICY, COMING OF AGE: TOWARD A NATIONAL RETIREMENT INCOME POLICY 42-43 (1981). *See* Adam Carasso & Jonathan Barry Forman, *Tax Considerations in a Universal Pension System*, (Urban-Brookings Tax Policy Center Disc. Paper No. 28, 2007), *available at* http://www.urban.org/UploadedPDF/411593_universal_pension_system.pdf.

Business leaders oppose and legislators have no stomach for a MUPS-type mandate. Recently a number of proposals have been developed that would go far toward achieving universal coverage in a more politically palatable manner, by using public moneys to fund savings on behalf of low-income workers. Two such programs are reviewed below.

Professors Daniel Halperin and Alicia Munnell "think it is time to acknowledge that today's voluntary employer-sponsored pension system is not capable of providing coverage for most of those individuals who end up in the lowest two quintiles of the retirement income distribution. . . . Reform is also needed to improve coverage and benefit adequacy for the rank and file."[283] Halperin and Munnell propose a two-pronged strategy.[284] First, government would directly fund retirement savings for low-income workers (those earning less than about $20,000 or $25,000 annually), who could be excluded from coverage under employer-sponsored retirement plans. "No longer would employers have to bribe lower-paid workers who have little interest in retirement saving to participate by increasing their total compensation."[285] Second, sponsorship of employer plans would remain voluntary, but if maintained, they would be required to cover virtually all workers not covered by the public program. As an inducement to do so, the employer would be allowed to provide higher benefits for top earners. If an employer sponsored a plan, all middle- and high-income employees working at least 500 hours per year would have to be covered, and benefits or contributions would have to constitute the same proportion of pay for all workers (without integration with Social Security). Therefore the complex coverage and amount nondiscrimination requirements of current law could be repealed.[286]

The key components of the Halperin and Munnell plan would greatly enlarge the portion of the U.S. labor force that accumulates meaningful retirement savings. Public funding would provide for the lowest-paid workers, while more mid-level

---

283   Daniel I. Halperin & Alicia H. Munnell, *Ensuring Retirement Income for All Workers, in* THE EVOLVING PENSION SYSTEM, *supra* Chapter 10 note 281, at 155, 180.

284   Halperin & Munnell, *supra* Chapter 10 note 283, at 179–85

285   Halperin & Munnell, *supra* Chapter 10 note 283, at 181. In return for diminished employer responsibility for covering low-income workers (reduced cost), Halperin and Munnell propose a 5 percent tax on private pension fund earnings, the revenue from which could be used to help fund the government contributions for low-wage workers. *Id.* at 182–83. The publicly funded retirement accounts for individuals earning less than $20,000 or $25,000 would be similar to the Clinton Administration's 1999 Universal Savings Account (USA) proposal, but withdrawals would be prohibited before age 65. The automatic government contribution would be phased out for individuals earning higher incomes, but dollar-for-dollar government matching contributions would apparently be available to workers earning somewhat higher amounts, perhaps up to about twice the income cutoff for the automatic grant (i.e., up to about $40,000 or $50,000 for single individuals). *See* Remarks on the Universal Savings Accounts Initiative (Apr. 14, 1999), *reprinted in* 1 PUBLIC PAPERS OF THE PRESIDENTS OF THE UNITED STATES: WILLIAM J. CLINTON, 1999, at 548 (2000).

286   Halperin & Munnell, *supra* Chapter 10 note 283, at 183. Current law permits the exclusion of part-time employees working less than 1,000 hours per year. In order to preserve retirement savings by the rank-and-file, Halperin and Munnell would also require full vesting within one year and mandatory rollover of lump-sum distributions to an IRA or another plan. In addition, all plans would have to offer an inflation-indexed annuity as a distribution option.

earners (rank-and-file employees) would be granted plan membership so that executives could amass higher benefits. Jettisoning the nondiscrimination rules would reduce administrative costs, yielding another inducement to plan sponsorship. (These features figure prominently in some other expert reform proposals.[287]) Yet because qualified plan sponsorship would remain voluntary, some workers would still be left out.

If universality is the goal, then a mandatory system like MUPS is the way. Politically, however, MUPS has always been a nonstarter. But would that necessarily be the fate of a mandatory program that offers government funding for low earners and that preserves significant inducements for employers to offer defined benefit pension plans? Professor Teresa Ghilarducci suggests just such a program.[288]

Like Halperin and Munnell, Ghilarducci agrees that the old ways aren't working. "To determine what is needed for effective pension reform, it is . . . crucial to stop pretending that the tax incentives for defined contribution plans do anything meaningful."[289] Professor Ghilarducci's proposal can be viewed as a version of add-on Social Security individual accounts, but with an important twist. There are three major components of her approach. First, she would repeal favorable tax treatment for all defined contribution plans, whether they are money purchase pension plans, profit-sharing plans, stock bonus plans, employee stock ownership plans (ESOPs), 401(k) plans, 403(b) tax-sheltered annuities, or otherwise.[290] As a substitute for defined contribution plans a "Guaranteed Retirement Account" (GRA) would be established for every worker. Like MUPS, GRAs entail compulsory savings: contributions of 5 percent of pay (up to the Social Security contribution and benefit base, $106,800 in 2009) would be required.[291] The contributions would be collected by withholding from the employee's pay and transferred to the Social Security Administration, whence they would be credited to individual accounts and invested by trustees as under the Federal Thrift Savings Plan.[292] GRA balances would earn a guaranteed minimum 3 percent real

---

287 PAMELA PERUN & C. EUGENE STEUERLE, WHY NOT A "SUPER SIMPLE" SAVING PLAN FOR THE UNITED STATES 8–13 (2008), http://www.urban.org/UploadedPDF/411676_simple_saving.pdf.

288 THERESA GHILARDUCCI, WHEN I'M SIXTY-FOUR 260–93 (2008) (quotation at 288).

289 Id. at 288.

290 See Id. at 264 (proposed $600 tax credit would substitute for current tax breaks granted 401(k) and other individual account plans).

291 Ghilarducci, supra Chapter 10 note 288, at 264. The features of the GRA plan are also explained in Teresa Ghilarducci, The Plan to Save American Workers' Retirement, in PENSIONS, SOCIAL SECURITY, AND THE PRIVATIZATION OF RISK 86, 95–101 (Mitchell A. Orenstein ed., 2009). All workers would be allowed to make voluntary additional contributions to their GRA out of after-tax income. This option would allow highly paid employees to contribute some of their earnings that exceed the Social Security contribution and benefit base (such excess earnings would not be subject to the 5 percent contribution requirement), and would also permit middle-income employees who want to replace more than 70 percent of their pre-retirement earnings to use their GRAs to do so.

292 GHILARDUCCI, supra Chapter 10 note 288, at 264–65. Curiously, Professor Ghilarducci does not explicitly address the tax status of the required 5 percent contributions. The assumption seems to be that they would come from the worker's after-tax income (i.e., withheld amounts not excludible from gross income), like the employee's share of Social Security taxes. See id. at 264 (voluntary additional contributions would be made with post-tax dollars; refundable tax credit would substitute for tax concessions granted defined contribution plans, presumably

rate of return. The earliest allowed withdrawal from a GRA would be at the earliest age for claiming Social Security benefits (62), at which point the balance would be converted to an inflation-adjusted life annuity. (Partial lump-sum payment of up to 10 percent of the account balance would be allowed.)[293] Ghilarducci calculates that the GRA accumulation over a full working career would produce retirement benefits equal to approximately 30 percent of pre-retirement compensation, which in combination with Social Security would yield a retirement income replacement rate for an average wage earner of about 70 percent.[294]

The second component of Ghilarducci's program is a refundable $600 tax credit for every worker contributing to GRA, regardless of income. This credit is set at a level that would ensure that the compulsory 5 percent contribution would not impose a reduction in take-home pay on full-time full-year minimum wage workers.[295] The revenue gained from repeal of the favorable treatment of defined contribution plans is projected to be more than enough to fund the tax credits.[296]

Finally, tax-favored defined benefit retirement plans (traditional pension plans) would still be permitted, and Ghilarducci proposes to allow employers to substitute coverage under a defined benefit plan for GRA contributions. An employer contributing at least 5 percent of payroll to a defined benefit plan each year would be excused from the obligation to withhold and pay over 5 percent of each worker's pay as GRA contributions.[297] This continuing role for traditional pension plans is founded upon their superior efficiency and risk allocation characteristics vis-à-vis defined contribution plans.[298] Compared to 401(k) plans and other defined contribution retirement savings programs, large defined benefit plans entail lower per-participant administrative costs, provide better diversification, insulate workers from the adverse effects of sharp market downturns on the eve of retirement, and can be designed to assure that workers

---

including the exclusion of contributions from employee income), *id.* at 276. The tax treatment of GRA distributions is also left entirely unspecified. If contributions are to be included in gross income, then distributions should at least be eligible for tax-free return of capital to that extent, presumably by application of the exclusion ratio approach to annuity taxation. *Cf.* I.R.C. §§ 402(a), 72 (2006). Alternatively, the GRA could be accorded Roth-style preferential tax treatment: contributions subject to tax with an exclusion for all amounts distributed. Because the value of such a yield exemption depends on the employee's tax rate (income level), preferential tax treatment might necessitate the imposition of some limits on voluntary additional contributions. *See supra* Chapter 10 note 291.

293   GHILARDUCCI, *supra* Chapter 10 note 288, at 265. In lieu of a single life annuity, the GRA owner would be permitted to elect actuarially equivalent (reduced) survivor annuity benefits.

294   *Id.* at 265.

295   *Id.* at 268.

296   *Id.* at 276.

297   *Id.* at 271–72, 292.

298   The declining prevalence of defined benefit plans, despite their superiority as a means to retirement security, is a main theme of Professor Ghilarducci's book. The same phenomenon is explored from another perspective by Edward A. Zelinsky, *The Origins of the Ownership Society* (2007), which is subtitled, "How the Defined Contribution Paradigm Changed America."

do not outlive their savings. These desirable attributes arguably support permitting at least some defined benefit plans to substitute for GRA coverage.

The defined benefit plan opt-out is an intriguing suggestion, but this feature of Ghilarducci's program is not fully developed. Not all defined benefit plans share the desiderata that are crucial to a sound national retirement policy. Presumably, traditional pension coverage would not be an adequate substitute for GRA contributions if the plan permitted pre-retirement[299] or lump-sum distributions, for instance, and the five-year cliff vesting that ERISA currently tolerates could leave a mobile worker with no retirement savings to show for many years of his career. Even if a participant is vested on separation from service, the limited portability of defined benefit pensions would need to be addressed.[300] Perhaps because of these difficulties, in a subsequent version of the GRA proposal Professor Ghilarducci does not mention the defined benefit plan alternative.[301]

Despite such complications, the defined benefit plan opt-out deserves further study, and for a reason that Professor Ghilarducci does not address. Tax advantages are not the only reason employers sponsor deferred compensation programs. Historically, many qualified plans were instituted in large part to advance the sponsoring company's personnel policy, whether the goal was to reduce turnover, encourage early retirement, offer a productivity incentive, or otherwise. ERISA allows pension plans that satisfy minimum standards of quality to be tailored to serve business objectives; this residual employer flexibility was deliberately preserved to encourage the continued growth of private plans.[302] If designed with care, allowing private plan coverage to substitute for GRA contributions in specified circumstances could benefit both employers and employees. That increased flexibility might reduce business opposition to the GRA proposal and enhance economic efficiency as well.

Some likely features of a composite qualified plan-GRA system can be sketched without getting mired in minutia. First, consider a defined benefit plan opt-out. As indicated earlier, defined benefit plan coverage should be allowed to substitute for mandatory GRA contributions only if plan characteristics provide at least as much savings with comparable security. Retirement distributions should take the form of an inflation-indexed life or joint life annuity; lump-sum payouts would be barred apart from permitting a single distribution of not more than 10 percent of the actuarial present value of the employee's accrued benefit. Pre-retirement distributions upon separation from service or plan termination could not be made either directly to the participant or to her IRA, but in these circumstances the value of the participant's accrued benefits could be rolled over into the employee's GRA. The requirement that a substitute plan provide

---

299 Under current law, pension plan distributions are permitted upon plan termination or separation from service.

300 *See* Halperin & Munnell, *supra* Chapter 10 note 283, at 169–73. One approach might be to require that upon separation from service before attaining Social Security retirement age a defined benefit plan transfer the actuarial present value of the departing employee's accrued benefits to his GRA.

301 *See* Ghilarducci, *The Plan to Save American Workers' Retirement*, *supra* Chapter 10 note 291.

302 *See generally supra* Chapter 1C.

savings at least as great as the 5 percent of pay that would otherwise be deposited in a participant's GRA would seem to demand an outright ban on forfeitures, or at least a reduction of the maximum acceptable vesting period to a year or two. Alternatively, however, the vesting schedules currently permitted (five-year cliff or three-to-seven-year graded vesting for defined benefit plans) could still be allowed, but subject to the stipulation that upon separation from service, the plan's forfeiture rules would apply only to the extent that the present value of the participant's accrued benefit under the terms of the plan exceeds the amount that would have accumulated in the participant's GRA but for the plan (i.e., periodic contributions of 5 percent of the wages or salary paid by the sponsor plus the guaranteed investment return of 3 percent thereon). This limited forfeiture would maintain some marginal incentive to continued employment with the plan sponsor, and a benefit formula based on final average compensation could also be used to encourage longer job tenure. Benefits based on final average compensation accrue disproportionately in the later years of a worker's career, inflicting substantial pension losses in the event of mid-career employment change, but so long as the present value of accrued benefits upon separation from service is equal to or greater than the amount that an outgoing participant would have accumulated under a GRA, there is no reason to prohibit an employer from designing a plan to reward service longevity. Early retirement incentives should also be acceptable, provided that the benefits are paid as a life or joint-life annuity, and the actuarial value of benefits that will be paid after the normal retirement date (recall that GRA distributions could commence no earlier than the youngest age for claiming Social Security benefits) is at least equal to the amount that, in the absence of the plan, the participant would have accumulated in her GRA based upon her employment with the plan sponsor.

Allowing coverage under an acceptable defined benefit plan to excuse the employer from making 5 percent contributions to an employee's GRA could be taken even further. One might allow an employer to establish a defined benefit plan that grants past-service credit and also permit the sponsor to immediately fund those retroactive benefits by claiming a refund of prior-year GRA contributions (and earnings thereon) that the employer made on behalf of plan participants in years before the plan was instituted. Prospectively, this retroactive take-up of prior-year GRA contributions would go far toward eliminating underfunding problems with defined benefit plans, and would reduce the exposure of the PBGC.

The GRA compulsory saving system proposed by Professor Ghilarducci is in effect a mandatory federally-administered cash balance plan under which every American worker is entitled to annual pay credits of 5 percent of current compensation, along with guaranteed interest credits of 3 percent of the account balance. The cash balance plan is a hybrid design; technically it is categorized as a defined benefit program (because a specified level of benefits is guaranteed regardless of the actual investment performance of the fund), but it promises an accrued benefit that mimics a defined contribution plan (specifically, a 5 percent money purchase pension plan that invests in inflation-protected bonds earning a 3 percent real return).[303] The androgynous nature

---

303   *See supra* Chapter 7 notes 25–26 and accompanying text.

of the GRA system offers a hint that some defined contribution plans might also be acceptable substitutes. Historically, defined contribution plans served a number of important employer objectives, many of which have been overlooked as 401(k) plans rose to dominance. In particular, profit-sharing and stock bonus plans were traditionally used to provide a productivity incentive to participating employees. The aggregate annual contribution to a profit-sharing plan could be tied to some measure of business performance, such as profits or sales, for example, with the overall contribution allocated among participants' accounts in proportion to their current compensation. There appears to be no reason to prohibit an employer from rewarding performance by making productivity-based contributions to its workers' GRAs so long as the minimum annual contribution is 5 percent of pay and the contributions are nondiscriminatory. By using the GRA as the savings vehicle, most of the threats to retirement security often posed by defined contribution plans would be alleviated: funds would obtain low-cost professional management and be broadly diversified, the guaranteed return would protect workers from sharp declines in retirement living standards caused by market volatility, and restrictions on GRA distributions would prevent employees from squandering or outliving their savings.

Replicating the incentives created by investments in employer stock would be antithetical to retirement income security, and so employer contributions under a stock bonus plan or ESOP should not be treated as meeting GRA obligations. Here again, however, the amount going into an employee's broadly diversified and professionally managed GRA could safely be fixed by reference to some measure of enterprise value or stock price movement if the contribution is subject to a 5 percent floor and satisfies nondiscrimination standards. Indeed, even the aversive aspects of investments in employer stock might be partially incorporated in a GRA-based savings program by allowing stock price declines in a given year to reduce or eliminate the employer's required GRA contribution, but only to the extent that the employer's total contributions to an employee's GRA exceed the aggregate minimum required for all years.[304]

The lesson here is that a system of compulsory minimum saving such as Ghilarducci's GRA proposal need not entirely homogenize retirement plans nor displace all work-related incentives. If the savings mandate is thoughtfully coordinated with other employer objectives, then the system could preserve or reclaim many of the personnel management functions that deferred compensation programs traditionally embraced.

E. CONCLUSION

Where taxes meet pensions, policies conflict and law is unstable. Evaluated exclusively as a problem of income tax policy, the principle of economic neutrality counsels

---

304 Actually, earnings on prior-year excess contributions could also be reclaimed (that is, subject to loss in the event of poor stock performance) without jeopardizing baseline GRA protections. Put another way, current year contributions could be reduced (perhaps even below zero) by any amount up to the amount by which the employer's total contributions to date plus guaranteed earnings thereon exceeds the amount that would have been accumulated if the employer had contributed only the minimum each year (5 percent of pay plus earnings thereon).

that taxes should not bias the choice between current and deferred compensation. Historically, the matching principle of Code section 404(a)(5) largely achieved neutrality between current and *nonqualified* deferred compensation by suspending the employer's business expense deduction until such time as the employee includes the deferred compensation in gross income. While that approach still generally prevails, in 2004 Congress enacted rules requiring employees to include nonqualified deferred compensation in advance of receipt unless the program satisfies certain criteria. Such advance inclusion by itself would not undermine tax neutrality, but Congress larded new section 409A with ill-conceived interest and penalty provisions that can upset the balance.

Once pension policy is added to the mix, matters become far more complex. All but the very lowest-paid workers must save to supplement Social Security if they are to have more than a subsistence-level standard of living in retirement. Low and moderate-income workers, however, simply do not save adequately when left to their own devices. Consequently, Congress encourages retirement saving by deliberately tilting the balance between current and deferred compensation, granting preferential tax treatment to qualified deferred compensation and to savings that are committed to an individual retirement account. The tax preference takes the form of deferral (which under certain conditions is equivalent to exemption from tax of the investment yield), which makes the value of the subsidy depend on the worker's marginal tax rate. Because individual income tax rates are progressive, tax deferral (or yield exemption) by itself provides the largest saving incentive to the highest income employees and offers no assistance to the many American workers (almost 40 percent of U.S. households) whose income is low enough that they incur no federal income tax liability. Left undisturbed, this state of affairs would clearly produce a perverse distribution of tax benefits: low- and middle-income workers who most need help saving would get little or no incentive, while highly paid workers who can and do save on their own would get a substantial tax reduction simply by shifting their saving into a tax-advantaged account. Under such circumstances, tax deferral is not an effective incentive that induces additional retirement saving—rather than offering assistance to those who need it, the tax concession is so much wasted revenue. There should be little wonder that year after year, IRA contributions are overwhelmingly made by high income individuals.

Many analysts assail the "upside-down" nature of our retirement savings tax subsidy,[305] but in doing so, they overlook the impact of the qualified retirement plan nondiscrimination rules, which are intended to mitigate the perverse distribution of tax benefits that would otherwise occur. When they operate correctly, the nondiscrimination rules funnel the tax benefits from highly paid workers who wish to save into

---

305 *E.g.*, SPERLING, *supra* Chapter 10 note 266, at 183–88 (taking no notice of the nondiscrimination rules, author asserts that the "reason our system is so upside-down is that the only way we encourage savings is through tax deductions"); GHILARDUCCI, *supra* Chapter 10 note 288, at 275–77 (asserting that 70 percent of the tax subsidy goes to those in the top 20 percent of the income distribution).

additional retirement saving by middle- and low-paid employees who cannot afford the reduction in their current take-home pay that unassisted plan participation would otherwise entail. Often, highly paid workers must give up a portion of their tax benefits by allowing the employer to reduce their compensation; that compensation cost savings is then used to finance additional compensation for rank-and-file employees whose participation is necessary to satisfy the nondiscrimination rules and who would not otherwise be willing to save. In this way, the nondiscrimination rules create a covert redistribution mechanism that is generally underappreciated or misunderstood. The common assertion that the $100+ billion annual tax expenditure for qualified retirement plans overwhelmingly benefits high-income employees is at best misleading because it ignores the fact that a large share of the tax savings may be recaptured from the apparent beneficiaries (high-income plan participants) by means of an implicit tax exacted by the employer via a reduction in their compensation.[306] To get any tax benefit from retirement savings, executives may have to consent to earning less than they would in the absence of a qualified plan, while low-wage workers may be getting paid more than they otherwise would. As has been shown, one can fairly criticize the efficacy of the nondiscrimination rules in shifting the tax subsidy from a windfall for highly paid executive and professional employees into retirement savings for rank-and-file workers. Yet even though the existing nondiscrimination regime is admittedly a makeshift, haphazard, and clunky redistribution device, it should not be dismissed or ignored. Indeed, under an income tax, the preferential treatment of qualified plan savings could not be justified without some such means of targeting the subsidy.

The future of qualified retirement plans depends upon the future of the income tax, which can no longer be taken for granted. Under a consumption tax base, the whole complex edifice would crumble because there would be no special advantage to employer-sponsored programs—all saving would be taxable only when withdrawn and applied to consumption. (If low-income workers needed help saving for retirement under a consumption tax, then forthright redistribution in the form of direct government assistance would be necessary. Social Security benefits might be made more generous for the low-income elderly, or a system of federal matching contributions to restricted retirement savings accounts might be established.) Assuming the income tax abides in something like its current (hybrid) form, the effectiveness of the nondiscrimination regime could be enhanced with a number of incremental reforms. Those refinements, however desirable, would not solve the central problem of national retirement policy, namely, the stubborn fact that at any time, only about one-half of the

---

306 *See supra* Chapter 10 note 305. Leonard E. Burman et al., *Distributional Effects of Defined Contribution Plans and Individual Retirement Accounts*, 8 (Tax Policy Center Disc. Paper No. 16, 2004), *available at* http://www.taxpolicycenter.org/UploadedPDF/311029_TPC_DP16. pdf (authors "do not make any adjustments for the presence or operation of nondiscrimination rules" in estimating distributional effects). *But see* Halperin & Munnell, *supra* Chapter 10 note 283, at 159 (due to nondiscrimination rules "plan sponsors may have to use some of the tax benefits to increase total compensation 'reluctant savers,' those employees who do not much value this deferred compensation").

American labor force is covered by any kind of employment-based retirement savings program. This coverage gap is concentrated among lower-paid workers and small business employees. Something more than rejiggering intra-firm compensation levels is needed to make long-term investors out of these reluctant savers. Quite a number of proposals have been advanced, but they mostly boil down to either contributing public monies to retirement accounts for low-wage workers, or imposing a compulsory minimum savings requirement on all American workers (or both).

Chapter 11

Taxes and Health Care

According to the Kaiser Family Foundation, 61 percent of nonelderly Americans (meaning people under 65 years old, the threshold for Medicare coverage) received health insurance coverage through an employer-sponsored program in 2007; 17 percent were uninsured; 16 percent were covered by Medicaid or another public program; and only 6 percent had private non-group health insurance.[1] The dominance of employer-mediated health insurance coverage in the United States is attributable to two factors. First, group insurance is necessary to overcome the problem of adverse selection.[2] The people most likely to buy individual insurance are those with private information

---

[1] Henry J. Kaiser Family Foundation, Health Insurance Coverage in America, 2007, at 1 (2008), http://facts.kff.org/chartbooks/Health%20Insurance%20Coverage%20in%20America, %202007.pdf; Paul Fronstin, *Sources of Health Insurance and Characteristics of the Uninsured: Analysis of the March 2008 Current Population Survey*, EBRI Issue Brief No. 321, Sep 2008, *available at* http://www.ebri.org/pdf/briefspdf/EBRI_IB_09a-2008.pdf.

[2] For a definition and explanation of the phenomenon of adverse selection, see Kenneth S. Abraham, Distributing Risk 15 (1986).

indicating that they are more likely than average to incur covered expenses; the resulting higher claims cause insurers to raise prices, which may induce relatively healthy insured individuals to drop coverage, triggering a further premium increase and shrinking of the insurance pool. Insuring a group, the membership of which is unrelated to health status, avoids this problem, and in modern America, the workforce offers a convenient preexisting group to which most households have access.[3]

The second reason for the prevalence of employer-provided health care coverage is that this fringe benefit can qualify for complete exemption from tax.[4] In contrast to qualified retirement savings, where the tax preference is limited to deferral (or equivalently yield exemption),[5] employer-provided health care receives outright tax forgiveness even though health care is a major component of spending. Like personal maintenance expenditures for food, shelter, and clothing, all of which are taxable,[6] health care costs may be considered consumption.[7] The combination of complete tax exemption and rising health care costs has made employer-provided health care the

---

3   Trade unions, professional organizations, churches, or various community groups could (and sometimes do) serve this function, but the employment relation offers a ubiquitous convenient group to which most people belong (and cannot afford to opt out of). Of course, employer group insurance is reinforced by tradition and the tax advantages discussed below. Membership in a political community (local, state, or national) could also serve to define the risk pool, but in the United States (in contrast to many other countries), political traditions seem to preclude government-run health insurance.

4   I.R.C. § 106(a) (2006) (value of employer-provided health insurance coverage excluded from gross income), *id.* § 105(b) (proceeds of employer-provided health insurance excluded if expended for medical care of the taxpayer, his spouse, or dependents).

5   The present tax treatment of qualified pension, profit-sharing, stock bonus, and annuity plans permits tax deferral on both employer contributions and investment earnings until such amounts are actually distributed to the employee or his beneficiary. *See* I.R.C. § 404(a)(1)-(3) (2006) (employer deduction upon contribution), *id.* §§ 83(e)(2) (employee not taxed on contribution), 501(a) (qualified trust exempt from tax), 402(a) (taxation upon actual distribution), 403(a)(1) (same for qualified annuity). Deferral of tax on an item of income is financially equivalent to exempting from tax the yield from the investment of that item throughout the period of deferral. For a demonstration of the equivalence of tax deferral and yield exemption, see *supra* Chapter 10 note 43.

6   *See* I.R.C. § 262(a) (2006) (except as otherwise expressly provided "no deduction shall be allowed for personal, living, or family expenses"). Quantitatively and practically, consumption is the core of the federal income tax base. Theoretically, of course, income is the sum of the taxpayer's consumption and the change in her wealth over the relevant period, but taxing wealth increases in anything like a comprehensive systematic fashion is extraordinarily difficult, both administratively and politically.

7   For tax policy analyses of the medical expense deduction and the exclusion of employer-provided health insurance, *see generally* William D. Andrews, *Personal Deductions in an Ideal Income Tax*, 86 HARV. L. REV. 309 (1972); Mark G. Kelman, *Personal Deductions Revisited: Why They Fit Poorly in an "Ideal" Income Tax and Why They Fit Worse in a Far from Ideal World*, 31 STAN. L. REV. 831 (1979); RICHARD GOODE, THE INDIVIDUAL INCOME TAX 156–60 (rev. ed. 1976); Thomas D. Griffith, *Theories of Personal Deductions in the Income Tax*, 40 HAST. L.J. 343 (1989); Louis Kaplow, *The Income Tax as Insurance: The Casualty Loss and Medical Expense Deductions and the Exclusion of Medical Insurance Premiums*, 79 CALIF. L. REV. 1485 (1991).

---

largest tax expenditure. The revenue loss attributable to the favorable tax treatment of health care has recently overtaken qualified retirement savings, and is estimated as $127.4 billion in fiscal year 2009.[8]

Despite the huge amount of money at stake, employer-provided health care is not subject to generally applicable nondiscrimination requirements.[9] Therefore, the tax rules governing health care plans are far less complex than the conditions for preferential tax treatment of retirement plans.[10] (In this respect the tax treatment of employer-provided health care is similar to ERISA's historically light touch when it comes to the labor law regulation of welfare plans.[11]) In other ways, however, tax law has had a pervasive influence on the structure of health care financing in the United States.

This chapter begins with an examination of the preferential tax treatment accorded employer-financed health care. It looks at the tax consequences of employee cost-sharing techniques, such as premium contributions and out-of-pocket expenditures required by the plan (co-pays and deductibles), and explores recent cost-containment initiatives, including health savings accounts and health reimbursement arrangements. The major trade-offs presented by several important health care tax reform proposals are briefly reviewed, as are special rules that come into play where employers provide retiree medical care coverage.

---

8   STAFF OF THE JOINT COMM. ON TAXATION, ESTIMATES OF FEDERAL TAX EXPENDITURES FOR FISCAL YEARS 2008–2012, at 14–15, 56 (2008), *available at* http://www.jct.gov/publications.html?func=startdown&id=1192. By way of comparison, the net exclusion for qualified retirement plans (both defined benefit and defined contribution) is estimated to cost $107.8 billion in lost revenue for FY 2009, or $126.5 billion if the cost of IRAs (both traditional and Roth) is included. *Id.* at 57.

9   As will be explained later, nondiscrimination requirements do come into play if the employer's health care plan is either self-insured or offered as an option under a cafeteria plan. In addition, employer contributions to health savings accounts are subject to comparability requirements. *See infra* Chapter 11 notes 54–66 and accompanying text.

10   *See supra* Chapter 10B.

11   *See supra* Chapter 1B and introductions to Parts II and III. Health care plans are classified as welfare plans under ERISA, and like other welfare plans, their terms were originally unregulated. That laissez-faire approach to health plan content was displaced by the enactment of the Health Insurance Portability and Accountability Act of 1996. The content of group health plans must now conform to numerous requirements set forth in Part 7 of ERISA Title I, including the regulation of plan terms relating to portability and preexisting conditions, health status discrimination, maternal and newborn care, and mental health parity. ERISA §§ 701-34, 29 U.S.C. §§ 1181–1191c (2006). The health plan content controls imposed by HIPAA were foreshadowed by the initial inroads on laissez faire, the COBRA continuation coverage requirements (enacted in 1986), and the qualified medical child support order rules (enacted in 1993). ERISA sections 601–609, 29 U.S.C. sections 1161–1169 (2006). *See supra* Chapter 1E. As is the case with the pension plan content controls, parallel tax sanctions backstop the health plan content controls, Chapter 1 note 105.

A. TAX ADVANTAGES OF EMPLOYER FINANCING[12]

"We already have a national health insurance program and it's being run by the Internal Revenue Service."[13]

Medical Care Expenditures—General Rules

Apart from public programs like Medicare and Medicaid, there are three common ways to finance the cost of medical care.[14] Many taxpayers participate in employer-provided group health care plans,[15] others purchase individual health insurance policies, and some, the uninsured, simply pay for their health care expenses (to the extent they are able) out of their salary, savings, or other resources as they are incurred. (Going without insurance is also known as self insurance.[16]) Table 11-1 summarizes the tax treatment of these alternative private funding methods, with citations to statutory authority.

---

12   A portion of the explanation in Chapter 11A is derived from WILLIAM D. ANDREWS & PETER J. WIEDENBECK, BASIC FEDERAL INCOME TAXATION 119–26 (6th ed. 2009), and is used with the permission of Aspen Publishers.

13   Edward M. Kennedy, *Second Thoughts—The IRS Health Insurance Program*, HUMAN BEHAVIOR (Sept. 1976).

14   As used here, medical care "means amounts paid for the diagnosis, cure, mitigation, treatment, or prevention of disease, or for the purpose of affecting any structure or function of the body" as well as the cost of transportation to obtain such care, such as by ambulance. I.R.C. § 213(d) (1)(A), (B) (2006).

15   Employers may finance health care either by purchasing third-party insurance coverage, thereby transferring the actuarial risk to an independent insurer, or by directly paying or reimbursing eligible health care costs of covered workers and dependents. Large employers commonly choose the latter option, known as employer self-insurance, in large part to avoid state insurance regulation via ERISA preemption. *See infra* Chapter 11 note 60 and accompanying text. Nevertheless, self-insured employers are apt to purchase high-attachment stop loss insurance coverage to protect against rare catastrophic claims. Under a stop loss policy, a third-party insurer agrees to take over responsibility for paying claims once a covered individual's expenses reach a specified level ($500,000, for example).

   From the standpoint of an employee covered by her employer's health care plan, there is often no apparent difference between an insured and a self-insured plan because companies that self insure frequently hire a traditional health insurance company to administer the plan, communicate with workers, and evaluate and pay claims. An insurance company hired as such a third party administrator, however, is only providing expert services for a fee; it is not bearing the ultimate risk of loss due to accident or disease of plan participants and their beneficiaries.

16   As used here, "self insurance" refers to individuals who have no health insurance coverage, either voluntarily or through circumstances beyond their control. This usage should not be confused with employer self insurance, as defined *supra* note 15, which refers to a company that provides its workers with health care benefits and chooses to bear ultimate responsibility for paying covered costs instead of paying premiums to shift the risk to an insurer.

Table 11-1

| Funding Method | Tax Treatment of Medical Care Financing Modes | |
	Premiums	Proceeds
Employer-Provided Coverage	Excluded, I.R.C. § 106	Excluded, § 105(b)
Individual Insurance Policy	Limited Ded'n, § 213(d)(1)(D)	Excluded, § 104(a)(3)
Uninsured (a/k/a self-insured)	n/a	Limited Ded'n, § 213(a)

Both exclusions and deductions reduce taxes by removing an amount from taxable income, which suggests an underlying theme in these approaches. Observe that if one could ignore the limits of the medical expense deduction of section 213, then all amounts used to pay for or reimburse the cost of medical care would be tax-free. The proceeds of employer-provided health insurance are excluded from the employee's income; the proceeds of an individual health insurance policy are excluded from the policyholder's income; and, absent the limits of section 213, an uninsured taxpayer could "exclude," via a deduction from gross income, her out-of-pocket payments for medical care.

The section 213 medical expense deduction is subject to two important limits that disrupt the tax equivalence of these three approaches, however. First, a deduction is allowed only to the extent that the aggregate of all medical expenses within the year exceed 7.5 percent of adjusted gross income (AGI). Second, the medical expense deduction is itemized, so that no tax saving results unless the aggregate of all itemized deductions exceeds the standard deduction ($5,700 for an unmarried individual and $11,400 for a joint return in 2009).[17] By virtue of these limits, the self-insured taxpayer can deduct only extraordinary medical expenses, not routine health care costs. Moreover, the same limits prevent a taxpayer who buys an individual health insurance policy from deducting a large part (or all) of the premiums paid for that coverage. In 2008, the average annual premiums for employer-sponsored insurance were $4,704 for single coverage and $12,680 for family coverage.[18] Although the cost of insurance is included in the definition of "medical care," a taxpayer earning $42,000 (roughly the national average wage in 2008) with no other significant sources of income would find that $3,150 of premiums paid (7.5 percent of $42,000) are entirely nondeductible, and the rest of the premiums save taxes only if his other itemized deductions (including home mortgage interest, state and local taxes, and charitable contributions) total more

---

17   I.R.C. §§ 62, 63 (2006).

18   KAISER FAMILY FOUNDATION & HEALTH RESEARCH AND EDUCATIONAL TRUST, EMPLOYER HEALTH BENEFITS: 2008 ANNUAL SURVEY at 1, *available at* http://ehbs.kff.org/pdf/7790.pdf [hereinafter EMPLOYER HEALTH BENEFITS 2008]. Due to adverse selection, individual policies are more expensive than employer-provided group insurance providing comparable coverage. To keep individual policies affordable, they typically provide less coverage than employer-sponsored group plans. Consequently, the cost of employer-provided coverage gives only a rough estimate of the price of more limited individual health insurance policies.

than the standard deduction. Because most itemizers are homeowners, the combined effect of the limits is to allow middle-income homeowners who purchase health insurance in the individual market to deduct *part* of their premiums.[19] In contrast, employer-paid premiums are excludible in full. Clearly, coverage under an employer-provided group health insurance program is the most advantageous alternative because both ends of the transaction—premiums *and* proceeds—are entirely tax-free. Hence it is hardly surprising that employment-based health benefits are the most prevalent form of health care coverage in the United States.[20] Furthermore, the income tax advantage is amplified by corresponding payroll tax preferences. Employer payments (both premiums for insurance and amounts paid for health care) under a plan that makes provision for employees generally or for one or more classes of employees are excluded from wages and so exempt from Social Security and Medicare taxes. For workers earning less than the Social Security wage and benefit base ($106,800 in 2009), this exclusion saves 15.3 percent, while for higher-paid employees it saves 2.9 percent.[21]

Employer-provided group insurance is the clear favorite, tax-wise. As between the remaining alternatives (individually purchased health insurance and self-insurance), the tax Code actually favors self-insurance. Over the long haul and on average, policyholders will pay about as much in premiums as the amount of their covered medical expenses (ignoring the insurer's administrative costs and profit), but of course that is not the case each year. Suppose a taxpayer pays premiums of $6,000 per year for five years but has no covered expenses until year five, in which she incurs $30,000 in medical bills. If she buys insurance, the nondeductible 7.5 percent AGI floor under the section 213 deduction affects this taxpayer every year as she pays her premiums, but if she self insures, she is caught by it only once, in year five when she pays the medical bills out of her own pocket. This artifact of annual tax reckoning reinforces the high cost of individual coverage to create what many observers view as a perverse incentive to go without insurance where employment-based coverage is unavailable. The deterrent is eliminated for self-employed taxpayers (meaning sole proprietors and partners), who since 2003 have been allowed to deduct as a business expense 100 percent of the premiums they pay for insurance for medical care for themselves and their spouses

---

19   Mortgage interest and real property tax obligations commonly push total itemized deductions above the standard deduction threshold. Low-income taxpayers typically do not itemize (they are not homeowners or owe no federal income tax), while high-income individuals find that the floor on the medical expense deduction (7.5 percent of AGI) approaches or exceeds the cost of coverage.

20   *See supra* Chapter 11 note 1 and accompanying text. In addition to the favorable tax treatment, employer coverage is also typically lower priced because the employment-based group mitigates the problem of adverse selection.

21   I.R.C. § 3121(a)(2) (2006). The Social Security tax of 6.2 percent of wages is imposed on both the employer and the employee but does not apply to wages in excess of the maximum taxable earnings. *Id.* §§ 3101(a), 3111(a), 3121(a)(1). The tax to fund the Medicare hospital insurance program (1.45 percent of wages imposed on both the employer and the employee, *id.* §§ 3101(b), 3111(b)) is not subject to an earnings cap. The same exclusion applies for purposes of the federal unemployment tax. *Id.* § 3306(b)(2).

and dependents.[22] No AGI floor applies to this deduction, and as a business expense, it is a nonitemized ("above the line") deduction, so every dollar of premiums paid reduces the taxable income of the unincorporated business owner regardless of whether she claims itemized deductions.[23] Hence for income tax purposes, self-employed individuals who buy health insurance coverage are taxed on neither the premiums nor any policy proceeds, which is functionally equivalent to the treatment of employer-provided coverage.[24] Employees are not eligible for the self-employed health insurance deduction even if their employer does not offer any health care benefits—instead, they are stuck with only a partial deduction for premiums (at best), and from a tax standpoint, their best option is going uninsured.[25]

Cost-Sharing

For many years, health care spending has grown faster than the overall economy. Total national health expenditures increased from 13.7 percent of U.S. gross domestic product (GDP) in 1993 to 16.0 percent in 2006 and are projected to rise to 19.5 percent in 2017.[26] Consequently, the cost of employer-sponsored health insurance is increasing dramatically. In 2008, health care benefits contributed 7.1 percent of total compensation cost for workers in private industry (10.0 percent of average wages).[27] The national

---

22   I.R.C. § 162(*l*) (2006). The deduction is not available for any month in which the self-employed taxpayer is eligible to participate in a health care plan maintained by an employer of the taxpayer or the taxpayer's spouse.

Absent the special business expense deduction, an unincorporated business could provide tax-favored employer-provided health care benefits to its employees, but not to the business owner(s) (sole proprietor or partners) even if they worked side-by-side with their employees, because the exclusions for the value of health care coverage and benefits apply only to taxpayers who are common-law employees. *Id.* §§ 105(g), 106. Prior to the enactment of section 162(*l*), that disparity created a tax-based incentive to incorporate so that the owner(s) could also qualify for the exclusions as corporate employees. If the corporation elected conduit tax treatment as an S corporation, however, shareholder-employees were still treated as partners, and the incorporation strategy was unavailing. *Id.* § 1372; *see id.* § 162(*l*)(5).

23   I.R.C. §§ 62(a)(1), 63(a), (b) (2006).

24   The premiums do not, however, reduce the self-employment tax obligation of the business owner, and so up to 15.3 percent of the amount paid may be owed in Social Security and Medicare hospital insurance taxes. I.R.C. §§ 162(*l*)(4), 1401, 1402 (2006).

25   Before 1983, taxpayers were allowed to deduct one-half of their health insurance premiums up to a maximum of $150 without regard to the AGI floor on the medical expense deduction. This special rule was apparently intended to partially counteract the tax incentive to forgo insurance.

26   Sean Keehan et al., *Health Spending Projections Through 2017: The Baby Boom Generation is Coming to Medicare*, HEALTH AFFAIRS 27, no. 2, w145, w146 (2008), *available at* http://content.healthaffairs.org/cgi/reprint/27/2/w145?maxtoshow=&HITS=10&hits=10&RESULTFORMAT=&fulltext=health+share+gdp&andorexactfulltext=and&searchid=1&FIRSTINDEX=0&resourcetype=HWCIT.

27   EMPLOYEE BENEFIT RESEARCH INSTITUTE, EBRI DATABOOK ON EMPLOYEE BENEFITS, Table 3.2c (May 2009), http://www.ebri.org/pdf/publications/books/databook/DB.Chapter%2003.pdf.

average cost of family health insurance coverage increased from $8,281 in 2001 to $10,728 in 2005, a 30 percent increase over a four-year period, during which the median income of those with family health insurance coverage increased only 3 percent.[28] Careful micro-simulation modeling predicts that absent health care reform, employer spending on health premiums will grow between 72 percent and 106 percent in the period between 2009 and 2019 (depending on assumptions concerning level of employment and growth rates of income and health care costs).[29]

Surging health care costs have led employers to require workers to contribute part of the expense of coverage, generally by wage withholding. The Kaiser Family Foundation reports that the average annual total health care premium contribution for covered workers in 2008 was $12,680 for family coverage, and that workers contributed $3,354 toward that total cost (26 percent) while employers paid $9,325 (74 percent).[30] Employee-only coverage cost on average $4,704 in 2008, of which workers contributed $721 (15 percent).[31] To the extent of his contribution, an employee is not receiving excludible employer-provided coverage under an accident or health plan, but is instead viewed as purchasing his own health insurance policy. So viewed, the employee's share of the cost of coverage qualifies as an insurance premium for which a medical expense deduction may be allowed, but the presence of insurance makes it unlikely that the employee will have other substantial unreimbursed medical care expenses for the year, with the result that her contribution toward the premiums will generate little or no medical expense deduction (i.e., will not surpass 7.5 percent of AGI). Accordingly, cost-sharing under a contributory health plan creates the potential to render otherwise-excludible health plan coverage partially taxable. Nevertheless, if the employer has a written plan that allows employees to elect to pay their share of premiums by salary reduction, then the arrangement may qualify as a "cafeteria plan," and payments made pursuant to such an election are treated as pre-tax employer contributions rather than after-tax employee contributions.[32] This device is sometimes called a premium conversion arrangement or a premium-only cafeteria plan.

Regardless of who pays the premiums, most employer-sponsored health care plans do not offer complete protection; instead they include coinsurance features to reduce moral hazard (that is, encourage cost consciousness in utilization of medical services). Covered individuals may bear part of the cost of their care because the plan imposes "deductibles" (e.g., first $200 per person of annual expenses not insured), requires fixed co-payments for certain services or goods (e.g., patient pays $20 per physician

---

28   State Health Access Data Assistance Center, *Squeezed: How Costs for Insuring Families are Outpacing Income* (April 2008), *available at* http://www.rwjf.org/coverage/product.jsp?id=28711.

29   John Holahan et al., *Health Reform: The Cost of Failure* 2, 20–22 (2009), *available at* http://www.rwjf.org/files/research/costoffailure20090529.pdf.

30   EMPLOYER HEALTH BENEFITS 2008, *supra* Chapter 11 note 18, at 2.

31   *Id.*

32   I.R.C. § 125 (2006); Prop. Treas. Reg. §§ 1.125-1(a)(5), -1(b)(4)(ii), -7(a)(13), -7(f), 72 Fed, Reg. 43,938 (2007). That is, employee premium contributions are treated as excludible employer-provided coverage under section 106 rather than as employee payments for insurance that are eligible only for the limited medical expense deduction of section 213.

office visit, $75 per emergency room visit, or $15 per prescription), or pays only a specified percentage of certain costs (e.g., 80 percent of inpatient hospital charges). Such out-of-pocket costs constitute medical care expenses, but they are unlikely to exceed the nondeductible floor of 7.5 percent of AGI precisely because insurance will pay for most of the employee's health care costs for the year. Here again, with proper planning, the cafeteria plan rules of section 125 can come to the rescue, magically transforming nondeductible employee out-of-pocket expenses into excludible employer-provided health benefits.

The cafeteria plan regulations authorize an employer-created program known as a flexible spending arrangement (FSA), which can be used to pay or reimburse otherwise uninsured out-of-pocket employee medical care expenses. The FSA is typically funded by participating employees, who elect to forego a portion of their pay for the upcoming year, directing it instead to their FSA accounts, although the employer may make nonelective contributions as well. (The salary reduction election, which is a choice between cash and a qualified benefit (health care), satisfies the definition of a cafeteria plan.) A health FSA—often called a medical or health care spending account—generally may reimburse only substantiated out-of-pocket medical expenses (as defined for purposes of the medical expense deduction[33]) incurred during a 12-month coverage period, although the plan may allow unused amounts to be paid for medical expenses incurred during a grace period of not more than two months and fifteen days following the close of the plan year. Adequate substantiation usually means a receipt or other written statement from an independent third party showing the expense that was incurred (i.e., nature, date, and amount of medical care provided), together with a written statement from the participant that the expense is not covered by any other health insurance. If special substantiation rules are followed, participants may be issued debit cards to pay for medical services and eligible drug store and pharmacy purchases directly, instead of requesting reimbursement by submitting receipts to the plan administrator after the fact.[34] The amount of coverage selected for the year

---

33   A health care spending account may be used to purchase non-prescription drugs that satisfy the general definition of medical care ("for the diagnosis, cure, mitigation, treatment, or prevention of disease, or for the purpose of affecting any structure or function of the body"), such as over-the-counter pain relievers or cold or allergy medicines, even though the medical expense deduction for pharmaceuticals is restricted to the cost of prescription drugs and insulin. Rev. Rul. 2003-102, 2003-2 C.B. 559; see I.R.C. § 213(b), (d)(3) (2006). The July 2009 version of the House Ways and Means Committee health care reform bill would exclude over-the-counter medications from eligibility for tax-free reimbursement. *Some House Democrats Want FSA Cuts Reconsidered Before Health Bill Gets to Floor*, 36 Pens. & Ben. Rep. (BNA) 1696 (2009).

34   The IRS requires that an item be preapproved as an eligible expense (an inventory information approval system) before it can be purchased with health care spending account funds via a payment card. I.R.S. Notice 2006-69, 2006-2 C.B. 107; see Rev. Rul. 2003-43, 2003-1 C.B. 935 (substantiation of debit card purchases via merchant code or verification at point of sale). This has led to the development of various lists of qualified purchases, and discrepancies in the treatment of some products, including competing products of different manufactures (e.g., bed-wetting diapers). Amy S. Elliot, *Plans Struggle to Define Health Expenses Under Flexible Accounts*, 123 Tax Notes 1072 (2009).

(generally, the amount of salary reduction) must be available to reimburse eligible expenses without regard to the time they are incurred during the year, and so an employee who elects $600 in coverage and has major uninsured dental work in January must be reimbursed up to the annual account limit ($600) even though she is funding her account by salary reduction only at the rate of $50 per month. Any unused amount remaining in the account at the end of the coverage period (12-month plan year, plus grace period, if applicable) must be forfeited under a use-it-or-lose-it rule; the residue cannot be carried over to the following period or refunded to the account holder. The election to contribute to the FSA generally must be made in advance of the coverage year and is irrevocable, but mid-year changes in response to certain family and employment status changes are permitted.[35] Although used to pay out-of-pocket health care costs, FSA contributions are characterized for tax purposes as employer-provided health care coverage (excludible under section 106), while payments from the account are viewed as proceeds of employer-provided medical care insurance (excludible under section 105(b)). In 2009, 55 percent of individuals working in private industry for an establishment having at least 100 employees were offered medical spending accounts, but only 18 percent of those working for firms with fewer than 100 employees had access to such accounts.[36]

Cost-Containment

Many analysts are convinced that widespread group insurance has contributed significantly to health care cost inflation by stimulating excessive demand due to the phenomenon known as "moral hazard." Moral hazard refers to the tendency of insurance to induce excessive risk-taking as a result of the insured's insulation from the full cost of his actions. An individual with comprehensive health insurance coverage might see a specialist, obtain a second opinion, undergo additional tests or procedures, or purchase high-priced name-brand pharmaceuticals without incurring any direct financial cost from those choices.[37] (Generous insurance, in other words, breeds a health care entitlement mentality.[38]) The coinsurance features in health care plans (deductibles and required co-payments) are one common device to instill some measure of consumer discipline in health care decision making by forcing insured individuals to bear part of the cost. Still, full coverage beyond a small admission charge (as in the

---

35   Prop. Treas. Reg. §§ 1.125-5 (general FSA requirements), -1(e) (grace period), -6 (substantiation, including debit card rules), -2 (election rules), 72 Fed, Reg. 43,938 (2007).

36   BUREAU OF LABOR STATISTICS, U.S. DEPARTMENT OF LABOR, NATIONAL COMPENSATION SURVEY: EMPLOYEE BENEFITS IN THE UNITED STATES, March 2009, Table 36, at 306, available at http://www.bls.gov/ncs/ebs/benefits/2009/ebbl0044.pdf.

37   For an explanation of moral hazard, see ABRAHAM, supra Chapter 11 note 2, at 14–15

38   In addition to excessive claiming of covered goods or services, moral hazard can also refer to behavioral choices that influence health status in the first place. A fully insured individual has little incentive to take precautions that would reduce the need for medical care, like quitting smoking, controlling weight through diet and exercise, or limiting participation in risky activities such as certain sports.

case of prescription drug co-pays), or an 80 percent subsidy of major expenditures (in the case of 20 percent coinsurance on hospitalization), tilts the scales in favor of purchase whenever the expected benefit of the health care in question exceeds the relatively small share of the cost that the insured must bear.[39] In recent years, two new techniques have emerged that are designed to encourage consumers to take into account the full cost of health care in their purchasing decisions. These devices, health savings accounts and health reimbursement arrangements, function by allowing consumers who conserve on health care now to use the savings for another purpose, including more essential health care later. Consequently, instead of facing the choice between claiming insured care of dubious net value and leaving money on the table (i.e., not utilizing available insurance), abstention frees up resources that can be applied to higher-priority needs.

An individual who has only high deductible health plan coverage (major medical insurance covering only extraordinary costs) is permitted to save for routine medical care expenses through a tax-preferred health savings account (HSA).[40] A high deductible health plan is a plan with an annual deductible that is not less than $1,200 for self-only coverage or $2,400 for family coverage (in 2010), and which provides that the maximum annual out-of-pocket expenses (deductibles, co-payments, and other amounts, but not premiums) may not exceed $5,950 for self-only coverage or $11,900 for family coverage.[41] In 2010, an individual with self-only coverage under a high deductible heath plan may deduct up to $3,050 in contributions to an HSA, while an individual with family coverage under a high deductible health plan can make up to $6,150 in deductible HSA contributions[42]. The deduction for HSA contributions is not subject to the floor on medical expense deductions (7.5 percent of AGI) and is available regardless of whether the taxpayer itemizes.[43] Investments earnings of an HSA are not taxed, and distributions used to pay for uninsured medical care for the account beneficiary or his spouse or dependents are not included in gross income.[44]

---

39   The dramatic increase in the prevalence of managed care plans in the early 1990s was one response to the wedge between private and social costs. Managed care plans insert a primary care physician or another expert third party as a gatekeeper whose approval is required for the patient to obtain insurance coverage of medical specialist charges or expensive tests or therapies. The function of the gatekeeper, of course, is to compare total costs (not just the insured's out-of-pocket expense) with expected benefits.

40   I.R.C. § 223 (2006). IRS technical guidance on HSA requirements, in question-and-answer form, appears in I.R.S. Notice 2008-59, 2008-29 I.R.B. 123, I.R.S. Notice 2004-50, 2004-2 C.B. 196, and I.R.S. Notice 2004-2, 2004-1 C.B 269.

41   I.R.C. § 223(c)(2)(A) (2006); Rev. Proc. 2009-29, 2009-22 I.R.B. 1050 (HSA inflation adjustments for 2010). The absence of a deductible for preventive care does not cause a plan to fail the high deductible condition. I.R.C. § 223(c)(2)(C) (2006).

42   I.R.C. § 223(b)(2) (2006); Rev. Proc. 2009-29, 2009-22 I.R.B. 1050 (HSA inflation adjustments for 2010). If at the end of the taxable year the HSA owner is age 55 or older, the applicable contribution limit (for either self-only or family coverage) is increased by $1,000. I.R.C. § 223(b)(3) (2006).

43   I.R.C. §§ 223(b)(2), 62(a)(19) (2006). Rev. Proc. 2009-29, 2009-22 I.R.B. 1050 (HSA inflation adjustments for 2010).

44   I.R.C. §223(e)(1), (f)(1) (2006).

In other words, both HSA contributions and proceeds may be entirely tax-free. Cost consciousness (consumer discipline) is achieved in two ways: first, amounts saved on health care now continue to be available to fund more urgent needs in the future, and second, amounts not ultimately needed for health care can be used for other purposes. Distributions not used to pay for medical care are included in gross income, and an additional (penalty) tax of 10 percent is imposed to discourage use of an HSA as a tax-deferral vehicle, but the penalty tax is waived once the account beneficiary is eligible for Medicare (i.e., attains age 65), becomes disabled, or dies.[45]

Instead of (or in addition to) the account beneficiary contributing his own resources, an employer may contribute to an eligible employee's HSA, and such employer funding may be treated as employer-provided health care coverage that is excludible from the employee's gross income and exempt from withholding and certain employment taxes.[46] This coordination between the tax treatment of employee and employer funding (deduction versus exclusion) provides flexibility. A company concerned about rising health care costs (as many small businesses are) can provide its employees with only low-cost catastrophic medical care coverage under a high-deductible plan and let each worker decide whether to put some of his own money aside in an HSA to pay for routine health care with pre-tax dollars. Another employer that is committed to providing generous health care benefits can offer the combination of high-deductible insurance paired with employer-funded HSA contributions, and let workers choose between that combination and plans that offer traditional comprehensive health care coverage.[47]

In 2002, the IRS announced that a new type of medical expense reimbursement program, called a "health reimbursement arrangement" (HRA), would be treated as an employer-provided accident or health plan, with the result that HRA coverage and benefits are excludible from gross income.[48] An HRA reimburses the employee for medical care expenses (as defined under the medical expense deduction rules of section 213) incurred by the employee or her spouse or dependents up to a maximum dollar amount per coverage period, and provides that any unused allowance at the end of the period is carried forward to increase the maximum reimbursement amount

---

45   I.R.C. § 223(f)(2), (f)(4) (2006).

46   I.R.C. §§ 106(d), 223(b)(4)(B) (2006), *id.* § 3401(a)(22) (exemption from employer's income tax withholding obligations). Employer contributions in excess of the limit on deductible HSA contributions are not excludible from gross income, and the limit on deductible employee contributions is reduced by the amount of any employer contributions for the year. To qualify for exclusion, the employer must make comparable contributions to HSAs of similarly situated employees, *id.* § 4980G, as discussed below in connection with health care plan nondiscrimination rules.

    Explicit statutory exceptions were added to exclude employer HSA contributions from the base of railroad retirement taxes and the federal unemployment tax. *Id.* §§ 3231(e)(11), 3306(b) (18). Curiously, no corresponding statutory language was added to the definition of wages for purposes of the most significant employment taxes, those that fund Social Security and Medicare. *Id.* § 3121(a).

47   *See* I.R.C. § 106(d)(2), (b)(2) (2006) (no constructive receipt where employee offered choice between traditional health care plan and HSA contribution).

48   Rev. Rul. 2002-41, 2002-2 C.B. 75; I.R.S. Notice 2002-45, 2002-2 C.B. 93.

in subsequent periods. This carry-forward may even continue past the worker's retirement or other termination of employment, and the resulting savings feature creates the incentive to economize (that is, it induces participants to act as price-sensitive health care consumers). Unlike a health care spending account, an HRA is not subject to the use-it-or-lose-it principle,[49] and unlike an HSA, HRA balances may not be used for any purpose other than medical care.[50] An HRA must be funded solely by the employer,[51] but it may be combined with other employer-provided health benefit programs, such as major medical insurance or other limited or catastrophic coverage.

Both HSAs and HRAs tend to instill an incentive to shop wisely. They are not without skeptics, however. Some observers question whether consumers have access to adequate information about the quality of medical services, or the ability to evaluate price-quality trade-offs. Concerns also have been raised about companies that allow their workers to choose a high-deductible health plan combined with coverage under either HSA or HRA as an alternative to traditional, broad-based health coverage. Optional institution of such "consumer-driven health plans" (as the combination of high-deductible coverage with an HSA or HRA program is sometimes called) could lead to adverse selection: healthy workers can be expected to select the consumer-driven plan, leaving a group of employees covered under the traditional plan that is likely to make greater than average demands on the health care system. Insuring the pool of higher-risk employees raises the cost of traditional coverage, inducing more workers to select the consumer-driven alternative, which some fear could lead to the eventual unraveling of the traditional health insurance coverage. A 2008 survey found that adults in consumer-driven health plans were significantly more likely than those with traditional health coverage to have high household income, to be in better health, and to exhibit healthy behavior.[52] The survey indicates that 11 percent of firms with 500 or more workers offered an HRA- or HSA-eligible plan, but the acceptance rate (market penetration) has been slow: only 3 percent of the adults age 21 to 64 with private insurance were actually enrolled in a consumer-driven health plan.[53]

Nondiscrimination in Health Benefits

Unlike retirement savings, employer-sponsored health care coverage is not subject to generally applicable nondiscrimination requirements. Legislation prescribing

---

49 Contrast I.R.C. §125(d)(2) (2006) and Prop. Treas. Reg. §1.125-5(c), 72 Fed, Reg. 43,938 (2007).

50 Contrast I.R.C. § 223(f) (2006).

51 I.R.S. Notice 2002-45, Parts I, IV, 2002-2 C.B. 93, 94. This stems from the fact that elective salary reduction would trigger the cafeteria plan rules and their prohibition on deferred compensation (which is the source of the use-it-or-lose-it rule).

52 Paul Fronstin, *Findings from the 2008 EBRI Consumer Engagement in Health Care Survey*, EBRI Issue Brief No. 323, Nov. 2008, at 7, *available at* http://www.ebri.org/pdf/briefspdf/EBRI_IB_11-20081.pdf.

53 *Id.* at 5; Paul Fronstin, *Availability, Contributions, Account Balances, and Rollovers in Account-Based Health Plans*, 29 EBRI Notes 1, 2 (2008).

comprehensive health plan nondiscrimination rules was enacted in 1986, but the business community complained that the rules were costly, complex, and unworkable, and they were retroactively repealed in 1989.[54] Even in the absence of mandated nondiscrimination, some 60 percent of American workers receive employer-provided health benefits, and in 2008, fully 80 percent of workers in firms offering health benefits were eligible for the coverage offered by their employer.[55] By way of comparison, less than half of the workforce is covered by qualified retirement plans, including pension, profit-sharing, stock bonus, and annuity plans, to which stringent nondiscrimination requirements apply. These data suggest that workers place a higher value on health benefits than retirement savings. Relative to pensions, more low- and moderate-income workers are apparently willing to pay for health plan coverage (by accepting less cash compensation) even though they derive little or no benefit from the preferential tax treatment of employer-sponsored health care. Yet despite the higher level of employee demand, firms with a higher proportion of low-paid or part-time employees are substantially less likely to offer their workers health benefits.[56]

Although the tax exemption of employer-provided health care is largely unregulated, prohibitions on favoring highly paid workers do come into play in three circumstances. First, and most importantly, a self-insured medical expense reimbursement program (that is, a program under which the employer pays benefits directly out of its own assets rather than paying premiums to shift the risk to an insurance company) must not discriminate in favor of highly compensated individuals with respect to coverage or benefits.[57] The suspect group, highly compensated individuals, consists of employees who are one of the five highest-paid officers, 10 percent shareholders, or among the highest-paid 25 percent of the workforce. The coverage tests track the pre-1986 version of the qualified retirement plan coverage nondiscrimination rules, but the categories of excludible employees are even broader (employees who have not completed three years of service or who have not attained age 25 may be ignored).[58] Violation of the nondiscrimination standard does not cause all benefits received under a self-insured plan to be taxable, nor even trigger taxation of all amounts paid to the highly compensated individuals; instead, only the "excess reimbursement," defined as the discriminatory portion of the benefits, is taxable to a recipient highly compensated individual. Thus Congress did not threaten overall plan disqualification, and in the absence of that "big stick" sanction, one might question how much incentive firms

---

54   I.R.C. § 89 (repealed 1989), described in STAFF OF THE JOINT COMM. ON TAXATION, 100TH CONG., GENERAL EXPLANATION OF THE TAX REFORM ACT OF 1986, at 778–815 (1987). *See generally*, Rosina B. Barker, *Lessons from a Legislative Disaster*, 47 TAX NOTES 843 (1990). Section 89 grew out of President Reagan's 1985 tax reform proposals, THE PRESIDENT'S TAX PROPOSALS TO THE CONGRESS FOR FAIRNESS, GROWTH, AND SIMPLICITY 33–46 (1985).

55   EMPLOYER HEALTH BENEFITS 2008, *supra* Chapter 11 note 18, at 46.

56   *Id.* at 34.

57   I.R.C. § 105(h) (2006); Treas. Reg. § 1.105-11(c) (1981).

58   *Compare* I.R.C. § 105(h)(3) (2006), *with id.* § 410(b)(1) (1982) (as in effect before amendment by the Tax Reform Act of 1986).

have to steer clear of health plan favoritism. Some experts contend that IRS enforcement of these nondiscrimination rules has been minimal to nonexistent.[59] Many large employers provide health benefits through self-insured plans (typically employing an insurance company as third-party administrator but not risk-bearer), thereby avoiding state insurance regulation and state-mandated benefit laws that would apply under ERISA's insurance savings clause.[60] Apparently, the tax law nondiscrimination standard applicable to such self-insured plans is not a very dear price to pay for exemption from insurance regulation.

Second, health benefits offered as an option (an alternative to cash or other taxable benefits) under a cafeteria plan become subject to the cafeteria plan nondiscrimination rules and a special amount nondiscrimination safe harbor.[61] (Where the employer offers a self-insured medical expense reimbursement plan as a cafeteria plan option, two sets of nondiscrimination rules come into play.[62])

Third, if an employer makes contributions to one or more employees' health savings accounts (HSAs) but fails to make comparable contributions to the HSAs of similarly situated employees (meaning those with the same type of high-deductible health plan coverage), then it is subject to an excise tax of 35 percent of the amount contributed to employee HSAs.[63] Recall that employer contributions to employees' health savings accounts (HSAs) are treated as excludible employer-provided health care coverage.[64] Distributions from an employee's HSA, even if partly employer-funded, apparently would not be classified as proceeds of an accident or health plan for employees, and so the nondiscrimination rule for self-insured medical expense reimbursement plans would not apply. The comparable contribution requirement fills this gap. Where the employer's HSA contributions are not evenhanded, the excise tax withdraws preferential tax treatment—it functions like disallowance of the employer's business expense deduction for selective contributions.[65] An exception to the comparability rule betrays an underlying concern with discrimination: if an employer makes contributions to HSAs of its rank-and-file employees, comparable contributions are *not* required for highly compensated employees.[66]

---

59   Mary B.H. Hevener & Charles K. Kerby, *Administrative Issues: Challenges of the Current System, in* USING TAXES TO REFORM HEALTH INSURANCE 147, 150, 154–55 (Henry J. Aaron & Leonard E. Burman eds. 2008); Daniel Halperin, *Comment, in id.* at 57.

60   *See supra* Chapter 6E.

61   I.R.C. § 125(b), (c), (g) (2006); Prop. Treas. Reg. § 1.125-7, 72 Fed. Reg. 43,938 (2007).

62   *See* Prop. Treas. Reg. § 1.125-1(a)(3)(B), -1(b)(2), 72 Fed. Reg. 43,938 (2007).

63   I.R.C. §§ 4980G, 4980E (2006); Treas. Reg. §§ 54.4980G-0 to -5 (as amended in 2008).

64   I.R.C. § 106(d) (2006).

65   H.R. CONF. REP. NO. 108-391, at 836, 843 (2003) ("The excise tax is designed as a proxy for the denial of the deduction for employer contributions."). Currently, the top income tax rate applicable to both individuals and corporations is 35 percent, I.R.C. §§ 1, 11(b) (2006).

66   I.R.C. § 4980G(d) (2006).

Taxation of Sick Pay and Disability Insurance

This discussion has focused on the tax treatment of medical care expenses, including the costs of insurance to pay for such expenses. Some insurance provides income replacement benefits in the event of sickness or disability. An individual health insurance policy, for example, might pay $100 per day that the insured is hospitalized or unable to work, with that "sick pay" allowance being in addition to the insurer's obligation to pay or reimburse hospital bills, doctor's charges, pharmaceutical costs, etc. Many employers sponsor separate disability insurance plans that pay a specified portion (commonly in the range of 60 to 67 percent) of an employee's regular salary during periods when he is away from work due to disability. The tax regime outlined in Table 11-1 and discussed above does not apply to such income-replacement insurance despite its connection with disease or injury. Instead—and in brief—the rules are as follows. The value of employer-provided disability insurance coverage is excluded from the employee's gross income, but any benefits received under the plan (insurance proceeds) are included in gross income.[67] In contrast, the cost of individually purchased sick pay or disability insurance is not deductible at all, but any proceeds received under such individual coverage are excluded from gross income.[68] Accordingly, while employer-provided health care can be entirely tax-free, not so for income protection—when it comes to disability insurance, one end of the transaction or the other is taxed. The difference between taxing premiums (in the case of individually purchased coverage), and taxing proceeds (in the case of employer-provided insurance) generally makes employer-provided insurance preferable, because most insured workers never receive disability benefits.

B. PROPOSED HEALTH CARE TAX REFORMS

"Projected growth in per-capita health care spending, not retirement of the baby boomers, is the principal cause of the [federal government's] long-term fiscal problem."[69]

Health system reform is back on the public agenda, fueled by concerns over the unsustainable rate of growth of health care spending (which has on average outstripped economic growth by 2.7 percentage points annually since 1960[70]) and the large and

---

67 I.R.C. §§ 106(a), 105(a) (2006). A tax credit of 15 percent of disability benefits is granted to certain totally disabled low-income taxpayers. Disability benefits in excess of $5,000 per year are generally not eligible for the credit, and may contribute (along with income from other sources) to the phase-out of the credit. *Id.* § 22.

68 I.R.C. § 104(a)(3) (2006) (exclusion of proceeds); *see id.* § 213(d)(1)(D) (amounts paid for income replacement insurance do not qualify as medical care for purposes of medical expense deduction).

69 Henry J. Aaron, *Budget Crisis, Entitlement Crisis, Health Care Financing Problem—Which Is It?*, 26 HEALTH AFFAIRS 1622, 1625 (2007).

70 *Id.* at 1626 & n.6.

growing number of uninsured Americans (more than 45 million[71]). Fundamental reform of health care financing is likely to have a major impact on both public programs (including Medicare, Medicaid, the State Children's Health Insurance Program, and the military and veterans' health system) and private sector health insurance. Changes in the tax treatment of employer-sponsored health insurance have repeatedly been proposed as incremental improvements in health care financing and could be a component of systemic reform. Nevertheless, the current tax rules have had remarkable staying power even in the face of sustained criticism. While an in-depth treatment of health care tax reform is beyond the scope of this report,[72] this part takes a brief look at a few distinctive recommendations to illustrate the complex interaction between taxes and health insurance coverage.

Capping the Coverage Exclusion and Related Approaches

The Treasury's 1984 tax reform study included a proposal to limit the exclusion of employee medical coverage to $70 per month for individual medical coverage and $175 per month for family coverage.[73] The thinking was that limiting the preferential tax treatment of health care coverage would create pressure to keep employer contributions under the cap, because workers would prefer additional wages to nonessential health benefits if the cost of the latter were, like wages, fully taxable. This pressure would induce cost-saving changes that would re-orient health benefit programs to focus on the core function of insurance, protection from extraordinary and unpredictable medical care needs. Plans might be amended by dropping some coverage (e.g., vision or dental care), by increasing employee out-of-pocket expenses (raising insurance deductibles and co-payments), or by encouraging preventive care. While not enacted in 1986, similar proposals have been advanced by succeeding Administrations, both Republican and Democratic. A recent version, offered by the President's Advisory Panel on Tax Reform, would have placed an annual cap on the section 106 exclusion set at $5,000 for individual coverage and $11,500 for family coverage in 2006.[74] Simple as it sounds, however, a cap on the coverage exclusion (or outright repeal) presents some formidable implementation problems, the foremost of which concerns the

---

71   John Holahan & Allison Cook, *The Decline in the Uninsured in 2007: Why Did It Happen and Can It Last?*, (Kaiser Commission on Medicaid and the Uninsured Pub. No. 7826, 2008), *available at* http://www.kff.org/uninsured/upload/7826.pdf.

72   *See generally*, USING TAXES TO REFORM HEALTH INSURANCE (Henry J. Aaron & Leonard E. Burman eds. 2008).

73   2 U.S. DEPARTMENT OF THE TREASURY, TAX REFORM FOR FAIRNESS, SIMPLICITY, AND ECONOMIC GROWTH 23–27 (1984). *See generally* Bradley W. Joondeph, *Tax Policy and Health Care Reform: Rethinking the Tax Treatment of Employer-Sponsored Health Insurance*, 1995 B.Y.U. L. REV. 1229.

74   PRESIDENT'S ADVISORY PANEL ON FEDERAL TAX REFORM, SIMPLE, FAIR, AND PRO-GROWTH 78–82 (2005), *available at* http://permanent.access.gpo.gov/lps64969/TaxReformwholedoc.pdf.

measurement of the value received by individual employees.[75] Health insurance coverage is more valuable to older and sicker individuals, and there are substantial regional variations in the cost of health care.[76]

The valuation difficulty could be sidestepped by imposing a tax on the employer in lieu of the employees. One such approach would deny the employer a deduction for the cost of employee health insurance or health care benefits to the extent that it exceeds the per capita cost of a specified baseline package of benefits multiplied by the number of individuals covered under the company's plan.[77] Besides avoiding individual valuation, this technique may be politically attractive because it hides the burden from workers who are used to receiving tax-free health benefits.[78] Disallowing the deduction, however, would cause profitable large corporations to pay a 35 percent rate on excess benefits—arguably a poor proxy for individual taxation that would generally occur at substantially lower rates.

Standard Deduction for Health Insurance

In 2007, the Bush Administration proposed a radical change in the tax treatment of health care. Its plan would repeal the existing exclusion for employment-based health benefits, the itemized deduction for extraordinary medical expenses, as well as the provision that allows self-employed individuals to deduct their health insurance premiums as a business expense. Those allowances would be replaced with a new "standard deduction for health insurance" in the amount of $15,000 for family coverage or $7,500 for single coverage. The standard deduction would be allowed only to individuals who have

---

75   Indeed, the exclusion of employer-provided health benefits originated during World War II when, as a matter of administrative practice, the IRS concluded that the difficulty of allocating the cost of group insurance premiums to individual employees justified ignoring the benefit since the amounts at stake were then quite small. The statutory exclusion in section 106 was enacted with the Internal Revenue Code of 1954.

76   Paul Fronstin, *Capping the Tax Exclusion for Employment-Based Health Coverage: Implications for Employers and Workders*, EBRI Issue Brief No. 325, Jan. 2009, *available at* http://www.ebri.org/pdf/briefspdf/EBRI_IB_1-2009_TaxCap1.pdf. Outright repeal of the exclusion has been suggested as a possible source of tax revenue that could be used to fund health care reform. A Congressional Research Service study recommends that repeal proposals be approached with caution. Bob Lyke, *The Tax Exclusion for Employer-Provided Health Insurance: Policy Issues Regarding the Repeal Debate*, CRS Report to Congress (Nov. 21, 2008), *available at* http://www.allhealth.org/BriefingMaterials/RL34767-1359.pdf.

77   A roughly similar alternative would impose an excise tax on insurers (with a corresponding levy on self-insured employer plans) applicable to premiums received in excess of the cost of insurance covering the prescribed baseline package of benefits.

78   As of mid-2009, the Obama Administration says it opposes capping or repealing the tax exclusion for employer-sponsored health insurance, as does Congressman Rangel (chair of House Ways and Means Committee) and Senator Baucus (chair of Senate Finance Committee). *See Public Plan Option Would Stabilize Private Insurance Market, Sebelius says*, 36 Pens. & Ben. Rep. (BNA) 1140 (2009); *Repeal of Health Care Tax Exclusion Not an Option, Baucus Tells Roundtable*, 36 Pens. & Ben. Rep. (BNA) 1216 (2009); *but see* Sam Goldfarb, *CBO Testimony Renews Interest in Capping Healthcare Tax Exclusion*, 124 Tax Notes 208 (2009).

certain qualifying health insurance coverage (determined on a monthly basis, with one-twelfth of the specified annual deduction granted per month), whether that coverage is individually purchased or employer-provided (the value of employer coverage would be included in gross income due to the repeal of section 106). The amount deductible, however, would not be tied to the actual cost of insurance—the deduction would be set at the specified dollar amount ($15,000/$7,500) regardless of whether the taxpayer (or her employer) actually spent more or less than that amount on health insurance.

> The new SDHI [Standard Deduction for Health Insurance] would address the rising cost of health insurance by removing the tax bias for more expensive insurance, while also providing a potent incentive for the uninsured to purchase insurance. The proposal would break the link between the value of the tax subsidy and the amount of insurance a worker purchases. The proposal also would level the playing field between less expensive and more expensive health insurance, and between wages and employer-provided health insurance.
>
> Individuals and families would have a strong incentive to purchase insurance under the proposal. However, the insurance they choose to purchase would be based on their needs and circumstances rather than the tax bias in favor of health insurance and against wages. The tax bias for overly generous insurance would be eliminated. This change would translate into greater price sensitivity for health care consumers. Many of those with employer-based insurance would take advantage of the level playing field between wages and health insurance by receiving higher wages in exchange for less expensive health insurance.[79]

The proposed standard deduction for health insurance, like capping the coverage exclusion, would end the incentive to purchase relatively low-value coverage because in each case the tax subsidy would not increase with spending. (That is, at the margin, an additional dollar devoted to health insurance would be taxed the same as spending on other consumption.) Unlike capping the exclusion, the standard deduction would allow people to better tailor their coverage to their individual and family circumstances because the tax benefit would be available if they bought their own policy. There is a downside to extending the tax benefit to individually purchased coverage, however: if employers dropped group coverage, workers who present higher health risks (older or sicker) might find that coverage in the non-group market is unaffordable.

Tax Credits

Besides the incentive to over-insure, the current unlimited exclusion from gross income of the value of employer-provided health insurance favors high-income taxpayers. Low-income workers get little or no assistance with health insurance costs while their highly paid coworkers get a tax windfall. Neither capping the exclusion nor the standard deduction for health insurance would address this situation. (Because the value of both

---

79 U.S. Department of the Treasury, General Explanation of the Administration's Fiscal Year 2008 Revenue Proposals 20 (Feb. 2007), *available at* http://www.ustreas.gov/offices/tax-policy/library/bluebk07.pdf.

exclusions and deductions depends upon the taxpayer's marginal rate.) For that reason some have proposed repealing the exclusion and granting all taxpayers a refundable tax credit for the purchase of insurance, either through employment or in the individual non-group market. The amount of the credit could be fixed without regard to the cost of the insurance coverage actually selected so as to remove the bias for excessive coverage. Unfortunately, the tax credit approach, like the proposed standard deduction for health care, could tend to undermine the group market via adverse selection, as individuals who present lower health risks migrate to the non-group market. That concern leads other analysts to support continuance of the current employer-based group system, supplemented with coverage mandates (directed either at firms or individuals) and subsidies to assist in handling the costs of insuring low-income individuals.

C. RETIREE HEALTH BENEFITS

From the 1950s through the 1980s, it became common for state and local governments and large private employers to promise workers employer-sponsored retiree health insurance. That trend reversed in the early 1990s, as a historically low-cost, "throw away" benefit became dramatically more expensive, while changes in financial accounting standards simultaneously forced firms to disclose the magnitude of the unfunded liability associated with retiree health coverage.[80] The result was a large negative impact on financial statements because retiree health benefits were traditionally financed on a pay-as-you-go basis; advance funding was uncommon. Many private companies responded by drastically curtailing or discontinuing retiree health programs, which led to a torrent of ERISA disclosure litigation, as disappointed retirees claimed that their health benefits had been withdrawn in violation of the terms of the plan or an extrinsic binding commitment.[81] Among large firms (200 or more workers) offering health benefits to active employees, 66 percent also offered retiree health benefits in 1988, but that number had fallen to only 31 percent in 2008.[82] Cutbacks seem to have leveled off of late, perhaps because studies show that in the face of rising health care costs, the availability of employer coverage is often crucial to inducing early retirement, as workers dare not brave the gap between loss of employer coverage and Medicare eligibility (at age 65) without the help of a significant subsidy.[83] In an effort to stabilize the situation and "ensure that all retirees have

---

80   Financial Accounting Standards Board, Statement of Financial Accounting Standards No. 106, Employers' Accounting for Postretirement Benefits Other Than Pensions (1990). Paul Fronstin, *The Impact of the Erosion of Retiree Health Benefits on Workers and Retirees*, EBRI ISSUE BRIEF No. 279, Mar. 2005, *available at* http://www.ebri.org/pdf/briefspdf/0305ib.pdf; Paul Fronstin, *Retiree Health Benefits: Trends and Outlook*, EBRI ISSUE BRIEF No. 236, Aug. 2001, *available at* http://www.ebri.org/pdf/briefspdf/0801ib.pdf.

81   *See supra* Chapter 3B–D.

82   EMPLOYER HEALTH BENEFITS 2008, *supra* Chapter 11 note 18, at 162, 163.

83   Employee Benefit Research Institute, *Retiree Health Benefits: Public Perceptions vs. National Reality* (2002), http://www.ebri.org/pdf/surveys/hcs/2002/hcs-ret.pdf (health confidence survey reveals that "[s]ixty percent of workers who expect both to receive retiree health benefits and to retire before age 65 would not retire before becoming eligible for Medicare if their

access to some health care coverage," the Equal Employment Opportunity Commission issued a rule under the Age Discrimination in Employment Act in December 2007 providing that "the ADEA will not prohibit employer and unions from providing retiree health coverage only to those retirees who are not yet eligible for Medicare. They also may supplement a retiree's Medicare coverage without having to demonstrate that the coverage is identical to that of non-Medicare eligible retirees."[84]

The tax treatment of employer-sponsored retiree health care is straightforward and just as favorable as the tax treatment of health benefits provided active employees. Even though the statute speaks to the income of an "employee," the IRS rules that health insurance coverage provided to former employees and their spouses and dependents is excludible from the former employee's gross income under section 106, as is the amount of any medical care reimbursements (insurance or plan proceeds) under section 105(b). Coverage and medical care reimbursements provided to the spouse and dependents of a deceased former employee are also granted complete tax exemption.[85] On the other side of the transaction, if the retiree health benefits are provided on a pay-as-you-go basis, then the employer can deduct amounts paid for insurance coverage of retirees and their dependents, or in the case of a self-insured plan the actual medical expense reimbursements, as an ordinary and necessary business expense.[86]

The timing of the employer's deduction becomes an issue where retiree health benefits are advance funded. Allowing a deduction upon contribution to a trust or segregated fund would provide employers a tax-favored means to save for future retiree health care expenses. Tax-favored saving for tax-exempt future expenses clashes with income tax norms on several dimensions. Code section 419 limits the employer's deduction of contributions to a welfare benefit fund to an amount equal to the qualified direct cost for the taxable year plus certain additions to a qualified asset account.[87] Qualified direct cost means the cost of providing benefits during the taxable year, including administrative expenses, reduced by the fund's after-tax income for the year.[88] In the case of retiree medical benefits, the permitted addition to a qualified asset account is defined to allow the deduction of both (1) claims incurred but unpaid as of the end of the taxable year (and administrative expenses relating thereto), and

---

former employer or union did not provide retiree health benefits."); *but see* James Marton & Stephen A. Woodbury, *Retiree Health Benefits and the Decision to Retire* (Andrew Young School of Policy Studies Research Paper Series No. 09-08, 2009), *available at* http://papers.ssrn.com/sol3/papers.cfm?abstract_id=1372829 (finding retiree health benefits associated with a 5 percentage point increase in the probability of retirement among men aged 60 to 64, and concluding that once employee sorting into firms that offer such benefits is taken into account, retiree health benefits have a relatively small effect on the decision to retire).

84   72 Fed. Reg. 72,938, 72,939 (Dec. 26, 2007), 29 C.F.R. § 1625.32 (2009). The Third Circuit rejected a challenge to the validity of the proposed rule in *AARP v. EEOC*, 489 F.3d 558 (2007).

85   Rev. Rul. 82-196, 1982-2 C.B. 53; Rev. Rul. 2002-41, 2002-2 C.B. 75. *See also* Rev. Rul. 85-121, 1985-2 C.B. 57 (exclusions also extend to laid-off employees).

86   I.R.C. § 162(a) (2006).

87   I.R.C. § 419(a), (b), (c)(1) (2006). *See generally*, Michael J. Canan & William D. Mitchell, Employee Fringe and Welfare Benefit Plans §§ 9:1–9:17 (2008).

88   I.R.C. § 419(c) (2006).

(2) limited advance funding of future benefits, determined on the basis of level actuarial funding over the working lives of covered employees but with projected obligations valued according to current medical costs.[89] As to covered employees who have already retired, the Tax Court has allowed full funding upon retirement, rejecting the IRS's interpretation that funding must be spread over the working lives of *active* employees.[90] The actuarial funding limit does not apply to a medical benefit fund maintained under a collective bargaining agreement, nor to certain plans to which 10 or more employers contribute.[91]

In addition to the advance funding deduction, if the welfare benefit fund qualifies as a tax-exempt voluntary employee beneficiary association (VEBA)[92] and does not accumulate a reserve that is greater than the amount reasonably and actuarially necessary to fund claims that are incurred but unpaid at the close of the taxable year, then the VEBA's investment income will be tax-free. To the extent that the VEBA accumulates a larger reserve to fund future retiree medical benefits, however, some or all of the fund's investment income will be taxed as unrelated business taxable income.[93]

---

89   I.R.C. §§ 419(c)(1)(B), 419A(a), (b), (c)(1), (c)(2) (2006). An annual actuarial certification is required to fund the reserve for future benefits. Absent such certification, the deduction is limited to qualified direct costs for the taxable year plus an amount equal to 35 percent of qualified direct costs for the preceding taxable year, *id.* § 419A(c)(5). The additional 35 percent is apparently intended to approximate incurred but unpaid claims, and may not be allowable if it exceeds a reasonable estimate of those claims. H.R. CONF. REP. NO. 98-861, at 1158 (1984); Gen. Signal Corp. v. Comm'r, 103 T.C. 216, *aff'd*, 142 F.3d 546 (2d Cir. 1998); Square D Co. v. Comm'r, 109 T.C. 200 (1997).

    If the welfare benefit fund is a taxable entity (such as a trust or corporation that is not a voluntary employees' beneficiary association exempt from tax under I.R.C. § 501(c)(9) (2006), the employer is allowed to deduct contributions to accumulate a reserve for retiree health care benefits only if the fund would satisfy the VEBA nondiscrimination requirements. *Id.* § 419A (e)(1). As is typical for qualified retirement plans, the welfare benefit fund nondiscrimination rules do not apply to a plan or fund maintained under a collective bargaining agreement that is the product of good faith bargaining. *Id.* §§ 505(a)(2), 419A(e)(1).

90   Wells Fargo & Co. v. Comm'r, 120 T.C. 69 (2003). This implies that contributions determined under the terminal funding actuarial cost method would be deductible under the account limits of section 419A.

91   I.R.C. § 419A(f)(5), (f)(6), (h)(2) (2006). The exception for collective bargaining agreements was essential to agreements reached in fall 2007 between the United Auto Workers and General Motors, Ford, and Chrysler, under which the automobile companies were relieved of retiree health care liabilities in exchange for billions of dollars in contributions to voluntary employee beneficiary associations established to pay those liabilities insofar as funding permits. *See* Kathryn L. Moore, *The New Retiree Health VEBAs*, N.Y.U. REV. EMP. BEN. Chapter 7 (2008).

92   I.R.C. § 419(e)(3)(A) (2006) (welfare benefit fund includes VEBA), *id.* §§ 501(c)(9) (VEBA definition and exemption), 505 (VEBA tax exempt only if benefits provided to classification of employees that does not discriminate in favor of HCEs, and amount and type of benefits also must not discriminate).

93   I.R.C. § 512(a)(3)(A), (B), (E)(i) (2006); Treas. Reg. § 1.512(a)-5T, Q&A-3(b) (1986); CANAN & MITCHELL, *supra* Chapter 11 note 87, § 9:16. The Joint Committee on Taxation explained this restriction as follows:

        The limit on the amount set aside as exempt function income does not include a reserve for post-retirement medical benefits because, in view of the advance deductions provided to

In addition, the employer is subject to a 100 percent excise tax on the amount of certain disqualified benefits paid by a welfare benefit fund, including (i) any post-retirement medical benefits paid with respect to a key employee if the fund does not provide such key employee benefits out of a separate account, and (ii) any payment of benefits to a highly compensated employee if the plan does not comply with the VEBA non-discrimination rules.[94]

The scope of the advance funding limitation deserves careful attention. The principal purpose of the welfare benefit fund rules "is to prevent employers from taking premature deductions for expenses that have not yet been incurred."[95] And indeed, the scope of the welfare benefit fund rules is defined to include employer-provided benefits that are not otherwise subject to advance deduction limitations under the rules governing deferred compensation.[96] Health savings accounts, health reimbursement arrangements, and long-term care insurance can each provide future medical benefits and may be employer-financed.[97] Are these devices subject to the welfare benefit fund advance deduction limits? HSAs seem pretty clearly to fall outside section 419's definition of a welfare benefit fund.[98] The cost of qualified long-term care insurance purchased by the employer also seems to escape the advance deduction limitation, provided that significant current risk is transferred to an independent insurance company.[99] Whether HRAs could trigger the welfare benefit fund advance deduction limitation is a murkier question; the IRS has at least suggested that section 419 could apply.[100]

One further mechanism for tax-favored saving to meet future retiree health care costs is available to some employers. The sponsor of a qualified defined benefit pension plan or a qualified annuity plan is permitted to maintain a separate account under the plan to provide for the payment of medical benefits to retired employees and their

---

employers for these benefits, it was determined that the allowance of such a tax-exempt reserve would provide an unnecessary tax incentive with respect to these benefits. STAFF OF THE JOINT COMM. ON TAXATION, 98TH CONG., GENERAL EXPLANATION OF THE REVENUE PROVISIONS OF THE TAX REFORM ACT OF 1984, at 791 (1984).

94 I.R.C. § 4976 (2006) (excise tax), *id.* §§ 419A(d) (separate account requirement), 416(i) (definition of key employee). The excise tax also captures any reversion of welfare benefit funds to the employer. *Id.* § 4976(b)(1)(C).

95 H.R. CONF. REP. NO. 99-841, at II-850 (1986).

96 I.R.C. § 419(e)(2) (2006).

97 Employer-provided coverage and benefits under a qualified long-term care insurance contract can be excluded from gross income under sections 105(b) and 106, provided that the coverage of qualified long-term care services is not provided through a flexible spending arrangement. I.R.C. § 7702B(a)(2), (a)(3), 106(c) (2006).

98 Specifically, an HSA is exempt from tax and, because the HSA is owned by the employee, it is not an account held for the employer. I.R.C. §§ 223(a), (d)(1), (e)(1), 419(e)(3) (2006).

99 I.R.C. § 419(e)(4) (2006); H.R. CONF. REP. NO. 99-841, at II-850 (1986) ("experience-rated insurance arrangements with a significant current risk of economic loss" do not involve significant premature deductions and are intended to be excluded from the definition of welfare benefit fund under the exception for qualified nonguaranteed contracts).

100 I.R.S. Notice 2002-45, Part VIII, 2002-2 C.B. 93, 95.

spouses and dependents.[101] The medical benefits must be subordinate to the retirement benefits provided by the plan, which requirement is violated if the aggregate contributions for medical benefits and life insurance protection under the plan exceed 25 percent of the total actual contributions to plan (ignoring contributions to fund past-service credits).[102] The employer's actual deduction for contributions to the medical benefit account must be determined by application of a reasonable and generally accepted actuarial method and is subject to a specified annual limit.[103] (The 25 percent test for subordinate benefits does not establish the amount allowable as a deduction for contributions.) Amounts contributed to the medical benefit account must be devoted solely to providing such benefits, and any excess funds remaining in the account after all medical benefit liabilities are satisfied must revert to the employer.[104] Because the medical benefits are provided under a qualified retirement plan, any discrimination in favor of highly compensated employees with respect to coverage of medical expenses or the amount or type of medical benefits available will disqualify the entire pension or annuity plan.[105] Tax-wise, financing retiree health benefits through a 401(h) account is the most beneficial alternative because the employer is allowed to deduct contributions, and the fund's investment return is entirely tax-free.[106] Finally, if a defined benefit pension plan is overfunded and certain additional conditions are satisfied, a special rule allows excess pension assets to be transferred into a section 401(h) account to be used to pay for retiree health benefit liabilities for the year of the transfer.[107]

---

101   I.R.C. § 404(a)(2) (2006) (deductible contributions under qualified annuity plan), *id.* § 401(h); Treas. Reg. § 1.401-1(b)(1)(i) (as amended in 1976) (pension plan may not provide medical benefits except under an account that satisfies section 401(h)), *id.* § 1.401-14 (1964).

102   I.R.C. § 401(h) (2006) (final sentence).

103   Treas. Reg. § 1.404(a)-3(f)(2) (as amended in 1972). The annual limit is set as the greater of (i) level funding (either as a level amount or a level percentage of compensation) over the remaining future service of each employee, or (ii) 10 percent of the cost that would be required to completely fund the promised medical benefits. Observe that the first measure is comparable to the funding permitted under section 419A(c)(2).

104   I.R.C. § 401(h)(4), (h)(5) (2006).

105   Treas. Reg. § 1.401-14(b)(2) (1964), § 1.401(a)(4)-4 (as amended in 2004). Also, a separate account must be maintained for each covered key employee, and medical benefit payments on behalf of a key employee must be restricted to the amount available in his account. I.R.C. § 401(h)(6) (2006).

106   In contrast, recall that the unrelated business income tax takes a bite out of the investment return if a reserve to fund retiree health benefits is accumulated in a VEBA. I.R.C. § 512(a)(3) (E)(i) (2006). *See supra* Chapter 11 note 93 and accompanying text. While a section 401(h) medical benefit account under a defined benefit plan is subject to nondiscrimination requirements, a reserve for retiree health benefits accumulated under a welfare benefit fund must also be nondiscriminatory. I.R.C. §§ 419A(e)(1), 505 (2006).

107   I.R.C. 420 (2006); *see generally* 1 MICHAEL J. CANAN, QUALIFIED RETIREMENT PLANS § 3:69 (2008). This rule is currently set to expire at the end of 2013. I.R.C. § 420(b)(5), (f)(2)(A) (2006). *See also id.* § 402(*l*), enacted in 2006, which allows the annual exclusion of up to $3,000 of otherwise-taxable distributions from a governmental plan that are used to pay health or long-term care insurance premiums for the coverage of a retired public safety officer (including police, firefighters, and emergency medical technicians), his spouse, and dependents.

D. CONCLUSION

For more than half a century, the tax law has strongly favored employer-sponsored health care over other financing methods. The tax advantage comes in the form of complete exemption of employer-provided health care coverage and benefits, and so its value depends upon the worker's marginal tax rate. Unlike the retirement savings tax incentive, however, the health care tax preference is not conditioned on satisfaction of generally applicable nondiscrimination requirements. Nevertheless, a large majority (60 percent of more) of the nonelderly population obtains employment-based health insurance.

Widespread employment-based group coverage has its advantages. In particular, the employment nexus limits adverse selection and helps keep health insurance available to high risk individuals at affordable prices. The current system has some obvious defects as well. Insurance that is employment-based does not help the unemployed; a tax subsidy that increases with income leaves many workers in low-wage industries uninsured; and older workers who have insurance experience job lock, as the prospect of losing coverage deters them from retiring early or starting their own business. Moreover the current system, while it mitigates adverse selection, tends to aggravate the problem of moral hazard. Widespread generous group insurance stimulates over-utilization of health care, and that excess demand drives up prices.

Since the 1980s, employers have responded to prolonged rapid health care cost escalation by amending their health care plans to shift some of the cost to workers. By making employees pay a share of the premiums for their insurance coverage and requiring patients to pay out-of-pocket charges to obtain health care (co-payments, deductibles, and coinsurance features), a certain amount of cost consciousness is encouraged (especially compared to the first-dollar indemnity insurance that was common in an earlier period). Such cost-sharing initiatives make workers pay, but do they pay in after-tax or pre-tax dollars? Following the 1978 enactment of the cafeteria plan rules, strategies were developed that allow employers to force workers to contribute to the cost of health care and still have the program treated, for tax purposes, as entirely employer-financed, so that the benefits remain entirely tax-free. By utilizing these mechanisms (including premium conversion plans and flexible spending arrangements) the employee's share of health care costs can be paid in pre-tax dollars, which leaves a preference for additional health care spending over other (after-tax) consumption, blunting the force of insurance limits.

Health savings accounts and health reimbursement arrangements, the latest innovations in tax-favored health care, seek to instill cost consciousness by introducing a trade-off between current and future spending, while maintaining high-deductible health insurance to protect against unpredictable catastrophic expenses. These mechanisms have thus far failed to wean many workers from traditional low-deductible coverage, and they still leave health spending tax advantaged. Proposals have been developed that would equate the tax treatment of marginal health care spending with other consumption. To date, these health care tax reforms, such as capping the exclusion for employer-provided coverage or substituting a standard deduction for health insurance, have not found political traction. In part, that is because they address health care demand by insured workers without confronting the problem of 45 million uninsured Americans.

Retiree health care benefits, especially during the gap between retirement and Medicare eligibility at age 65, were an important and once-common adjunct to employer-sponsored health care plans for current workers. Traditionally, retiree health care was nearly always provided on an unfunded (pay-as-you-go) basis. Since the early 1990s, the combination of escalating costs and new accounting rules mandating disclosure of the unfunded liability have taken their toll, inducing many companies to reduce or eliminate retiree health benefits. Other sponsors, in an effort to preserve retiree health coverage while brightening the balance sheet, have sought tax-favored means of advance funding future benefits. Prospectively, the fate of employer-sponsored retiree health care seems particularly sensitive to choices that may be made in the course of comprehensive health care reform.

ERISA's Legislative History

Background

James A. Wooten, The Employee Retirement Income Security Act of 1974 (2004).

James A. Wooten, *"The Most Glorious Story of Failure in the Business": The Studebaker-Packard Corporation and the Origins of ERISA*, 49 Buff. L. Rev. 683 (2001).

Michael S. Gordon, *Overview: Why Was ERISA Enacted?*, in S. Spec. Comm. on Aging, 98th Cong., 2d Sess., The Employee Retirement Income Security Act of 1974: The First Decade 1 (Comm. Print 1984).

Merton C. Bernstein, The Future of Private Pensions (1964).

William M. Lieber, *An IRS Insider's View of ERISA*, 65 Tax Notes 751 (1994).

ERISA Precursors (in chronological order)

U.S. Department of Labor, Legislative History of the Welfare and Pension Plans Disclosure Act of 1958, *as Amended by* Pub. L. 87-420 of 1962 (Washington, D.C., GPO; 1962). Compilation includes the legislative history of the 1962 amendments.

President's Comm. on Corporate Pension Funds and Other Private Retirement and Welfare Programs, Public Policy and Private Pension Programs, A Report to the President on Private Employee Retirement Plans (Washington, D.C., GPO; 1965).

S. Comm. on Government Operations, Diversion of Union Welfare-Pension Funds of Allied Trades Council and Teamsters Local 815, S. Rep. No. 89-1348, 89th Cong., 2d Sess. (1966).

Private Pension Plans: Hearings Before the Subcomm. on Fiscal Policy of the J. Economic Comm., 89th Cong., 2d Sess. (1966) (background study of pension plans).

S. 1024, 90th Cong., 1st Sess. (1967). This is the Johnson Administration fiduciary responsibility bill, the principal provisions of which are described at 113 Cong. Rec. 3924–25 (1967) (statement of Sen. Yarborough).

S. 1103, 90th Cong., 1st Sess. (1967). This is the original comprehensive pension regulatory proposal of Senator Jacob Javits (R–N.Y.). The proposal is printed, together with Senator Javits's introductory statement and explanatory notes, at 113 Cong. Rec. 4650–61 (1967). According to those notes, the proposal was in large measure derived from the Ontario Pension Benefits Act, 1965, S.O. 1965, ch. 96, 4 R.S.O. 1970, ch. 342. See the remarks of Senator Javits at pp. 4–27 of the 1966 Joint Economic Committee hearings.

H.R. 16462, 91st Cong., 2d Sess. (1970). This is the Nixon Administration fiduciary responsibility bill, which is printed, together with an introductory statement and section-by-section analysis, at 116 Cong. Rec. 7566–78 (1970).

S. 2, 92d Cong., 1st Sess. (1971). This is a revised version of Senator Javits's comprehensive regulatory proposal, which is printed, together with introductory and explanatory statements, at 117 Cong. Rec. 274–84 (1971), and in *Private Welfare and Pension Plan Study, 1971: Hearings Before the Subcomm. on Labor of the S. Comm. on Labor and Public Welfare*, 92d Cong., 1st Sess. 11–92 (1971).

S. 3598, 92d Cong., 2d Sess. (1972). This is a comprehensive reform bill jointly sponsored by Senators Williams and Javits, chair and ranking minority member, respectively, of the Senate Committee on Labor and Public Welfare, which is printed, together with introductory statements, at 118 Cong. Rec. 16904-22 (1972).

S. Rᴇᴘ. Nᴏ. 1150, 92d Cong., 2d Sess. (1972) (Comm. on Labor and Public Welfare report on S. 3598).

S. Rᴇᴘ. Nᴏ. 1224, 92d Cong., 2d Sess. (1972) (Finance Comm. report on S. 3598, stripping the bill of its coverage, vesting, funding, termination insurance, and portability provisions, leaving only fiduciary standards and additional disclosure requirements).

ERISA in the 93d Congress

Sᴜʙᴄᴏᴍᴍ. ᴏɴ Lᴀʙᴏʀ ᴏғ ᴛʜᴇ S. Cᴏᴍᴍ. ᴏɴ Lᴀʙᴏʀ ᴀɴᴅ Pᴜʙʟɪᴄ Wᴇʟғᴀʀᴇ, 94ᴛʜ Cᴏɴɢ., 2ᴅ Sᴇss., Lᴇɢɪsʟᴀᴛɪᴠᴇ Hɪsᴛᴏʀʏ ᴏғ ᴛʜᴇ Eᴍᴘʟᴏʏᴇᴇ Rᴇᴛɪʀᴇᴍᴇɴᴛ Iɴᴄᴏᴍᴇ Sᴇᴄᴜʀɪᴛʏ Aᴄᴛ ᴏғ 1974 (Washington, D.C., GPO; Comm. Print 1976) (3 volumes) (ERISA Lᴇɢɪsʟᴀᴛɪᴠᴇ Hɪsᴛᴏʀʏ).

Richard M. Nixon, Recommendations for Pension Reform, H.R. Dᴏᴄ. Nᴏ. 82, 93d Cong., 1st Sess. (Apr. 11, 1973) *in* Pᴜʙʟɪᴄ Pᴀᴘᴇʀs ᴏғ ᴛʜᴇ Pʀᴇsɪᴅᴇɴᴛs ᴏғ ᴛʜᴇ Uɴɪᴛᴇᴅ Sᴛᴀᴛᴇs: Rɪᴄʜᴀʀᴅ Nɪxᴏɴ, 1973, entry no. 115, at 273 (1975) (presidential message outlining the components of bills subsequently introduced as S. 1557 and S. 1631, 93d Cong., 1st Sess. (1973)). Although the bills introduced in the 93d Congress, together with introductory and explanatory statements, are reprinted in the compiled ERISA Lᴇɢɪsʟᴀᴛɪᴠᴇ Hɪsᴛᴏʀʏ (preceding source), the presidential message does not appear therein.

Table of Cases

Table of Statutes

UNITED STATES

STATE STATUTES

Table of Rules and Regulations

FEDERAL RULES

CODE OF FEDERAL REGULATIONS

Index

content controls
Congress and, 13, 210, 282
generally, 209–10, 282–83
health care plans, 209n1
See also accumulation of pension savings;
distribution of pension benefits; security of
pension benefits
contractors, independent, 40–42
corporate takeovers, 128–30
Coverdell education savings
accounts (ESA), 302

death
COBRA continuation coverage, 24
community property rights, 254–55
denial of health benefits and, 180, 182
divorce and death benefits, 178, 243n32, 246
early distribution of benefits and, 237n3
fixed-term deferred compensation and, 44
forfeiture of benefits at, 226–27, 244n37, 257
spousal protection, 12, 244, 252–53
survivor benefits, 244–45
taxes and death benefits, 356, 357
welfare plans, 46
wrongful death, 103n221
deferred compensation, nonqualified, 295–96
deferred compensation plans
complexity of, 363–64
efficiency of, 364–65
expensive nature of, 364
mandatory plan terms, 19
nonqualified deferred compensation, 295–96
preferential tax treatment for, 20–23
profit sharing plans, 236n2
qualified vs. nonqualified, 6
taxation and, 6, 43n98
welfare benefits, 47
See also pension plans
defined benefit plans
administrative costs, 364n253
annuity due formulae, 8–9
cash balance plans, 217n25
defined contribution plans as substitute
for, 282–83
defined in ERISA, 7
distribution of funds, 236
employee vs. employer risk, 7
funding, 9
legislative limits on standing and, 157–58
number of, 350f
proposed plan for, 376–77
retroactive benefits feature of, 9
*See also Specific types of defined
benefit plans*

defined contribution plans, 364n253
defined in ERISA, 7
distribution of funds, 236
employee vs. employer risk, 7
grounds for stopping benefit accrual, 216
number of, 350f
proposed plan for, 375
as substitute for defined benefit plans, 282–83
survivor protection, 250–51, 257
vs. defined benefit plans, 376–77
*See also Specific types of defined
contribution plans*
de novo review, 162–63, 163n41, 165, 165n50
dependent care benefits, 48
disability insurance, 398
disability pensions, 356, 357
disclosure obligations
fiduciary disclosure, 93–98
fiduciary silence, 101–2
liability, 103–7, 108
misleading information, 99–101
financial decision making and, 14–16, 106–7
funded status of pension plans, 270
mandated, 24
overview, 14–15, 57–58
regarding future benefits, 97n183, 100–101
statutory, 58
individual status, 60–61
plan finances, 59–60
plan instruments, 61–65
plan terms, 59
See also informal communications; summary
plan description (SPD)
discretionary benefits, 34–35, 110–11
distribution of pension benefits
anti-alienation, 238–41, 256, 358n234
IRS and, 239n16
overriding beneficiary designations, 244–50
qualified domestic relations orders, 241–44
overriding beneficiary designations, 244–50
overview, 235, 256–57
phased retirement programs, 236n1
qualified domestic relations orders, 241–44
rollovers, 222, 297, 359–63
spousal rights, 257
community property, 254–56
crimes committed by spouse and, 240
survivor protection, 226, 250–54
state and local laws, 297n32
timing of plan distributions, 235–37, 353
late distributions, 353–58
plan loans, 358–59
rollovers, 359–63
See also pension plans

health reimbursement arrangement, 394–95, 405, 407
health savings accounts, 393–95, 405, 407
high deductible, 393–95
managed care, 393*n*39
proposed health care tax reforms, 398–402
regulation of, 24–25
for retirees, 70–71, 281, 402–6, 408
workers covered by, 4, 383–84
See also taxes and health care
health care reform and ERISA's remedial balance, 180–81
health care spending, 389–90, 398–99
health maintenance organizations (HMOs), fiduciary acts, 102, 103, 115–16
health reimbursement arrangement (HRA), 394–95, 405, 407
health savings accounts (HSA), 393–95, 405, 407
highly compensated employees (HCEs)
  access to workplace retirement plans, 368
  defined, 317, 321–22
  discrimination in contributions or benefits, 324–32, 338
  discrimination in coverage, 311–17
  disqualified plans and tax consequences, 324
  401(k) plans, 339–43
  health benefits, 396
  income limits and tax-exempt IRAs, 371
  IRA contributions by, 380
  maximum amount rule and, 345–46
  minimum coverage requirement, 322–23
  nondiscrimination and redistribution, 306–11, 364, 365–67, 380–81
  proposed plans for, 374
  Social Security and, 332–37
  See also employees; nonhighly compensated employees (NHCEs)
HRA (health reimbursement arrangement), 394–95, 405, 407
HSA (health savings accounts), 393–95, 405, 407
Hurricane Katrina, 358

implied terms, standardization of, 15–16
income tax
  early distributions, 236
  household income tax liability, 305*n*63
  independent contractors and, 42*n*88
  IRAs and, 299–302
  plan classification and, 6
  principle of economic neutrality, 379–80
  See also taxes and health care; taxes and retirement saving

independent contractors, 40–42
Indian tribal governments, 23*n*96, 311*n*70
individual account plans *See* defined contribution plans
individual retirement accounts (IRA)
  assets held in, 358
  direct deposit with default contributions, 369
  distributions, 222–23
  early withdrawals, 357–58
  minimum distribution rule and, 354
  participation in, 298
  rollovers, 222, 297, 359–63
  Roth IRAs, 299–302, 354–55, 358*n*233, 364*n*253, 371*nn*274–275
  tax deferral and, 21, 298–302
  tax-free rollovers, 222, 297
  tax revenue and, 364*n*253
  vs. Lifetime Savings Accounts, 371*n*274
  See also 401(k) plans; 403(b) plans
informal communications
  estoppel and, 84, 86–88, 89–90, 108
  inconsistent oral statements, 84–85, 99
  liability for, 83–84
  plan amendments, 88–93
  plan clarification, 86–88
  vesting language, 72
  written, 84, 88, 90
  See also disclosure obligations; summary plan description (SPD)
insurance savings clause, 203–5
Internal Revenue Code
  on advance funding contributions, 264
  on the anti-alienation rule, 239*n*16
  deferred compensation plans, 6–8
  minimum funding standards and plan amendments, 267–68
  minimum funding waivers, 267, 275
  plan loans under the, 239
  property defined in the, 291–92
  qualification criteria for preferential tax treatment, 20–23
  qualified plan provisions funding requirements, 269
  qualified retirement plan provisions, 223*n*93
  transfer in the, 290–91
Internal Revenue Service
  on actuarial assumptions for minimum funding obligations, 265–66
  on governmental and church plans, 51
  interpretation of nondiscrimination rules, 325
  on plan disqualification, 338
investment advisers, 111
IRAs *See* individual retirement accounts
IRS Form 5500, 59